JAMES BOND
007

TROUBLE SPOT

JAMES BOND 007:
TROUBLE SPOT
ISBN 1 84576 269 X
ISBN-13: 9781845762698

Published by Titan Books,
a division of Titan Publishing Group Ltd.
144 Southwark St
London SE1 0UP

A CIP catalogue record for this title is available from the British Library.

First edition: September 2006
3 5 7 9 10 8 6 4 2

Printed in Italy.

Also available from Titan Books:
James Bond: Casino Royale (ISBN: 1 84023 843 7)
James Bond: Dr No (ISBN: 1 84576 089 1)
James Bond: Goldfinger (ISBN: 1 84023 908 5)
James Bond: On Her Majesty's Secret Service (ISBN: 1 84023 674 4)
James Bond: The Man with the Golden Gun (ISBN: 1 84023 690 6)
James Bond: Octopussy (ISBN: 1 84023 743 0)
James Bond: The Spy Who Loved Me (ISBN: 1 84576 174 X)
James Bond: Colonel Sun (ISBN: 1 84576 175 8)
James Bond: The Golden Ghost (ISBN: 1 84576 261 4)

Huge thanks to John Abbott at the *Daily Express*, everyone at http://www.mi6.co.uk, Peter Knight at
Knight Features, Gareth Owen, Zoe Watkins and Fleur Gooch, without whom this book would never
have happened.

Introduction © Martine Beswicke 2006.

Feature and story introductions © James Wheatley, Matthias Garretway & James Page 2006.

What did you think of this book? We love to hear from our readers. Please email us at:
readerfeedback@titanemail.com, or write to us at the above address. You can also visit us at
www.titanbooks.com

**Much of the comic strip material used by Titan in this edition is
exceedingly rare. As such, we hope that readers appreciate that the
quality of the materials can be variable.**

JAMES BOND
007

TROUBLE SPOT

IAN FLEMING
JIM LAWRENCE ◆ YAROSLAV HORAK

TITAN BOOKS

YOUNG PROTÈGÈE

Introduction by
MARTINE BESWICKE

Although I was born and bred in Jamaica, I had never heard of Ian Fleming, perhaps due to my having moved to England in the early 1950s and spending my formative years here. In fact, I didn't know Fleming's work until 1961, when my first agent sent me to meet Terence Young for my first audition — the role of Honey Ryder in *Dr No*. Green as I was, Terence was very straight with me: he told me to go to work and gain some experience. After *Dr No* had been completed, I met Terence again through Christopher Blackwell, who had co-ordinated the Jamaican shoot. Terence — who had a habit of taking people under his wing, and of referring to his friends as 'his children' — told me to keep working, because he was going to cast me in the next *James Bond* film as one of the fighting gypsies. True to his word — so rare in the movie industry! — I was cast as Zora in *From Russia With Love*. This was my real introduction to Ian Fleming, and the beginning of my film career.

Two years later, an 'island girl' was needed to be Bond's liaison in *Thunderball*. At that time, the hard and fast rule was that no actress was allowed to appear in more than one *Bond* film playing different characters. However, Terence convinced Cubby Broccoli and Harry Saltzman that I was the real 'island girl', Paula Caplan. I became the first actress to break that rule, Maud Adams being the only other.

Working on the production of *Thunderball* in Nassau was probably one of the most exciting and fun experiences of my entire career. It was 1965, the British Invasion was in full swing and *James Bond* was now a worldwide phenomenon. Unfortunately, even though Ian Fleming had initially raised objections regarding the big-screen portrayal of 007, he did not get to see the extent to which his character captured the world.

It is interesting to note that there were definite background similarities between Ian Fleming and Terence Young, particularly the fact that they have both been described as 'stylish, witty and charming.' Terence was the most debonair gentleman I have ever met, and he used these attributes to great effect when he took Sean Connery under his wing and helped to create the cinematic James Bond who still captures and thrills audiences today.

It seems that there is no end to this phenomenon which Ian Fleming created; the cameras are rolling again for *Casino Royale*, with Daniel Craig as the new James Bond, and the comic strips continue to entertain fans around the world.

Enjoy.

Martine Beswicke
March 2006

Martine Beswicke is an actress of silver and small-screen, having appeared on TV in *Quincy*, *The Fall Guy*, *Days of Our Lives*, *Hart to Hart* and many others. Her film career includes *One Million Years BC*, *Dr Jekyll and Sister Hyde*, *Miami Blues* and *Wide Sargasso Sea*.

CURVES, CHARM & COOL:
THE WOMEN OF JAMES BOND – STRIPPED!

Readers with a depth of knowledge encompassing not only the published *Bond*, but also Fleming's own life, will notice a correlation between the characters and the numerous women, both married and single, with whom Fleming had relationships. Every writer needs some form of inspiration to develop characters: Fleming had his close to hand... Typically, every *Bond* girl has roughly the same qualities; aspects which make them not only attractive to Bond but also appealing to Fleming. Almost always, the girls have curves and a body to die for, even though a slight imperfection is generally a plus for Bond — Honeychile Rider has a broken nose, for example.

However, physical aspects are only one part of the *Bond* girl appeal, as without emotional resonance, the characters would merely be shells. The general formula for a *Bond* girl is one that has some emotional need from 007, yet at the same time has just enough confidence within herself to put on enough of a show to attract him in the first place. This attraction occurs in many forms: whereas Comtesse Teresa Di Vicenzo enrages Bond when her car speeds past him, leaving him almost unable to catch up, Gala Brand blanks Bond at the dinner table and intrigues him. It is this confidence that not only agitates Bond, but also shows up the sexist streak in Fleming himself. How could Bond allow a *woman* to overtake him, or decline his advances over dinner?

Fleming's writing style remained largely consistent throughout his series of novels, but the visual style of the strip adaptations altered over time. As fashions developed and the public's attitude to sex changed over the two decades during which his novels would be adapted into comic strip form, the appearance of the *Bond* girls also evolved. Whereas the opening story *Casino Royale* (adapted in 1958) depicts Gala Brand conservatively, a couple of years later and five adventures into the series, Honeychile Rider in *Dr No* (adapted in 1960) is the first *Bond* girl to appear semi-nude. By the time the run of Fleming-based comic strip adventures was nearing its end, and 'Bond fever' was spreading the globe with the cinematic release of *Thunderball* in the swinging sixties, nudity abounded in the comic strip version of *You Only Live Twice* (adapted in 1965). *Bond* girl sexuality was taken to new heights when artist Yaroslav Horak took over from John McLusky with *The Man With The Golden Gun* in 1966. As writer Jim Lawrence said in *Comics Interview* #69, published in 1989, "You've got to have T and A, you can't just have long sequences of taking heads."

James Page and James Wheatley

VESPER LYND
Casino Royale

Vesper is known as Agent 3030 within MI6. During World War II she was in love with a Polish RAF officer, who was captured by the Russians, and Vesper was blackmailed into becoming a double agent — a fact unbeknownst to Bond until the final strip. Vesper is Bond's first lover in both the prose and comic strip series. In *Casino Royale* we see a very cocky and immature Bond, and there are no initially obvious sparks flying between the two; the sexual charge slowly builds between them as the adventure unfolds.

"Behaving like a millionaire occasionally is a wonderful treat."

In the strip, Vesper's dress sense remains identical to Fleming's description in the novel, particularly the black velvet evening dress that she wears to dinner and the casino. Add some witty conversation to her stylish fashion sense and classic beauty and it is easy to see why Vesper and Bond build such a strong relationship. It is made plain throughout the story that Vesper knows more than she is letting on to Bond, and it is the cause of tension between them, which remains unresolved until it is too late. This key aspect of Lynd's character is carried over faithfully from the novel, as is her untimely death, as Vesper's guilt over her duplicity drives her to commit suicide. However, unlike Fleming's novel, Bond does not seem as eager to leave the immediate vicinity...

MISS SOLITAIRE
Live and Let Die

Solitaire – real name Simone Latrelle – is portrayed in the early part of the comic strip as being a weak character, who constantly relies on Bond to help her. To paraphrase 007, she 'hangs off his gun arm' for the most part. In Fleming's novel, the reader gets a different impression of her, as she seems capable of looking after herself without Bond's aid.

The strip is more faithful to the novel in the description of the character's former life as a cabaret star, although the strip does not go into any detail about how Mr Big trapped her into working for him, leaving this to the reader's imagination. As Solitaire is an unwilling recruit for Mr. Big, she switches sides part-way through the adventure and falls in love with Bond very easily. Solitaire's physical appearance in the strip is more of a caricature, in comparison to the realistic depiction of Vesper Lynd in the first adventure. The appearance of the *Bond* girls in the strips would settle down in to a happy middle-ground in the later stories.

Towards the end of the story her portrayal becomes closer to that in the novel; stronger and more independent. Even when their own deaths are seemingly apparent, she manages to sum up enough stiff upper lip to tell Bond, "Don't worry about me, my darling, I am just happy to be with you again. Although death is very close, I'm not afraid."

"James! Oh, James!"

GALA BRAND
Moonraker

Gala Brand is a rarity among *Bond* girls, as throughout the strip she shows little or no romantic attraction to 007. Bond even struggles to maintain a conversation with her, but she eventually succumbs to his charms – in a platonic manner.

Gala's character in the strip is faithfully adapted from the novel, with her loyalty and hard-working qualities shining through. After a sequence when their lives are threatened by a cliff collapse, Gala almost concedes to Bond's forced kiss, but she quickly regains her cold and professional demeanour.

Gala's main interest lies in getting her job done, and her almost fanatical work with the Moonraker project almost doesn't allow her to see Drax's true intentions. Her opinion of him is summed up nicely in strip #266: "He's a ruthless man with deplorable manners and not a very nice face. But I love working for him and I'm longing for the Moonraker to be a success." When she eventually sees the true Drax, it is largely left to Bond to get them both to safety and to foil his plot to destroy London, but Gala still plays a useful role.

At the end of the strip we understand why Gala has been shirking Bond's advances when she makes a rather surprising announcement. There are no 'bedtime privileges' for Bond at the end of this adventure, as Gala walks off into the sunset — accompanied by her fiancé!

"If you must know, Mr. Bond, these are gyro settings."

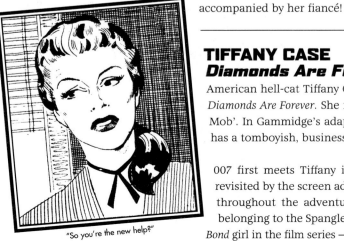

"So you're the new help?"

TIFFANY CASE
Diamonds Are Forever

American hell-cat Tiffany Case, a short-haired beauty, is instrumental throughout the plot of *Diamonds Are Forever*. She is quickly introduced in the strip as 007's contact to the 'Spangled Mob'. In Gammidge's adaptation, which is faithful to Fleming's novel, this tough-talking gal has a tomboyish, businesslike quality in both character and appearance.

007 first meets Tiffany in her apartment while she is half-naked, in a scene which was revisited by the screen adaptation over ten years later. As in Fleming's novel, Tiffany smokes throughout the adventure, and when in Las Vegas she works as a croupier for a hotel belonging to the Spangled Mob. Her ability to stack a deck of cards would be granted to a later *Bond* girl in the film series – Lupe Lamora in *Licence To Kill*.

During the showdown at the Wild West-themed Spectreville, Case appears as a cowgirl. She and Bond then set a trap together for the pursuing hoods. After the three-day cruise from New York, Bond and Tiffany finally settle in his London flat. Tiffany was the first *Bond* girl to bridge more than one adventure, as she appears in the opening panels of *From Russia With Love.* In Fleming's novel, Tiffany returns to America for the love of another man. However, in the strip adaptation, she becomes homesick, returning to Las Vegas.

TATIANA ROMANOVA
From Russia With Love

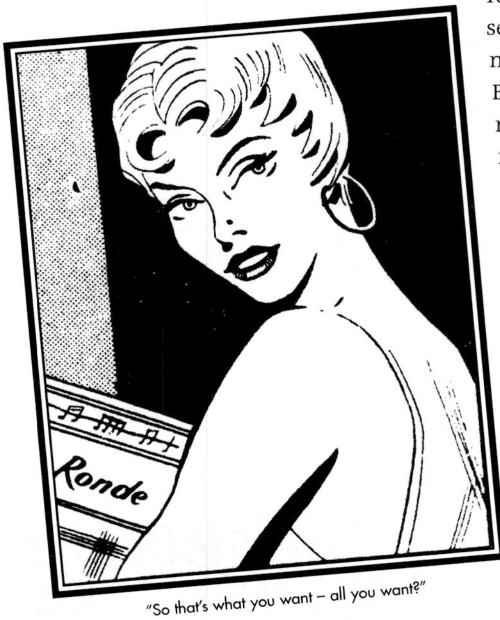
Ronde
"So that's what you want – all you want?"

Tatiana Romanova was the first girl to go after Bond deliberately intending to seduce him, as per her orders from Rosa Klebb. Due to the nature of Fleming's novel – the opening third of which details the SMERSH plan, in the absence of Bond – the narrative in the strip adaptation is condensed. With 007 narrating most of the story, a lot of Tatiana's dialogue is missing, so her character is not fully conveyed to the reader.

Tatiana (nicknamed Tania) is a stunning young lady working as a clerk for the Russian secret service in Moscow. Fleming's plot promotes Tania to a Captain upon her learning of her new assignment, an omission from the strip, though Gammidge and McLusky's adaptation otherwise stays close to Fleming's description, with Tania featuring shoulder-length wavy hair and smoking with a filter – like most of the early Bond girls. However, many of the edgier, key character moments have suffered due to the condensed format. One such instance is Tania's interview with Rosa Klebb, where the strip does not deliver the same level of tension.

When 007 meets Tania she quickly works her charm, luring him into bed four strips later, for the benefit of the SMERSH cameras. Appearing only thirty-nine times in total, Tania is last seen when Bond drops her off at the British embassy in Paris.

HONEYCHILE RIDER
Dr No

Honeychile Rider (Honey to her friends) first appeared in 1958 in Fleming's sixth novel, *Dr No*, which was adapted to strip form in 1960. Artist John McLusky and one-time *Bond* writer Peter O'Donnell (creator of one of comics' strongest ever female characters, Modesty Blaise) developed Honey for the daily strip.

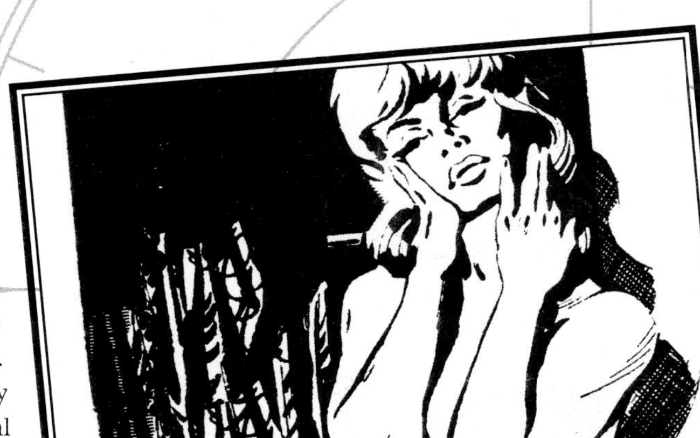
"Would you like me in white, with pale blue birds flying all over me?"

First seen in an iconic introduction foreshadowing that in the movie (which followed two years later), it is difficult not to picture Ursula Andress, due to the striking familiarity of McClusky's artwork. This beautiful girl has wavy, shoulder-length hair, but most notably she has a broken nose; a feature carried over from Fleming's original backstory, setting Honey apart from all the other *Bond* girls.

Compared to her original literary incarnation, Honey appears in the strips semi-clothed most of the time, although her penchant for nudity can be seen later, as she catches 007 off-guard after showering. A very earthy girl in every respect, Honey's knowledge of the natural world proves invaluable to Bond and Quarrel as they hide from patrolling guards, and later as she escapes harm from Dr No's giant land crabs — a scene from the novel that was cut from the film.

A keen canoeist, Honey paddles 007 back to Jamaica, quite possibly saving his life. After their traumatic adventure, she comforts Bond on the beach as he recovers from his various injuries. Honey then heads to New York with 007 to get her nose straightened and forget about her memories of Crab Key.

JILL MASTERTON
Goldfinger

Appearing only five times at the beginning of the adventure, Jill Masterton is the first *Bond* girl we meet in *Goldfinger*. A personal aide to Goldfinger, this blonde beauty helps her employer cheat at canasta in a Miami resort.

Jill first encounters 007 as he breaks into her hotel room to stop Goldfinger cheating. She is quickly taken by Bond's charm and agrees to ditch her boss. Jill is last seen planning to escape to New York with 007.

The most notable change to the character is her death. After fleeing to New York with Bond in the original novel, Jill dies of skin asphyxiation after Goldfinger catches up with her (he covers her with gold paint, as in the filmed version). In the strip, Bond learns of her death at Goldfinger's hands from Tilly, and Jill leaves a ring for her sister to give to Bond should they ever meet.

"Goldfinger loves gold, really loves it.
Like people love jewels or stamps or – well, women..."

TILLY SOAMES
Goldfinger

Tilly Soames, sister of Jill Masterton, meets Bond midway through the adventure after a forced rendezvous. 007 is immediately taken by her fiery temperament and determination, which are carried through from Fleming's original work.

With wavy, light-coloured hair, this strong-willed feminist is out for revenge. Tilly's failed assassination of Goldfinger results in her and Bond being put to work for him. As she works alongside Bond we learn about her clerical abilities. Tilly appears twenty-one times in the strip, making her the leading female role. As established in the novel, Tilly does not succumb to Bond's charms — even in extreme situations.

Escaping with 007 proves fatal for Tilly, as for her sister, as she is struck by Oddjob's deadly hat. However, just before her death, Tilly exclaims that she would prefer to stay with Pussy Galore — not Bond — hinting at her lesbianism, as per the novel.

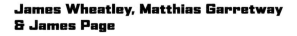

"You damn fool! What d'you think you're doing?"

PUSSY GALORE
Goldfinger

The third *Bond* girl in the strip – and the only survivor – Pussy Galore first appears two-thirds into the adventure. McLusky created a tomboy look for Pussy, similar in style to Tiffany Case from *Diamonds Are Forever*. This 'boyish' look was presumably influenced by the suggestion in Fleming's novel that she is a lesbian.

Pussy is the leader of the notorious "Cement Mixers" gang, based in New York's Harlem. Over her thirteen appearances in the strips, Pussy appears in two disguises: a nurse and stewardess. As in Fleming's novel, Pussy Galore changes both her sexual orientation and loyalty at the last minute. Thus, at the end of the story, Bond defeats the villain and gets the girl — however unlikely it may seem...

**James Wheatley, Matthias Garretway
& James Page**

"Me an' my gals got to eat..."

TROUBLE SPOT

Following a run of high-tech and fantastical stories penned by Lawrence, *Trouble Spot* brings Bond back down to earth in a straightforward espionage tale – the only exception being the machine-gun mounted in the wing of 007's car.

Once the reader can get past the implausibility of a blind woman accepting Bond as her dead husband by only the similarity of his voice, writer Jim Lawrence and artist Yaroslav Horak cook up a story packed with plenty of sex, sadism and snobbery.

From the opening panel, scantily-clad ladies abound in this adventure, with a touch of sado-masochism thrown in for good measure in the shape of Olga, the villain's whip-toting sidekick. Add to the mix some exotic locales, a thrilling car chase, a cold-blooded killing, and a Bond girl 'with a wing down' and it's a recipe of which Fleming would have heartily approved.

Trouble Spot is the first comic strip in the series not to feature M, but Miss Moneypenny and chief of staff Bill Tanner make their usual appearances. The telephone gadget Bond uses to disable a goon with a high-pitched shrill over the line would be echoed two years later in the Roger Moore film *Live and Let Die*, where villains use a similar device at the United Nations.

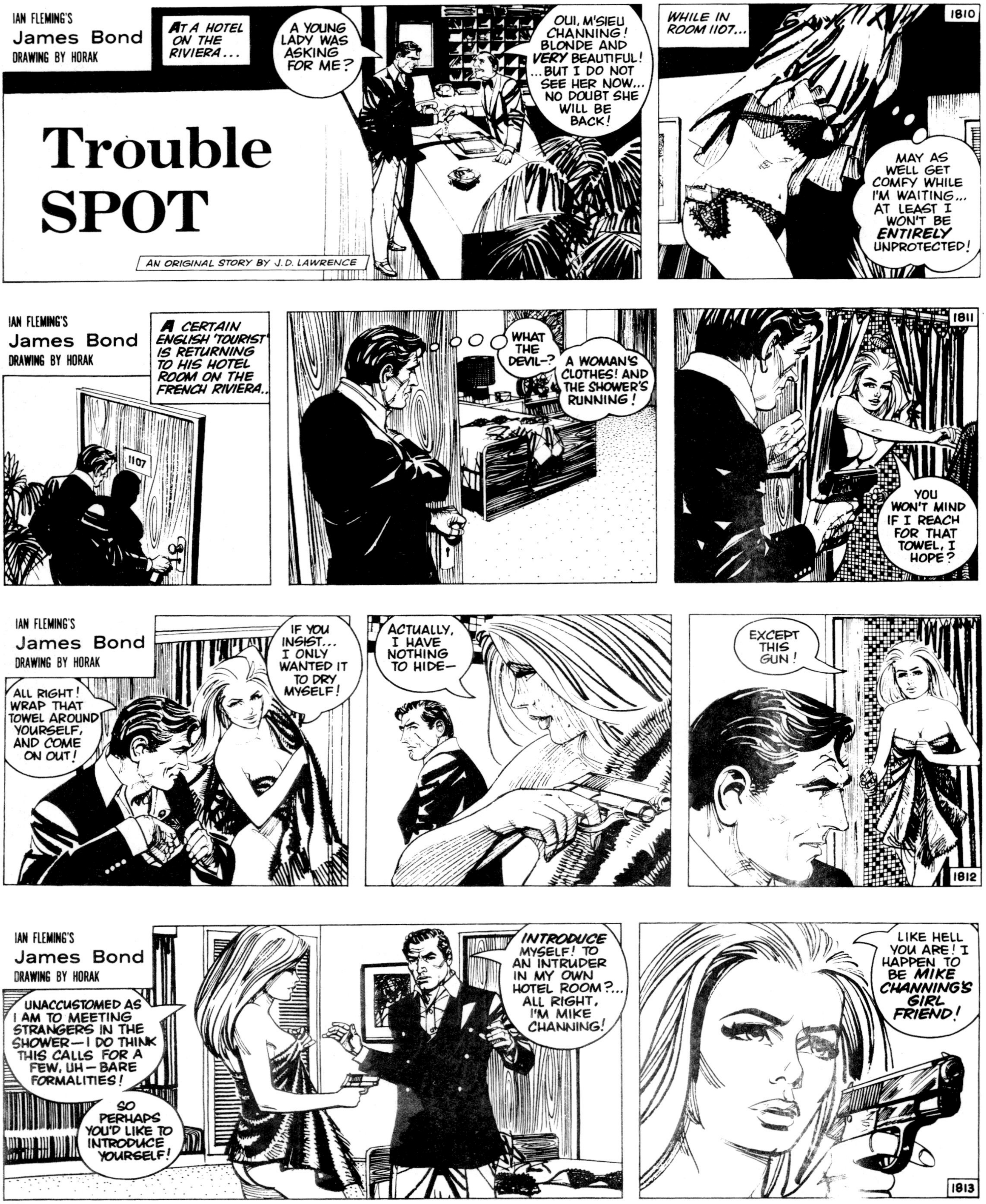
IAN FLEMING'S
James Bond
DRAWING BY HORAK
Trouble SPOT
AN ORIGINAL STORY BY J. D. LAWRENCE
AT A HOTEL ON THE RIVIERA...
A YOUNG LADY WAS ASKING FOR ME?
OUI, M'SIEU CHANNING! BLONDE AND VERY BEAUTIFUL! ...BUT I DO NOT SEE HER NOW... NO DOUBT SHE WILL BE BACK!
1810
WHILE IN ROOM 1107...
MAY AS WELL GET COMFY WHILE I'M WAITING... AT LEAST I WON'T BE ENTIRELY UNPROTECTED!
IAN FLEMING'S
James Bond
DRAWING BY HORAK
A CERTAIN ENGLISH 'TOURIST' IS RETURNING TO HIS HOTEL ROOM ON THE FRENCH RIVIERA..
1107
WHAT THE DEVIL-?
A WOMAN'S CLOTHES! AND THE SHOWER'S RUNNING!
1811
YOU WON'T MIND IF I REACH FOR THAT TOWEL, I HOPE?
IAN FLEMING'S
James Bond
DRAWING BY HORAK
ALL RIGHT! WRAP THAT TOWEL AROUND YOURSELF, AND COME ON OUT!
IF YOU INSIST... I ONLY WANTED IT TO DRY MYSELF!
ACTUALLY, I HAVE NOTHING TO HIDE-
EXCEPT THIS GUN!
1812
IAN FLEMING'S
James Bond
DRAWING BY HORAK
UNACCUSTOMED AS I AM TO MEETING STRANGERS IN THE SHOWER—I DO THINK THIS CALLS FOR A FEW, UH—BARE FORMALITIES!
SO PERHAPS YOU'D LIKE TO INTRODUCE YOURSELF!
INTRODUCE MYSELF! TO AN INTRUDER IN MY OWN HOTEL ROOM?... ALL RIGHT, I'M MIKE CHANNING!
LIKE HELL YOU ARE! I HAPPEN TO BE MIKE CHANNING'S GIRL FRIEND!
1813

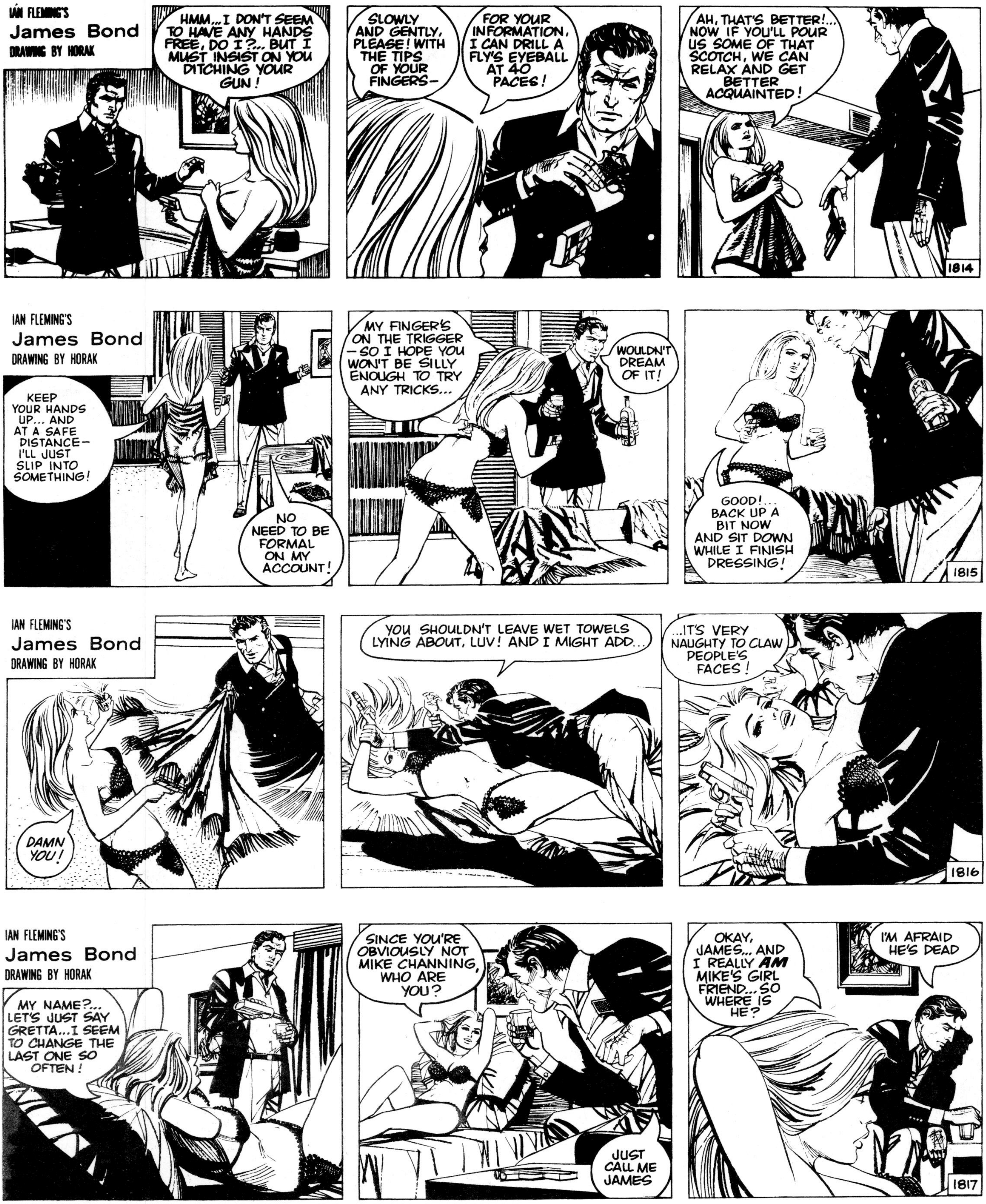
IAN FLEMING'S
James Bond
DRAWING BY HORAK
HMM... I DON'T SEEM TO HAVE ANY HANDS FREE, DO I?... BUT I MUST INSIST ON YOU DITCHING YOUR GUN!
SLOWLY AND GENTLY, PLEASE! WITH THE TIPS OF YOUR FINGERS—
FOR YOUR INFORMATION, I CAN DRILL A FLY'S EYEBALL AT 40 PACES!
AH, THAT'S BETTER!... NOW IF YOU'LL POUR US SOME OF THAT SCOTCH, WE CAN RELAX AND GET BETTER ACQUAINTED!
1814
IAN FLEMING'S
James Bond
DRAWING BY HORAK
KEEP YOUR HANDS UP... AND AT A SAFE DISTANCE—I'LL JUST SLIP INTO SOMETHING!
NO NEED TO BE FORMAL ON MY ACCOUNT!
MY FINGER'S ON THE TRIGGER —SO I HOPE YOU WON'T BE SILLY ENOUGH TO TRY ANY TRICKS...
WOULDN'T DREAM OF IT!
GOOD!... BACK UP A BIT NOW AND SIT DOWN WHILE I FINISH DRESSING!
1815
IAN FLEMING'S
James Bond
DRAWING BY HORAK
DAMN YOU!
YOU SHOULDN'T LEAVE WET TOWELS LYING ABOUT, LUV! AND I MIGHT ADD...
...IT'S VERY NAUGHTY TO CLAW PEOPLE'S FACES!
1816
IAN FLEMING'S
James Bond
DRAWING BY HORAK
MY NAME?... LET'S JUST SAY GRETTA... I SEEM TO CHANGE THE LAST ONE SO OFTEN!
SINCE YOU'RE OBVIOUSLY NOT MIKE CHANNING, WHO ARE YOU?
JUST CALL ME JAMES
OKAY, JAMES... AND I REALLY AM MIKE'S GIRL FRIEND... SO WHERE IS HE?
I'M AFRAID HE'S DEAD
1817

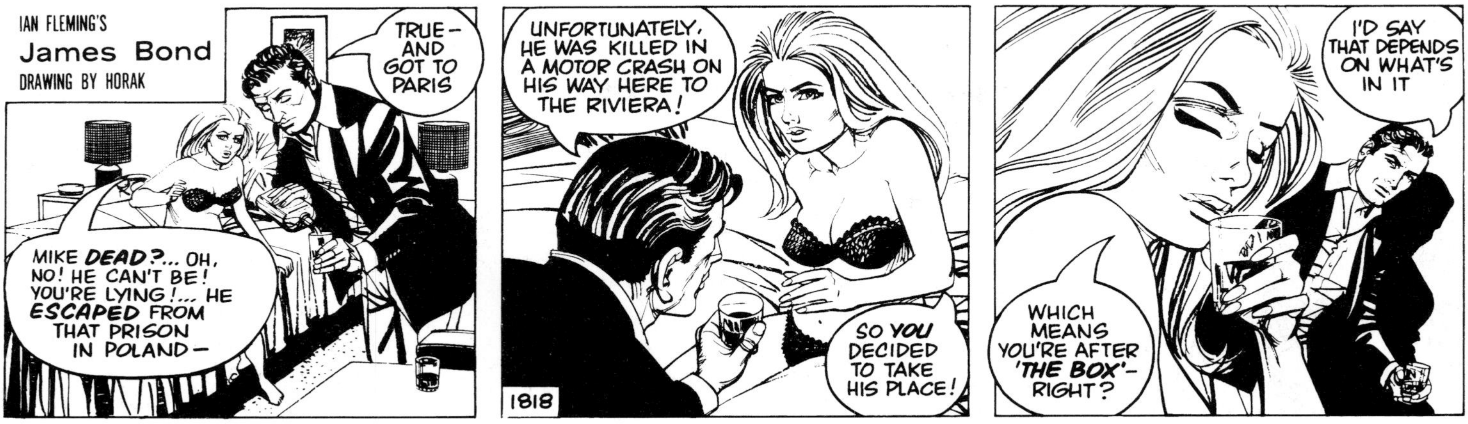
IAN FLEMING'S
James Bond
DRAWING BY HORAK
TRUE— AND GOT TO PARIS
MIKE DEAD?... OH, NO! HE CAN'T BE! YOU'RE LYING!... HE ESCAPED FROM THAT PRISON IN POLAND—
UNFORTUNATELY, HE WAS KILLED IN A MOTOR CRASH ON HIS WAY HERE TO THE RIVIERA!
SO YOU DECIDED TO TAKE HIS PLACE!
1818
I'D SAY THAT DEPENDS ON WHAT'S IN IT
WHICH MEANS YOU'RE AFTER 'THE BOX'— RIGHT?

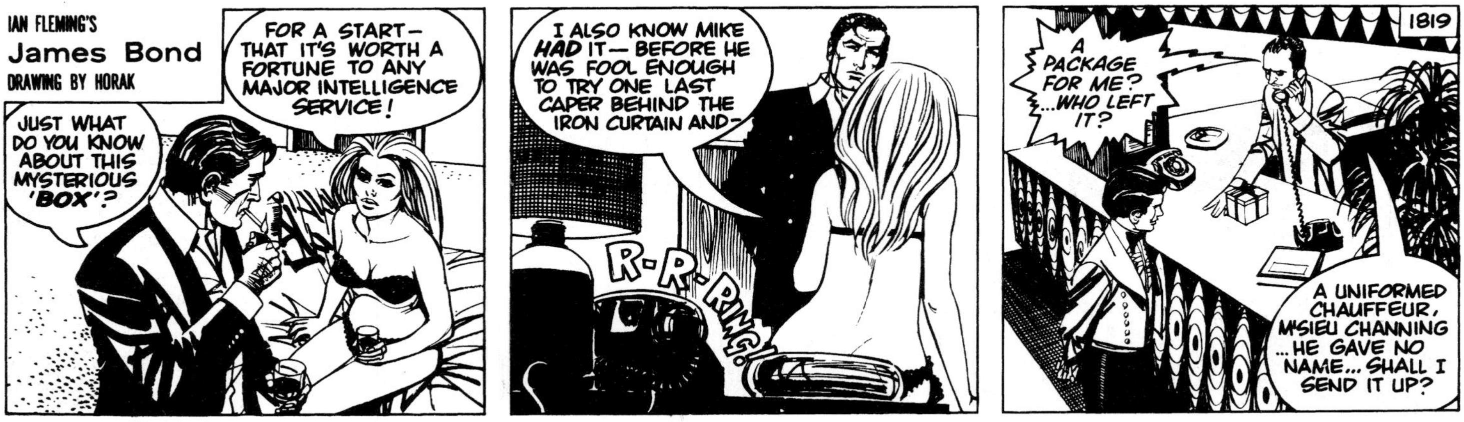
IAN FLEMING'S
James Bond
DRAWING BY HORAK
JUST WHAT DO YOU KNOW ABOUT THIS MYSTERIOUS 'BOX'?
FOR A START— THAT IT'S WORTH A FORTUNE TO ANY MAJOR INTELLIGENCE SERVICE!
I ALSO KNOW MIKE HAD IT— BEFORE HE WAS FOOL ENOUGH TO TRY ONE LAST CAPER BEHIND THE IRON CURTAIN AND—
R-R-RING!
1819
A PACKAGE FOR ME? ...WHO LEFT IT?
A UNIFORMED CHAUFFEUR, M'SIEU CHANNING ...HE GAVE NO NAME... SHALL I SEND IT UP?

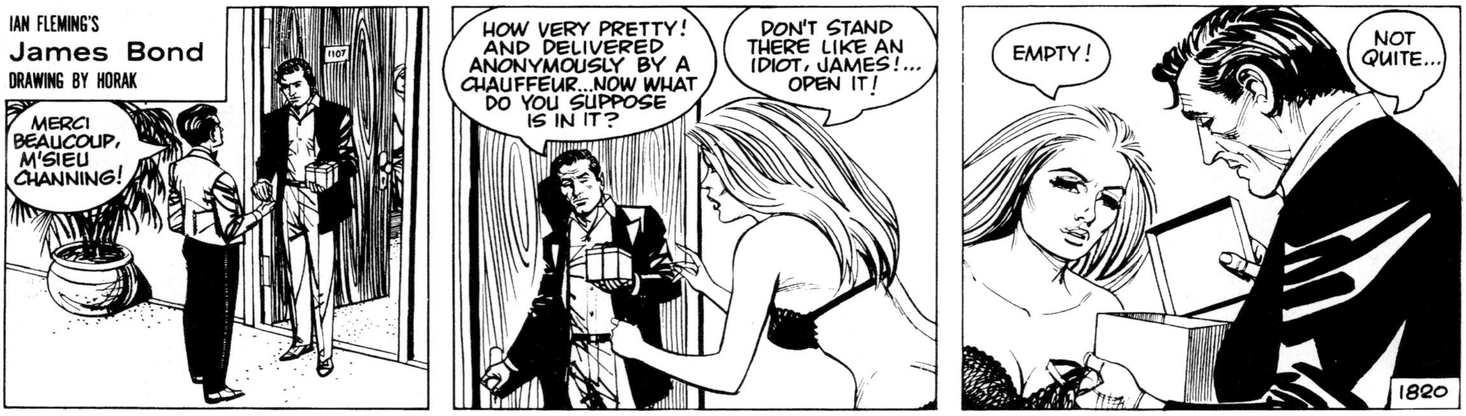
IAN FLEMING'S
James Bond
DRAWING BY HORAK
MERCI BEAUCOUP, M'SIEU CHANNING!
1107
HOW VERY PRETTY! AND DELIVERED ANONYMOUSLY BY A CHAUFFEUR...NOW WHAT DO YOU SUPPOSE IS IN IT?
DON'T STAND THERE LIKE AN IDIOT, JAMES!... OPEN IT!
EMPTY!
NOT QUITE...
1820

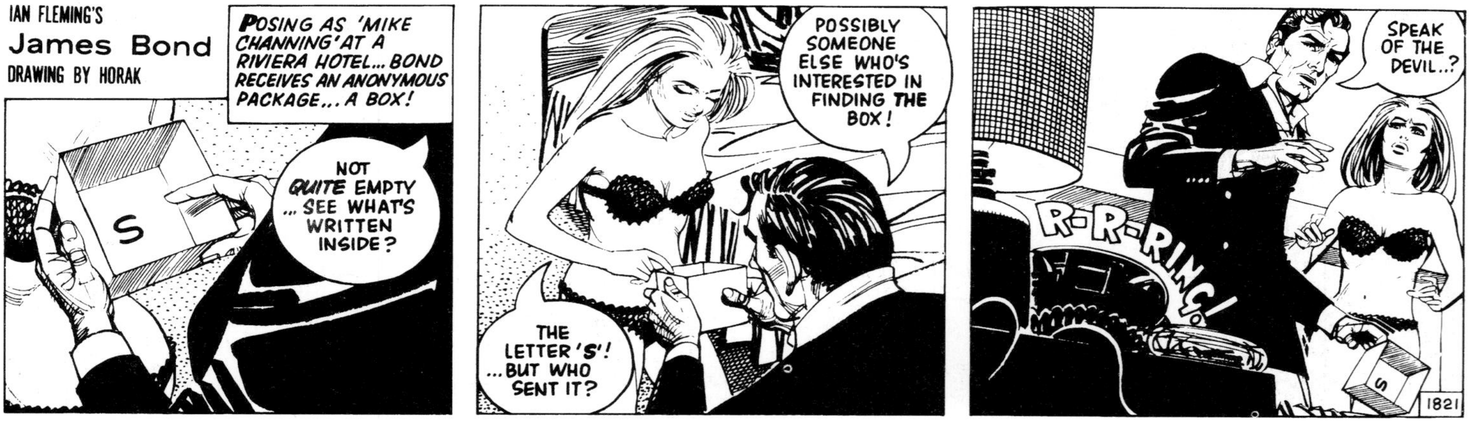
IAN FLEMING'S
James Bond
DRAWING BY HORAK
POSING AS 'MIKE CHANNING' AT A RIVIERA HOTEL... BOND RECEIVES AN ANONYMOUS PACKAGE... A BOX!
S
NOT QUITE EMPTY ... SEE WHAT'S WRITTEN INSIDE?
POSSIBLY SOMEONE ELSE WHO'S INTERESTED IN FINDING THE BOX!
THE LETTER 'S'! ...BUT WHO SENT IT?
SPEAK OF THE DEVIL..?
R-R-RING!
1821

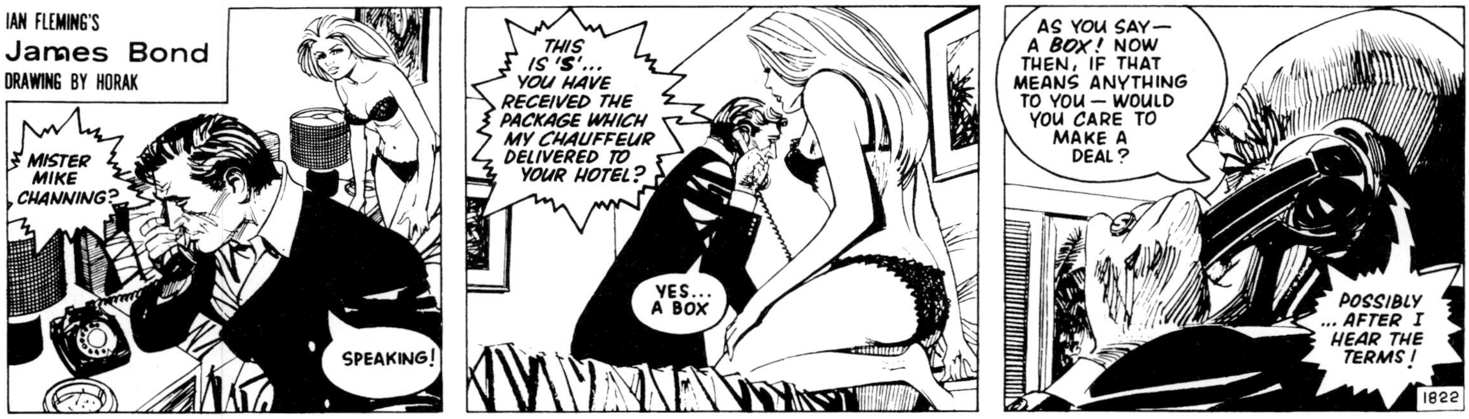
IAN FLEMING'S
James Bond
DRAWING BY HORAK
MISTER MIKE CHANNING?
SPEAKING!
THIS IS 'S'... YOU HAVE RECEIVED THE PACKAGE WHICH MY CHAUFFEUR DELIVERED TO YOUR HOTEL?
YES... A BOX
AS YOU SAY— A BOX! NOW THEN, IF THAT MEANS ANYTHING TO YOU — WOULD YOU CARE TO MAKE A DEAL?
POSSIBLY ... AFTER I HEAR THE TERMS!
1822

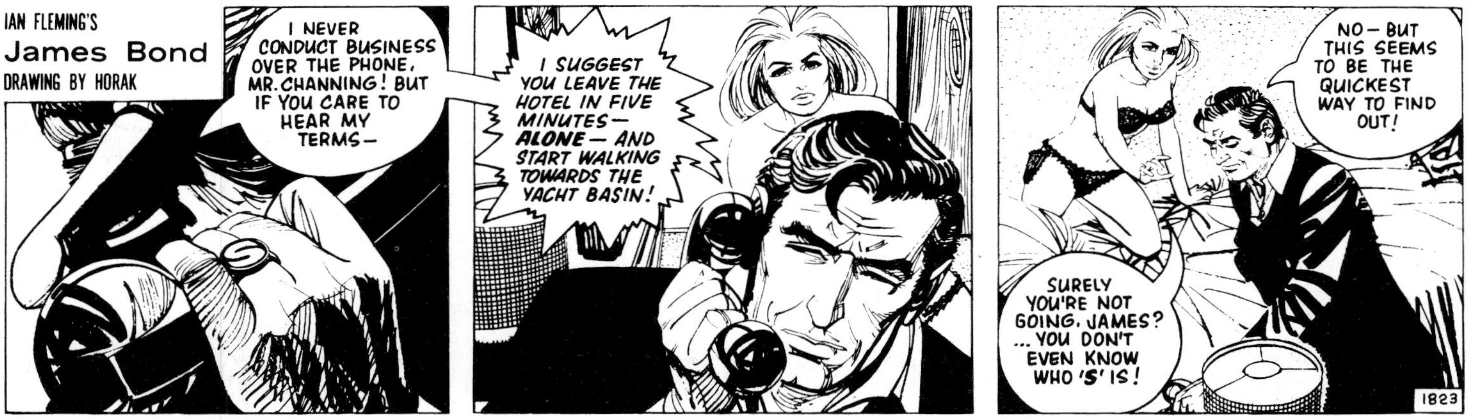
IAN FLEMING'S
James Bond
DRAWING BY HORAK
I NEVER CONDUCT BUSINESS OVER THE PHONE, MR. CHANNING! BUT IF YOU CARE TO HEAR MY TERMS—
I SUGGEST YOU LEAVE THE HOTEL IN FIVE MINUTES— ALONE— AND START WALKING TOWARDS THE YACHT BASIN!
NO— BUT THIS SEEMS TO BE THE QUICKEST WAY TO FIND OUT!
SURELY YOU'RE NOT GOING, JAMES? ... YOU DON'T EVEN KNOW WHO 'S' IS!
1823

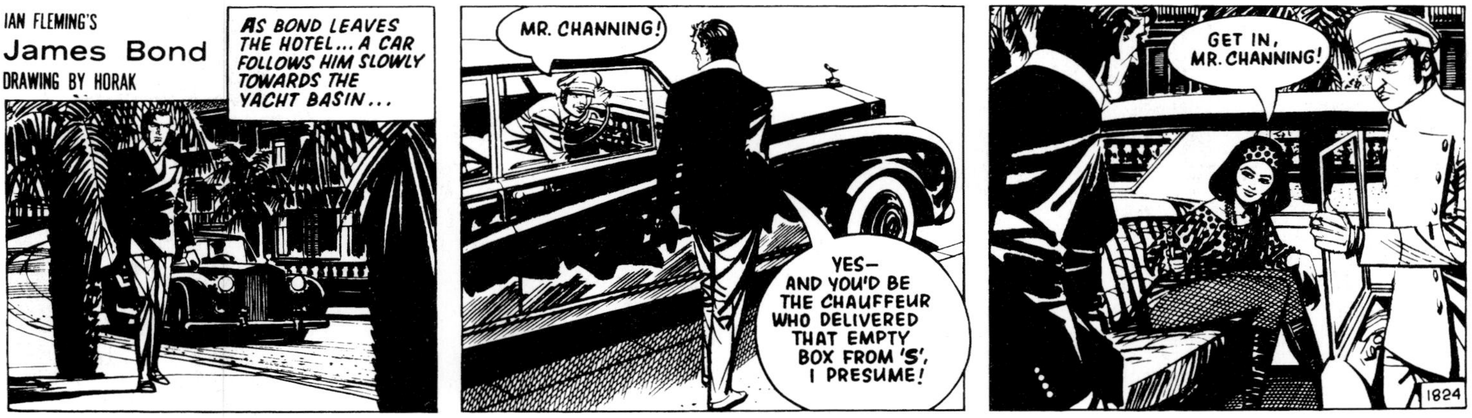
IAN FLEMING'S
James Bond
DRAWING BY HORAK
AS BOND LEAVES THE HOTEL... A CAR FOLLOWS HIM SLOWLY TOWARDS THE YACHT BASIN...
MR. CHANNING!
YES— AND YOU'D BE THE CHAUFFEUR WHO DELIVERED THAT EMPTY BOX FROM 'S', I PRESUME!
GET IN, MR. CHANNING!
1824

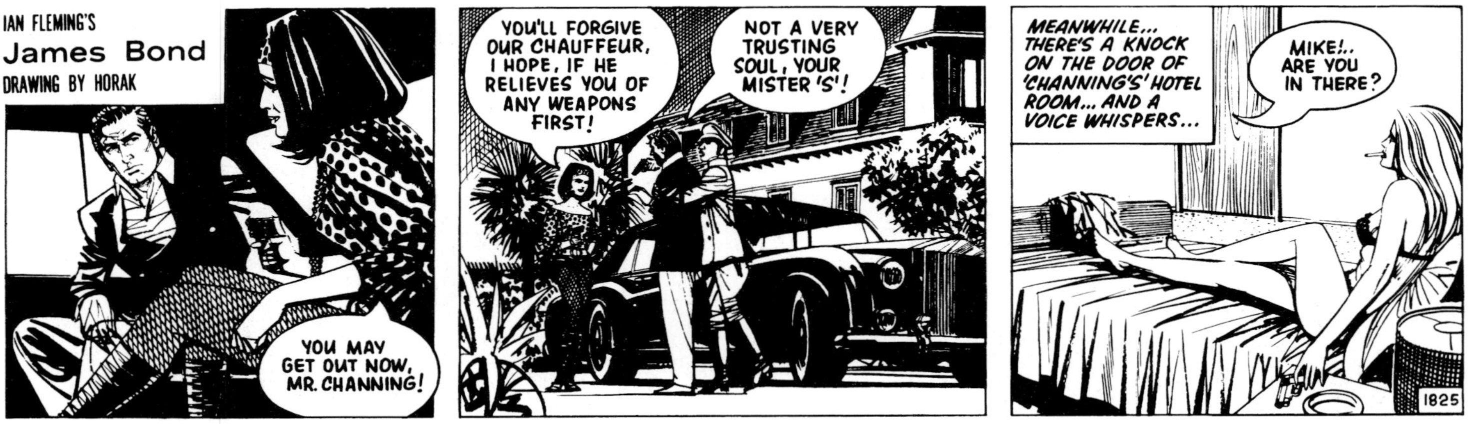
IAN FLEMING'S
James Bond
DRAWING BY HORAK
YOU MAY GET OUT NOW, MR. CHANNING!
YOU'LL FORGIVE OUR CHAUFFEUR, I HOPE, IF HE RELIEVES YOU OF ANY WEAPONS FIRST!
NOT A VERY TRUSTING SOUL, YOUR MISTER 'S'!
MEANWHILE... THERE'S A KNOCK ON THE DOOR OF 'CHANNING'S' HOTEL ROOM... AND A VOICE WHISPERS...
MIKE!.. ARE YOU IN THERE?
1825

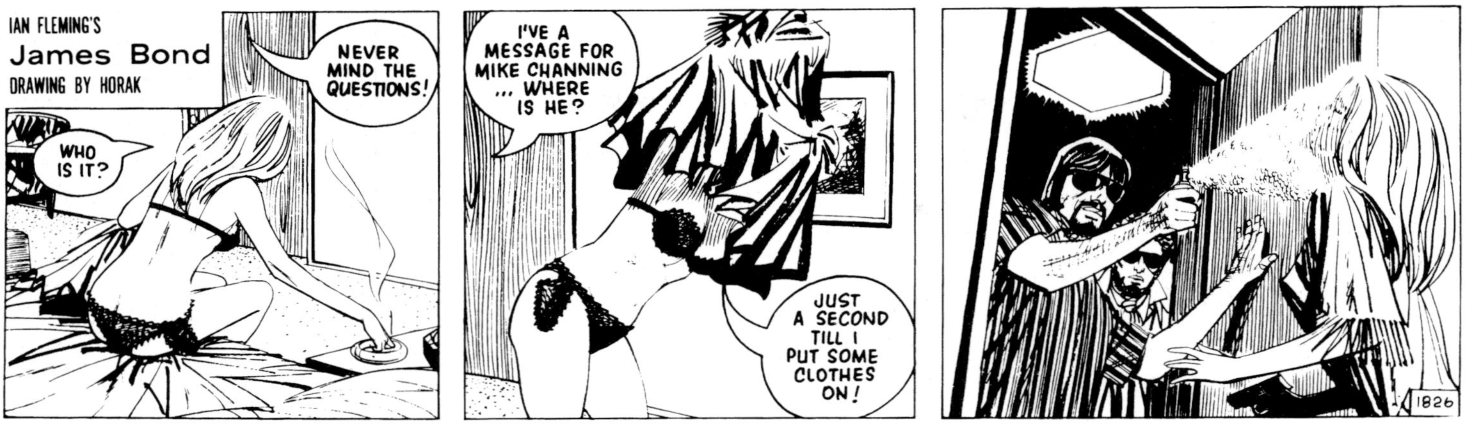

IAN FLEMING'S
James Bond
DRAWING BY HORAK
WHO IS IT?
NEVER MIND THE QUESTIONS!
I'VE A MESSAGE FOR MIKE CHANNING ... WHERE IS HE?
JUST A SECOND TILL I PUT SOME CLOTHES ON!
1826

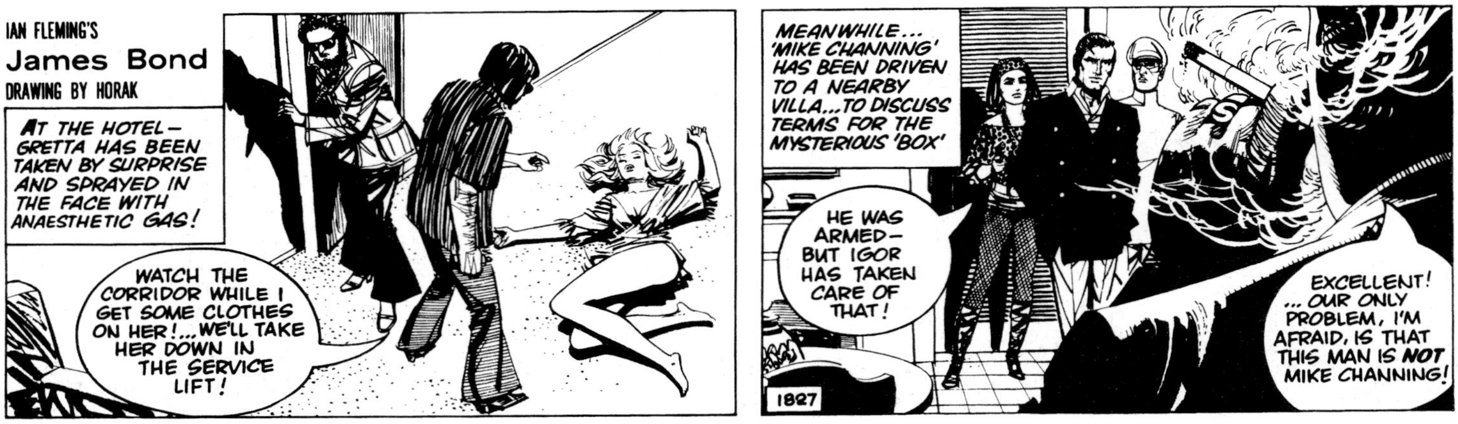

IAN FLEMING'S
James Bond
DRAWING BY HORAK
AT THE HOTEL—GRETTA HAS BEEN TAKEN BY SURPRISE AND SPRAYED IN THE FACE WITH ANAESTHETIC GAS!
WATCH THE CORRIDOR WHILE I GET SOME CLOTHES ON HER!... WE'LL TAKE HER DOWN IN THE SERVICE LIFT!
MEANWHILE... 'MIKE CHANNING' HAS BEEN DRIVEN TO A NEARBY VILLA... TO DISCUSS TERMS FOR THE MYSTERIOUS 'BOX'
HE WAS ARMED—BUT IGOR HAS TAKEN CARE OF THAT!
EXCELLENT! ... OUR ONLY PROBLEM, I'M AFRAID, IS THAT THIS MAN IS NOT MIKE CHANNING!
1827

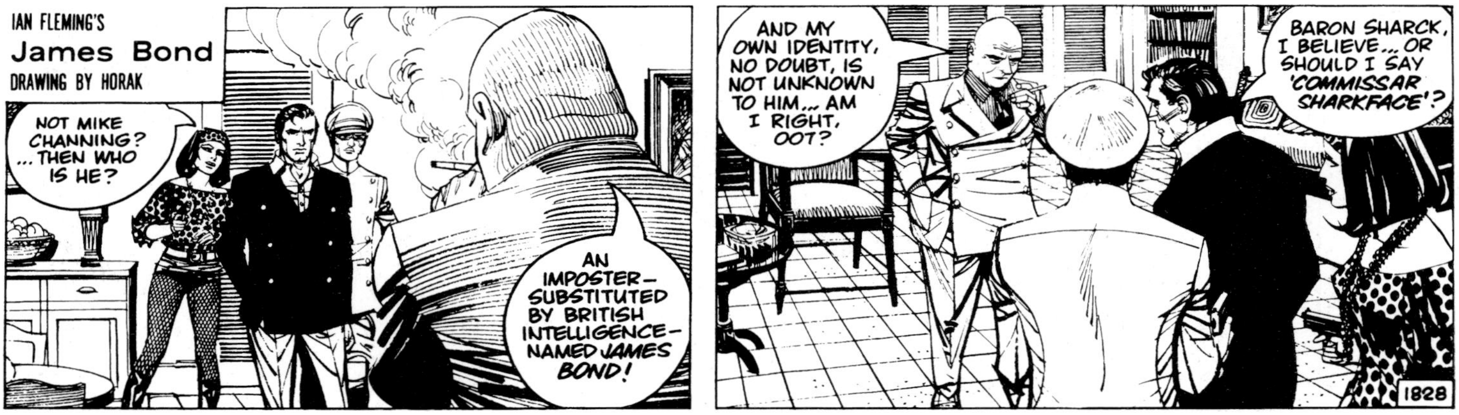

IAN FLEMING'S
James Bond
DRAWING BY HORAK
NOT MIKE CHANNING? ... THEN WHO IS HE?
AN IMPOSTER—SUBSTITUTED BY BRITISH INTELLIGENCE—NAMED JAMES BOND!
AND MY OWN IDENTITY, NO DOUBT, IS NOT UNKNOWN TO HIM... AM I RIGHT, OOT?
BARON SHARCK, I BELIEVE... OR SHOULD I SAY 'COMMISSAR SHARKFACE'?
1828

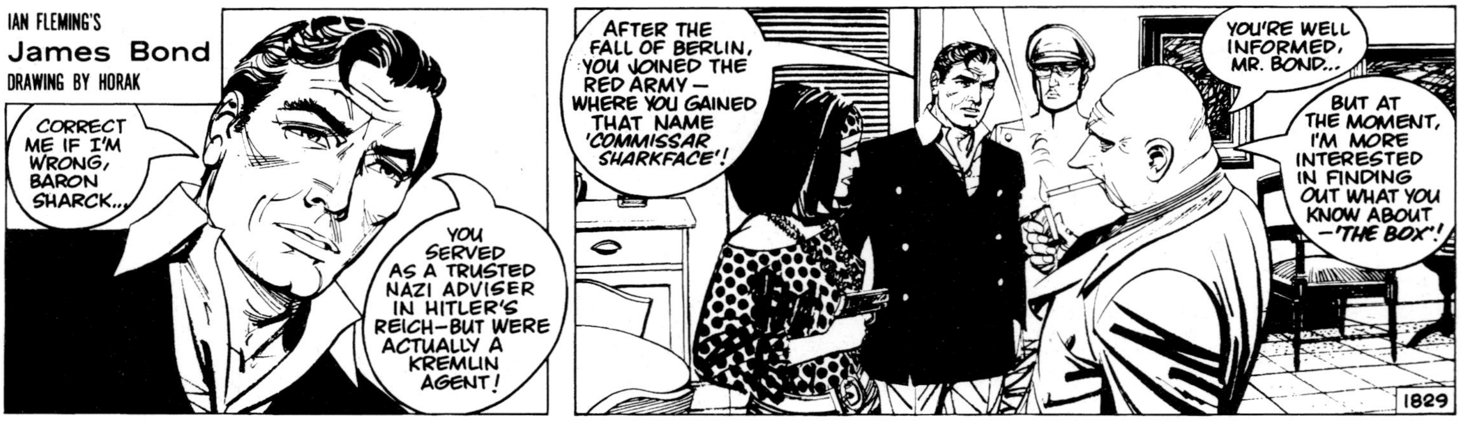

IAN FLEMING'S
James Bond
DRAWING BY HORAK
CORRECT ME IF I'M WRONG, BARON SHARCK...
YOU SERVED AS A TRUSTED NAZI ADVISER IN HITLER'S REICH—BUT WERE ACTUALLY A KREMLIN AGENT!
AFTER THE FALL OF BERLIN, YOU JOINED THE RED ARMY—WHERE YOU GAINED THAT NAME 'COMMISSAR SHARKFACE'!
YOU'RE WELL INFORMED, MR. BOND...
BUT AT THE MOMENT, I'M MORE INTERESTED IN FINDING OUT WHAT YOU KNOW ABOUT—'THE BOX'!
1829

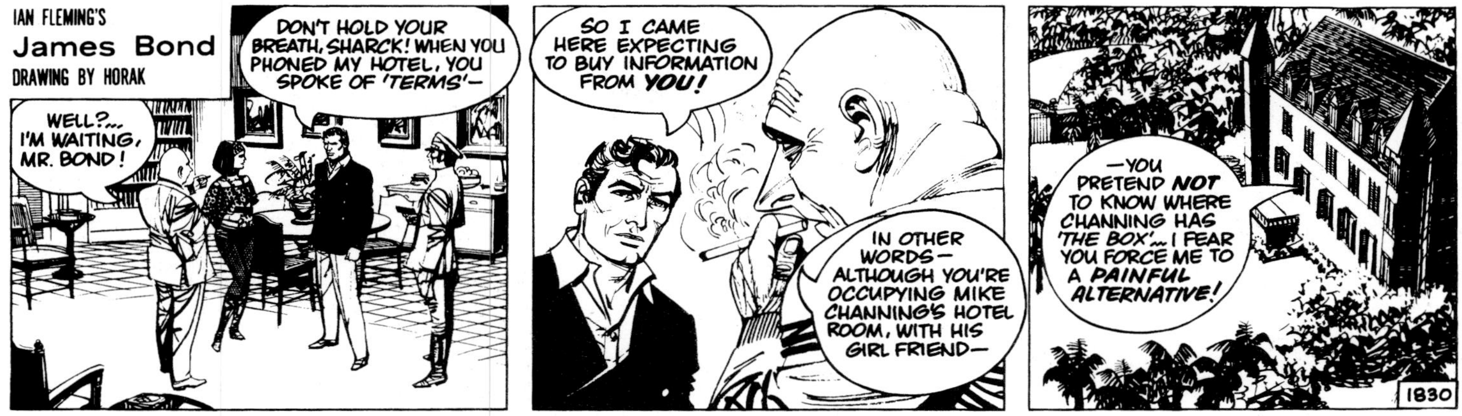
IAN FLEMING'S
James Bond
DRAWING BY HORAK
WELL?... I'M WAITING, MR. BOND!
DON'T HOLD YOUR BREATH, SHARCK! WHEN YOU PHONED MY HOTEL, YOU SPOKE OF 'TERMS'—
SO I CAME HERE EXPECTING TO BUY INFORMATION FROM YOU!
IN OTHER WORDS— ALTHOUGH YOU'RE OCCUPYING MIKE CHANNING'S HOTEL ROOM, WITH HIS GIRL FRIEND—
—YOU PRETEND NOT TO KNOW WHERE CHANNING HAS 'THE BOX'... I FEAR YOU FORCE ME TO A PAINFUL ALTERNATIVE!
1830

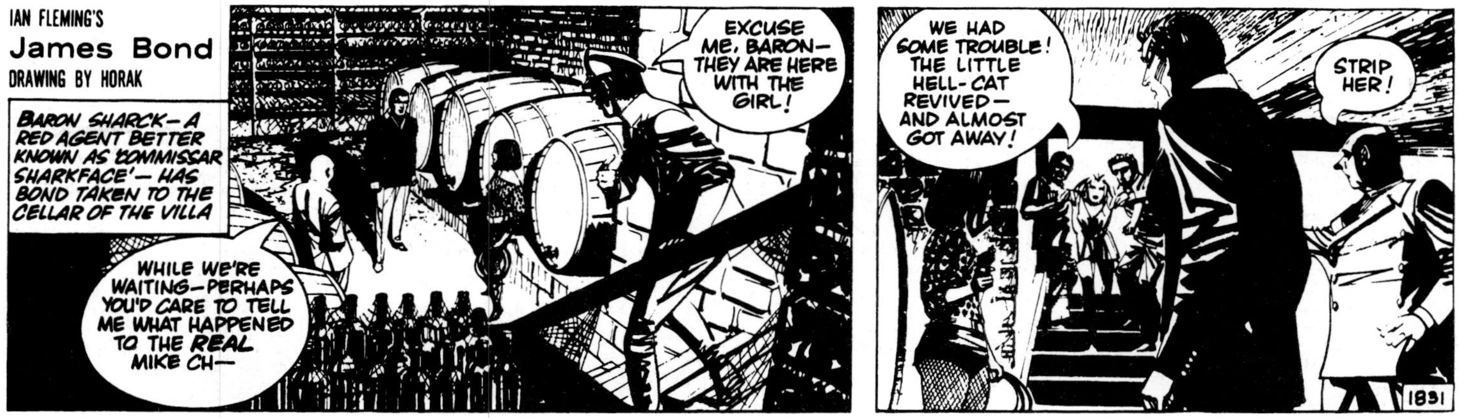
IAN FLEMING'S
James Bond
DRAWING BY HORAK
BARON SHARCK—A RED AGENT BETTER KNOWN AS 'COMMISSAR SHARKFACE'—HAS BOND TAKEN TO THE CELLAR OF THE VILLA
WHILE WE'RE WAITING—PERHAPS YOU'D CARE TO TELL ME WHAT HAPPENED TO THE REAL MIKE CH—
EXCUSE ME, BARON— THEY ARE HERE WITH THE GIRL!
WE HAD SOME TROUBLE! THE LITTLE HELL-CAT REVIVED— AND ALMOST GOT AWAY!
STRIP HER!
1831

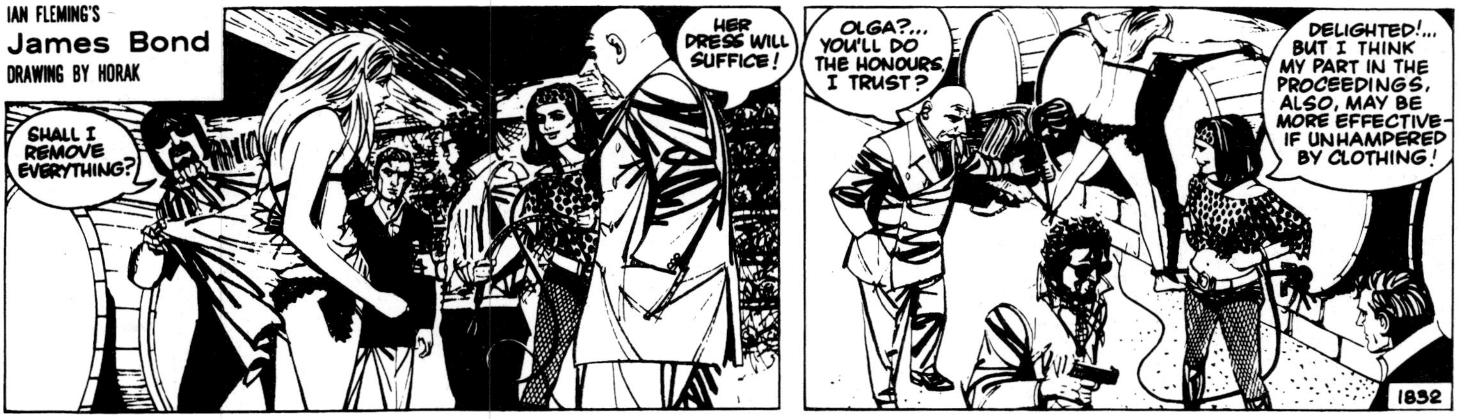
IAN FLEMING'S
James Bond
DRAWING BY HORAK
SHALL I REMOVE EVERYTHING?
HER DRESS WILL SUFFICE!
OLGA?... YOU'LL DO THE HONOURS, I TRUST?
DELIGHTED!... BUT I THINK MY PART IN THE PROCEEDINGS, ALSO, MAY BE MORE EFFECTIVE— IF UNHAMPERED BY CLOTHING!
1832

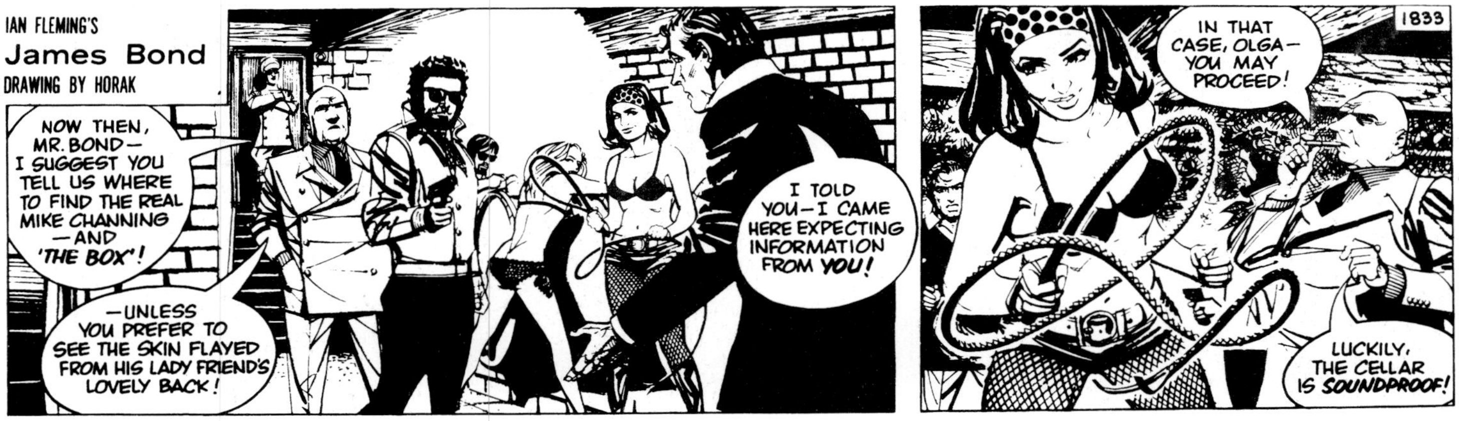
IAN FLEMING'S
James Bond
DRAWING BY HORAK
NOW THEN, MR. BOND— I SUGGEST YOU TELL US WHERE TO FIND THE REAL MIKE CHANNING —AND 'THE BOX'!
—UNLESS YOU PREFER TO SEE THE SKIN FLAYED FROM HIS LADY FRIEND'S LOVELY BACK!
I TOLD YOU—I CAME HERE EXPECTING INFORMATION FROM YOU!
1833
IN THAT CASE, OLGA— YOU MAY PROCEED!
LUCKILY, THE CELLAR IS SOUNDPROOF!

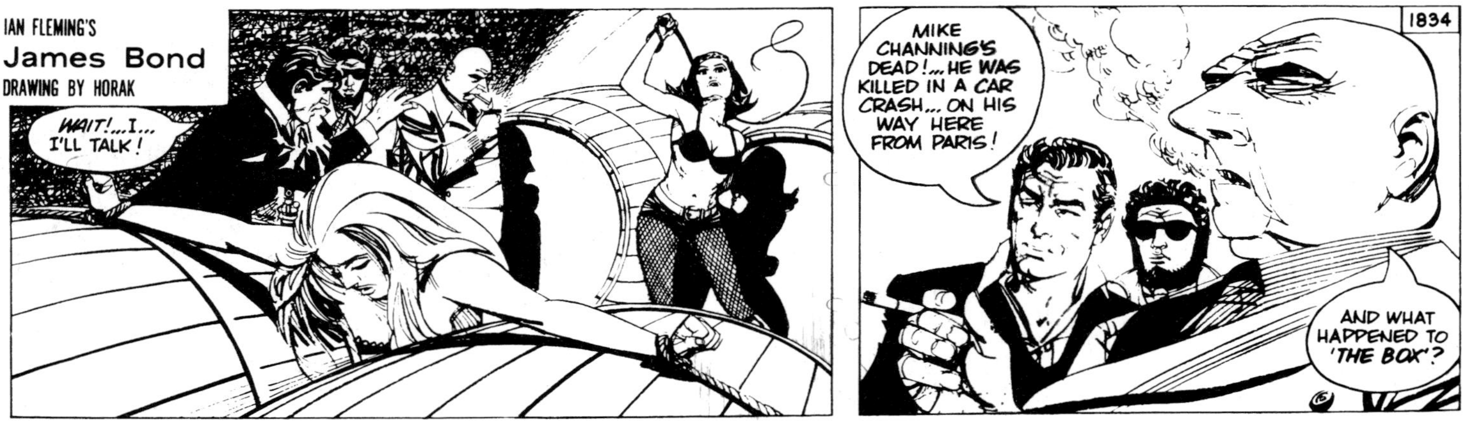
IAN FLEMING'S
James Bond
DRAWING BY HORAK
WAIT!... I... I'LL TALK!
1834
MIKE CHANNING'S DEAD!... HE WAS KILLED IN A CAR CRASH... ON HIS WAY HERE FROM PARIS!
AND WHAT HAPPENED TO 'THE BOX'?

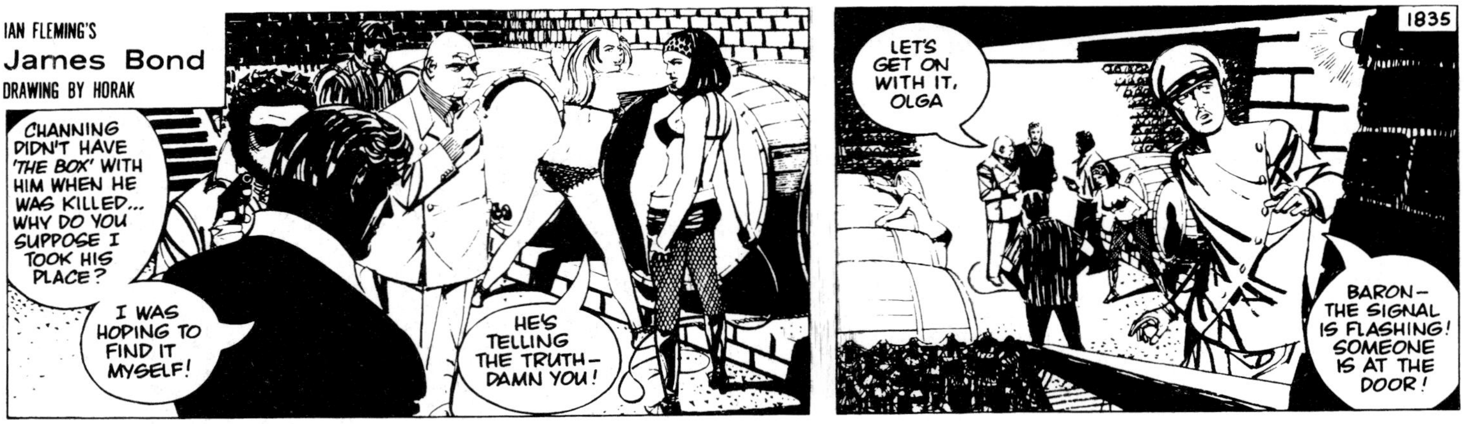
IAN FLEMING'S
James Bond
DRAWING BY HORAK
CHANNING DIDN'T HAVE 'THE BOX' WITH HIM WHEN HE WAS KILLED... WHY DO YOU SUPPOSE I TOOK HIS PLACE?
I WAS HOPING TO FIND IT MYSELF!
HE'S TELLING THE TRUTH - DAMN YOU!
1835
LET'S GET ON WITH IT, OLGA
BARON - THE SIGNAL IS FLASHING! SOMEONE IS AT THE DOOR!

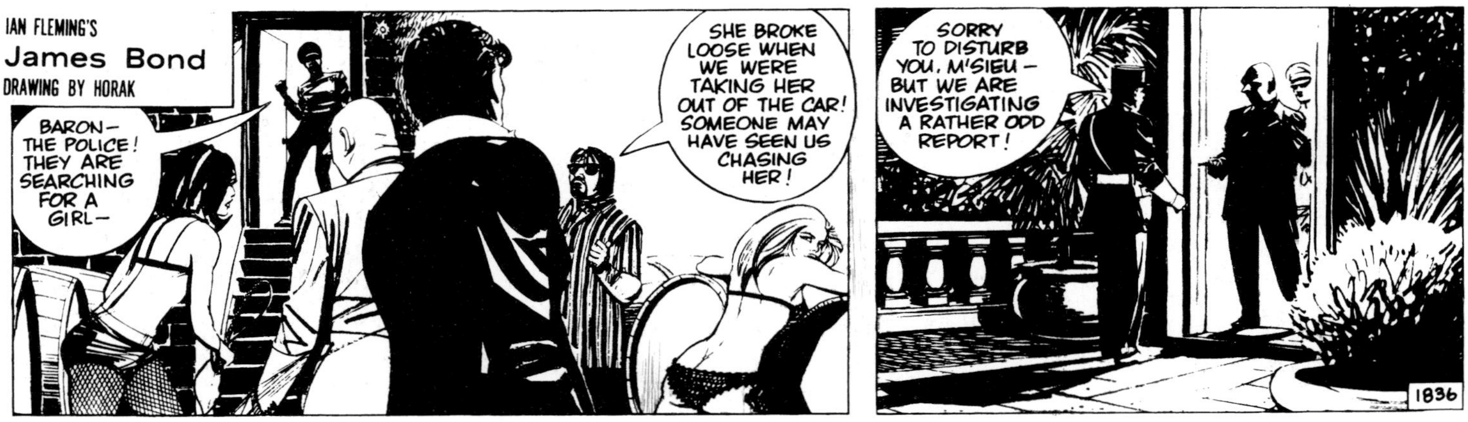
IAN FLEMING'S
James Bond
DRAWING BY HORAK
BARON - THE POLICE! THEY ARE SEARCHING FOR A GIRL -
SHE BROKE LOOSE WHEN WE WERE TAKING HER OUT OF THE CAR! SOMEONE MAY HAVE SEEN US CHASING HER!
SORRY TO DISTURB YOU, M'SIEU - BUT WE ARE INVESTIGATING A RATHER ODD REPORT!
1836

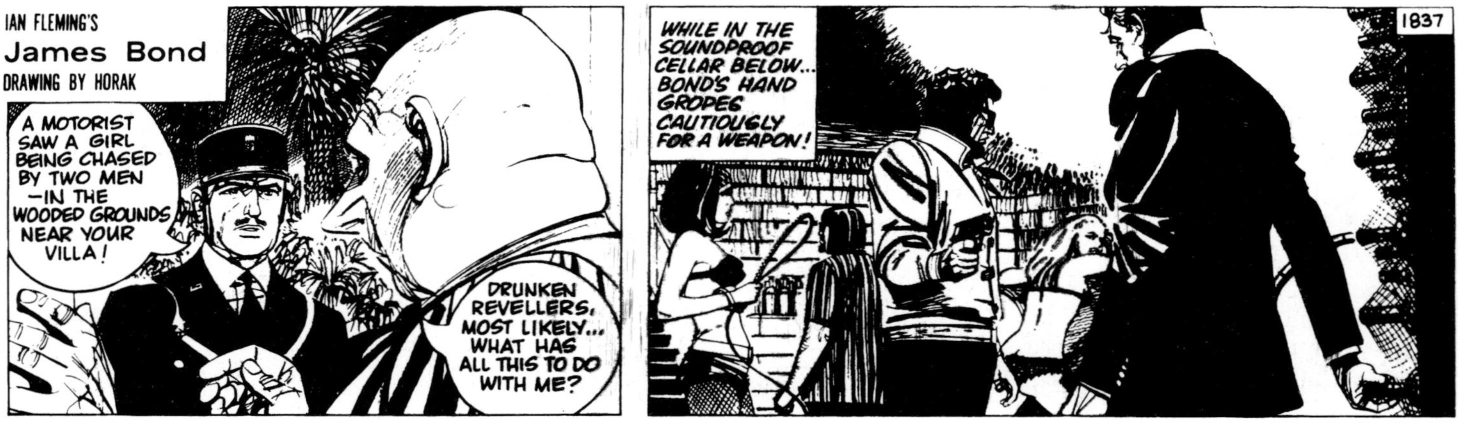
IAN FLEMING'S
James Bond
DRAWING BY HORAK
A MOTORIST SAW A GIRL BEING CHASED BY TWO MEN - IN THE WOODED GROUNDS NEAR YOUR VILLA!
DRUNKEN REVELLERS, MOST LIKELY... WHAT HAS ALL THIS TO DO WITH ME?
1837
WHILE IN THE SOUNDPROOF CELLAR BELOW... BOND'S HAND GROPES CAUTIOUSLY FOR A WEAPON!

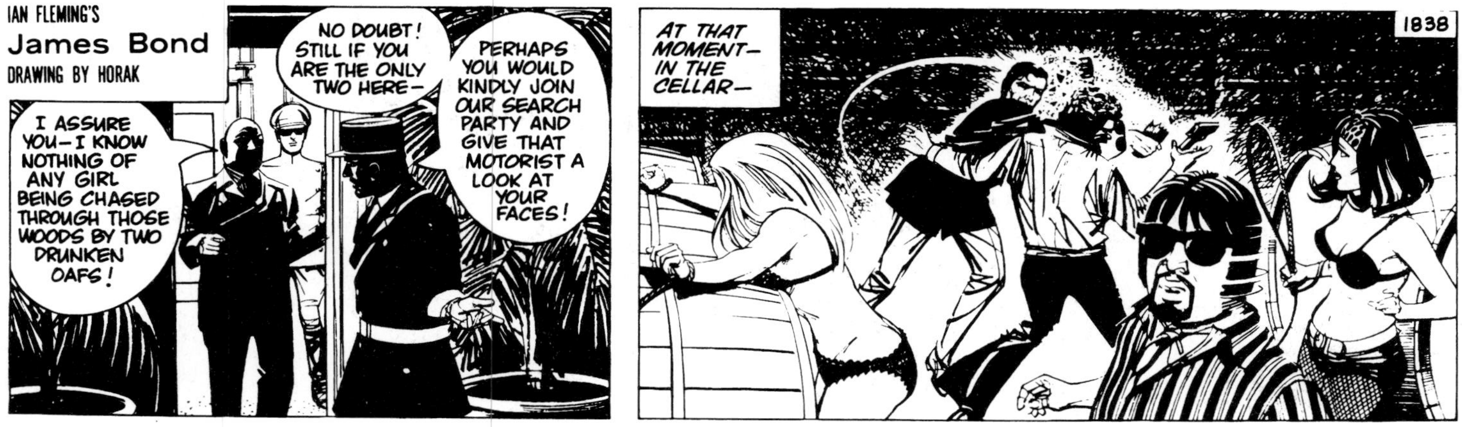

IAN FLEMING'S
James Bond
DRAWING BY HORAK
I ASSURE YOU—I KNOW NOTHING OF ANY GIRL BEING CHASED THROUGH THOSE WOODS BY TWO DRUNKEN OAFS!
NO DOUBT! STILL IF YOU ARE THE ONLY TWO HERE—
PERHAPS YOU WOULD KINDLY JOIN OUR SEARCH PARTY AND GIVE THAT MOTORIST A LOOK AT YOUR FACES!
AT THAT MOMENT—IN THE CELLAR—
1838

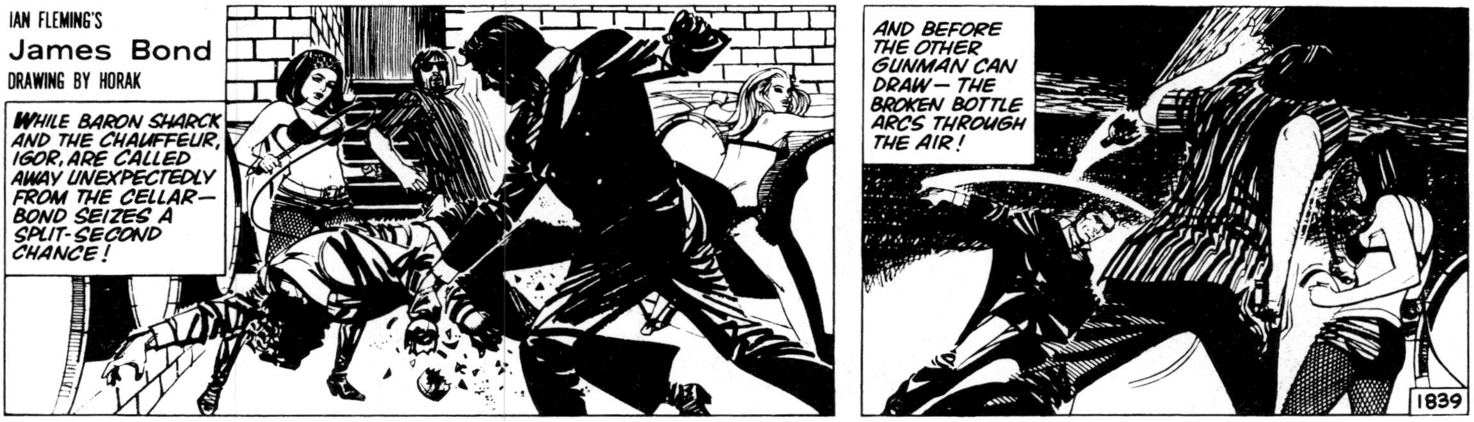

IAN FLEMING'S
James Bond
DRAWING BY HORAK
WHILE BARON SHARCK AND THE CHAUFFEUR, IGOR, ARE CALLED AWAY UNEXPECTEDLY FROM THE CELLAR—BOND SEIZES A SPLIT-SECOND CHANCE!
AND BEFORE THE OTHER GUNMAN CAN DRAW—THE BROKEN BOTTLE ARCS THROUGH THE AIR!
1839

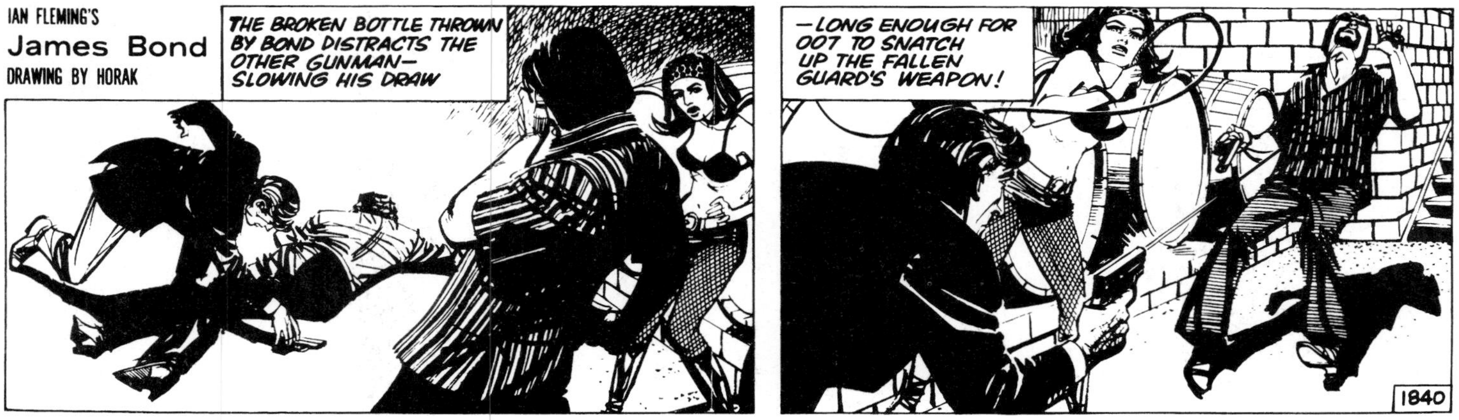

IAN FLEMING'S
James Bond
DRAWING BY HORAK
THE BROKEN BOTTLE THROWN BY BOND DISTRACTS THE OTHER GUNMAN—SLOWING HIS DRAW
—LONG ENOUGH FOR 007 TO SNATCH UP THE FALLEN GUARD'S WEAPON!
1840

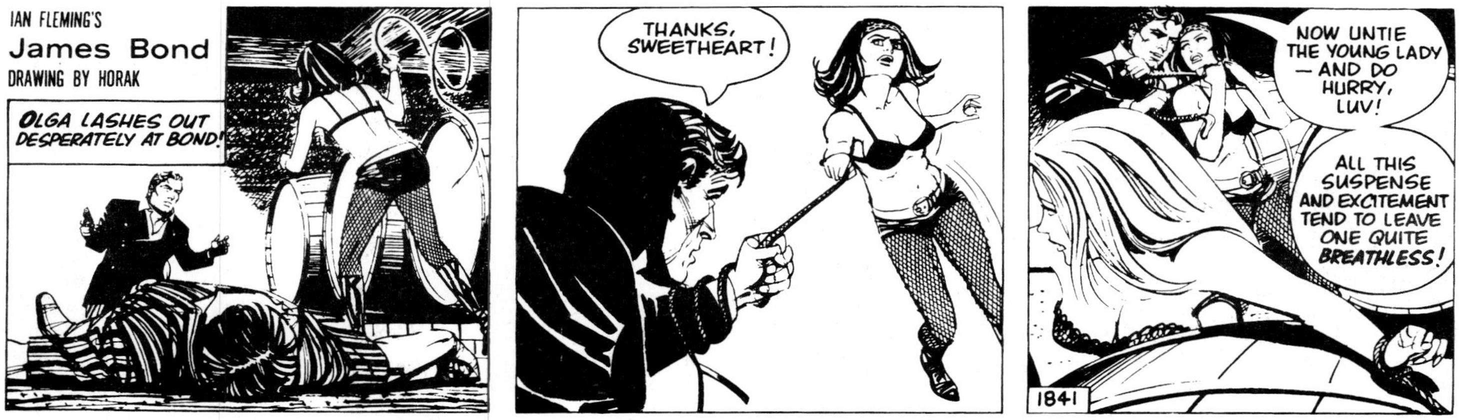

IAN FLEMING'S
James Bond
DRAWING BY HORAK
OLGA LASHES OUT DESPERATELY AT BOND!
THANKS, SWEETHEART!
NOW UNTIE THE YOUNG LADY—AND DO HURRY, LUV!
ALL THIS SUSPENSE AND EXCITEMENT TEND TO LEAVE ONE QUITE BREATHLESS!
1841

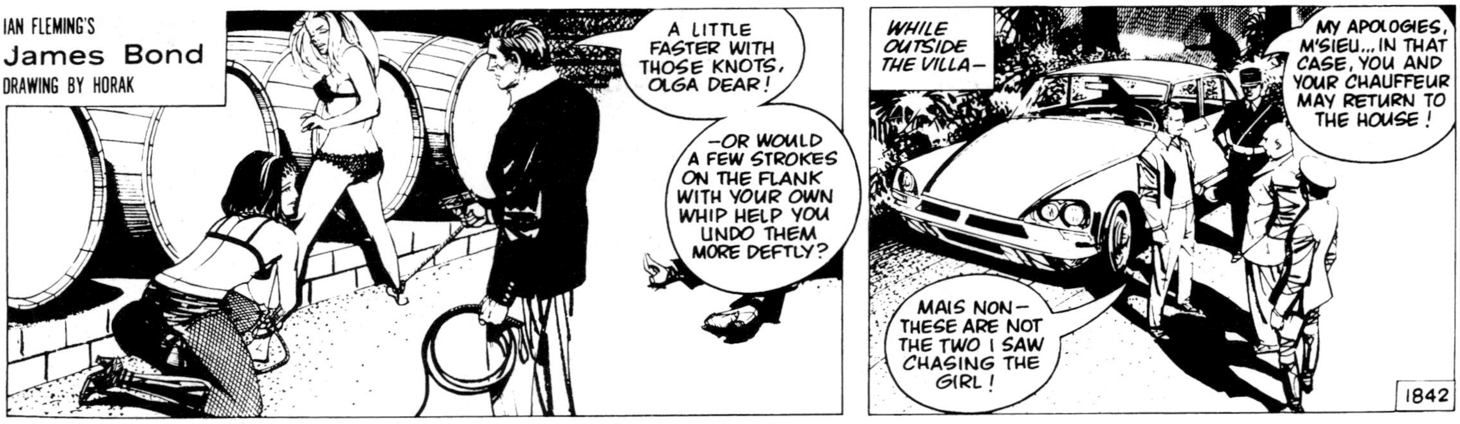
IAN FLEMING'S
James Bond
DRAWING BY HORAK
A LITTLE FASTER WITH THOSE KNOTS, OLGA DEAR!
—OR WOULD A FEW STROKES ON THE FLANK WITH YOUR OWN WHIP HELP YOU UNDO THEM MORE DEFTLY?
WHILE OUTSIDE THE VILLA—
MAIS NON— THESE ARE NOT THE TWO I SAW CHASING THE GIRL!
MY APOLOGIES, M'SIEU... IN THAT CASE, YOU AND YOUR CHAUFFEUR MAY RETURN TO THE HOUSE!
1842

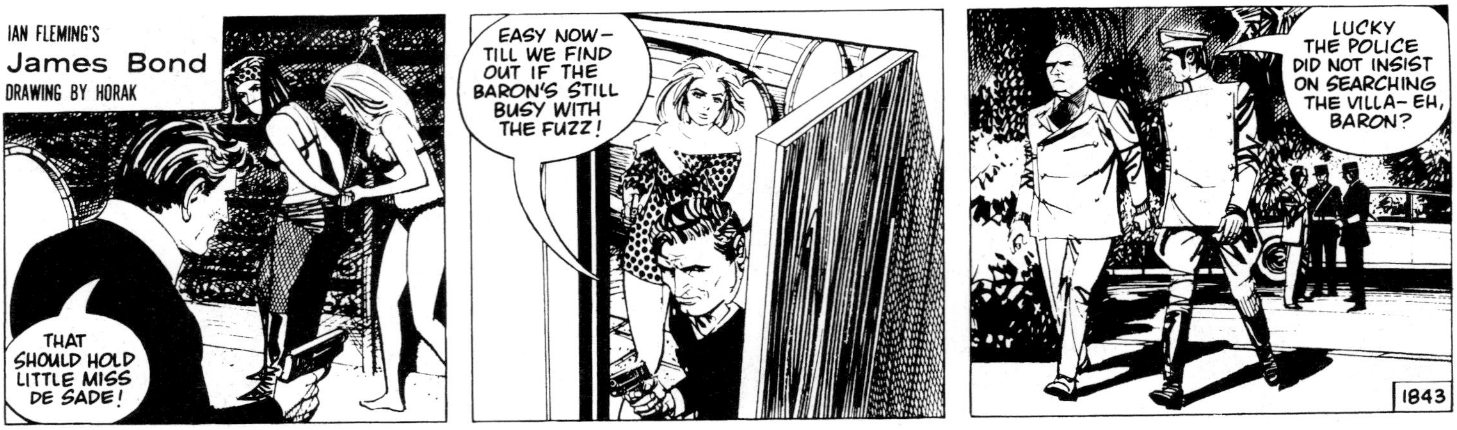
IAN FLEMING'S
James Bond
DRAWING BY HORAK
THAT SHOULD HOLD LITTLE MISS DE SADE!
EASY NOW— TILL WE FIND OUT IF THE BARON'S STILL BUSY WITH THE FUZZ!
LUCKY THE POLICE DID NOT INSIST ON SEARCHING THE VILLA— EH, BARON?
1843

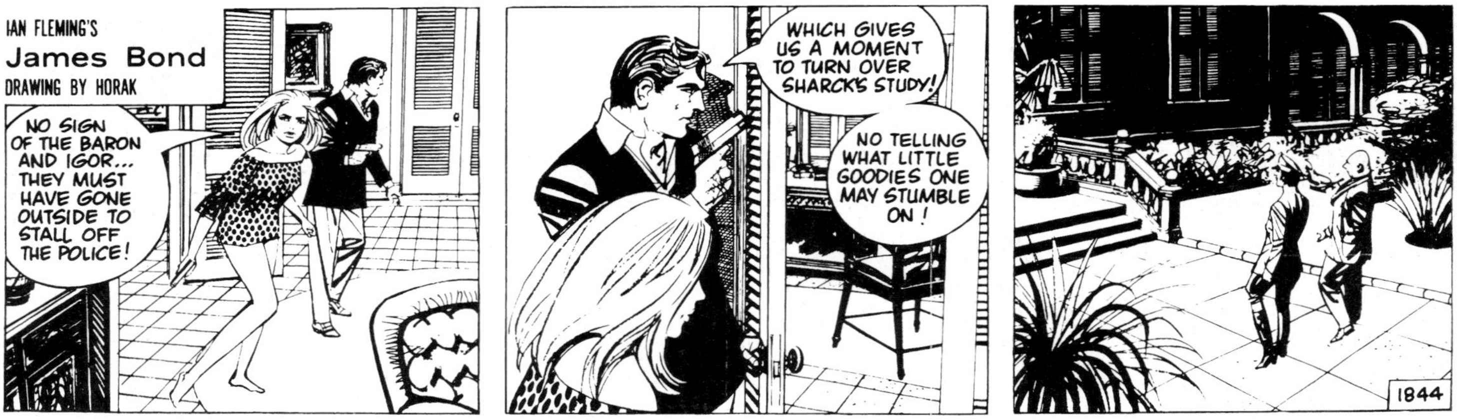
IAN FLEMING'S
James Bond
DRAWING BY HORAK
NO SIGN OF THE BARON AND IGOR... THEY MUST HAVE GONE OUTSIDE TO STALL OFF THE POLICE!
WHICH GIVES US A MOMENT TO TURN OVER SHARCK'S STUDY!
NO TELLING WHAT LITTLE GOODIES ONE MAY STUMBLE ON!
1844

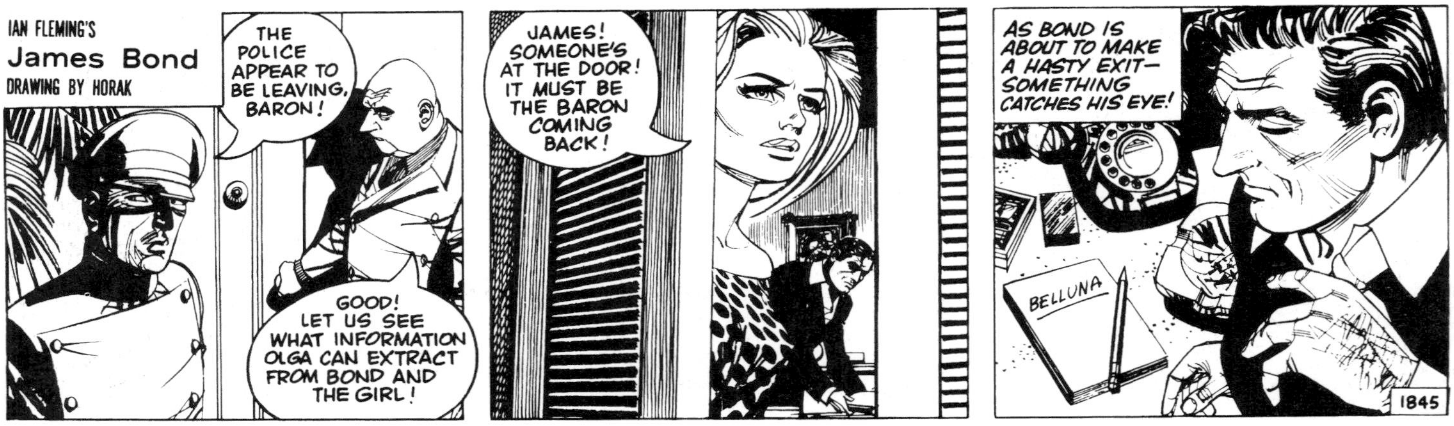
IAN FLEMING'S
James Bond
DRAWING BY HORAK
THE POLICE APPEAR TO BE LEAVING, BARON!
GOOD! LET US SEE WHAT INFORMATION OLGA CAN EXTRACT FROM BOND AND THE GIRL!
JAMES! SOMEONE'S AT THE DOOR! IT MUST BE THE BARON COMING BACK!
AS BOND IS ABOUT TO MAKE A HASTY EXIT— SOMETHING CATCHES HIS EYE!
BELLUNA
1845

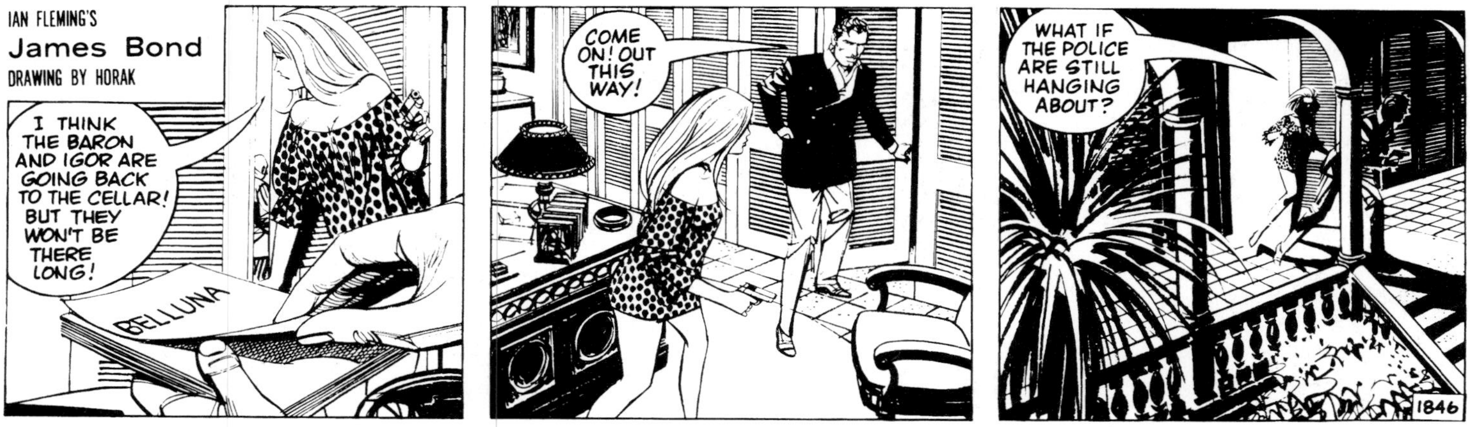
IAN FLEMING'S
James Bond
DRAWING BY HORAK
I THINK THE BARON AND IGOR ARE GOING BACK TO THE CELLAR! BUT THEY WON'T BE THERE LONG!
BELLUNA
COME ON! OUT THIS WAY!
WHAT IF THE POLICE ARE STILL HANGING ABOUT?
1846

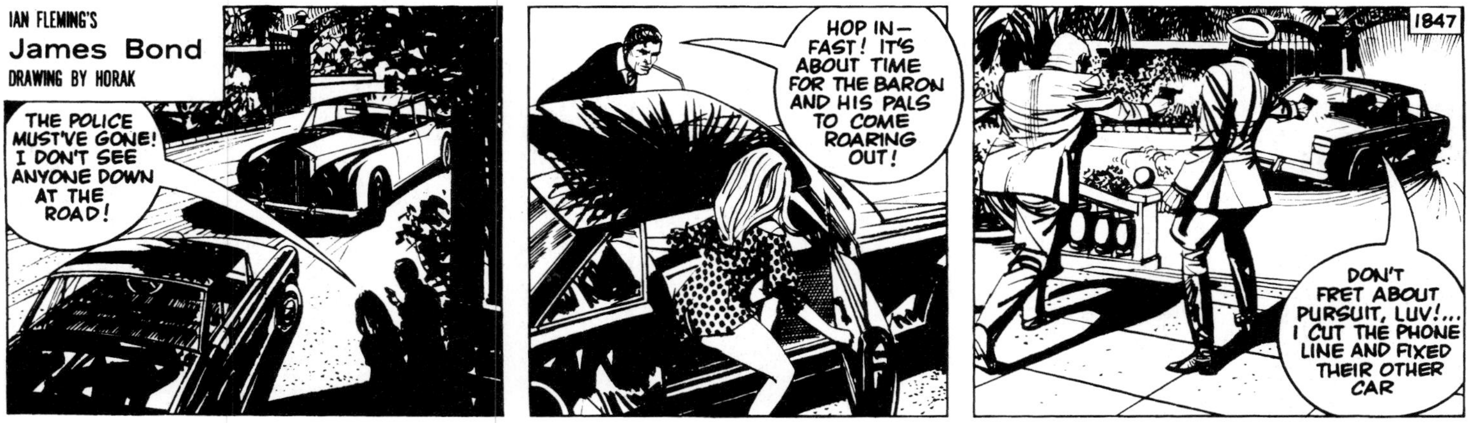
IAN FLEMING'S
James Bond
DRAWING BY HORAK
THE POLICE MUST'VE GONE! I DON'T SEE ANYONE DOWN AT THE ROAD!
HOP IN—FAST! IT'S ABOUT TIME FOR THE BARON AND HIS PALS TO COME ROARING OUT!
1847
DON'T FRET ABOUT PURSUIT, LUV!... I CUT THE PHONE LINE AND FIXED THEIR OTHER CAR

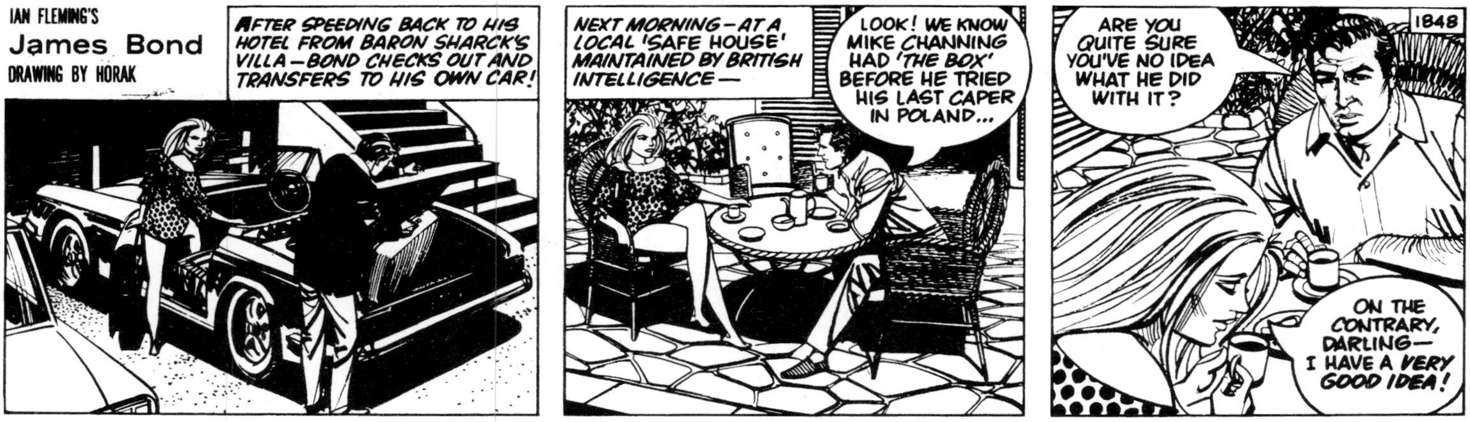
IAN FLEMING'S
James Bond
DRAWING BY HORAK
AFTER SPEEDING BACK TO HIS HOTEL FROM BARON SHARCK'S VILLA—BOND CHECKS OUT AND TRANSFERS TO HIS OWN CAR!
NEXT MORNING—AT A LOCAL 'SAFE HOUSE' MAINTAINED BY BRITISH INTELLIGENCE—
LOOK! WE KNOW MIKE CHANNING HAD 'THE BOX' BEFORE HE TRIED HIS LAST CAPER IN POLAND...
1848
ARE YOU QUITE SURE YOU'VE NO IDEA WHAT HE DID WITH IT?
ON THE CONTRARY, DARLING—I HAVE A VERY GOOD IDEA!

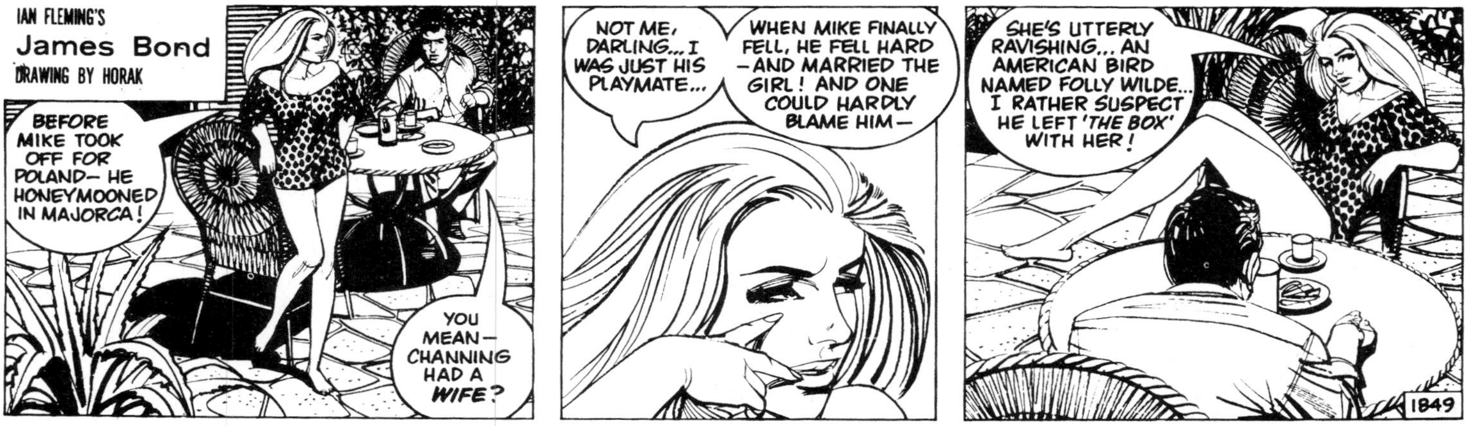
IAN FLEMING'S
James Bond
DRAWING BY HORAK
BEFORE MIKE TOOK OFF FOR POLAND—HE HONEYMOONED IN MAJORCA!
YOU MEAN—CHANNING HAD A WIFE?
NOT ME, DARLING... I WAS JUST HIS PLAYMATE...
WHEN MIKE FINALLY FELL, HE FELL HARD—AND MARRIED THE GIRL! AND ONE COULD HARDLY BLAME HIM—
SHE'S UTTERLY RAVISHING... AN AMERICAN BIRD NAMED FOLLY WILDE... I RATHER SUSPECT HE LEFT 'THE BOX' WITH HER!
1849

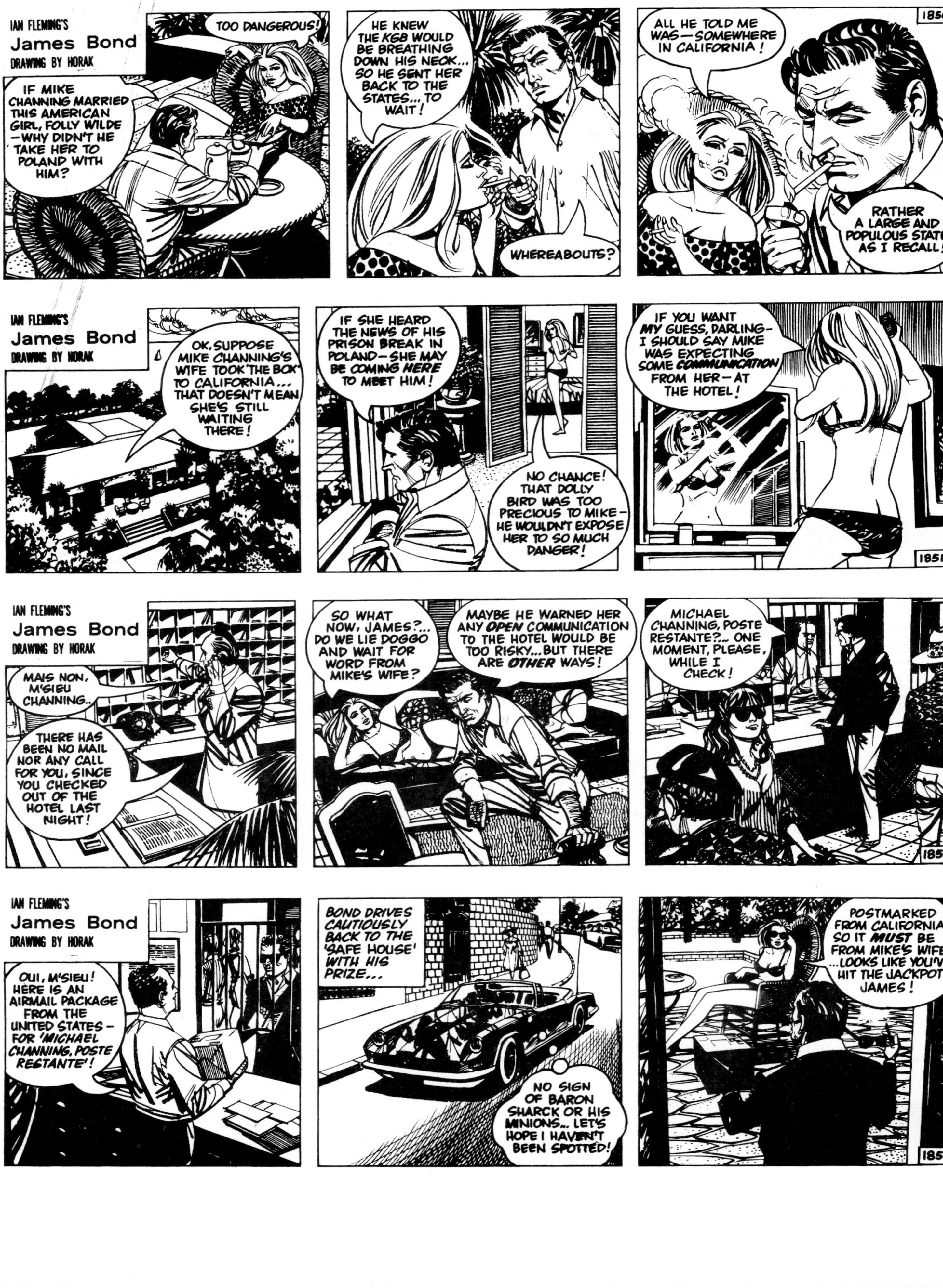
IAN FLEMING'S
James Bond
DRAWING BY HORAK
TOO DANGEROUS!
IF MIKE CHANNING MARRIED THIS AMERICAN GIRL, FOLLY WILDE —WHY DIDN'T HE TAKE HER TO POLAND WITH HIM?
HE KNEW THE KGB WOULD BE BREATHING DOWN HIS NECK... SO HE SENT HER BACK TO THE STATES... TO WAIT!
WHEREABOUTS?
1850
ALL HE TOLD ME WAS—SOMEWHERE IN CALIFORNIA!
RATHER A LARGE AND POPULOUS STATE, AS I RECALL!
IAN FLEMING'S
James Bond
DRAWING BY HORAK
OK, SUPPOSE MIKE CHANNING'S WIFE TOOK 'THE BOX' TO CALIFORNIA... THAT DOESN'T MEAN SHE'S STILL WAITING THERE!
IF SHE HEARD THE NEWS OF HIS PRISON BREAK IN POLAND—SHE MAY BE COMING HERE TO MEET HIM!
NO CHANCE! THAT DOLLY BIRD WAS TOO PRECIOUS TO MIKE—HE WOULDN'T EXPOSE HER TO SO MUCH DANGER!
IF YOU WANT MY GUESS, DARLING—I SHOULD SAY MIKE WAS EXPECTING SOME COMMUNICATION FROM HER—AT THE HOTEL!
1851
IAN FLEMING'S
James Bond
DRAWING BY HORAK
MAIS NON, M'SIEU CHANNING..
THERE HAS BEEN NO MAIL NOR ANY CALL FOR YOU, SINCE YOU CHECKED OUT OF THE HOTEL LAST NIGHT!
SO WHAT NOW, JAMES?... DO WE LIE DOGGO AND WAIT FOR WORD FROM MIKE'S WIFE?
MAYBE HE WARNED HER ANY OPEN COMMUNICATION TO THE HOTEL WOULD BE TOO RISKY... BUT THERE ARE OTHER WAYS!
MICHAEL CHANNING, POSTE RESTANTE?... ONE MOMENT, PLEASE, WHILE I CHECK!
1852
IAN FLEMING'S
James Bond
DRAWING BY HORAK
OUI, M'SIEU! HERE IS AN AIRMAIL PACKAGE FROM THE UNITED STATES—FOR 'MICHAEL CHANNING, POSTE RESTANTE'!
BOND DRIVES CAUTIOUSLY BACK TO THE 'SAFE HOUSE' WITH HIS PRIZE...
NO SIGN OF BARON SHARCK OR HIS MINIONS... LET'S HOPE I HAVEN'T BEEN SPOTTED!
POSTMARKED FROM CALIFORNIA! SO IT MUST BE FROM MIKE'S WIFE! ...LOOKS LIKE YOU'VE HIT THE JACKPOT, JAMES!
1853

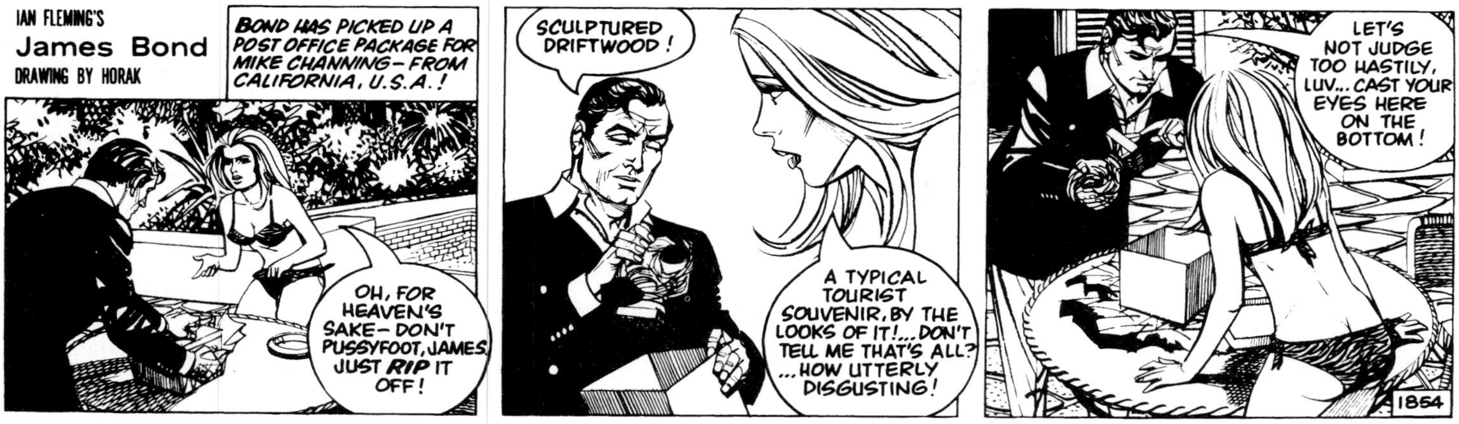
IAN FLEMING'S
James Bond
DRAWING BY HORAK
BOND HAS PICKED UP A POST OFFICE PACKAGE FOR MIKE CHANNING – FROM CALIFORNIA, U.S.A.!
OH, FOR HEAVEN'S SAKE – DON'T PUSSYFOOT, JAMES, JUST RIP IT OFF!
SCULPTURED DRIFTWOOD!
A TYPICAL TOURIST SOUVENIR, BY THE LOOKS OF IT!... DON'T TELL ME THAT'S ALL?... HOW UTTERLY DISGUSTING!
LET'S NOT JUDGE TOO HASTILY, LUV... CAST YOUR EYES HERE ON THE BOTTOM!
1854

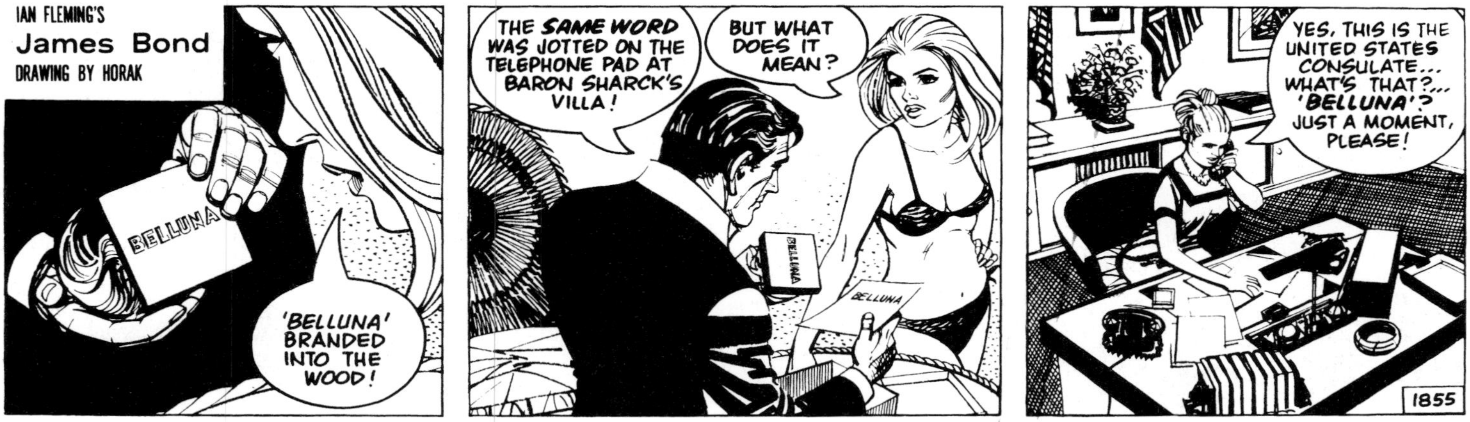
IAN FLEMING'S
James Bond
DRAWING BY HORAK
BELLUNA
'BELLUNA' BRANDED INTO THE WOOD!
THE SAME WORD WAS JOTTED ON THE TELEPHONE PAD AT BARON SHARCK'S VILLA!
BUT WHAT DOES IT MEAN?
BELLUNA
BELLUNA
YES, THIS IS THE UNITED STATES CONSULATE... WHAT'S THAT?... 'BELLUNA'? JUST A MOMENT, PLEASE!
1855

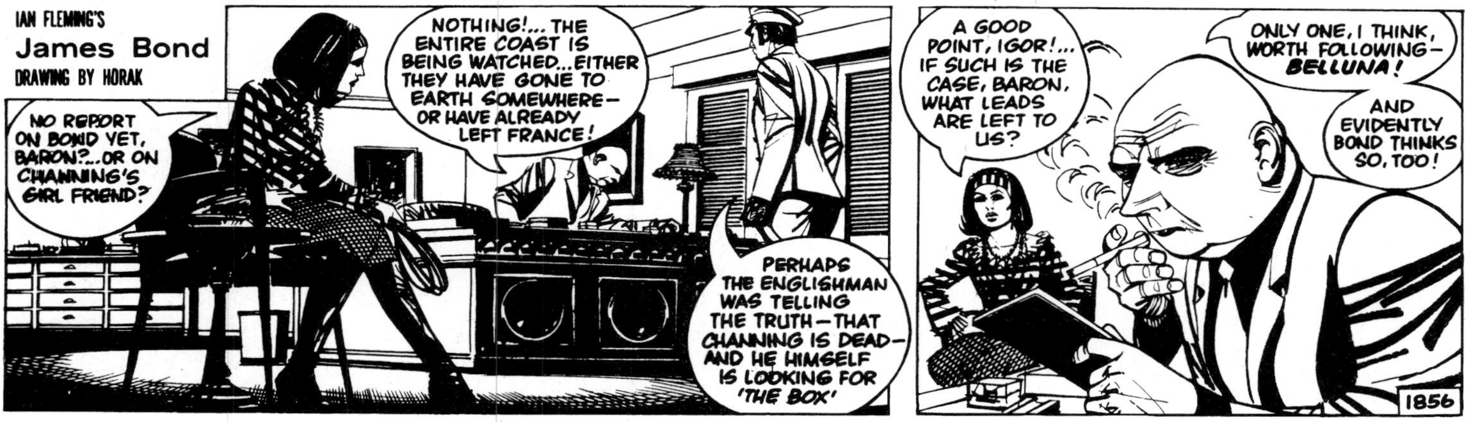
IAN FLEMING'S
James Bond
DRAWING BY HORAK
NO REPORT ON BOND YET, BARON?... OR ON CHANNING'S GIRL FRIEND?
NOTHING!... THE ENTIRE COAST IS BEING WATCHED... EITHER THEY HAVE GONE TO EARTH SOMEWHERE – OR HAVE ALREADY LEFT FRANCE!
PERHAPS THE ENGLISHMAN WAS TELLING THE TRUTH – THAT CHANNING IS DEAD – AND HE HIMSELF IS LOOKING FOR 'THE BOX'
A GOOD POINT, IGOR!... IF SUCH IS THE CASE, BARON, WHAT LEADS ARE LEFT TO US?
ONLY ONE, I THINK, WORTH FOLLOWING – BELLUNA!
AND EVIDENTLY BOND THINKS SO, TOO!
1856

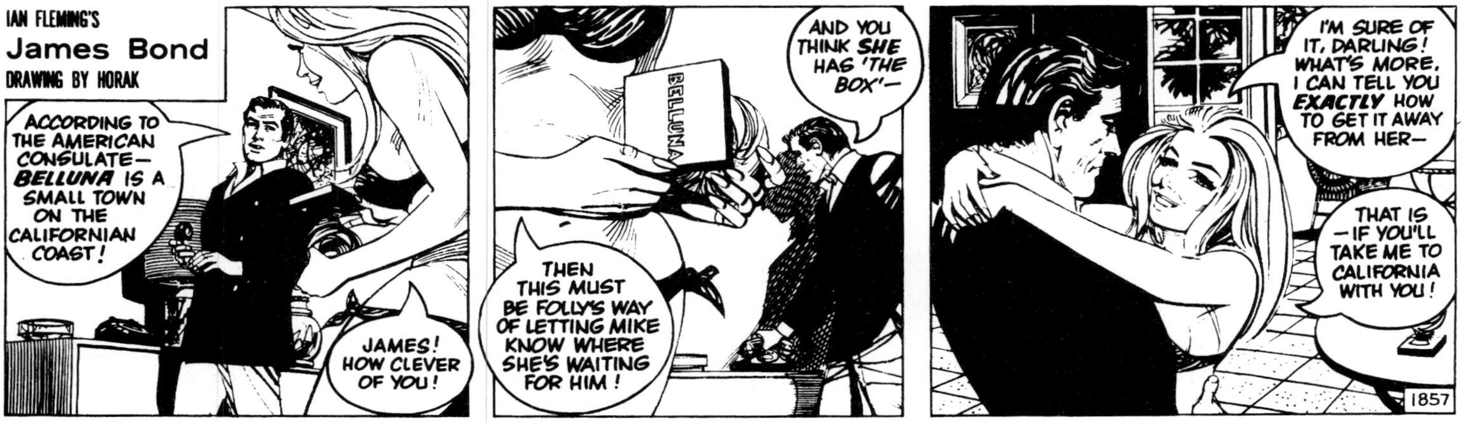
IAN FLEMING'S
James Bond
DRAWING BY HORAK
ACCORDING TO THE AMERICAN CONSULATE – BELLUNA IS A SMALL TOWN ON THE CALIFORNIAN COAST!
JAMES! HOW CLEVER OF YOU!
BELLUNA
AND YOU THINK SHE HAS 'THE BOX' –
THEN THIS MUST BE FOLLY'S WAY OF LETTING MIKE KNOW WHERE SHE'S WAITING FOR HIM!
I'M SURE OF IT, DARLING! WHAT'S MORE, I CAN TELL YOU EXACTLY HOW TO GET IT AWAY FROM HER –
THAT IS – IF YOU'LL TAKE ME TO CALIFORNIA WITH YOU!
1857

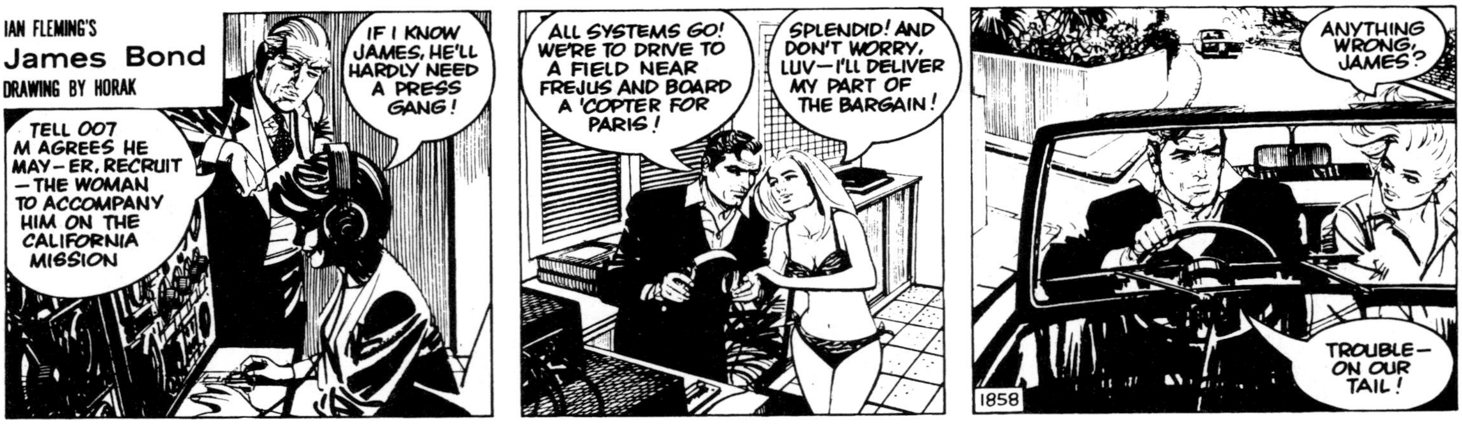
IAN FLEMING'S
James Bond
DRAWING BY HORAK
TELL 007 M AGREES HE MAY–ER, RECRUIT –THE WOMAN TO ACCOMPANY HIM ON THE CALIFORNIA MISSION
IF I KNOW JAMES, HE'LL HARDLY NEED A PRESS GANG!
ALL SYSTEMS GO! WE'RE TO DRIVE TO A FIELD NEAR FREJUS AND BOARD A 'COPTER FOR PARIS!
SPLENDID! AND DON'T WORRY, LUV–I'LL DELIVER MY PART OF THE BARGAIN!
ANYTHING WRONG, JAMES?
TROUBLE– ON OUR TAIL!
1858

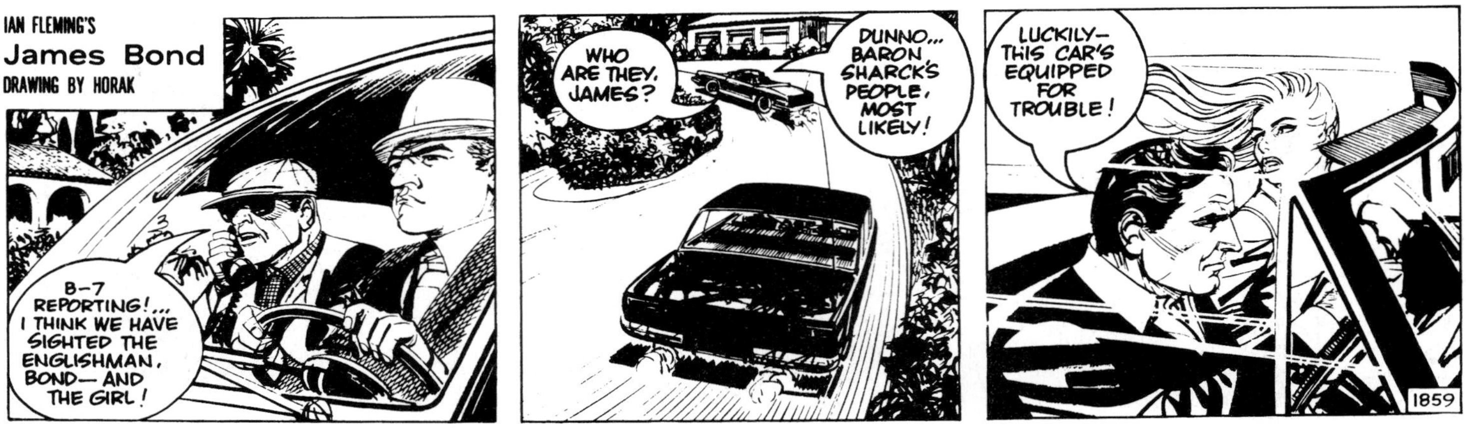
IAN FLEMING'S
James Bond
DRAWING BY HORAK
B-7 REPORTING!... I THINK WE HAVE SIGHTED THE ENGLISHMAN, BOND– AND THE GIRL!
WHO ARE THEY, JAMES?
DUNNO... BARON SHARCK'S PEOPLE, MOST LIKELY!
LUCKILY– THIS CAR'S EQUIPPED FOR TROUBLE!
1859

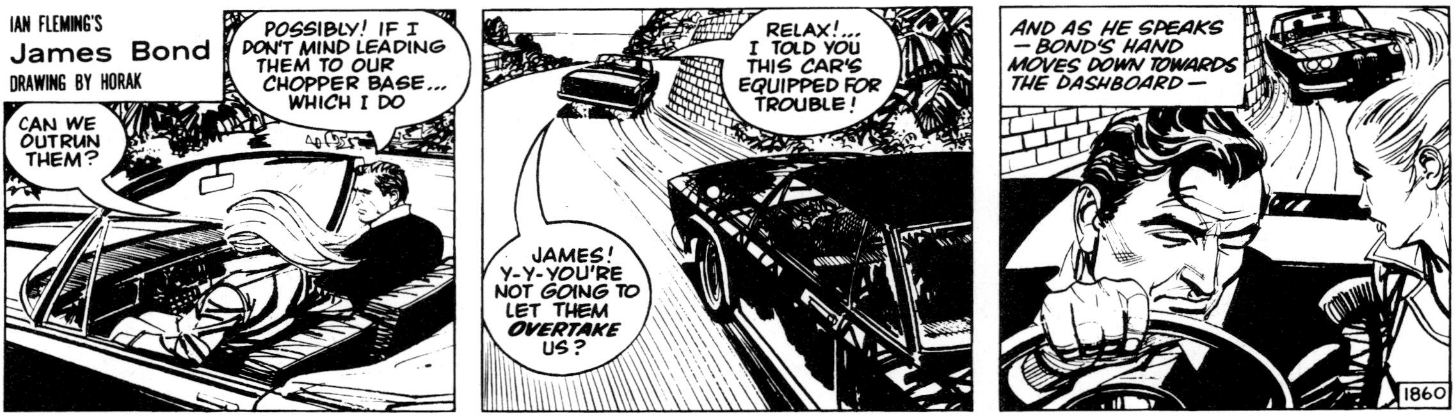
IAN FLEMING'S
James Bond
DRAWING BY HORAK
CAN WE OUTRUN THEM?
POSSIBLY! IF I DON'T MIND LEADING THEM TO OUR CHOPPER BASE... WHICH I DO
RELAX!... I TOLD YOU THIS CAR'S EQUIPPED FOR TROUBLE!
JAMES! Y-Y-YOU'RE NOT GOING TO LET THEM OVERTAKE US?
AND AS HE SPEAKS –BOND'S HAND MOVES DOWN TOWARDS THE DASHBOARD–
1860

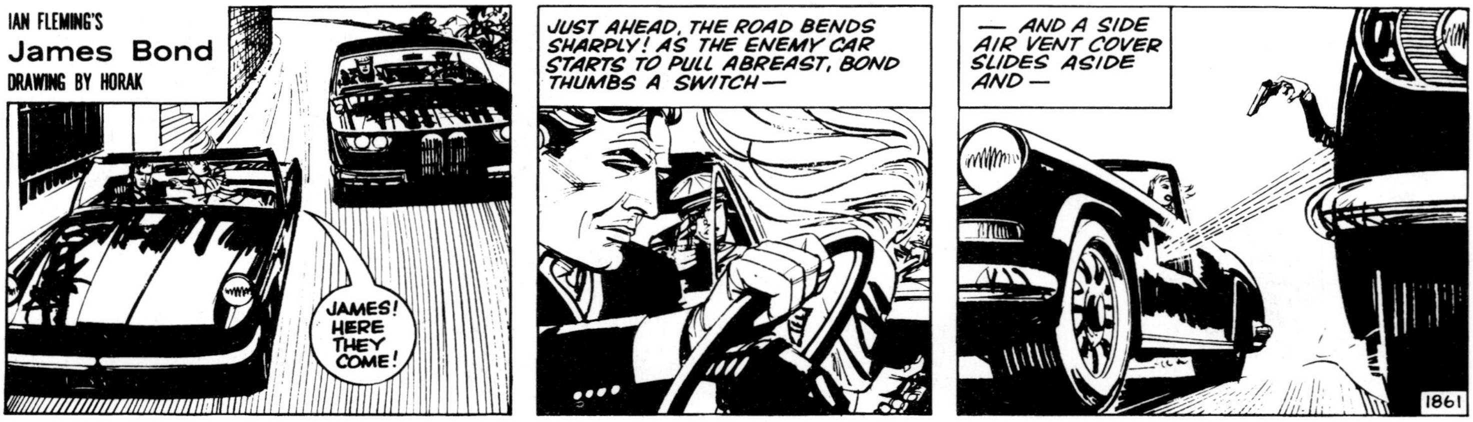
IAN FLEMING'S
James Bond
DRAWING BY HORAK
JAMES! HERE THEY COME!
JUST AHEAD, THE ROAD BENDS SHARPLY! AS THE ENEMY CAR STARTS TO PULL ABREAST, BOND THUMBS A SWITCH–
— AND A SIDE AIR VENT COVER SLIDES ASIDE AND–
1861

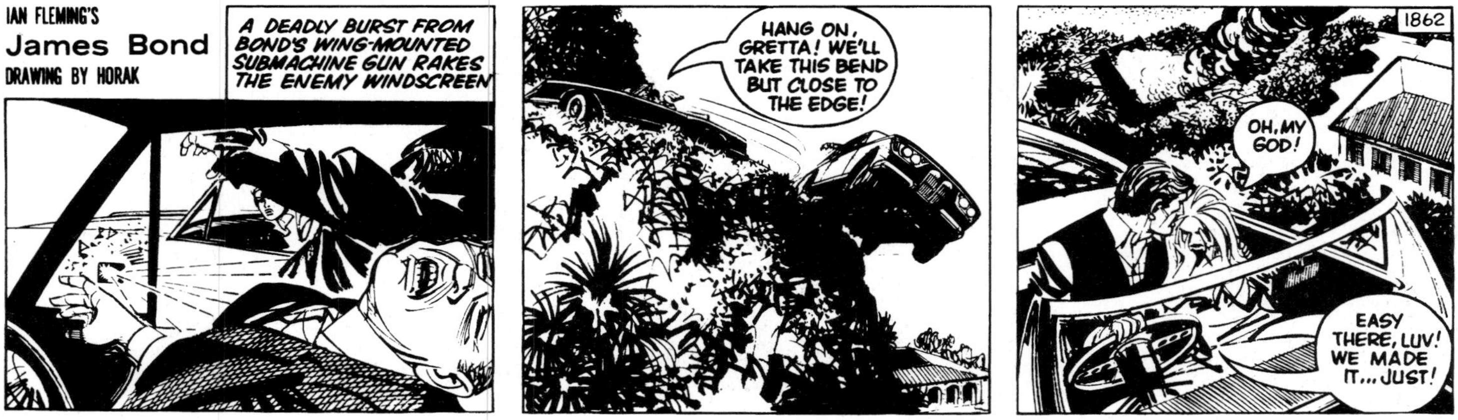
IAN FLEMING'S
James Bond
DRAWING BY HORAK
A DEADLY BURST FROM BOND'S WING-MOUNTED SUBMACHINE GUN RAKES THE ENEMY WINDSCREEN
HANG ON, GRETTA! WE'LL TAKE THIS BEND BUT CLOSE TO THE EDGE!
1862
OH, MY GOD!
EASY THERE, LUV! WE MADE IT... JUST!

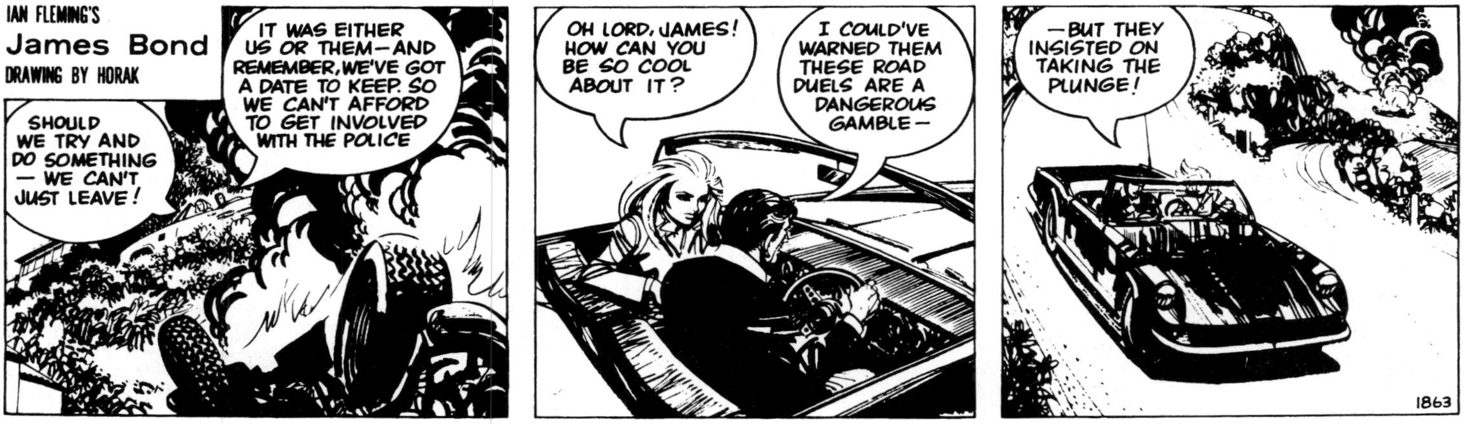
IAN FLEMING'S
James Bond
DRAWING BY HORAK
SHOULD WE TRY AND DO SOMETHING — WE CAN'T JUST LEAVE!
IT WAS EITHER US OR THEM—AND REMEMBER, WE'VE GOT A DATE TO KEEP. SO WE CAN'T AFFORD TO GET INVOLVED WITH THE POLICE
OH LORD, JAMES! HOW CAN YOU BE SO COOL ABOUT IT?
I COULD'VE WARNED THEM THESE ROAD DUELS ARE A DANGEROUS GAMBLE—
—BUT THEY INSISTED ON TAKING THE PLUNGE!
1863

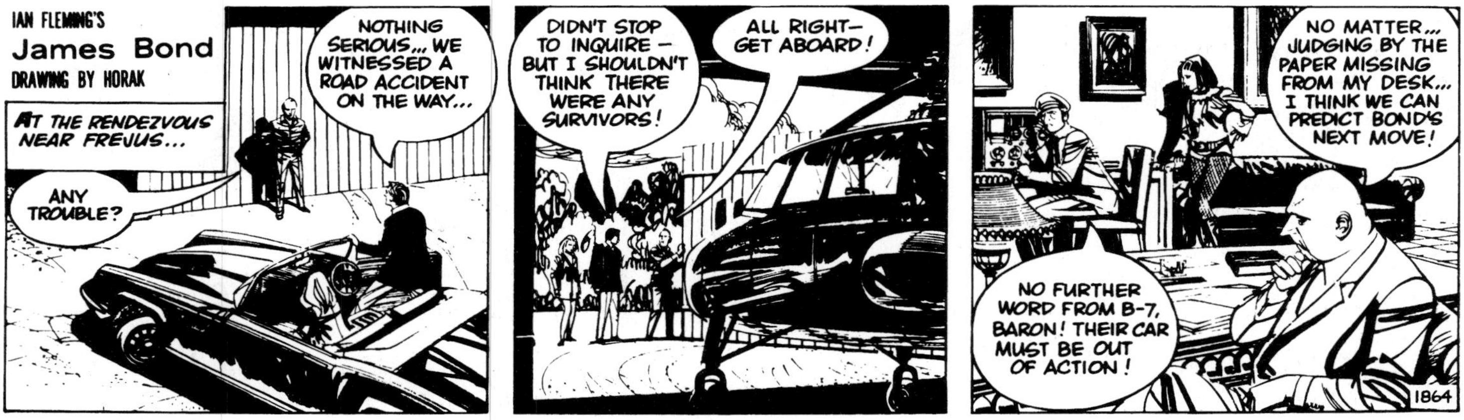
IAN FLEMING'S
James Bond
DRAWING BY HORAK
AT THE RENDEZVOUS NEAR FREJUS...
ANY TROUBLE?
NOTHING SERIOUS... WE WITNESSED A ROAD ACCIDENT ON THE WAY...
DIDN'T STOP TO INQUIRE — BUT I SHOULDN'T THINK THERE WERE ANY SURVIVORS!
ALL RIGHT— GET ABOARD!
NO FURTHER WORD FROM B-7, BARON! THEIR CAR MUST BE OUT OF ACTION!
NO MATTER... JUDGING BY THE PAPER MISSING FROM MY DESK... I THINK WE CAN PREDICT BOND'S NEXT MOVE!
1864

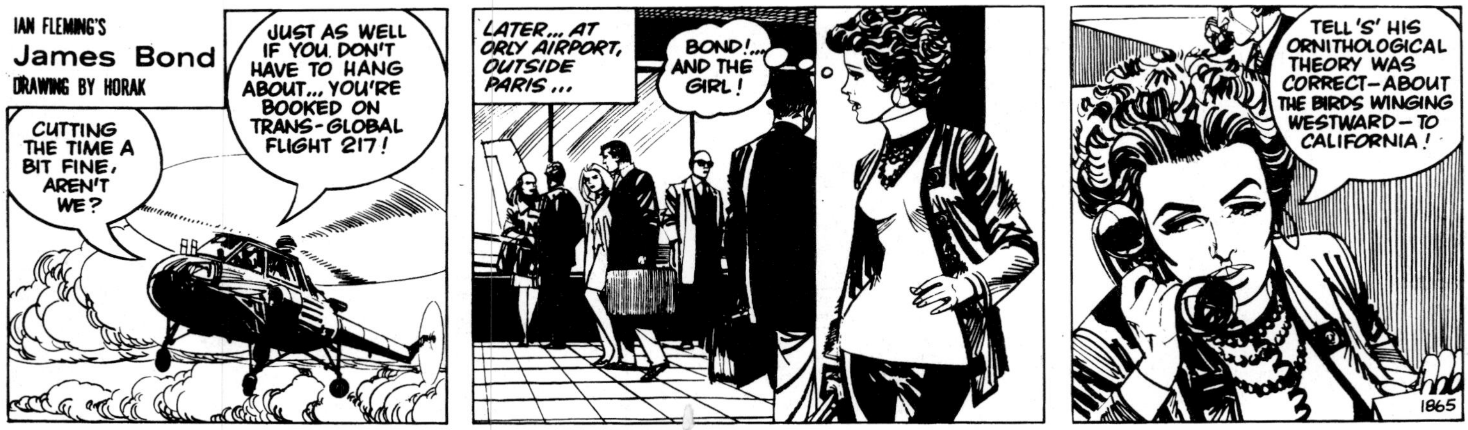
IAN FLEMING'S
James Bond
DRAWING BY HORAK
CUTTING THE TIME A BIT FINE, AREN'T WE?
JUST AS WELL IF YOU DON'T HAVE TO HANG ABOUT... YOU'RE BOOKED ON TRANS-GLOBAL FLIGHT 217!
LATER... AT ORLY AIRPORT, OUTSIDE PARIS...
BOND!... AND THE GIRL!
TELL 'S' HIS ORNITHOLOGICAL THEORY WAS CORRECT—ABOUT THE BIRDS WINGING WESTWARD—TO CALIFORNIA!
1865

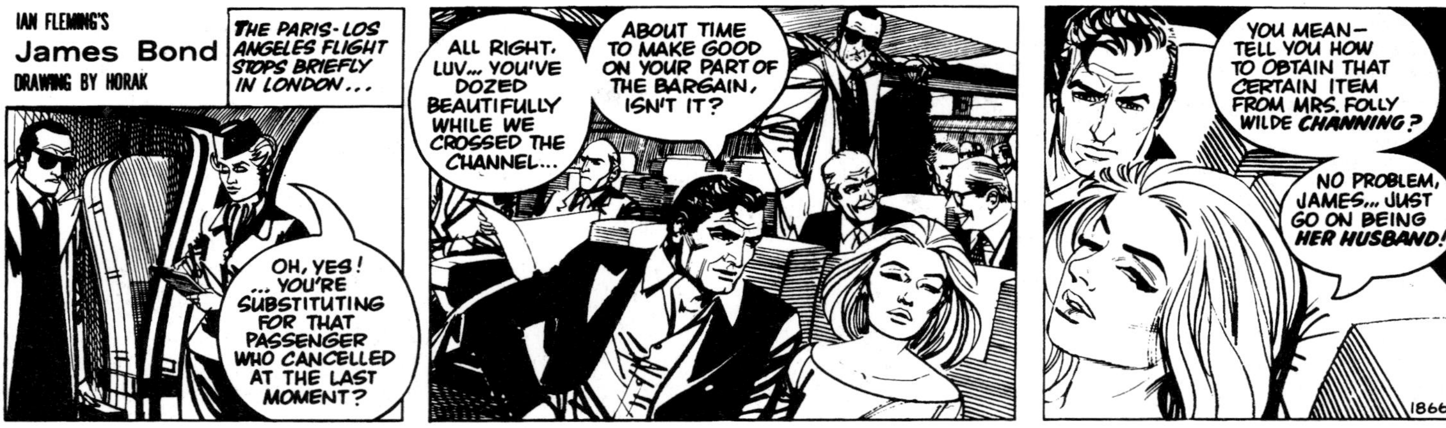
IAN FLEMING'S
James Bond
DRAWING BY HORAK
THE PARIS-LOS ANGELES FLIGHT STOPS BRIEFLY IN LONDON...
OH, YES! ...YOU'RE SUBSTITUTING FOR THAT PASSENGER WHO CANCELLED AT THE LAST MOMENT?
ALL RIGHT, LUV... YOU'VE DOZED BEAUTIFULLY WHILE WE CROSSED THE CHANNEL...
ABOUT TIME TO MAKE GOOD ON YOUR PART OF THE BARGAIN, ISN'T IT?
YOU MEAN— TELL YOU HOW TO OBTAIN THAT CERTAIN ITEM FROM MRS. FOLLY WILDE CHANNING?
NO PROBLEM, JAMES... JUST GO ON BEING HER HUSBAND!
1866

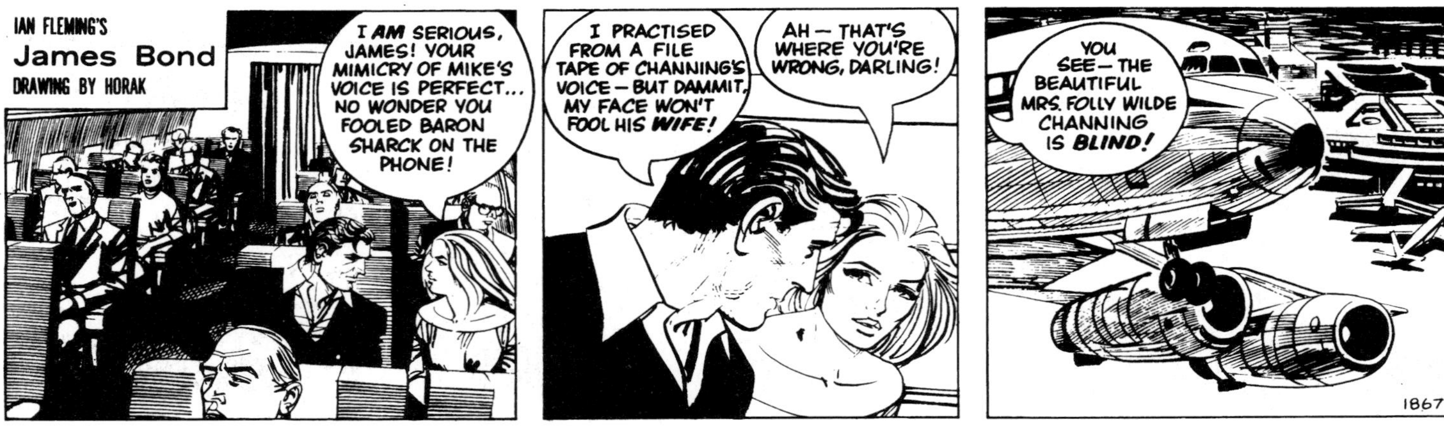
IAN FLEMING'S
James Bond
DRAWING BY HORAK
I AM SERIOUS, JAMES! YOUR MIMICRY OF MIKE'S VOICE IS PERFECT... NO WONDER YOU FOOLED BARON SHARCK ON THE PHONE!
I PRACTISED FROM A FILE TAPE OF CHANNING'S VOICE—BUT DAMMIT, MY FACE WON'T FOOL HIS WIFE!
AH—THAT'S WHERE YOU'RE WRONG, DARLING!
YOU SEE—THE BEAUTIFUL MRS. FOLLY WILDE CHANNING IS BLIND!
1867

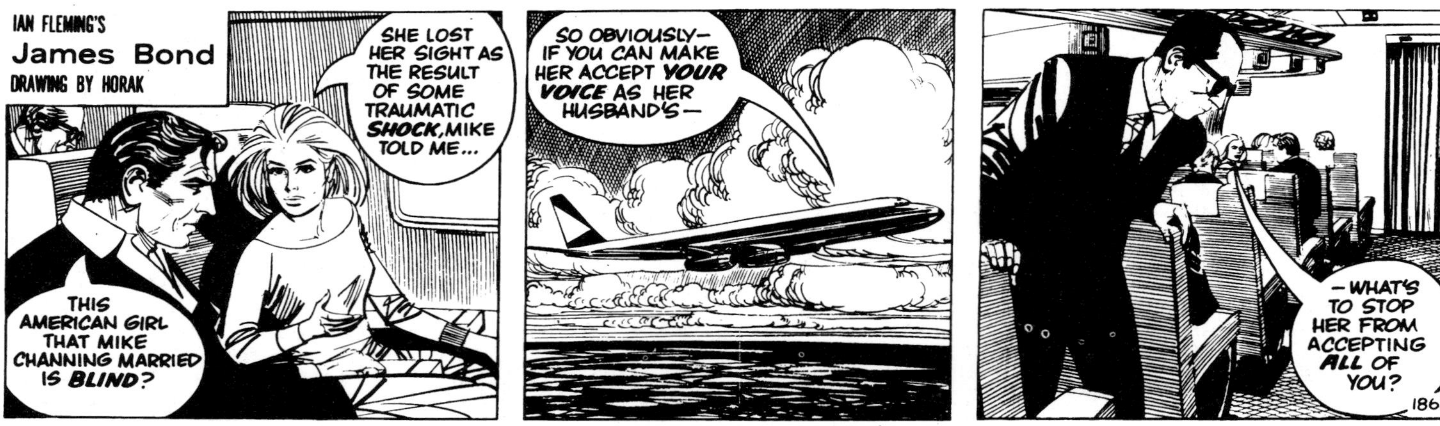
IAN FLEMING'S
James Bond
DRAWING BY HORAK
THIS AMERICAN GIRL THAT MIKE CHANNING MARRIED IS BLIND?
SHE LOST HER SIGHT AS THE RESULT OF SOME TRAUMATIC SHOCK, MIKE TOLD ME...
SO OBVIOUSLY— IF YOU CAN MAKE HER ACCEPT YOUR VOICE AS HER HUSBAND'S—
—WHAT'S TO STOP HER FROM ACCEPTING ALL OF YOU?
1868

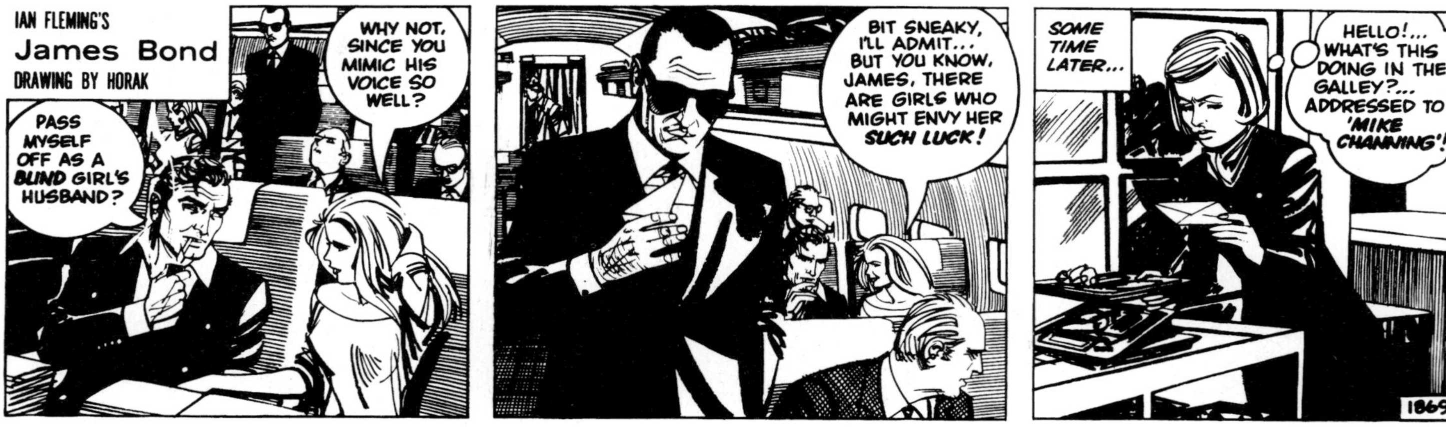
IAN FLEMING'S
James Bond
DRAWING BY HORAK
PASS MYSELF OFF AS A BLIND GIRL'S HUSBAND?
WHY NOT, SINCE YOU MIMIC HIS VOICE SO WELL?
BIT SNEAKY, I'LL ADMIT... BUT YOU KNOW, JAMES, THERE ARE GIRLS WHO MIGHT ENVY HER SUCH LUCK!
SOME TIME LATER...
HELLO!... WHAT'S THIS DOING IN THE GALLEY?... ADDRESSED TO 'MIKE CHANNING'!
1869

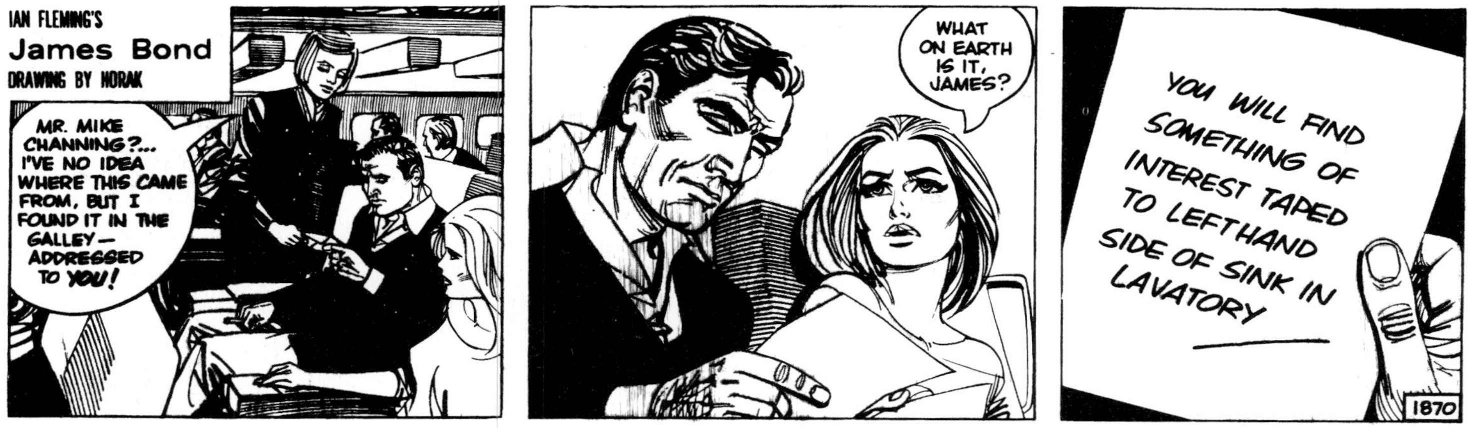
IAN FLEMING'S
James Bond
DRAWING BY HORAK
MR. MIKE CHANNING?... I'VE NO IDEA WHERE THIS CAME FROM, BUT I FOUND IT IN THE GALLEY— ADDRESSED TO YOU!
WHAT ON EARTH IS IT, JAMES?
YOU WILL FIND SOMETHING OF INTEREST TAPED TO LEFTHAND SIDE OF SINK IN LAVATORY
1870

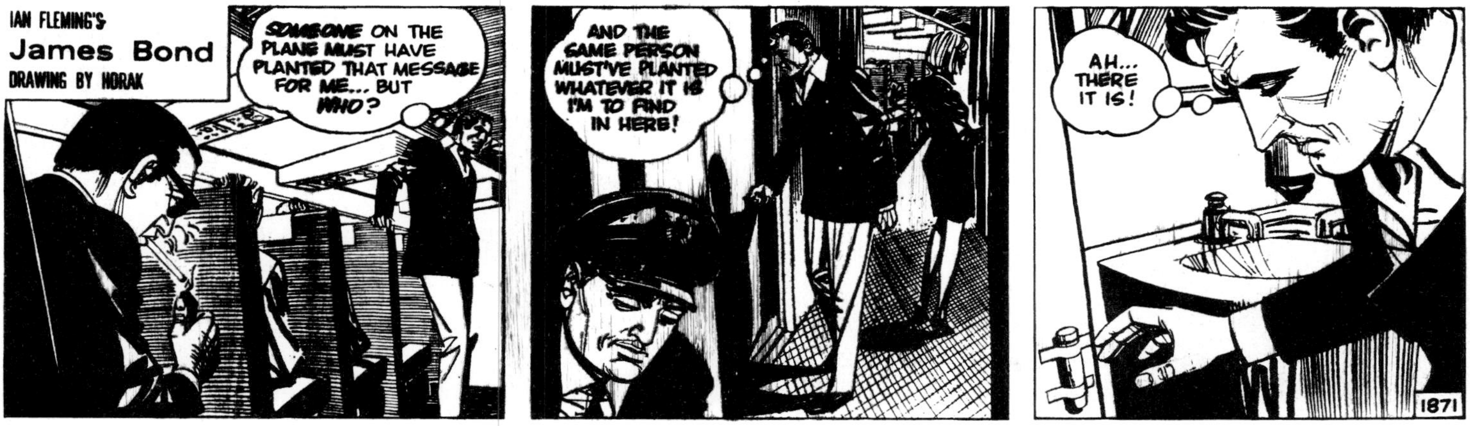
IAN FLEMING'S
James Bond
DRAWING BY HORAK
SOMEONE ON THE PLANE MUST HAVE PLANTED THAT MESSAGE FOR ME... BUT WHO?
AND THE SAME PERSON MUST'VE PLANTED WHATEVER IT IS I'M TO FIND IN HERE!
AH... THERE IT IS!
1871

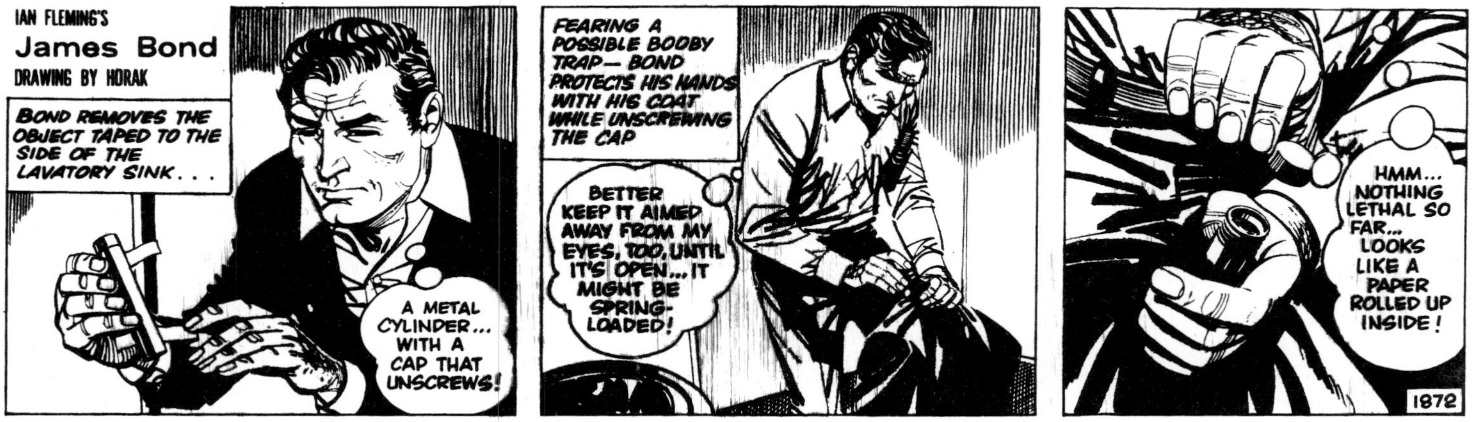
IAN FLEMING'S
James Bond
DRAWING BY HORAK
BOND REMOVES THE OBJECT TAPED TO THE SIDE OF THE LAVATORY SINK . . .
A METAL CYLINDER... WITH A CAP THAT UNSCREWS!
FEARING A POSSIBLE BOOBY TRAP— BOND PROTECTS HIS HANDS WITH HIS COAT WHILE UNSCREWING THE CAP
BETTER KEEP IT AIMED AWAY FROM MY EYES, TOO, UNTIL IT'S OPEN... IT MIGHT BE SPRING-LOADED!
HMM... NOTHING LETHAL SO FAR... LOOKS LIKE A PAPER ROLLED UP INSIDE!
1872

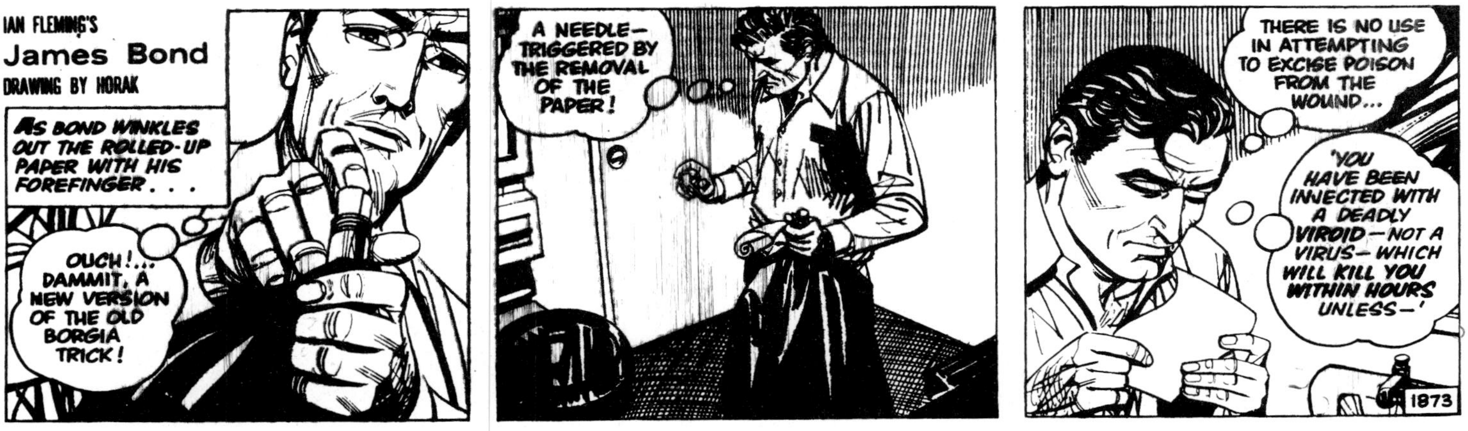
IAN FLEMING'S
James Bond
DRAWING BY HORAK
AS BOND WINKLES OUT THE ROLLED-UP PAPER WITH HIS FOREFINGER . . .
OUCH!... DAMMIT, A NEW VERSION OF THE OLD BORGIA TRICK!
A NEEDLE— TRIGGERED BY THE REMOVAL OF THE PAPER!
THERE IS NO USE IN ATTEMPTING TO EXCISE POISON FROM THE WOUND...
'YOU HAVE BEEN INJECTED WITH A DEADLY VIROID—NOT A VIRUS—WHICH WILL KILL YOU WITHIN HOURS UNLESS—'
1873

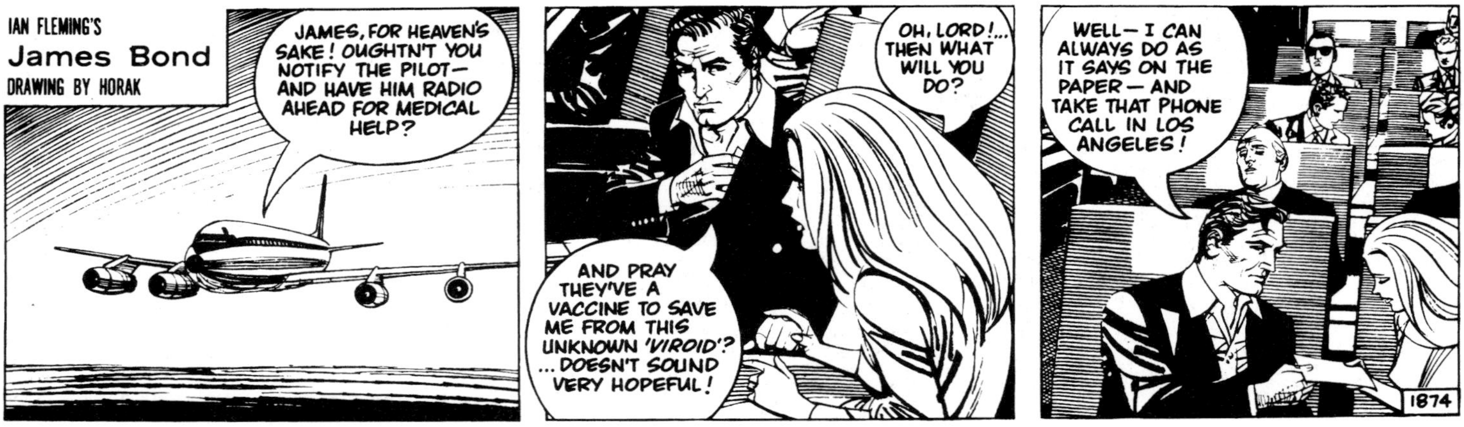
IAN FLEMING'S
James Bond
DRAWING BY HORAK
JAMES, FOR HEAVEN'S SAKE! OUGHTN'T YOU NOTIFY THE PILOT— AND HAVE HIM RADIO AHEAD FOR MEDICAL HELP?
OH, LORD!... THEN WHAT WILL YOU DO?
AND PRAY THEY'VE A VACCINE TO SAVE ME FROM THIS UNKNOWN 'VIROID'? ... DOESN'T SOUND VERY HOPEFUL!
WELL— I CAN ALWAYS DO AS IT SAYS ON THE PAPER — AND TAKE THAT PHONE CALL IN LOS ANGELES!
1874

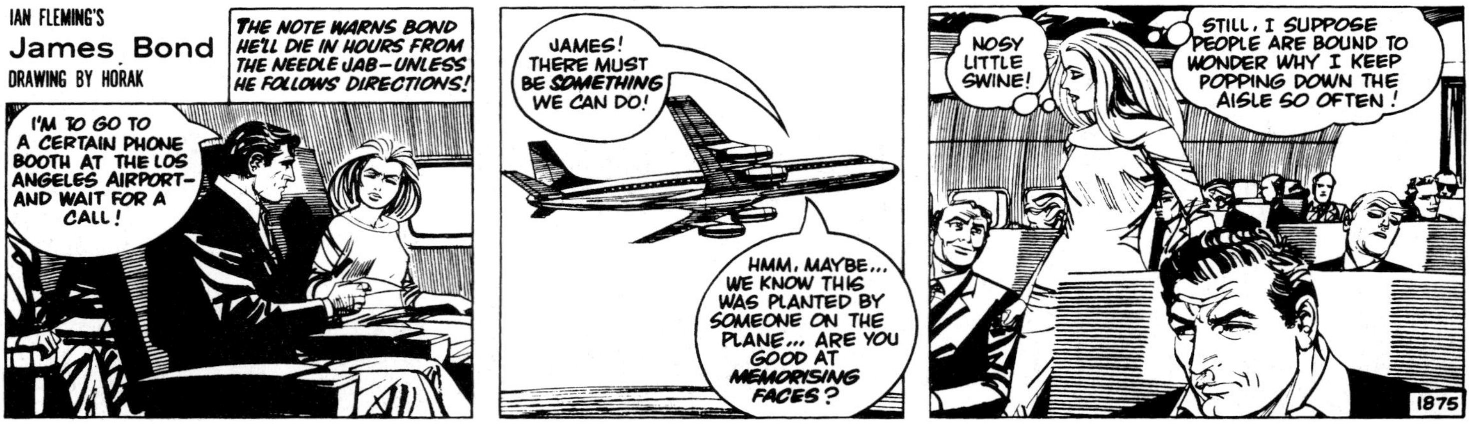
IAN FLEMING'S
James Bond
DRAWING BY HORAK
THE NOTE WARNS BOND HE'LL DIE IN HOURS FROM THE NEEDLE JAB—UNLESS HE FOLLOWS DIRECTIONS!
I'M TO GO TO A CERTAIN PHONE BOOTH AT THE LOS ANGELES AIRPORT— AND WAIT FOR A CALL!
JAMES! THERE MUST BE SOMETHING WE CAN DO!
HMM, MAYBE... WE KNOW THIS WAS PLANTED BY SOMEONE ON THE PLANE... ARE YOU GOOD AT MEMORISING FACES?
NOSY LITTLE SWINE!
STILL, I SUPPOSE PEOPLE ARE BOUND TO WONDER WHY I KEEP POPPING DOWN THE AISLE SO OFTEN!
1875

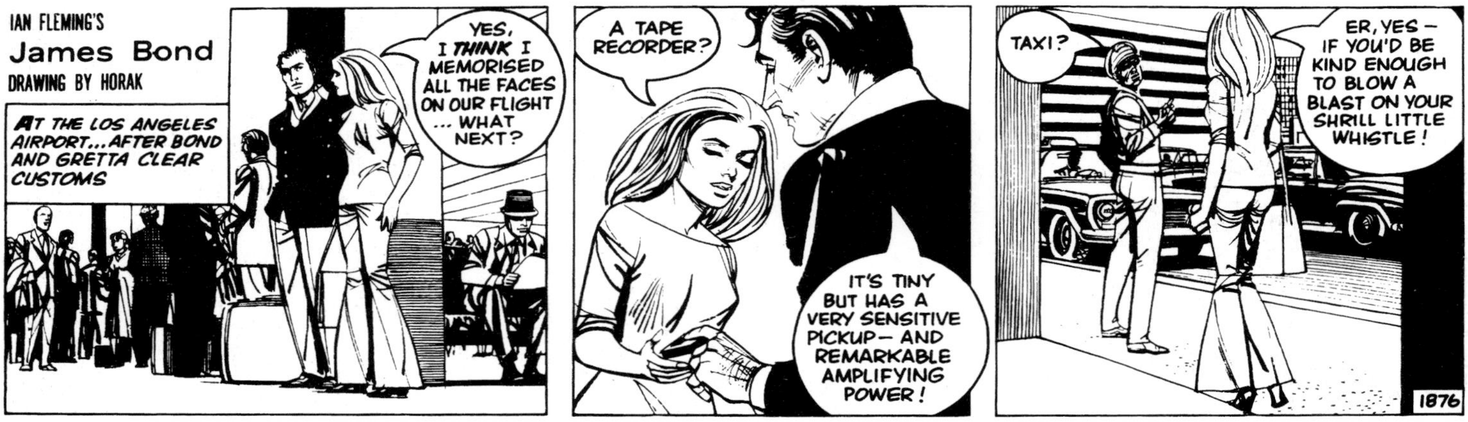
IAN FLEMING'S
James Bond
DRAWING BY HORAK
AT THE LOS ANGELES AIRPORT... AFTER BOND AND GRETTA CLEAR CUSTOMS
YES, I THINK I MEMORISED ALL THE FACES ON OUR FLIGHT ... WHAT NEXT?
A TAPE RECORDER?
IT'S TINY BUT HAS A VERY SENSITIVE PICKUP— AND REMARKABLE AMPLIFYING POWER!
TAXI?
ER, YES— IF YOU'D BE KIND ENOUGH TO BLOW A BLAST ON YOUR SHRILL LITTLE WHISTLE!
1876

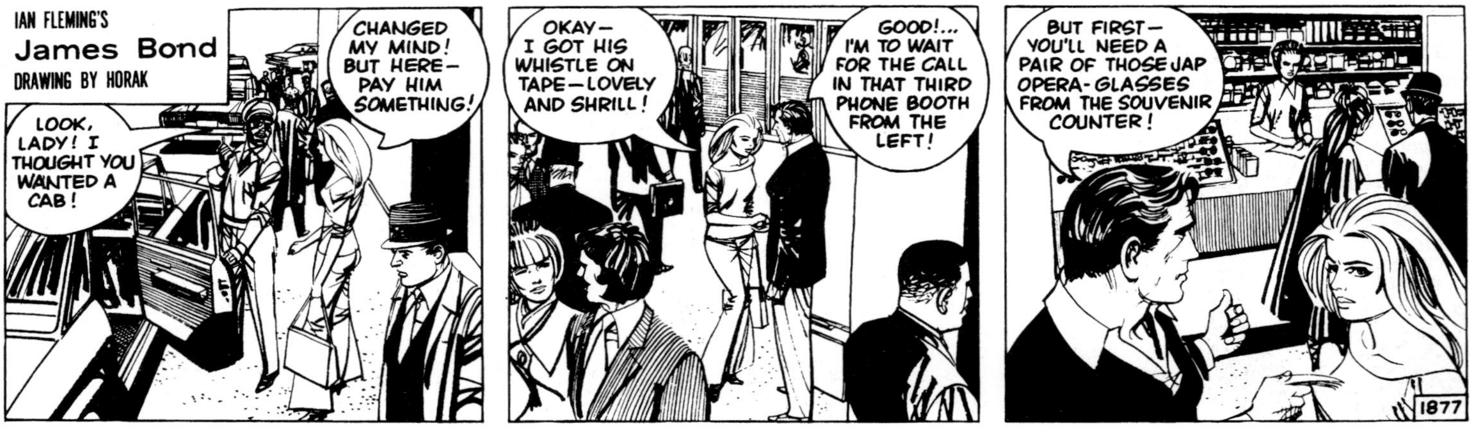
IAN FLEMING'S
James Bond
DRAWING BY HORAK
LOOK, LADY! I THOUGHT YOU WANTED A CAB!
CHANGED MY MIND! BUT HERE— PAY HIM SOMETHING!
OKAY— I GOT HIS WHISTLE ON TAPE—LOVELY AND SHRILL!
GOOD!... I'M TO WAIT FOR THE CALL IN THAT THIRD PHONE BOOTH FROM THE LEFT!
BUT FIRST— YOU'LL NEED A PAIR OF THOSE JAP OPERA-GLASSES FROM THE SOUVENIR COUNTER!
1877

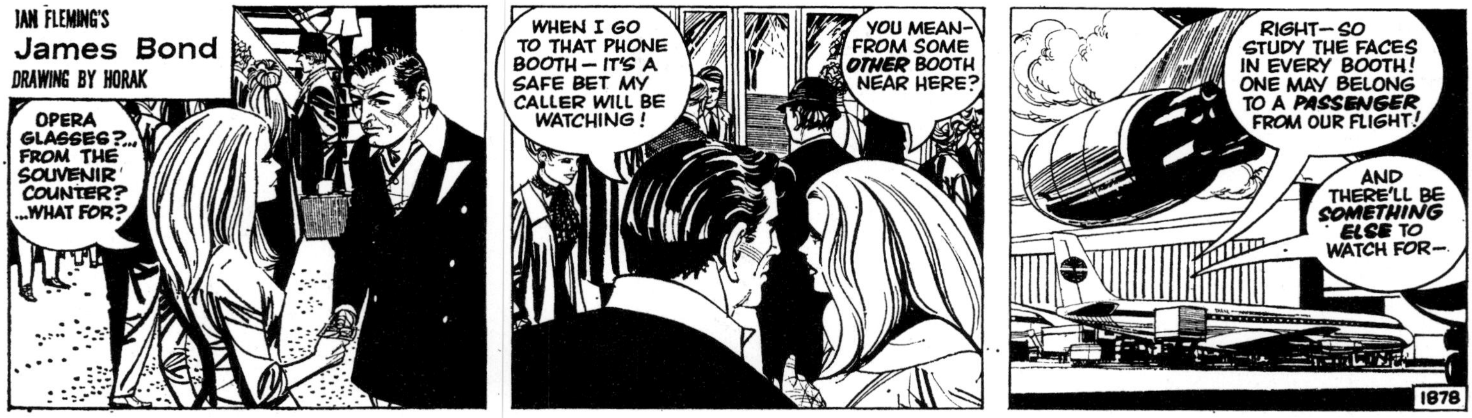
IAN FLEMING'S
James Bond
DRAWING BY HORAK
OPERA GLASSES?... FROM THE SOUVENIR COUNTER? ...WHAT FOR?
WHEN I GO TO THAT PHONE BOOTH — IT'S A SAFE BET MY CALLER WILL BE WATCHING!
YOU MEAN— FROM SOME OTHER BOOTH NEAR HERE?
RIGHT—SO STUDY THE FACES IN EVERY BOOTH! ONE MAY BELONG TO A PASSENGER FROM OUR FLIGHT!
AND THERE'LL BE SOMETHING ELSE TO WATCH FOR—
1878

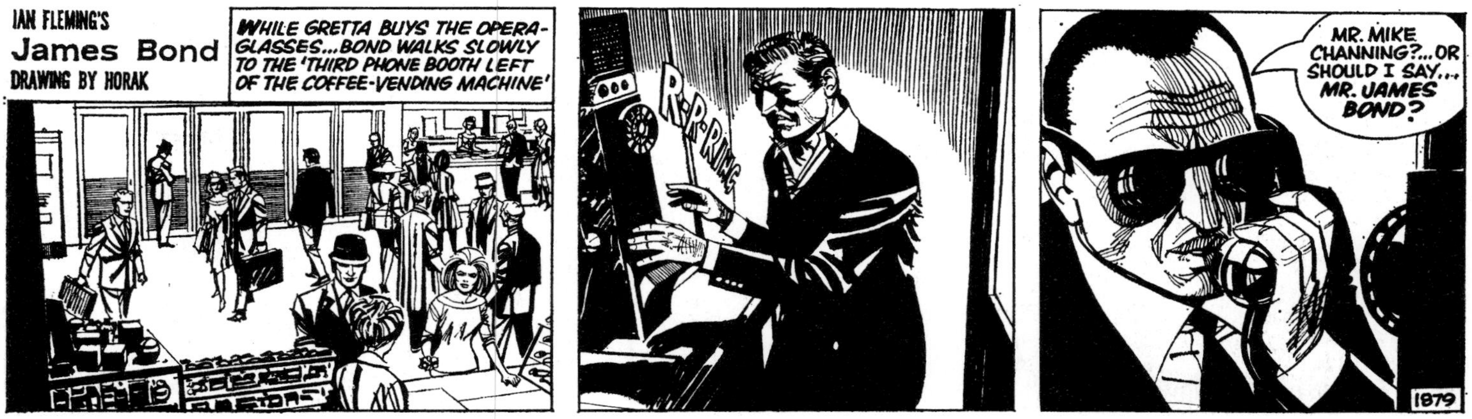
IAN FLEMING'S
James Bond
DRAWING BY HORAK
WHILE GRETTA BUYS THE OPERA-GLASSES...BOND WALKS SLOWLY TO THE 'THIRD PHONE BOOTH LEFT OF THE COFFEE-VENDING MACHINE'
R-R-RING
MR. MIKE CHANNING?...OR SHOULD I SAY... MR. JAMES BOND?
1879

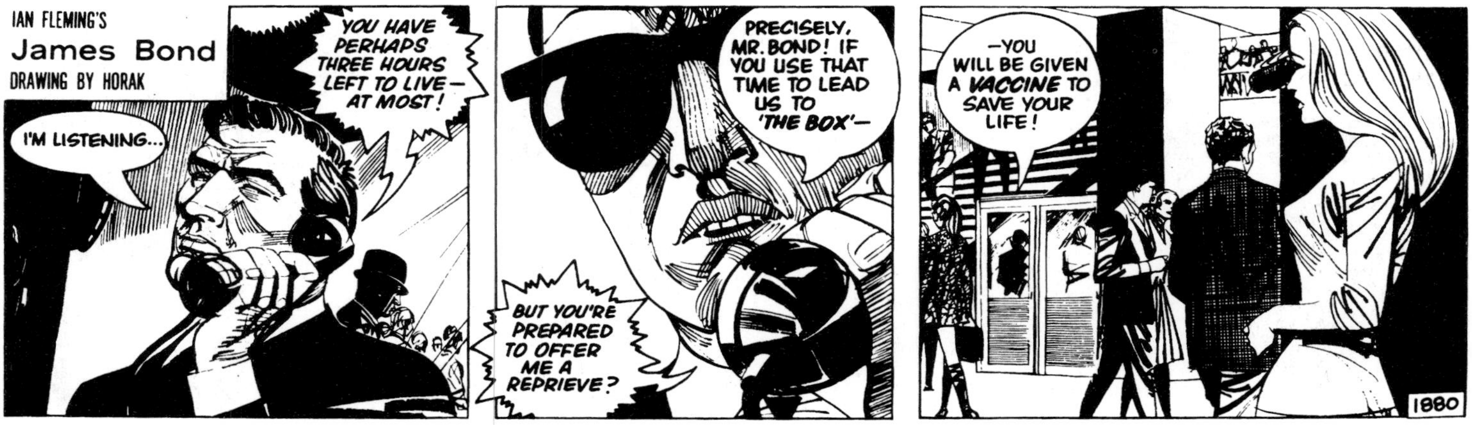
IAN FLEMING'S
James Bond
DRAWING BY HORAK
YOU HAVE PERHAPS THREE HOURS LEFT TO LIVE— AT MOST!
I'M LISTENING...
PRECISELY, MR. BOND! IF YOU USE THAT TIME TO LEAD US TO 'THE BOX'—
BUT YOU'RE PREPARED TO OFFER ME A REPRIEVE?
—YOU WILL BE GIVEN A VACCINE TO SAVE YOUR LIFE!
1880

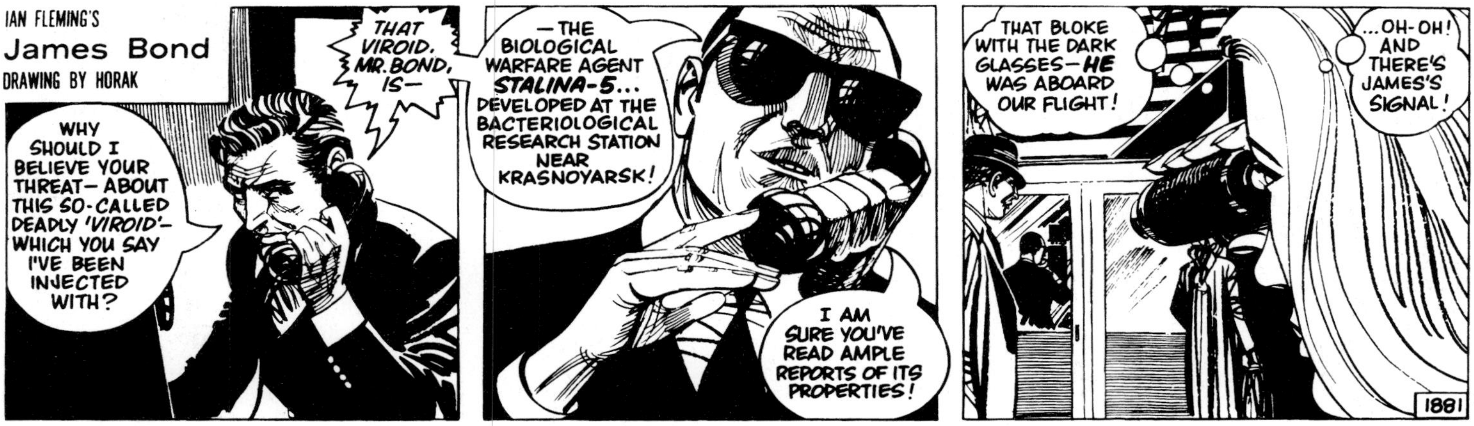
IAN FLEMING'S
James Bond
DRAWING BY HORAK
THAT VIROID, MR. BOND, IS—
WHY SHOULD I BELIEVE YOUR THREAT— ABOUT THIS SO-CALLED DEADLY 'VIROID'— WHICH YOU SAY I'VE BEEN INJECTED WITH?
—THE BIOLOGICAL WARFARE AGENT STALINA-5... DEVELOPED AT THE BACTERIOLOGICAL RESEARCH STATION NEAR KRASNOYARSK!
I AM SURE YOU'VE READ AMPLE REPORTS OF ITS PROPERTIES!
THAT BLOKE WITH THE DARK GLASSES—HE WAS ABOARD OUR FLIGHT!
...OH-OH! AND THERE'S JAMES'S SIGNAL!
1881

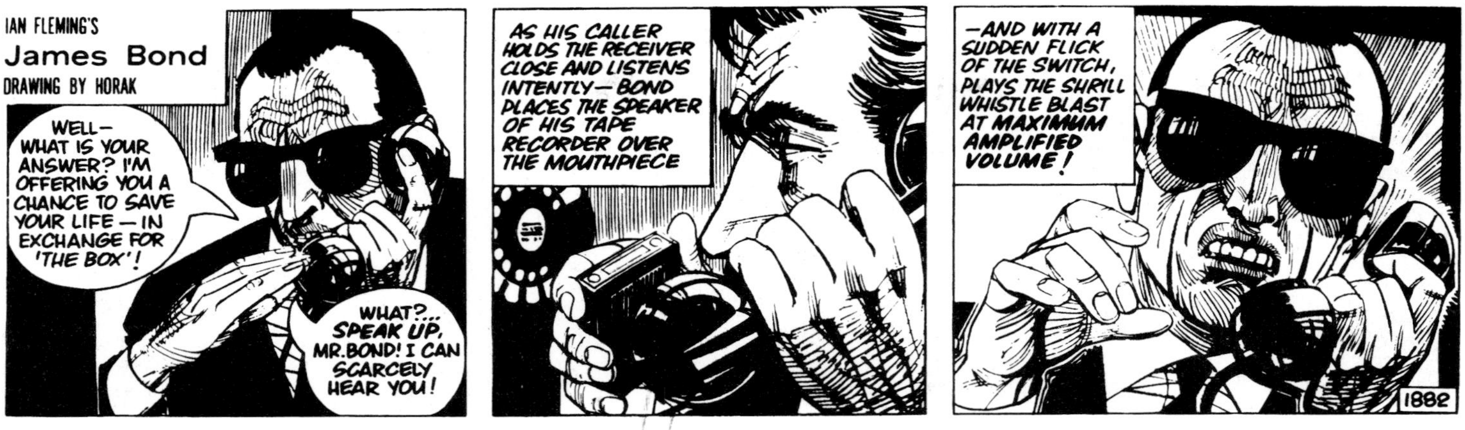
IAN FLEMING'S
James Bond
DRAWING BY HORAK
WELL— WHAT IS YOUR ANSWER? I'M OFFERING YOU A CHANCE TO SAVE YOUR LIFE — IN EXCHANGE FOR 'THE BOX'!
WHAT?... SPEAK UP, MR. BOND! I CAN SCARCELY HEAR YOU!
AS HIS CALLER HOLDS THE RECEIVER CLOSE AND LISTENS INTENTLY— BOND PLACES THE SPEAKER OF HIS TAPE RECORDER OVER THE MOUTHPIECE
—AND WITH A SUDDEN FLICK OF THE SWITCH, PLAYS THE SHRILL WHISTLE BLAST AT MAXIMUM AMPLIFIED VOLUME!
1882

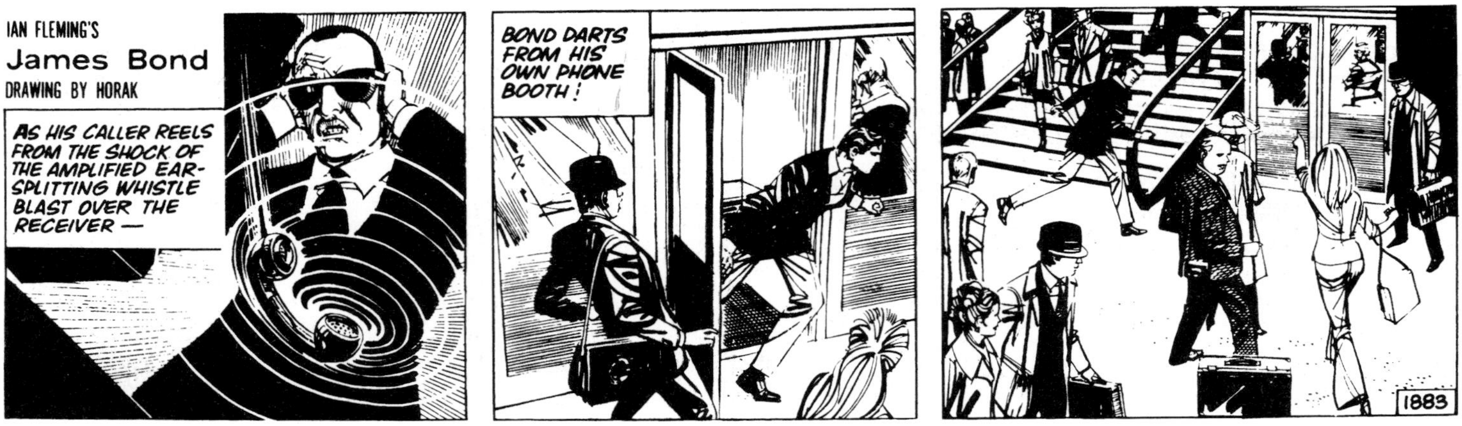
IAN FLEMING'S
James Bond
DRAWING BY HORAK
AS HIS CALLER REELS FROM THE SHOCK OF THE AMPLIFIED EAR-SPLITTING WHISTLE BLAST OVER THE RECEIVER —
BOND DARTS FROM HIS OWN PHONE BOOTH!
1883

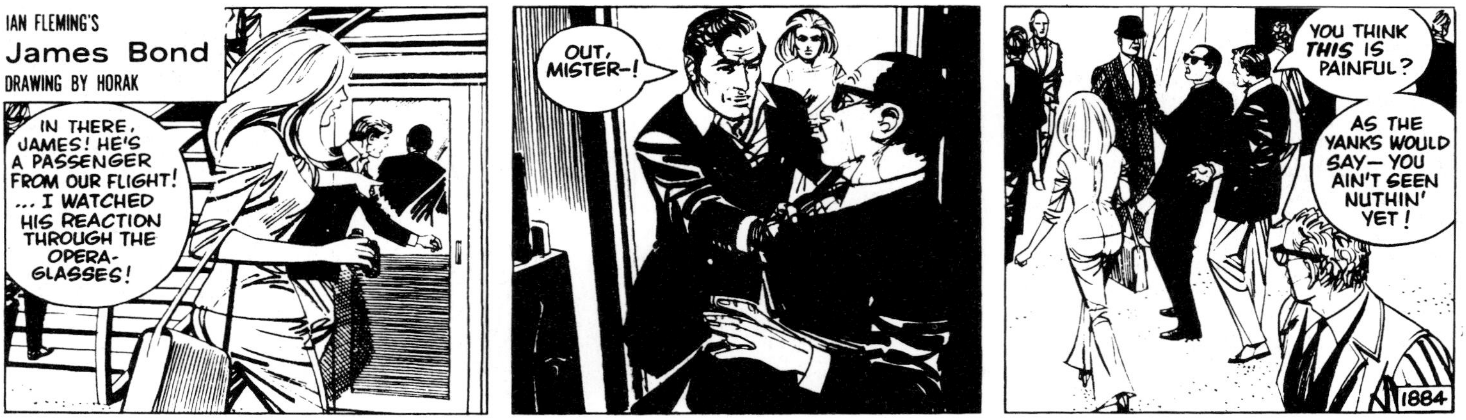
IAN FLEMING'S
James Bond
DRAWING BY HORAK
IN THERE, JAMES! HE'S A PASSENGER FROM OUR FLIGHT! ... I WATCHED HIS REACTION THROUGH THE OPERA-GLASSES!
OUT, MISTER—!
YOU THINK THIS IS PAINFUL?
AS THE YANKS WOULD SAY— YOU AIN'T SEEN NUTHIN' YET!
1884

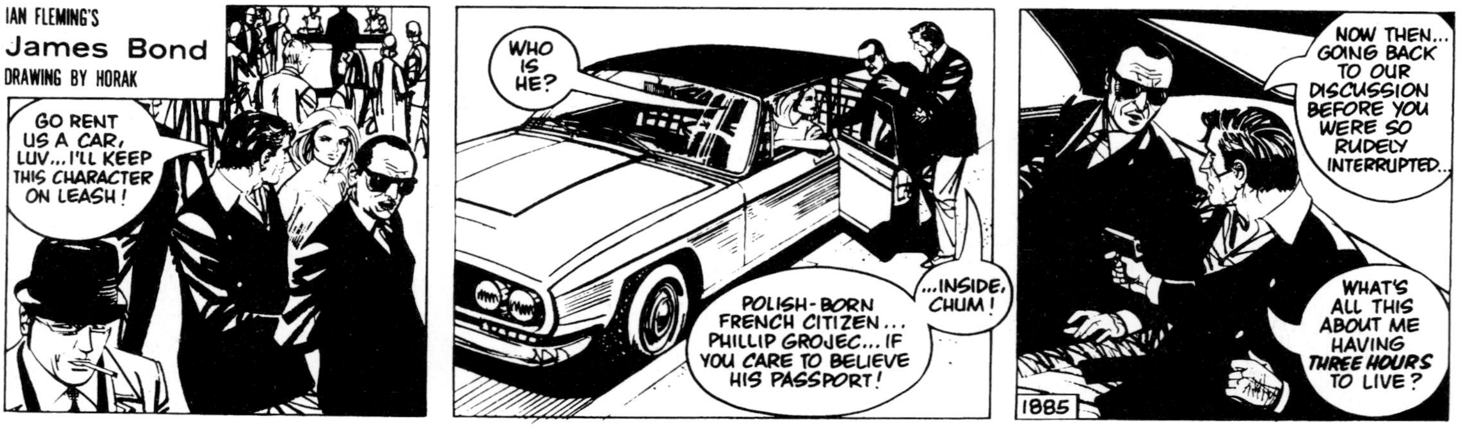
IAN FLEMING'S
James Bond
DRAWING BY HORAK
GO RENT US A CAR, LUV... I'LL KEEP THIS CHARACTER ON LEASH!
WHO IS HE?
POLISH-BORN FRENCH CITIZEN... PHILLIP GROJEC... IF YOU CARE TO BELIEVE HIS PASSPORT!
...INSIDE, CHUM!
NOW THEN... GOING BACK TO OUR DISCUSSION BEFORE YOU WERE SO RUDELY INTERRUPTED...
WHAT'S ALL THIS ABOUT ME HAVING THREE HOURS TO LIVE?
1885

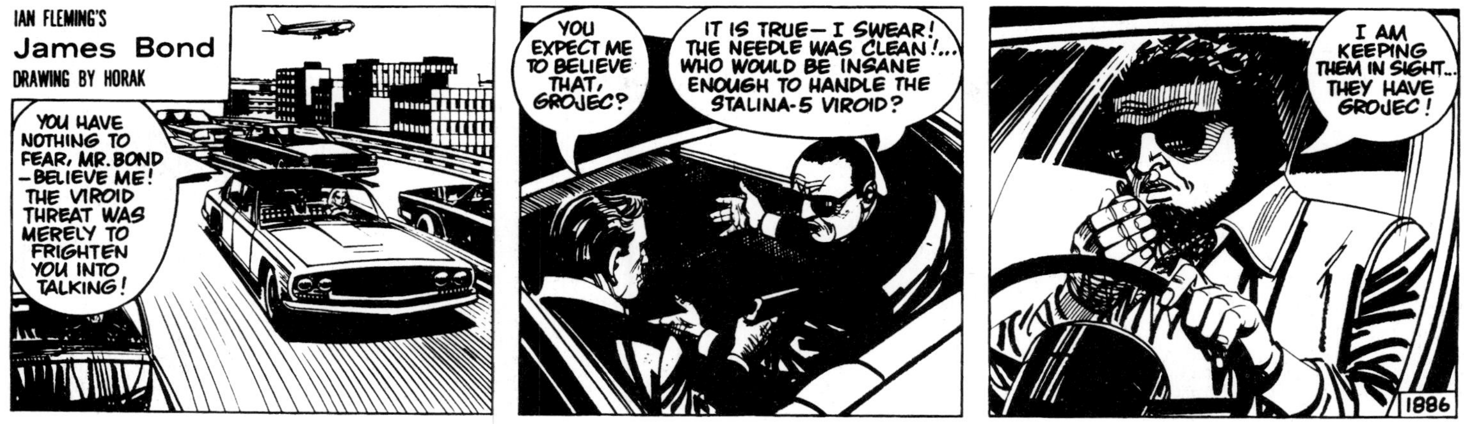
IAN FLEMING'S
James Bond
DRAWING BY HORAK
YOU HAVE NOTHING TO FEAR, MR. BOND – BELIEVE ME! THE VIROID THREAT WAS MERELY TO FRIGHTEN YOU INTO TALKING!
YOU EXPECT ME TO BELIEVE THAT, GROJEC?
IT IS TRUE – I SWEAR! THE NEEDLE WAS CLEAN!... WHO WOULD BE INSANE ENOUGH TO HANDLE THE STALINA-5 VIROID?
I AM KEEPING THEM IN SIGHT... THEY HAVE GROJEC!
1886

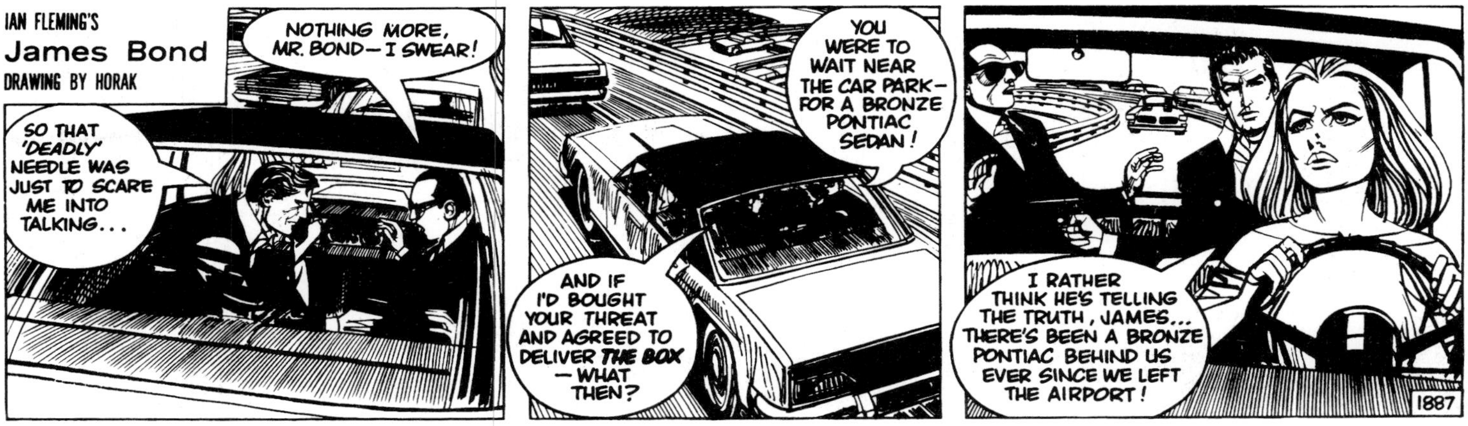
IAN FLEMING'S
James Bond
DRAWING BY HORAK
NOTHING MORE, MR. BOND – I SWEAR!
SO THAT 'DEADLY' NEEDLE WAS JUST TO SCARE ME INTO TALKING...
YOU WERE TO WAIT NEAR THE CAR PARK FOR A BRONZE PONTIAC SEDAN!
AND IF I'D BOUGHT YOUR THREAT AND AGREED TO DELIVER THE BOX – WHAT THEN?
I RATHER THINK HE'S TELLING THE TRUTH, JAMES... THERE'S BEEN A BRONZE PONTIAC BEHIND US EVER SINCE WE LEFT THE AIRPORT!
1887

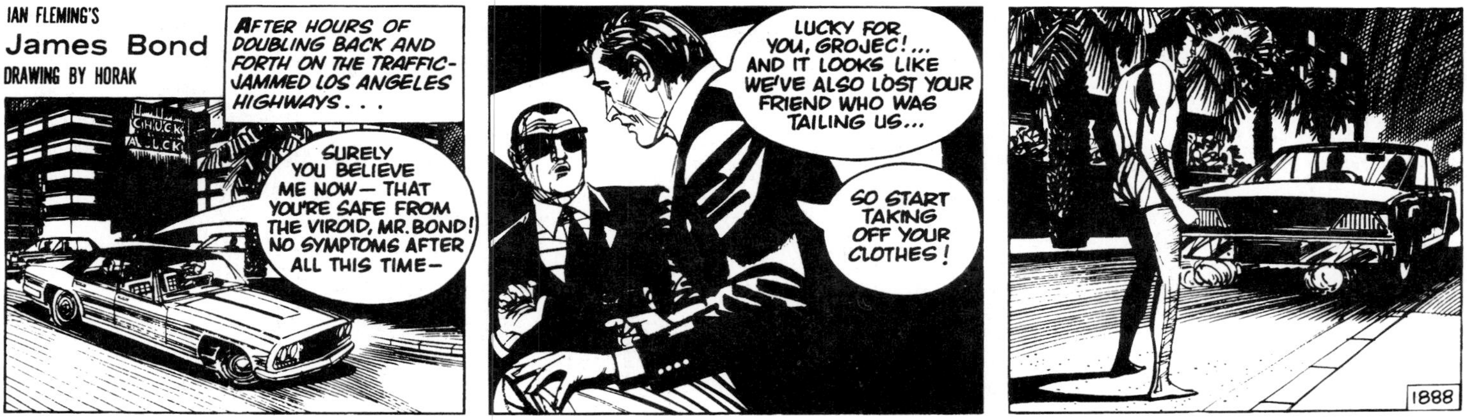
IAN FLEMING'S
James Bond
DRAWING BY HORAK
AFTER HOURS OF DOUBLING BACK AND FORTH ON THE TRAFFIC-JAMMED LOS ANGELES HIGHWAYS . . .
SURELY YOU BELIEVE ME NOW – THAT YOU'RE SAFE FROM THE VIROID, MR. BOND! NO SYMPTOMS AFTER ALL THIS TIME –
LUCKY FOR YOU, GROJEC!... AND IT LOOKS LIKE WE'VE ALSO LOST YOUR FRIEND WHO WAS TAILING US...
SO START TAKING OFF YOUR CLOTHES!
1888

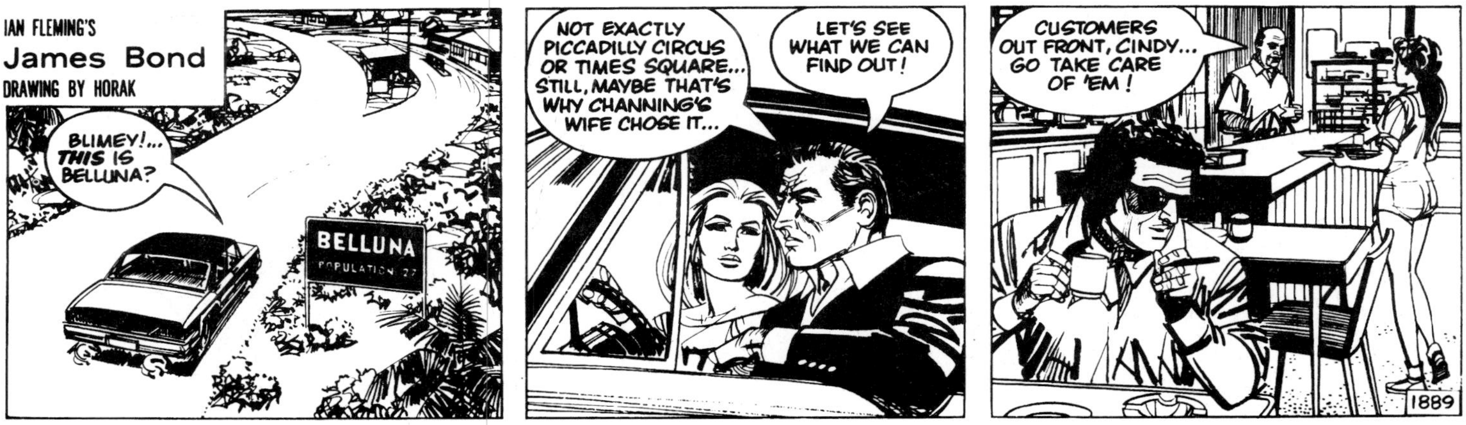
IAN FLEMING'S
James Bond
DRAWING BY HORAK
BLIMEY!... THIS IS BELLUNA?
BELLUNA
POPULATION 27
NOT EXACTLY PICCADILLY CIRCUS OR TIMES SQUARE... STILL, MAYBE THAT'S WHY CHANNING'S WIFE CHOSE IT...
LET'S SEE WHAT WE CAN FIND OUT!
CUSTOMERS OUT FRONT, CINDY... GO TAKE CARE OF 'EM!
1889

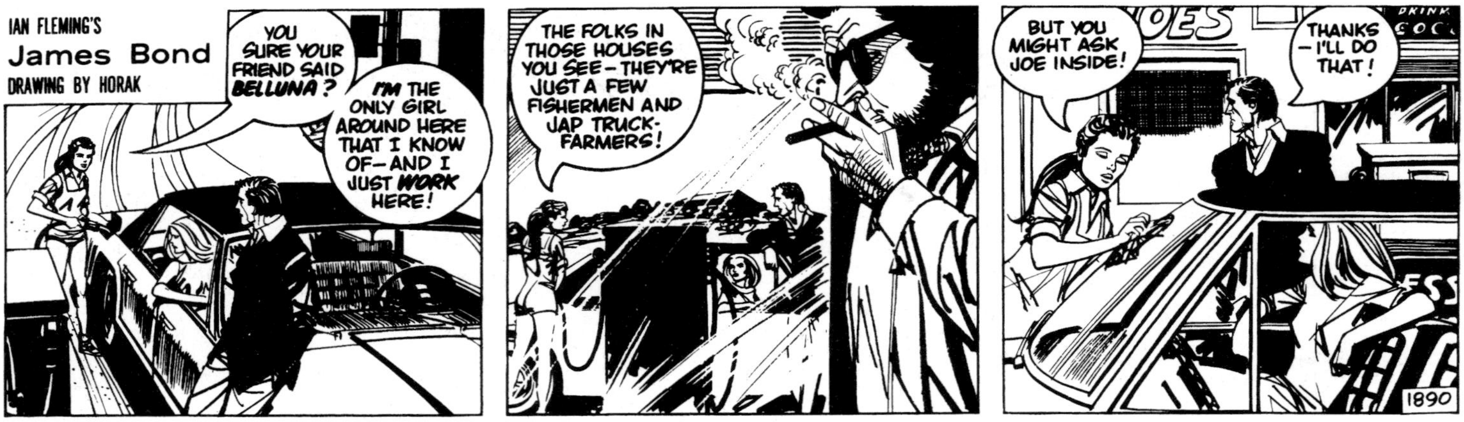
IAN FLEMING'S
James Bond
DRAWING BY HORAK
YOU SURE YOUR FRIEND SAID **BELLUNA?**
I'M THE ONLY GIRL AROUND HERE THAT I KNOW OF—AND I JUST **WORK** HERE!
THE FOLKS IN THOSE HOUSES YOU SEE—THEY'RE JUST A FEW FISHERMEN AND JAP TRUCK-FARMERS!
BUT YOU MIGHT ASK JOE INSIDE!
THANKS —I'LL DO THAT!
1890

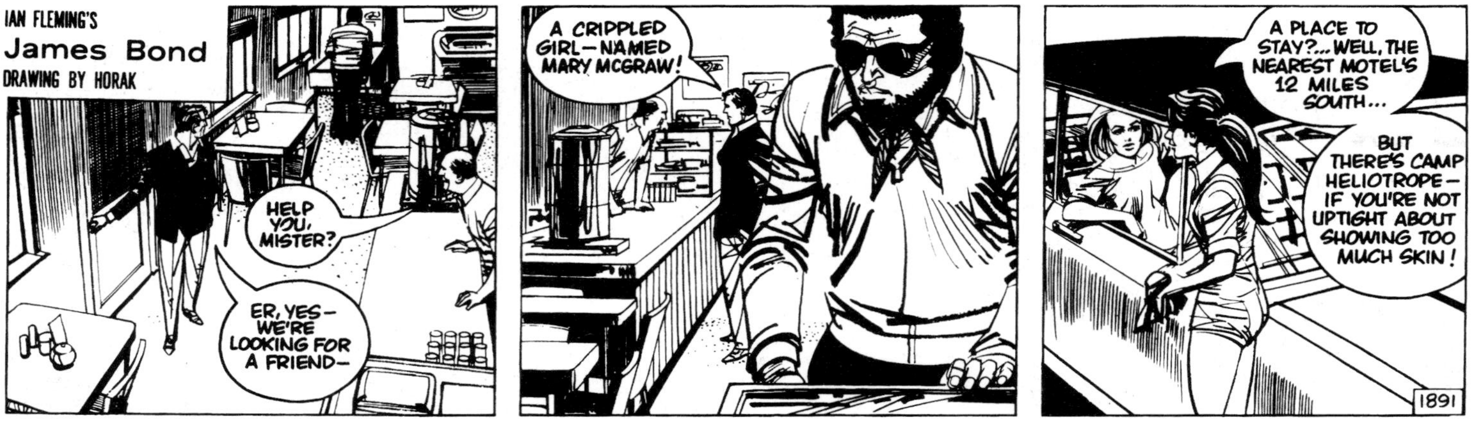
IAN FLEMING'S
James Bond
DRAWING BY HORAK
HELP YOU, MISTER?
ER, YES— WE'RE LOOKING FOR A FRIEND—
A CRIPPLED GIRL—NAMED MARY MCGRAW!
A PLACE TO STAY?... WELL, THE NEAREST MOTEL'S 12 MILES SOUTH...
BUT THERE'S CAMP HELIOTROPE— IF YOU'RE NOT UPTIGHT ABOUT SHOWING TOO MUCH SKIN!
1891

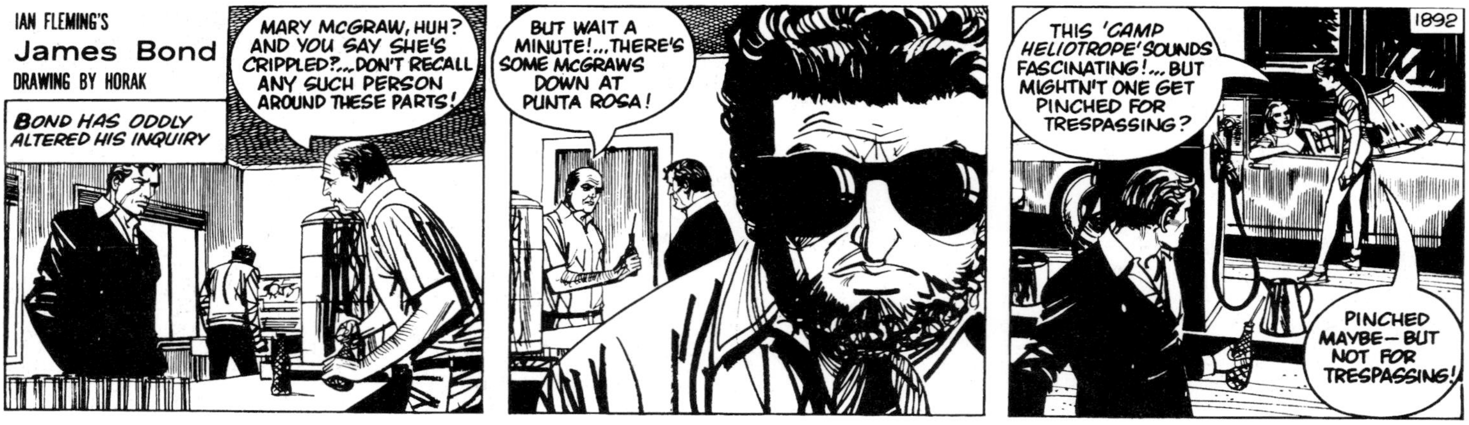
IAN FLEMING'S
James Bond
DRAWING BY HORAK
BOND HAS ODDLY ALTERED HIS INQUIRY
MARY MCGRAW, HUH? AND YOU SAY SHE'S CRIPPLED?... DON'T RECALL ANY SUCH PERSON AROUND THESE PARTS!
BUT WAIT A MINUTE!... THERE'S SOME MCGRAWS DOWN AT PUNTA ROSA!
1892
THIS 'CAMP HELIOTROPE' SOUNDS FASCINATING!... BUT MIGHTN'T ONE GET PINCHED FOR TRESPASSING?
PINCHED MAYBE—BUT NOT FOR TRESPASSING!

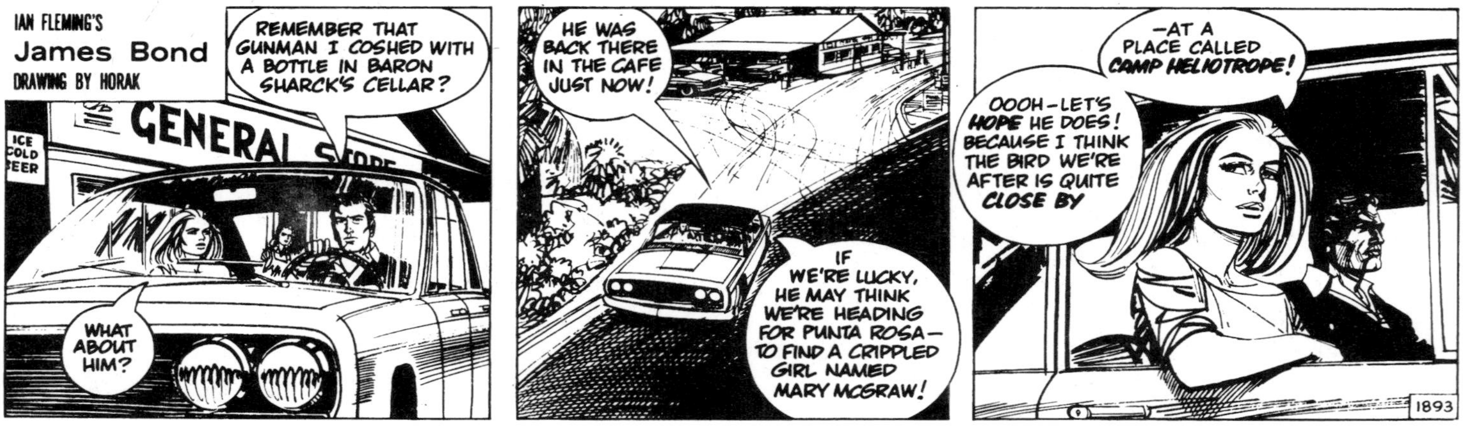
IAN FLEMING'S
James Bond
DRAWING BY HORAK
REMEMBER THAT GUNMAN I COSHED WITH A BOTTLE IN BARON SHARCK'S CELLAR?
WHAT ABOUT HIM?
HE WAS BACK THERE IN THE CAFE JUST NOW!
IF WE'RE LUCKY, HE MAY THINK WE'RE HEADING FOR PUNTA ROSA— TO FIND A CRIPPLED GIRL NAMED MARY MCGRAW!
OOOH—LET'S **HOPE** HE DOES! BECAUSE I THINK THE BIRD WE'RE AFTER IS QUITE **CLOSE BY**
—AT A PLACE CALLED **CAMP HELIOTROPE!**
1893

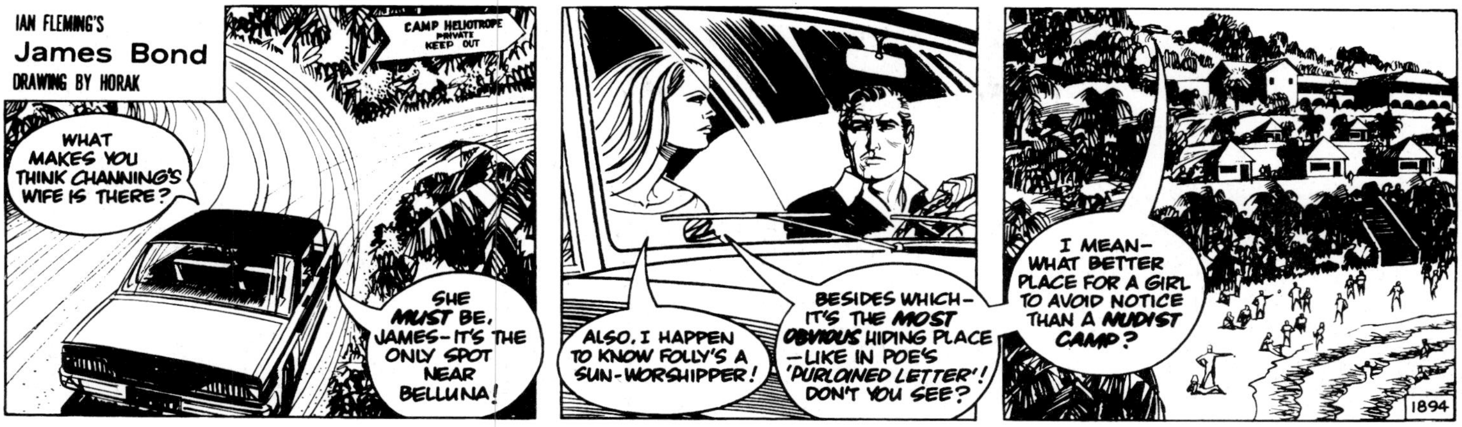
IAN FLEMING'S
James Bond
DRAWING BY HORAK
CAMP HELIOTROPE PRIVATE KEEP OUT
WHAT MAKES YOU THINK CHANNING'S WIFE IS THERE?
SHE MUST BE, JAMES—IT'S THE ONLY SPOT NEAR BELLUNA!
ALSO, I HAPPEN TO KNOW FOLLY'S A SUN-WORSHIPPER!
BESIDES WHICH—IT'S THE MOST OBVIOUS HIDING PLACE—LIKE IN POE'S 'PURLOINED LETTER'! DON'T YOU SEE?
I MEAN—WHAT BETTER PLACE FOR A GIRL TO AVOID NOTICE THAN A NUDIST CAMP?
1894

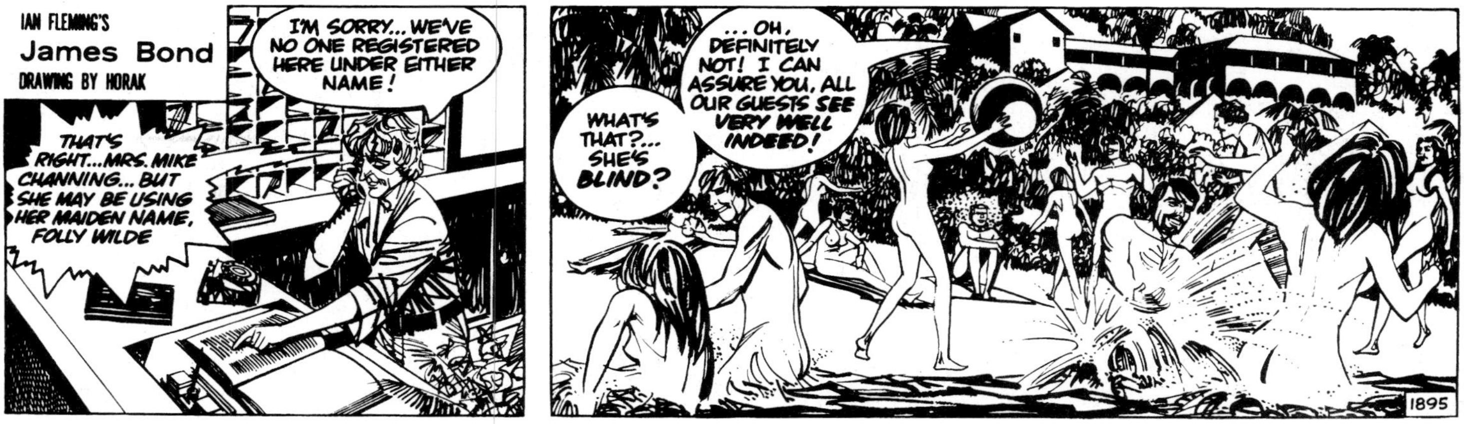
IAN FLEMING'S
James Bond
DRAWING BY HORAK
THAT'S RIGHT... MRS. MIKE CHANNING... BUT SHE MAY BE USING HER MAIDEN NAME, FOLLY WILDE
I'M SORRY... WE'VE NO ONE REGISTERED HERE UNDER EITHER NAME!
WHAT'S THAT?... SHE'S BLIND?
... OH, DEFINITELY NOT! I CAN ASSURE YOU, ALL OUR GUESTS SEE VERY WELL INDEED!
1895

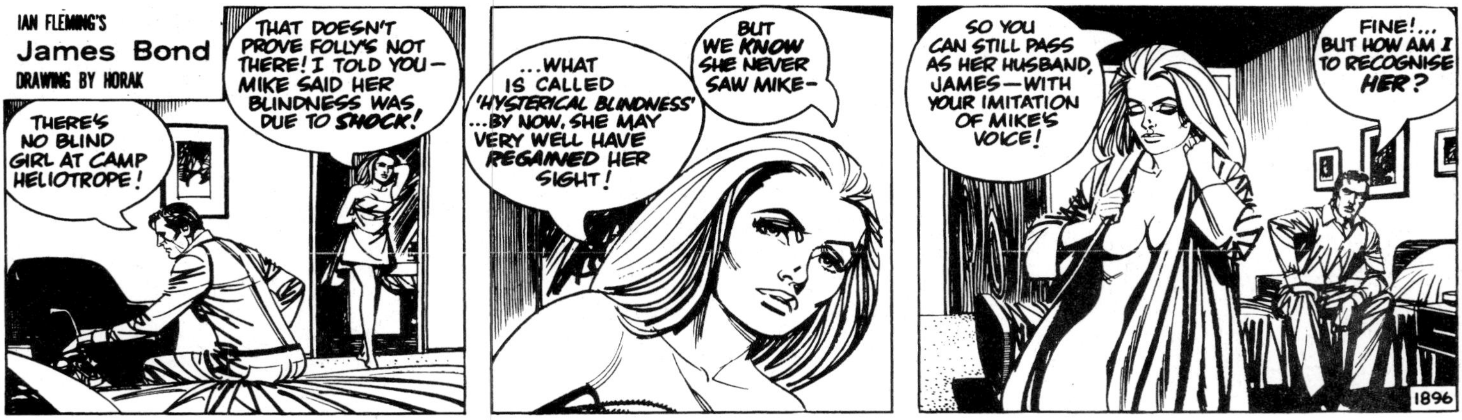
IAN FLEMING'S
James Bond
DRAWING BY HORAK
THERE'S NO BLIND GIRL AT CAMP HELIOTROPE!
THAT DOESN'T PROVE FOLLY'S NOT THERE! I TOLD YOU—MIKE SAID HER BLINDNESS WAS DUE TO SHOCK!
BUT WE KNOW SHE NEVER SAW MIKE—
...WHAT IS CALLED 'HYSTERICAL BLINDNESS' ...BY NOW, SHE MAY VERY WELL HAVE REGAINED HER SIGHT!
SO YOU CAN STILL PASS AS HER HUSBAND, JAMES—WITH YOUR IMITATION OF MIKE'S VOICE!
FINE!... BUT HOW AM I TO RECOGNISE HER?
1896

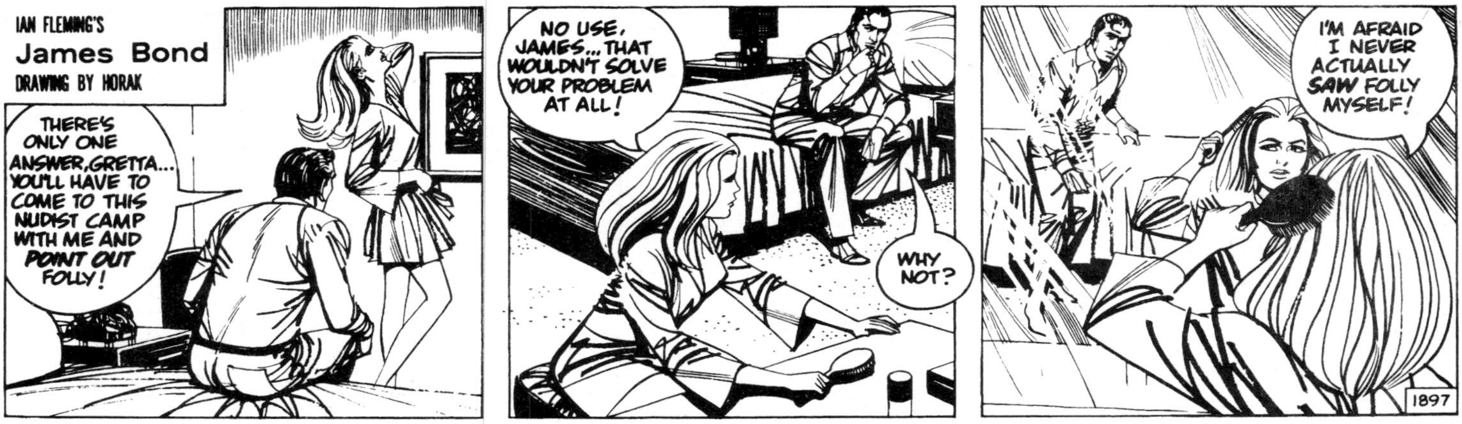
IAN FLEMING'S
James Bond
DRAWING BY HORAK
THERE'S ONLY ONE ANSWER, GRETTA... YOU'LL HAVE TO COME TO THIS NUDIST CAMP WITH ME AND POINT OUT FOLLY!
NO USE, JAMES... THAT WOULDN'T SOLVE YOUR PROBLEM AT ALL!
WHY NOT?
I'M AFRAID I NEVER ACTUALLY SAW FOLLY MYSELF!
1897

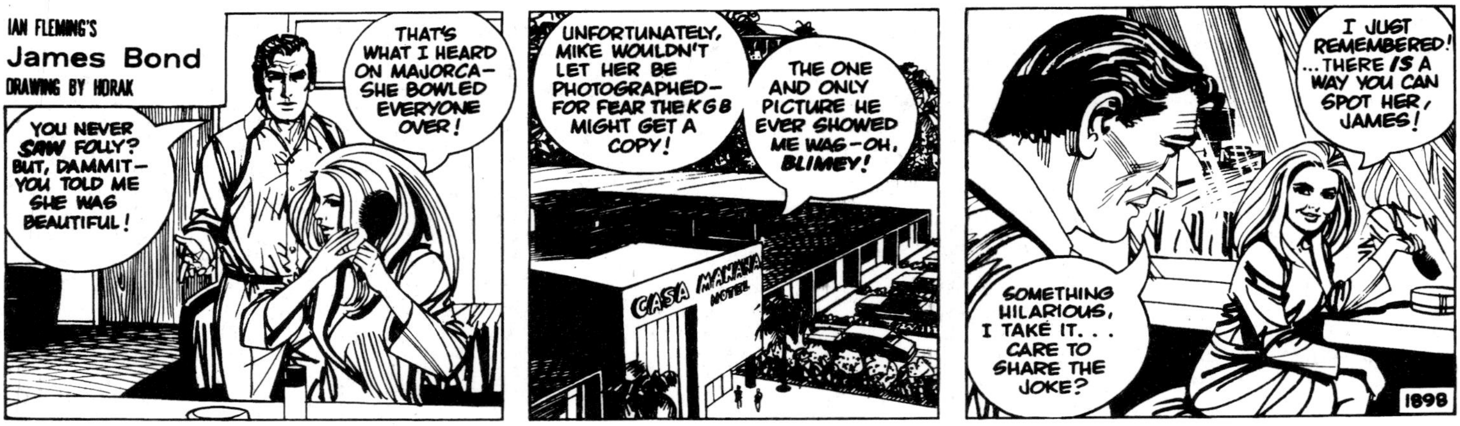
IAN FLEMING'S
James Bond
DRAWING BY HORAK
YOU NEVER SAW FOLLY? BUT, DAMMIT—YOU TOLD ME SHE WAS BEAUTIFUL!
THAT'S WHAT I HEARD ON MAJORCA—SHE BOWLED EVERYONE OVER!
UNFORTUNATELY, MIKE WOULDN'T LET HER BE PHOTOGRAPHED—FOR FEAR THE KGB MIGHT GET A COPY!
THE ONE AND ONLY PICTURE HE EVER SHOWED ME WAS—OH, BLIMEY!
CASA MANANA MOTEL
I JUST REMEMBERED! ...THERE IS A WAY YOU CAN SPOT HER, JAMES!
SOMETHING HILARIOUS, I TAKE IT. . . CARE TO SHARE THE JOKE?
1898

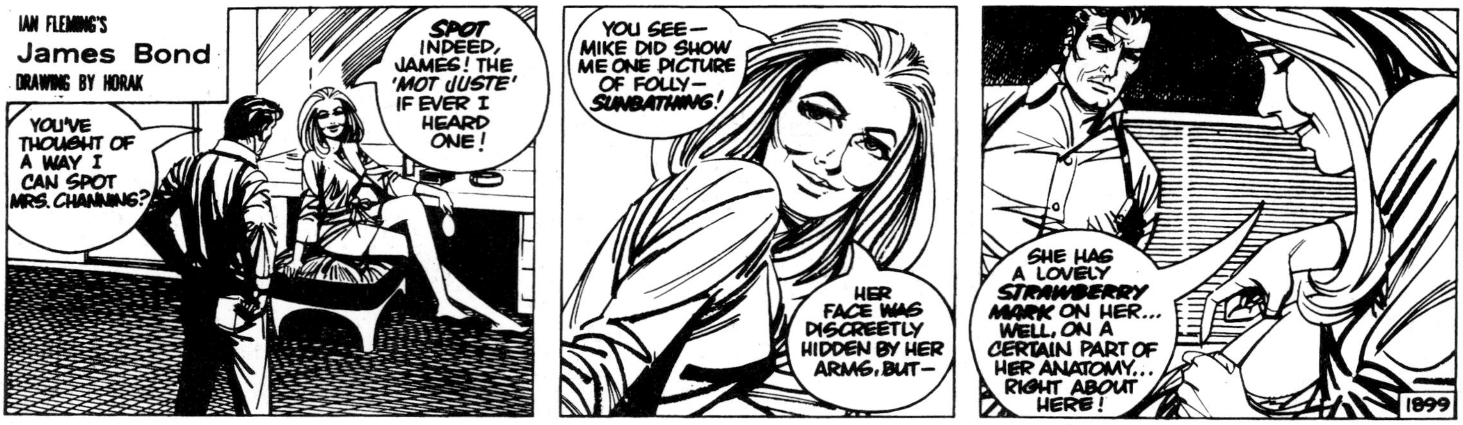
IAN FLEMING'S
James Bond
DRAWING BY HORAK
YOU'VE THOUGHT OF A WAY I CAN SPOT MRS. CHANNING?
SPOT INDEED, JAMES! THE 'MOT JUSTE' IF EVER I HEARD ONE!
YOU SEE—MIKE DID SHOW ME ONE PICTURE OF FOLLY—SUNBATHING!
HER FACE WAS DISCREETLY HIDDEN BY HER ARMS, BUT—
SHE HAS A LOVELY STRAWBERRY MARK ON HER... WELL, ON A CERTAIN PART OF HER ANATOMY... RIGHT ABOUT HERE!
1899

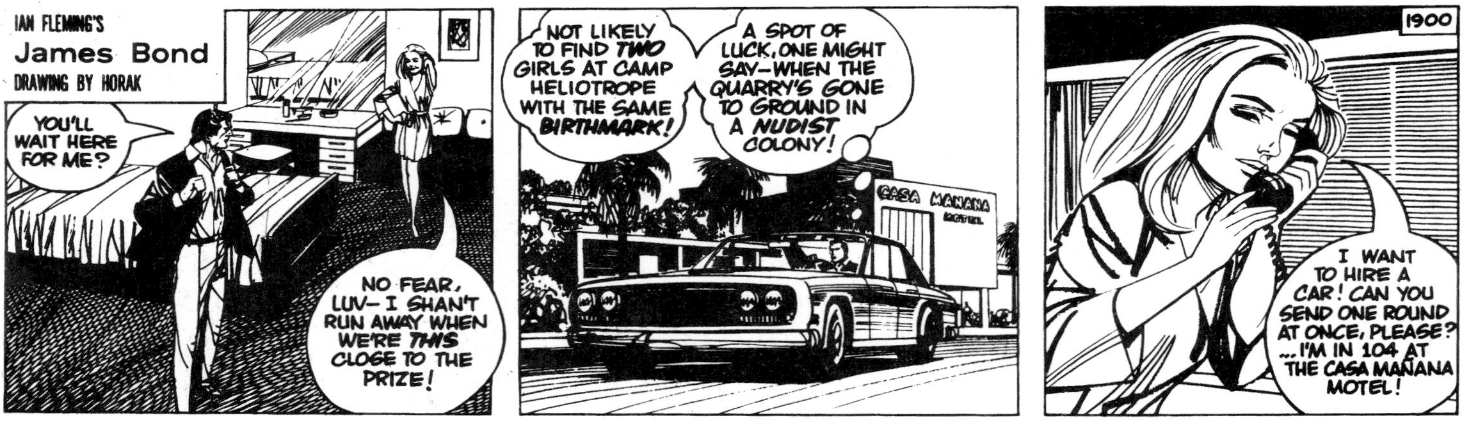
IAN FLEMING'S
James Bond
DRAWING BY HORAK
YOU'LL WAIT HERE FOR ME?
NO FEAR, LUV—I SHAN'T RUN AWAY WHEN WE'RE THIS CLOSE TO THE PRIZE!
NOT LIKELY TO FIND TWO GIRLS AT CAMP HELIOTROPE WITH THE SAME BIRTHMARK!
A SPOT OF LUCK, ONE MIGHT SAY—WHEN THE QUARRY'S GONE TO GROUND IN A NUDIST COLONY!
CASA MANANA MOTEL
1900
I WANT TO HIRE A CAR! CAN YOU SEND ONE ROUND AT ONCE, PLEASE? ...I'M IN 104 AT THE CASA MAÑANA MOTEL!

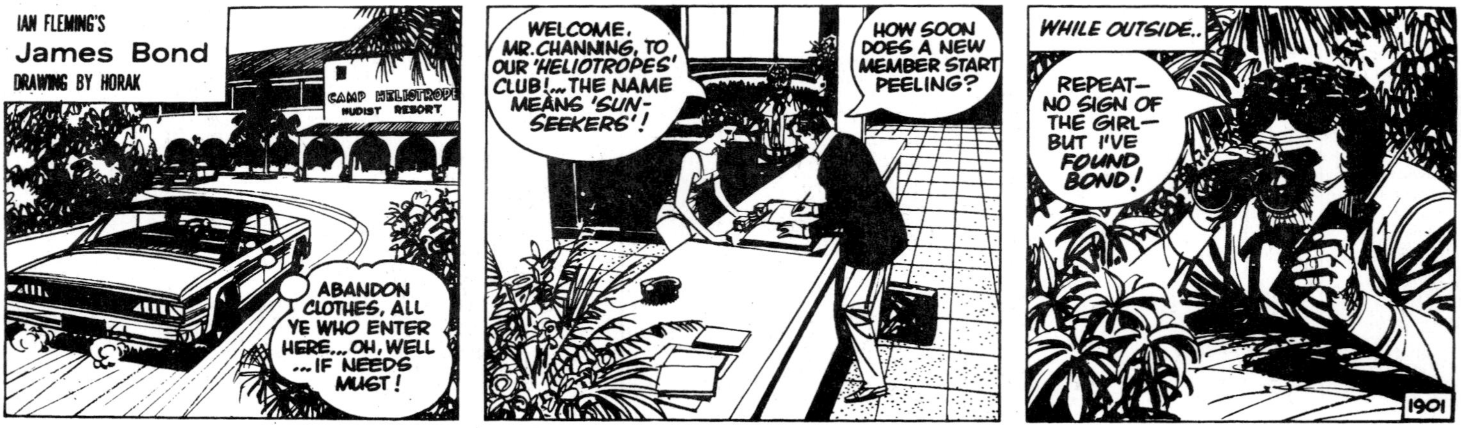
IAN FLEMING'S
James Bond
DRAWING BY HORAK
CAMP HELIOTROPE NUDIST RESORT
ABANDON CLOTHES, ALL YE WHO ENTER HERE... OH, WELL ...IF NEEDS MUST!
WELCOME, MR. CHANNING, TO OUR 'HELIOTROPES' CLUB!... THE NAME MEANS 'SUN-SEEKERS'!
HOW SOON DOES A NEW MEMBER START PEELING?
WHILE OUTSIDE..
REPEAT—NO SIGN OF THE GIRL—BUT I'VE FOUND BOND!
1901

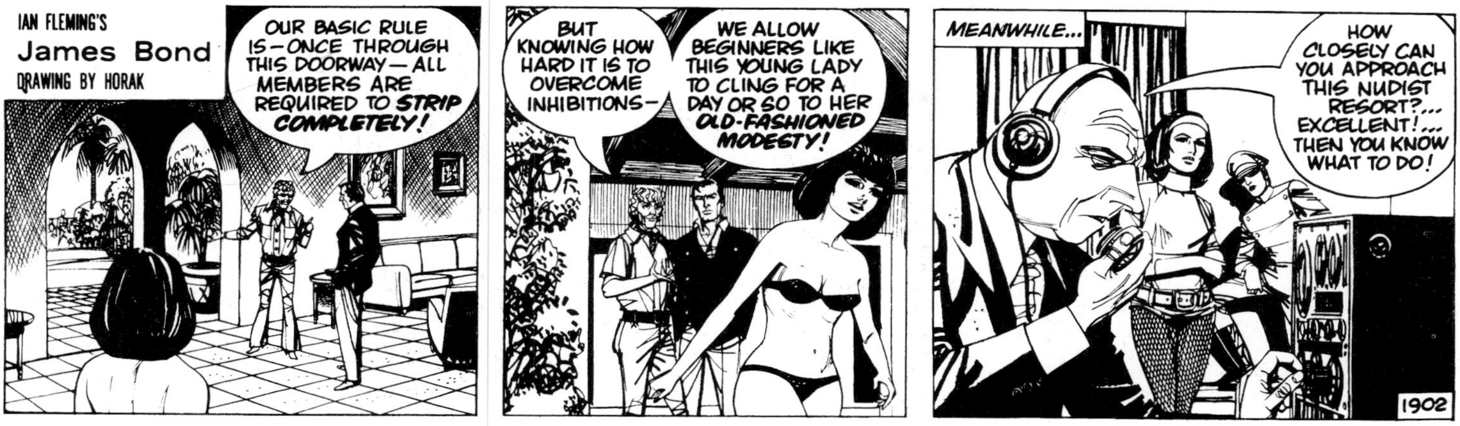
IAN FLEMING'S
James Bond
DRAWING BY HORAK
OUR BASIC RULE IS—ONCE THROUGH THIS DOORWAY—ALL MEMBERS ARE REQUIRED TO STRIP COMPLETELY!
BUT KNOWING HOW HARD IT IS TO OVERCOME INHIBITIONS—
WE ALLOW BEGINNERS LIKE THIS YOUNG LADY TO CLING FOR A DAY OR SO TO HER OLD-FASHIONED MODESTY!
MEANWHILE...
HOW CLOSELY CAN YOU APPROACH THIS NUDIST RESORT?... EXCELLENT!... THEN YOU KNOW WHAT TO DO!
1902

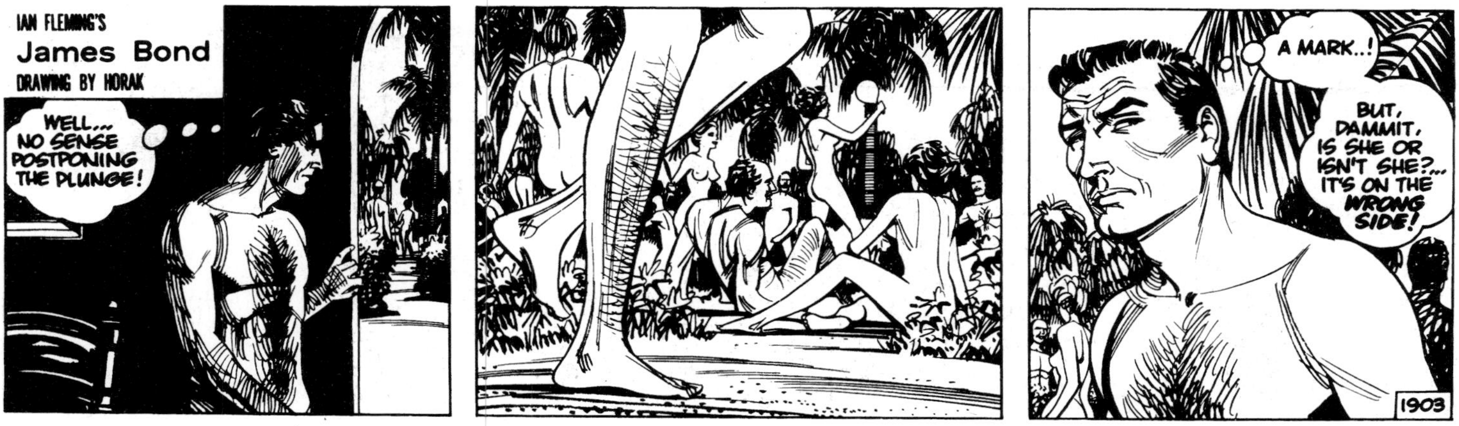
IAN FLEMING'S
James Bond
DRAWING BY HORAK
WELL... NO SENSE POSTPONING THE PLUNGE!
A MARK..!
BUT, DAMMIT, IS SHE OR ISN'T SHE?... IT'S ON THE WRONG SIDE!
1903

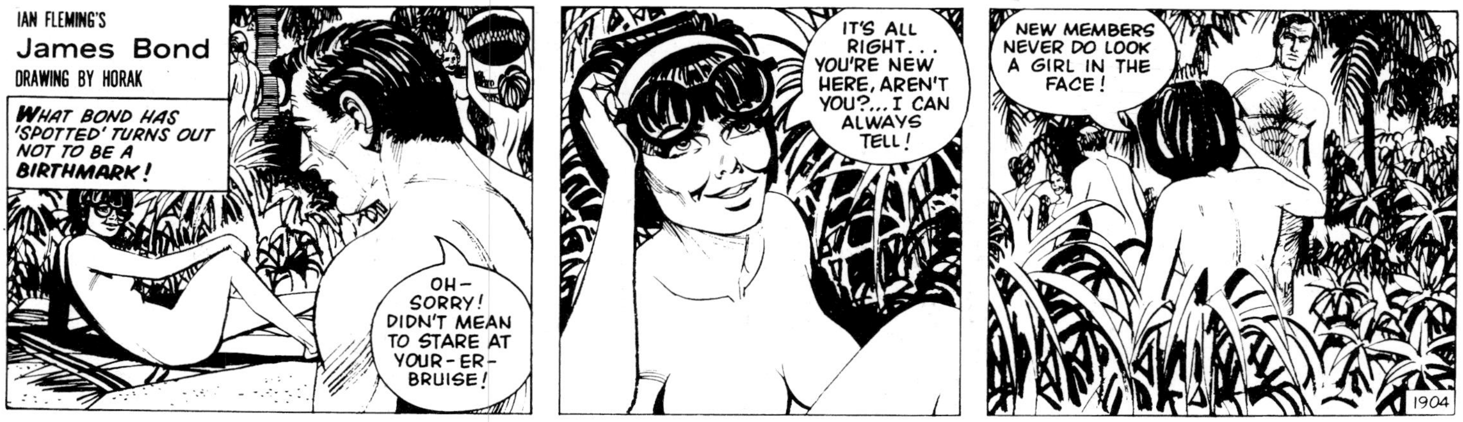
IAN FLEMING'S
James Bond
DRAWING BY HORAK
WHAT BOND HAS 'SPOTTED' TURNS OUT NOT TO BE A BIRTHMARK!
OH—SORRY! DIDN'T MEAN TO STARE AT YOUR-ER-BRUISE!
IT'S ALL RIGHT... YOU'RE NEW HERE, AREN'T YOU?... I CAN ALWAYS TELL!
NEW MEMBERS NEVER DO LOOK A GIRL IN THE FACE!
1904

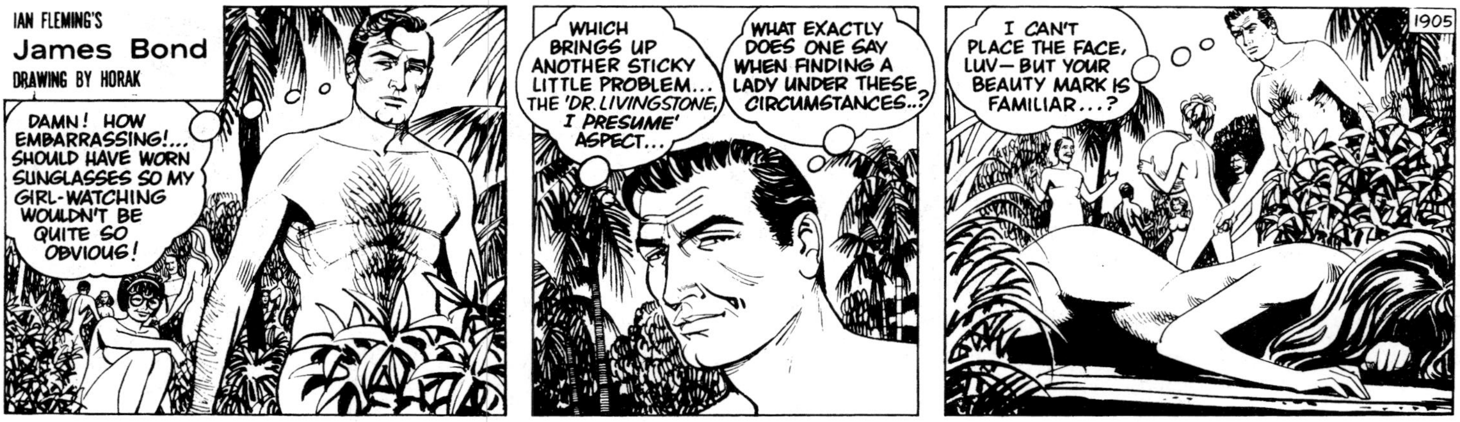
IAN FLEMING'S
James Bond
DRAWING BY HORAK
DAMN! HOW EMBARRASSING!... SHOULD HAVE WORN SUNGLASSES SO MY GIRL-WATCHING WOULDN'T BE QUITE SO OBVIOUS!
WHICH BRINGS UP ANOTHER STICKY LITTLE PROBLEM... THE 'DR. LIVINGSTONE, I PRESUME' ASPECT...
WHAT EXACTLY DOES ONE SAY WHEN FINDING A LADY UNDER THESE CIRCUMSTANCES..?
1905
I CAN'T PLACE THE FACE, LUV—BUT YOUR BEAUTY MARK IS FAMILIAR...?

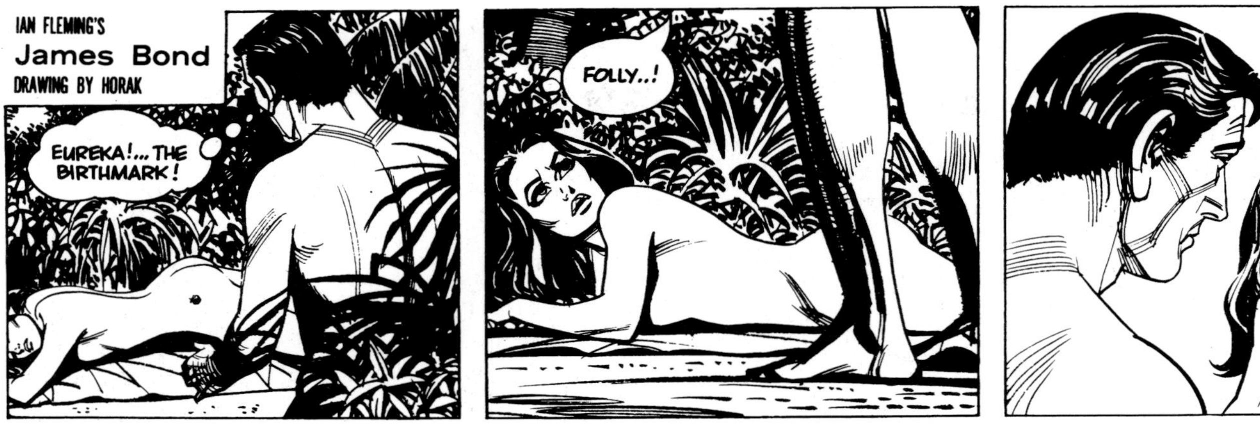
IAN FLEMING'S
James Bond
DRAWING BY HORAK
EUREKA!... THE BIRTHMARK!
FOLLY..!
1906
OH, MY GOD! ...MIKE!!

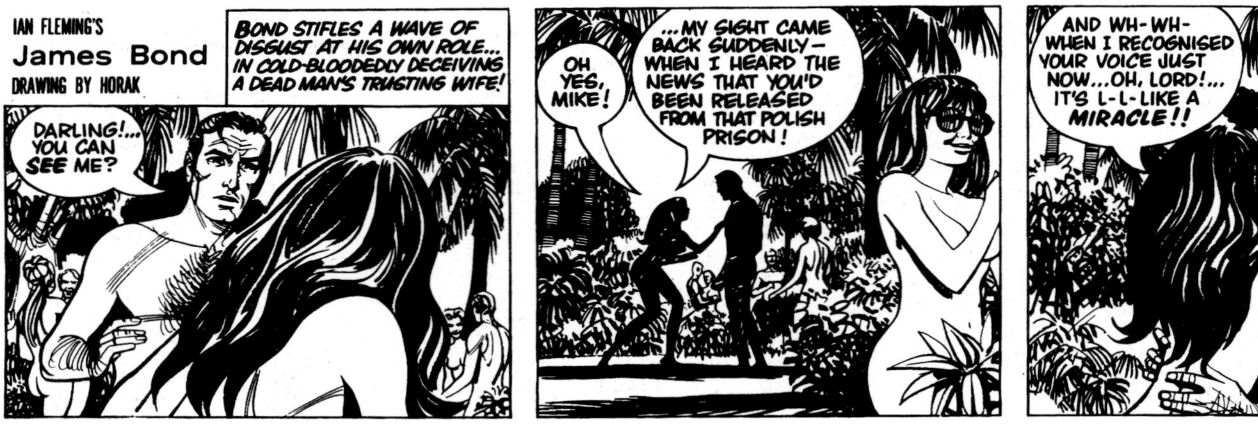
IAN FLEMING'S
James Bond
DRAWING BY HORAK
BOND STIFLES A WAVE OF DISGUST AT HIS OWN ROLE... IN COLD-BLOODEDLY DECEIVING A DEAD MAN'S TRUSTING WIFE!
DARLING!... YOU CAN SEE ME?
OH YES, MIKE!
...MY SIGHT CAME BACK SUDDENLY— WHEN I HEARD THE NEWS THAT YOU'D BEEN RELEASED FROM THAT POLISH PRISON!
AND WH-WH-WHEN I RECOGNISED YOUR VOICE JUST NOW...OH, LORD!... IT'S L-L-LIKE A MIRACLE!!
1907

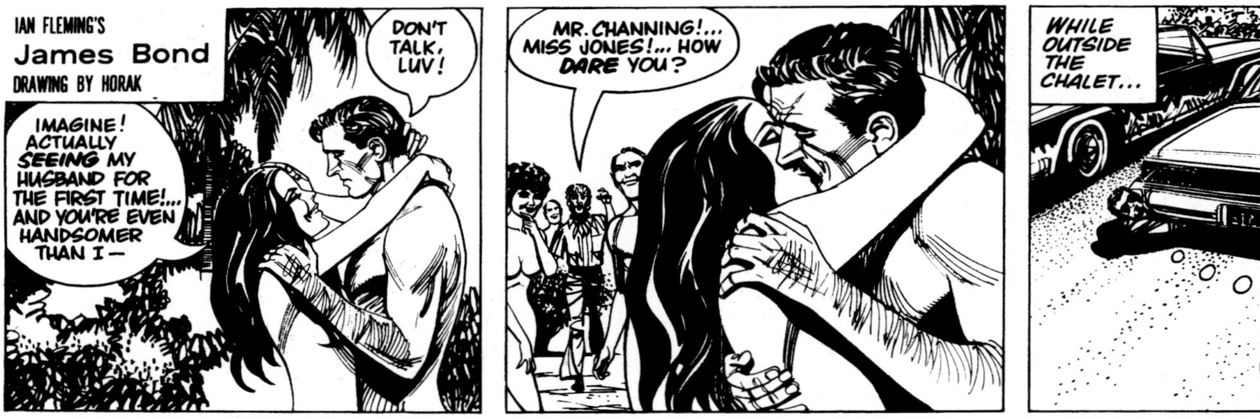
IAN FLEMING'S
James Bond
DRAWING BY HORAK
IMAGINE! ACTUALLY SEEING MY HUSBAND FOR THE FIRST TIME!... AND YOU'RE EVEN HANDSOMER THAN I—
DON'T TALK, LUV!
MR. CHANNING!... MISS JONES!... HOW DARE YOU?
1908
WHILE OUTSIDE THE CHALET...
AH! THAT DOES IT! THE ENGLISHMAN WILL BE IN FOR A SLIGHT SURPRISE WHEN HE LEAVES CAMP HELIOTROPE!

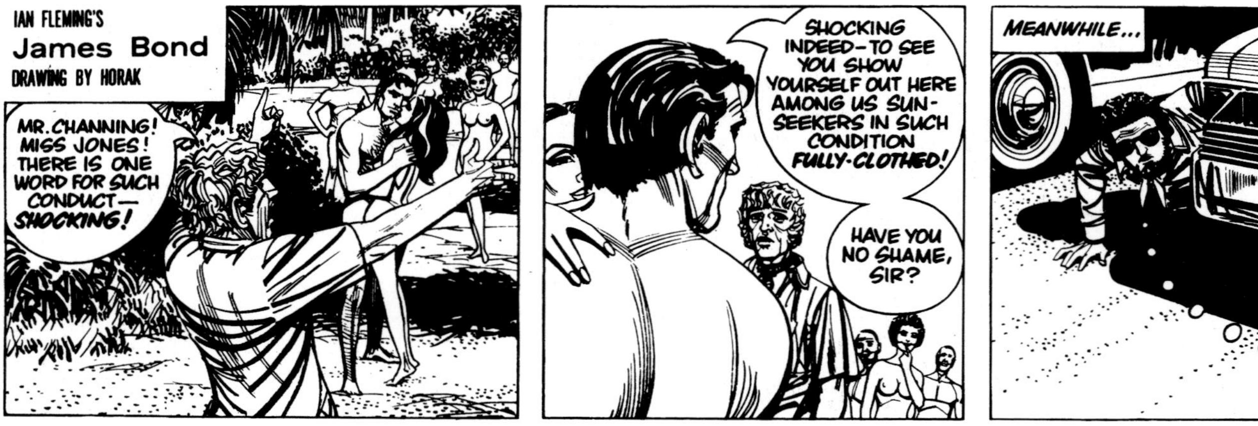
IAN FLEMING'S
James Bond
DRAWING BY HORAK
MR. CHANNING! MISS JONES! THERE IS ONE WORD FOR SUCH CONDUCT— SHOCKING!
SHOCKING INDEED—TO SEE YOU SHOW YOURSELF OUT HERE AMONG US SUN-SEEKERS IN SUCH CONDITION FULLY-CLOTHED!
HAVE YOU NO SHAME, SIR?
MEANWHILE...
1909
CHANNING'S GIRL FRIEND! ... AND SHE'S COMING THIS WAY! ... MUSTN'T LET HER SEE ME!

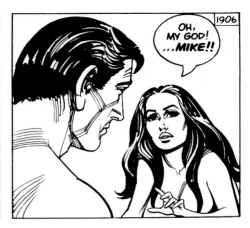

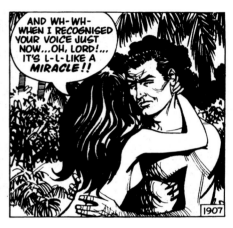

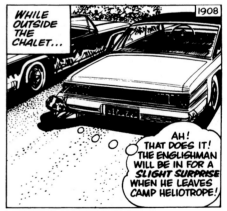

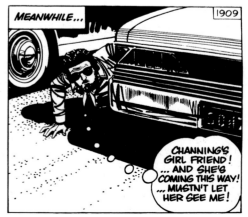

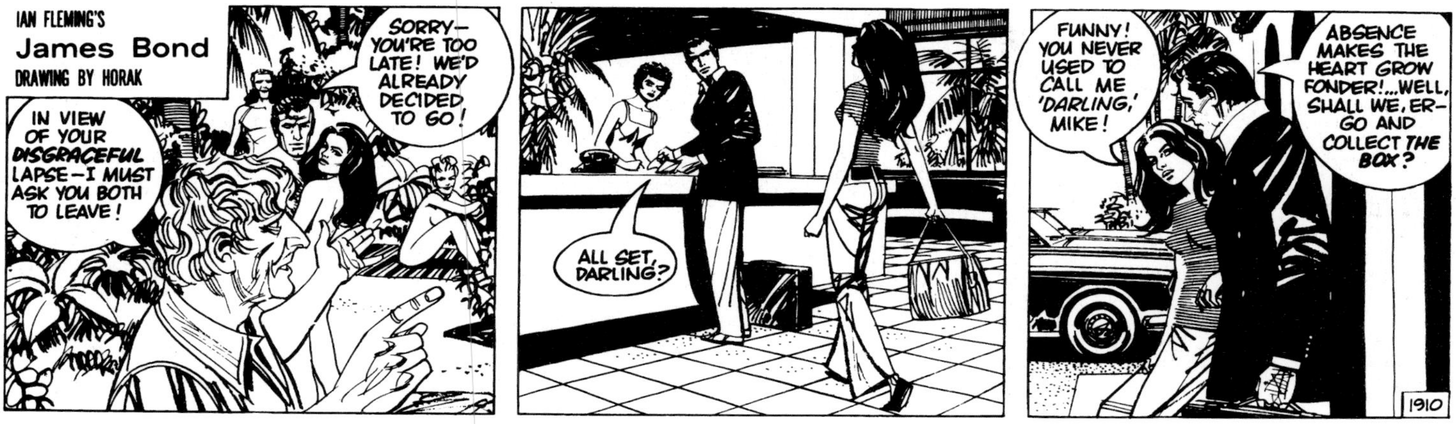
IAN FLEMING'S James Bond DRAWING BY HORAK
IN VIEW OF YOUR ***DISGRACEFUL*** LAPSE—I MUST ASK YOU BOTH TO LEAVE!
SORRY—YOU'RE TOO LATE! WE'D ALREADY DECIDED TO GO!
ALL SET, DARLING?
FUNNY! YOU NEVER USED TO CALL ME 'DARLING,' MIKE!
ABSENCE MAKES THE HEART GROW FONDER!...WELL, SHALL WE, ER—GO AND COLLECT ***THE BOX?***
1910

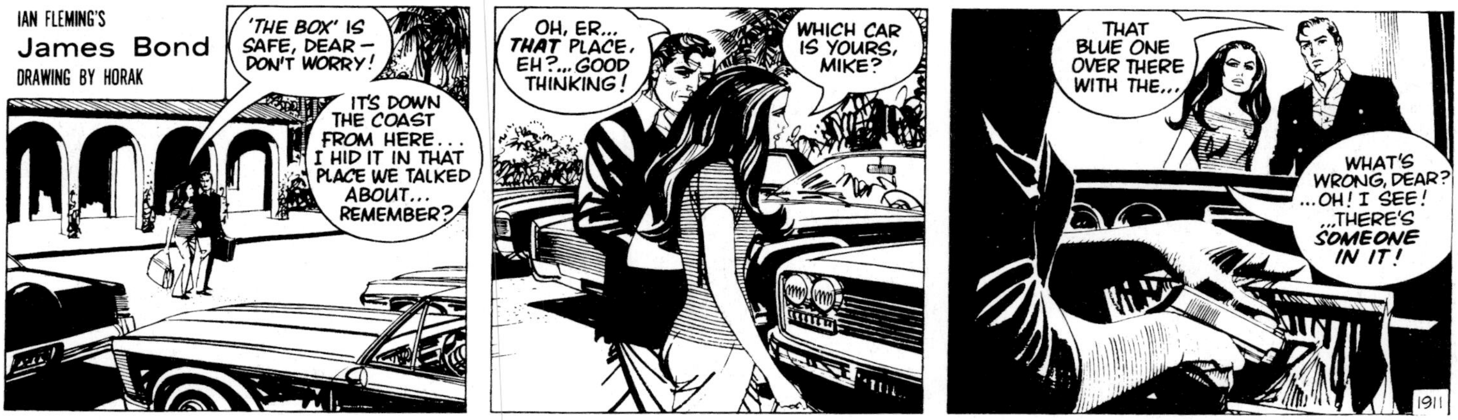
IAN FLEMING'S James Bond DRAWING BY HORAK
'THE BOX' IS SAFE, DEAR—DON'T WORRY!
IT'S DOWN THE COAST FROM HERE... I HID IT IN THAT PLACE WE TALKED ABOUT... REMEMBER?
OH, ER... ***THAT*** PLACE, EH?... GOOD THINKING!
WHICH CAR IS YOURS, MIKE?
THAT BLUE ONE OVER THERE WITH THE...
WHAT'S WRONG, DEAR? ...OH! I SEE! ...THERE'S ***SOMEONE IN IT!***
1911

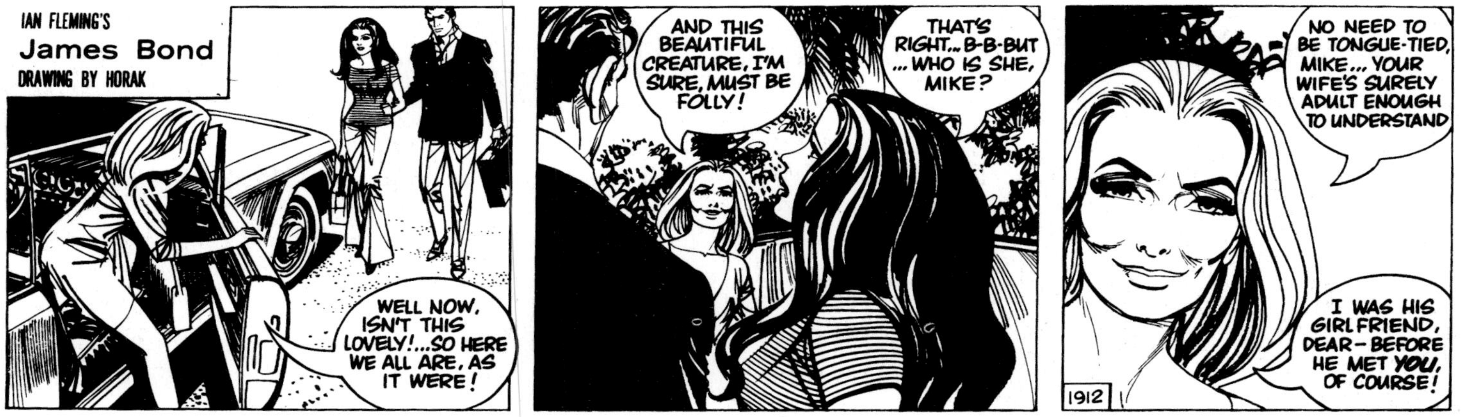
IAN FLEMING'S James Bond DRAWING BY HORAK
WELL NOW, ISN'T THIS LOVELY!...SO HERE WE ALL ARE, AS IT WERE!
AND THIS BEAUTIFUL CREATURE, I'M SURE, MUST BE FOLLY!
THAT'S RIGHT... B-B-BUT ...WHO IS SHE, MIKE?
1912
NO NEED TO BE TONGUE-TIED, MIKE... YOUR WIFE'S SURELY ADULT ENOUGH TO UNDERSTAND
I WAS HIS GIRLFRIEND, DEAR—BEFORE HE MET ***YOU,*** OF COURSE!

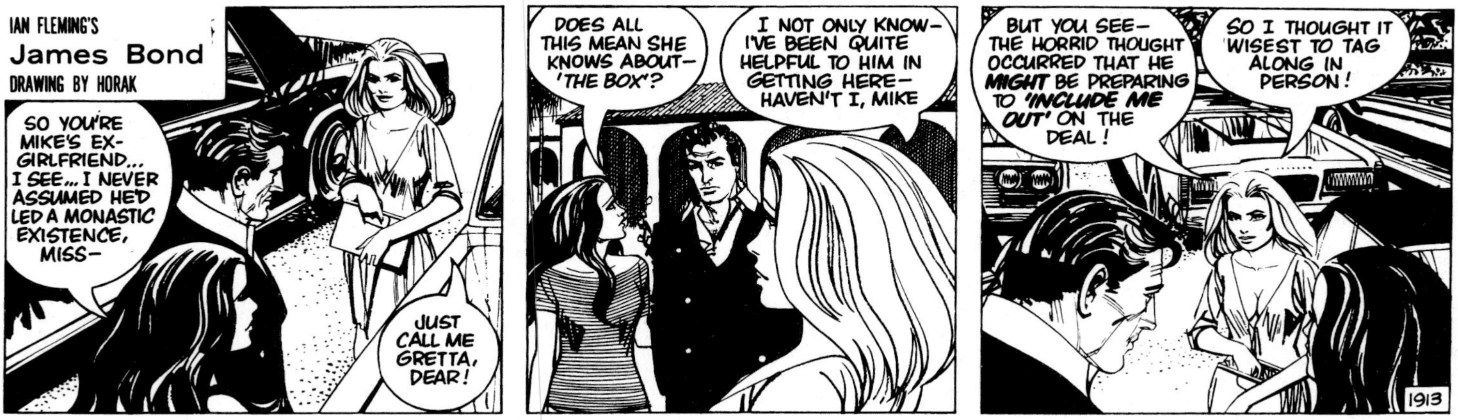
IAN FLEMING'S James Bond DRAWING BY HORAK
SO YOU'RE MIKE'S EX-GIRLFRIEND... I SEE... I NEVER ASSUMED HE'D LED A MONASTIC EXISTENCE, MISS—
JUST CALL ME GRETTA, DEAR!
DOES ALL THIS MEAN SHE KNOWS ABOUT—'THE BOX'?
I NOT ONLY KNOW—I'VE BEEN QUITE HELPFUL TO HIM IN GETTING HERE—HAVEN'T I, MIKE
BUT YOU SEE—THE HORRID THOUGHT OCCURRED THAT HE ***MIGHT*** BE PREPARING TO ***'INCLUDE ME OUT'*** ON THE DEAL!
SO I THOUGHT IT WISEST TO TAG ALONG IN PERSON!
1913

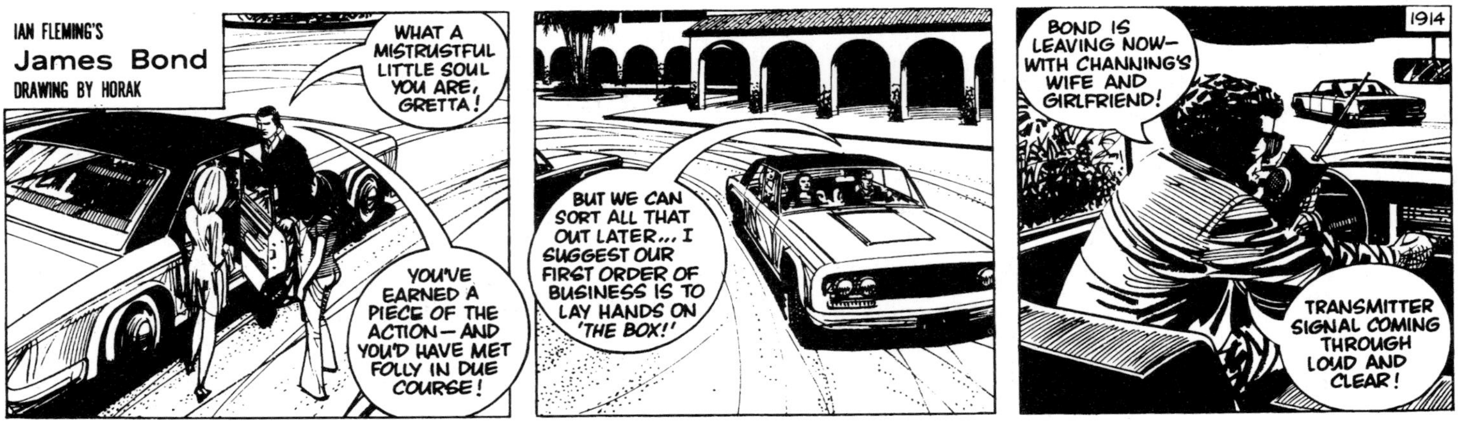
IAN FLEMING'S
James Bond
DRAWING BY HORAK
WHAT A MISTRUSTFUL LITTLE SOUL YOU ARE, GRETTA!
YOU'VE EARNED A PIECE OF THE ACTION—AND YOU'D HAVE MET FOLLY IN DUE COURSE!
BUT WE CAN SORT ALL THAT OUT LATER... I SUGGEST OUR FIRST ORDER OF BUSINESS IS TO LAY HANDS ON 'THE BOX!'
1914
BOND IS LEAVING NOW—WITH CHANNING'S WIFE AND GIRLFRIEND!
TRANSMITTER SIGNAL COMING THROUGH LOUD AND CLEAR!

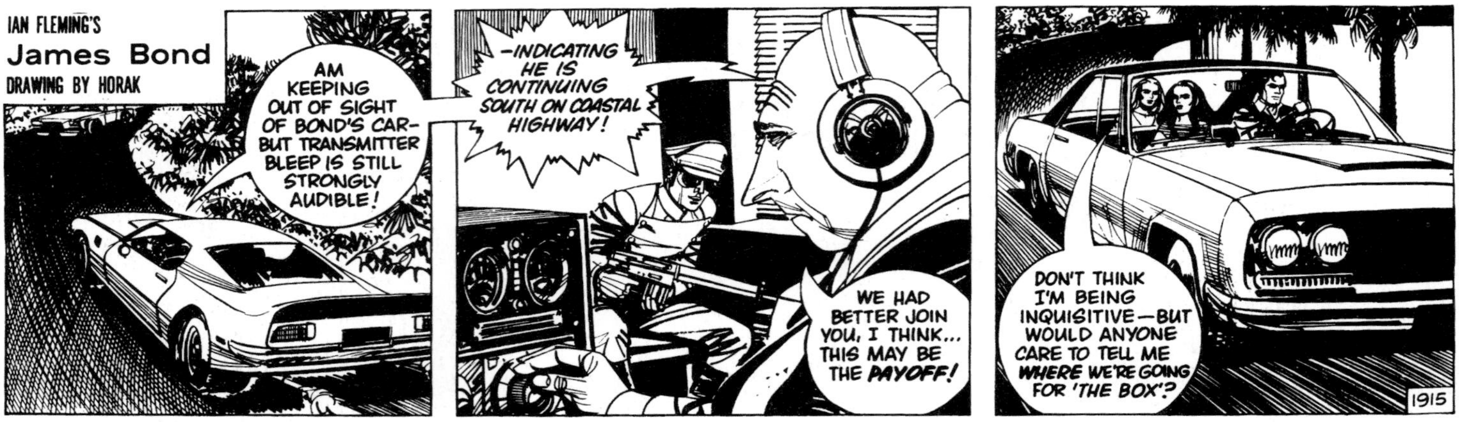
IAN FLEMING'S
James Bond
DRAWING BY HORAK
AM KEEPING OUT OF SIGHT OF BOND'S CAR-BUT TRANSMITTER BLEEP IS STILL STRONGLY AUDIBLE!
—INDICATING HE IS CONTINUING SOUTH ON COASTAL HIGHWAY!
WE HAD BETTER JOIN YOU, I THINK... THIS MAY BE THE PAYOFF!
DON'T THINK I'M BEING INQUISITIVE—BUT WOULD ANYONE CARE TO TELL ME WHERE WE'RE GOING FOR 'THE BOX'?
1915

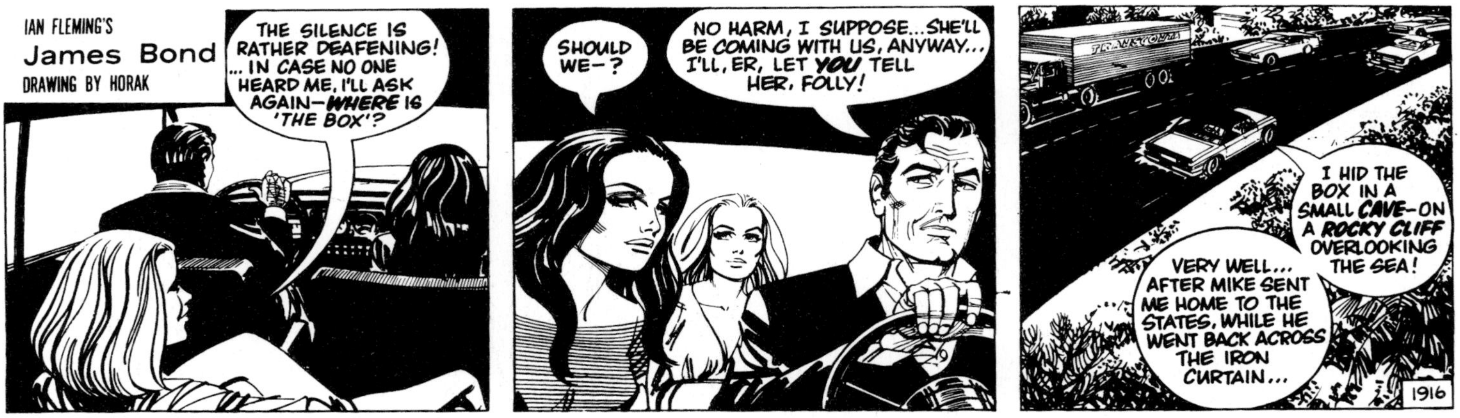
IAN FLEMING'S
James Bond
DRAWING BY HORAK
THE SILENCE IS RATHER DEAFENING! ... IN CASE NO ONE HEARD ME, I'LL ASK AGAIN—WHERE IS 'THE BOX'?
SHOULD WE—?
NO HARM, I SUPPOSE... SHE'LL BE COMING WITH US, ANYWAY... I'LL, ER, LET YOU TELL HER, FOLLY!
I HID THE BOX IN A SMALL CAVE—ON A ROCKY CLIFF OVERLOOKING THE SEA!
VERY WELL... AFTER MIKE SENT ME HOME TO THE STATES, WHILE HE WENT BACK ACROSS THE IRON CURTAIN...
1916

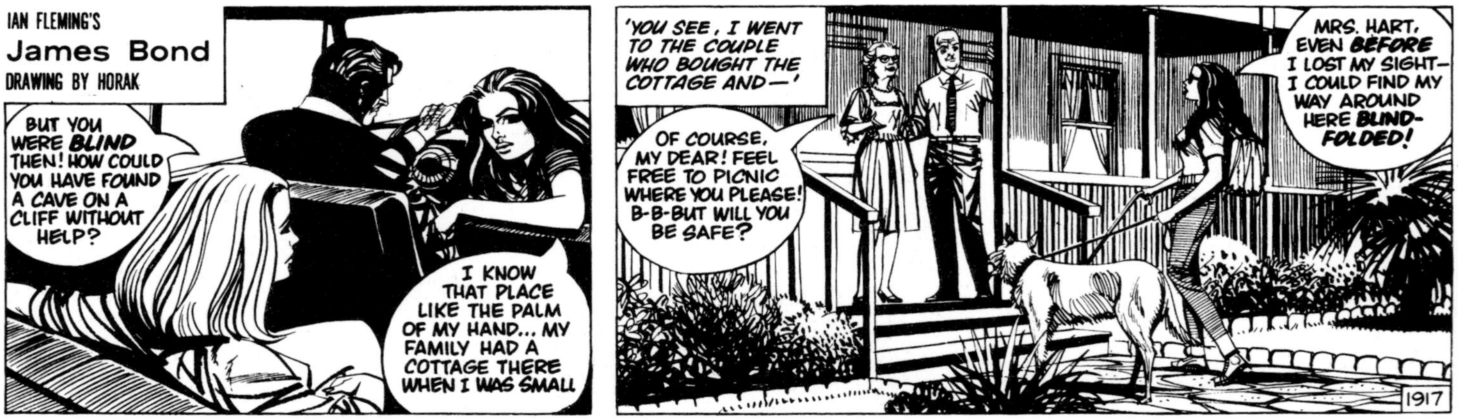
IAN FLEMING'S
James Bond
DRAWING BY HORAK
BUT YOU WERE BLIND THEN! HOW COULD YOU HAVE FOUND A CAVE ON A CLIFF WITHOUT HELP?
I KNOW THAT PLACE LIKE THE PALM OF MY HAND... MY FAMILY HAD A COTTAGE THERE WHEN I WAS SMALL
'YOU SEE, I WENT TO THE COUPLE WHO BOUGHT THE COTTAGE AND—'
OF COURSE, MY DEAR! FEEL FREE TO PICNIC WHERE YOU PLEASE! B-B-BUT WILL YOU BE SAFE?
MRS. HART, EVEN BEFORE I LOST MY SIGHT—I COULD FIND MY WAY AROUND HERE BLIND-FOLDED!
1917

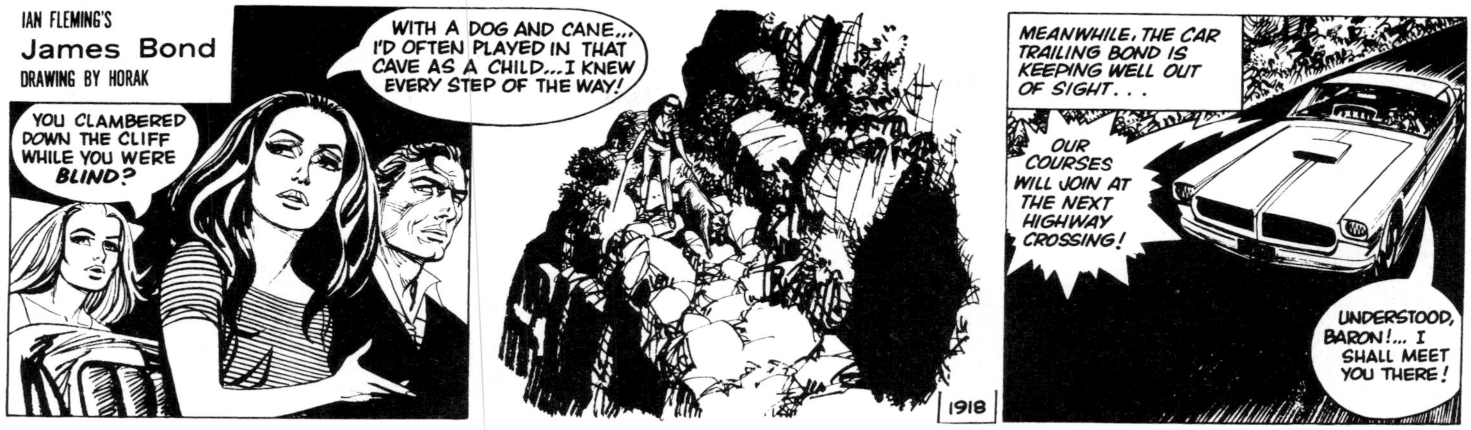
IAN FLEMING'S
James Bond
DRAWING BY HORAK
YOU CLAMBERED DOWN THE CLIFF WHILE YOU WERE BLIND?
WITH A DOG AND CANE... I'D OFTEN PLAYED IN THAT CAVE AS A CHILD... I KNEW EVERY STEP OF THE WAY!
MEANWHILE, THE CAR TRAILING BOND IS KEEPING WELL OUT OF SIGHT . . .
OUR COURSES WILL JOIN AT THE NEXT HIGHWAY CROSSING!
UNDERSTOOD, BARON!... I SHALL MEET YOU THERE!
1918

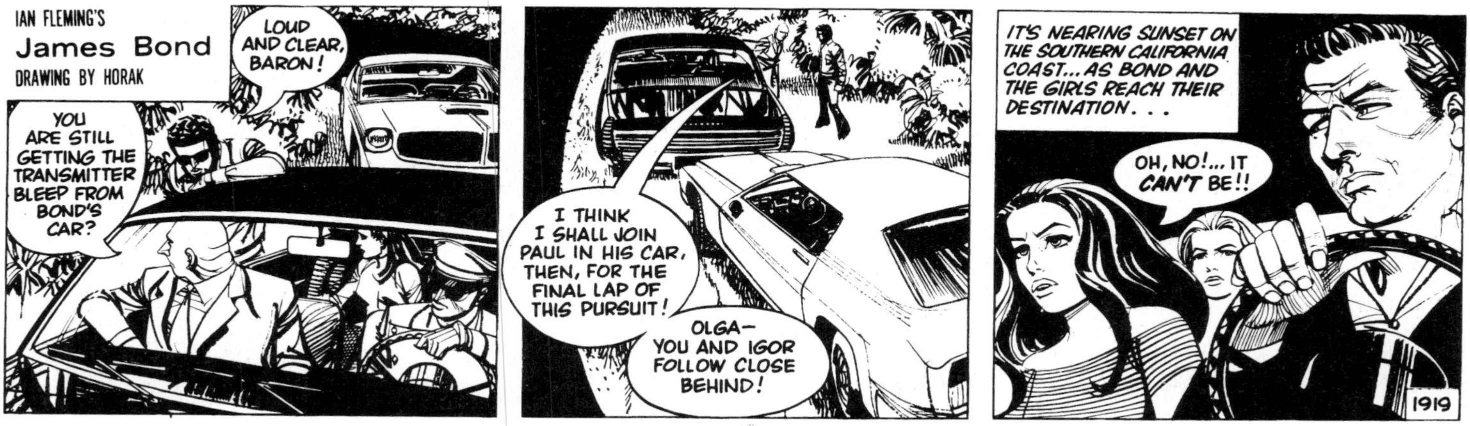
IAN FLEMING'S
James Bond
DRAWING BY HORAK
YOU ARE STILL GETTING THE TRANSMITTER BLEEP FROM BOND'S CAR?
LOUD AND CLEAR, BARON!
I THINK I SHALL JOIN PAUL IN HIS CAR, THEN, FOR THE FINAL LAP OF THIS PURSUIT!
OLGA— YOU AND IGOR FOLLOW CLOSE BEHIND!
IT'S NEARING SUNSET ON THE SOUTHERN CALIFORNIA COAST... AS BOND AND THE GIRLS REACH THEIR DESTINATION . . .
OH, NO!... IT CAN'T BE!!
1919

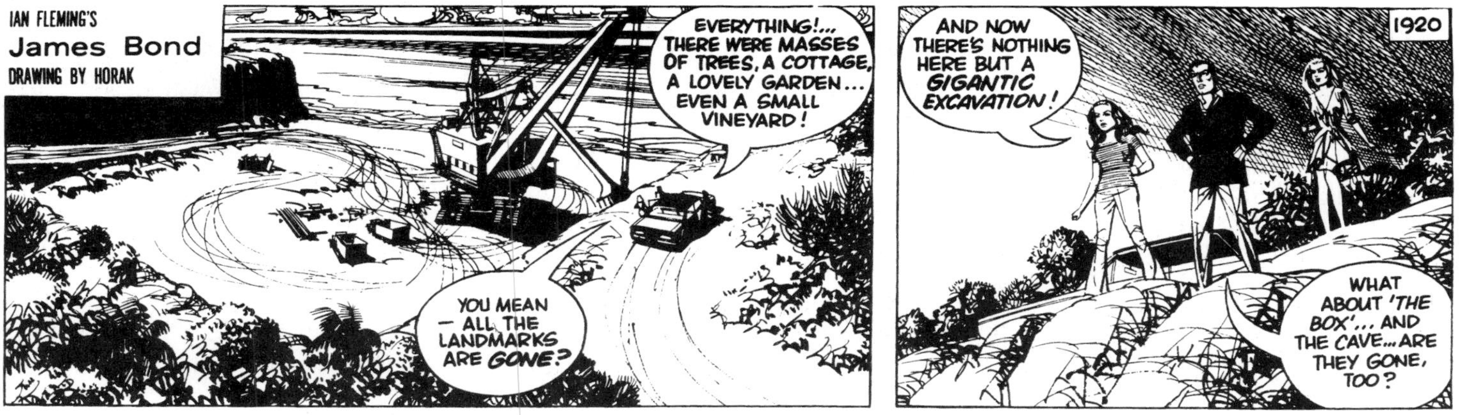
IAN FLEMING'S
James Bond
DRAWING BY HORAK
EVERYTHING!... THERE WERE MASSES OF TREES, A COTTAGE, A LOVELY GARDEN... EVEN A SMALL VINEYARD!
YOU MEAN — ALL THE LANDMARKS ARE GONE?
AND NOW THERE'S NOTHING HERE BUT A GIGANTIC EXCAVATION!
WHAT ABOUT 'THE BOX'... AND THE CAVE... ARE THEY GONE, TOO?
1920

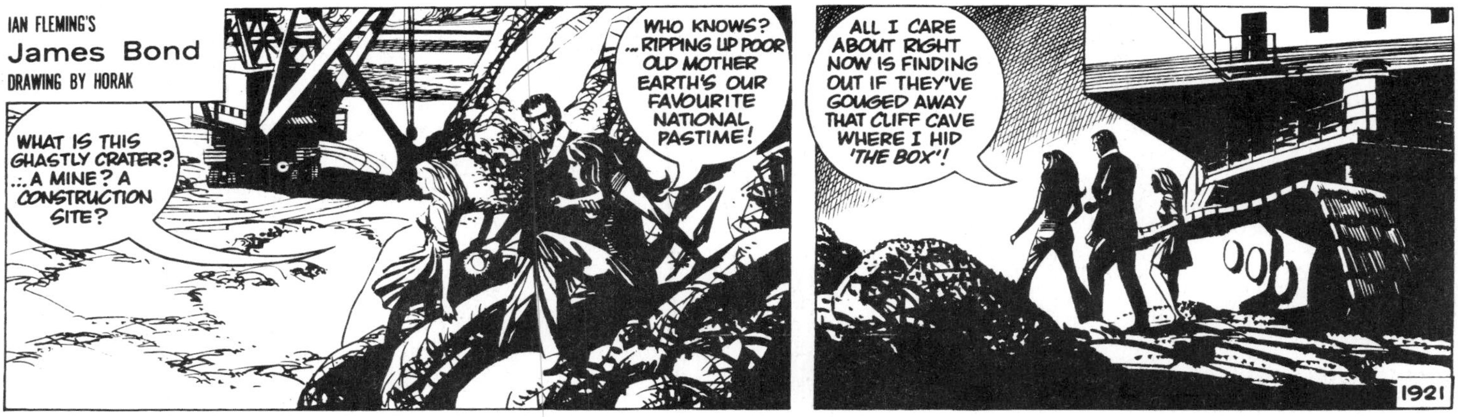
IAN FLEMING'S
James Bond
DRAWING BY HORAK
WHAT IS THIS GHASTLY CRATER? ... A MINE? A CONSTRUCTION SITE?
WHO KNOWS? ...RIPPING UP POOR OLD MOTHER EARTH'S OUR FAVOURITE NATIONAL PASTIME!
ALL I CARE ABOUT RIGHT NOW IS FINDING OUT IF THEY'VE GOUGED AWAY THAT CLIFF CAVE WHERE I HID 'THE BOX'!
1921

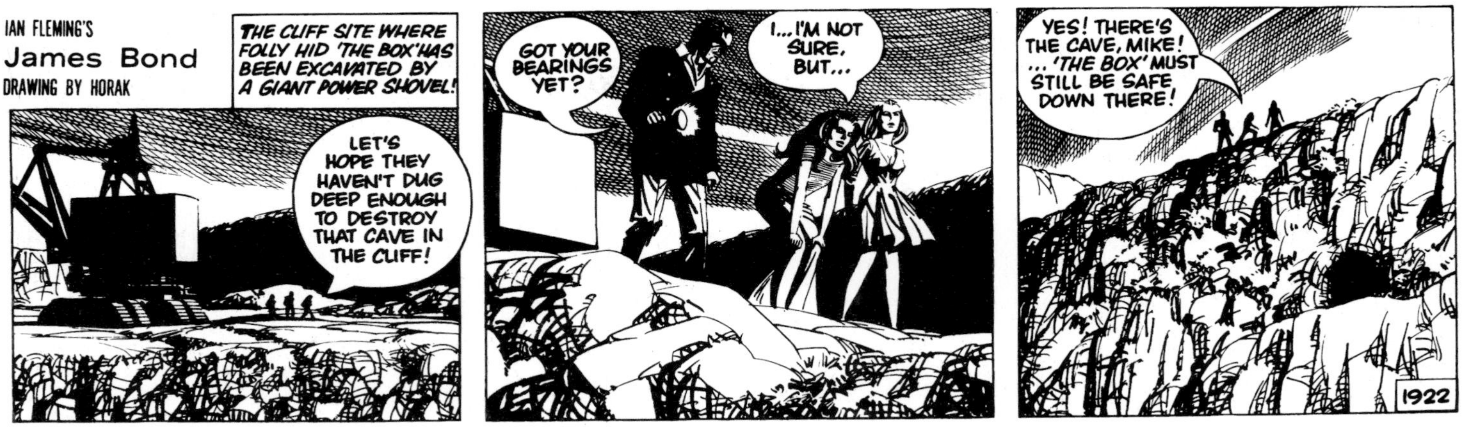
IAN FLEMING'S
James Bond
DRAWING BY HORAK
THE CLIFF SITE WHERE FOLLY HID 'THE BOX' HAS BEEN EXCAVATED BY A GIANT POWER SHOVEL!
LET'S HOPE THEY HAVEN'T DUG DEEP ENOUGH TO DESTROY THAT CAVE IN THE CLIFF!
GOT YOUR BEARINGS YET?
I... I'M NOT SURE, BUT...
YES! THERE'S THE CAVE, MIKE! ... 'THE BOX' MUST STILL BE SAFE DOWN THERE!
1922

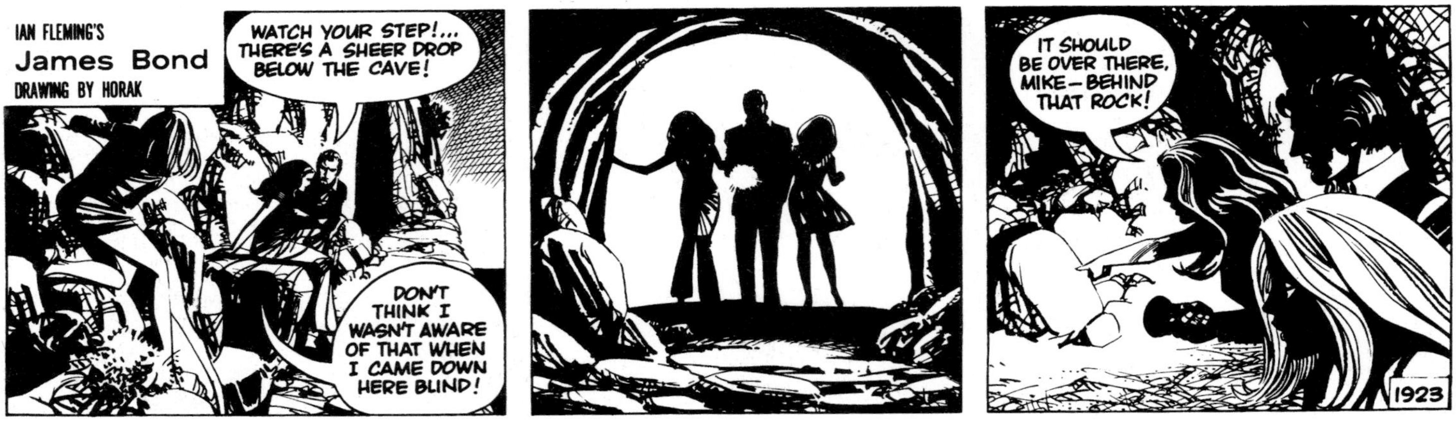
IAN FLEMING'S
James Bond
DRAWING BY HORAK
WATCH YOUR STEP!... THERE'S A SHEER DROP BELOW THE CAVE!
DON'T THINK I WASN'T AWARE OF THAT WHEN I CAME DOWN HERE BLIND!
IT SHOULD BE OVER THERE, MIKE—BEHIND THAT ROCK!
1923

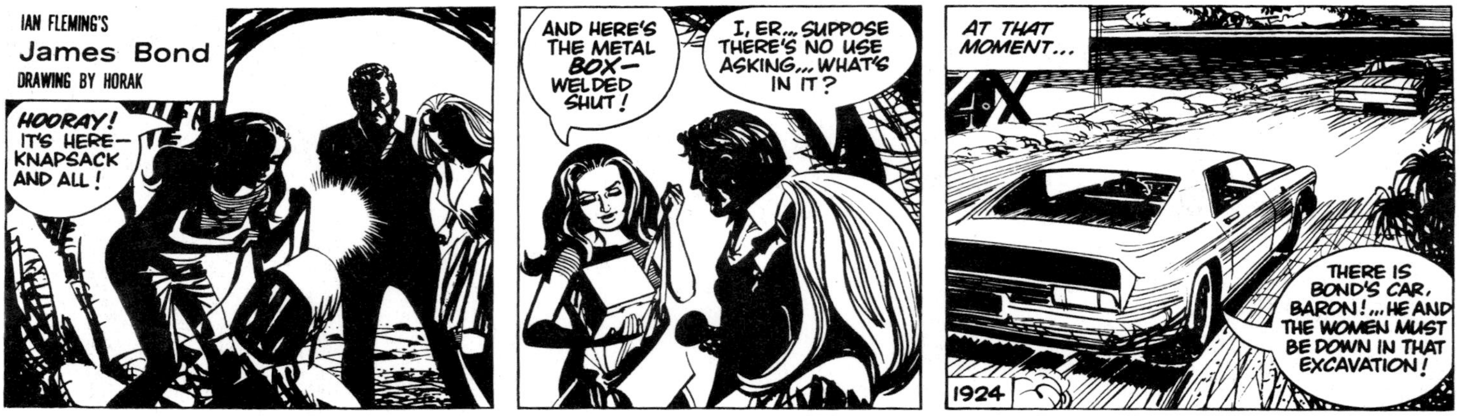
IAN FLEMING'S
James Bond
DRAWING BY HORAK
HOORAY! IT'S HERE—KNAPSACK AND ALL!
AND HERE'S THE METAL BOX—WELDED SHUT!
I, ER... SUPPOSE THERE'S NO USE ASKING... WHAT'S IN IT?
AT THAT MOMENT...
THERE IS BOND'S CAR, BARON!... HE AND THE WOMEN MUST BE DOWN IN THAT EXCAVATION!
1924

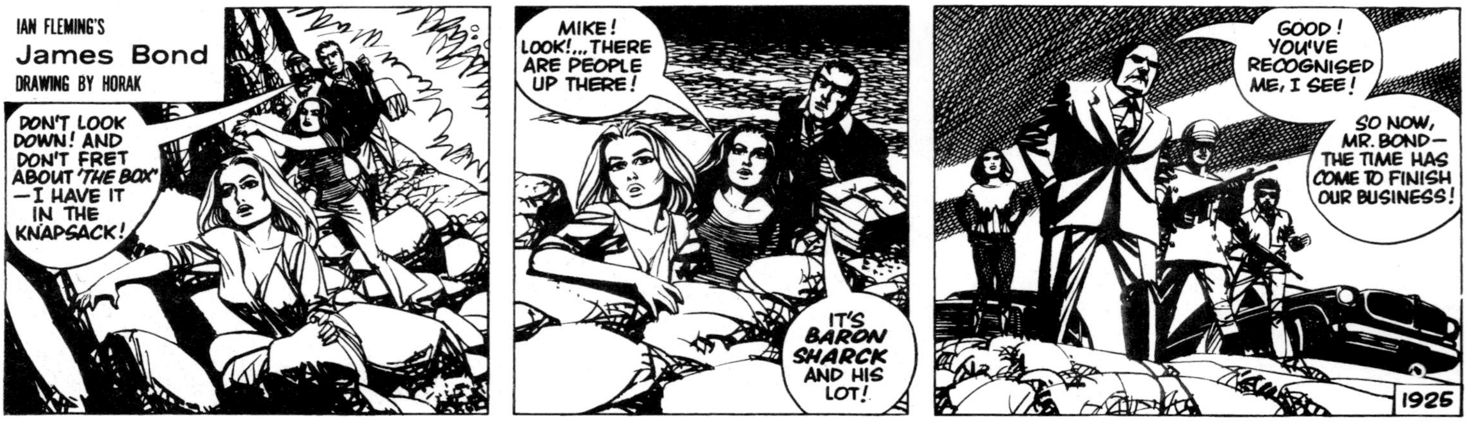
IAN FLEMING'S
James Bond
DRAWING BY HORAK
DON'T LOOK DOWN! AND DON'T FRET ABOUT 'THE BOX' —I HAVE IT IN THE KNAPSACK!
MIKE! LOOK!... THERE ARE PEOPLE UP THERE!
IT'S BARON SHARCK AND HIS LOT!
GOOD! YOU'VE RECOGNISED ME, I SEE!
SO NOW, MR. BOND—THE TIME HAS COME TO FINISH OUR BUSINESS!
1925

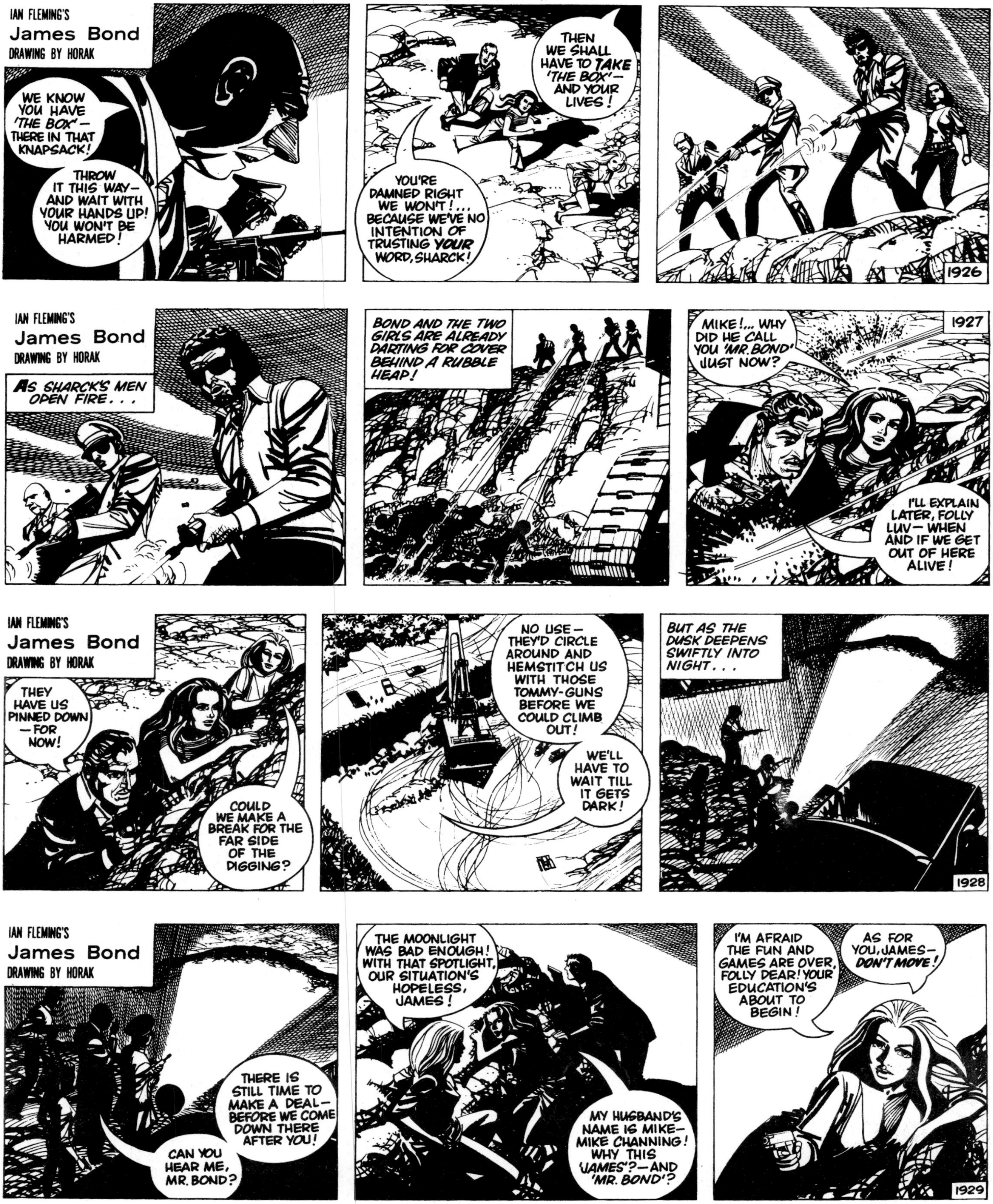
IAN FLEMING'S
James Bond
DRAWING BY HORAK
WE KNOW YOU HAVE 'THE BOX'— THERE IN THAT KNAPSACK!
THROW IT THIS WAY— AND WAIT WITH YOUR HANDS UP! YOU WON'T BE HARMED!
THEN WE SHALL HAVE TO TAKE 'THE BOX'— AND YOUR LIVES!
YOU'RE DAMNED RIGHT WE WON'T!... BECAUSE WE'VE NO INTENTION OF TRUSTING YOUR WORD, SHARCK!
1926
IAN FLEMING'S
James Bond
DRAWING BY HORAK
AS SHARCK'S MEN OPEN FIRE...
BOND AND THE TWO GIRLS ARE ALREADY DARTING FOR COVER BEHIND A RUBBLE HEAP!
1927
MIKE!... WHY DID HE CALL YOU 'MR. BOND' JUST NOW?
I'LL EXPLAIN LATER, FOLLY LUV— WHEN AND IF WE GET OUT OF HERE ALIVE!
IAN FLEMING'S
James Bond
DRAWING BY HORAK
THEY HAVE US PINNED DOWN —FOR NOW!
COULD WE MAKE A BREAK FOR THE FAR SIDE OF THE DIGGING?
NO USE— THEY'D CIRCLE AROUND AND HEMSTITCH US WITH THOSE TOMMY-GUNS BEFORE WE COULD CLIMB OUT!
WE'LL HAVE TO WAIT TILL IT GETS DARK!
BUT AS THE DUSK DEEPENS SWIFTLY INTO NIGHT...
1928
IAN FLEMING'S
James Bond
DRAWING BY HORAK
THERE IS STILL TIME TO MAKE A DEAL— BEFORE WE COME DOWN THERE AFTER YOU!
CAN YOU HEAR ME, MR. BOND?
THE MOONLIGHT WAS BAD ENOUGH! WITH THAT SPOTLIGHT, OUR SITUATION'S HOPELESS, JAMES!
MY HUSBAND'S NAME IS MIKE— MIKE CHANNING! WHY THIS 'JAMES'?— AND 'MR. BOND'?
I'M AFRAID THE FUN AND GAMES ARE OVER, FOLLY DEAR! YOUR EDUCATION'S ABOUT TO BEGIN!
AS FOR YOU, JAMES— DON'T MOVE!
1929

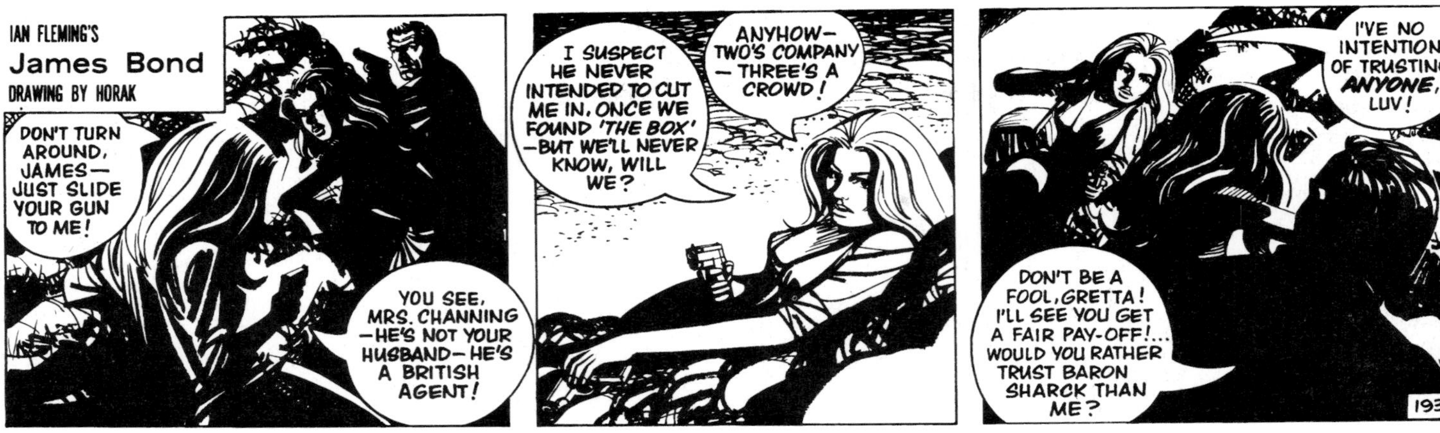
IAN FLEMING'S
James Bond
DRAWING BY HORAK
DON'T TURN AROUND, JAMES—JUST SLIDE YOUR GUN TO ME!
YOU SEE, MRS. CHANNING—HE'S NOT YOUR HUSBAND—HE'S A BRITISH AGENT!
I SUSPECT HE NEVER INTENDED TO CUT ME IN, ONCE WE FOUND 'THE BOX'—BUT WE'LL NEVER KNOW, WILL WE?
ANYHOW—TWO'S COMPANY—THREE'S A CROWD!
I'VE NO INTENTION OF TRUSTING ANYONE, LUV!
DON'T BE A FOOL, GRETTA! I'LL SEE YOU GET A FAIR PAY-OFF!... WOULD YOU RATHER TRUST BARON SHARCK THAN ME?
1930

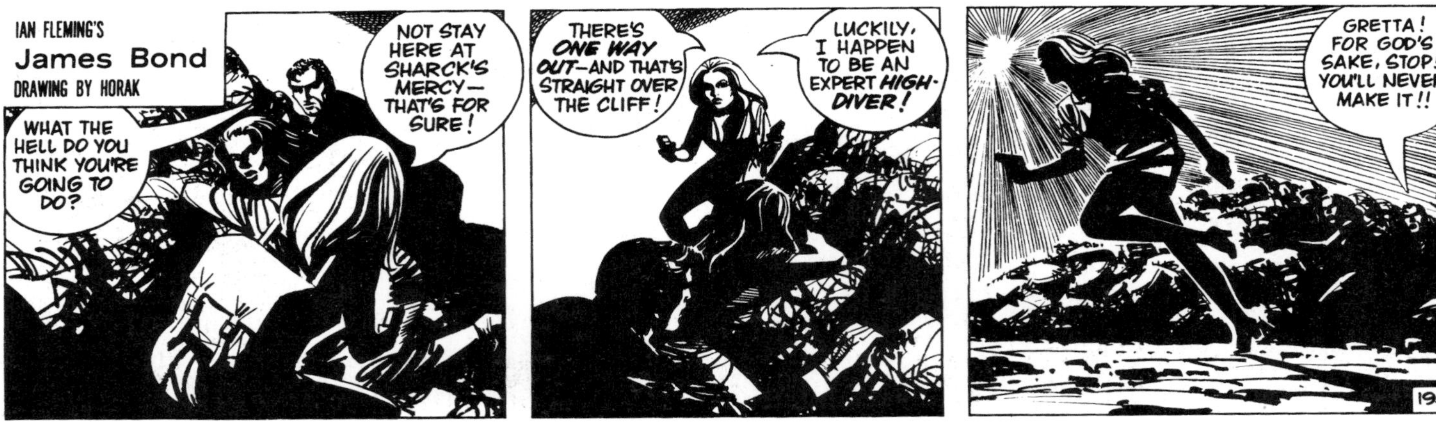
IAN FLEMING'S
James Bond
DRAWING BY HORAK
WHAT THE HELL DO YOU THINK YOU'RE GOING TO DO?
NOT STAY HERE AT SHARCK'S MERCY—THAT'S FOR SURE!
THERE'S ONE WAY OUT—AND THAT'S STRAIGHT OVER THE CLIFF!
LUCKILY, I HAPPEN TO BE AN EXPERT HIGH-DIVER!
GRETTA! FOR GOD'S SAKE, STOP!... YOU'LL NEVER MAKE IT!!
1931

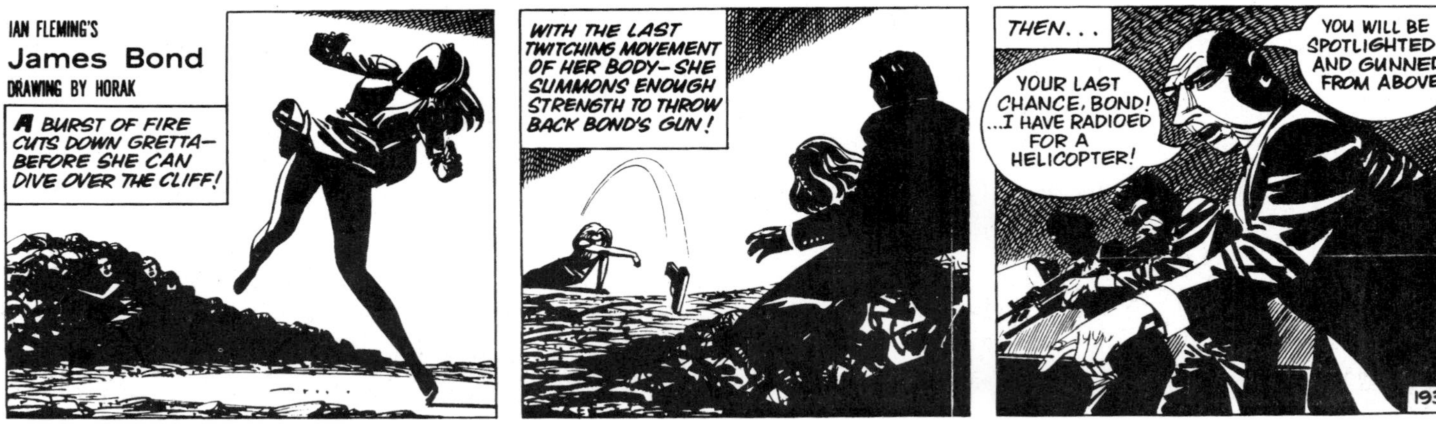
IAN FLEMING'S
James Bond
DRAWING BY HORAK
A BURST OF FIRE CUTS DOWN GRETTA—BEFORE SHE CAN DIVE OVER THE CLIFF!
WITH THE LAST TWITCHING MOVEMENT OF HER BODY—SHE SUMMONS ENOUGH STRENGTH TO THROW BACK BOND'S GUN!
THEN...
YOUR LAST CHANCE, BOND! ...I HAVE RADIOED FOR A HELICOPTER!
YOU WILL BE SPOTLIGHTED AND GUNNED FROM ABOVE!
1932

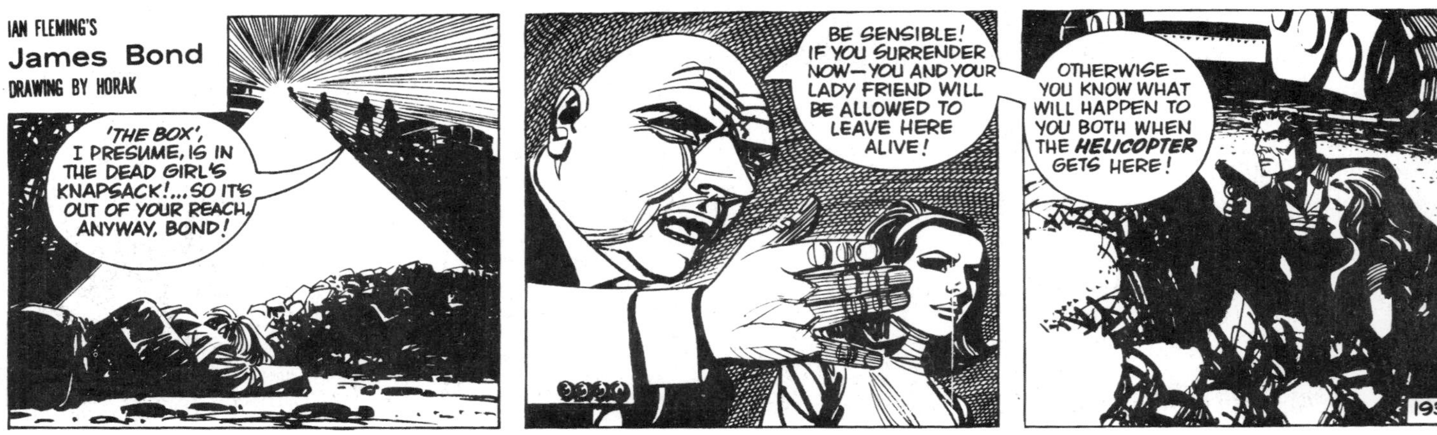
IAN FLEMING'S
James Bond
DRAWING BY HORAK
'THE BOX', I PRESUME, IS IN THE DEAD GIRL'S KNAPSACK!... SO IT'S OUT OF YOUR REACH, ANYWAY, BOND!
BE SENSIBLE! IF YOU SURRENDER NOW—YOU AND YOUR LADY FRIEND WILL BE ALLOWED TO LEAVE HERE ALIVE!
OTHERWISE—YOU KNOW WHAT WILL HAPPEN TO YOU BOTH WHEN THE HELICOPTER GETS HERE!
1933

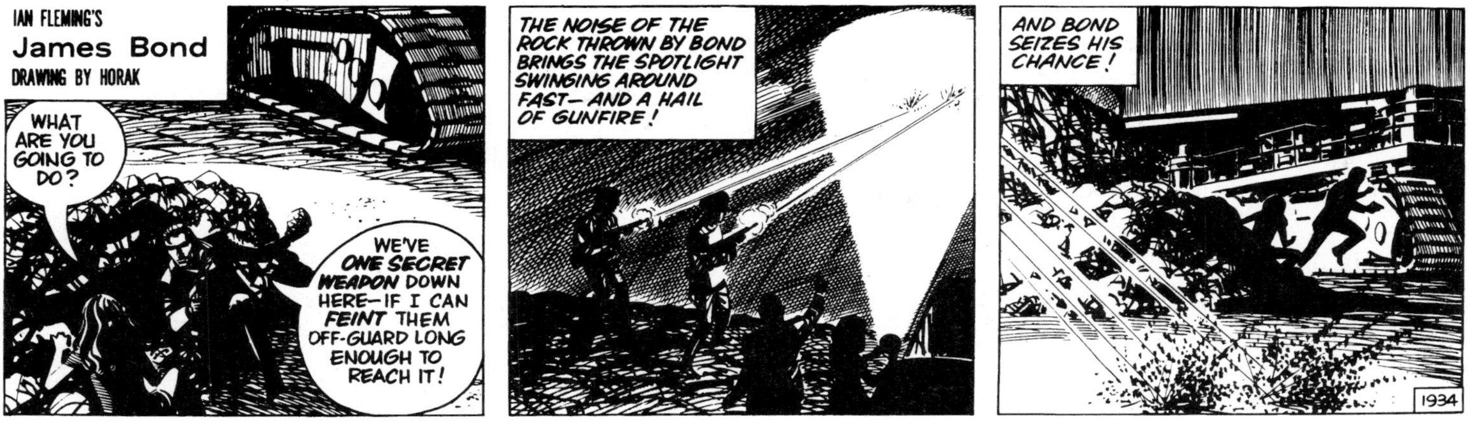
IAN FLEMING'S
James Bond
DRAWING BY HORAK
WHAT ARE YOU GOING TO DO?
WE'VE ONE SECRET WEAPON DOWN HERE—IF I CAN FEINT THEM OFF-GUARD LONG ENOUGH TO REACH IT!
THE NOISE OF THE ROCK THROWN BY BOND BRINGS THE SPOTLIGHT SWINGING AROUND FAST— AND A HAIL OF GUNFIRE!
AND BOND SEIZES HIS CHANCE!
1934

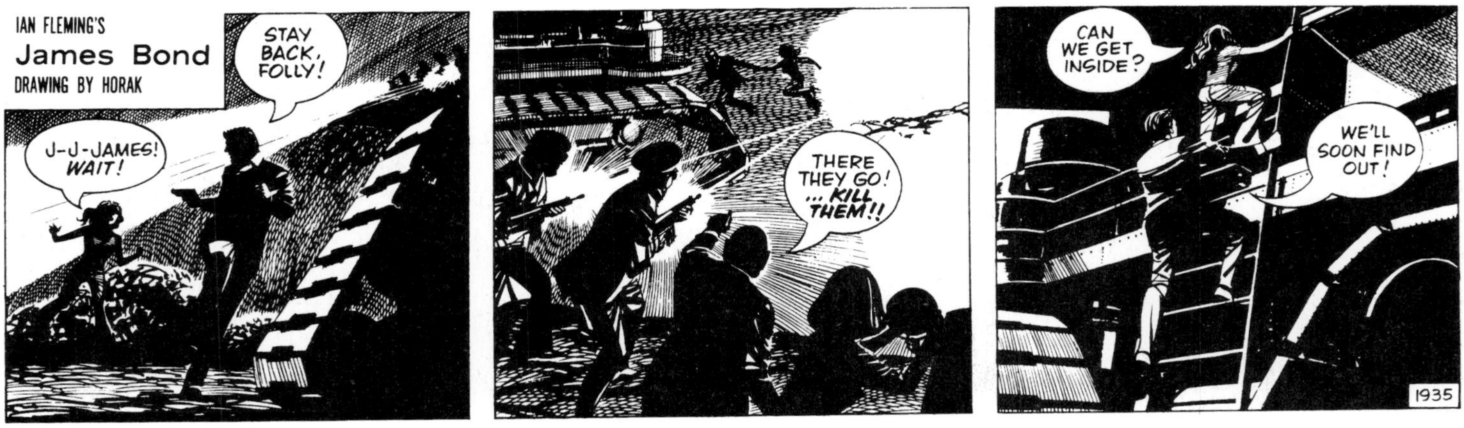
IAN FLEMING'S
James Bond
DRAWING BY HORAK
STAY BACK, FOLLY!
J-J-JAMES! WAIT!
THERE THEY GO! ... KILL THEM!!
CAN WE GET INSIDE?
WE'LL SOON FIND OUT!
1935

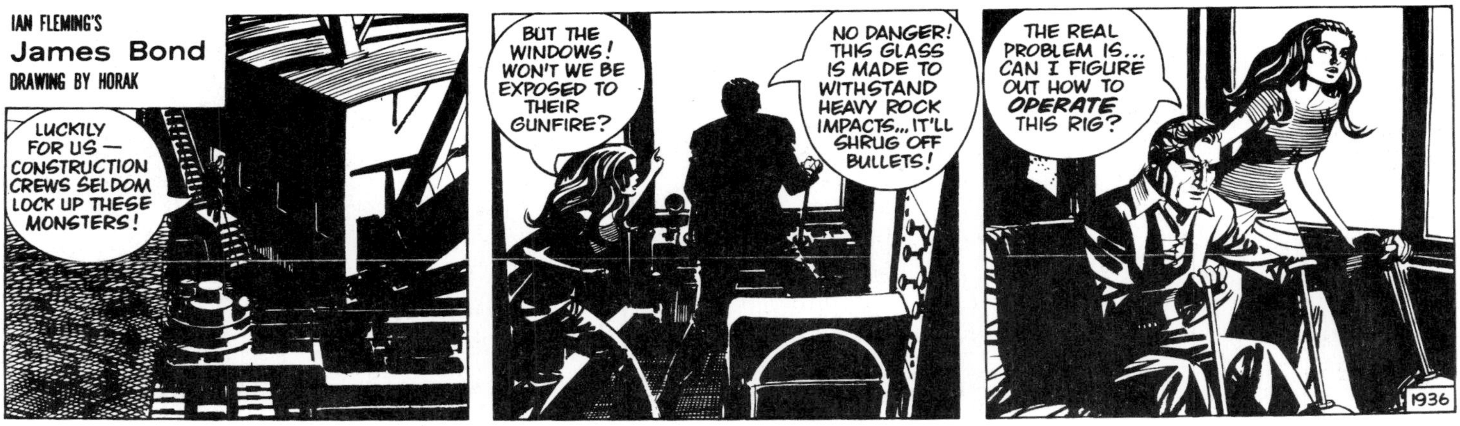
IAN FLEMING'S
James Bond
DRAWING BY HORAK
LUCKILY FOR US — CONSTRUCTION CREWS SELDOM LOCK UP THESE MONSTERS!
BUT THE WINDOWS! WON'T WE BE EXPOSED TO THEIR GUNFIRE?
NO DANGER! THIS GLASS IS MADE TO WITHSTAND HEAVY ROCK IMPACTS... IT'LL SHRUG OFF BULLETS!
THE REAL PROBLEM IS... CAN I FIGURE OUT HOW TO OPERATE THIS RIG?
1936

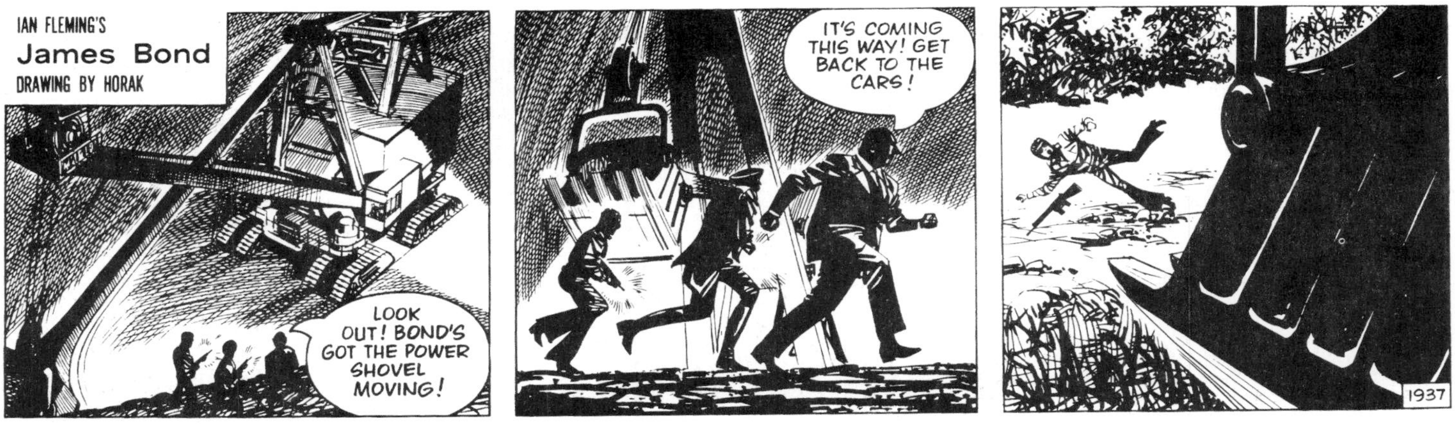
IAN FLEMING'S
James Bond
DRAWING BY HORAK
LOOK OUT! BOND'S GOT THE POWER SHOVEL MOVING!
IT'S COMING THIS WAY! GET BACK TO THE CARS!
1937

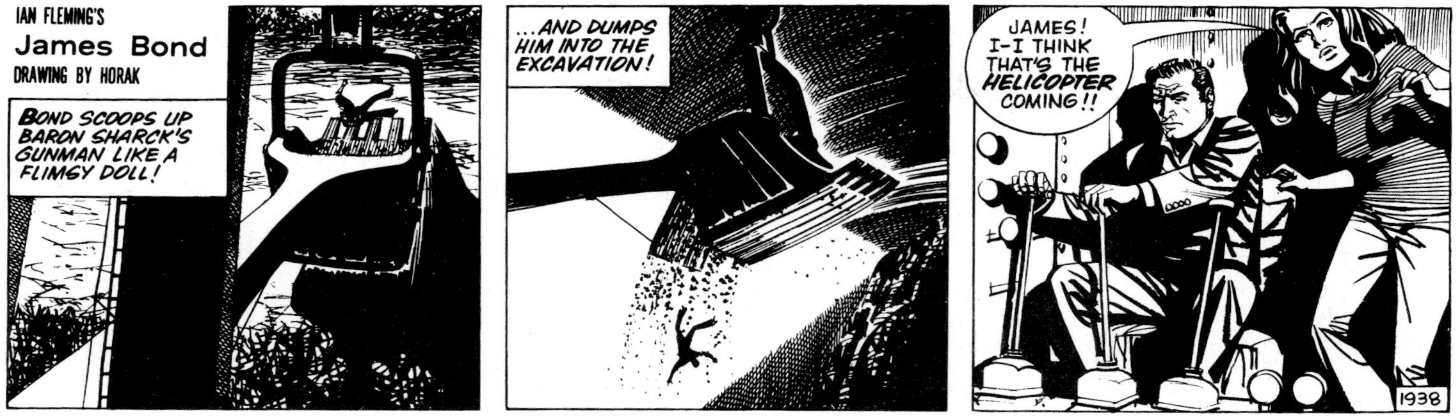
IAN FLEMING'S
James Bond
DRAWING BY HORAK
BOND SCOOPS UP BARON SHARCK'S GUNMAN LIKE A FLIMGY DOLL!
...AND DUMPS HIM INTO THE EXCAVATION!
JAMES! I-I THINK THAT'S THE HELICOPTER COMING!!
1938

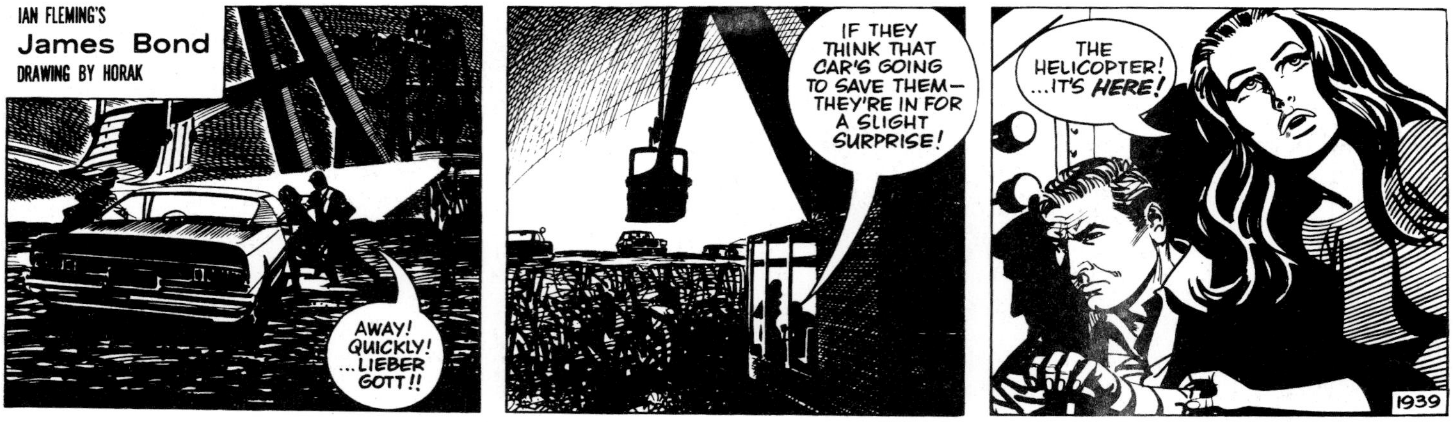
IAN FLEMING'S
James Bond
DRAWING BY HORAK
AWAY! QUICKLY! ...LIEBER GOTT!!
IF THEY THINK THAT CAR'S GOING TO SAVE THEM— THEY'RE IN FOR A SLIGHT SURPRISE!
THE HELICOPTER! ...IT'S HERE!
1939

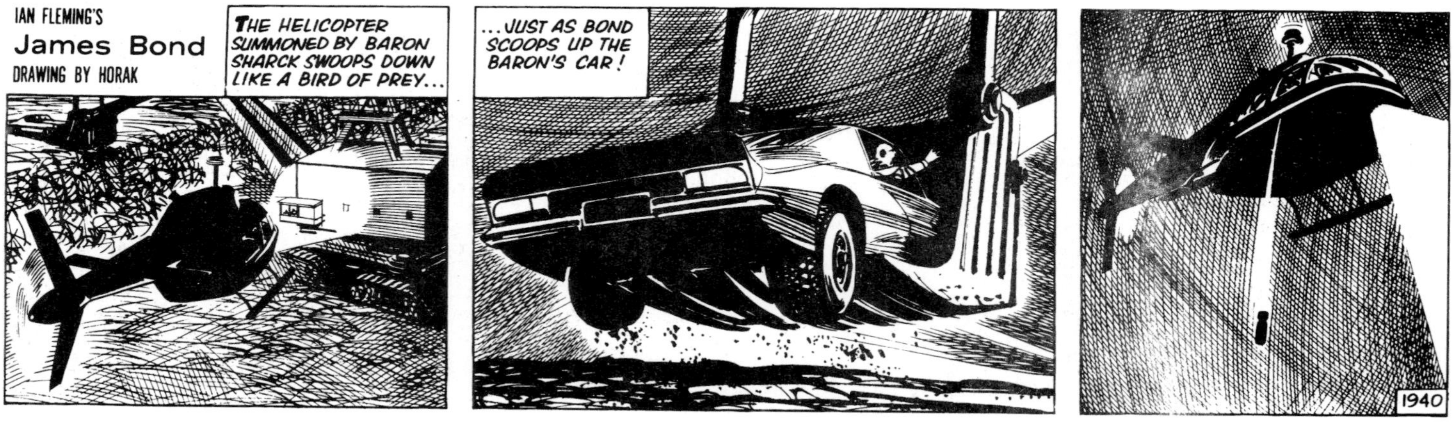
IAN FLEMING'S
James Bond
DRAWING BY HORAK
THE HELICOPTER SUMMONED BY BARON SHARCK SWOOPS DOWN LIKE A BIRD OF PREY...
...JUST AS BOND SCOOPS UP THE BARON'S CAR!
1940

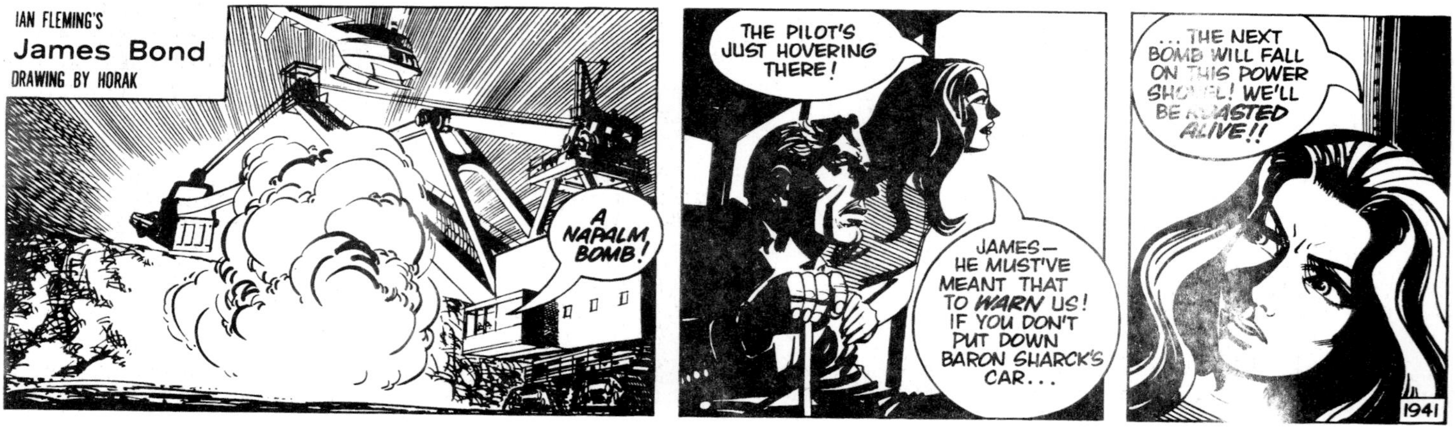
IAN FLEMING'S
James Bond
DRAWING BY HORAK
A NAPALM BOMB!
THE PILOT'S JUST HOVERING THERE!
JAMES— HE MUST'VE MEANT THAT TO WARN US! IF YOU DON'T PUT DOWN BARON SHARCK'S CAR...
... THE NEXT BOMB WILL FALL ON THIS POWER SHOVEL! WE'LL BE ROASTED ALIVE!!
1941

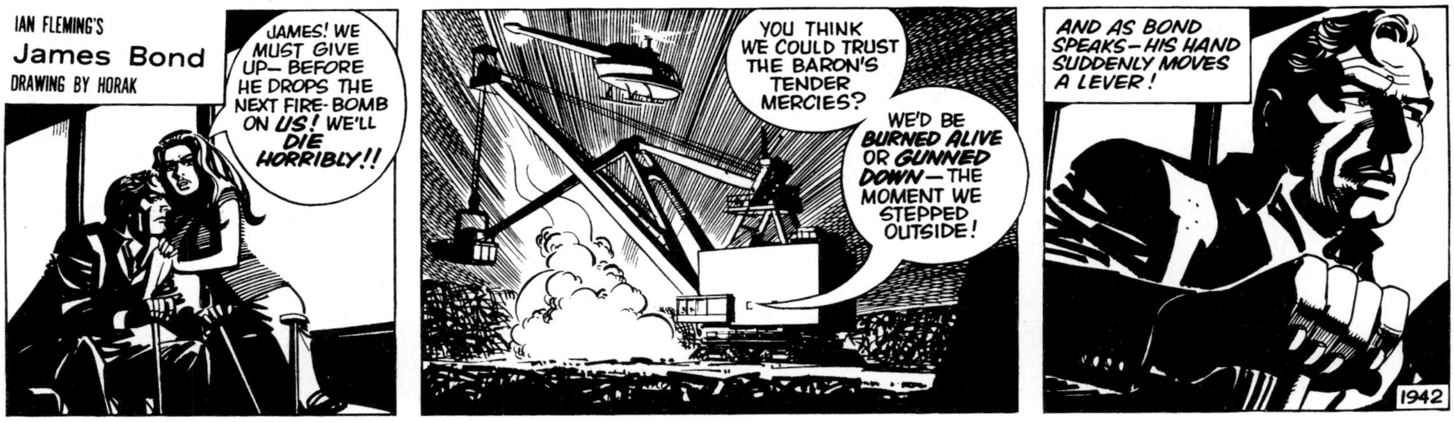
IAN FLEMING'S
James Bond
DRAWING BY HORAK
JAMES! WE MUST GIVE UP— BEFORE HE DROPS THE NEXT FIRE-BOMB ON US! WE'LL DIE HORRIBLY!!
YOU THINK WE COULD TRUST THE BARON'S TENDER MERCIES?
WE'D BE BURNED ALIVE OR GUNNED DOWN — THE MOMENT WE STEPPED OUTSIDE!
AND AS BOND SPEAKS— HIS HAND SUDDENLY MOVES A LEVER!
1942

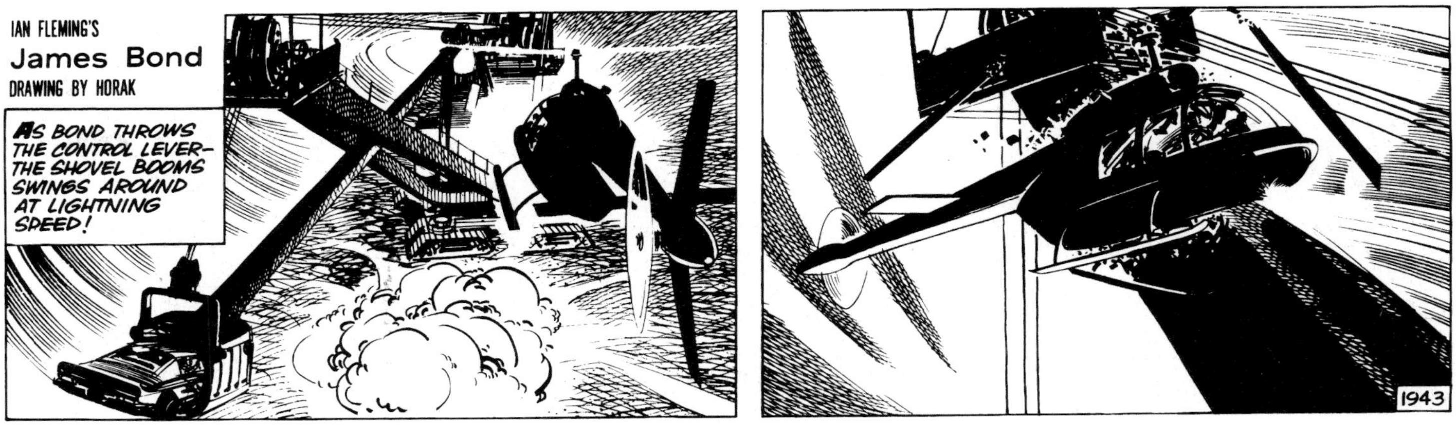
IAN FLEMING'S
James Bond
DRAWING BY HORAK
AS BOND THROWS THE CONTROL LEVER— THE SHOVEL BOOMS SWINGS AROUND AT LIGHTNING SPEED!
1943

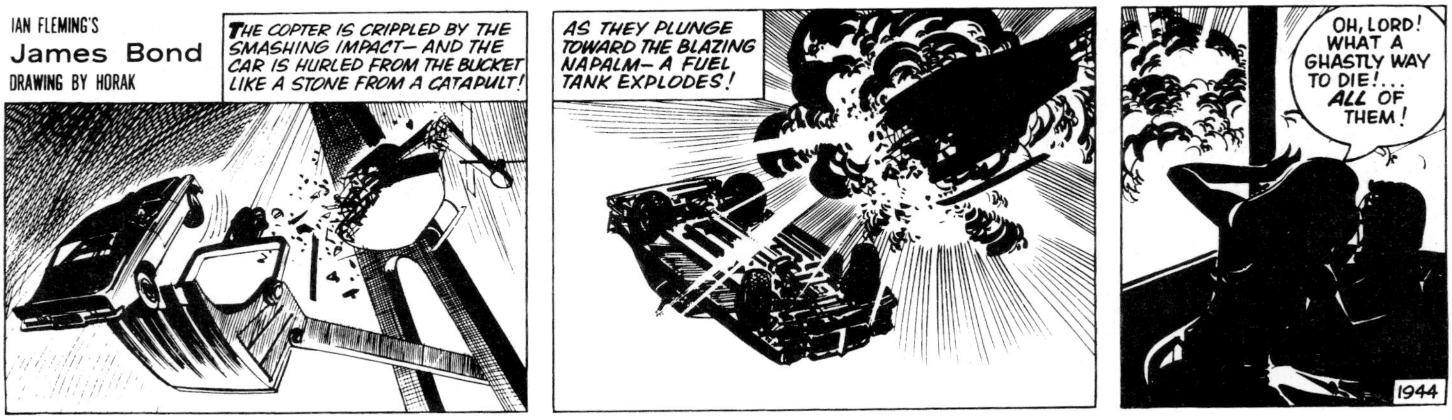
IAN FLEMING'S
James Bond
DRAWING BY HORAK
THE COPTER IS CRIPPLED BY THE SMASHING IMPACT— AND THE CAR IS HURLED FROM THE BUCKET LIKE A STONE FROM A CATAPULT!
AS THEY PLUNGE TOWARD THE BLAZING NAPALM— A FUEL TANK EXPLODES!
OH, LORD! WHAT A GHASTLY WAY TO DIE!... ALL OF THEM!
1944

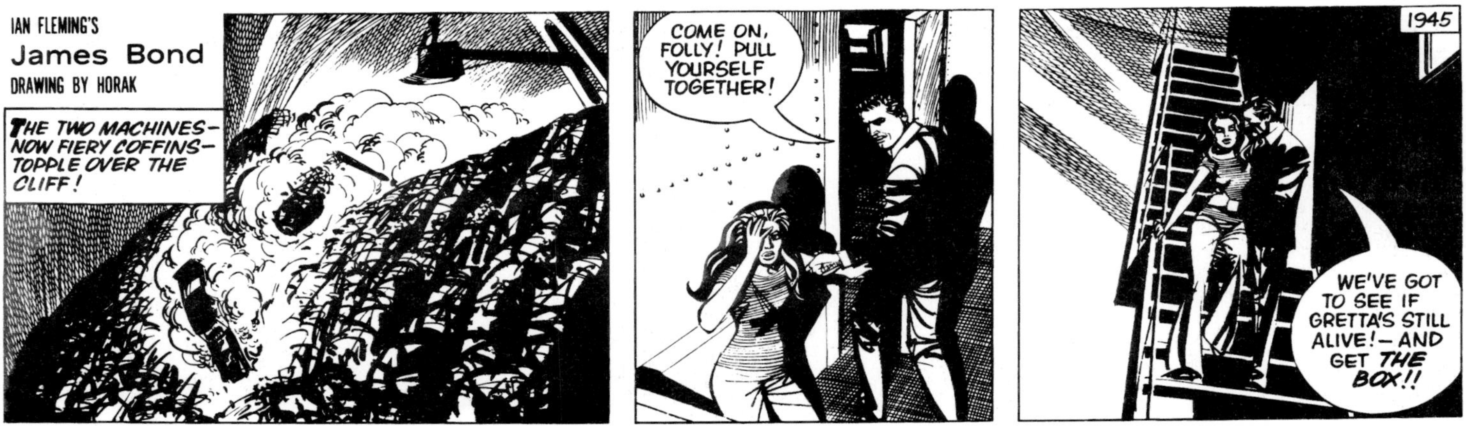
IAN FLEMING'S
James Bond
DRAWING BY HORAK
THE TWO MACHINES— NOW FIERY COFFINS— TOPPLE OVER THE CLIFF!
COME ON, FOLLY! PULL YOURSELF TOGETHER!
1945
WE'VE GOT TO SEE IF GRETTA'S STILL ALIVE!— AND GET THE BOX!!

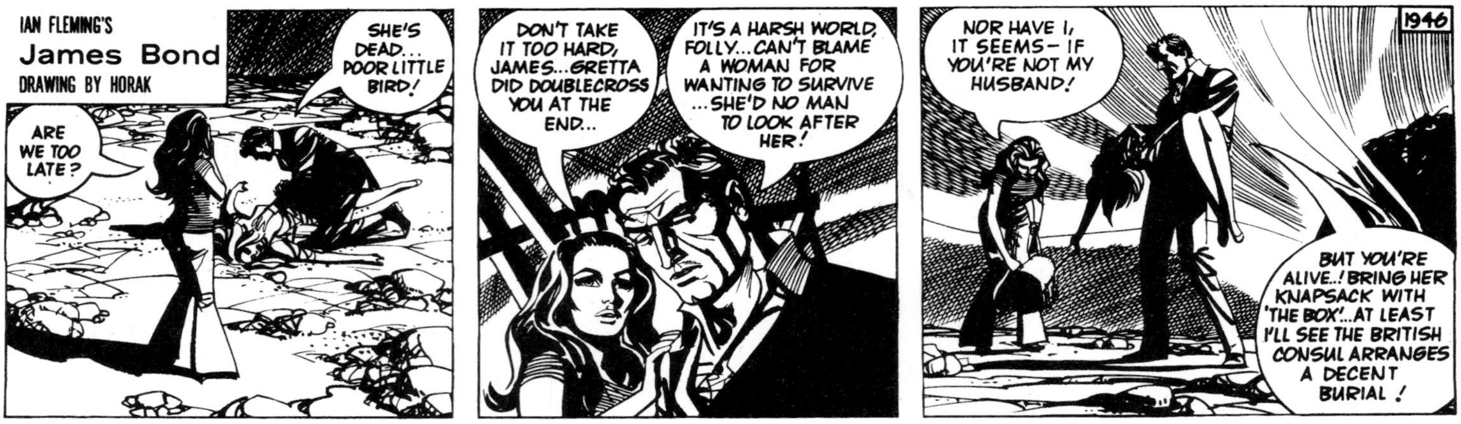
IAN FLEMING'S
James Bond
DRAWING BY HORAK
ARE WE TOO LATE?
SHE'S DEAD... POOR LITTLE BIRD!
DON'T TAKE IT TOO HARD, JAMES... GRETTA DID DOUBLECROSS YOU AT THE END...
IT'S A HARSH WORLD, FOLLY... CAN'T BLAME A WOMAN FOR WANTING TO SURVIVE ...SHE'D NO MAN TO LOOK AFTER HER!
1946
NOR HAVE I, IT SEEMS– IF YOU'RE NOT MY HUSBAND!
BUT YOU'RE ALIVE..! BRING HER KNAPSACK WITH 'THE BOX'...AT LEAST I'LL SEE THE BRITISH CONSUL ARRANGES A DECENT BURIAL!

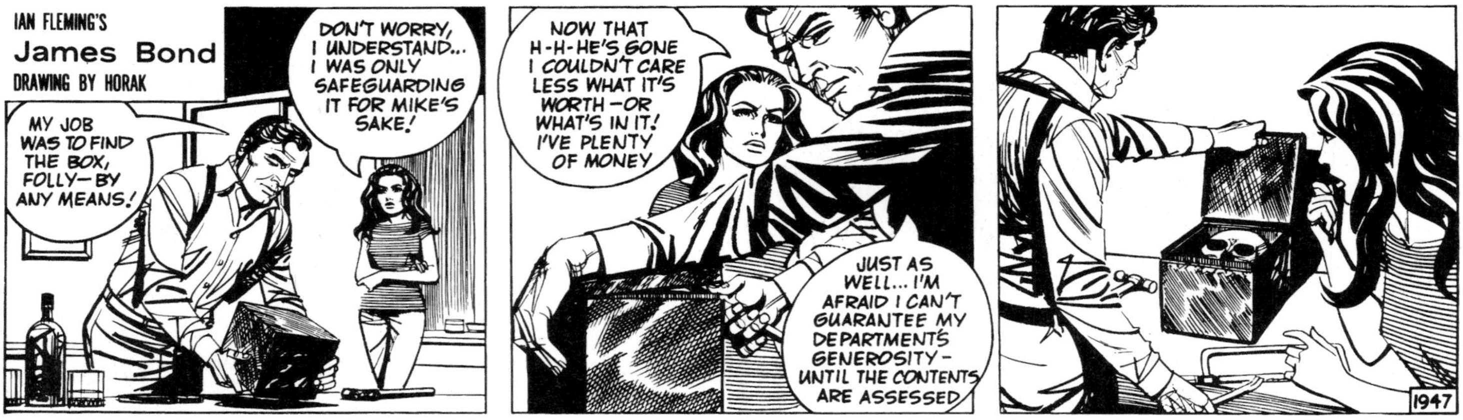
IAN FLEMING'S
James Bond
DRAWING BY HORAK
MY JOB WAS TO FIND THE BOX, FOLLY–BY ANY MEANS!
DON'T WORRY, I UNDERSTAND... I WAS ONLY SAFEGUARDING IT FOR MIKE'S SAKE!
NOW THAT H-H-HE'S GONE I COULDN'T CARE LESS WHAT IT'S WORTH –OR WHAT'S IN IT! I'VE PLENTY OF MONEY
JUST AS WELL... I'M AFRAID I CAN'T GUARANTEE MY DEPARTMENT'S GENEROSITY– UNTIL THE CONTENTS ARE ASSESSED
1947

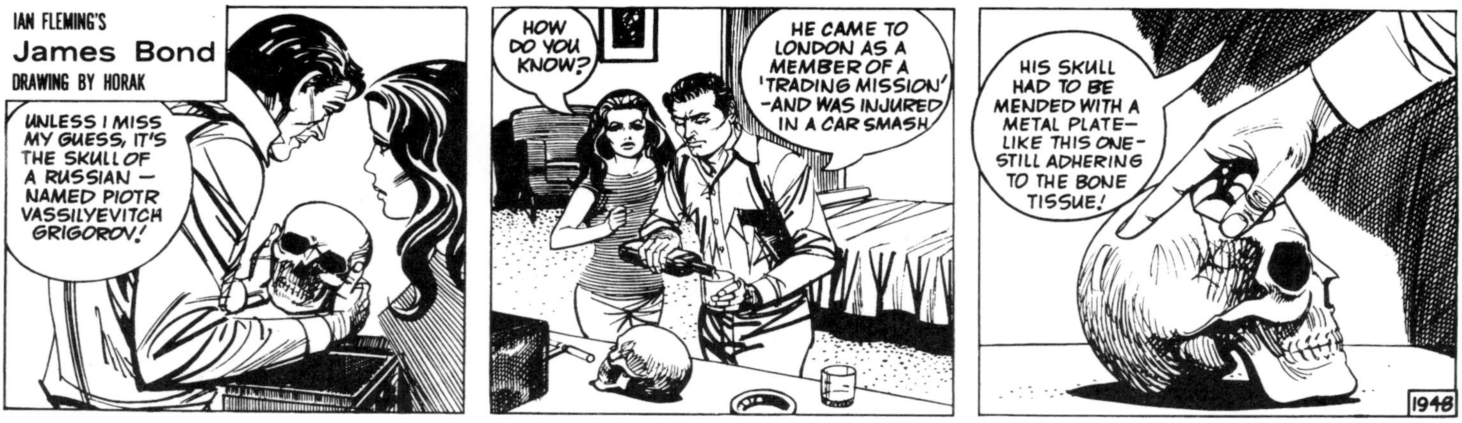
IAN FLEMING'S
James Bond
DRAWING BY HORAK
UNLESS I MISS MY GUESS, IT'S THE SKULL OF A RUSSIAN – NAMED PIOTR VASSILYEVITCH GRIGOROV!
HOW DO YOU KNOW?
HE CAME TO LONDON AS A MEMBER OF A 'TRADING MISSION' –AND WAS INJURED IN A CAR SMASH
HIS SKULL HAD TO BE MENDED WITH A METAL PLATE– LIKE THIS ONE– STILL ADHERING TO THE BONE TISSUE!
1948

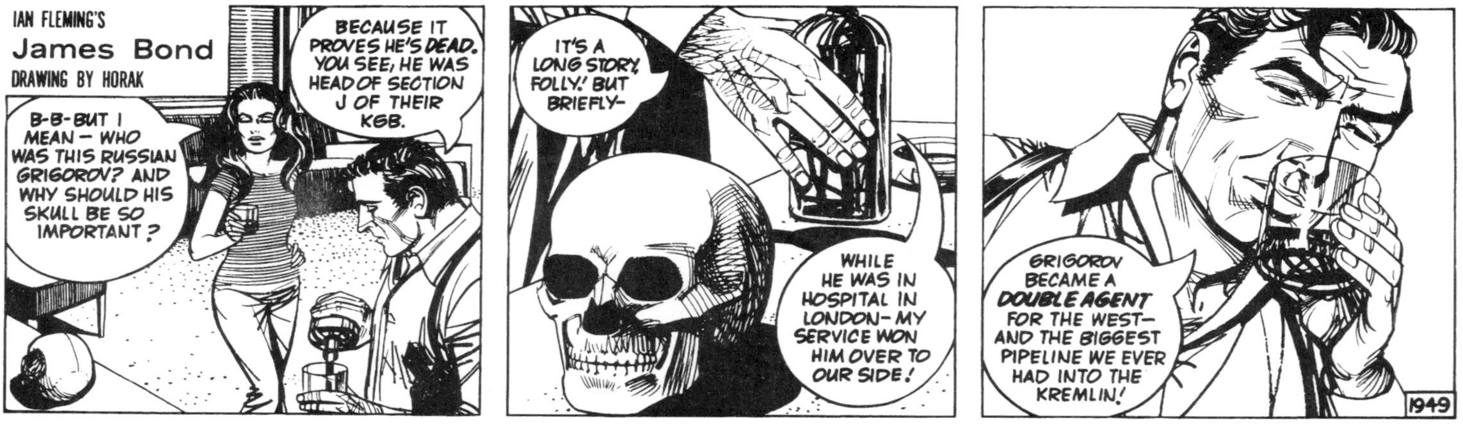
IAN FLEMING'S
James Bond
DRAWING BY HORAK
B-B-BUT I MEAN – WHO WAS THIS RUSSIAN GRIGOROV? AND WHY SHOULD HIS SKULL BE SO IMPORTANT?
BECAUSE IT PROVES HE'S DEAD. YOU SEE, HE WAS HEAD OF SECTION J OF THEIR KGB.
IT'S A LONG STORY, FOLLY! BUT BRIEFLY–
WHILE HE WAS IN HOSPITAL IN LONDON– MY SERVICE WON HIM OVER TO OUR SIDE!
GRIGOROV BECAME A DOUBLE AGENT FOR THE WEST– AND THE BIGGEST PIPELINE WE EVER HAD INTO THE KREMLIN!
1949

IAN FLEMING'S
James Bond
DRAWING BY HORAK
FOR TWO YEARS, OUR ALLIED SERVICES SUSPECTED THAT GRIGOROV MIGHT'VE BEEN RUMBLED—BUT WE COULDN'T BE SURE
AGENTS' LIVES—AND MAJOR POLITICAL MOVES—HAD TO BE STAKED ON THE INFORMATION HE WAS FEEDING US!
—YET WE'D NO CLUE TO WHETHER THE REAL GRIGOROV HAD BEEN REMOVED FROM SECTION J OR EXECUTED
WELL... NOW WE **KNOW!**
1950

IAN FLEMING'S
James Bond
DRAWING BY HORAK
IT'S GRIGOROV, ALL RIGHT, SIR! THE SKULL-TREPHINING DETAILS CHECK OUT PRECISELY—AND SO DO THE DENTAL X-RAYS
Q.E.D. EH? SO IT APPEARS 007 HAS EARNED HIS TWO WEEKS OF LEAVE IN THE STATES!
I KNOW OUR 'MARRIAGE' WAS JUST MAKE-BELIEVE, MIKE, ER JAMES! B-B-BUT I DON'T SUPPOSE YOU'D CARE TO MAKE IT REAL!
THIS SEEMS **VERY** REAL TO ME, FOLLY!
1951

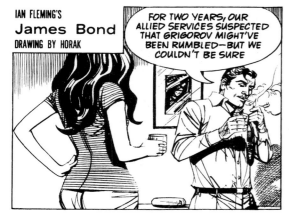

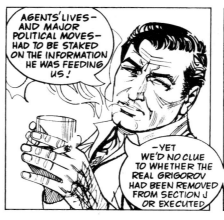

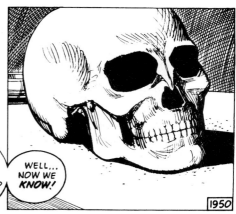

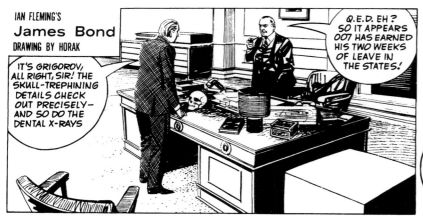

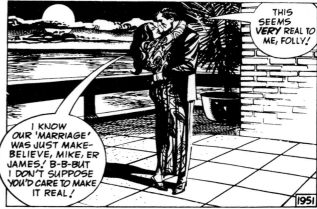

ISLE OF CONDORS

*I*sle of Condors can, in some respects, be seen as a signifier of changing social mores. Published in 1973 during the filming of Roger Moore's debut outing, *Live and Let Die*, the strip stars Crystal Kelly – a strong and sexy black female lead. The character, created by writer Jim Lawrence and artist Yaroslav Horak, closely resembles Rosie Carver from the 1973 film – the first black *Bond* girl on the silver screen. But unlike Rosie, Crystal Kelly earns 007's respect, indicating a sea-change in treatment of female characters in the strip series.

Isle of Condors continues the roller-coaster of original Lawrence and Horak adventures. As one of the stronger non-Fleming stories, it sees 007 return – in the guise of Mark Hazard – in order to investigate a kidnapping. Both Moneypenny and Bill Tanner make fleeting appearances, but M is once again missing from the adventure.

Horak's artwork in this strip is as striking as ever; his action is dynamic and well constructed – a style, and standard, regular readers should be well used to. But the strip is an important entry in the series for another reason, as it introduced a very rigid story structure that can be seen throughout the majority of the subsequent tales.

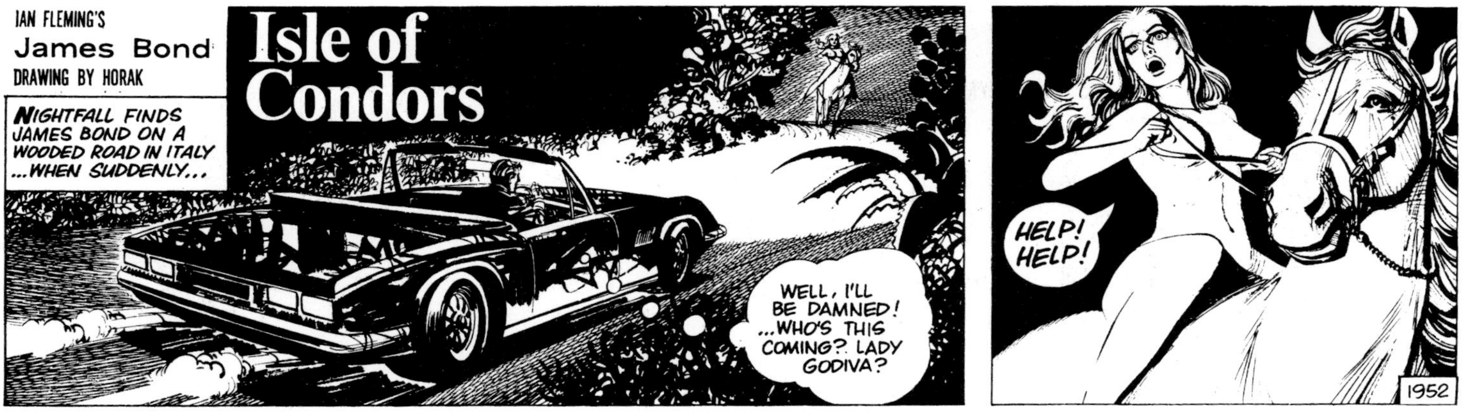
IAN FLEMING'S
James Bond
DRAWING BY HORAK
Isle of Condors
NIGHTFALL FINDS JAMES BOND ON A WOODED ROAD IN ITALY ...WHEN SUDDENLY...
WELL, I'LL BE DAMNED! ...WHO'S THIS COMING? LADY GODIVA?
HELP! HELP!
1952

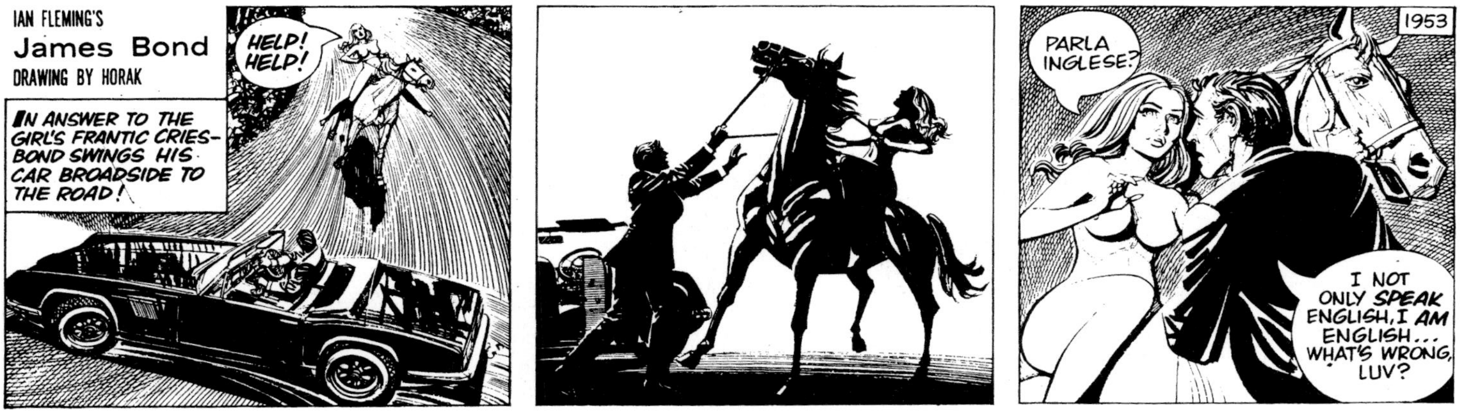
IAN FLEMING'S
James Bond
DRAWING BY HORAK
IN ANSWER TO THE GIRL'S FRANTIC CRIES-BOND SWINGS HIS CAR BROADSIDE TO THE ROAD!
HELP! HELP!
1953
PARLA INGLESE?
I NOT ONLY SPEAK ENGLISH, I AM ENGLISH... WHAT'S WRONG, LUV?

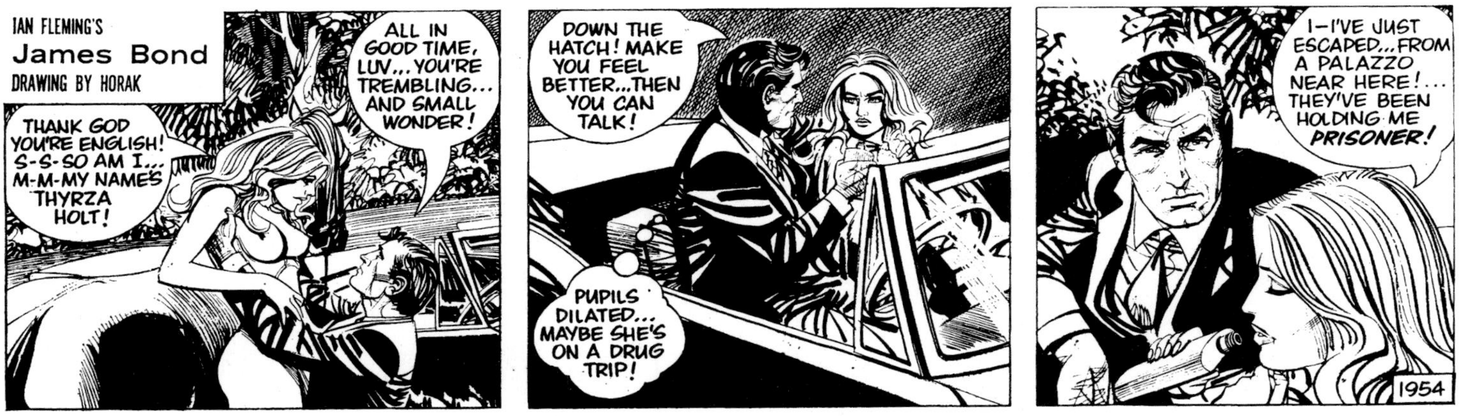
IAN FLEMING'S
James Bond
DRAWING BY HORAK
THANK GOD YOU'RE ENGLISH! S-S-SO AM I... M-M-MY NAME'S THYRZA HOLT!
ALL IN GOOD TIME, LUV... YOU'RE TREMBLING... AND SMALL WONDER!
DOWN THE HATCH! MAKE YOU FEEL BETTER... THEN YOU CAN TALK!
PUPILS DILATED... MAYBE SHE'S ON A DRUG TRIP!
I-I'VE JUST ESCAPED... FROM A PALAZZO NEAR HERE!... THEY'VE BEEN HOLDING ME PRISONER!
1954

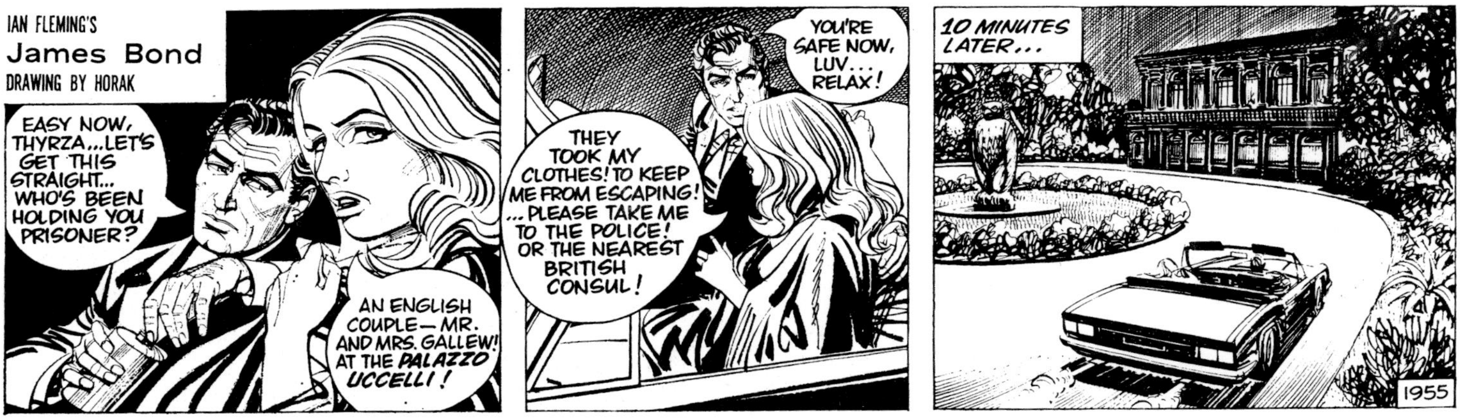
IAN FLEMING'S
James Bond
DRAWING BY HORAK
EASY NOW, THYRZA... LET'S GET THIS STRAIGHT... WHO'S BEEN HOLDING YOU PRISONER?
AN ENGLISH COUPLE—MR. AND MRS. GALLEW! AT THE PALAZZO UCCELLI!
YOU'RE SAFE NOW, LUV... RELAX!
THEY TOOK MY CLOTHES! TO KEEP ME FROM ESCAPING! ...PLEASE TAKE ME TO THE POLICE! OR THE NEAREST BRITISH CONSUL!
10 MINUTES LATER...
1955

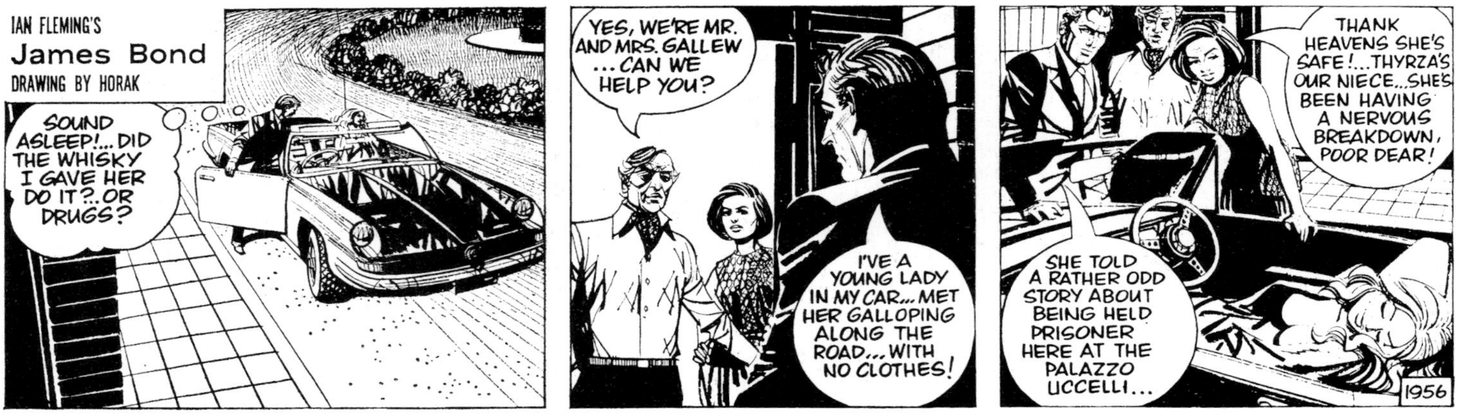
IAN FLEMING'S
James Bond
DRAWING BY HORAK
SOUND ASLEEP!... DID THE WHISKY I GAVE HER DO IT?..OR DRUGS?
YES, WE'RE MR. AND MRS. GALLEW ...CAN WE HELP YOU?
I'VE A YOUNG LADY IN MY CAR... MET HER GALLOPING ALONG THE ROAD... WITH NO CLOTHES!
THANK HEAVENS SHE'S SAFE!...THYRZA'S OUR NIECE...SHE'S BEEN HAVING A NERVOUS BREAKDOWN, POOR DEAR!
SHE TOLD A RATHER ODD STORY ABOUT BEING HELD PRISONER HERE AT THE PALAZZO UCCELLI...
1956

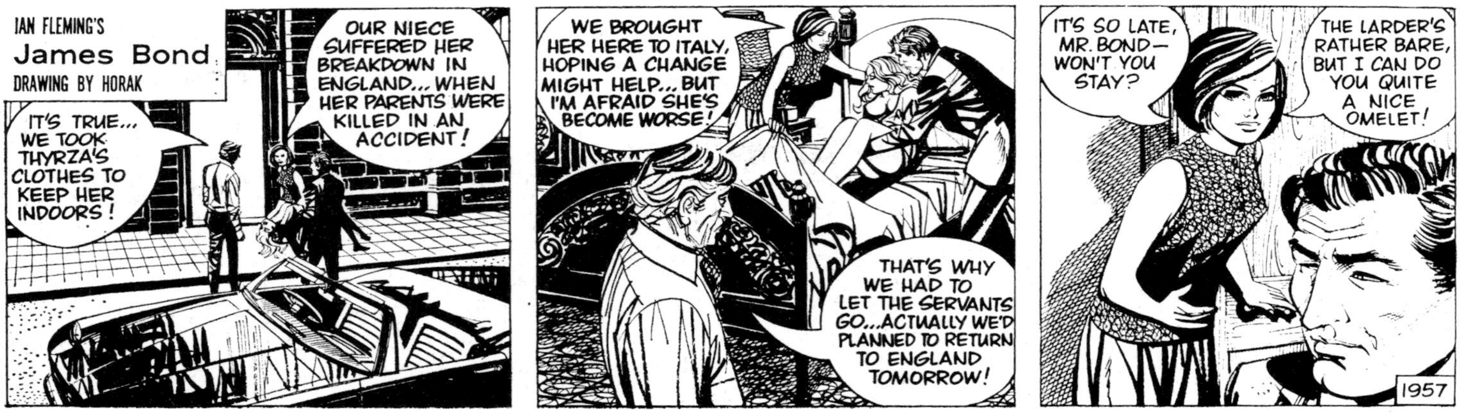
IAN FLEMING'S
James Bond
DRAWING BY HORAK
IT'S TRUE... WE TOOK THYRZA'S CLOTHES TO KEEP HER INDOORS!
OUR NIECE SUFFERED HER BREAKDOWN IN ENGLAND... WHEN HER PARENTS WERE KILLED IN AN ACCIDENT!
WE BROUGHT HER HERE TO ITALY, HOPING A CHANGE MIGHT HELP... BUT I'M AFRAID SHE'S BECOME WORSE!
THAT'S WHY WE HAD TO LET THE SERVANTS GO...ACTUALLY WE'D PLANNED TO RETURN TO ENGLAND TOMORROW!
IT'S SO LATE, MR. BOND— WON'T YOU STAY?
THE LARDER'S RATHER BARE, BUT I CAN DO YOU QUITE A NICE OMELET!
1957

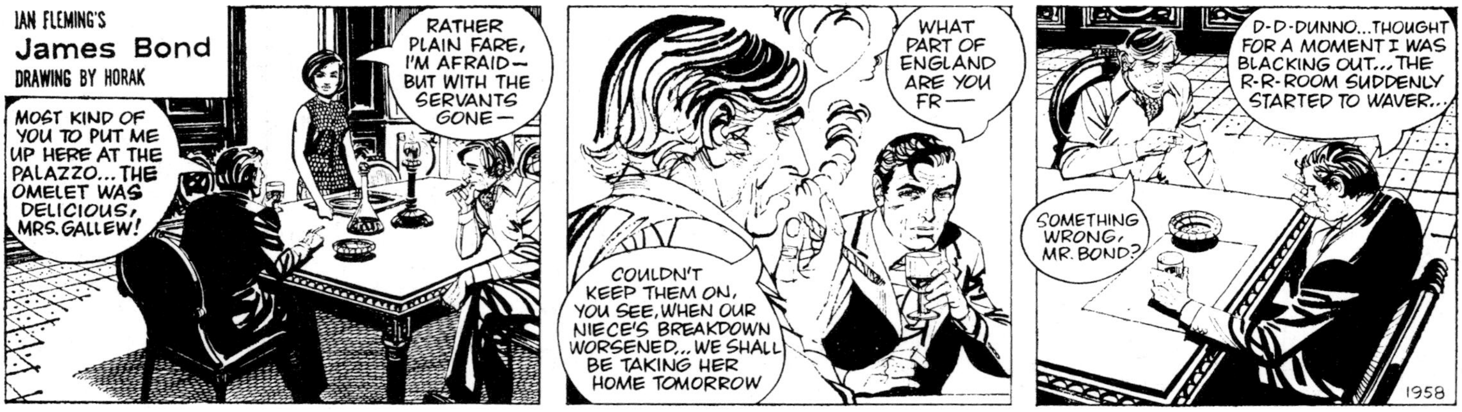
IAN FLEMING'S
James Bond
DRAWING BY HORAK
MOST KIND OF YOU TO PUT ME UP HERE AT THE PALAZZO... THE OMELET WAS DELICIOUS, MRS. GALLEW!
RATHER PLAIN FARE, I'M AFRAID— BUT WITH THE SERVANTS GONE—
COULDN'T KEEP THEM ON, YOU SEE, WHEN OUR NIECE'S BREAKDOWN WORSENED... WE SHALL BE TAKING HER HOME TOMORROW
WHAT PART OF ENGLAND ARE YOU FR—
D-D-DUNNO...THOUGHT FOR A MOMENT I WAS BLACKING OUT... THE R-R-ROOM SUDDENLY STARTED TO WAVER...
SOMETHING WRONG, MR. BOND?
1958

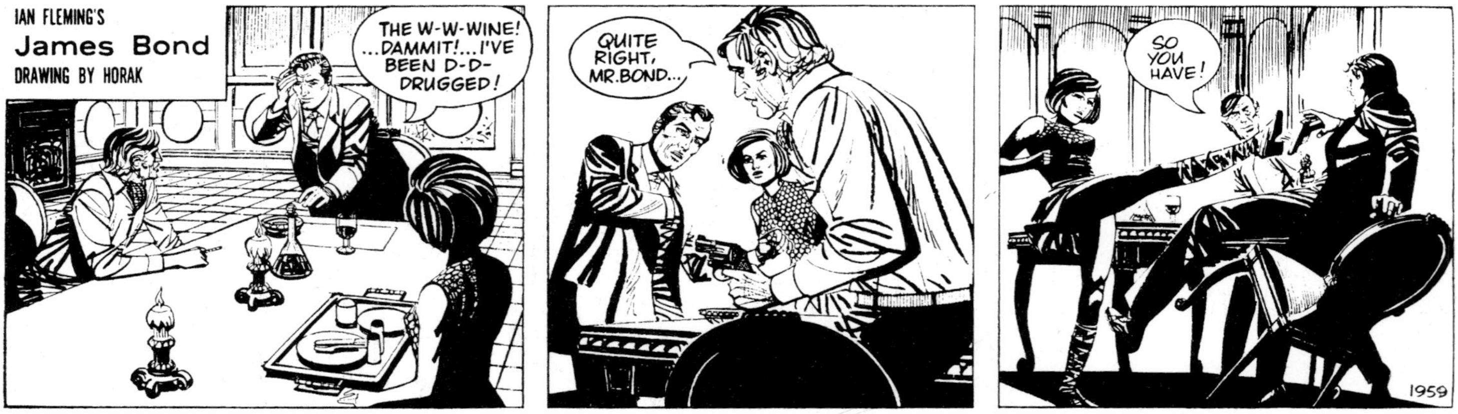
IAN FLEMING'S
James Bond
DRAWING BY HORAK
THE W-W-WINE! ...DAMMIT!...I'VE BEEN D-D-DRUGGED!
QUITE RIGHT, MR. BOND...
SO YOU HAVE!
1959

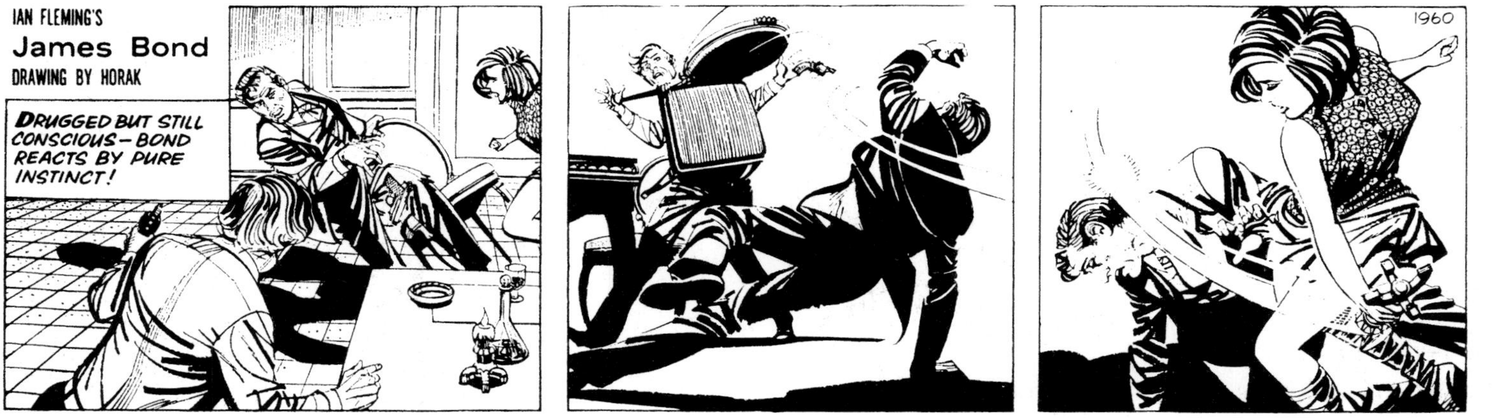
IAN FLEMING'S
James Bond
DRAWING BY HORAK
DRUGGED BUT STILL CONSCIOUS – BOND REACTS BY PURE INSTINCT!
1960

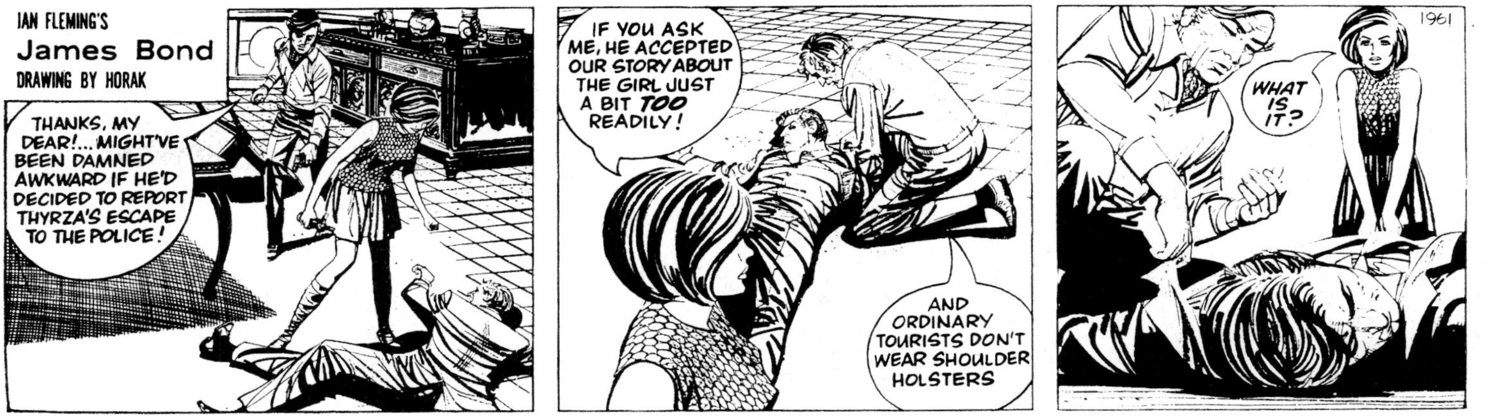
IAN FLEMING'S
James Bond
DRAWING BY HORAK
THANKS, MY DEAR!... MIGHT'VE BEEN DAMNED AWKWARD IF HE'D DECIDED TO REPORT THYRZA'S ESCAPE TO THE POLICE!
IF YOU ASK ME, HE ACCEPTED OUR STORY ABOUT THE GIRL JUST A BIT TOO READILY!
AND ORDINARY TOURISTS DON'T WEAR SHOULDER HOLSTERS
WHAT IS IT?
1961

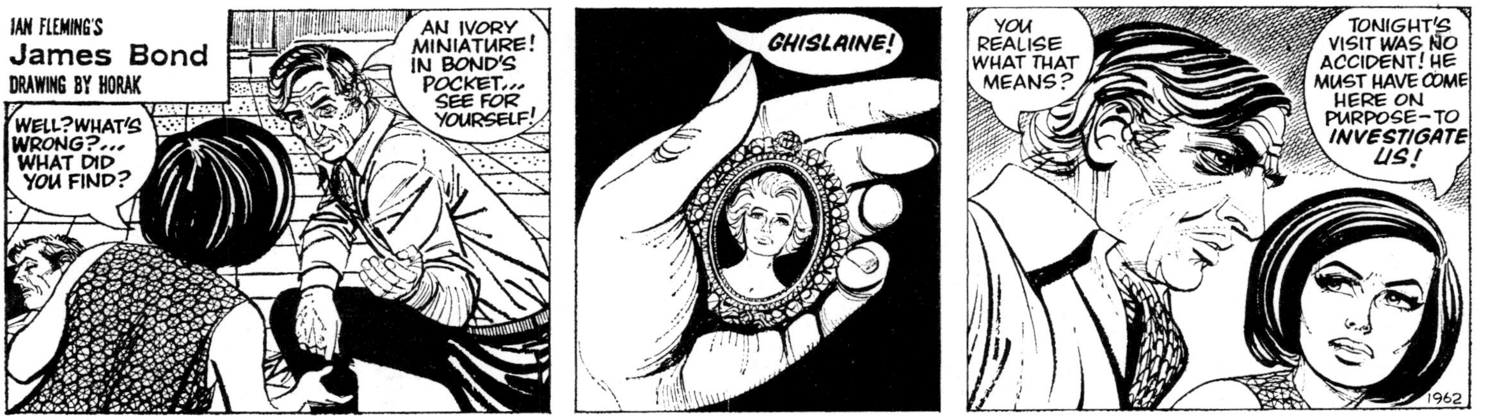
IAN FLEMING'S
James Bond
DRAWING BY HORAK
WELL? WHAT'S WRONG?... WHAT DID YOU FIND?
AN IVORY MINIATURE! IN BOND'S POCKET... SEE FOR YOURSELF!
GHISLAINE!
YOU REALISE WHAT THAT MEANS?
TONIGHT'S VISIT WAS NO ACCIDENT! HE MUST HAVE COME HERE ON PURPOSE – TO INVESTIGATE US!
1962

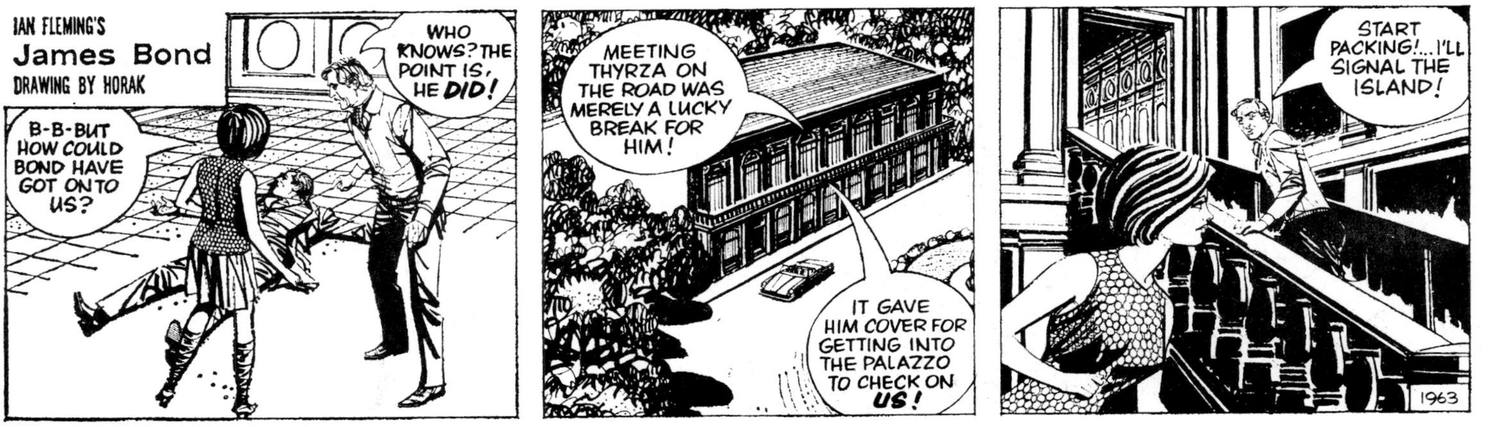
IAN FLEMING'S
James Bond
DRAWING BY HORAK
B-B-BUT HOW COULD BOND HAVE GOT ON TO US?
WHO KNOWS? THE POINT IS, HE DID!
MEETING THYRZA ON THE ROAD WAS MERELY A LUCKY BREAK FOR HIM!
IT GAVE HIM COVER FOR GETTING INTO THE PALAZZO TO CHECK ON US!
START PACKING!... I'LL SIGNAL THE ISLAND!
1963

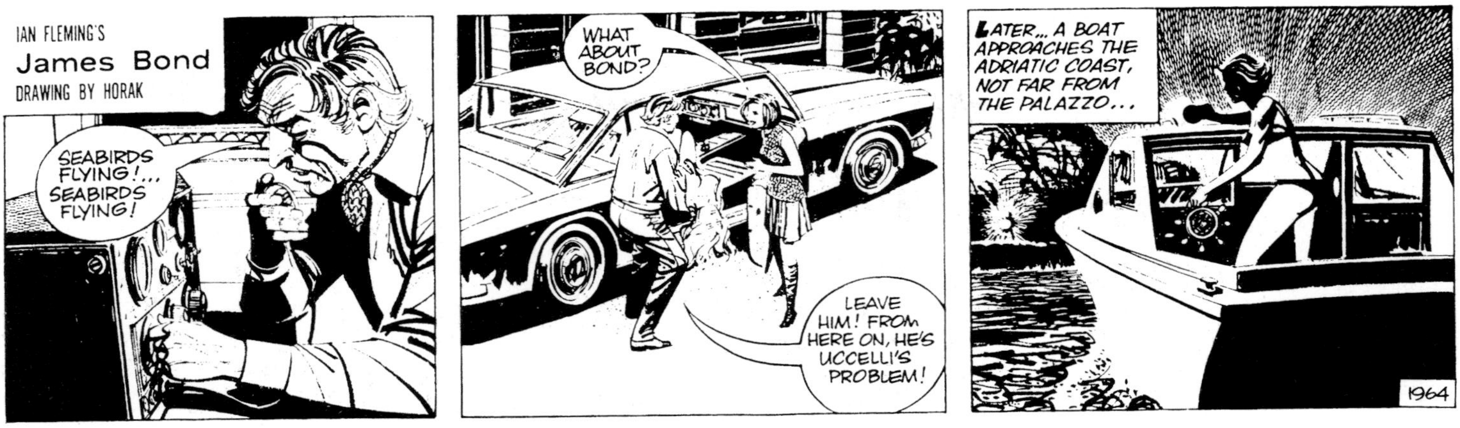
IAN FLEMING'S
James Bond
DRAWING BY HORAK
SEABIRDS FLYING!... SEABIRDS FLYING!
WHAT ABOUT BOND?
LEAVE HIM! FROM HERE ON, HE'S UCCELLI'S PROBLEM!
LATER... A BOAT APPROACHES THE ADRIATIC COAST, NOT FAR FROM THE PALAZZO...
1964

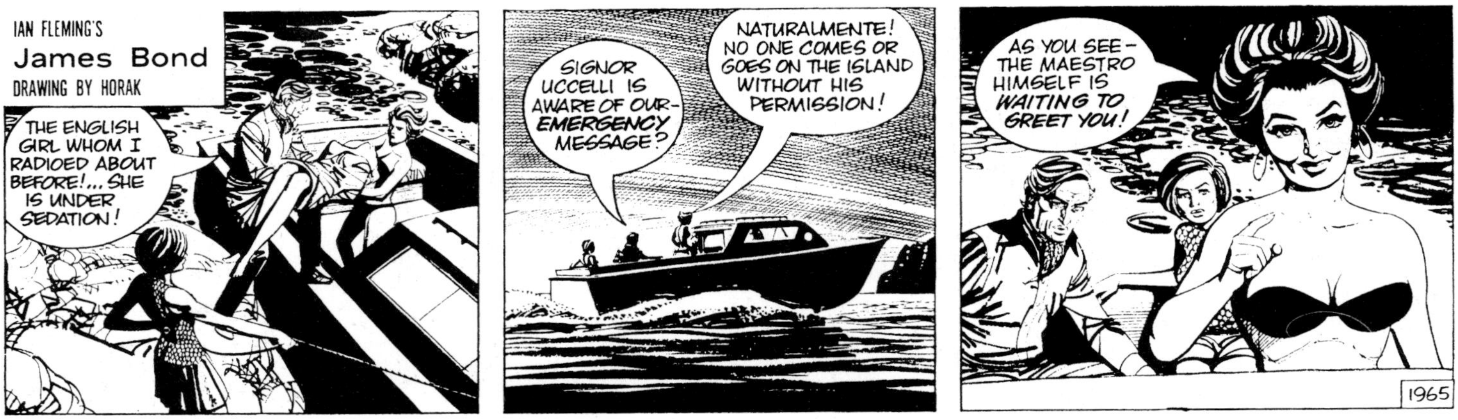
IAN FLEMING'S
James Bond
DRAWING BY HORAK
THE ENGLISH GIRL WHOM I RADIOED ABOUT BEFORE!... SHE IS UNDER SEDATION!
SIGNOR UCCELLI IS AWARE OF OUR EMERGENCY MESSAGE?
NATURALMENTE! NO ONE COMES OR GOES ON THE ISLAND WITHOUT HIS PERMISSION!
AS YOU SEE— THE MAESTRO HIMSELF IS WAITING TO GREET YOU!
1965

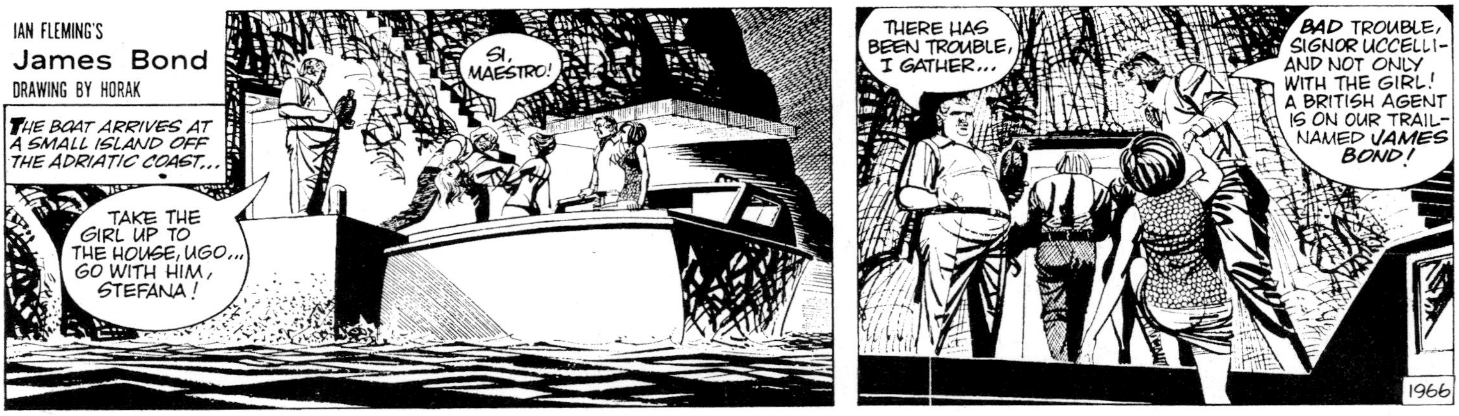
IAN FLEMING'S
James Bond
DRAWING BY HORAK
THE BOAT ARRIVES AT A SMALL ISLAND OFF THE ADRIATIC COAST...
TAKE THE GIRL UP TO THE HOUSE, UGO... GO WITH HIM, STEFANA!
SI, MAESTRO!
THERE HAS BEEN TROUBLE, I GATHER...
BAD TROUBLE, SIGNOR UCCELLI— AND NOT ONLY WITH THE GIRL! A BRITISH AGENT IS ON OUR TRAIL— NAMED JAMES BOND!
1966

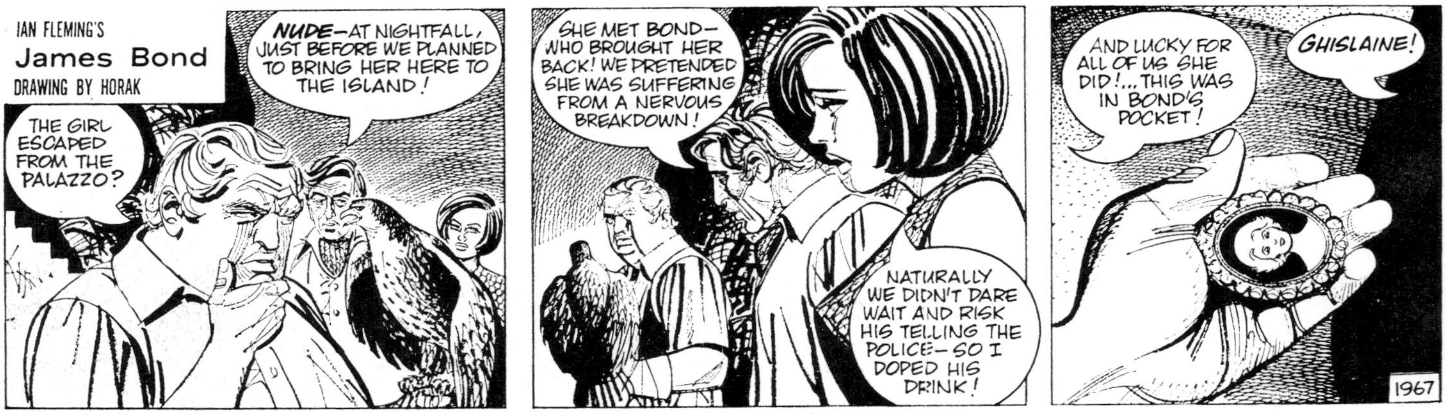
IAN FLEMING'S
James Bond
DRAWING BY HORAK
THE GIRL ESCAPED FROM THE PALAZZO?
NUDE—AT NIGHTFALL, JUST BEFORE WE PLANNED TO BRING HER HERE TO THE ISLAND!
SHE MET BOND— WHO BROUGHT HER BACK! WE PRETENDED SHE WAS SUFFERING FROM A NERVOUS BREAKDOWN!
NATURALLY WE DIDN'T DARE WAIT AND RISK HIS TELLING THE POLICE— SO I DOPED HIS DRINK!
AND LUCKY FOR ALL OF US SHE DID!... THIS WAS IN BOND'S POCKET!
GHISLAINE!
1967

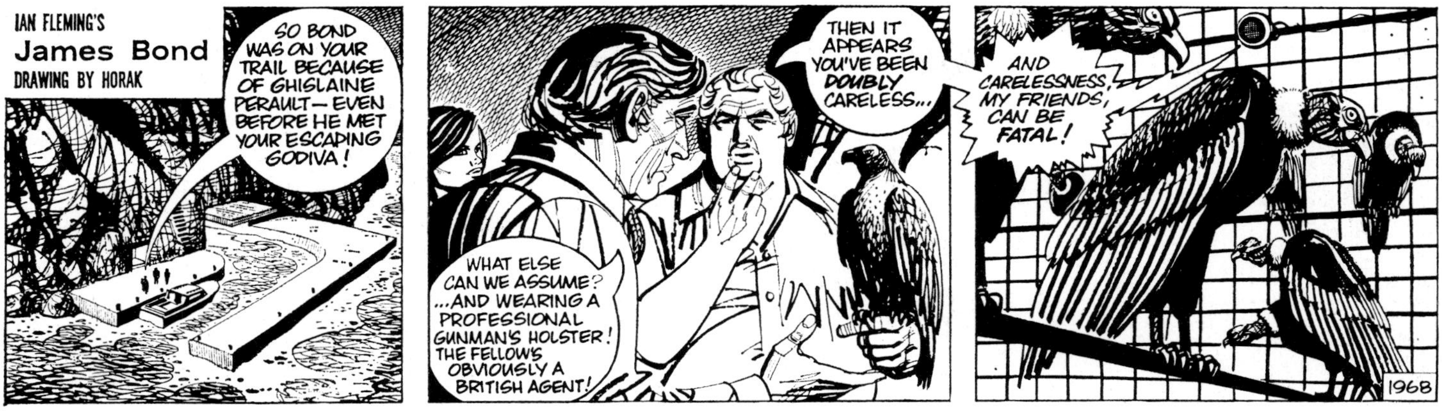
IAN FLEMING'S
James Bond
DRAWING BY HORAK
SO BOND WAS ON YOUR TRAIL BECAUSE OF GHISLAINE PERAULT— EVEN BEFORE HE MET YOUR ESCAPING GODIVA!
THEN IT APPEARS YOU'VE BEEN DOUBLY CARELESS...
WHAT ELSE CAN WE ASSUME? ...AND WEARING A PROFESSIONAL GUNMAN'S HOLSTER! THE FELLOW'S OBVIOUSLY A BRITISH AGENT!
AND CARELESSNESS, MY FRIENDS, CAN BE FATAL!
1968

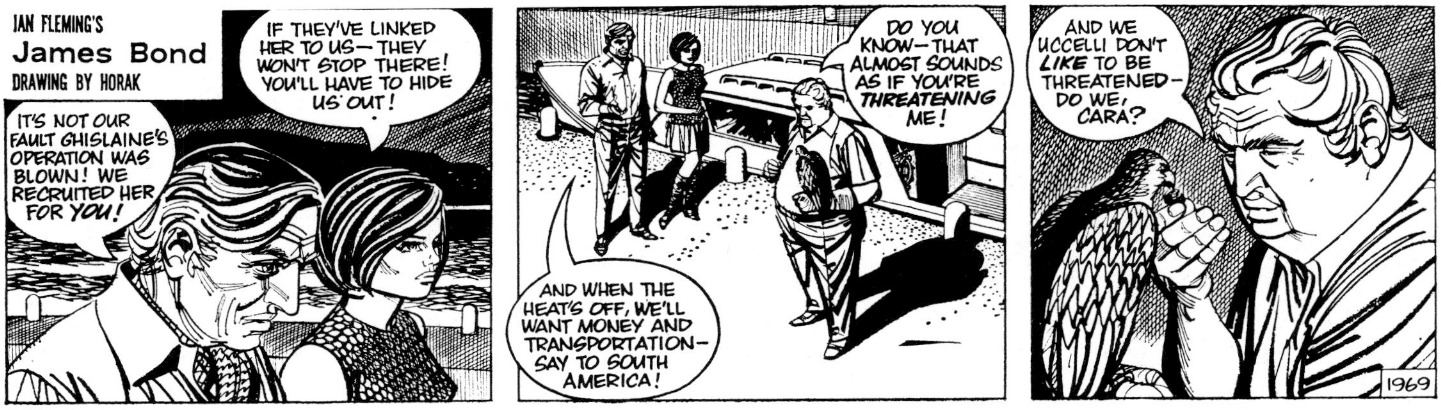
IAN FLEMING'S
James Bond
DRAWING BY HORAK
IF THEY'VE LINKED HER TO US— THEY WON'T STOP THERE! YOU'LL HAVE TO HIDE US OUT!
IT'S NOT OUR FAULT GHISLAINE'S OPERATION WAS BLOWN! WE RECRUITED HER FOR YOU!
DO YOU KNOW— THAT ALMOST SOUNDS AS IF YOU'RE THREATENING ME!
AND WHEN THE HEAT'S OFF, WE'LL WANT MONEY AND TRANSPORTATION— SAY TO SOUTH AMERICA!
AND WE UCCELLI DON'T LIKE TO BE THREATENED— DO WE, CARA?
1969

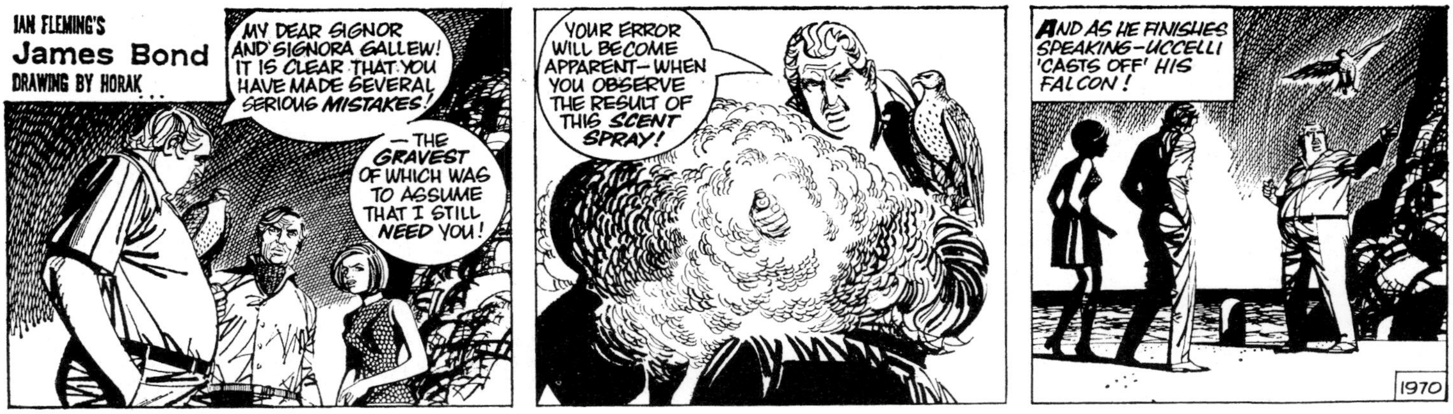
IAN FLEMING'S
James Bond
DRAWING BY HORAK
MY DEAR SIGNOR AND SIGNORA GALLEW! IT IS CLEAR THAT YOU HAVE MADE SEVERAL SERIOUS MISTAKES!
— THE GRAVEST OF WHICH WAS TO ASSUME THAT I STILL NEED YOU!
YOUR ERROR WILL BECOME APPARENT— WHEN YOU OBSERVE THE RESULT OF THIS SCENT SPRAY!
AND AS HE FINISHES SPEAKING— UCCELLI 'CASTS OFF' HIS FALCON!
1970

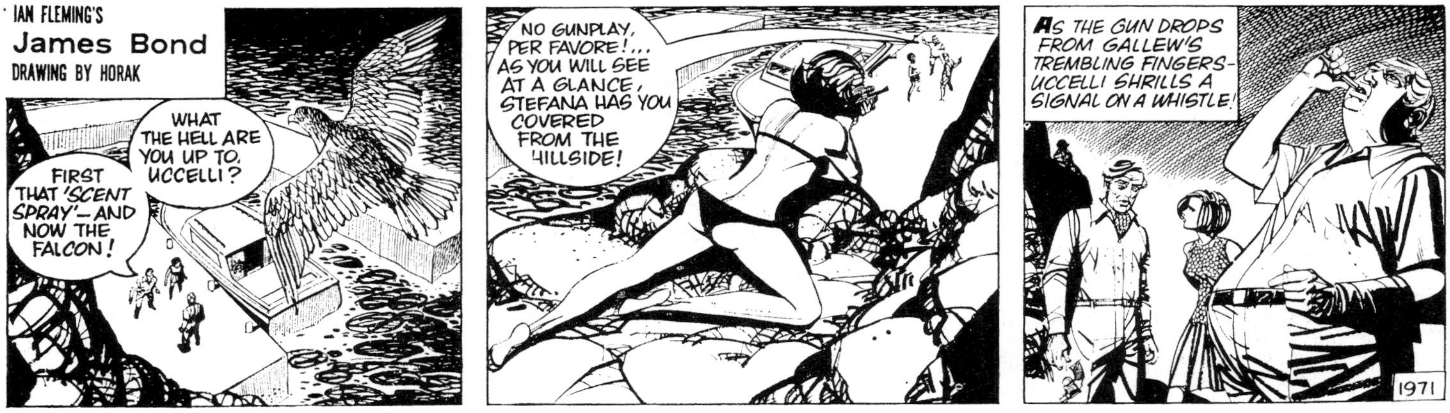
IAN FLEMING'S
James Bond
DRAWING BY HORAK
WHAT THE HELL ARE YOU UP TO, UCCELLI?
FIRST THAT 'SCENT SPRAY'— AND NOW THE FALCON!
NO GUNPLAY, PER FAVORE!... AS YOU WILL SEE AT A GLANCE, STEFANA HAS YOU COVERED FROM THE HILLSIDE!
AS THE GUN DROPS FROM GALLEW'S TREMBLING FINGERS— UCCELLI SHRILLS A SIGNAL ON A WHISTLE!
1971

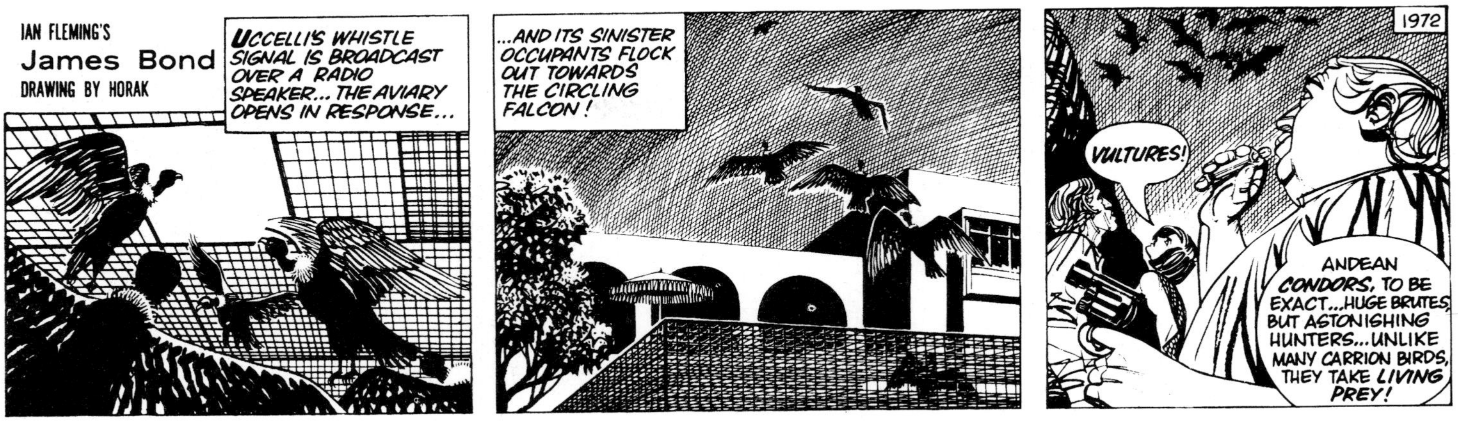
IAN FLEMING'S
James Bond
DRAWING BY HORAK
UCCELLI'S WHISTLE SIGNAL IS BROADCAST OVER A RADIO SPEAKER... THE AVIARY OPENS IN RESPONSE...
...AND ITS SINISTER OCCUPANTS FLOCK OUT TOWARDS THE CIRCLING FALCON!
1972
VULTURES!
ANDEAN CONDORS, TO BE EXACT...HUGE BRUTES, BUT ASTONISHING HUNTERS...UNLIKE MANY CARRION BIRDS, THEY TAKE LIVING PREY!

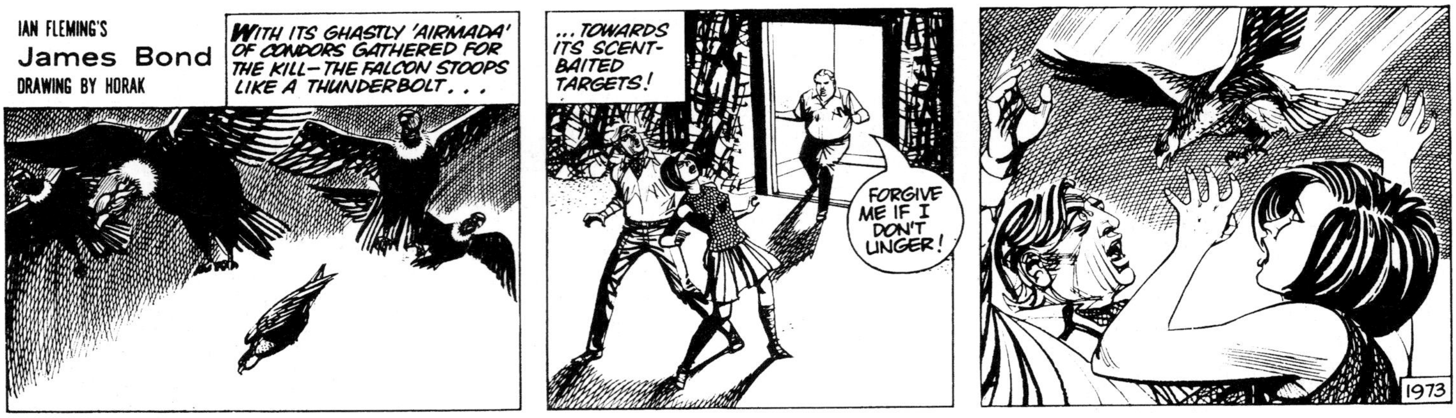
IAN FLEMING'S
James Bond
DRAWING BY HORAK
WITH ITS GHASTLY 'AIRMADA' OF CONDORS GATHERED FOR THE KILL—THE FALCON STOOPS LIKE A THUNDERBOLT...
...TOWARDS ITS SCENT-BAITED TARGETS!
FORGIVE ME IF I DON'T LINGER!
1973

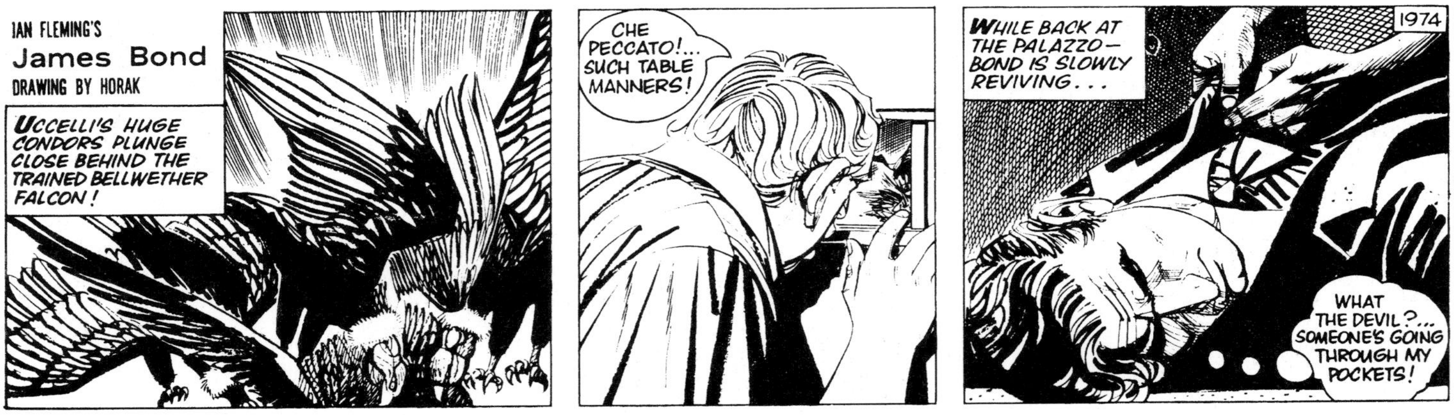
IAN FLEMING'S
James Bond
DRAWING BY HORAK
UCCELLI'S HUGE CONDORS PLUNGE CLOSE BEHIND THE TRAINED BELLWETHER FALCON!
CHE PECCATO!... SUCH TABLE MANNERS!
1974
WHILE BACK AT THE PALAZZO— BOND IS SLOWLY REVIVING...
WHAT THE DEVIL?... SOMEONE'S GOING THROUGH MY POCKETS!

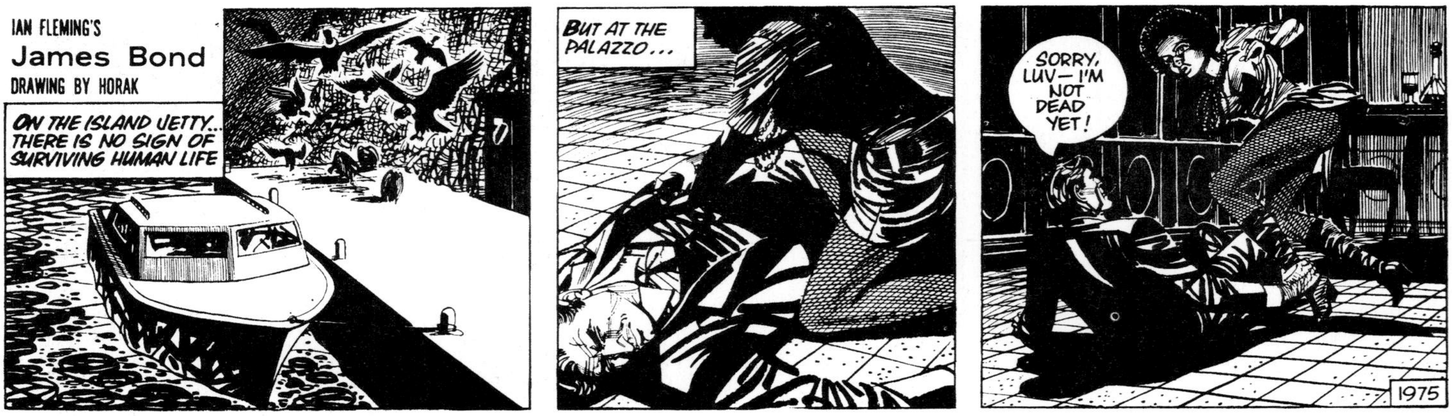
IAN FLEMING'S
James Bond
DRAWING BY HORAK
ON THE ISLAND JETTY... THERE IS NO SIGN OF SURVIVING HUMAN LIFE
BUT AT THE PALAZZO...
SORRY, LUV— I'M NOT DEAD YET!
1975

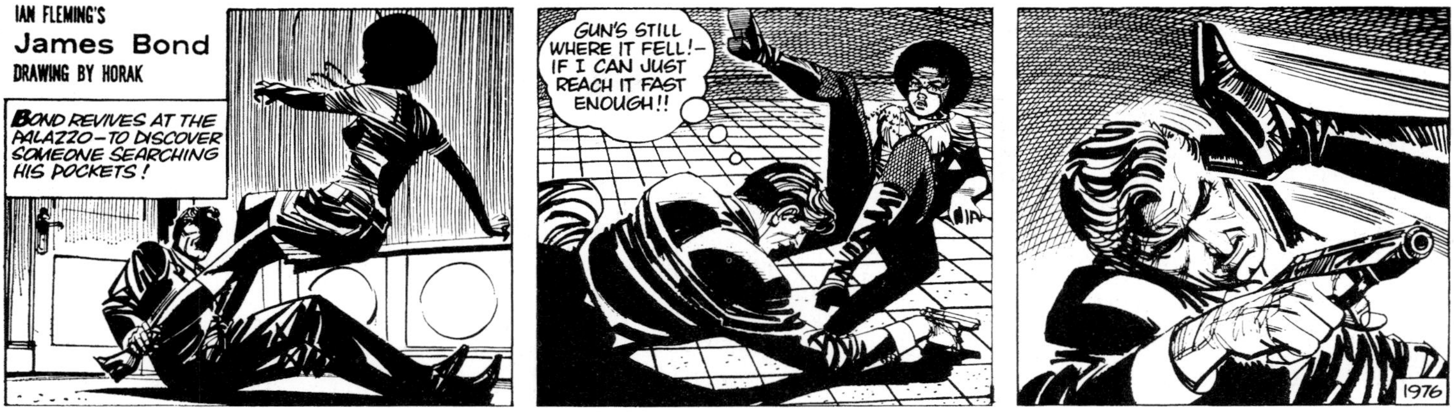
IAN FLEMING'S
James Bond
DRAWING BY HORAK
BOND REVIVES AT THE PALAZZO—TO DISCOVER SOMEONE SEARCHING HIS POCKETS!
GUN'S STILL WHERE IT FELL!—IF I CAN JUST REACH IT FAST ENOUGH!!
1976

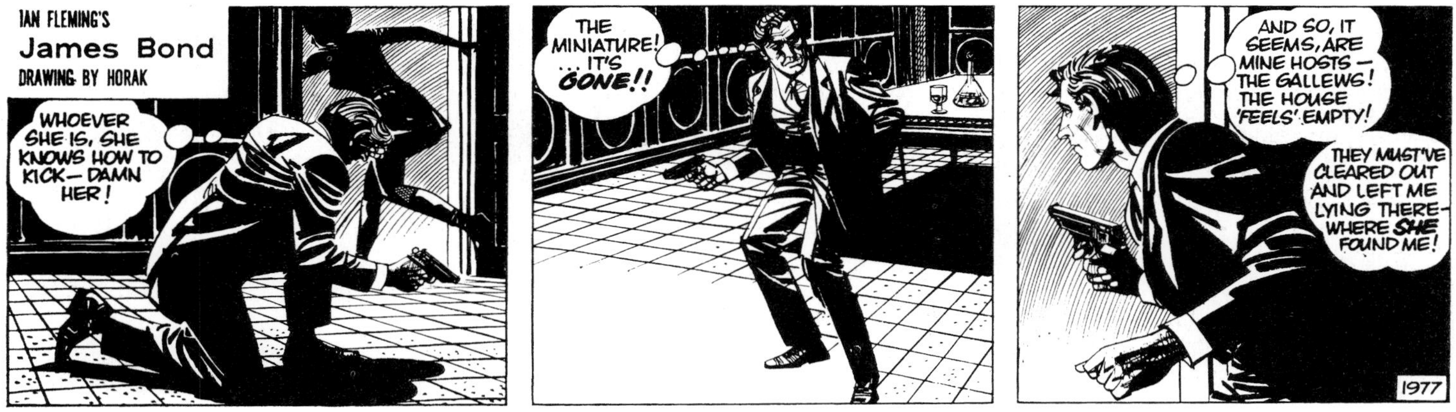
IAN FLEMING'S
James Bond
DRAWING BY HORAK
WHOEVER SHE IS, SHE KNOWS HOW TO KICK—DAMN HER!
THE MINIATURE! ... IT'S GONE!!
AND SO, IT SEEMS, ARE MINE HOSTS—THE GALLEWS! THE HOUSE 'FEELS' EMPTY!
THEY MUST'VE CLEARED OUT AND LEFT ME LYING THERE—WHERE SHE FOUND ME!
1977

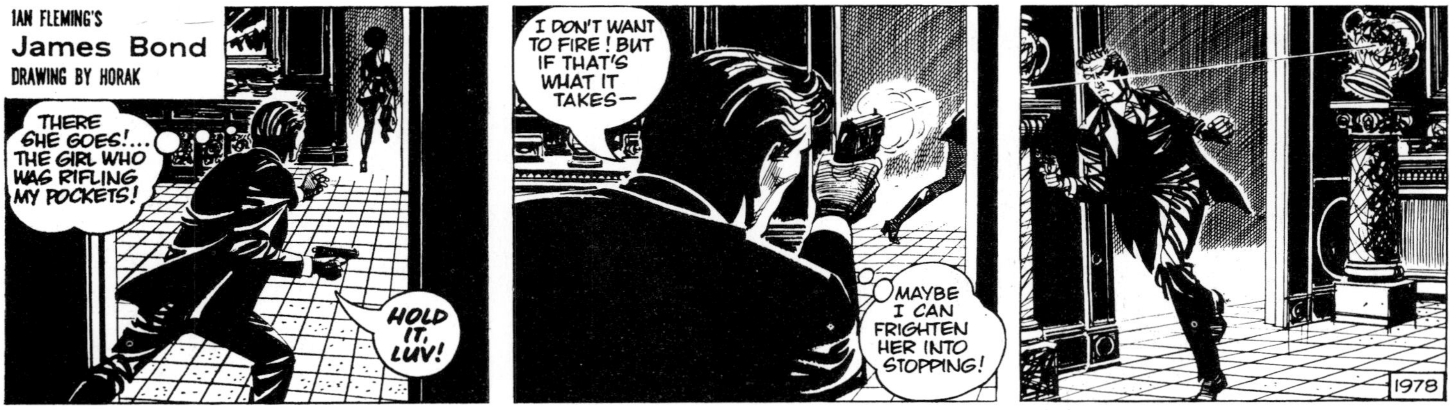
IAN FLEMING'S
James Bond
DRAWING BY HORAK
THERE SHE GOES!... THE GIRL WHO WAS RIFLING MY POCKETS!
HOLD IT, LUV!
I DON'T WANT TO FIRE! BUT IF THAT'S WHAT IT TAKES—
MAYBE I CAN FRIGHTEN HER INTO STOPPING!
1978

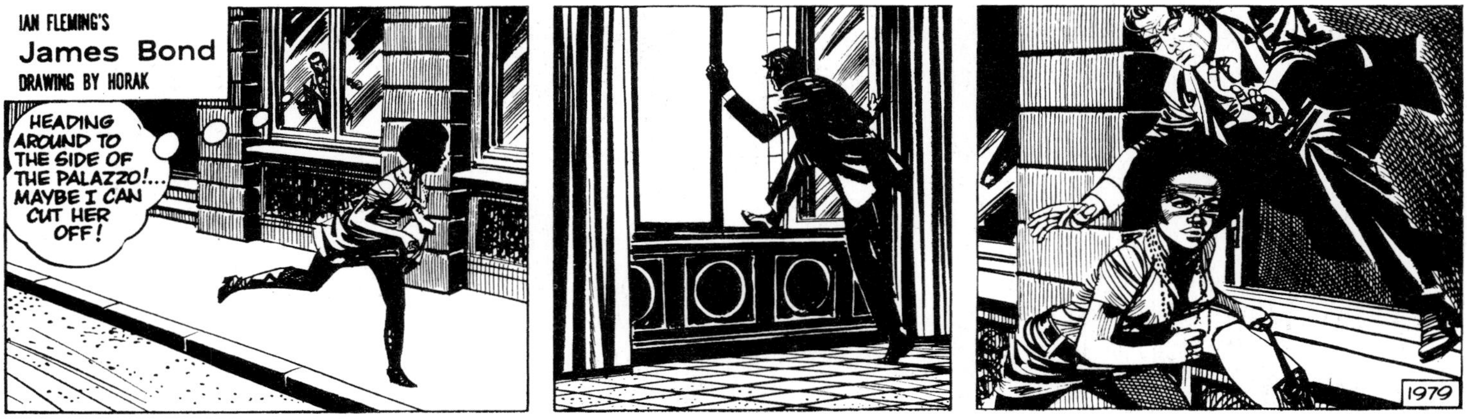
IAN FLEMING'S
James Bond
DRAWING BY HORAK
HEADING AROUND TO THE SIDE OF THE PALAZZO!... MAYBE I CAN CUT HER OFF!
1979

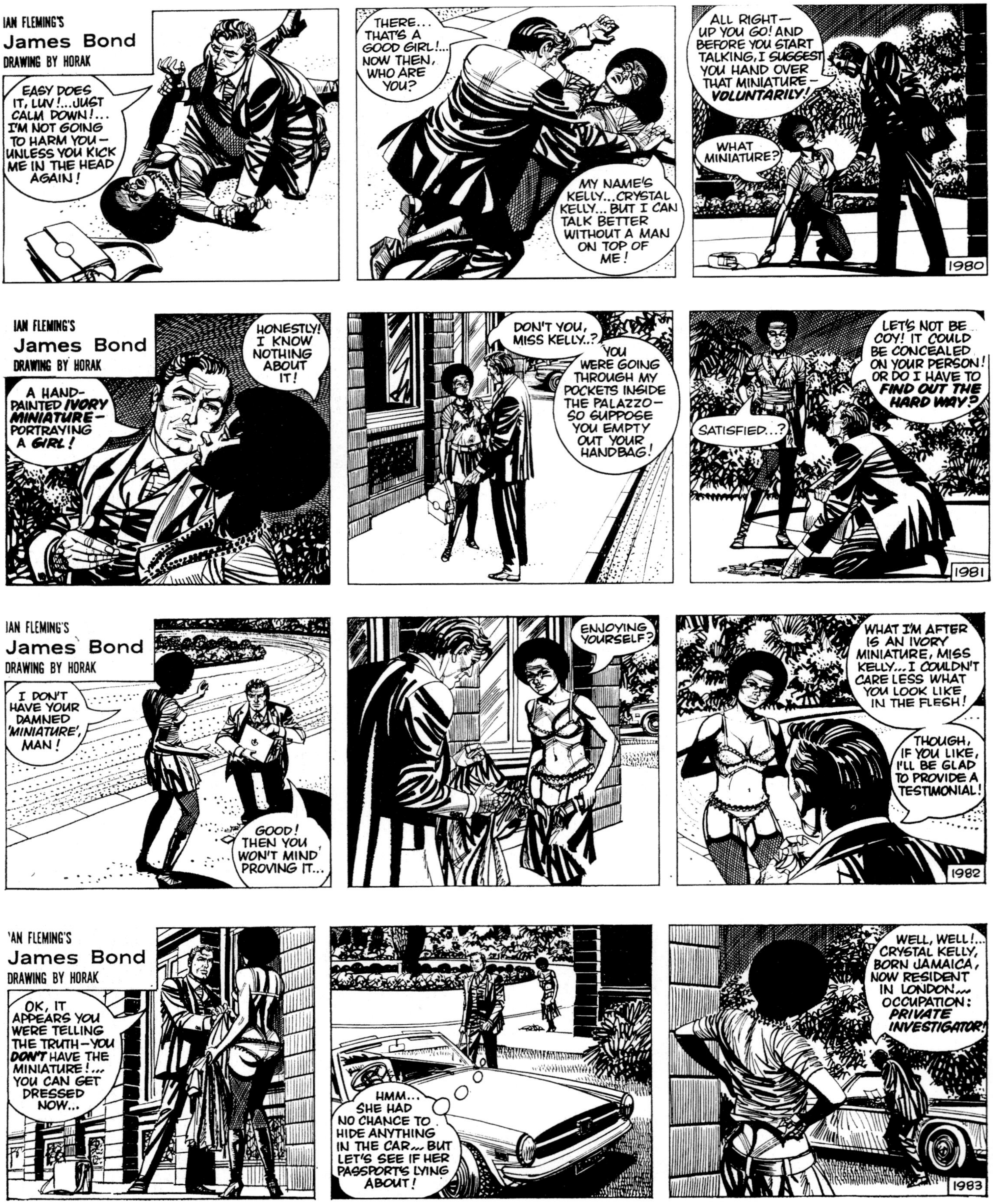
IAN FLEMING'S
James Bond
DRAWING BY HORAK
EASY DOES IT, LUV!...JUST CALM DOWN!... I'M NOT GOING TO HARM YOU—UNLESS YOU KICK ME IN THE HEAD AGAIN!
THERE... THAT'S A GOOD GIRL!... NOW THEN, WHO ARE YOU?
MY NAME'S KELLY...CRYSTAL KELLY... BUT I CAN TALK BETTER WITHOUT A MAN ON TOP OF ME!
ALL RIGHT—UP YOU GO! AND BEFORE YOU START TALKING, I SUGGEST YOU HAND OVER THAT MINIATURE—VOLUNTARILY!
WHAT MINIATURE?
1980
IAN FLEMING'S
James Bond
DRAWING BY HORAK
A HAND-PAINTED IVORY MINIATURE—PORTRAYING A GIRL!
HONESTLY! I KNOW NOTHING ABOUT IT!
DON'T YOU, MISS KELLY..?
YOU WERE GOING THROUGH MY POCKETS INSIDE THE PALAZZO—SO SUPPOSE YOU EMPTY OUT YOUR HANDBAG!
LET'S NOT BE COY! IT COULD BE CONCEALED ON YOUR PERSON! OR DO I HAVE TO FIND OUT THE HARD WAY?
SATISFIED...?
1981
IAN FLEMING'S
James Bond
DRAWING BY HORAK
I DON'T HAVE YOUR DAMNED 'MINIATURE', MAN!
GOOD! THEN YOU WON'T MIND PROVING IT...
ENJOYING YOURSELF?
WHAT I'M AFTER IS AN IVORY MINIATURE, MISS KELLY... I COULDN'T CARE LESS WHAT YOU LOOK LIKE IN THE FLESH!
THOUGH, IF YOU LIKE, I'LL BE GLAD TO PROVIDE A TESTIMONIAL!
1982
IAN FLEMING'S
James Bond
DRAWING BY HORAK
OK, IT APPEARS YOU WERE TELLING THE TRUTH—YOU DON'T HAVE THE MINIATURE!... YOU CAN GET DRESSED NOW...
HMM... SHE HAD NO CHANCE TO HIDE ANYTHING IN THE CAR... BUT LET'S SEE IF HER PASSPORT'S LYING ABOUT!
WELL, WELL!... CRYSTAL KELLY, BORN JAMAICA, NOW RESIDENT IN LONDON!... OCCUPATION: PRIVATE INVESTIGATOR!
1983

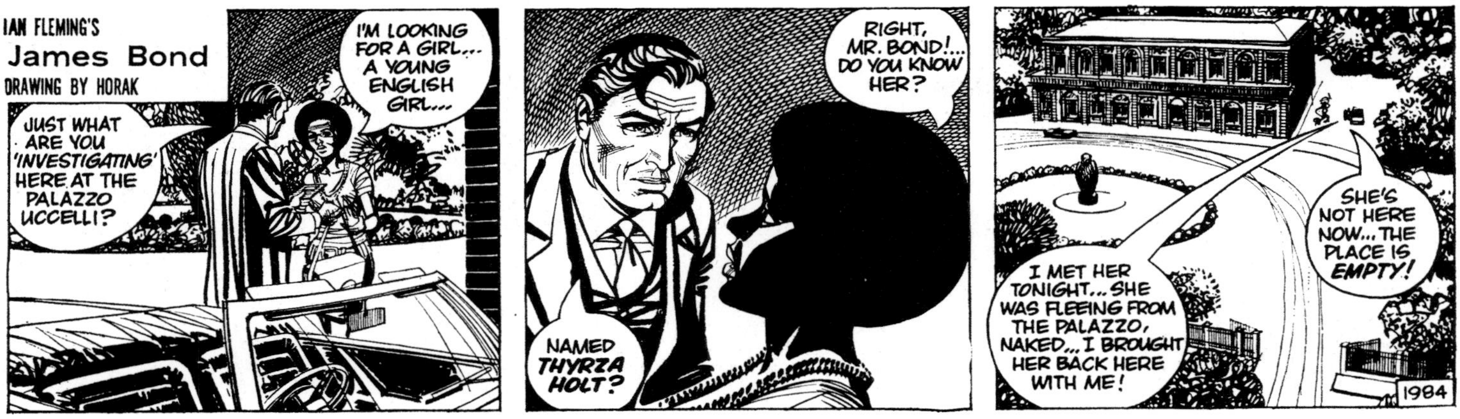
IAN FLEMING'S
James Bond
DRAWING BY HORAK
I'M LOOKING FOR A GIRL... A YOUNG ENGLISH GIRL...
JUST WHAT ARE YOU 'INVESTIGATING' HERE AT THE PALAZZO UCCELLI?
RIGHT, MR. BOND!... DO YOU KNOW HER?
NAMED **THYRZA HOLT**?
I MET HER TONIGHT... SHE WAS FLEEING FROM THE PALAZZO, NAKED... I BROUGHT HER BACK HERE WITH ME!
SHE'S NOT HERE NOW... THE PLACE IS **EMPTY!**
1984

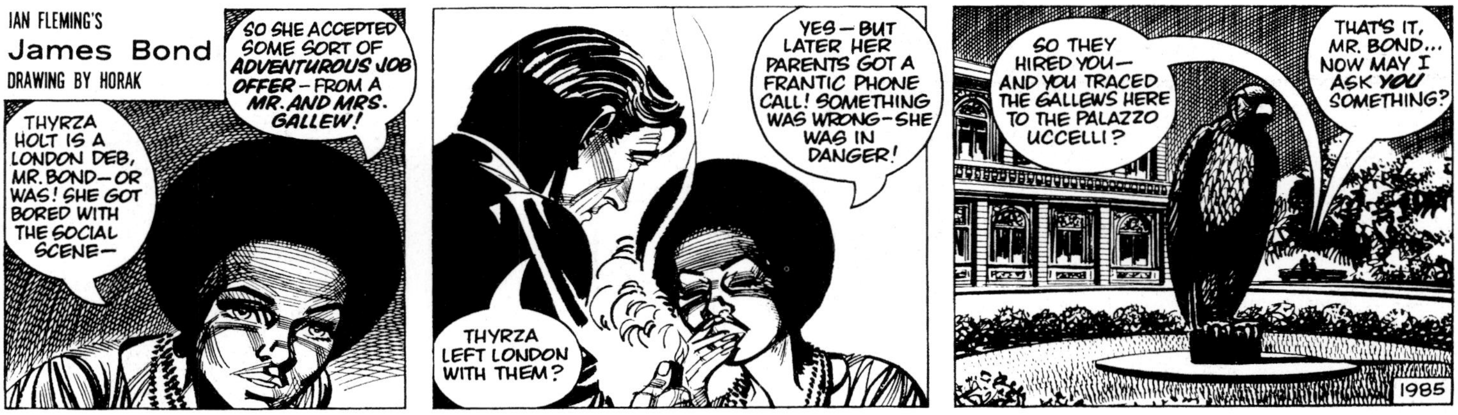
IAN FLEMING'S
James Bond
DRAWING BY HORAK
THYRZA HOLT IS A LONDON DEB, MR. BOND—OR WAS! SHE GOT BORED WITH THE SOCIAL SCENE—
SO SHE ACCEPTED SOME SORT OF **ADVENTUROUS JOB OFFER**—FROM A **MR. AND MRS. GALLEW!**
THYRZA LEFT LONDON WITH THEM?
YES—BUT LATER HER PARENTS GOT A FRANTIC PHONE CALL! SOMETHING WAS WRONG—SHE WAS IN DANGER!
SO THEY HIRED YOU—AND YOU TRACED THE GALLEWS HERE TO THE PALAZZO UCCELLI?
THAT'S IT, MR. BOND... NOW MAY I ASK **YOU** SOMETHING?
1985

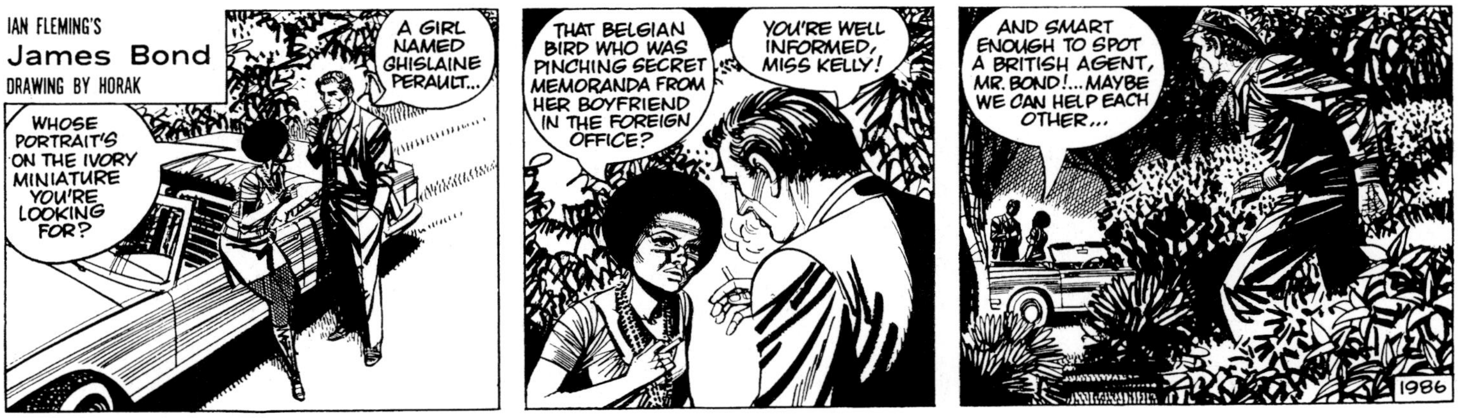
IAN FLEMING'S
James Bond
DRAWING BY HORAK
WHOSE PORTRAIT'S ON THE IVORY MINIATURE YOU'RE LOOKING FOR?
A GIRL NAMED GHISLAINE PERAULT...
THAT BELGIAN BIRD WHO WAS PINCHING SECRET MEMORANDA FROM HER BOYFRIEND IN THE FOREIGN OFFICE?
YOU'RE WELL INFORMED, MISS KELLY!
AND SMART ENOUGH TO SPOT A BRITISH AGENT, MR. BOND!... MAYBE WE CAN HELP EACH OTHER...
1986

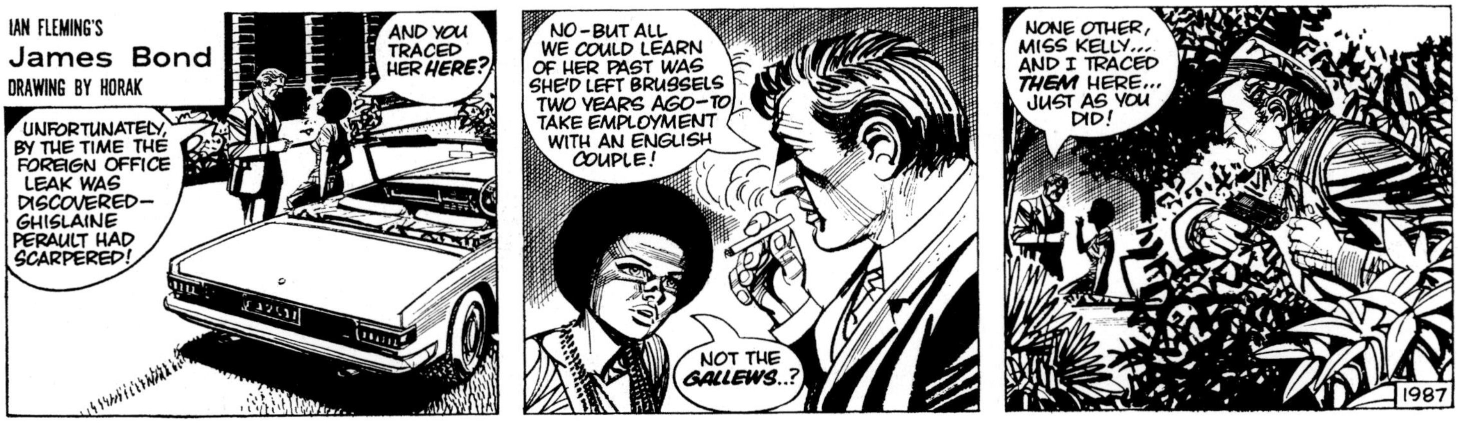
IAN FLEMING'S
James Bond
DRAWING BY HORAK
AND YOU TRACED HER **HERE?**
UNFORTUNATELY, BY THE TIME THE FOREIGN OFFICE LEAK WAS DISCOVERED—GHISLAINE PERAULT HAD SCARPERED!
NO—BUT ALL WE COULD LEARN OF HER PAST WAS SHE'D LEFT BRUSSELS TWO YEARS AGO—TO TAKE EMPLOYMENT WITH AN ENGLISH COUPLE!
NOT THE **GALLEWS**..?
NONE OTHER, MISS KELLY... AND I TRACED **THEM** HERE... JUST AS YOU DID!
1987

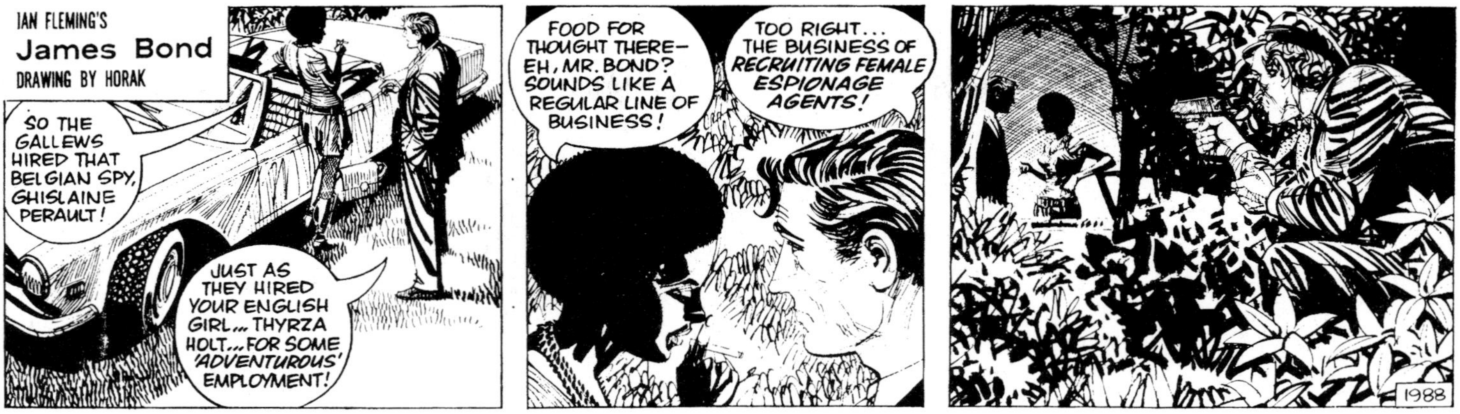
IAN FLEMING'S
James Bond
DRAWING BY HORAK
SO THE GALLEWS HIRED THAT BELGIAN SPY, GHISLAINE PERAULT!
JUST AS THEY HIRED YOUR ENGLISH GIRL... THYRZA HOLT... FOR SOME 'ADVENTUROUS' EMPLOYMENT!
FOOD FOR THOUGHT THERE— EH, MR. BOND? SOUNDS LIKE A REGULAR LINE OF BUSINESS!
TOO RIGHT... THE BUSINESS OF RECRUITING FEMALE ESPIONAGE AGENTS!
1988

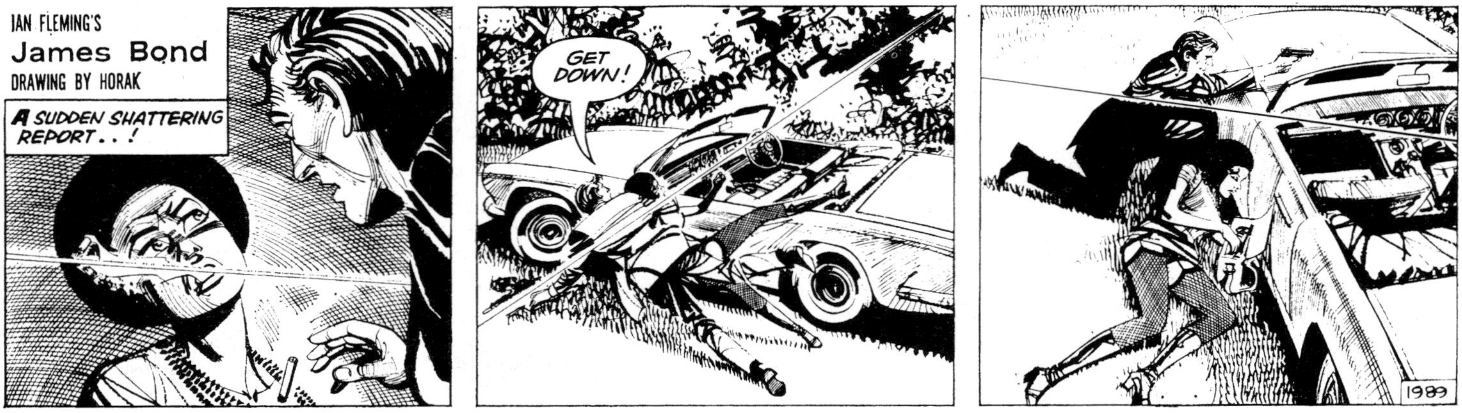
IAN FLEMING'S
James Bond
DRAWING BY HORAK
A SUDDEN SHATTERING REPORT..!
GET DOWN!
1989

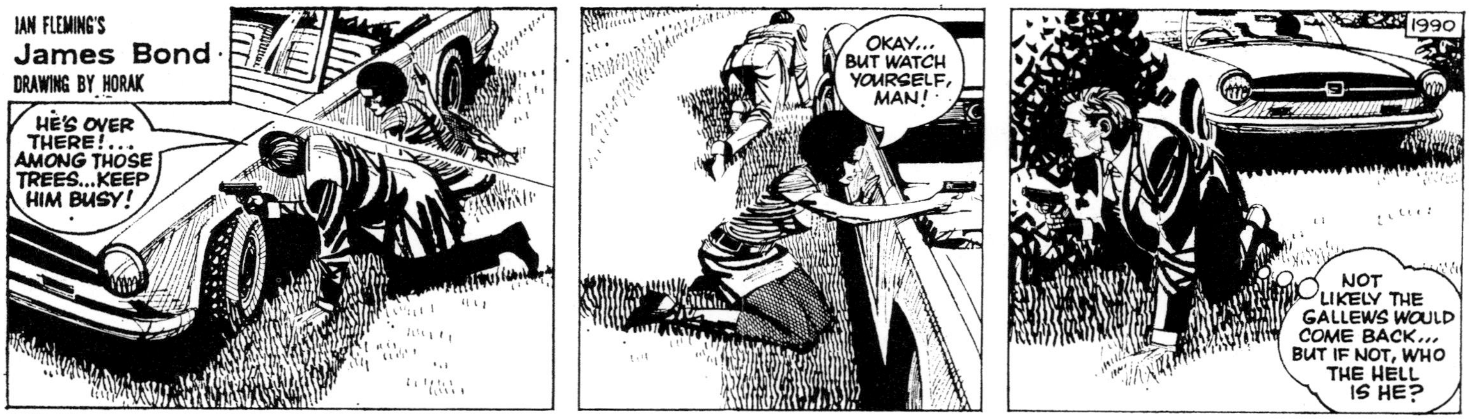
IAN FLEMING'S
James Bond
DRAWING BY HORAK
HE'S OVER THERE!... AMONG THOSE TREES... KEEP HIM BUSY!
OKAY... BUT WATCH YOURSELF, MAN!
1990
NOT LIKELY THE GALLEWS WOULD COME BACK... BUT IF NOT, WHO THE HELL IS HE?

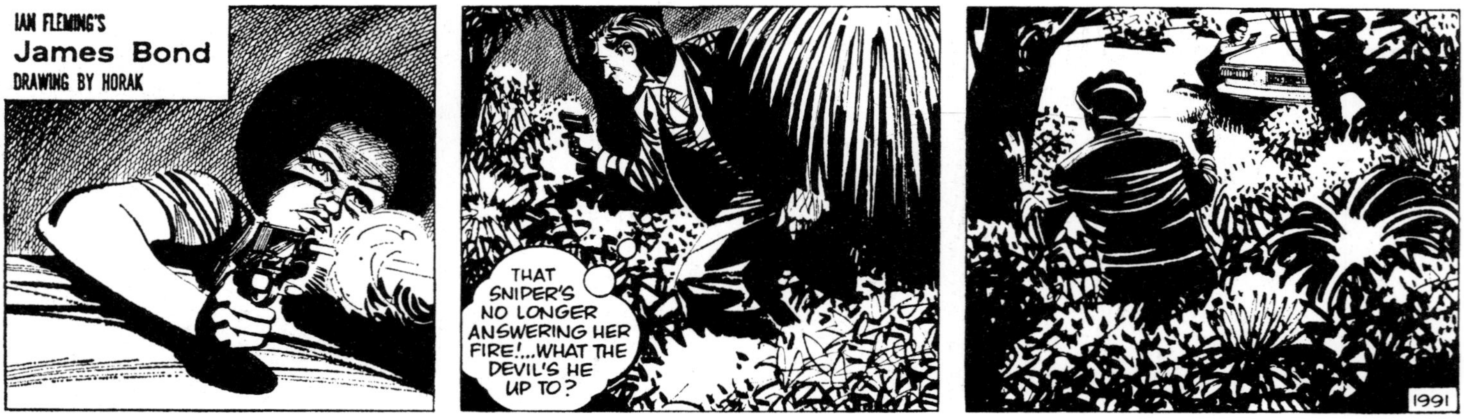
IAN FLEMING'S
James Bond
DRAWING BY HORAK
THAT SNIPER'S NO LONGER ANSWERING HER FIRE!... WHAT THE DEVIL'S HE UP TO?
1991

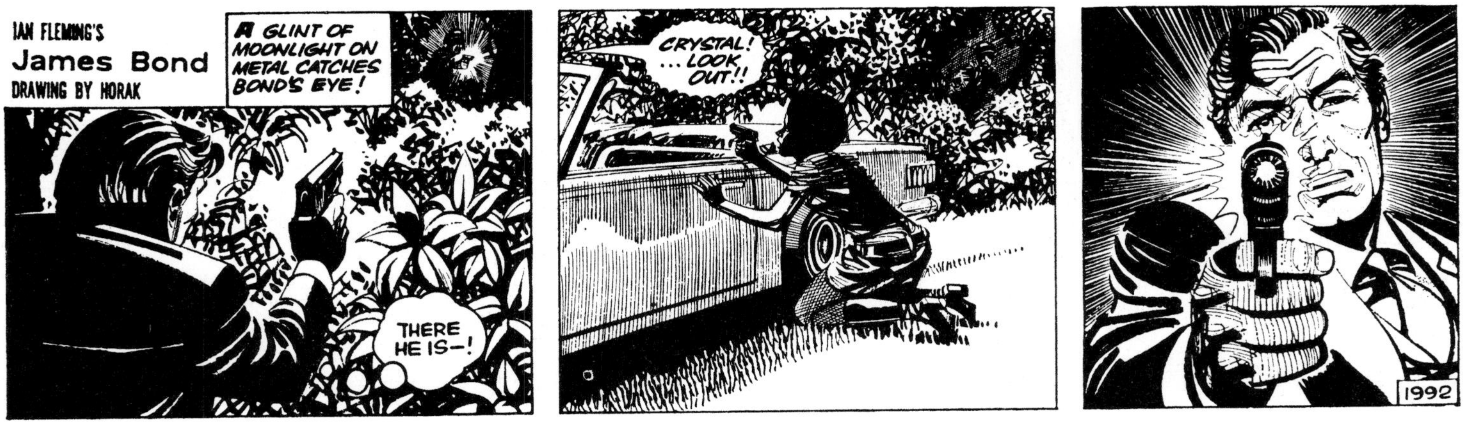
IAN FLEMING'S
James Bond
DRAWING BY HORAK
A GLINT OF MOONLIGHT ON METAL CATCHES BOND'S EYE!
THERE HE IS--!
CRYSTAL! ...LOOK OUT!!
1992

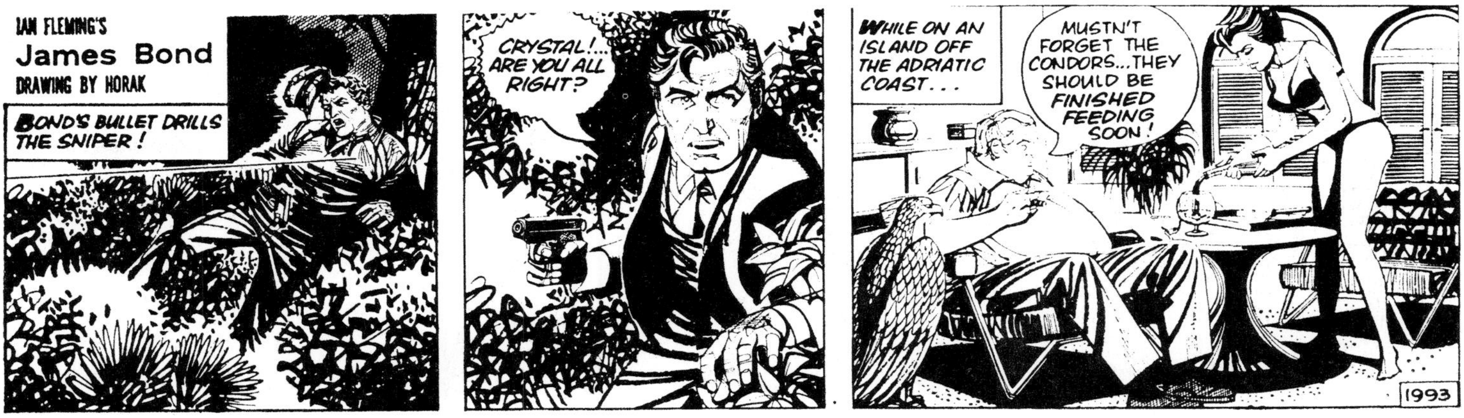
IAN FLEMING'S
James Bond
DRAWING BY HORAK
BOND'S BULLET DRILLS THE SNIPER!
CRYSTAL!... ARE YOU ALL RIGHT?
WHILE ON AN ISLAND OFF THE ADRIATIC COAST...
MUSTN'T FORGET THE CONDORS... THEY SHOULD BE FINISHED FEEDING SOON!
1993

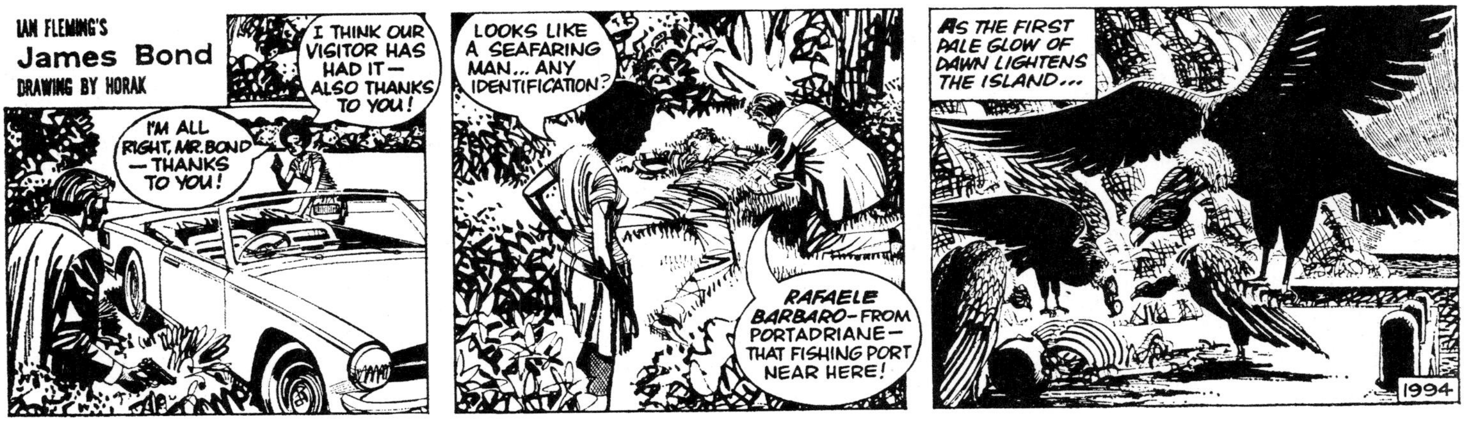
IAN FLEMING'S
James Bond
DRAWING BY HORAK
I THINK OUR VISITOR HAS HAD IT— ALSO THANKS TO YOU!
I'M ALL RIGHT, MR. BOND —THANKS TO YOU!
LOOKS LIKE A SEAFARING MAN... ANY IDENTIFICATION?
RAFAELE BARBARO—FROM PORTADRIANE— THAT FISHING PORT NEAR HERE!
AS THE FIRST PALE GLOW OF DAWN LIGHTENS THE ISLAND...
1994

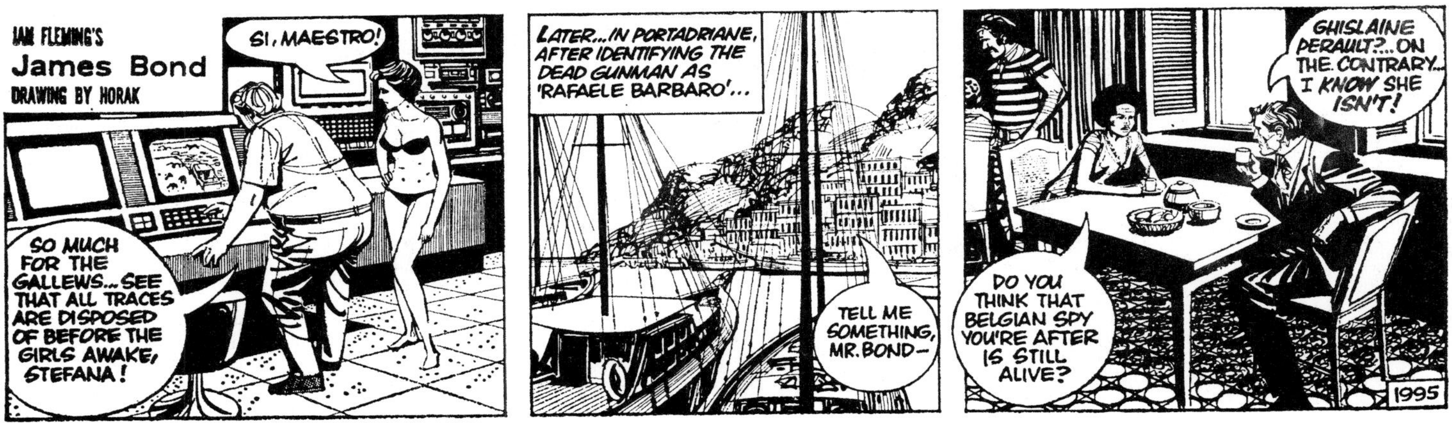
IAN FLEMING'S
James Bond
DRAWING BY HORAK
SI, MAESTRO!
SO MUCH FOR THE GALLEWS... SEE THAT ALL TRACES ARE DISPOSED OF BEFORE THE GIRLS AWAKE, STEFANA!
LATER... IN PORTADRIANE, AFTER IDENTIFYING THE DEAD GUNMAN AS 'RAFAELE BARBARO'...
TELL ME SOMETHING, MR. BOND—
DO YOU THINK THAT BELGIAN SPY YOU'RE AFTER IS STILL ALIVE?
GHISLAINE PERAULT?... ON THE CONTRARY... I KNOW SHE ISN'T!
1995

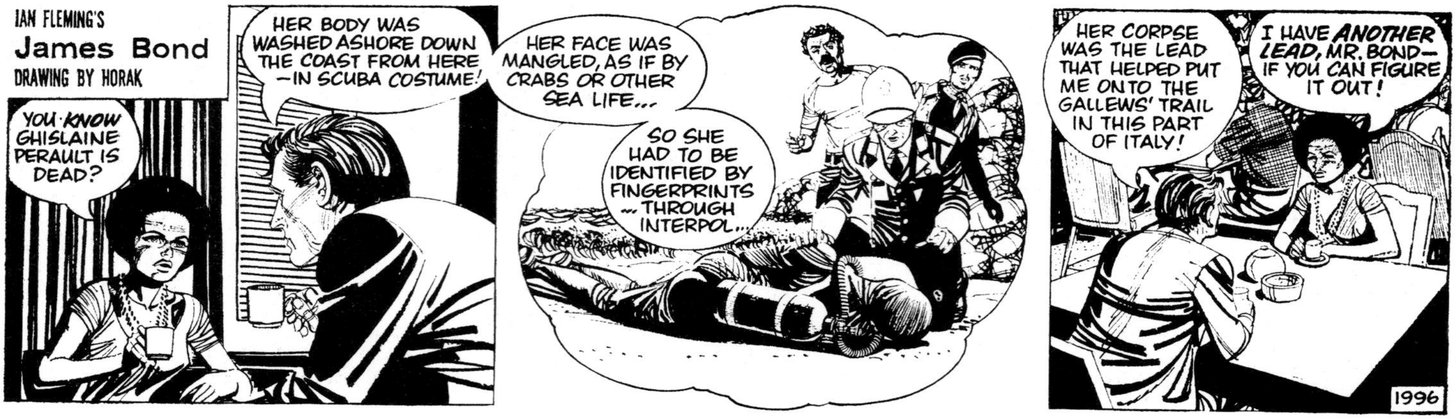

IAN FLEMING'S
James Bond
DRAWING BY HORAK
YOU KNOW GHISLAINE PERAULT IS DEAD?
HER BODY WAS WASHED ASHORE DOWN THE COAST FROM HERE —IN SCUBA COSTUME!
HER FACE WAS MANGLED, AS IF BY CRABS OR OTHER SEA LIFE...
SO SHE HAD TO BE IDENTIFIED BY FINGERPRINTS ...THROUGH INTERPOL...
HER CORPSE WAS THE LEAD THAT HELPED PUT ME ONTO THE GALLEWS' TRAIL IN THIS PART OF ITALY!
I HAVE ANOTHER LEAD, MR. BOND— IF YOU CAN FIGURE IT OUT!
1996

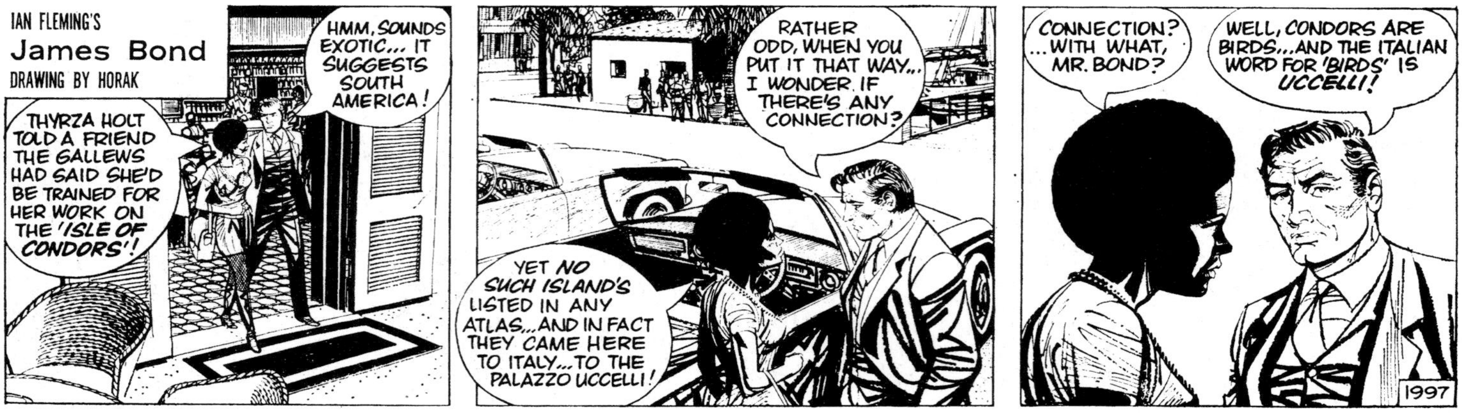

IAN FLEMING'S
James Bond
DRAWING BY HORAK
THYRZA HOLT TOLD A FRIEND THE GALLEWS HAD SAID SHE'D BE TRAINED FOR HER WORK ON THE 'ISLE OF CONDORS'!
HMM, SOUNDS EXOTIC... IT SUGGESTS SOUTH AMERICA!
YET NO SUCH ISLAND'S LISTED IN ANY ATLAS... AND IN FACT THEY CAME HERE TO ITALY... TO THE PALAZZO UCCELLI!
RATHER ODD, WHEN YOU PUT IT THAT WAY... I WONDER, IF THERE'S ANY CONNECTION?
CONNECTION? ...WITH WHAT, MR. BOND?
WELL, CONDORS ARE BIRDS... AND THE ITALIAN WORD FOR 'BIRDS' IS UCCELLI!
1997

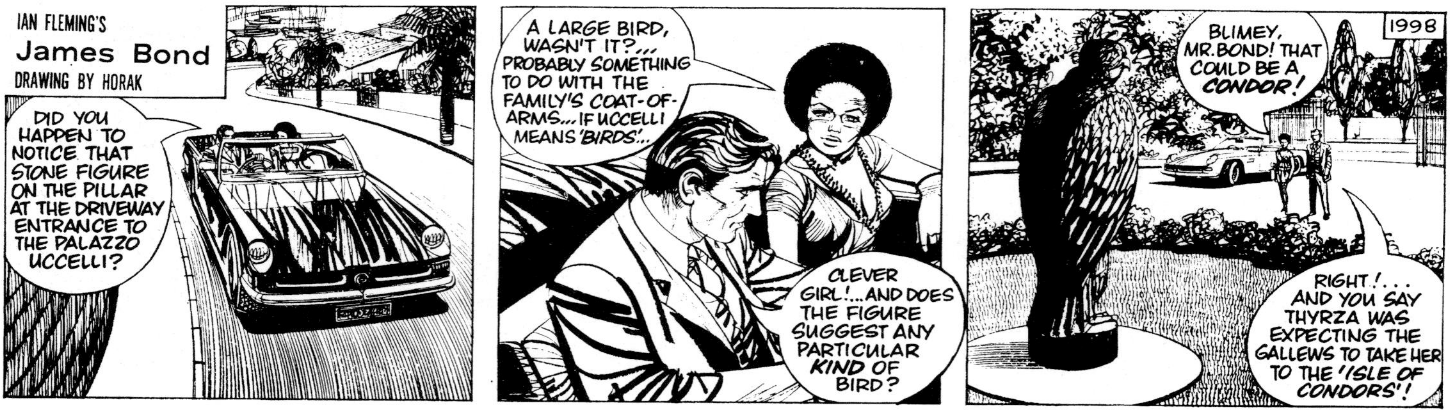

IAN FLEMING'S
James Bond
DRAWING BY HORAK
DID YOU HAPPEN TO NOTICE THAT STONE FIGURE ON THE PILLAR AT THE DRIVEWAY ENTRANCE TO THE PALAZZO UCCELLI?
A LARGE BIRD, WASN'T IT?... PROBABLY SOMETHING TO DO WITH THE FAMILY'S COAT-OF-ARMS... IF UCCELLI MEANS 'BIRDS'...
CLEVER GIRL!... AND DOES THE FIGURE SUGGEST ANY PARTICULAR KIND OF BIRD?
1998
BLIMEY, MR. BOND! THAT COULD BE A CONDOR!
RIGHT!... AND YOU SAY THYRZA WAS EXPECTING THE GALLEWS TO TAKE HER TO THE 'ISLE OF CONDORS'!

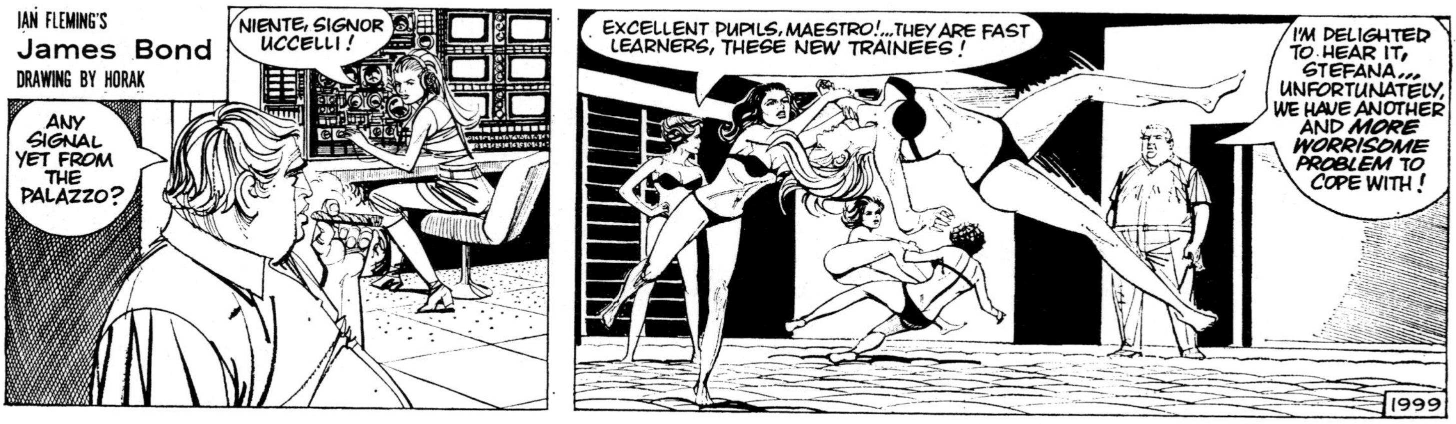

IAN FLEMING'S
James Bond
DRAWING BY HORAK
ANY SIGNAL YET FROM THE PALAZZO?
NIENTE, SIGNOR UCCELLI!
EXCELLENT PUPILS, MAESTRO!... THEY ARE FAST LEARNERS, THESE NEW TRAINEES!
I'M DELIGHTED TO HEAR IT, STEFANA... UNFORTUNATELY, WE HAVE ANOTHER AND MORE WORRISOME PROBLEM TO COPE WITH!
1999

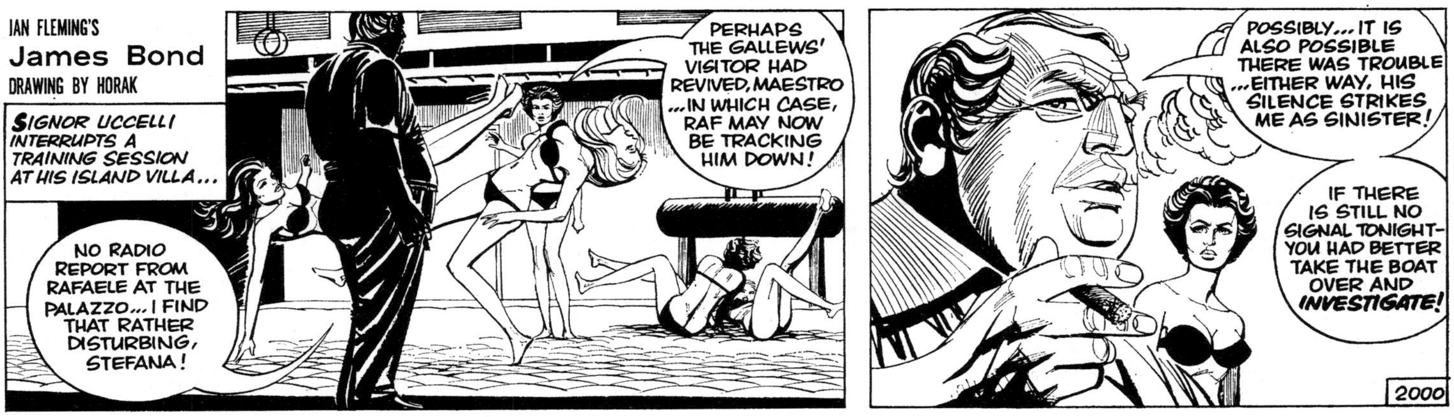
IAN FLEMING'S
James Bond
DRAWING BY HORAK
SIGNOR UCCELLI INTERRUPTS A TRAINING SESSION AT HIS ISLAND VILLA...
NO RADIO REPORT FROM RAFAELE AT THE PALAZZO... I FIND THAT RATHER DISTURBING, STEFANA!
PERHAPS THE GALLEWS' VISITOR HAD REVIVED, MAESTRO ...IN WHICH CASE, RAF MAY NOW BE TRACKING HIM DOWN!
POSSIBLY... IT IS ALSO POSSIBLE THERE WAS TROUBLE ...EITHER WAY, HIS SILENCE STRIKES ME AS SINISTER!
IF THERE IS STILL NO SIGNAL TONIGHT- YOU HAD BETTER TAKE THE BOAT OVER AND INVESTIGATE!
2000

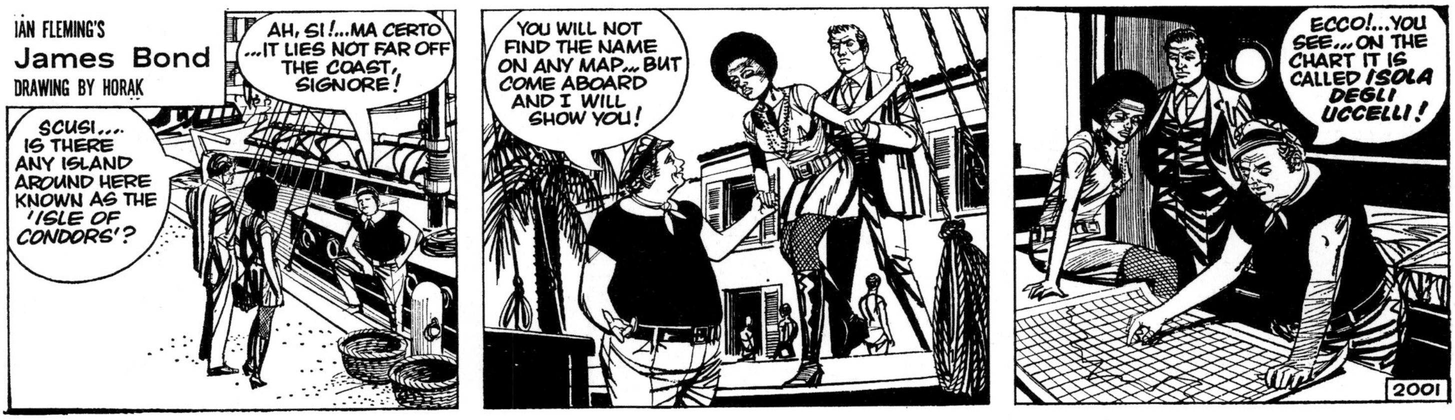
IAN FLEMING'S
James Bond
DRAWING BY HORAK
SCUSI... IS THERE ANY ISLAND AROUND HERE KNOWN AS THE 'ISLE OF CONDORS'?
AH, SI!...MA CERTO ...IT LIES NOT FAR OFF THE COAST, SIGNORE!
YOU WILL NOT FIND THE NAME ON ANY MAP... BUT COME ABOARD AND I WILL SHOW YOU!
ECCO!...YOU SEE... ON THE CHART IT IS CALLED ISOLA DEGLI UCCELLI!
2001

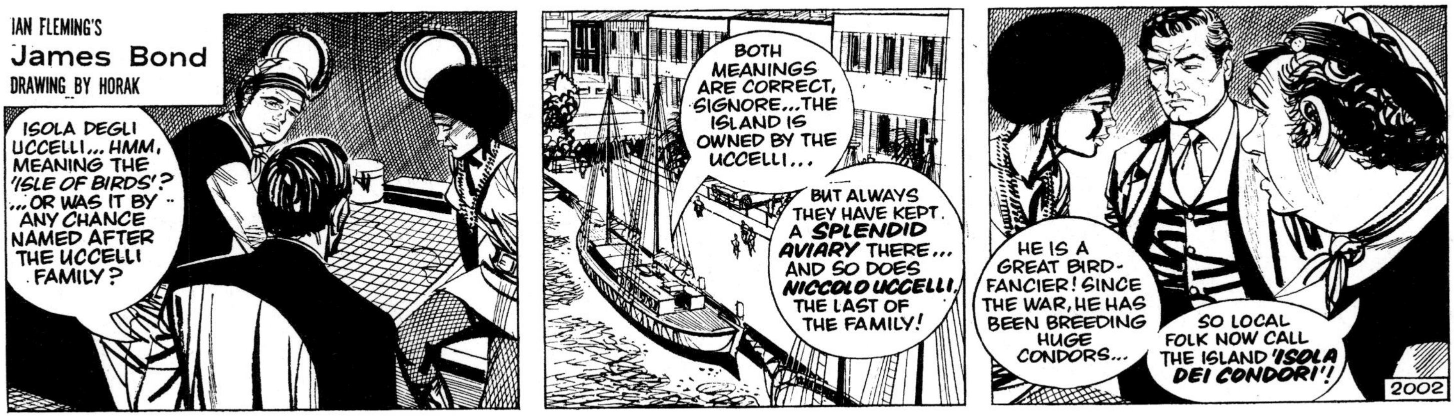
IAN FLEMING'S
James Bond
DRAWING BY HORAK
ISOLA DEGLI UCCELLI... HMM, MEANING THE 'ISLE OF BIRDS'? ...OR WAS IT BY ANY CHANCE NAMED AFTER THE UCCELLI FAMILY?
BOTH MEANINGS ARE CORRECT, SIGNORE... THE ISLAND IS OWNED BY THE UCCELLI...
BUT ALWAYS THEY HAVE KEPT A SPLENDID AVIARY THERE... AND SO DOES NICCOLO UCCELLI, THE LAST OF THE FAMILY!
HE IS A GREAT BIRD-FANCIER! SINCE THE WAR, HE HAS BEEN BREEDING HUGE CONDORS...
SO LOCAL FOLK NOW CALL THE ISLAND 'ISOLA DEI CONDORI'!
2002

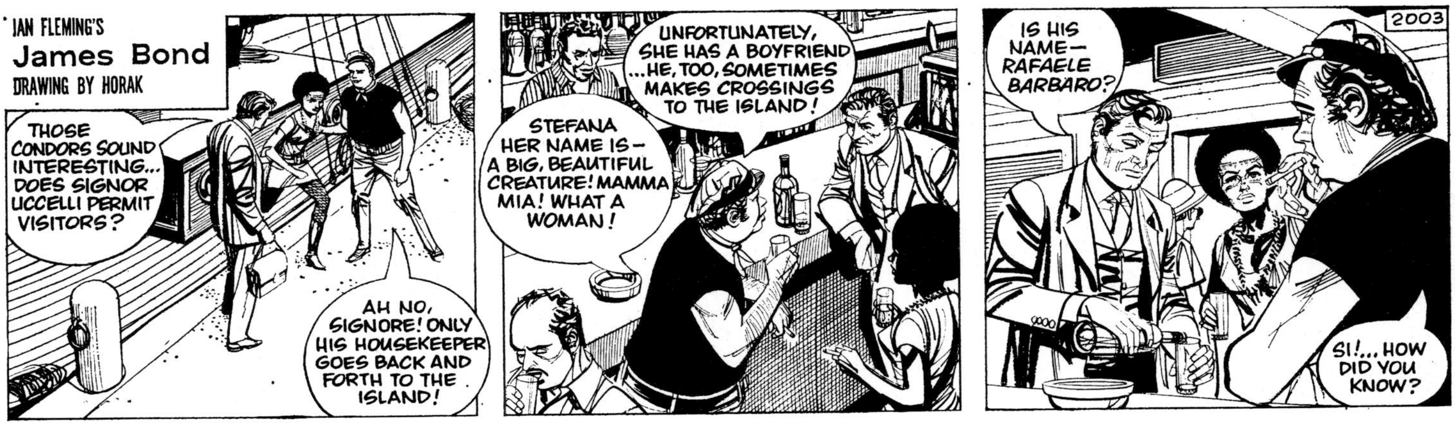
IAN FLEMING'S
James Bond
DRAWING BY HORAK
THOSE CONDORS SOUND INTERESTING... DOES SIGNOR UCCELLI PERMIT VISITORS?
AH NO, SIGNORE! ONLY HIS HOUSEKEEPER GOES BACK AND FORTH TO THE ISLAND!
STEFANA HER NAME IS- A BIG, BEAUTIFUL CREATURE! MAMMA MIA! WHAT A WOMAN!
UNFORTUNATELY, SHE HAS A BOYFRIEND ...HE, TOO, SOMETIMES MAKES CROSSINGS TO THE ISLAND!
2003
IS HIS NAME- RAFAELE BARBARO?
SI!... HOW DID YOU KNOW?

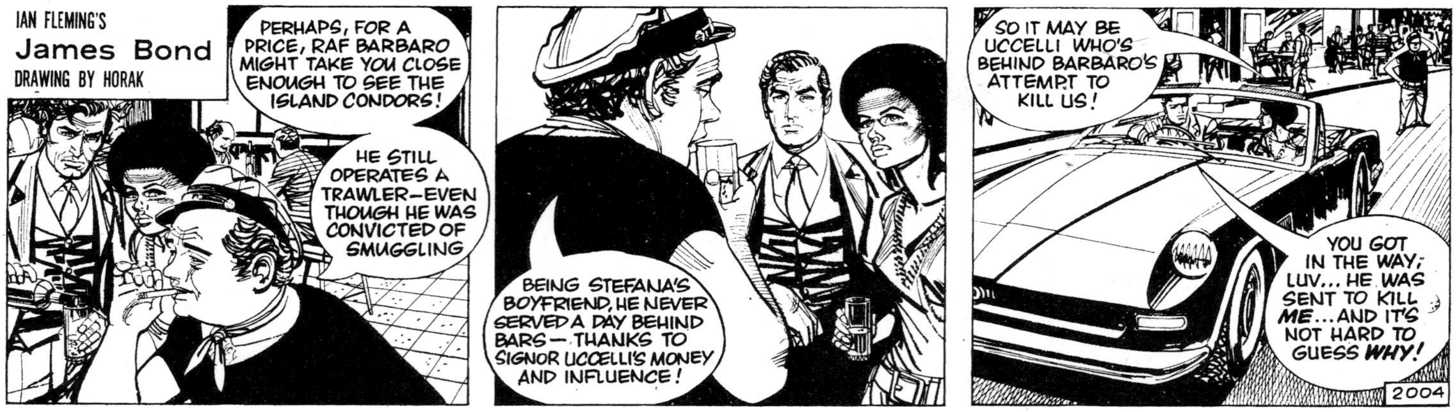
IAN FLEMING'S
James Bond
DRAWING BY HORAK
PERHAPS, FOR A PRICE, RAF BARBARO MIGHT TAKE YOU CLOSE ENOUGH TO SEE THE ISLAND CONDORS!
HE STILL OPERATES A TRAWLER—EVEN THOUGH HE WAS CONVICTED OF SMUGGLING
BEING STEFANIA'S BOYFRIEND, HE NEVER SERVED A DAY BEHIND BARS— THANKS TO SIGNOR UCCELLI'S MONEY AND INFLUENCE!
SO IT MAY BE UCCELLI WHO'S BEHIND BARBARO'S ATTEMPT TO KILL US!
YOU GOT IN THE WAY, LUV... HE WAS SENT TO KILL **ME**... AND IT'S NOT HARD TO GUESS **WHY**!
2004

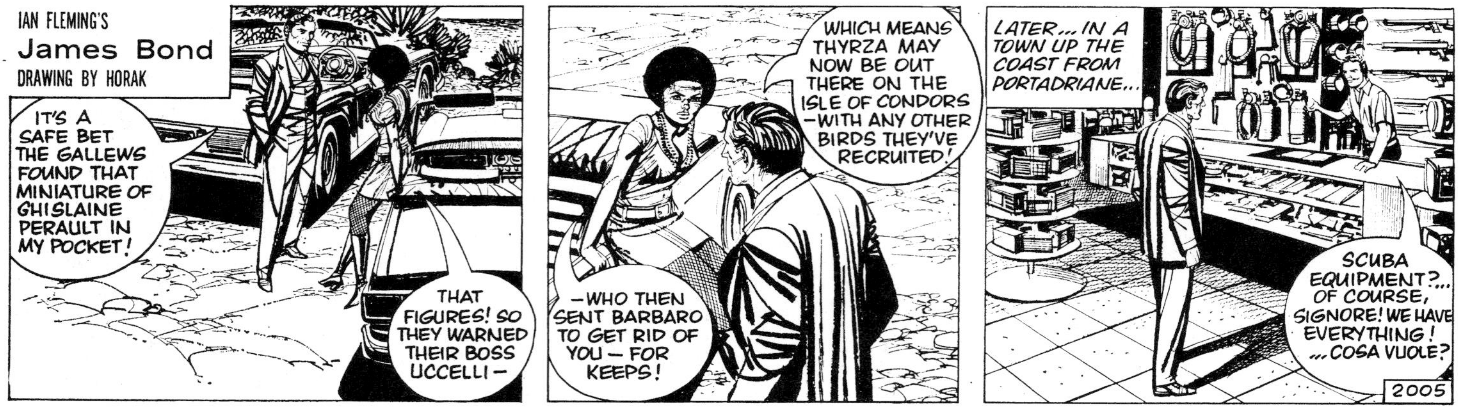
IAN FLEMING'S
James Bond
DRAWING BY HORAK
IT'S A SAFE BET THE GALLEWS FOUND THAT MINIATURE OF GHISLAINE PERAULT IN MY POCKET!
THAT FIGURES! SO THEY WARNED THEIR BOSS UCCELLI—
WHICH MEANS THYRZA MAY NOW BE OUT THERE ON THE ISLE OF CONDORS —WITH ANY OTHER BIRDS THEY'VE RECRUITED!
—WHO THEN SENT BARBARO TO GET RID OF YOU — FOR KEEPS!
LATER... IN A TOWN UP THE COAST FROM PORTADRIANE...
SCUBA EQUIPMENT?... OF COURSE, SIGNORE! WE HAVE EVERYTHING! ...COSA VUOLE?
2005

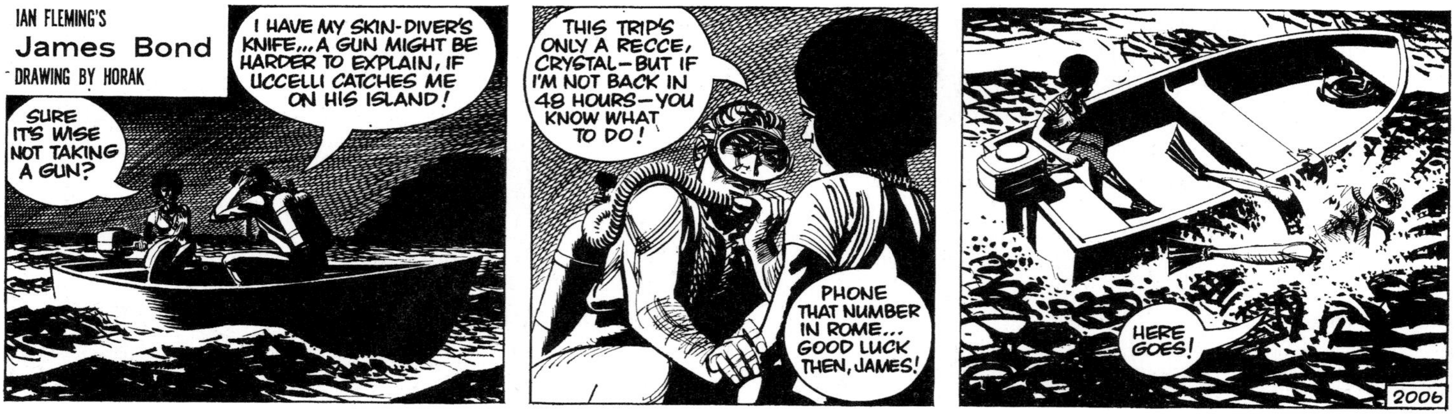
IAN FLEMING'S
James Bond
DRAWING BY HORAK
SURE IT'S WISE NOT TAKING A GUN?
I HAVE MY SKIN-DIVER'S KNIFE... A GUN MIGHT BE HARDER TO EXPLAIN, IF UCCELLI CATCHES ME ON HIS ISLAND!
THIS TRIP'S ONLY A RECCE, CRYSTAL—BUT IF I'M NOT BACK IN 48 HOURS—YOU KNOW WHAT TO DO!
PHONE THAT NUMBER IN ROME... GOOD LUCK THEN, JAMES!
HERE GOES!
2006

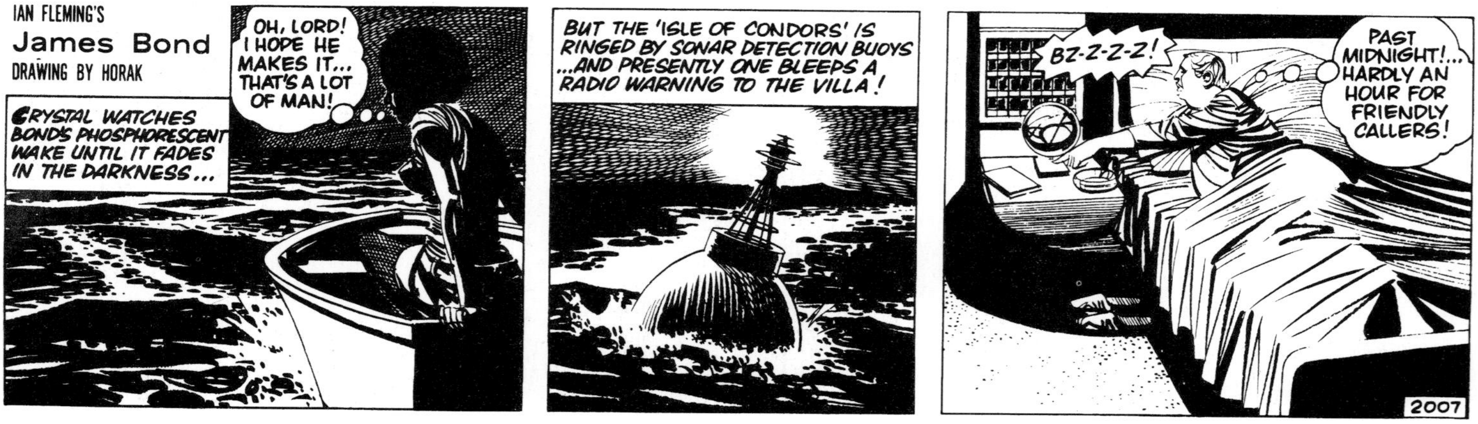
IAN FLEMING'S
James Bond
DRAWING BY HORAK
OH, LORD! I HOPE HE MAKES IT... THAT'S A LOT OF MAN!
CRYSTAL WATCHES BOND'S PHOSPHORESCENT WAKE UNTIL IT FADES IN THE DARKNESS...
BUT THE 'ISLE OF CONDORS' IS RINGED BY SONAR DETECTION BUOYS ...AND PRESENTLY ONE BLEEPS A RADIO WARNING TO THE VILLA!
BZ-Z-Z-Z!
PAST MIDNIGHT!... HARDLY AN HOUR FOR FRIENDLY CALLERS!
2007

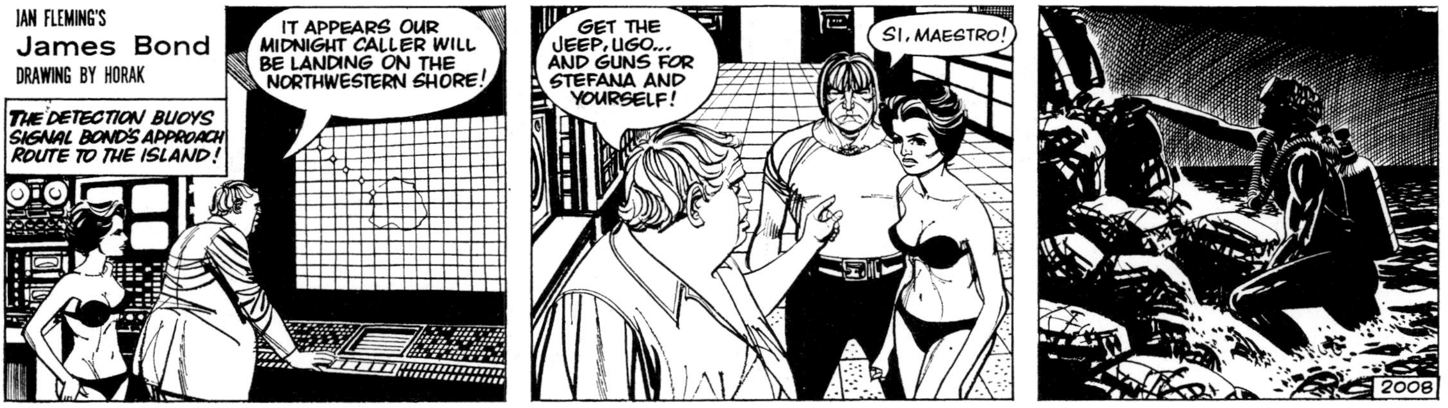
IAN FLEMING'S
James Bond
DRAWING BY HORAK
THE DETECTION BUOYS SIGNAL BOND'S APPROACH ROUTE TO THE ISLAND!
IT APPEARS OUR MIDNIGHT CALLER WILL BE LANDING ON THE NORTHWESTERN SHORE!
GET THE JEEP, UGO... AND GUNS FOR STEFANA AND YOURSELF!
SI, MAESTRO!
2008

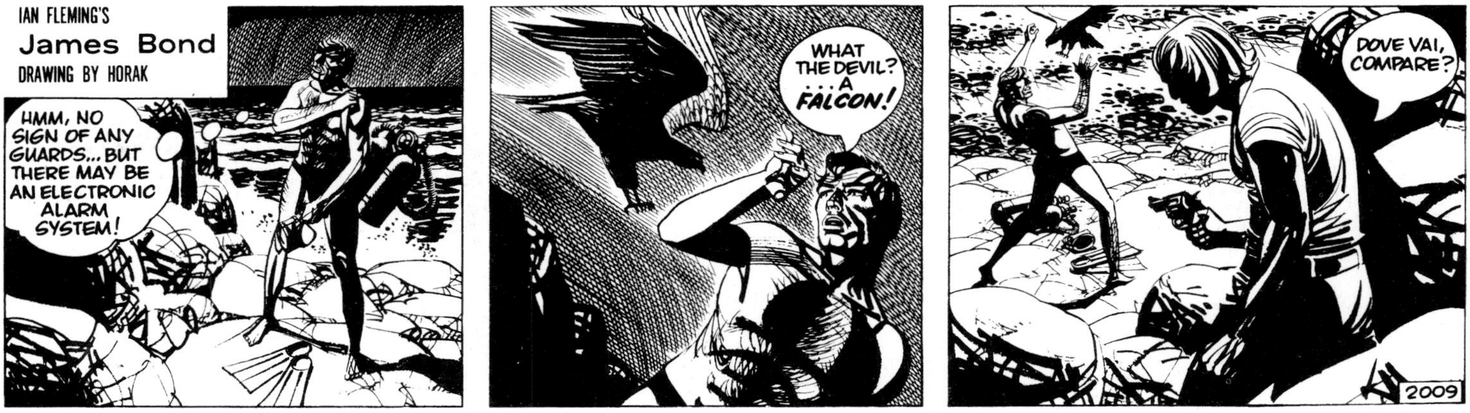
IAN FLEMING'S
James Bond
DRAWING BY HORAK
HMM, NO SIGN OF ANY GUARDS... BUT THERE MAY BE AN ELECTRONIC ALARM SYSTEM!
WHAT THE DEVIL? . . . A FALCON!
DOVE VAI, COMPARE?
2009

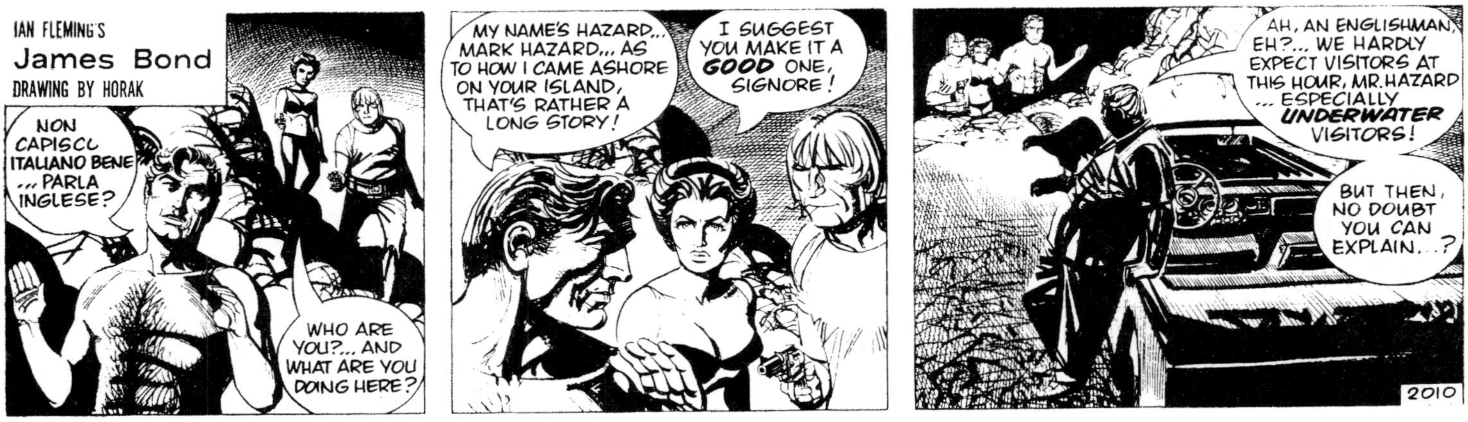
IAN FLEMING'S
James Bond
DRAWING BY HORAK
NON CAPISCO ITALIANO BENE ... PARLA INGLESE?
WHO ARE YOU?... AND WHAT ARE YOU DOING HERE?
MY NAME'S HAZARD... MARK HAZARD... AS TO HOW I CAME ASHORE ON YOUR ISLAND, THAT'S RATHER A LONG STORY!
I SUGGEST YOU MAKE IT A GOOD ONE, SIGNORE!
AH, AN ENGLISHMAN, EH?... WE HARDLY EXPECT VISITORS AT THIS HOUR, MR. HAZARD ... ESPECIALLY UNDERWATER VISITORS!
BUT THEN, NO DOUBT YOU CAN EXPLAIN...?
2010

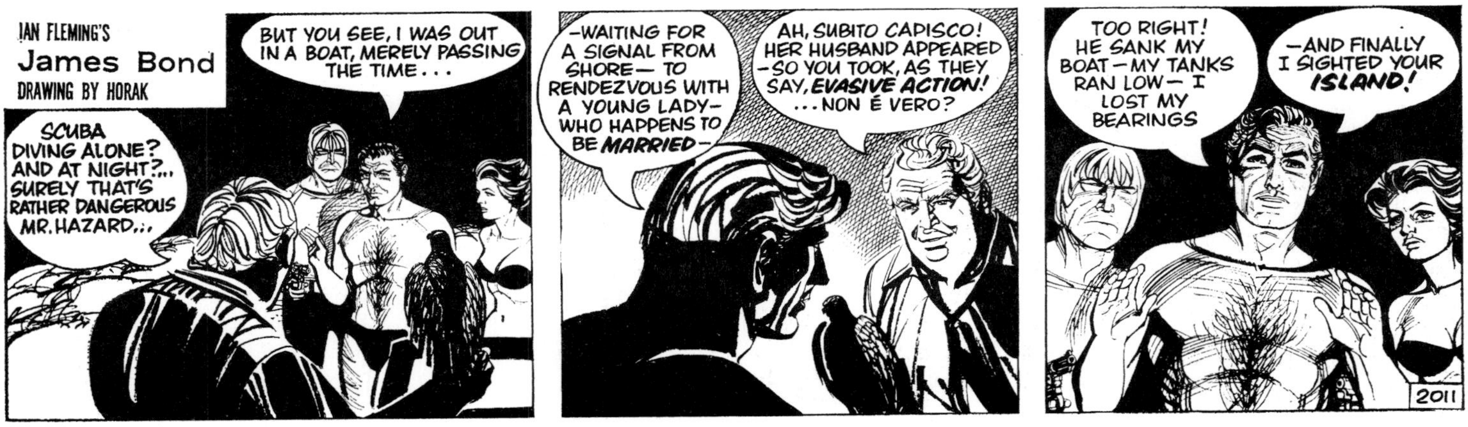
IAN FLEMING'S
James Bond
DRAWING BY HORAK
SCUBA DIVING ALONE? AND AT NIGHT?... SURELY THAT'S RATHER DANGEROUS MR. HAZARD...
BUT YOU SEE, I WAS OUT IN A BOAT, MERELY PASSING THE TIME . . .
—WAITING FOR A SIGNAL FROM SHORE— TO RENDEZVOUS WITH A YOUNG LADY— WHO HAPPENS TO BE MARRIED—
AH, SUBITO CAPISCO! HER HUSBAND APPEARED —SO YOU TOOK, AS THEY SAY, EVASIVE ACTION! . . . NON É VERO?
TOO RIGHT! HE SANK MY BOAT—MY TANKS RAN LOW— I LOST MY BEARINGS
—AND FINALLY I SIGHTED YOUR ISLAND!
2011

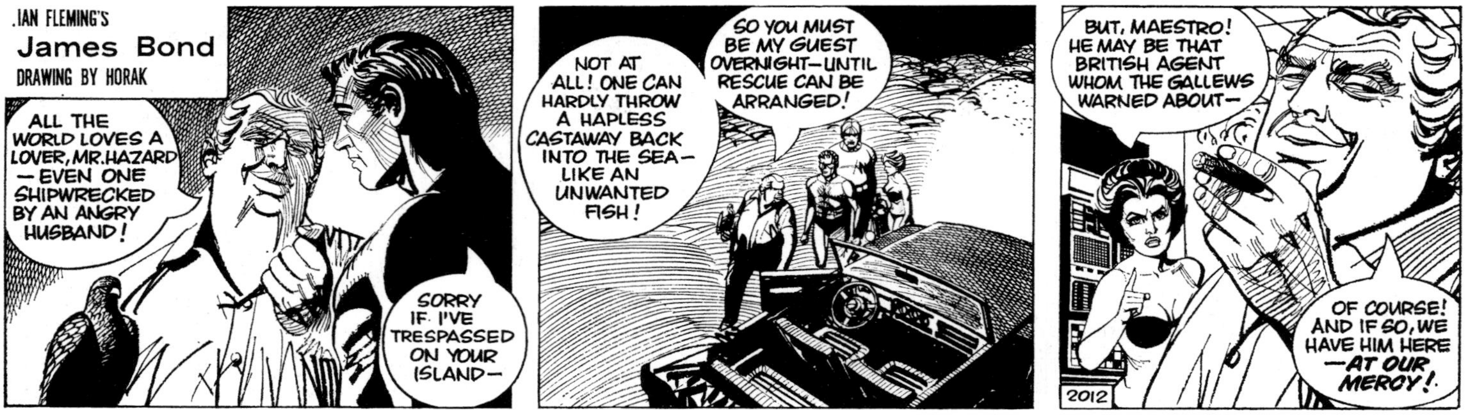
IAN FLEMING'S
James Bond
DRAWING BY HORAK
ALL THE WORLD LOVES A LOVER, MR. HAZARD—EVEN ONE SHIPWRECKED BY AN ANGRY HUSBAND!
SORRY IF I'VE TRESPASSED ON YOUR ISLAND—
NOT AT ALL! ONE CAN HARDLY THROW A HAPLESS CASTAWAY BACK INTO THE SEA—LIKE AN UNWANTED FISH!
SO YOU MUST BE MY GUEST OVERNIGHT—UNTIL RESCUE CAN BE ARRANGED!
BUT, MAESTRO! HE MAY BE THAT BRITISH AGENT WHOM THE GALLEWS WARNED ABOUT—
OF COURSE! AND IF SO, WE HAVE HIM HERE—AT OUR MERCY!
2012

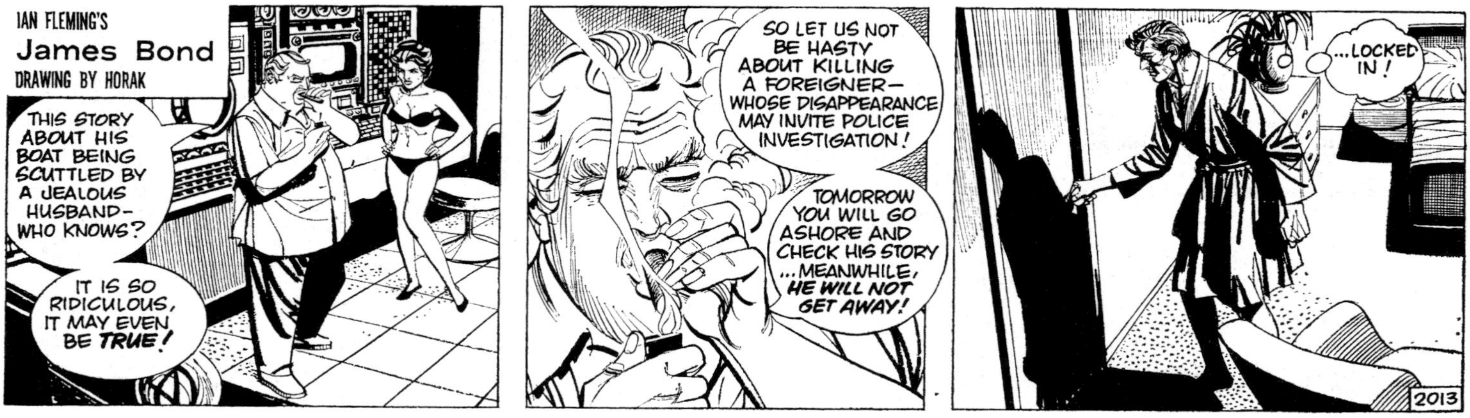
IAN FLEMING'S
James Bond
DRAWING BY HORAK
THIS STORY ABOUT HIS BOAT BEING SCUTTLED BY A JEALOUS HUSBAND—WHO KNOWS?
IT IS SO RIDICULOUS, IT MAY EVEN BE TRUE!
SO LET US NOT BE HASTY ABOUT KILLING A FOREIGNER—WHOSE DISAPPEARANCE MAY INVITE POLICE INVESTIGATION!
TOMORROW YOU WILL GO ASHORE AND CHECK HIS STORY ...MEANWHILE, HE WILL NOT GET AWAY!
...LOCKED IN!
2013

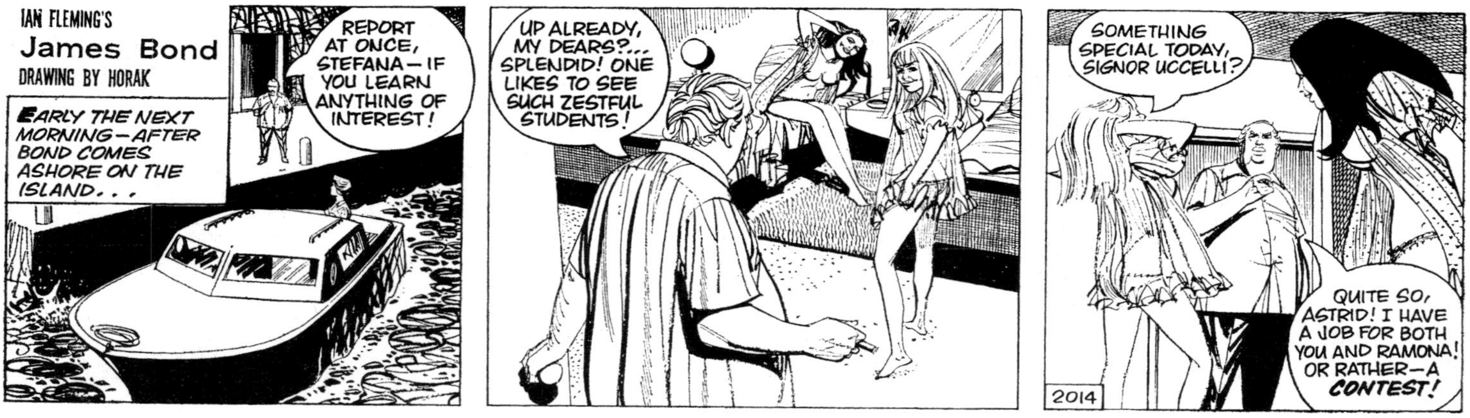
IAN FLEMING'S
James Bond
DRAWING BY HORAK
EARLY THE NEXT MORNING—AFTER BOND COMES ASHORE ON THE ISLAND...
REPORT AT ONCE, STEFANA—IF YOU LEARN ANYTHING OF INTEREST!
UP ALREADY, MY DEARS?... SPLENDID! ONE LIKES TO SEE SUCH ZESTFUL STUDENTS!
SOMETHING SPECIAL TODAY, SIGNOR UCCELLI?
QUITE SO, ASTRID! I HAVE A JOB FOR BOTH YOU AND RAMONA! OR RATHER—A CONTEST!
2014

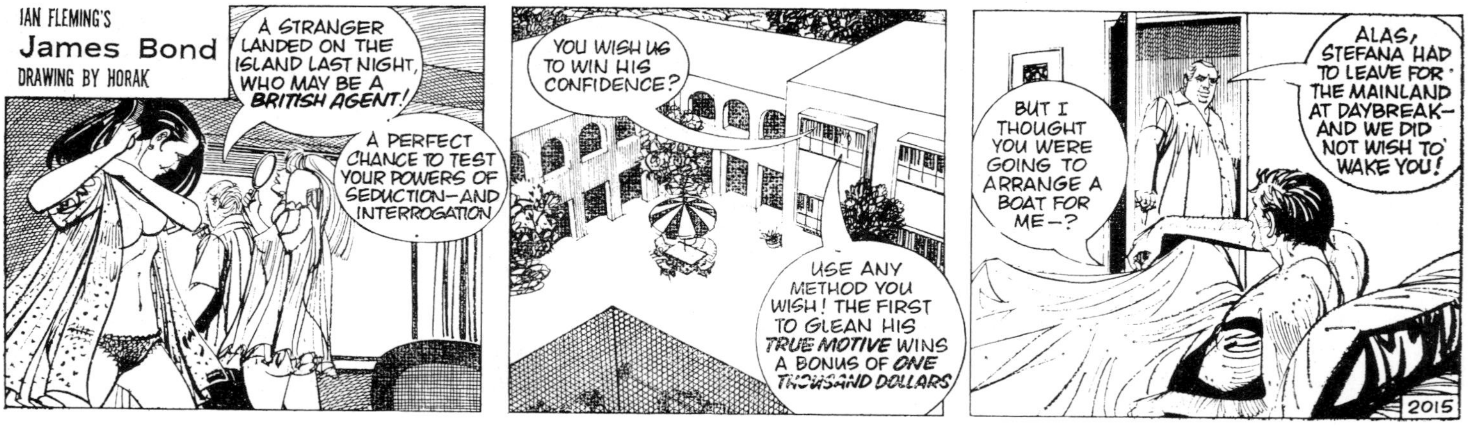
IAN FLEMING'S
James Bond
DRAWING BY HORAK
A STRANGER LANDED ON THE ISLAND LAST NIGHT, WHO MAY BE A BRITISH AGENT!
A PERFECT CHANCE TO TEST YOUR POWERS OF SEDUCTION—AND INTERROGATION
YOU WISH US TO WIN HIS CONFIDENCE?
USE ANY METHOD YOU WISH! THE FIRST TO GLEAN HIS TRUE MOTIVE WINS A BONUS OF ONE THOUSAND DOLLARS
BUT I THOUGHT YOU WERE GOING TO ARRANGE A BOAT FOR ME—?
ALAS, STEFANA HAD TO LEAVE FOR THE MAINLAND AT DAYBREAK—AND WE DID NOT WISH TO WAKE YOU!
2015

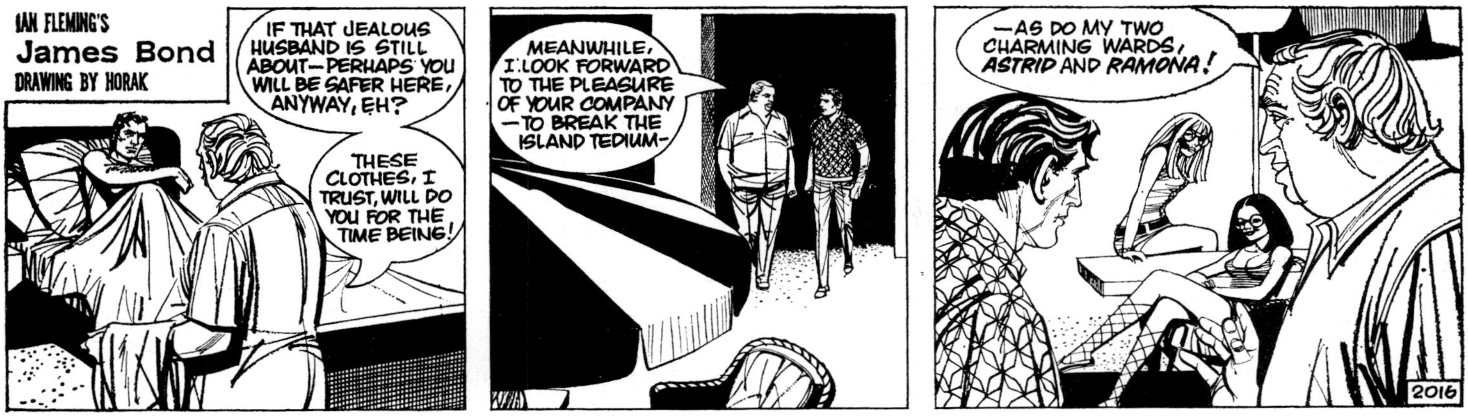
IAN FLEMING'S
James Bond
DRAWING BY HORAK
IF THAT JEALOUS HUSBAND IS STILL ABOUT—PERHAPS YOU WILL BE SAFER HERE, ANYWAY, EH?
THESE CLOTHES, I TRUST, WILL DO YOU FOR THE TIME BEING!
MEANWHILE, I LOOK FORWARD TO THE PLEASURE OF YOUR COMPANY—TO BREAK THE ISLAND TEDIUM—
—AS DO MY TWO CHARMING WARDS, ASTRID AND RAMONA!
2016

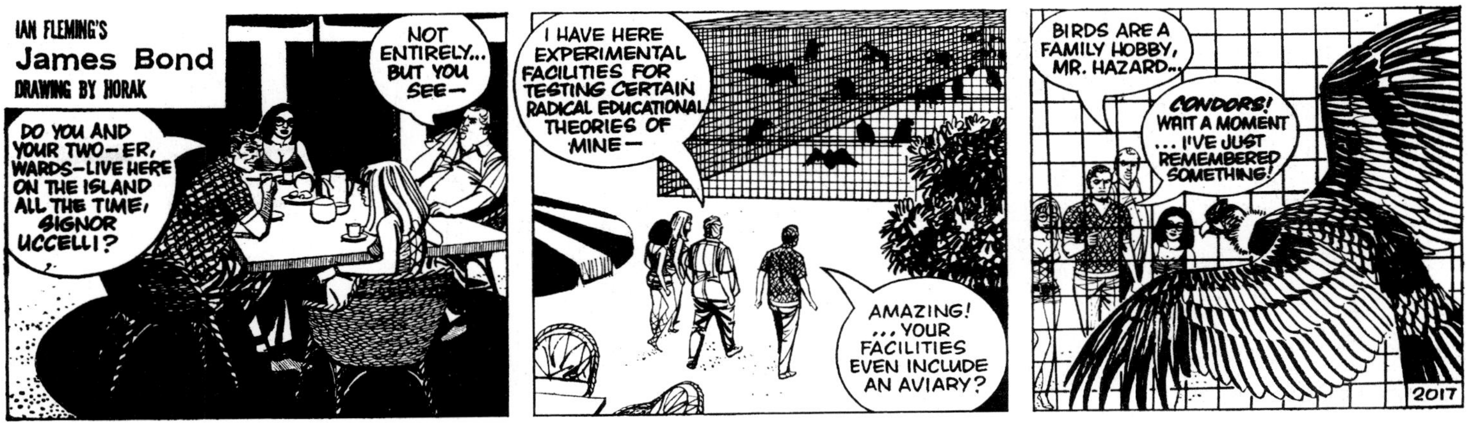
IAN FLEMING'S
James Bond
DRAWING BY HORAK
DO YOU AND YOUR TWO—ER, WARDS—LIVE HERE ON THE ISLAND ALL THE TIME, SIGNOR UCCELLI?
NOT ENTIRELY... BUT YOU SEE—
I HAVE HERE EXPERIMENTAL FACILITIES FOR TESTING CERTAIN RADICAL EDUCATIONAL THEORIES OF MINE—
AMAZING! ... YOUR FACILITIES EVEN INCLUDE AN AVIARY?
BIRDS ARE A FAMILY HOBBY, MR. HAZARD...
CONDORS! WAIT A MOMENT ... I'VE JUST REMEMBERED SOMETHING!
2017

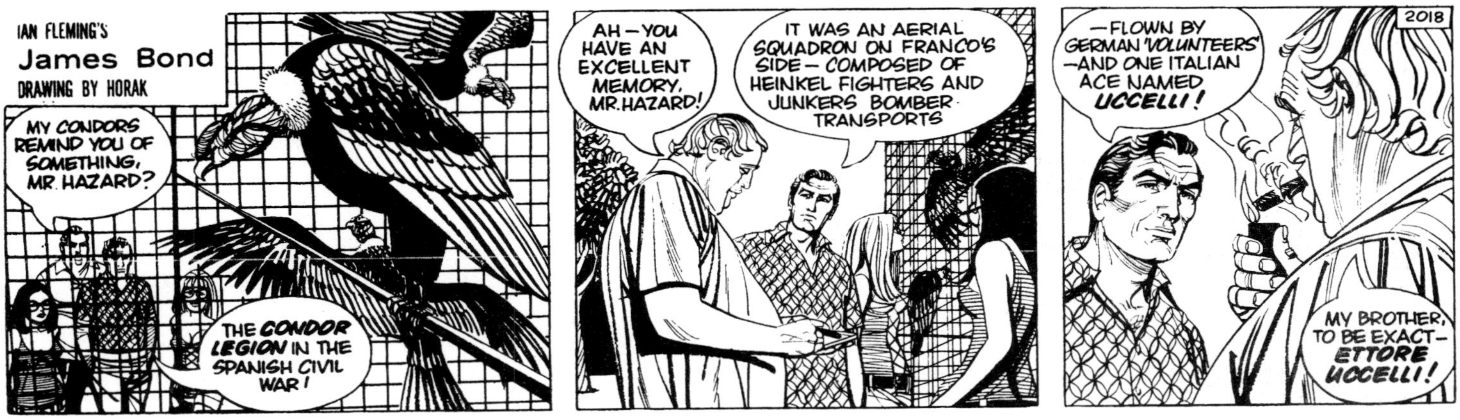
IAN FLEMING'S
James Bond
DRAWING BY HORAK
MY CONDORS REMIND YOU OF SOMETHING, MR. HAZARD?
THE CONDOR LEGION IN THE SPANISH CIVIL WAR!
AH—YOU HAVE AN EXCELLENT MEMORY, MR. HAZARD!
IT WAS AN AERIAL SQUADRON ON FRANCO'S SIDE—COMPOSED OF HEINKEL FIGHTERS AND JUNKERS BOMBER TRANSPORTS
2018
—FLOWN BY GERMAN 'VOLUNTEERS' —AND ONE ITALIAN ACE NAMED UCCELLI!
MY BROTHER, TO BE EXACT—ETTORE UCCELLI!

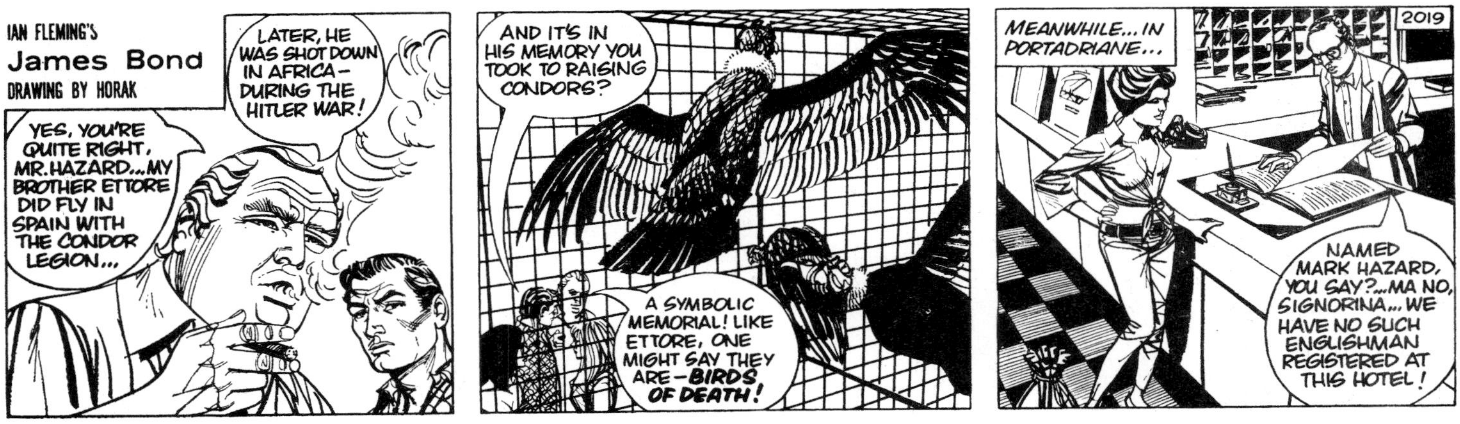
IAN FLEMING'S
James Bond
DRAWING BY HORAK
YES, YOU'RE QUITE RIGHT, MR. HAZARD... MY BROTHER ETTORE DID FLY IN SPAIN WITH THE CONDOR LEGION...
LATER, HE WAS SHOT DOWN IN AFRICA—DURING THE HITLER WAR!
AND IT'S IN HIS MEMORY YOU TOOK TO RAISING CONDORS?
A SYMBOLIC MEMORIAL! LIKE ETTORE, ONE MIGHT SAY THEY ARE—BIRDS OF DEATH!
MEANWHILE... IN PORTADRIANE...
2019
NAMED MARK HAZARD, YOU SAY?... MA NO, SIGNORINA... WE HAVE NO SUCH ENGLISHMAN REGISTERED AT THIS HOTEL!

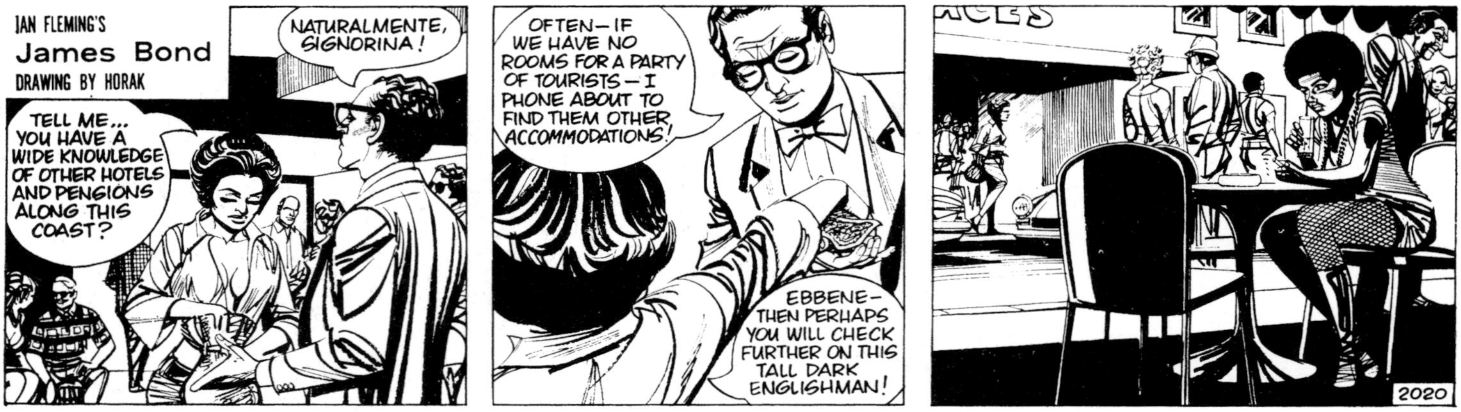
IAN FLEMING'S
James Bond
DRAWING BY HORAK
TELL ME... YOU HAVE A WIDE KNOWLEDGE OF OTHER HOTELS AND PENSIONS ALONG THIS COAST?
NATURALMENTE, SIGNORINA!
OFTEN—IF WE HAVE NO ROOMS FOR A PARTY OF TOURISTS—I PHONE ABOUT TO FIND THEM OTHER ACCOMMODATIONS!
EBBENE—THEN PERHAPS YOU WILL CHECK FURTHER ON THIS TALL DARK ENGLISHMAN!
2020

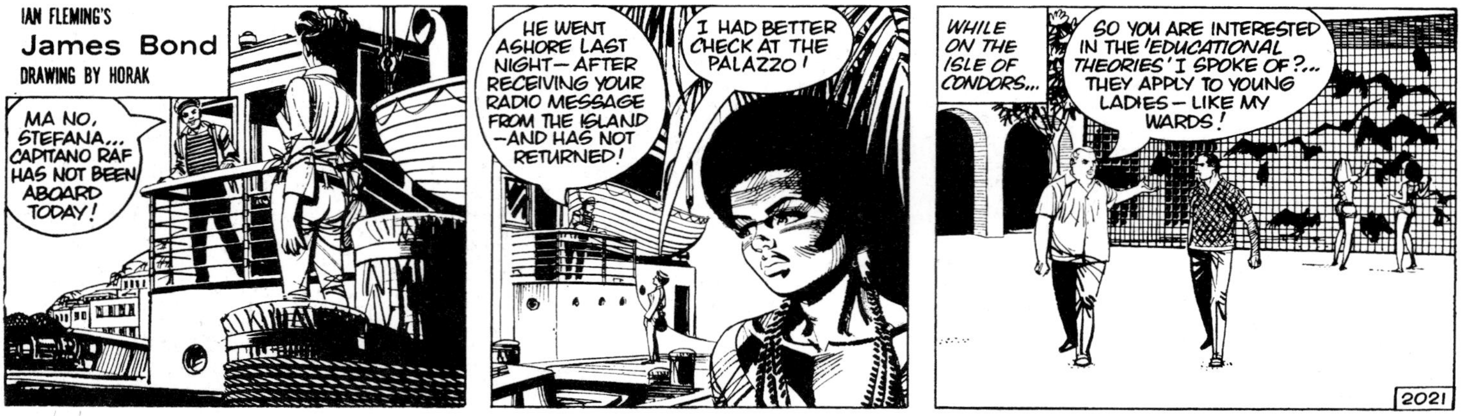
IAN FLEMING'S
James Bond
DRAWING BY HORAK
MA NO, STEFANA... CAPITANO RAF HAS NOT BEEN ABOARD TODAY!
HE WENT ASHORE LAST NIGHT—AFTER RECEIVING YOUR RADIO MESSAGE FROM THE ISLAND—AND HAS NOT RETURNED!
I HAD BETTER CHECK AT THE PALAZZO!
WHILE ON THE ISLE OF CONDORS...
SO YOU ARE INTERESTED IN THE 'EDUCATIONAL THEORIES' I SPOKE OF?... THEY APPLY TO YOUNG LADIES—LIKE MY WARDS!
2021

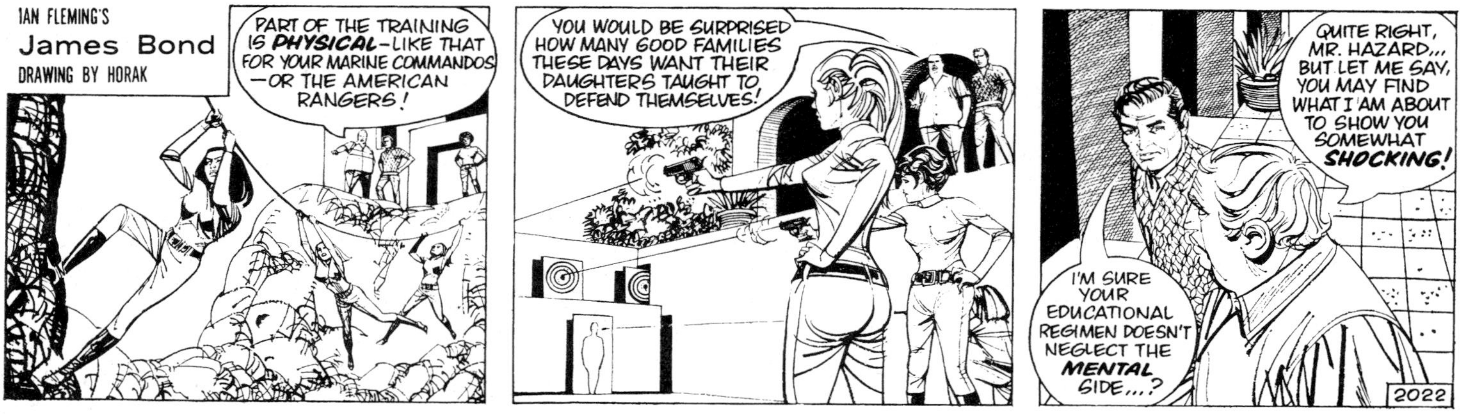
IAN FLEMING'S
James Bond
DRAWING BY HORAK
PART OF THE TRAINING IS PHYSICAL—LIKE THAT FOR YOUR MARINE COMMANDOS—OR THE AMERICAN RANGERS!
YOU WOULD BE SURPRISED HOW MANY GOOD FAMILIES THESE DAYS WANT THEIR DAUGHTERS TAUGHT TO DEFEND THEMSELVES!
I'M SURE YOUR EDUCATIONAL REGIMEN DOESN'T NEGLECT THE MENTAL SIDE...?
QUITE RIGHT, MR. HAZARD... BUT LET ME SAY, YOU MAY FIND WHAT I AM ABOUT TO SHOW YOU SOMEWHAT SHOCKING!
2022

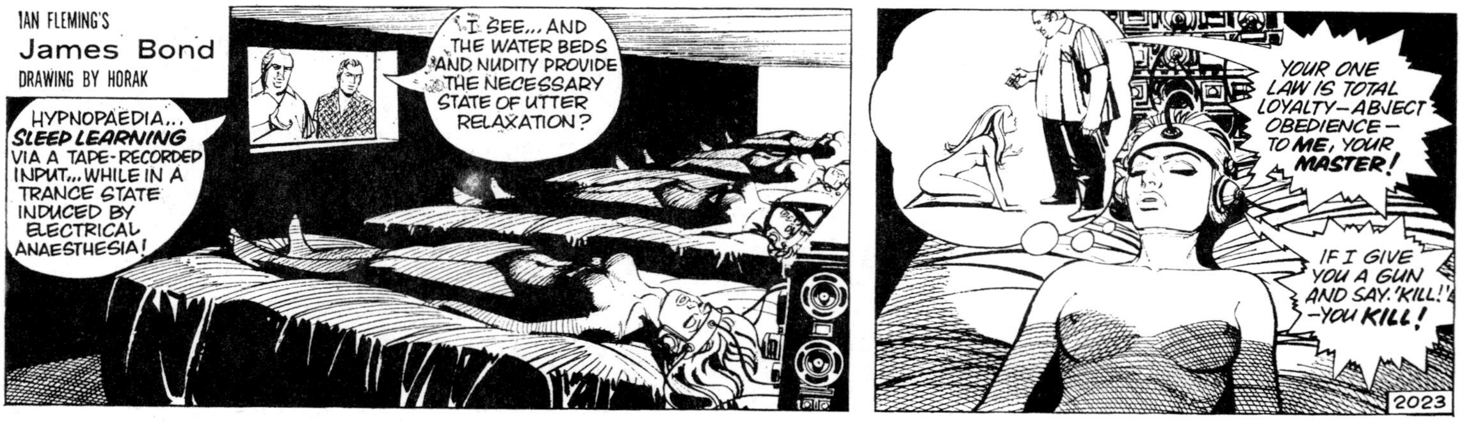
IAN FLEMING'S
James Bond
DRAWING BY HORAK
HYPNOPAEDIA... SLEEP LEARNING VIA A TAPE-RECORDED INPUT... WHILE IN A TRANCE STATE INDUCED BY ELECTRICAL ANAESTHESIA!
I SEE... AND THE WATER BEDS AND NUDITY PROVIDE THE NECESSARY STATE OF UTTER RELAXATION?
YOUR ONE LAW IS TOTAL LOYALTY—ABJECT OBEDIENCE—TO ME, YOUR MASTER!
IF I GIVE YOU A GUN AND SAY 'KILL!'—YOU KILL!
2023

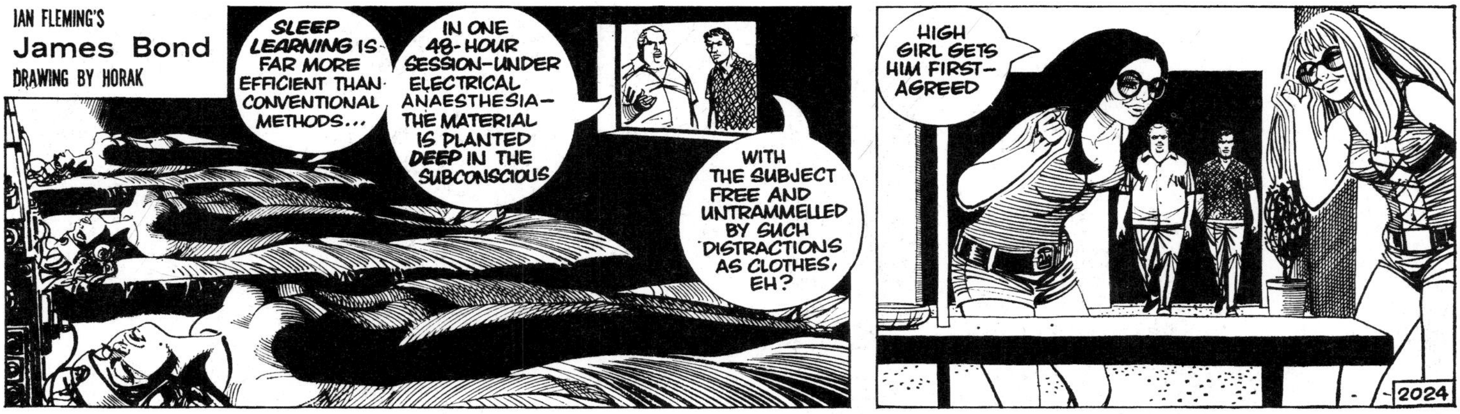
IAN FLEMING'S
James Bond
DRAWING BY HORAK
SLEEP LEARNING IS FAR MORE EFFICIENT THAN CONVENTIONAL METHODS...
IN ONE 48-HOUR SESSION—UNDER ELECTRICAL ANAESTHESIA—THE MATERIAL IS PLANTED DEEP IN THE SUBCONSCIOUS
WITH THE SUBJECT FREE AND UNTRAMMELLED BY SUCH DISTRACTIONS AS CLOTHES, EH?
HIGH GIRL GETS HIM FIRST—AGREED
2024

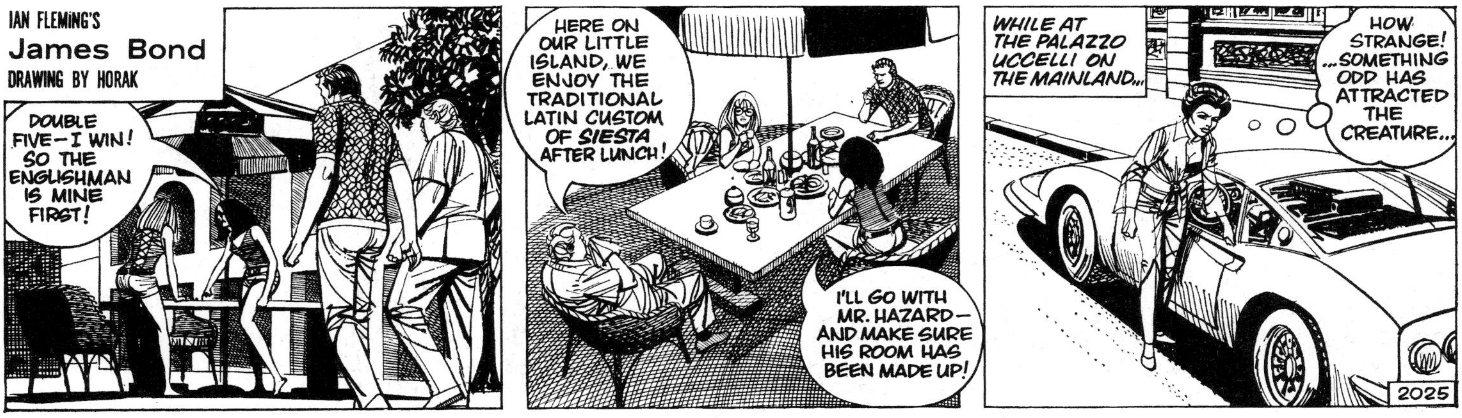
IAN FLEMING'S
James Bond
DRAWING BY HORAK
DOUBLE FIVE—I WIN! SO THE ENGLISHMAN IS MINE FIRST!
HERE ON OUR LITTLE ISLAND, WE ENJOY THE TRADITIONAL LATIN CUSTOM OF SIESTA AFTER LUNCH!
I'LL GO WITH MR. HAZARD—AND MAKE SURE HIS ROOM HAS BEEN MADE UP!
WHILE AT THE PALAZZO UCCELLI ON THE MAINLAND...
HOW STRANGE! ...SOMETHING ODD HAS ATTRACTED THE CREATURE...
2025

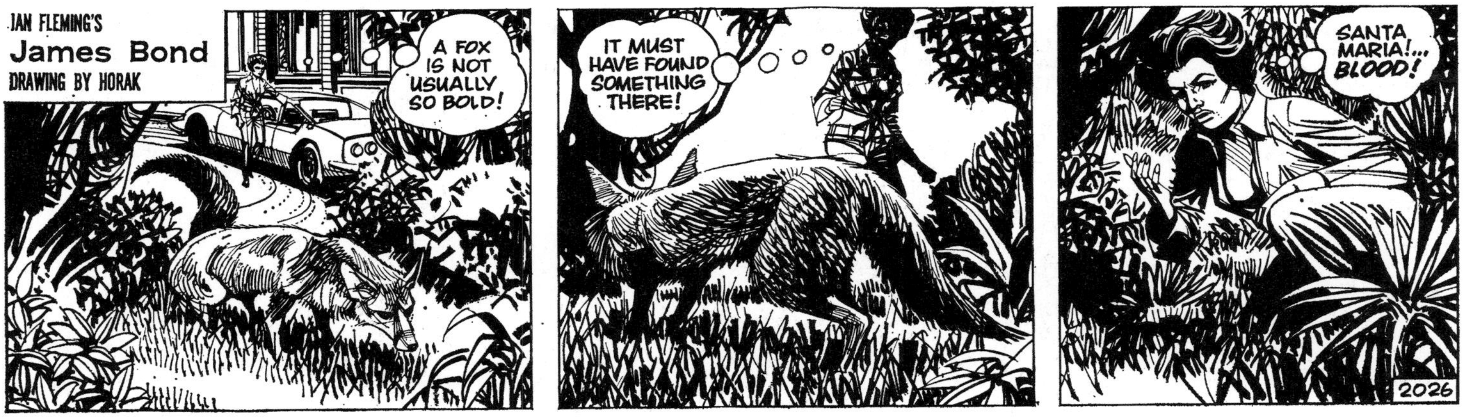
IAN FLEMING'S
James Bond
DRAWING BY HORAK
A FOX IS NOT USUALLY SO BOLD!
IT MUST HAVE FOUND SOMETHING THERE!
SANTA MARIA!... BLOOD!
2026

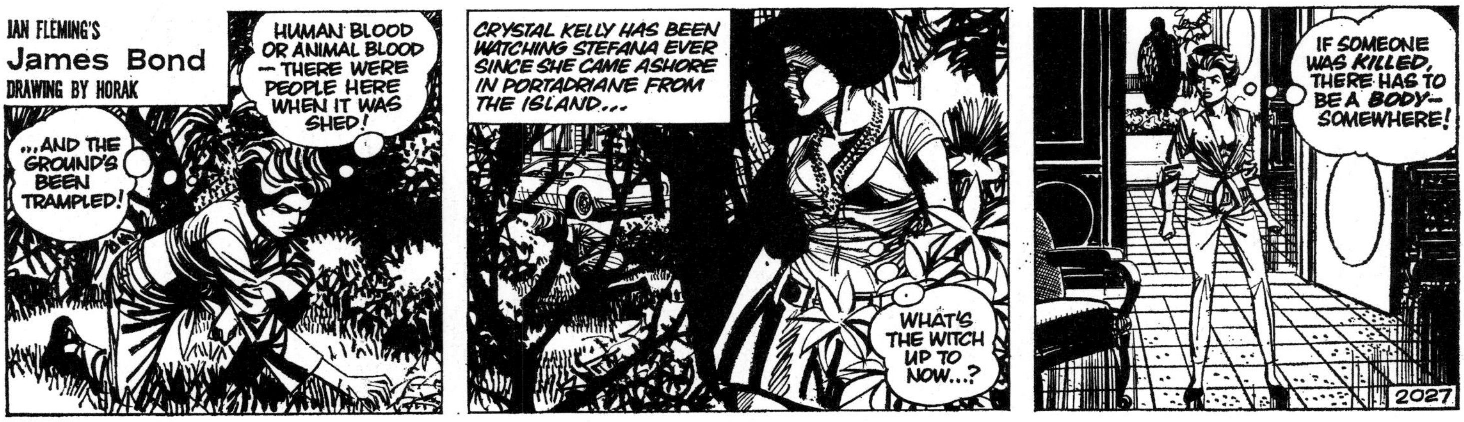
IAN FLEMING'S
James Bond
DRAWING BY HORAK
HUMAN BLOOD OR ANIMAL BLOOD—THERE WERE PEOPLE HERE WHEN IT WAS SHED!
...AND THE GROUND'S BEEN TRAMPLED!
CRYSTAL KELLY HAS BEEN WATCHING STEFANA EVER SINCE SHE CAME ASHORE IN PORTADRIANE FROM THE ISLAND...
WHAT'S THE WITCH UP TO NOW...?
IF SOMEONE WAS KILLED, THERE HAS TO BE A BODY—SOMEWHERE!
2027

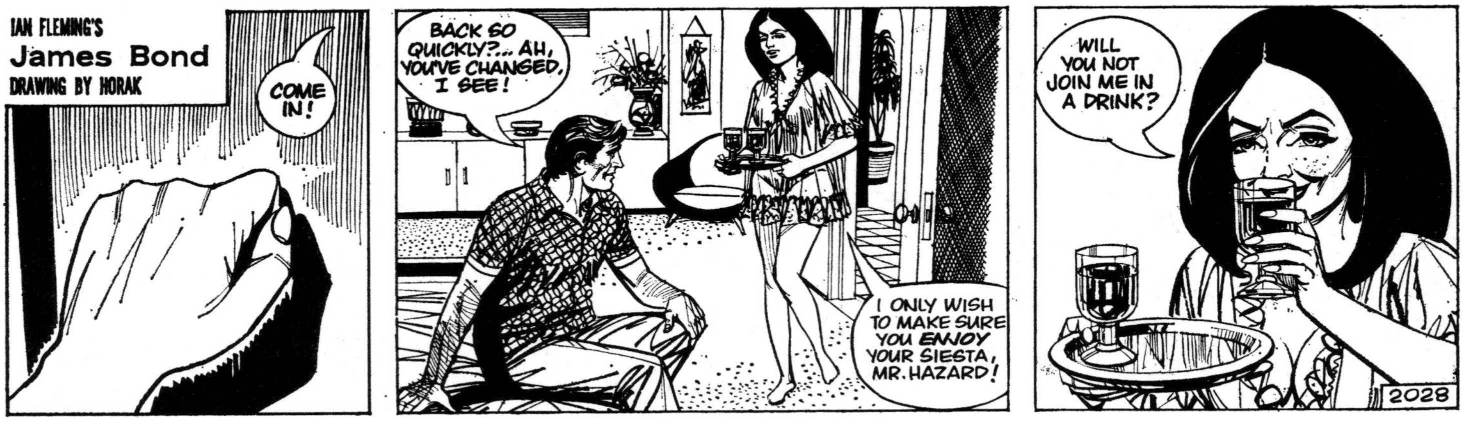
IAN FLEMING'S
James Bond
DRAWING BY HORAK
COME IN!
BACK SO QUICKLY?... AH, YOU'VE CHANGED, I SEE!
I ONLY WISH TO MAKE SURE YOU ENJOY YOUR SIESTA, MR. HAZARD!
WILL YOU NOT JOIN ME IN A DRINK?
2028

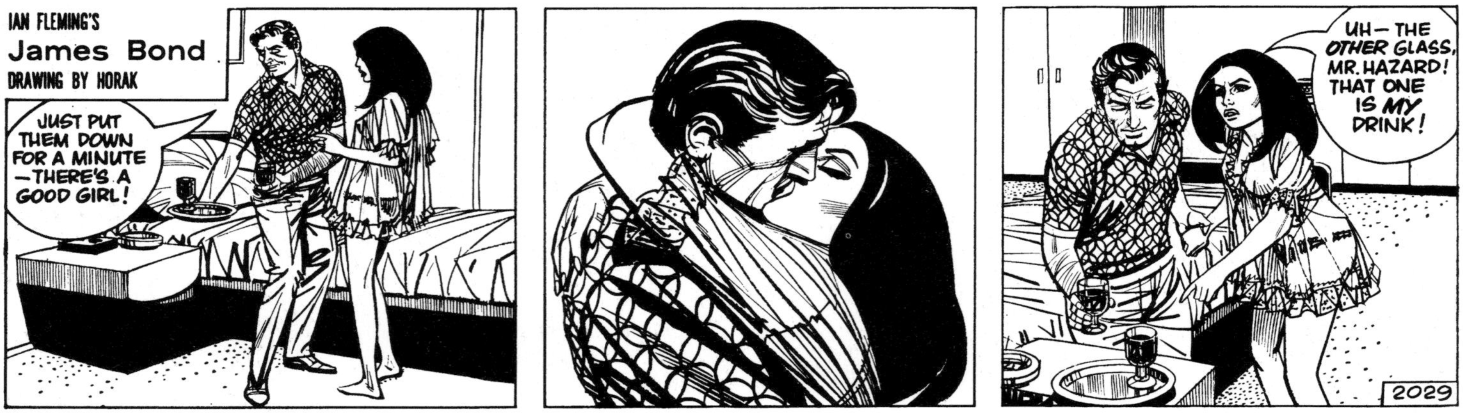
IAN FLEMING'S
James Bond
DRAWING BY HORAK
JUST PUT THEM DOWN FOR A MINUTE —THERE'S A GOOD GIRL!
UH— THE OTHER GLASS, MR. HAZARD! THAT ONE IS MY DRINK!
2029

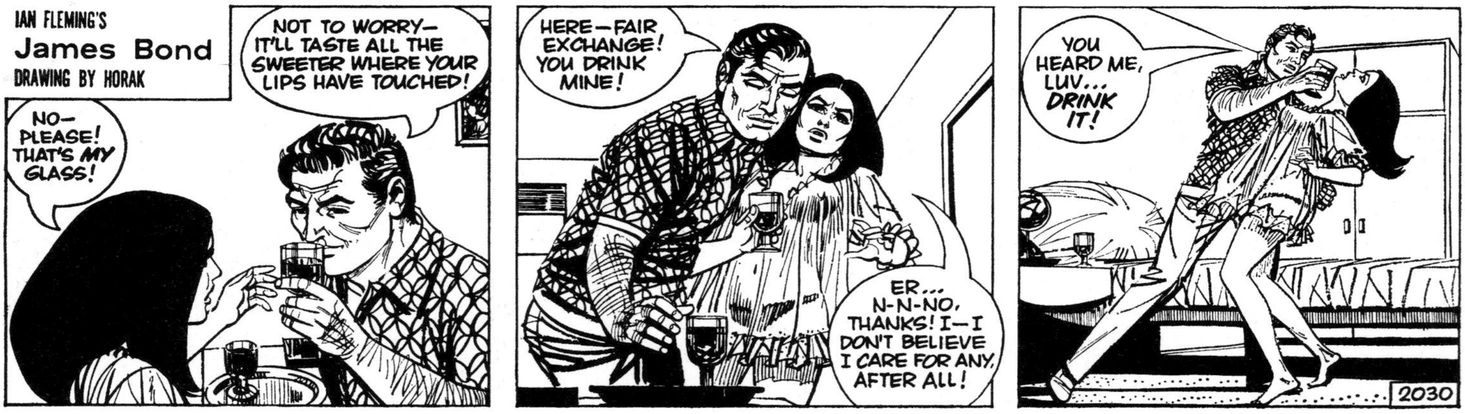
IAN FLEMING'S
James Bond
DRAWING BY HORAK
NO— PLEASE! THAT'S MY GLASS!
NOT TO WORRY— IT'LL TASTE ALL THE SWEETER WHERE YOUR LIPS HAVE TOUCHED!
HERE—FAIR EXCHANGE! YOU DRINK MINE!
ER... N-N-NO, THANKS! I—I DON'T BELIEVE I CARE FOR ANY, AFTER ALL!
YOU HEARD ME, LUV... DRINK IT!
2030

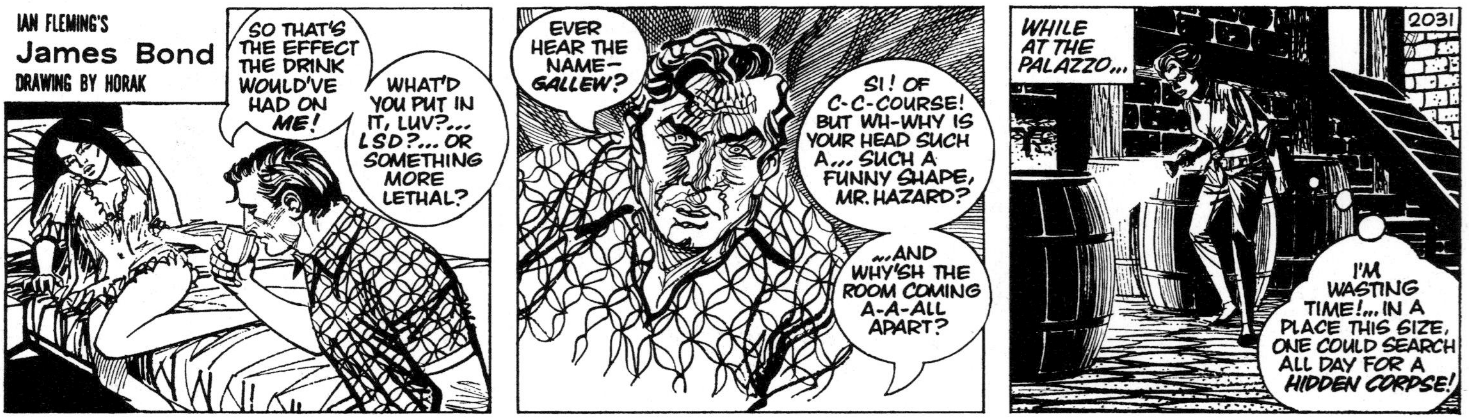
IAN FLEMING'S
James Bond
DRAWING BY HORAK
SO THAT'S THE EFFECT THE DRINK WOULD'VE HAD ON ME!
WHAT'D YOU PUT IN IT, LUV?... LSD?... OR SOMETHING MORE LETHAL?
EVER HEAR THE NAME— GALLEW?
SI! OF C-C-COURSE! BUT WH-WHY IS YOUR HEAD SUCH A... SUCH A FUNNY SHAPE, MR. HAZARD?
...AND WHY'SH THE ROOM COMING A-A-ALL APART?
WHILE AT THE PALAZZO...
2031
I'M WASTING TIME!... IN A PLACE THIS SIZE, ONE COULD SEARCH ALL DAY FOR A HIDDEN CORPSE!

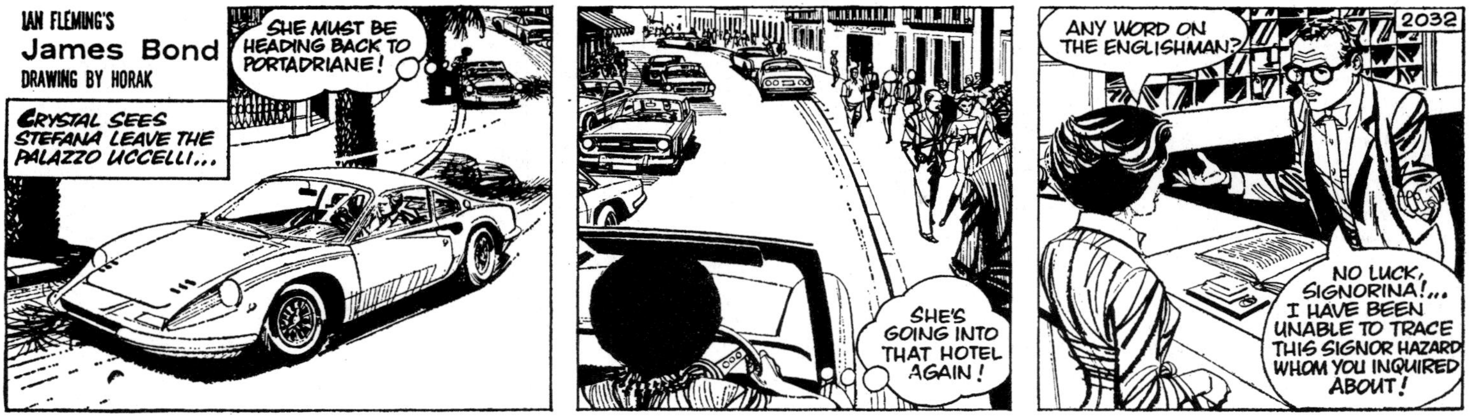
IAN FLEMING'S
James Bond
DRAWING BY HORAK
CRYSTAL SEES STEFANA LEAVE THE PALAZZO UCCELLI...
SHE MUST BE HEADING BACK TO PORTADRIANE!
SHE'S GOING INTO THAT HOTEL AGAIN!
2032
ANY WORD ON THE ENGLISHMAN?
NO LUCK, SIGNORINA!... I HAVE BEEN UNABLE TO TRACE THIS SIGNOR HAZARD WHOM YOU INQUIRED ABOUT!

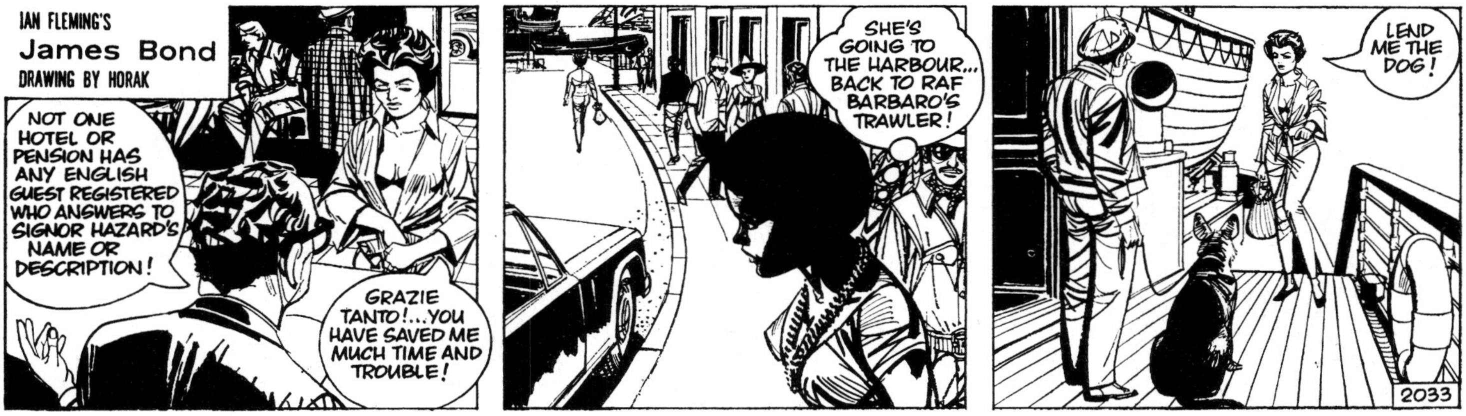
IAN FLEMING'S
James Bond
DRAWING BY HORAK
NOT ONE HOTEL OR PENSION HAS ANY ENGLISH GUEST REGISTERED WHO ANSWERS TO SIGNOR HAZARD'S NAME OR DESCRIPTION!
GRAZIE TANTO!...YOU HAVE SAVED ME MUCH TIME AND TROUBLE!
SHE'S GOING TO THE HARBOUR... BACK TO RAF BARBARO'S TRAWLER!
LEND ME THE DOG!
2033

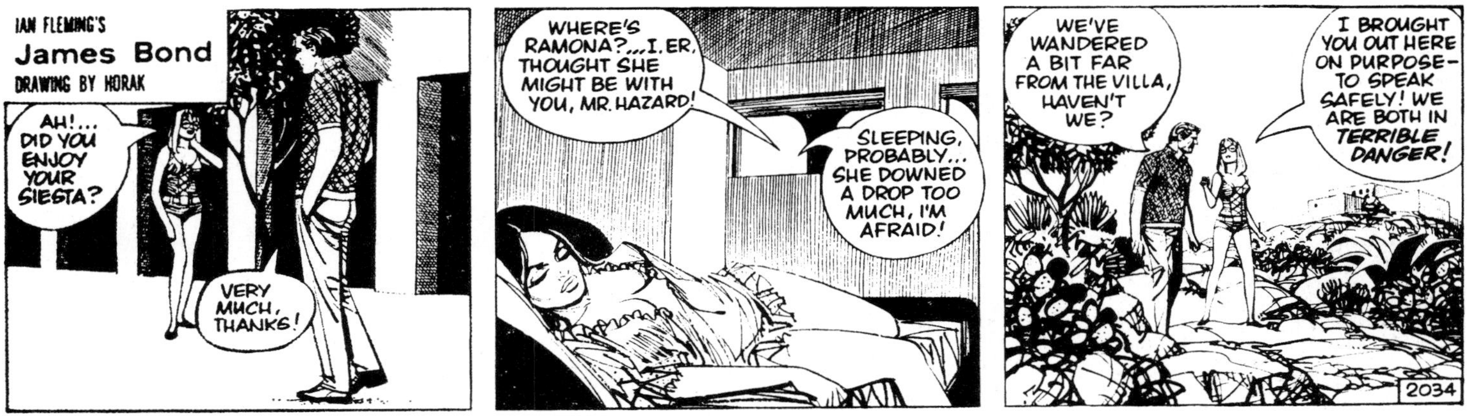
IAN FLEMING'S
James Bond
DRAWING BY HORAK
AH!... DID YOU ENJOY YOUR SIESTA?
VERY MUCH, THANKS!
WHERE'S RAMONA?... I. ER, THOUGHT SHE MIGHT BE WITH YOU, MR. HAZARD!
SLEEPING, PROBABLY... SHE DOWNED A DROP TOO MUCH, I'M AFRAID!
WE'VE WANDERED A BIT FAR FROM THE VILLA, HAVEN'T WE?
I BROUGHT YOU OUT HERE ON PURPOSE-TO SPEAK SAFELY! WE ARE BOTH IN TERRIBLE DANGER!
2034

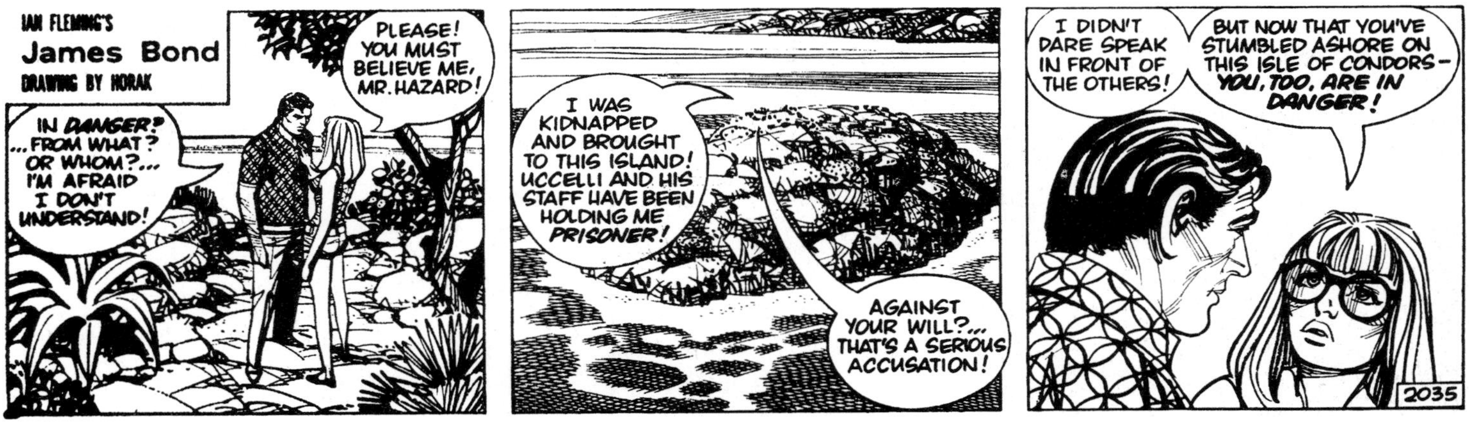
IAN FLEMING'S
James Bond
DRAWING BY HORAK
IN DANGER? ...FROM WHAT? OR WHOM?... I'M AFRAID I DON'T UNDERSTAND!
PLEASE! YOU MUST BELIEVE ME, MR. HAZARD!
I WAS KIDNAPPED AND BROUGHT TO THIS ISLAND! UCCELLI AND HIS STAFF HAVE BEEN HOLDING ME PRISONER!
AGAINST YOUR WILL?... THAT'S A SERIOUS ACCUSATION!
I DIDN'T DARE SPEAK IN FRONT OF THE OTHERS!
BUT NOW THAT YOU'VE STUMBLED ASHORE ON THIS ISLE OF CONDORS- YOU, TOO, ARE IN DANGER!
2035

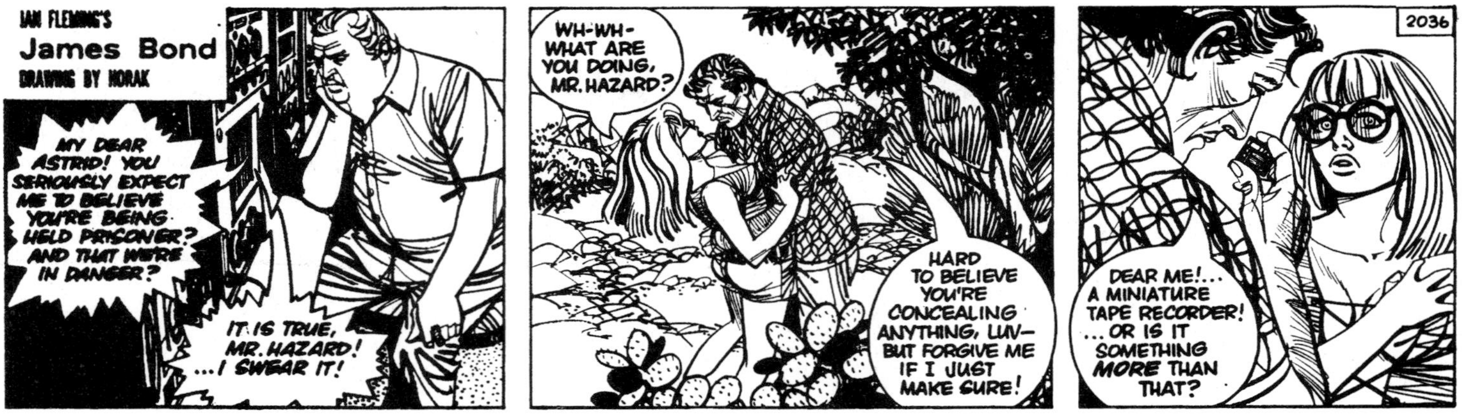
IAN FLEMING'S
James Bond
DRAWING BY HORAK
MY DEAR ASTRID! YOU SERIOUSLY EXPECT ME TO BELIEVE YOU'RE BEING HELD PRISONER? AND THAT WE'RE IN DANGER?
IT IS TRUE, MR. HAZARD! ...I SWEAR IT!
WH-WH-WHAT ARE YOU DOING, MR. HAZARD?
HARD TO BELIEVE YOU'RE CONCEALING ANYTHING, LUV– BUT FORGIVE ME IF I JUST MAKE SURE!
2036
DEAR ME!... A MINIATURE TAPE RECORDER! ...OR IS IT SOMETHING MORE THAN THAT?

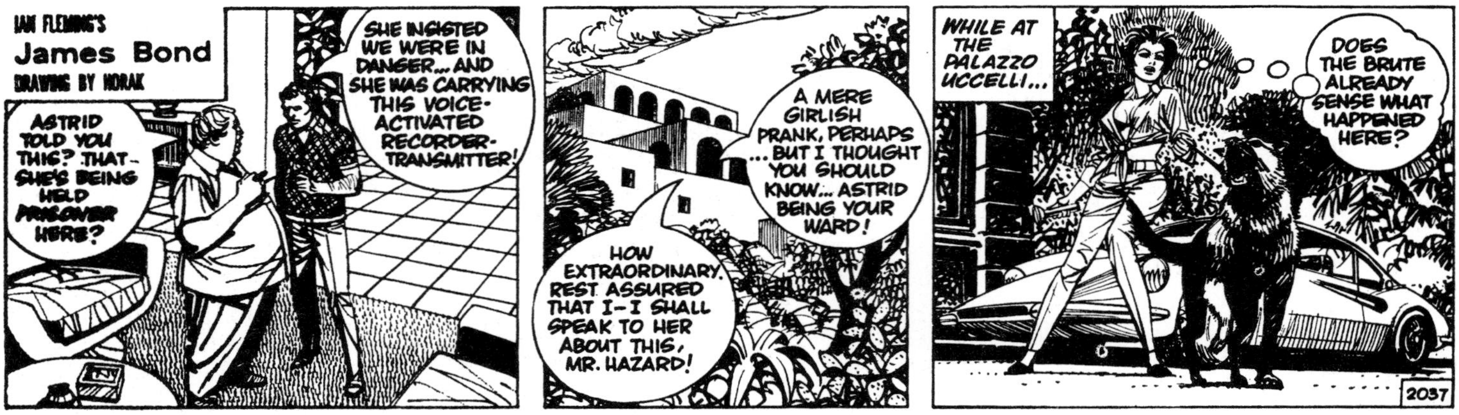
IAN FLEMING'S
James Bond
DRAWING BY HORAK
ASTRID TOLD YOU THIS? THAT SHE'S BEING HELD PRISONER HERE?
SHE INSISTED WE WERE IN DANGER... AND SHE WAS CARRYING THIS VOICE-ACTIVATED RECORDER-TRANSMITTER!
A MERE GIRLISH PRANK, PERHAPS ...BUT I THOUGHT YOU SHOULD KNOW... ASTRID BEING YOUR WARD!
HOW EXTRAORDINARY. REST ASSURED THAT I-I SHALL SPEAK TO HER ABOUT THIS, MR. HAZARD!
WHILE AT THE PALAZZO UCCELLI...
DOES THE BRUTE ALREADY SENSE WHAT HAPPENED HERE?
2037

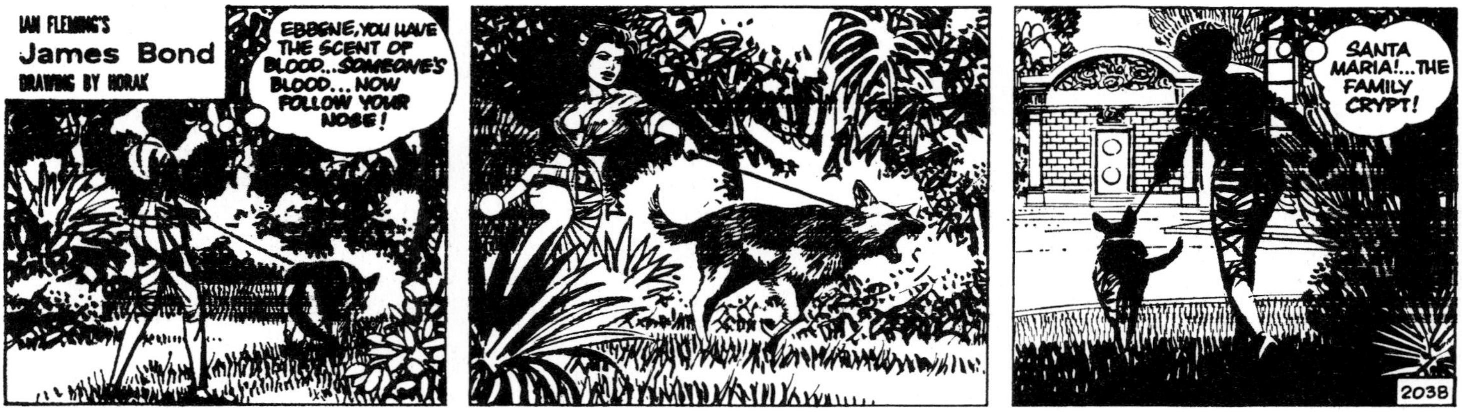
IAN FLEMING'S
James Bond
DRAWING BY HORAK
EBBENE, YOU HAVE THE SCENT OF BLOOD... SOMEONE'S BLOOD... NOW FOLLOW YOUR NOSE!
SANTA MARIA!... THE FAMILY CRYPT!
2038

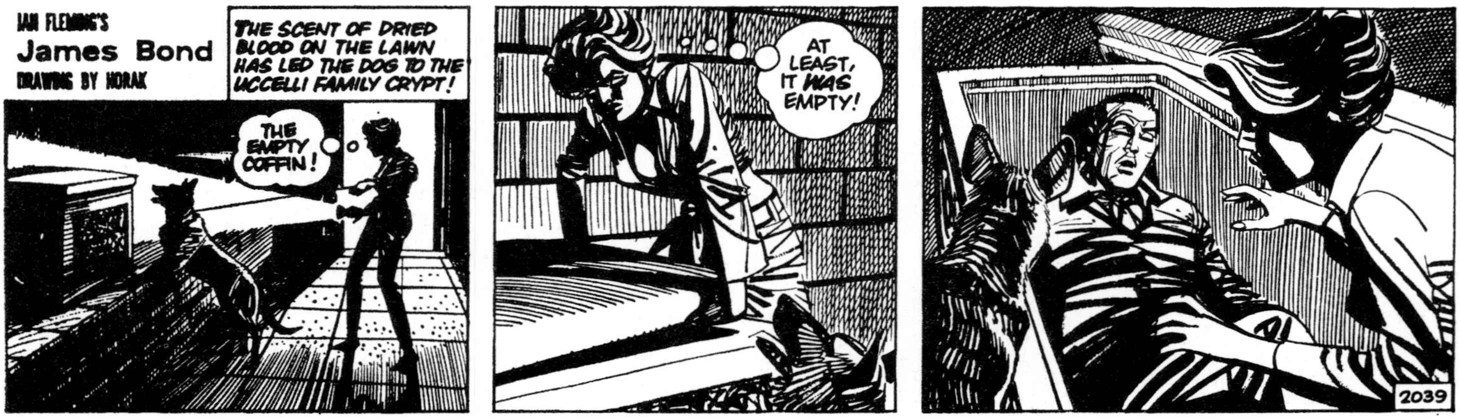
IAN FLEMING'S
James Bond
DRAWING BY HORAK
THE SCENT OF DRIED BLOOD ON THE LAWN HAS LED THE DOG TO THE UCCELLI FAMILY CRYPT!
THE EMPTY COFFIN!
AT LEAST, IT WAS EMPTY!
2039

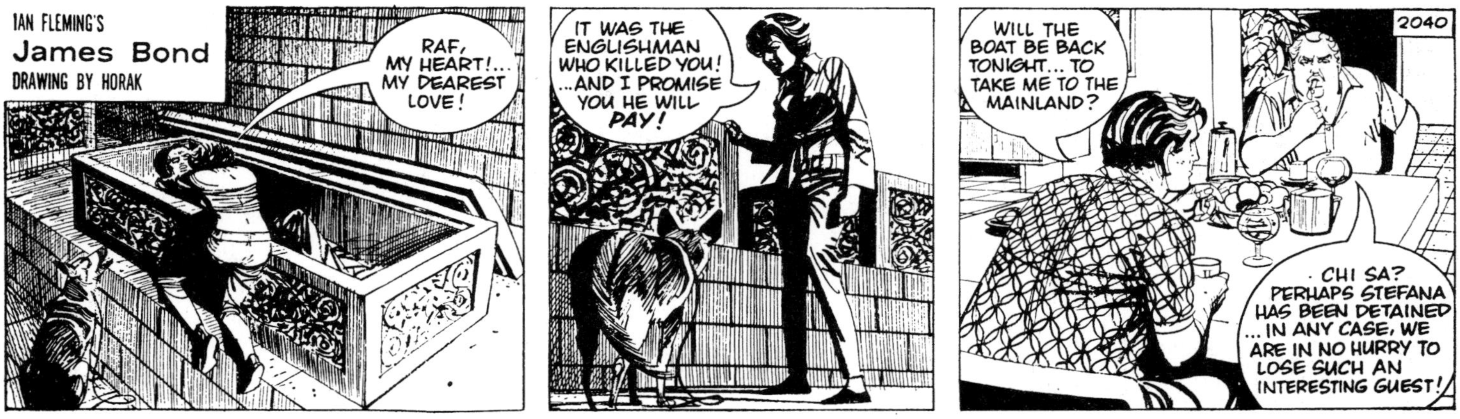
IAN FLEMING'S
James Bond
DRAWING BY HORAK
RAF, MY HEART!... MY DEAREST LOVE!
IT WAS THE ENGLISHMAN WHO KILLED YOU! ...AND I PROMISE YOU HE WILL PAY!
2040
WILL THE BOAT BE BACK TONIGHT... TO TAKE ME TO THE MAINLAND?
CHI SA? PERHAPS STEFANA HAS BEEN DETAINED ...IN ANY CASE, WE ARE IN NO HURRY TO LOSE SUCH AN INTERESTING GUEST!

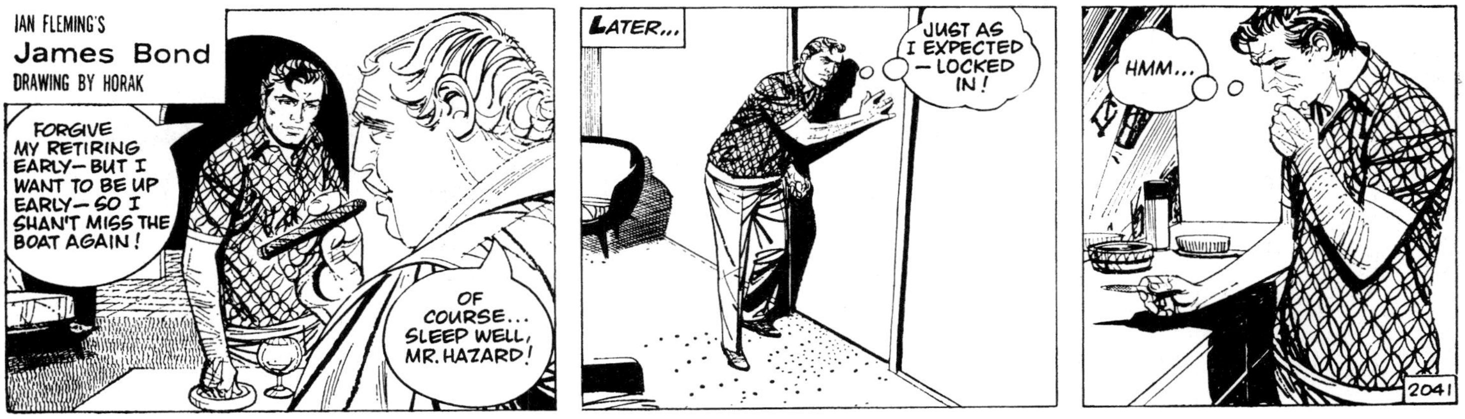
IAN FLEMING'S
James Bond
DRAWING BY HORAK
FORGIVE MY RETIRING EARLY—BUT I WANT TO BE UP EARLY—SO I SHAN'T MISS THE BOAT AGAIN!
OF COURSE... SLEEP WELL, MR. HAZARD!
LATER...
JUST AS I EXPECTED —LOCKED IN!
HMM...
2041

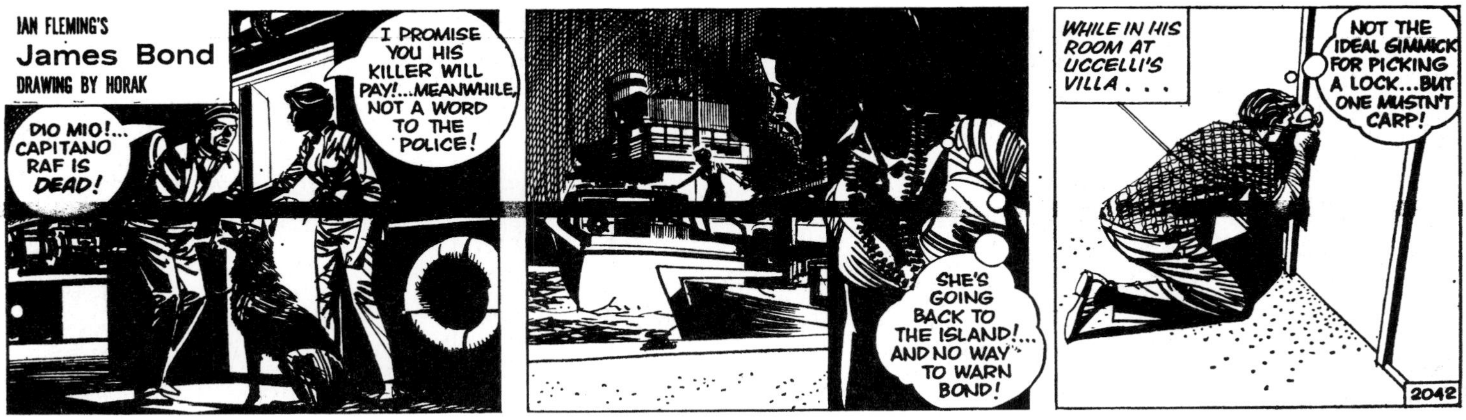
IAN FLEMING'S
James Bond
DRAWING BY HORAK
DIO MIO!... CAPITANO RAF IS DEAD!
I PROMISE YOU HIS KILLER WILL PAY!...MEANWHILE, NOT A WORD TO THE POLICE!
SHE'S GOING BACK TO THE ISLAND!... AND NO WAY TO WARN BOND!
WHILE IN HIS ROOM AT UCCELLI'S VILLA . . .
NOT THE IDEAL GIMMICK FOR PICKING A LOCK...BUT ONE MUSTN'T CARP!
2042

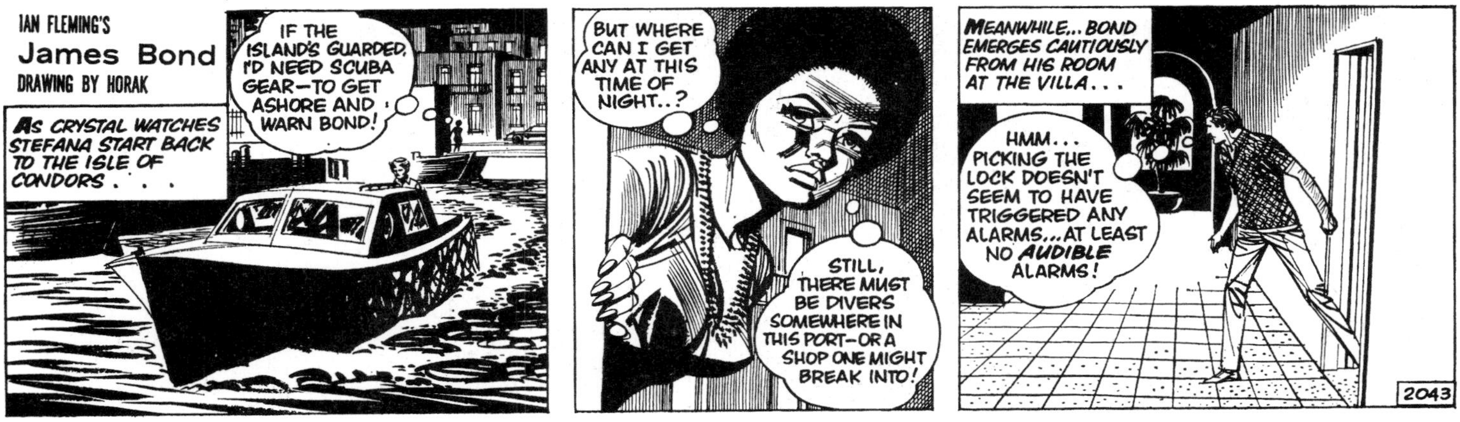
IAN FLEMING'S
James Bond
DRAWING BY HORAK
AS CRYSTAL WATCHES STEFANA START BACK TO THE ISLE OF CONDORS . . .
IF THE ISLAND'S GUARDED, I'D NEED SCUBA GEAR—TO GET ASHORE AND WARN BOND!
BUT WHERE CAN I GET ANY AT THIS TIME OF NIGHT..?
STILL, THERE MUST BE DIVERS SOMEWHERE IN THIS PORT—OR A SHOP ONE MIGHT BREAK INTO!
MEANWHILE... BOND EMERGES CAUTIOUSLY FROM HIS ROOM AT THE VILLA . . .
HMM... PICKING THE LOCK DOESN'T SEEM TO HAVE TRIGGERED ANY ALARMS... AT LEAST NO AUDIBLE ALARMS!
2043

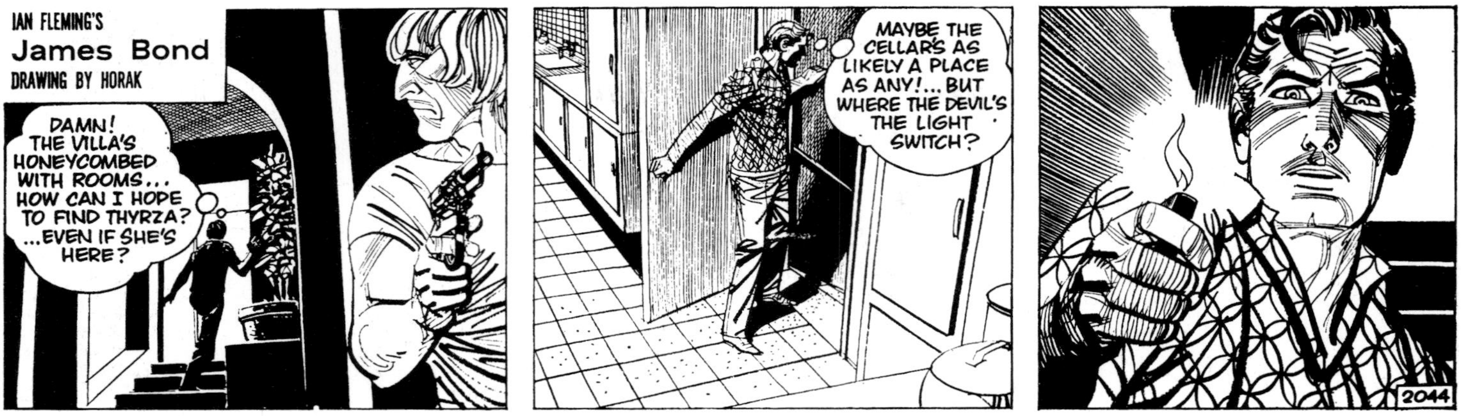
IAN FLEMING'S
James Bond
DRAWING BY HORAK
DAMN! THE VILLA'S HONEYCOMBED WITH ROOMS... HOW CAN I HOPE TO FIND THYRZA? ...EVEN IF SHE'S HERE?
MAYBE THE CELLAR'S AS LIKELY A PLACE AS ANY!... BUT WHERE THE DEVIL'S THE LIGHT SWITCH?
2044

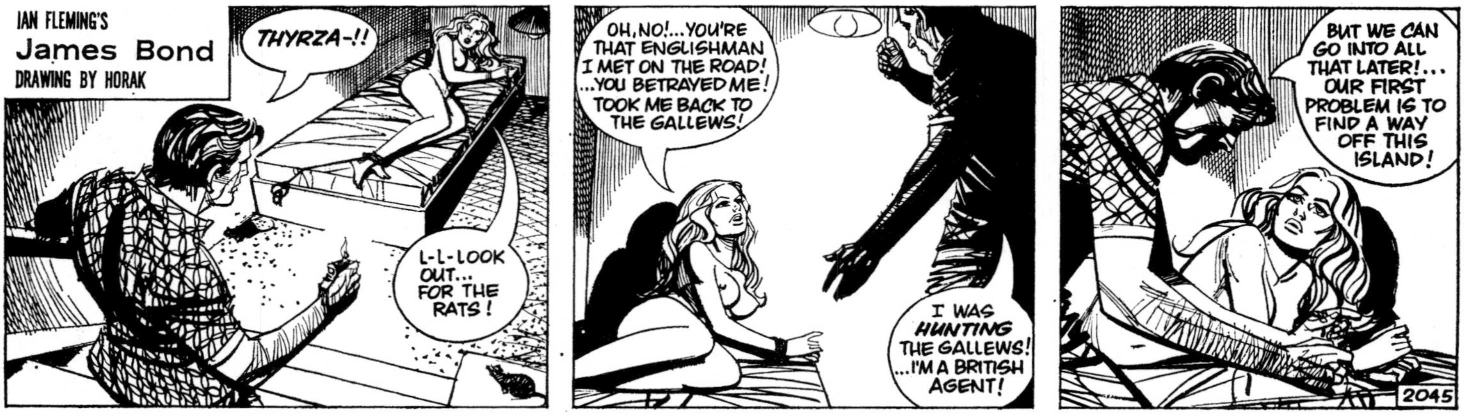
IAN FLEMING'S
James Bond
DRAWING BY HORAK
THYRZA-!!
L-L-LOOK OUT... FOR THE RATS!
OH, NO!... YOU'RE THAT ENGLISHMAN I MET ON THE ROAD! ...YOU BETRAYED ME! TOOK ME BACK TO THE GALLEWS!
I WAS HUNTING THE GALLEWS! ...I'M A BRITISH AGENT!
BUT WE CAN GO INTO ALL THAT LATER!... OUR FIRST PROBLEM IS TO FIND A WAY OFF THIS ISLAND!
2045

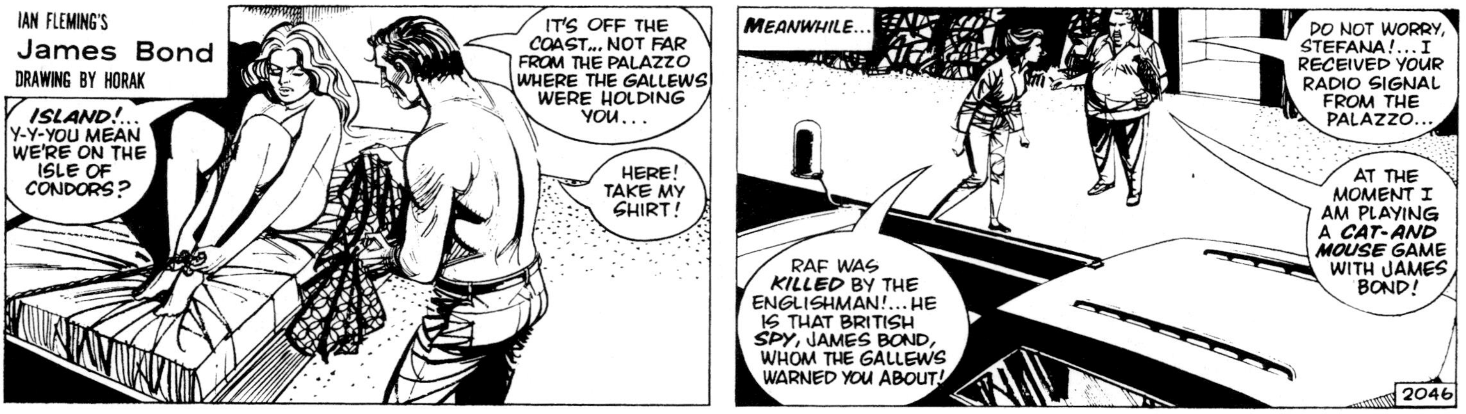
IAN FLEMING'S
James Bond
DRAWING BY HORAK
ISLAND!... Y-Y-YOU MEAN WE'RE ON THE ISLE OF CONDORS?
IT'S OFF THE COAST... NOT FAR FROM THE PALAZZO WHERE THE GALLEWS WERE HOLDING YOU...
HERE! TAKE MY SHIRT!
MEANWHILE...
RAF WAS KILLED BY THE ENGLISHMAN!... HE IS THAT BRITISH SPY, JAMES BOND, WHOM THE GALLEWS WARNED YOU ABOUT!
DO NOT WORRY, STEFANA!... I RECEIVED YOUR RADIO SIGNAL FROM THE PALAZZO...
AT THE MOMENT I AM PLAYING A CAT-AND MOUSE GAME WITH JAMES BOND!
2046

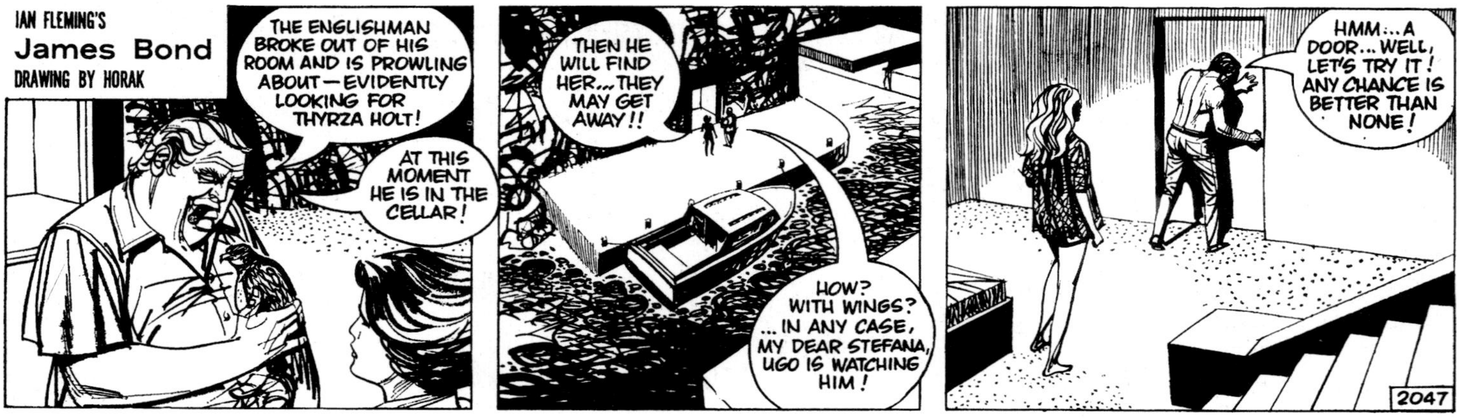
IAN FLEMING'S
James Bond
DRAWING BY HORAK
THE ENGLISHMAN BROKE OUT OF HIS ROOM AND IS PROWLING ABOUT—EVIDENTLY LOOKING FOR THYRZA HOLT!
AT THIS MOMENT HE IS IN THE CELLAR!
THEN HE WILL FIND HER... THEY MAY GET AWAY!!
HOW? WITH WINGS? ... IN ANY CASE, MY DEAR STEFANA, UGO IS WATCHING HIM!
HMM... A DOOR... WELL, LET'S TRY IT! ANY CHANCE IS BETTER THAN NONE!
2047

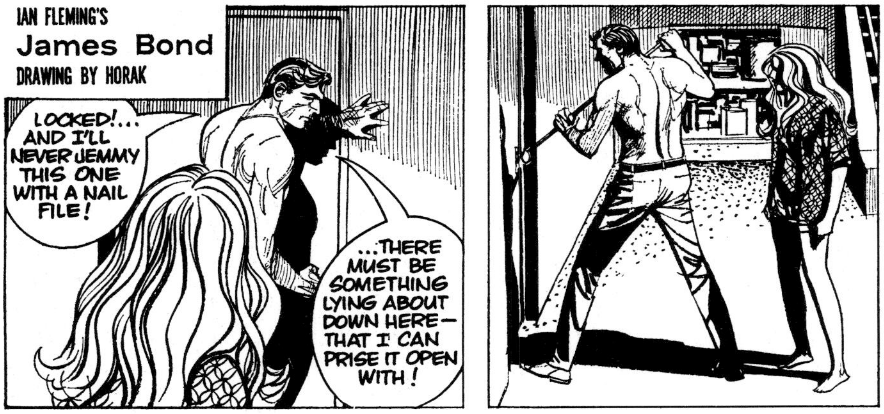
IAN FLEMING'S
James Bond
DRAWING BY HORAK
LOCKED!... AND I'LL NEVER JEMMY THIS ONE WITH A NAIL FILE!
...THERE MUST BE SOMETHING LYING ABOUT DOWN HERE—THAT I CAN PRISE IT OPEN WITH!
2048

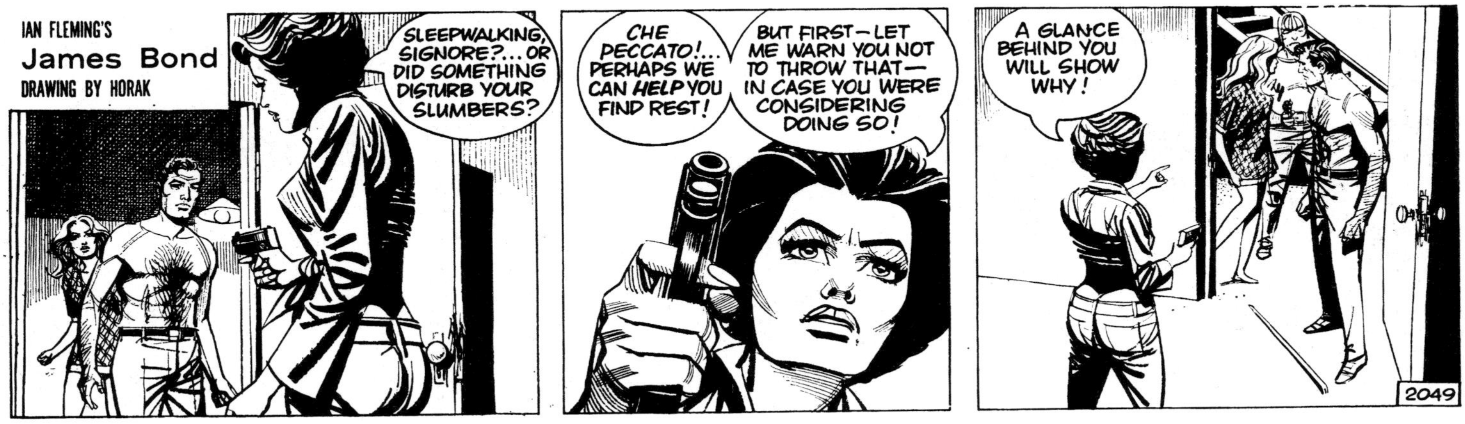
IAN FLEMING'S
James Bond
DRAWING BY HORAK
SLEEPWALKING, SIGNORE?... OR DID SOMETHING DISTURB YOUR SLUMBERS?
CHE PECCATO!... PERHAPS WE CAN HELP YOU FIND REST!
BUT FIRST—LET ME WARN YOU NOT TO THROW THAT—IN CASE YOU WERE CONSIDERING DOING SO!
A GLANCE BEHIND YOU WILL SHOW WHY!
2049

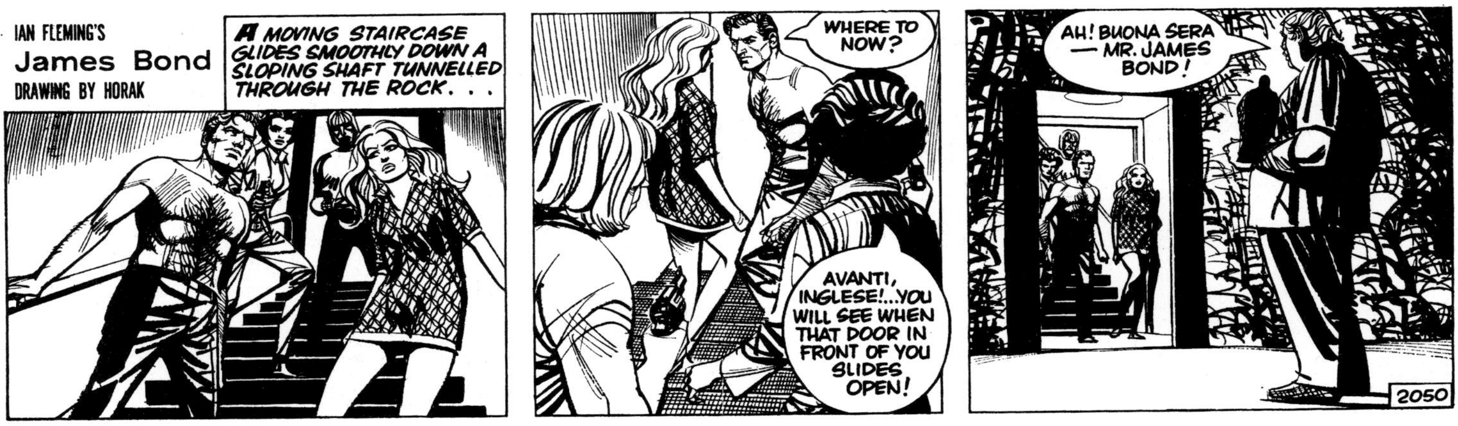
IAN FLEMING'S
James Bond
DRAWING BY HORAK
A MOVING STAIRCASE GLIDES SMOOTHLY DOWN A SLOPING SHAFT TUNNELLED THROUGH THE ROCK. . .
WHERE TO NOW?
AVANTI, INGLESE!...YOU WILL SEE WHEN THAT DOOR IN FRONT OF YOU SLIDES OPEN!
AH! BUONA SERA —MR. JAMES BOND!
2050

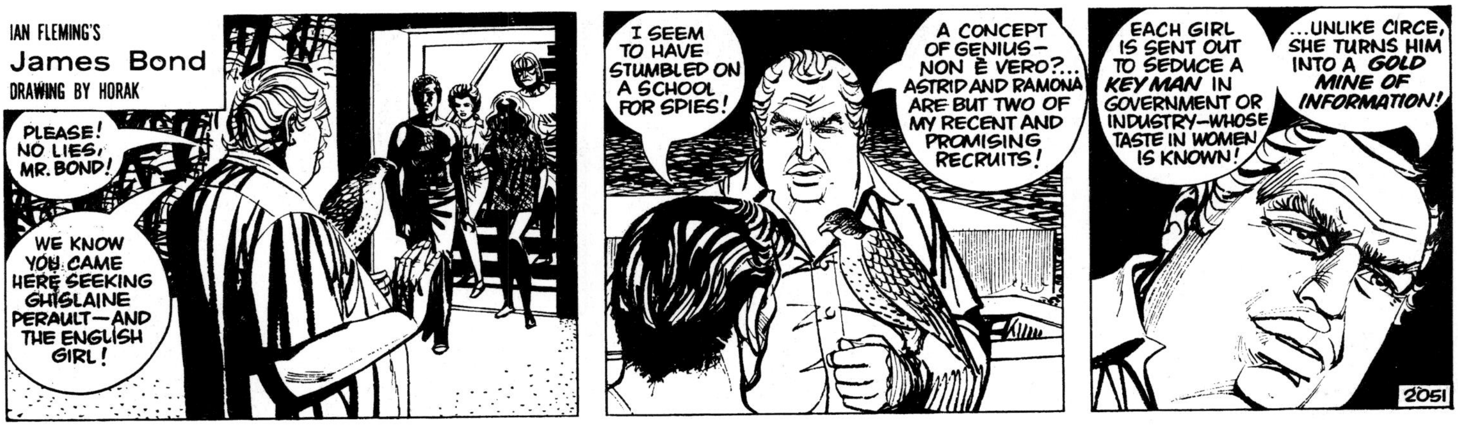
IAN FLEMING'S
James Bond
DRAWING BY HORAK
PLEASE! NO LIES, MR. BOND!
WE KNOW YOU CAME HERE SEEKING GHISLAINE PERAULT—AND THE ENGLISH GIRL!
I SEEM TO HAVE STUMBLED ON A SCHOOL FOR SPIES!
A CONCEPT OF GENIUS—NON È VERO?... ASTRID AND RAMONA ARE BUT TWO OF MY RECENT AND PROMISING RECRUITS!
EACH GIRL IS SENT OUT TO SEDUCE A KEY MAN IN GOVERNMENT OR INDUSTRY—WHOSE TASTE IN WOMEN IS KNOWN!
...UNLIKE CIRCE, SHE TURNS HIM INTO A GOLD MINE OF INFORMATION!
2051

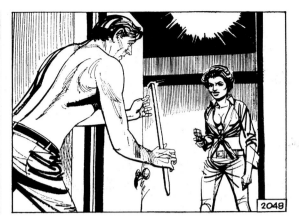

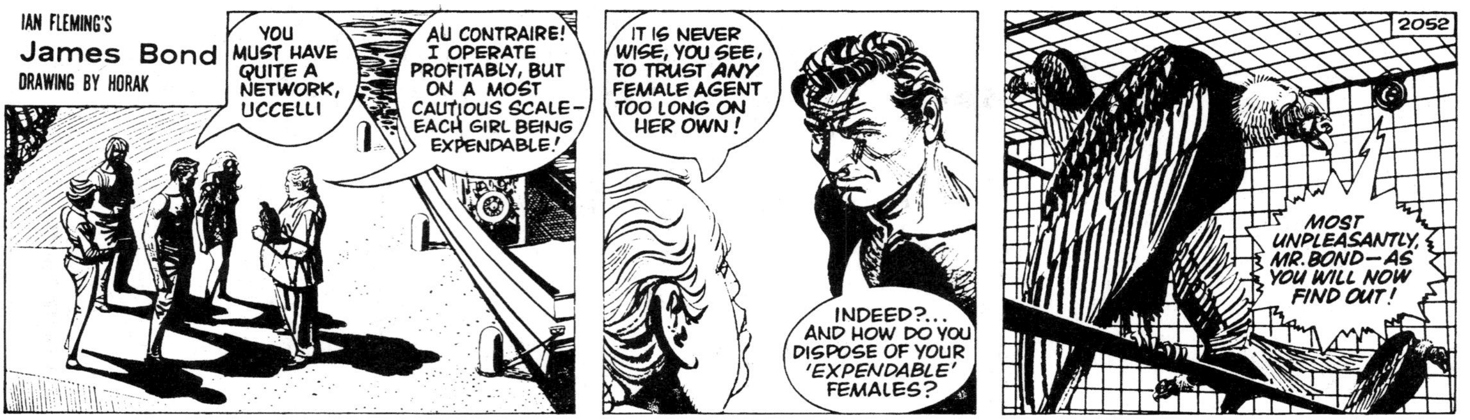
IAN FLEMING'S
James Bond
DRAWING BY HORAK
YOU MUST HAVE QUITE A NETWORK, UCCELLI
AU CONTRAIRE! I OPERATE PROFITABLY, BUT ON A MOST CAUTIOUS SCALE—EACH GIRL BEING EXPENDABLE!
IT IS NEVER WISE, YOU SEE, TO TRUST ANY FEMALE AGENT TOO LONG ON HER OWN!
INDEED?... AND HOW DO YOU DISPOSE OF YOUR 'EXPENDABLE' FEMALES?
2052
MOST UNPLEASANTLY, MR. BOND—AS YOU WILL NOW FIND OUT!

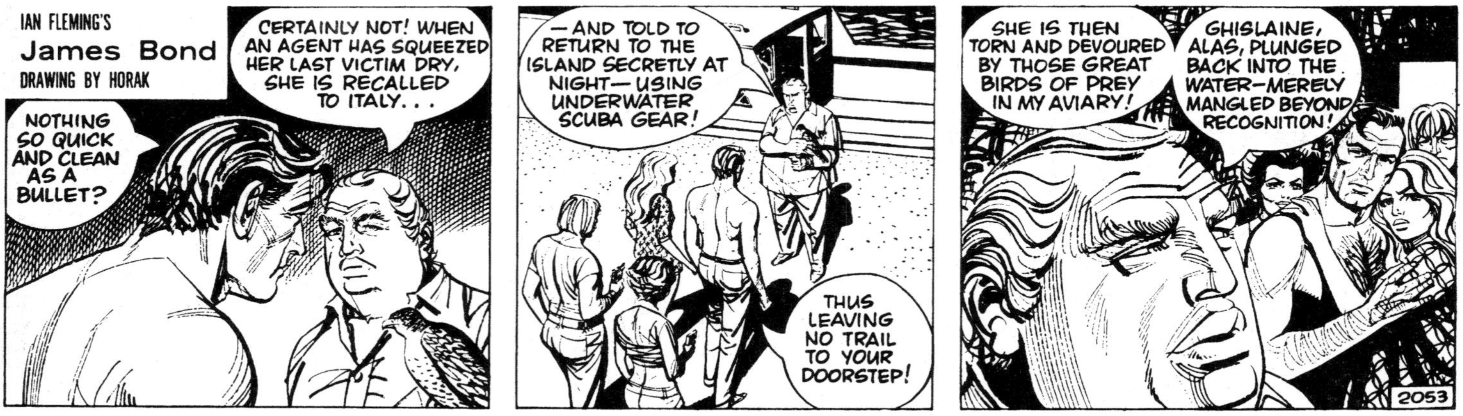
IAN FLEMING'S
James Bond
DRAWING BY HORAK
NOTHING SO QUICK AND CLEAN AS A BULLET?
CERTAINLY NOT! WHEN AN AGENT HAS SQUEEZED HER LAST VICTIM DRY, SHE IS RECALLED TO ITALY...
—AND TOLD TO RETURN TO THE ISLAND SECRETLY AT NIGHT—USING UNDERWATER SCUBA GEAR!
THUS LEAVING NO TRAIL TO YOUR DOORSTEP!
SHE IS THEN TORN AND DEVOURED BY THOSE GREAT BIRDS OF PREY IN MY AVIARY!
GHISLAINE, ALAS, PLUNGED BACK INTO THE WATER—MERELY MANGLED BEYOND RECOGNITION!
2053

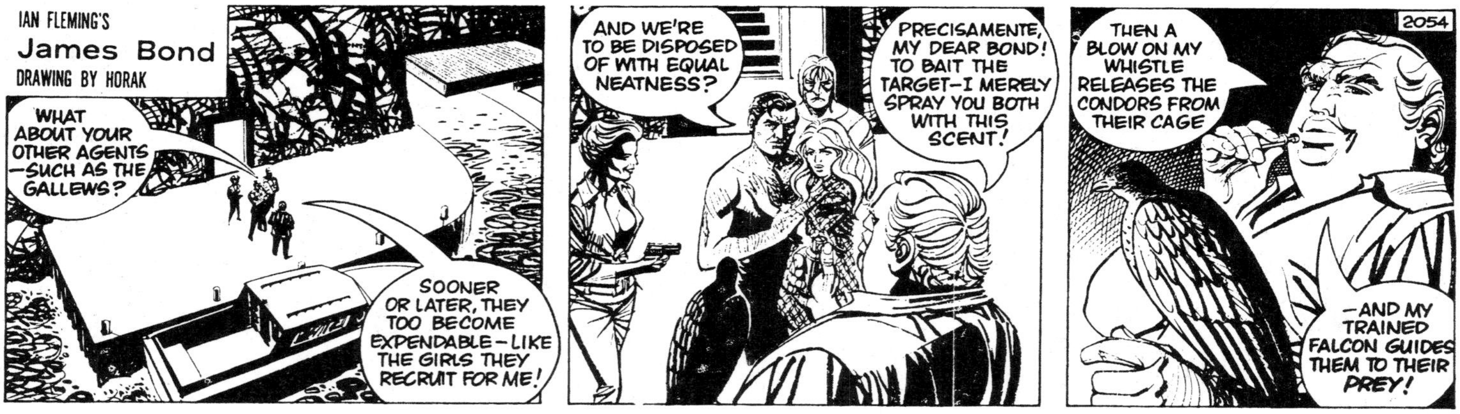
IAN FLEMING'S
James Bond
DRAWING BY HORAK
WHAT ABOUT YOUR OTHER AGENTS—SUCH AS THE GALLEWS?
SOONER OR LATER, THEY TOO BECOME EXPENDABLE—LIKE THE GIRLS THEY RECRUIT FOR ME!
AND WE'RE TO BE DISPOSED OF WITH EQUAL NEATNESS?
PRECISAMENTE, MY DEAR BOND! TO BAIT THE TARGET—I MERELY SPRAY YOU BOTH WITH THIS SCENT!
2054
THEN A BLOW ON MY WHISTLE RELEASES THE CONDORS FROM THEIR CAGE
—AND MY TRAINED FALCON GUIDES THEM TO THEIR PREY!

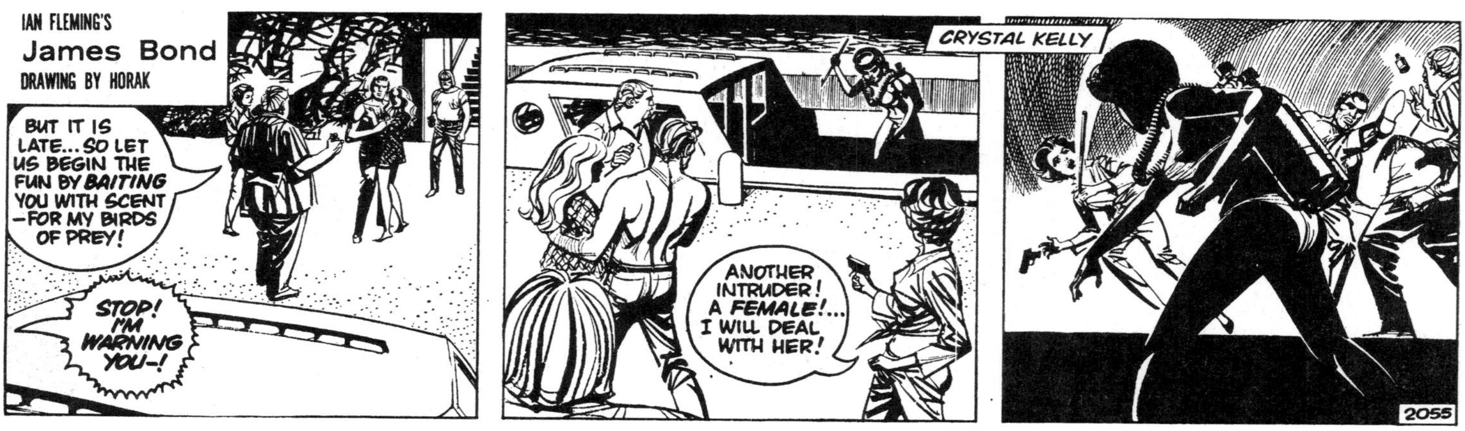
IAN FLEMING'S
James Bond
DRAWING BY HORAK
BUT IT IS LATE... SO LET US BEGIN THE FUN BY BAITING YOU WITH SCENT—FOR MY BIRDS OF PREY!
STOP! I'M WARNING YOU-!
CRYSTAL KELLY
ANOTHER INTRUDER! A FEMALE!... I WILL DEAL WITH HER!
2055

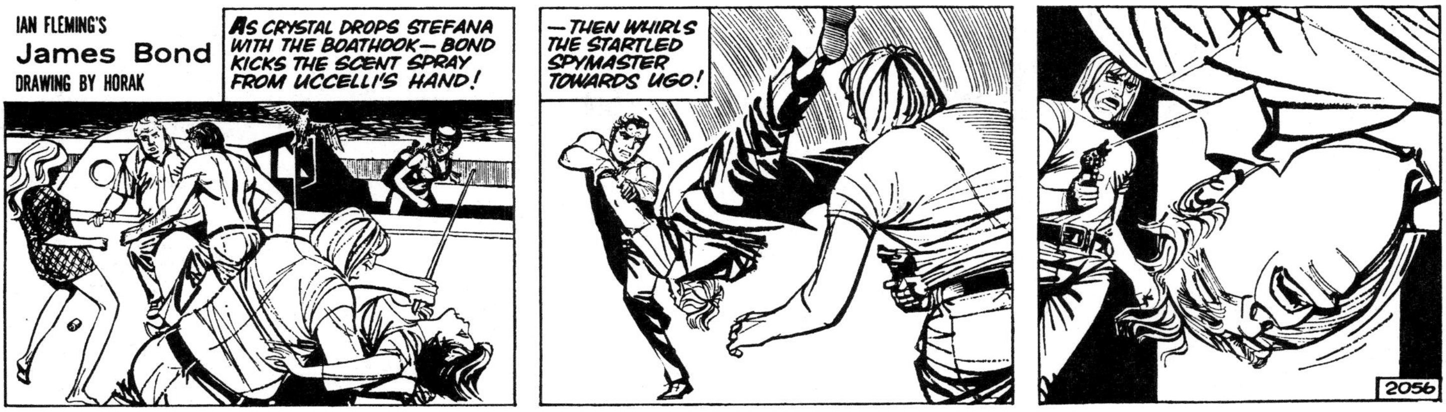
IAN FLEMING'S
James Bond
DRAWING BY HORAK
AS CRYSTAL DROPS STEFANA WITH THE BOATHOOK—BOND KICKS THE SCENT SPRAY FROM UCCELLI'S HAND!
—THEN WHIRLS THE STARTLED SPYMASTER TOWARDS UGO!
2056

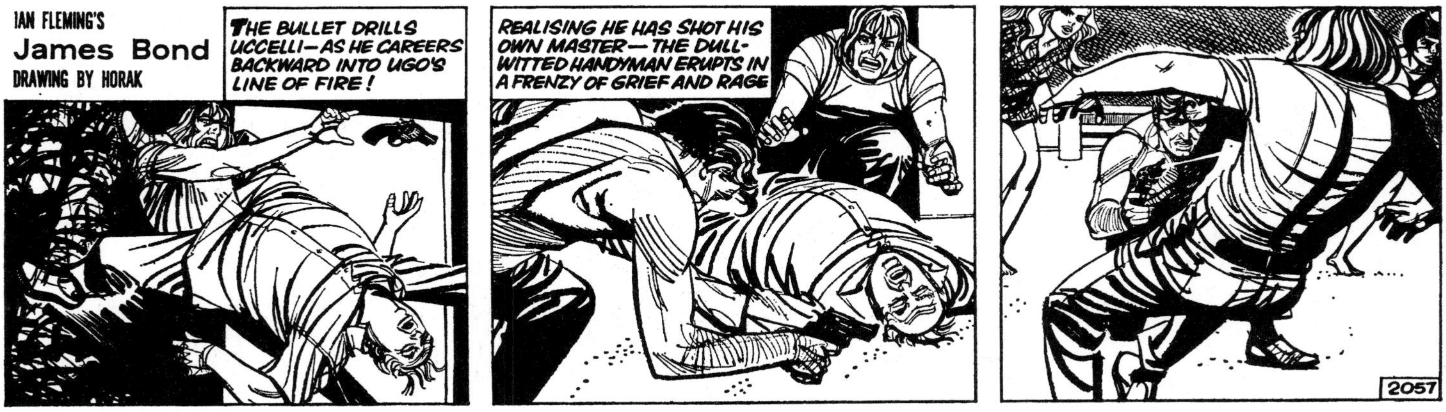
IAN FLEMING'S
James Bond
DRAWING BY HORAK
THE BULLET DRILLS UCCELLI—AS HE CAREERS BACKWARD INTO UGO'S LINE OF FIRE!
REALISING HE HAS SHOT HIS OWN MASTER—THE DULL-WITTED HANDYMAN ERUPTS IN A FRENZY OF GRIEF AND RAGE
2057

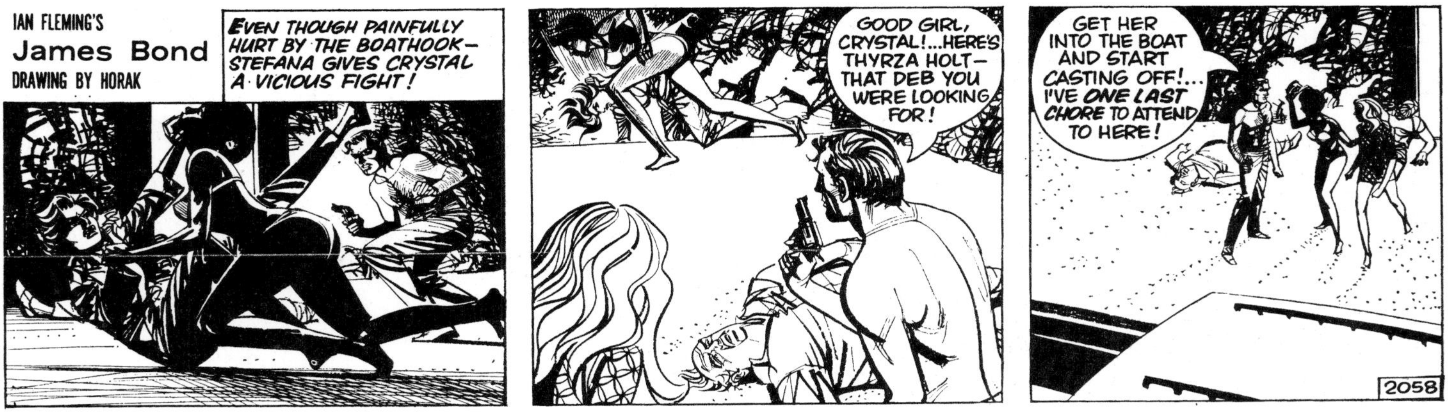
IAN FLEMING'S
James Bond
DRAWING BY HORAK
EVEN THOUGH PAINFULLY HURT BY THE BOATHOOK—STEFANA GIVES CRYSTAL A VICIOUS FIGHT!
GOOD GIRL, CRYSTAL!...HERE'S THYRZA HOLT—THAT DEB YOU WERE LOOKING FOR!
GET HER INTO THE BOAT AND START CASTING OFF!... I'VE ONE LAST CHORE TO ATTEND TO HERE!
2058

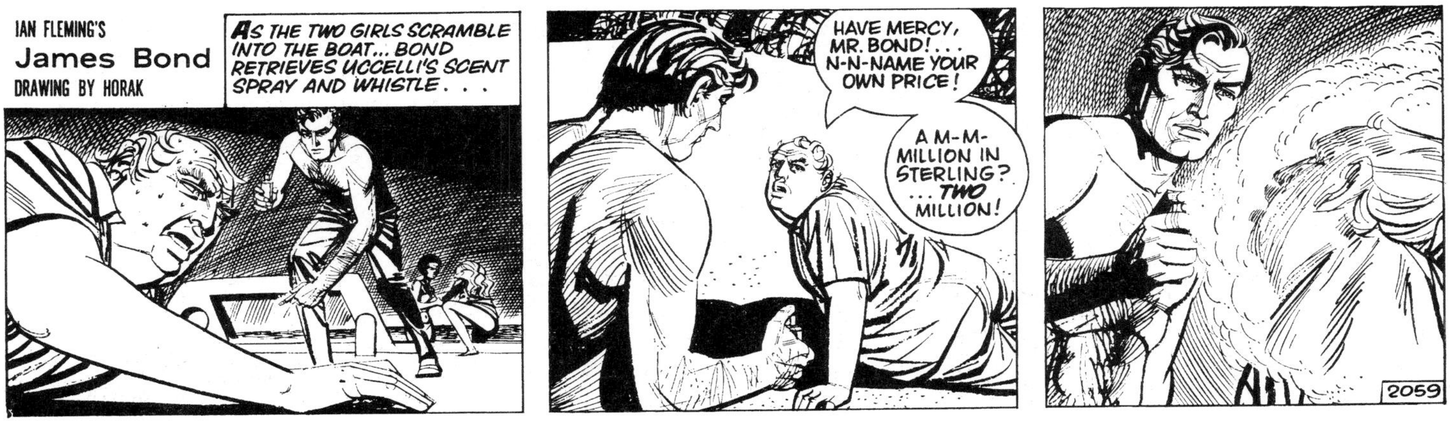
IAN FLEMING'S
James Bond
DRAWING BY HORAK
AS THE TWO GIRLS SCRAMBLE INTO THE BOAT... BOND RETRIEVES UCCELLI'S SCENT SPRAY AND WHISTLE . . .
HAVE MERCY, MR. BOND!... N-N-NAME YOUR OWN PRICE!
A M-M-MILLION IN STERLING? ... TWO MILLION!
2059

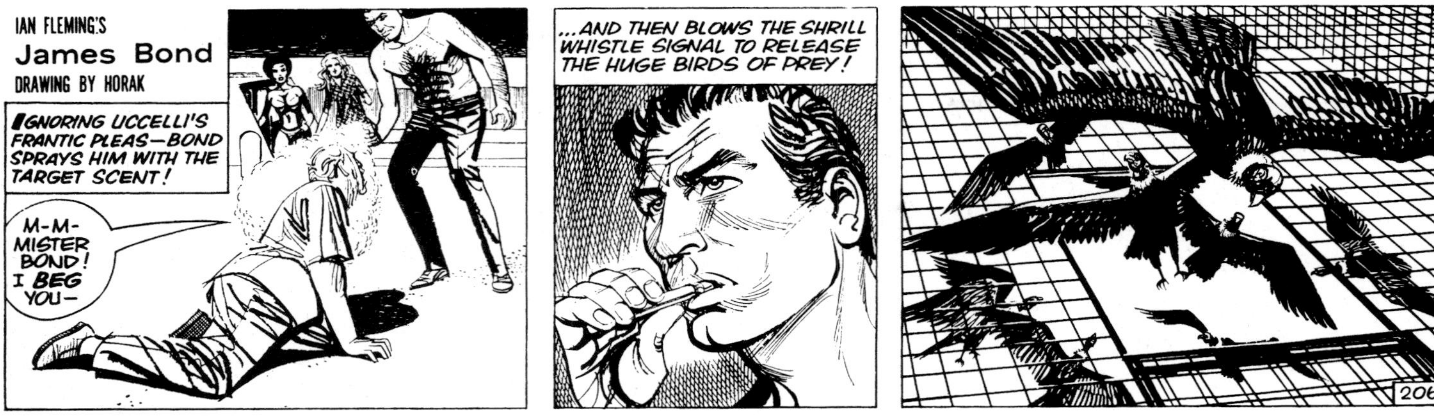
IAN FLEMING'S
James Bond
DRAWING BY HORAK
IGNORING UCCELLI'S FRANTIC PLEAS—BOND SPRAYS HIM WITH THE TARGET SCENT!
M-M-MISTER BOND! I BEG YOU—
...AND THEN BLOWS THE SHRILL WHISTLE SIGNAL TO RELEASE THE HUGE BIRDS OF PREY!
2060

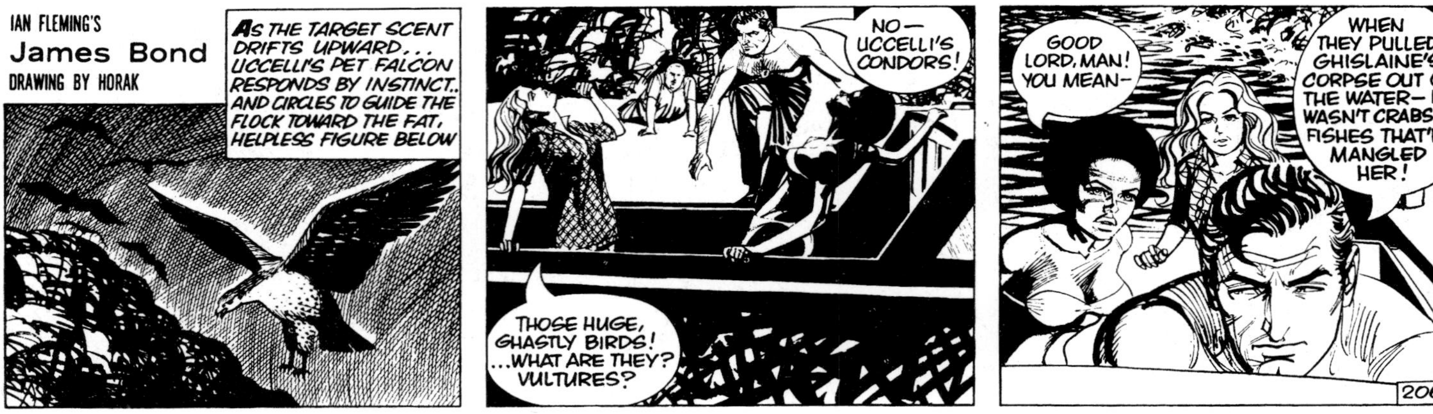
IAN FLEMING'S
James Bond
DRAWING BY HORAK
AS THE TARGET SCENT DRIFTS UPWARD... UCCELLI'S PET FALCON RESPONDS BY INSTINCT.. AND CIRCLES TO GUIDE THE FLOCK TOWARD THE FAT, HELPLESS FIGURE BELOW
NO—UCCELLI'S CONDORS!
THOSE HUGE, GHASTLY BIRDS! ...WHAT ARE THEY? VULTURES?
GOOD LORD, MAN! YOU MEAN—
WHEN THEY PULLED GHISLAINE'S CORPSE OUT OF THE WATER—IT WASN'T CRABS OR FISHES THAT'D MANGLED HER!
2061

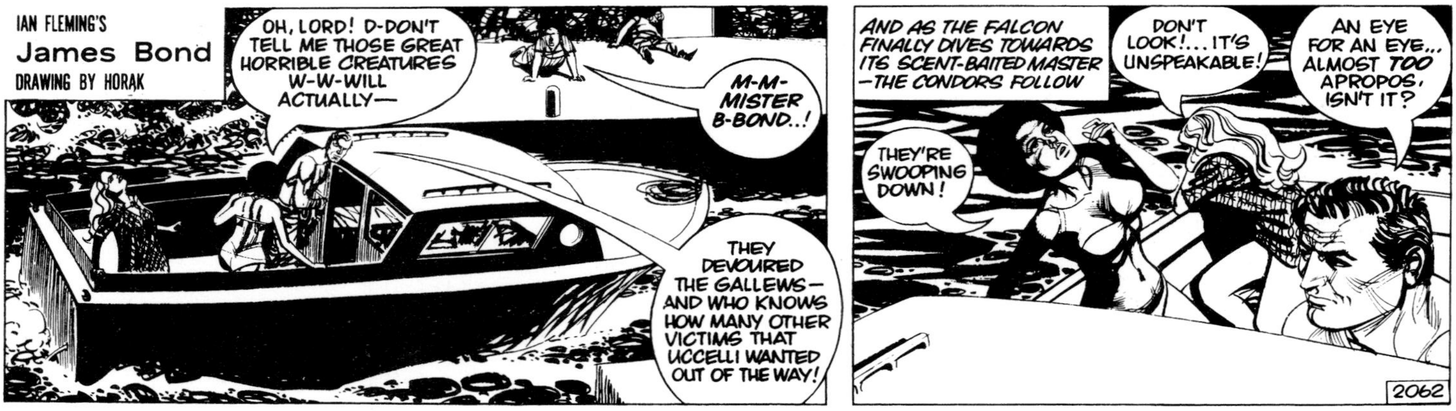
IAN FLEMING'S
James Bond
DRAWING BY HORAK
OH, LORD! D-DON'T TELL ME THOSE GREAT HORRIBLE CREATURES W-W-WILL ACTUALLY—
M-M-MISTER B-BOND..!
THEY DEVOURED THE GALLEWS—AND WHO KNOWS HOW MANY OTHER VICTIMS THAT UCCELLI WANTED OUT OF THE WAY!
AND AS THE FALCON FINALLY DIVES TOWARDS ITS SCENT-BAITED MASTER—THE CONDORS FOLLOW
THEY'RE SWOOPING DOWN!
DON'T LOOK!... IT'S UNSPEAKABLE!
AN EYE FOR AN EYE... ALMOST TOO APROPOS, ISN'T IT?
2062

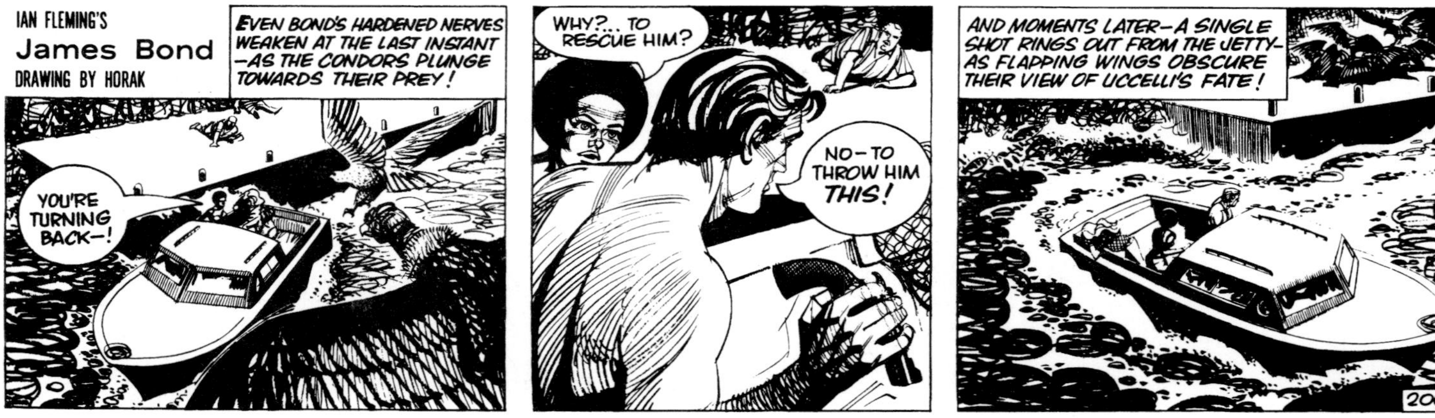
IAN FLEMING'S
James Bond
DRAWING BY HORAK
EVEN BOND'S HARDENED NERVES WEAKEN AT THE LAST INSTANT—AS THE CONDORS PLUNGE TOWARDS THEIR PREY!
YOU'RE TURNING BACK—!
WHY?... TO RESCUE HIM?
NO—TO THROW HIM THIS!
AND MOMENTS LATER—A SINGLE SHOT RINGS OUT FROM THE JETTY—AS FLAPPING WINGS OBSCURE THEIR VIEW OF UCCELLI'S FATE!
2063

IAN FLEMING'S
James Bond
DRAWING BY HORAK
NO ONE'S STIRRING YET- FORTUNATELY! WE'LL GET OUR CARS AND ROLL- BEFORE THE PORT WAKES UP!
WHAT ABOUT ALL THOSE OTHER GIRLS, STILL ON CONDOR ISLAND?
WE'D BEST LEAVE THAT SMALL DETAIL TO NATO INTELLIGENCE!
RATHER A TERSE SIGNAL ...AND WHAT'S THIS LAST BIT, ABOUT UCCELLI?
JAMES DIDN'T EXPLAIN... I ASKED HIM TO REPEAT, BUT THAT WAS THE END OF MESSAGE - "STRICTLY FOR THE BIRDS"!
2064

IAN FLEMING'S
James Bond
DRAWING BY HORAK
THYRZA IS DELIVERED SAFELY TO HER PARENTS IN LONDON. . .
MY DEAR MISS KELLY! WHATEVER YOUR FEE- WE CAN NEVER ADEQUATELY EXPRESS OUR GRATITUDE!
WE'LL MEET AGAIN, I HOPE...
ME TOO, JAMES - ESPECIALLY IF YOU MISLAY ANY MORE IVORY MINIATURES!
TWO GIRLS! DEAR ME - AND THYRZA HOLT'S A BLUE-BLOODED LONDON DEB... WHAT ABOUT THE OTHER?
CRYSTAL KELLY- BLACK IRISH!
2065
END OF STORY

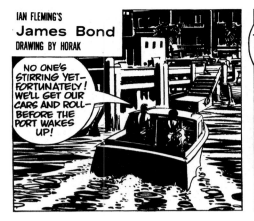

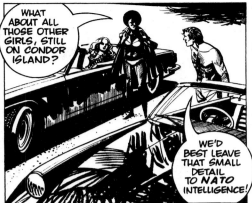

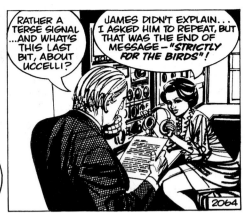

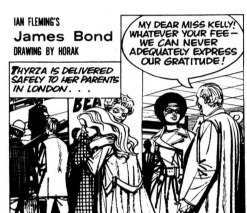

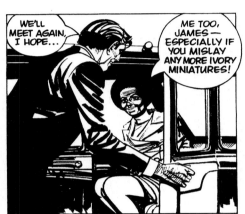

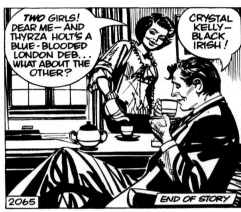

THE LEAGUE OF VAMPIRES

*T*he League of Vampires is different in many ways to other strips in the series. Although all the elements of a good Bond adventure are present, the story's tone may initially strike readers as too far-fetched — the title alone may scare off fans of Fleming's prose!

However, when the plot starts to thicken and the finer details become apparent, *The League of Vampires* takes its place as one of the most enjoyable stories in the strip series. Many similarities can be seen between the villain's plot in this strip and the cinematic versions of *Goldfinger* (destruction of an asset to increase the value of his own), *Live and Let Die* (cults used for nefarious purposes) and *Moonraker* (detonating a nuclear missile on English soil).

Whilst some of the earlier strips by Jim Lawrence & Yaroslav Horak may have pushed the boundaries with regards to nudity, *The League of Vampires* – evidently a product of a less censorious editorial policy – smashes through them and is rather graphic in places. Of course, in true *Bond* style, what is shown is done so in the best possible taste...

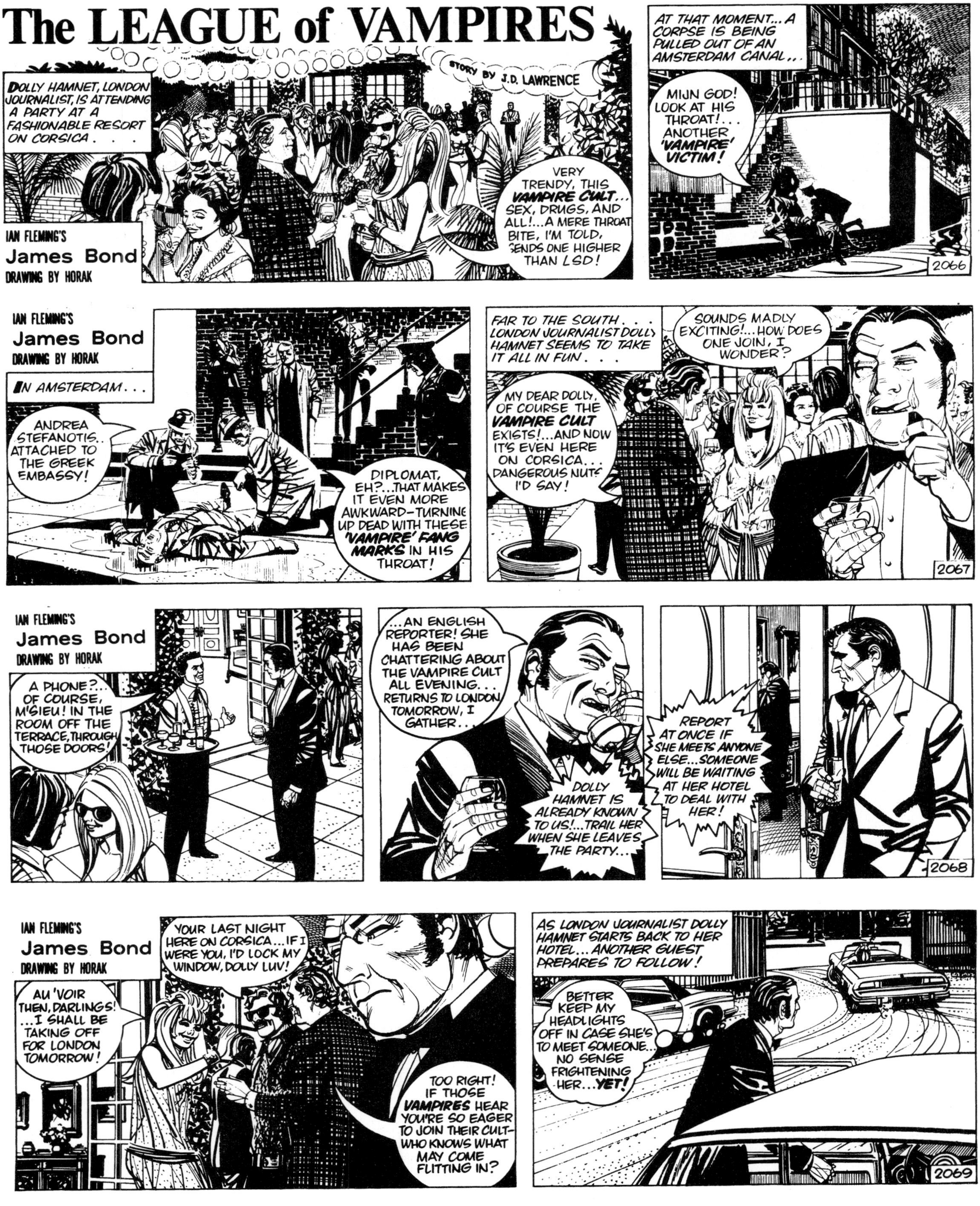

The LEAGUE of VAMPIRES
STORY BY J.D. LAWRENCE
DOLLY HAMNET, LONDON JOURNALIST, IS ATTENDING A PARTY AT A FASHIONABLE RESORT ON CORSICA . . .
IAN FLEMING'S James Bond DRAWING BY HORAK
VERY TRENDY, THIS VAMPIRE CULT... SEX, DRUGS, AND ALL!... A MERE THROAT BITE, I'M TOLD, SENDS ONE HIGHER THAN LSD!
AT THAT MOMENT... A CORPSE IS BEING PULLED OUT OF AN AMSTERDAM CANAL...
MIJN GOD! LOOK AT HIS THROAT!... ANOTHER 'VAMPIRE' VICTIM!
2066
IAN FLEMING'S James Bond DRAWING BY HORAK
IN AMSTERDAM . . .
ANDREA STEFANOTIS.. ATTACHED TO THE GREEK EMBASSY!
DIPLOMAT, EH?... THAT MAKES IT EVEN MORE AWKWARD—TURNING UP DEAD WITH THESE 'VAMPIRE' FANG MARKS IN HIS THROAT!
FAR TO THE SOUTH . . . LONDON JOURNALIST DOLLY HAMNET SEEMS TO TAKE IT ALL IN FUN . . .
SOUNDS MADLY EXCITING!... HOW DOES ONE JOIN, I WONDER?
MY DEAR DOLLY, OF COURSE THE VAMPIRE CULT EXISTS!... AND NOW IT'S EVEN HERE ON CORSICA... DANGEROUS NUTS I'D SAY!
2067
IAN FLEMING'S James Bond DRAWING BY HORAK
A PHONE?... OF COURSE, M'SIEU! IN THE ROOM OFF THE TERRACE, THROUGH THOSE DOORS!
...AN ENGLISH REPORTER! SHE HAS BEEN CHATTERING ABOUT THE VAMPIRE CULT ALL EVENING... RETURNS TO LONDON TOMORROW, I GATHER...
DOLLY HAMNET IS ALREADY KNOWN TO US!... TRAIL HER WHEN SHE LEAVES THE PARTY...
REPORT AT ONCE IF SHE MEETS ANYONE ELSE... SOMEONE WILL BE WAITING AT HER HOTEL TO DEAL WITH HER!
2068
IAN FLEMING'S James Bond DRAWING BY HORAK
YOUR LAST NIGHT HERE ON CORSICA... IF I WERE YOU, I'D LOCK MY WINDOW, DOLLY LUV!
AU 'VOIR THEN, DARLINGS! ...I SHALL BE TAKING OFF FOR LONDON TOMORROW!
TOO RIGHT! IF THOSE VAMPIRES HEAR YOU'RE SO EAGER TO JOIN THEIR CULT— WHO KNOWS WHAT MAY COME FLITTING IN?
AS LONDON JOURNALIST DOLLY HAMNET STARTS BACK TO HER HOTEL... ANOTHER GUEST PREPARES TO FOLLOW!
BETTER KEEP MY HEADLIGHTS OFF IN CASE SHE'S TO MEET SOMEONE... NO SENSE FRIGHTENING HER... YET!
2069

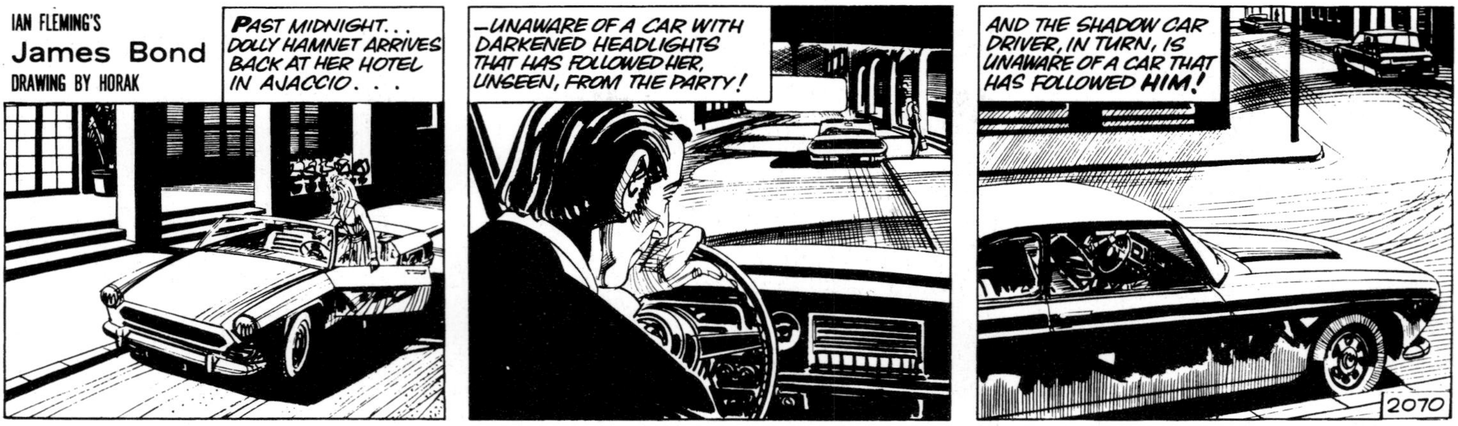
IAN FLEMING'S
James Bond
DRAWING BY HORAK
PAST MIDNIGHT... DOLLY HAMNET ARRIVES BACK AT HER HOTEL IN AJACCIO...
—UNAWARE OF A CAR WITH DARKENED HEADLIGHTS THAT HAS FOLLOWED HER, UNSEEN, FROM THE PARTY!
AND THE SHADOW CAR DRIVER, IN TURN, IS UNAWARE OF A CAR THAT HAS FOLLOWED HIM!
2070

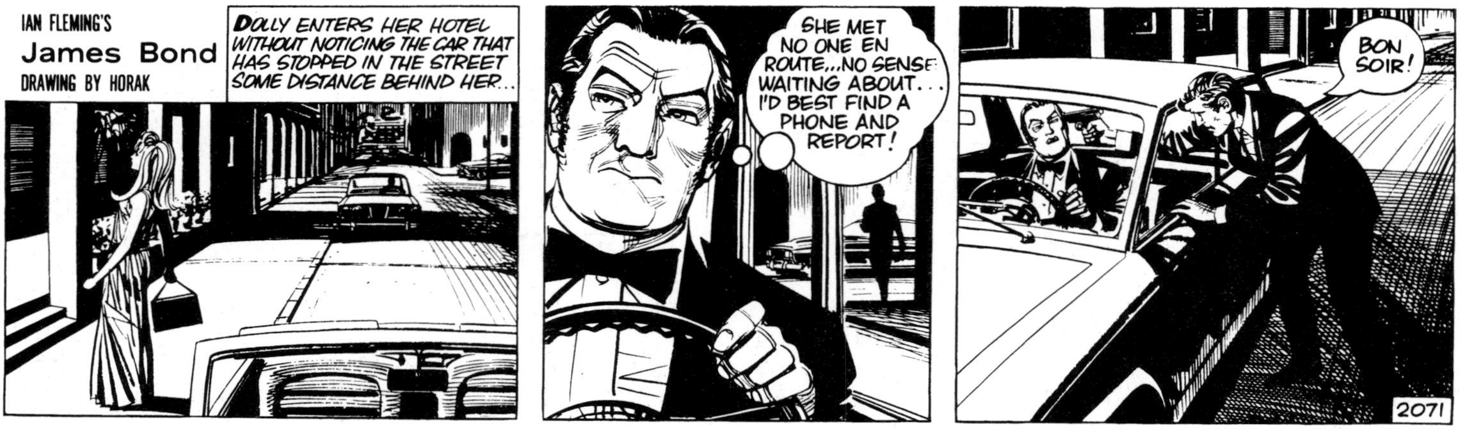
IAN FLEMING'S
James Bond
DRAWING BY HORAK
DOLLY ENTERS HER HOTEL WITHOUT NOTICING THE CAR THAT HAS STOPPED IN THE STREET SOME DISTANCE BEHIND HER...
SHE MET NO ONE EN ROUTE,..NO SENSE WAITING ABOUT... I'D BEST FIND A PHONE AND REPORT!
BON SOIR!
2071

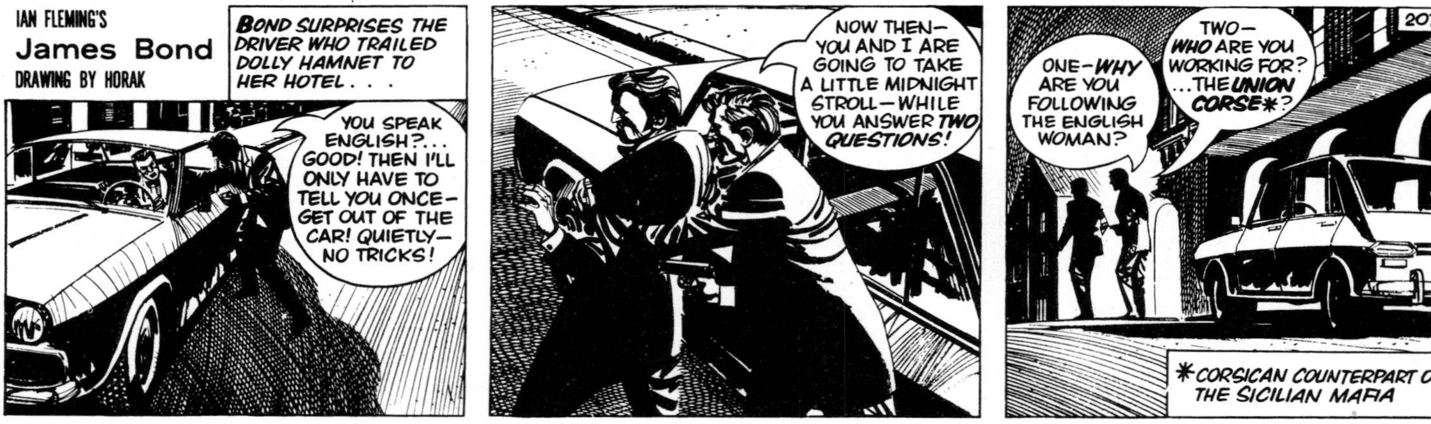
IAN FLEMING'S
James Bond
DRAWING BY HORAK
BOND SURPRISES THE DRIVER WHO TRAILED DOLLY HAMNET TO HER HOTEL...
YOU SPEAK ENGLISH?... GOOD! THEN I'LL ONLY HAVE TO TELL YOU ONCE-GET OUT OF THE CAR! QUIETLY—NO TRICKS!
NOW THEN—YOU AND I ARE GOING TO TAKE A LITTLE MIDNIGHT STROLL—WHILE YOU ANSWER TWO QUESTIONS!
2072
ONE—WHY ARE YOU FOLLOWING THE ENGLISH WOMAN?
TWO—WHO ARE YOU WORKING FOR? ...THE UNION CORSE*?
*CORSICAN COUNTERPART OF THE SICILIAN MAFIA

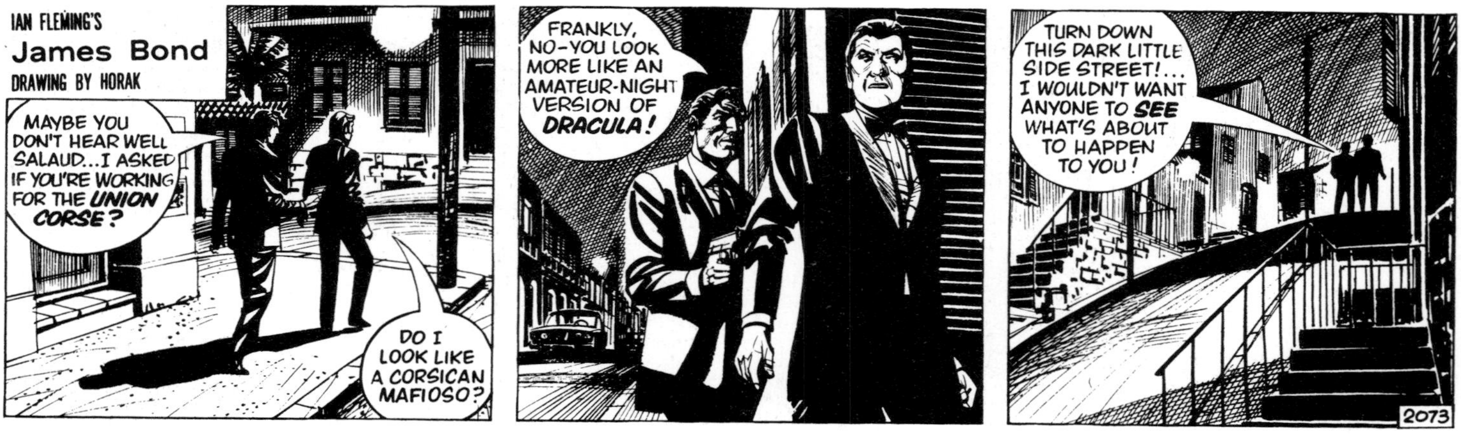
IAN FLEMING'S
James Bond
DRAWING BY HORAK
MAYBE YOU DON'T HEAR WELL SALAUD...I ASKED IF YOU'RE WORKING FOR THE UNION CORSE?
DO I LOOK LIKE A CORSICAN MAFIOSO?
FRANKLY, NO-YOU LOOK MORE LIKE AN AMATEUR-NIGHT VERSION OF DRACULA!
TURN DOWN THIS DARK LITTLE SIDE STREET!... I WOULDN'T WANT ANYONE TO SEE WHAT'S ABOUT TO HAPPEN TO YOU!
2073

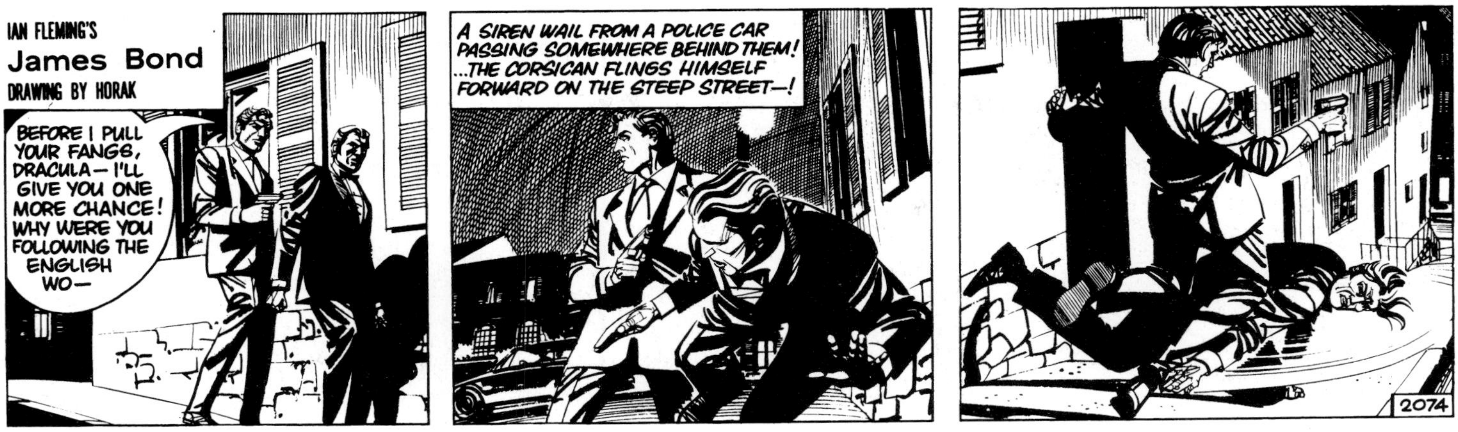
IAN FLEMING'S
James Bond
DRAWING BY HORAK
BEFORE I PULL YOUR FANGS, DRACULA— I'LL GIVE YOU ONE MORE CHANCE! WHY WERE YOU FOLLOWING THE ENGLISH WO—
A SIREN WAIL FROM A POLICE CAR PASSING SOMEWHERE BEHIND THEM! ...THE CORSICAN FLINGS HIMSELF FORWARD ON THE STEEP STREET—!
2074

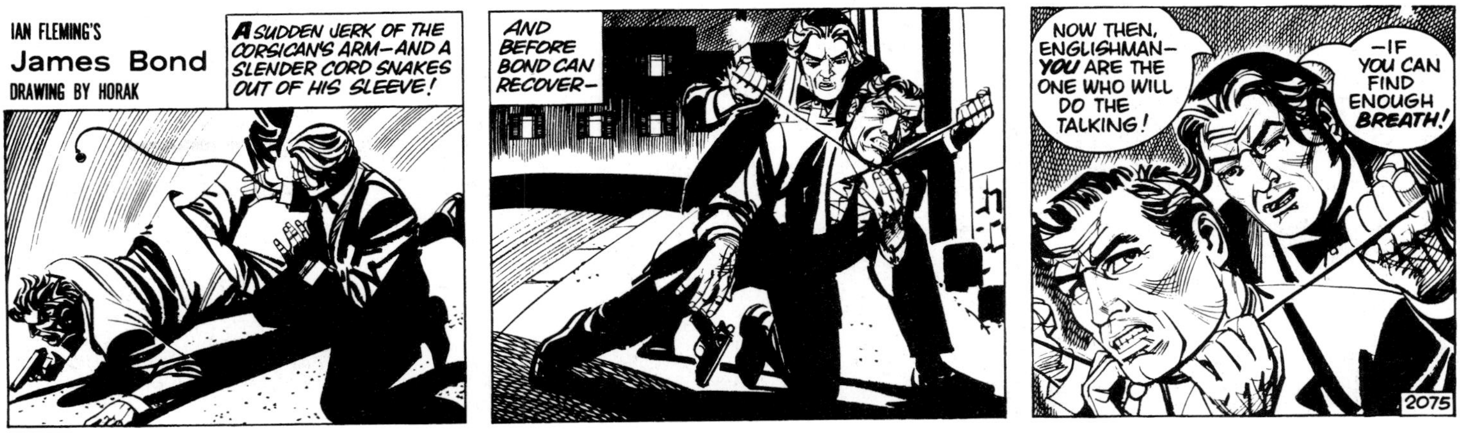
IAN FLEMING'S
James Bond
DRAWING BY HORAK
A SUDDEN JERK OF THE CORSICAN'S ARM—AND A SLENDER CORD SNAKES OUT OF HIS SLEEVE!
AND BEFORE BOND CAN RECOVER—
NOW THEN, ENGLISHMAN— YOU ARE THE ONE WHO WILL DO THE TALKING!
—IF YOU CAN FIND ENOUGH BREATH!
2075

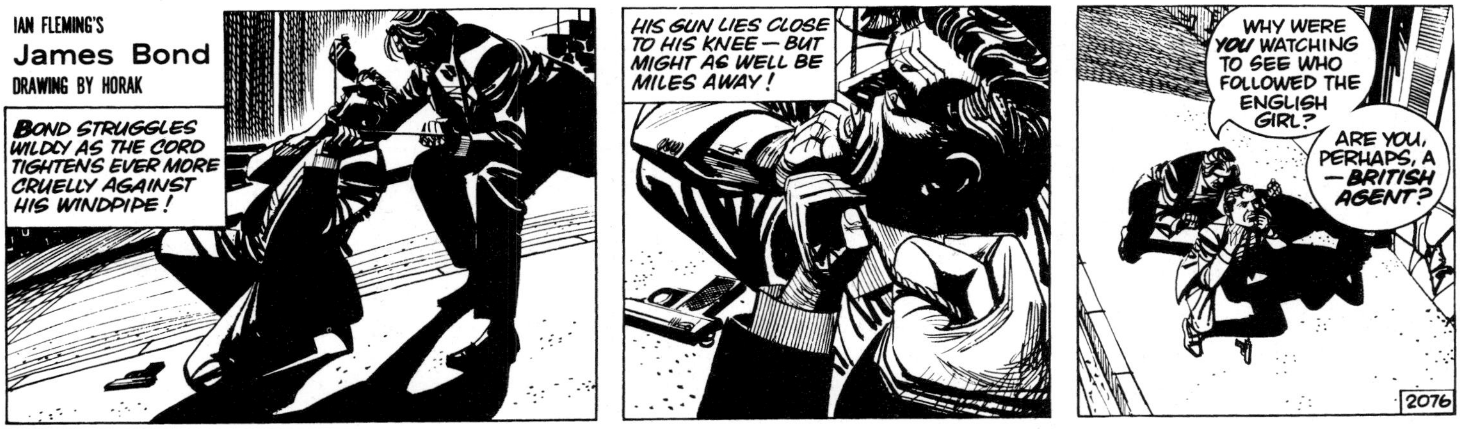
IAN FLEMING'S
James Bond
DRAWING BY HORAK
BOND STRUGGLES WILDLY AS THE CORD TIGHTENS EVER MORE CRUELLY AGAINST HIS WINDPIPE!
HIS GUN LIES CLOSE TO HIS KNEE — BUT MIGHT AS WELL BE MILES AWAY!
WHY WERE YOU WATCHING TO SEE WHO FOLLOWED THE ENGLISH GIRL?
ARE YOU, PERHAPS, A —BRITISH AGENT?
2076

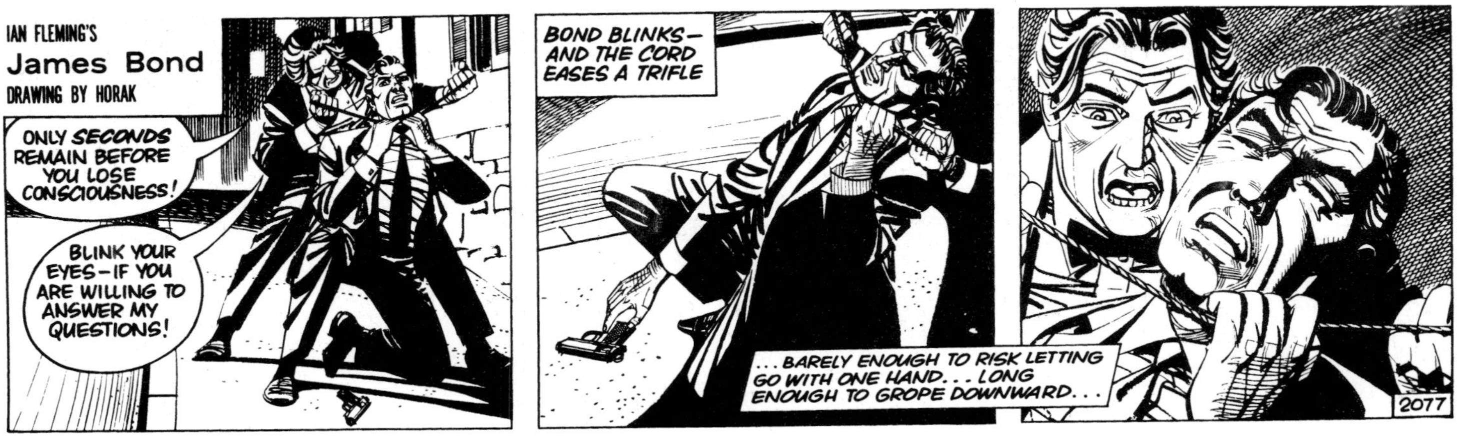
IAN FLEMING'S
James Bond
DRAWING BY HORAK
ONLY SECONDS REMAIN BEFORE YOU LOSE CONSCIOUSNESS!
BLINK YOUR EYES—IF YOU ARE WILLING TO ANSWER MY QUESTIONS!
BOND BLINKS— AND THE CORD EASES A TRIFLE
...BARELY ENOUGH TO RISK LETTING GO WITH ONE HAND... LONG ENOUGH TO GROPE DOWNWARD...
2077

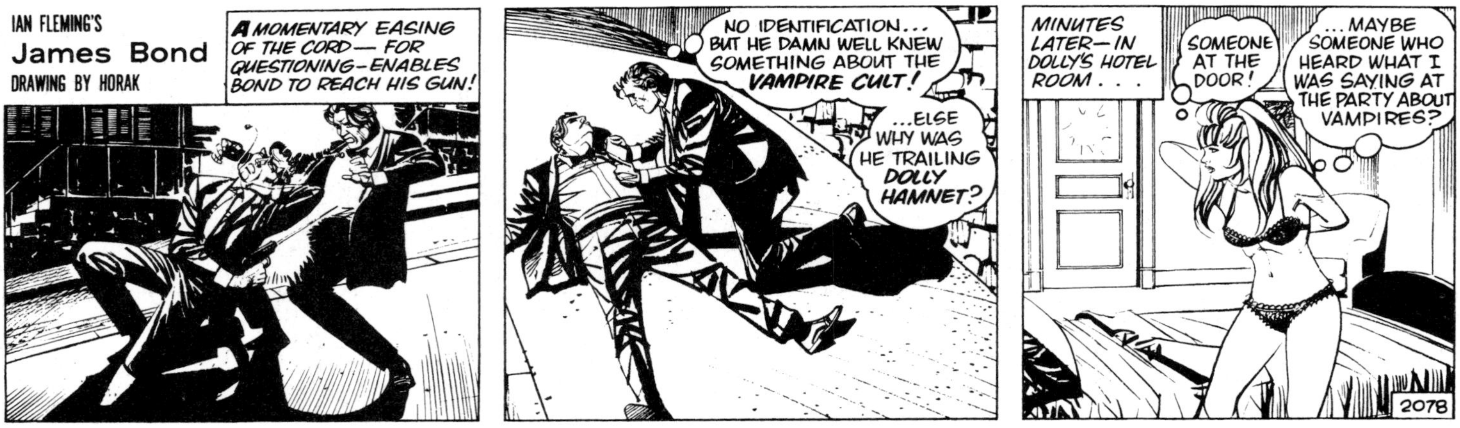
IAN FLEMING'S
James Bond
DRAWING BY HORAK
A MOMENTARY EASING OF THE CORD — FOR QUESTIONING - ENABLES BOND TO REACH HIS GUN!
NO IDENTIFICATION... BUT HE DAMN WELL KNEW SOMETHING ABOUT THE VAMPIRE CULT!
...ELSE WHY WAS HE TRAILING DOLLY HAMNET?
MINUTES LATER— IN DOLLY'S HOTEL ROOM . . .
SOMEONE AT THE DOOR!
... MAYBE SOMEONE WHO HEARD WHAT I WAS SAYING AT THE PARTY ABOUT VAMPIRES?
2078

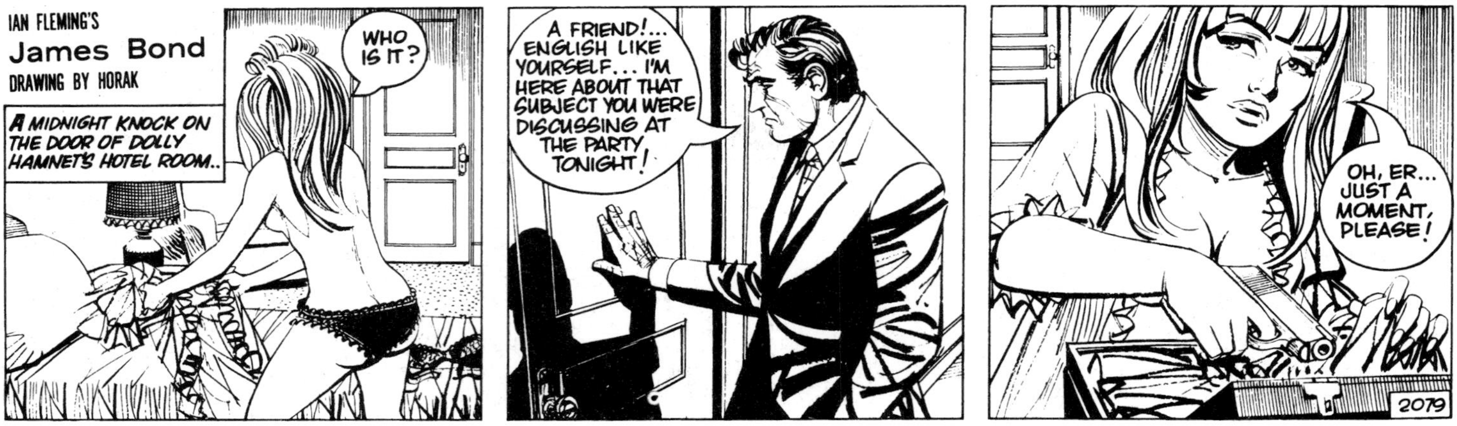
IAN FLEMING'S
James Bond
DRAWING BY HORAK
A MIDNIGHT KNOCK ON THE DOOR OF DOLLY HAMNET'S HOTEL ROOM..
WHO IS IT?
A FRIEND!... ENGLISH LIKE YOURSELF... I'M HERE ABOUT THAT SUBJECT YOU WERE DISCUSSING AT THE PARTY TONIGHT!
OH, ER... JUST A MOMENT, PLEASE!
2079

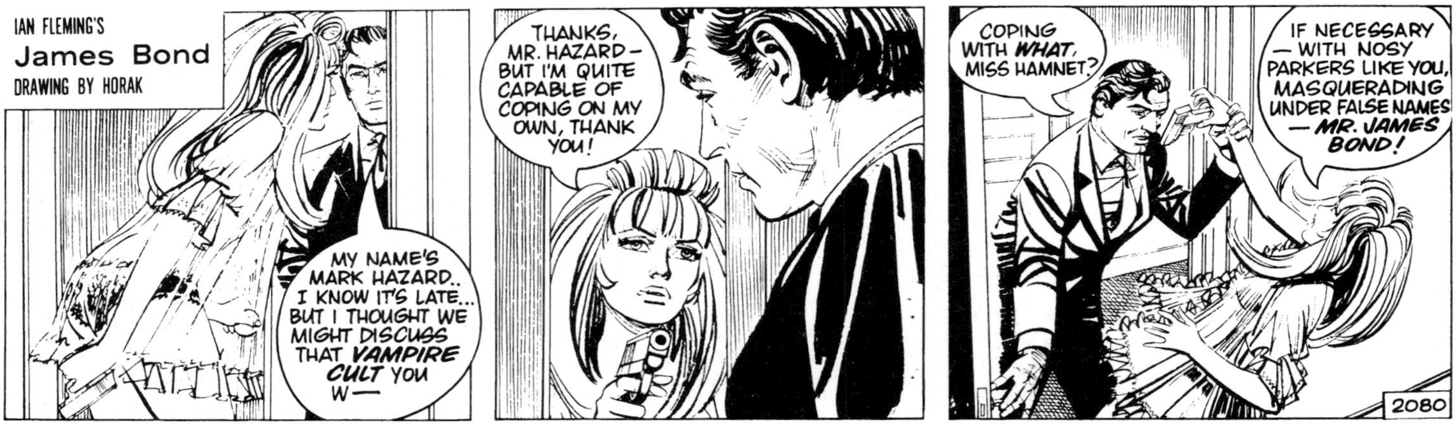
IAN FLEMING'S
James Bond
DRAWING BY HORAK
MY NAME'S MARK HAZARD.. I KNOW IT'S LATE... BUT I THOUGHT WE MIGHT DISCUSS THAT VAMPIRE CULT YOU W—
THANKS, MR. HAZARD— BUT I'M QUITE CAPABLE OF COPING ON MY OWN, THANK YOU!
COPING WITH WHAT, MISS HAMNET?
IF NECESSARY — WITH NOSY PARKERS LIKE YOU, MASQUERADING UNDER FALSE NAMES — MR. JAMES BOND!
2080

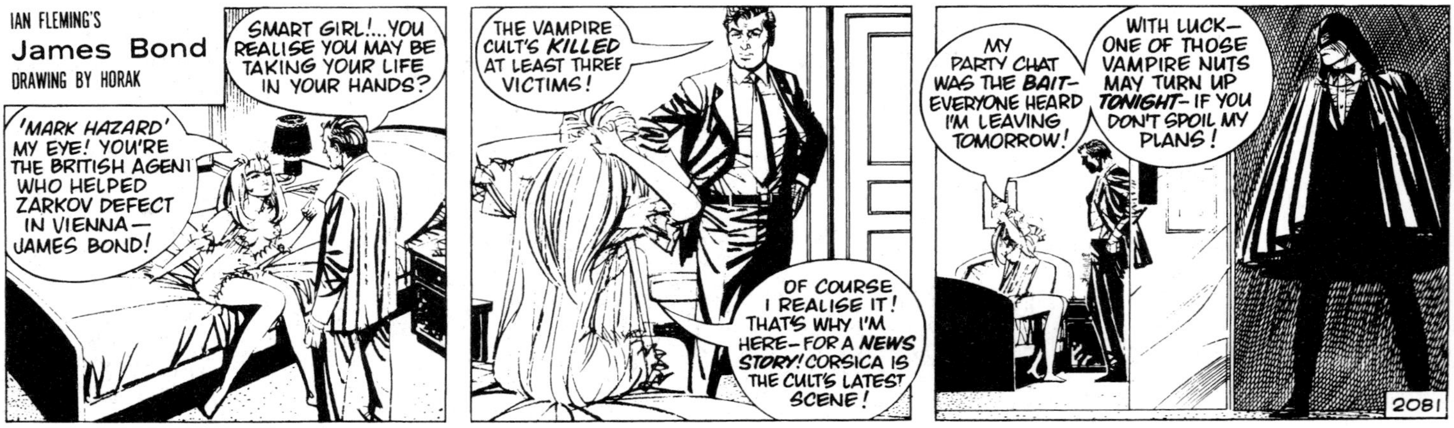
IAN FLEMING'S
James Bond
DRAWING BY HORAK
'MARK HAZARD' MY EYE! YOU'RE THE BRITISH AGENT WHO HELPED ZARKOV DEFECT IN VIENNA— JAMES BOND!
SMART GIRL!... YOU REALISE YOU MAY BE TAKING YOUR LIFE IN YOUR HANDS?
THE VAMPIRE CULT'S KILLED AT LEAST THREE VICTIMS!
OF COURSE I REALISE IT! THAT'S WHY I'M HERE— FOR A NEWS STORY! CORSICA IS THE CULT'S LATEST SCENE!
MY PARTY CHAT WAS THE BAIT— EVERYONE HEARD I'M LEAVING TOMORROW!
WITH LUCK— ONE OF THOSE VAMPIRE NUTS MAY TURN UP TONIGHT— IF YOU DON'T SPOIL MY PLANS!
2081

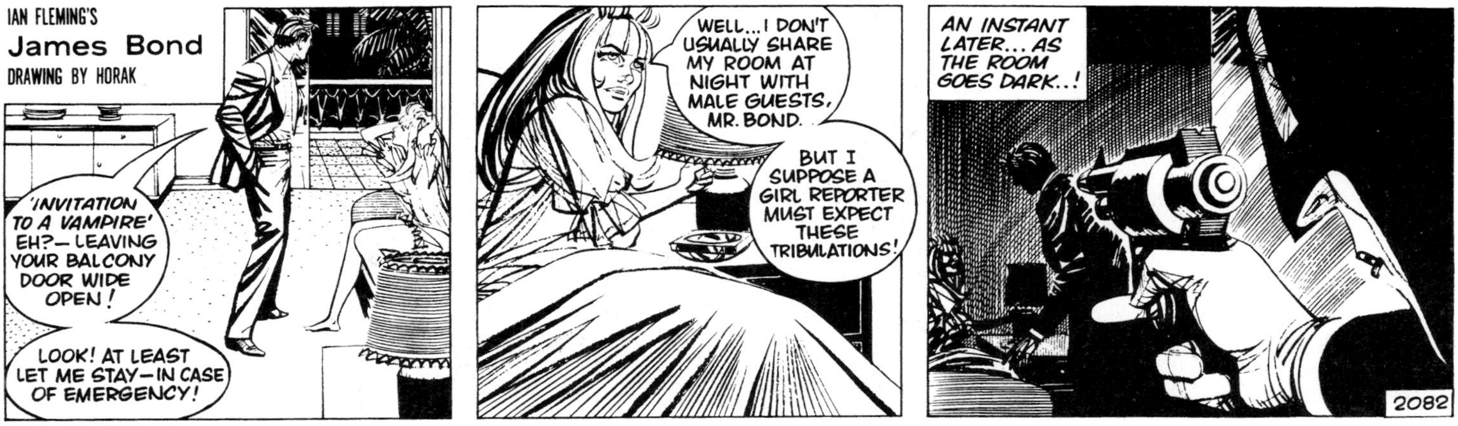
IAN FLEMING'S
James Bond
DRAWING BY HORAK
'INVITATION TO A VAMPIRE' EH?— LEAVING YOUR BALCONY DOOR WIDE OPEN!
LOOK! AT LEAST LET ME STAY—IN CASE OF EMERGENCY!
WELL... I DON'T USUALLY SHARE MY ROOM AT NIGHT WITH MALE GUESTS, MR. BOND.
BUT I SUPPOSE A GIRL REPORTER MUST EXPECT THESE TRIBULATIONS!
AN INSTANT LATER... AS THE ROOM GOES DARK..!
2082

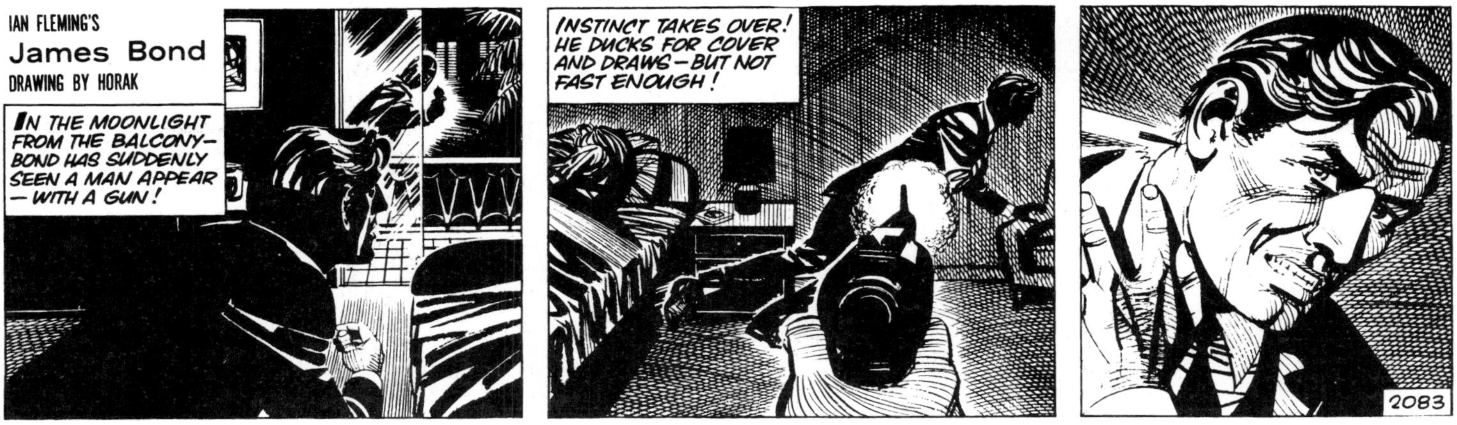
IAN FLEMING'S
James Bond
DRAWING BY HORAK
IN THE MOONLIGHT FROM THE BALCONY— BOND HAS SUDDENLY SEEN A MAN APPEAR —WITH A GUN!
INSTINCT TAKES OVER! HE DUCKS FOR COVER AND DRAWS—BUT NOT FAST ENOUGH!
2083

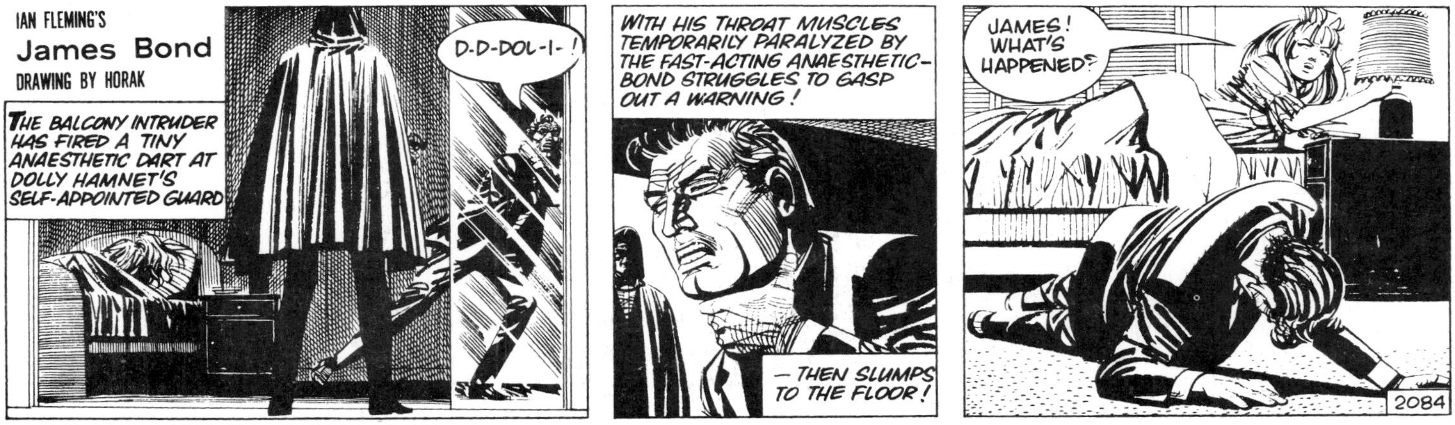
IAN FLEMING'S
James Bond
DRAWING BY HORAK
THE BALCONY INTRUDER HAS FIRED A TINY ANAESTHETIC DART AT DOLLY HAMNET'S SELF-APPOINTED GUARD
D-D-DOL-I-!
WITH HIS THROAT MUSCLES TEMPORARILY PARALYZED BY THE FAST-ACTING ANAESTHETIC- BOND STRUGGLES TO GASP OUT A WARNING!
—THEN SLUMPS TO THE FLOOR!
JAMES! WHAT'S HAPPENED?
2084

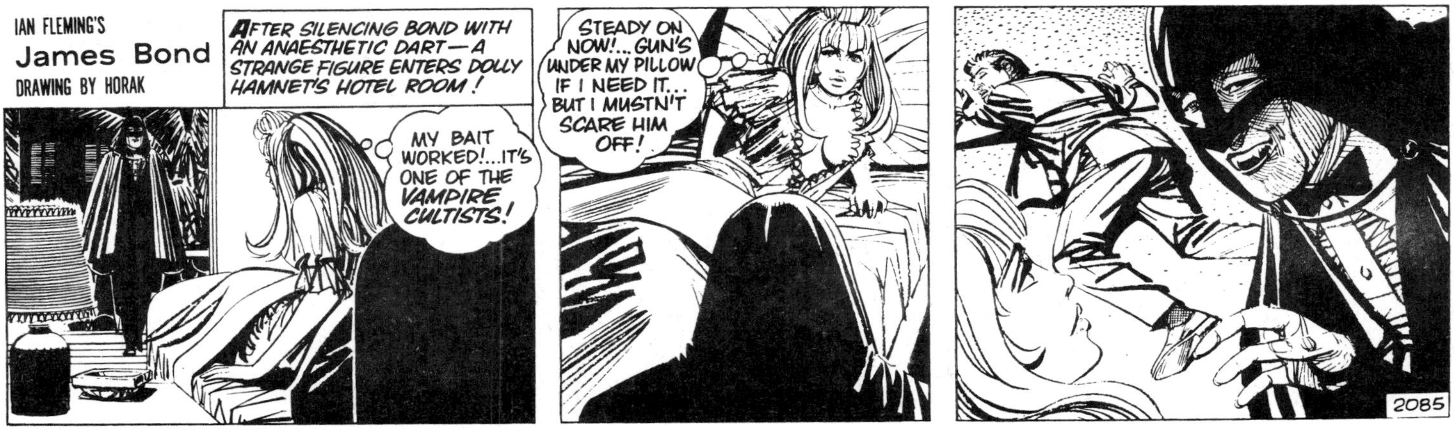
IAN FLEMING'S
James Bond
DRAWING BY HORAK
AFTER SILENCING BOND WITH AN ANAESTHETIC DART—A STRANGE FIGURE ENTERS DOLLY HAMNET'S HOTEL ROOM!
MY BAIT WORKED!... IT'S ONE OF THE VAMPIRE CULTISTS!
STEADY ON NOW!... GUN'S UNDER MY PILLOW IF I NEED IT... BUT I MUSTN'T SCARE HIM OFF!
2085

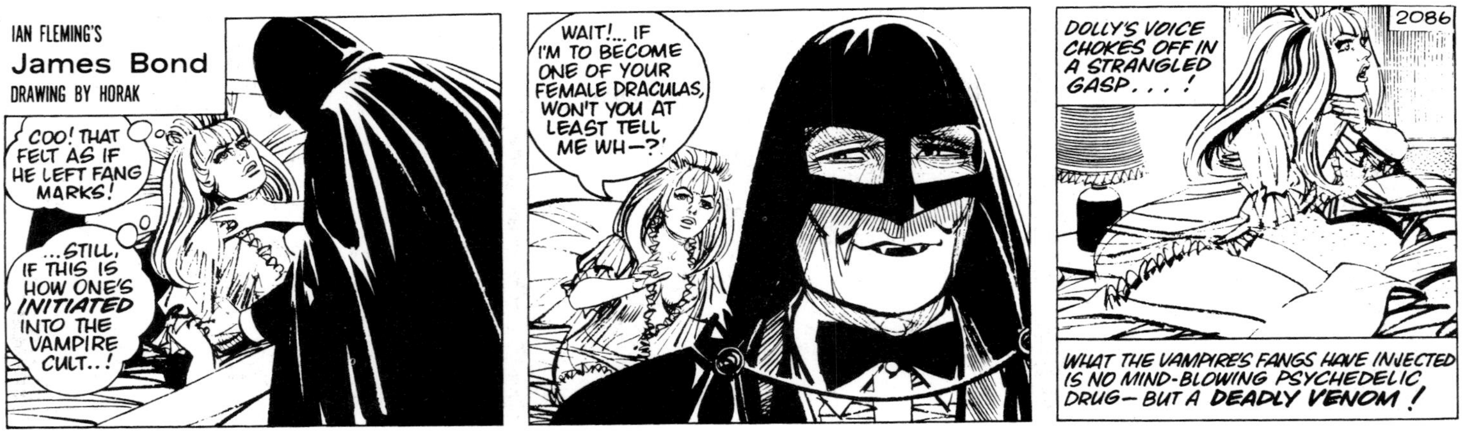
IAN FLEMING'S
James Bond
DRAWING BY HORAK
COO! THAT FELT AS IF HE LEFT FANG MARKS!
...STILL, IF THIS IS HOW ONE'S INITIATED INTO THE VAMPIRE CULT..!
WAIT!... IF I'M TO BECOME ONE OF YOUR FEMALE DRACULAS, WON'T YOU AT LEAST TELL ME WH—?'
2086
DOLLY'S VOICE CHOKES OFF IN A STRANGLED GASP . . . !
WHAT THE VAMPIRE'S FANGS HAVE INJECTED IS NO MIND-BLOWING PSYCHEDELIC DRUG— BUT A DEADLY VENOM !

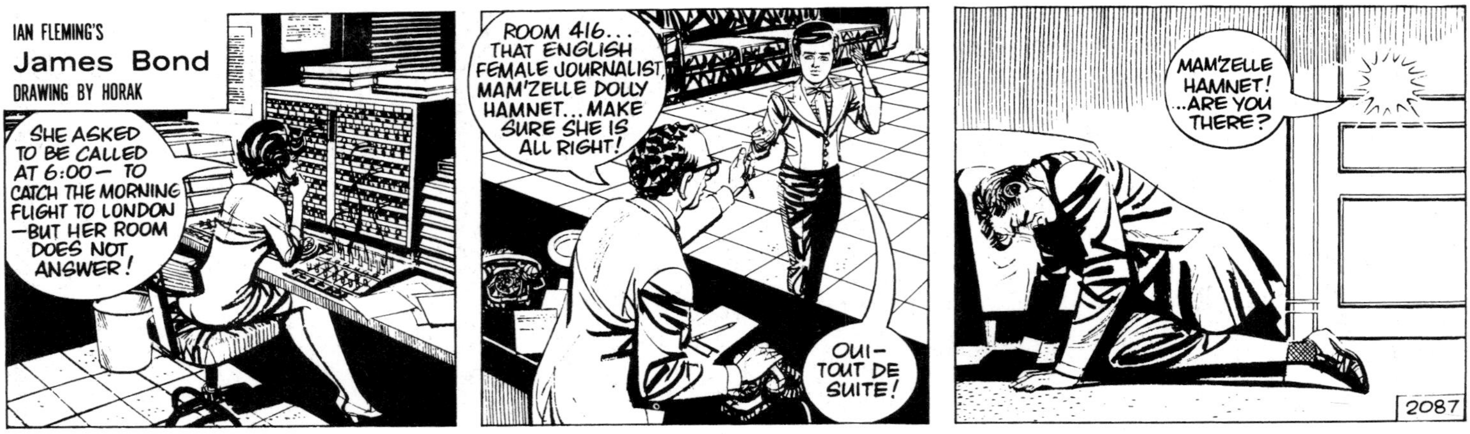
IAN FLEMING'S
James Bond
DRAWING BY HORAK
SHE ASKED TO BE CALLED AT 6:00— TO CATCH THE MORNING FLIGHT TO LONDON —BUT HER ROOM DOES NOT ANSWER!
ROOM 416... THAT ENGLISH FEMALE JOURNALIST, MAM'ZELLE DOLLY HAMNET... MAKE SURE SHE IS ALL RIGHT!
OUI— TOUT DE SUITE!
MAM'ZELLE HAMNET! ...ARE YOU THERE?
2087

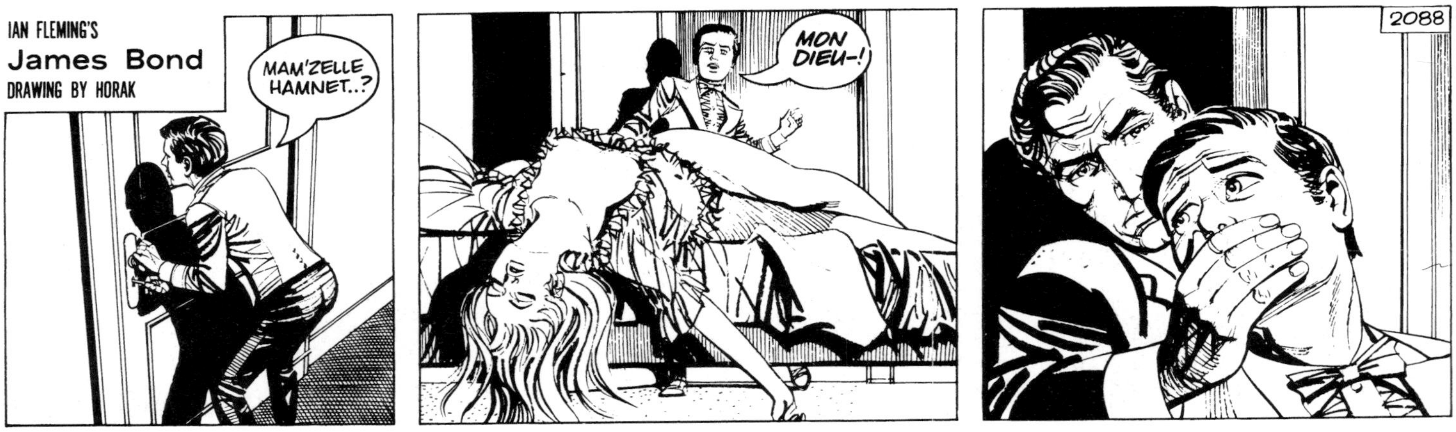
IAN FLEMING'S
James Bond
DRAWING BY HORAK
MAM'ZELLE HAMNET..?
MON DIEU-!
2088

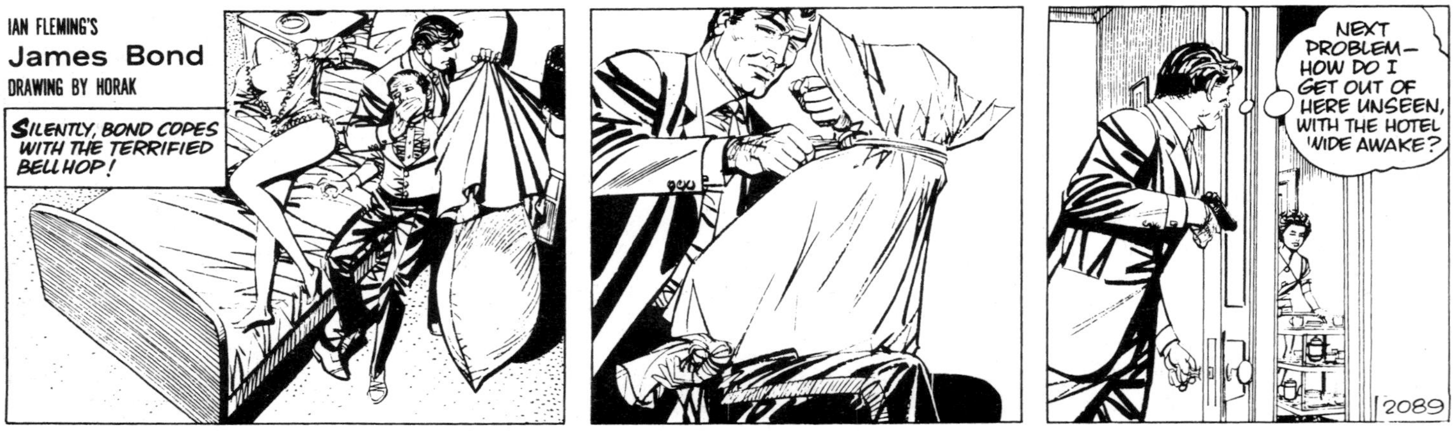
IAN FLEMING'S
James Bond
DRAWING BY HORAK
SILENTLY, BOND COPES WITH THE TERRIFIED BELLHOP!
NEXT PROBLEM— HOW DO I GET OUT OF HERE UNSEEN, WITH THE HOTEL WIDE AWAKE?
2089

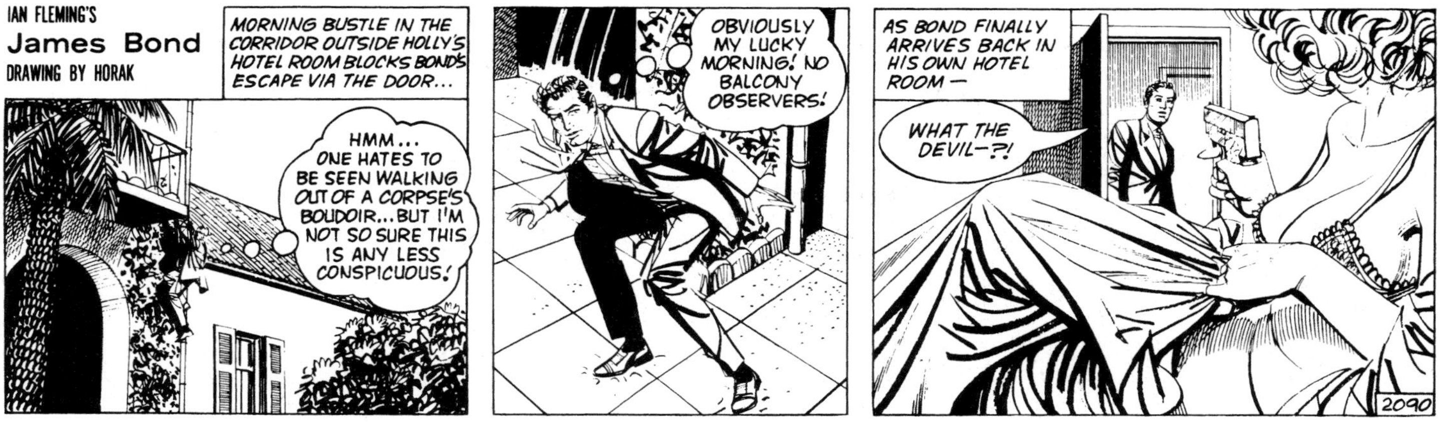
IAN FLEMING'S
James Bond
DRAWING BY HORAK
MORNING BUSTLE IN THE CORRIDOR OUTSIDE HOLLY'S HOTEL ROOM BLOCKS BOND'S ESCAPE VIA THE DOOR...
HMM... ONE HATES TO BE SEEN WALKING OUT OF A CORPSE'S BOUDOIR... BUT I'M NOT SO SURE THIS IS ANY LESS CONSPICUOUS!
OBVIOUSLY MY LUCKY MORNING! NO BALCONY OBSERVERS!
AS BOND FINALLY ARRIVES BACK IN HIS OWN HOTEL ROOM —
WHAT THE DEVIL—?!
2090

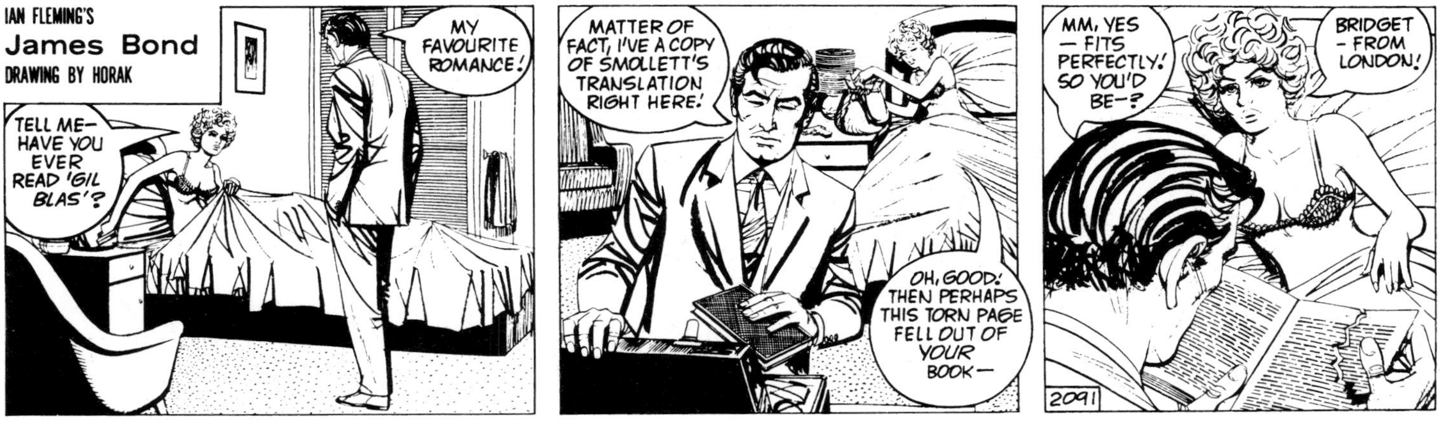
IAN FLEMING'S
James Bond
DRAWING BY HORAK
TELL ME— HAVE YOU EVER READ 'GIL BLAS'?
MY FAVOURITE ROMANCE!
MATTER OF FACT, I'VE A COPY OF SMOLLETT'S TRANSLATION RIGHT HERE!
OH, GOOD! THEN PERHAPS THIS TORN PAGE FELL OUT OF YOUR BOOK—
MM, YES — FITS PERFECTLY! SO YOU'D BE—?
BRIDGET - FROM LONDON!
2091

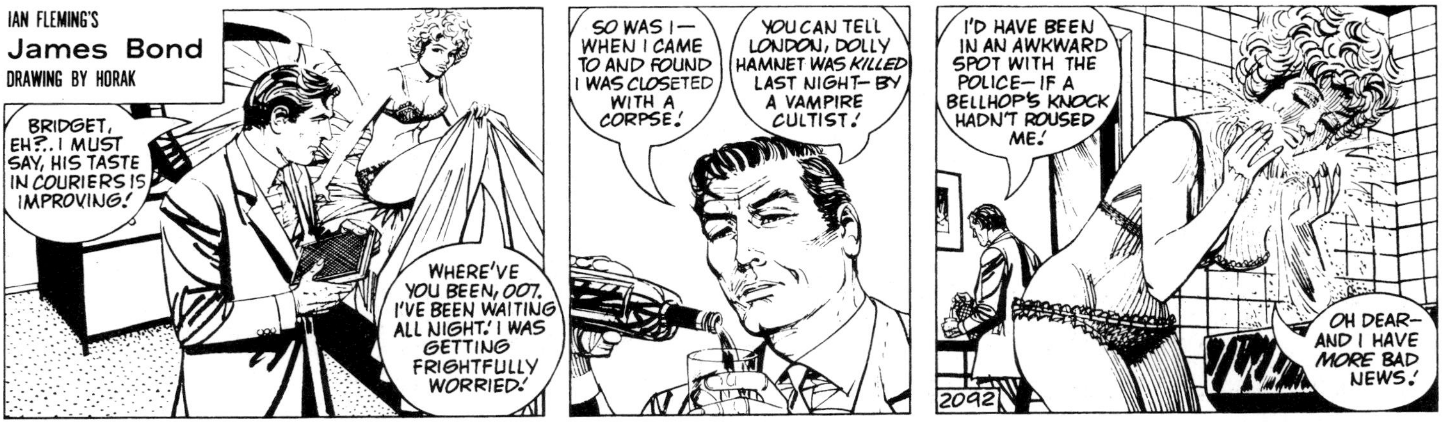
IAN FLEMING'S
James Bond
DRAWING BY HORAK
BRIDGET, EH?.. I MUST SAY, HIS TASTE IN COURIERS IS IMPROVING!
WHERE'VE YOU BEEN, 007. I'VE BEEN WAITING ALL NIGHT! I WAS GETTING FRIGHTFULLY WORRIED!
SO WAS I — WHEN I CAME TO AND FOUND I WAS CLOSETED WITH A CORPSE!
YOU CAN TELL LONDON, DOLLY HAMNET WAS KILLED LAST NIGHT— BY A VAMPIRE CULTIST!
I'D HAVE BEEN IN AN AWKWARD SPOT WITH THE POLICE— IF A BELLHOP'S KNOCK HADN'T ROUSED ME!
OH DEAR— AND I HAVE MORE BAD NEWS!
2092

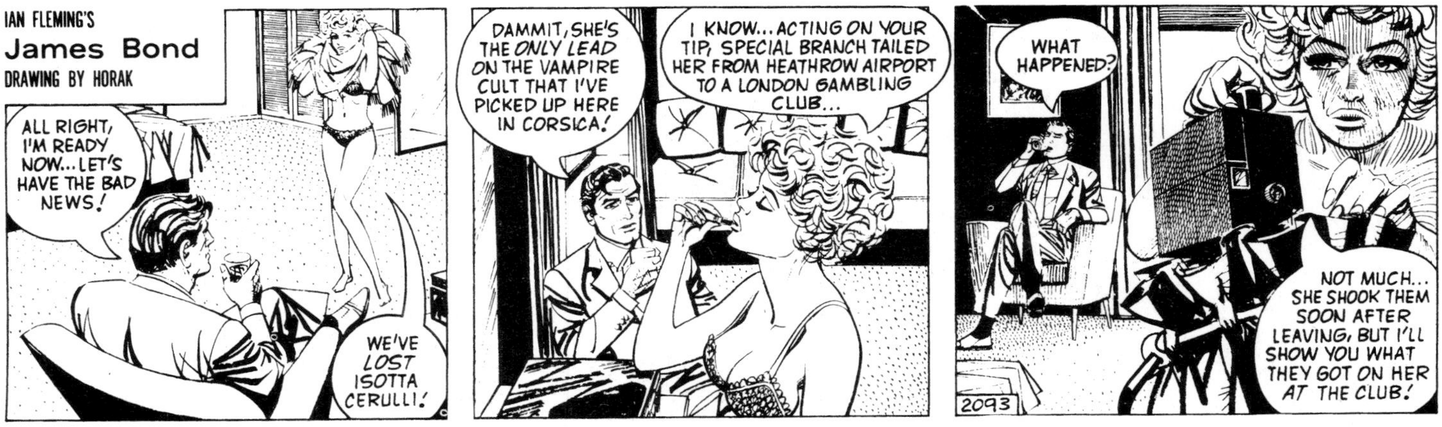
IAN FLEMING'S
James Bond
DRAWING BY HORAK
ALL RIGHT, I'M READY NOW... LET'S HAVE THE BAD NEWS!
WE'VE LOST ISOTTA CERULLI!
DAMMIT, SHE'S THE ONLY LEAD ON THE VAMPIRE CULT THAT I'VE PICKED UP HERE IN CORSICA!
I KNOW... ACTING ON YOUR TIP, SPECIAL BRANCH TAILED HER FROM HEATHROW AIRPORT TO A LONDON GAMBLING CLUB...
WHAT HAPPENED?
NOT MUCH... SHE SHOOK THEM SOON AFTER LEAVING, BUT I'LL SHOW YOU WHAT THEY GOT ON HER AT THE CLUB!
2093

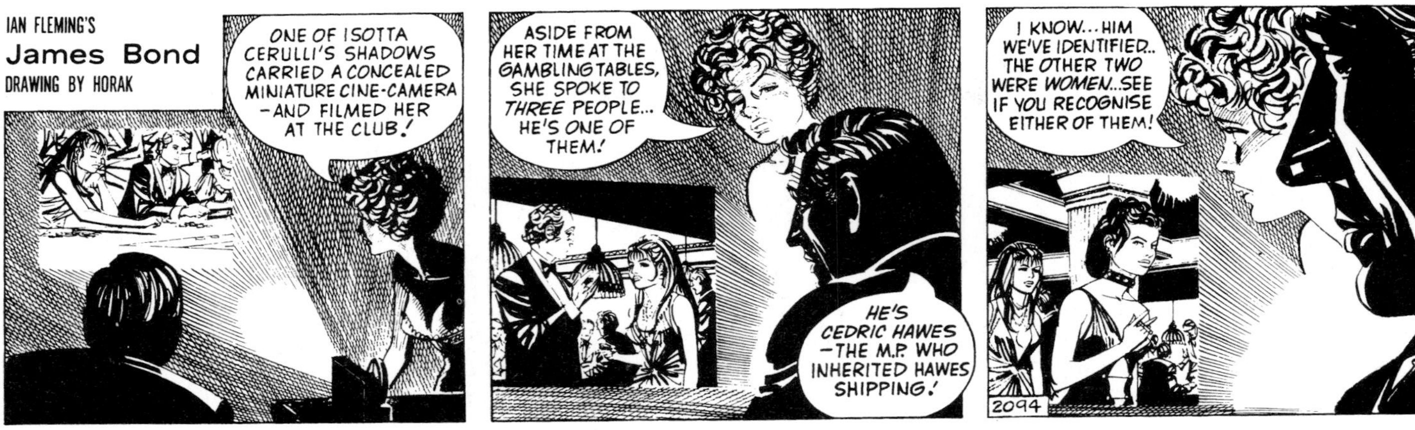
IAN FLEMING'S
James Bond
DRAWING BY HORAK
ONE OF ISOTTA CERULLI'S SHADOWS CARRIED A CONCEALED MINIATURE CINE-CAMERA —AND FILMED HER AT THE CLUB!
ASIDE FROM HER TIME AT THE GAMBLING TABLES, SHE SPOKE TO THREE PEOPLE... HE'S ONE OF THEM!
HE'S CEDRIC HAWES —THE M.P. WHO INHERITED HAWES SHIPPING!
I KNOW... HIM WE'VE IDENTIFIED.. THE OTHER TWO WERE WOMEN...SEE IF YOU RECOGNISE EITHER OF THEM!
2094

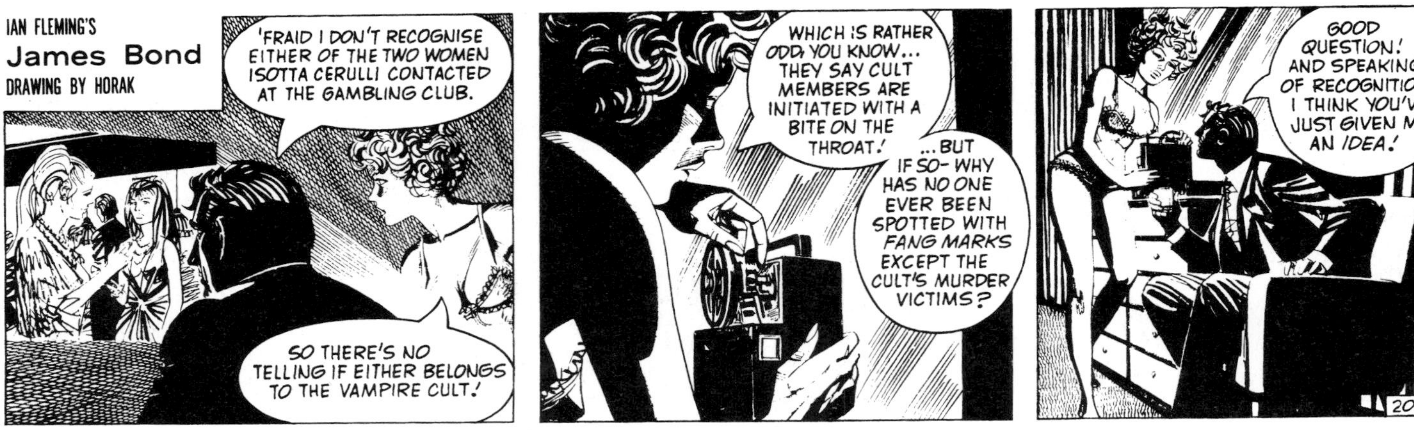
IAN FLEMING'S
James Bond
DRAWING BY HORAK
'FRAID I DON'T RECOGNISE EITHER OF THE TWO WOMEN ISOTTA CERULLI CONTACTED AT THE GAMBLING CLUB.
SO THERE'S NO TELLING IF EITHER BELONGS TO THE VAMPIRE CULT!
WHICH IS RATHER ODD, YOU KNOW... THEY SAY CULT MEMBERS ARE INITIATED WITH A BITE ON THE THROAT!
...BUT IF SO- WHY HAS NO ONE EVER BEEN SPOTTED WITH FANG MARKS EXCEPT THE CULT'S MURDER VICTIMS?
GOOD QUESTION! AND SPEAKING OF RECOGNITION- I THINK YOU'VE JUST GIVEN ME AN IDEA!
2095

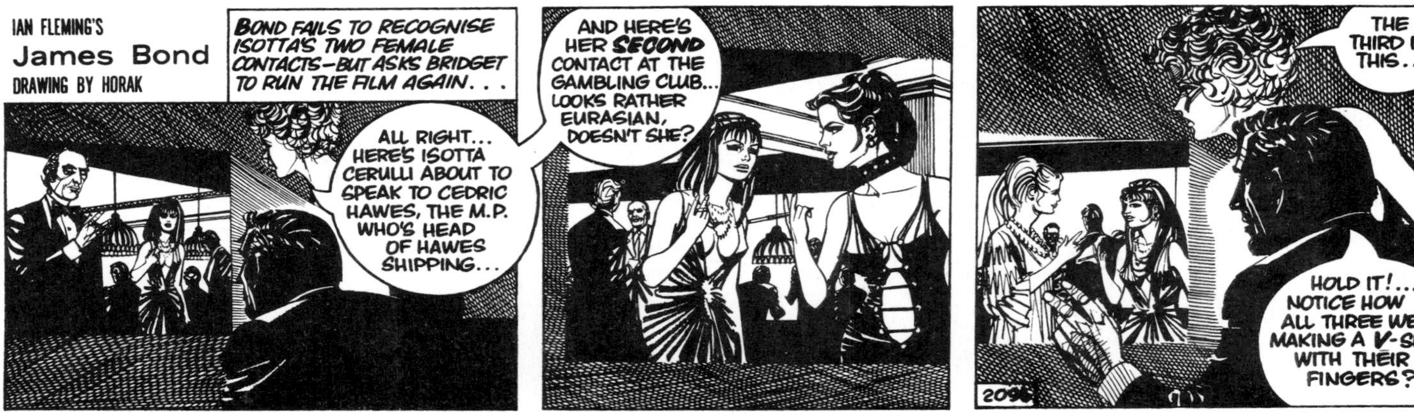
IAN FLEMING'S
James Bond
DRAWING BY HORAK
BOND FAILS TO RECOGNISE ISOTTA'S TWO FEMALE CONTACTS—BUT ASKS BRIDGET TO RUN THE FILM AGAIN...
ALL RIGHT... HERE'S ISOTTA CERULLI ABOUT TO SPEAK TO CEDRIC HAWES, THE M.P. WHO'S HEAD OF HAWES SHIPPING...
AND HERE'S HER SECOND CONTACT AT THE GAMBLING CLUB... LOOKS RATHER EURASIAN, DOESN'T SHE?
THE THIRD IS THIS...
HOLD IT!... NOTICE HOW ALL THREE WERE MAKING A V-SIGN WITH THEIR FINGERS?

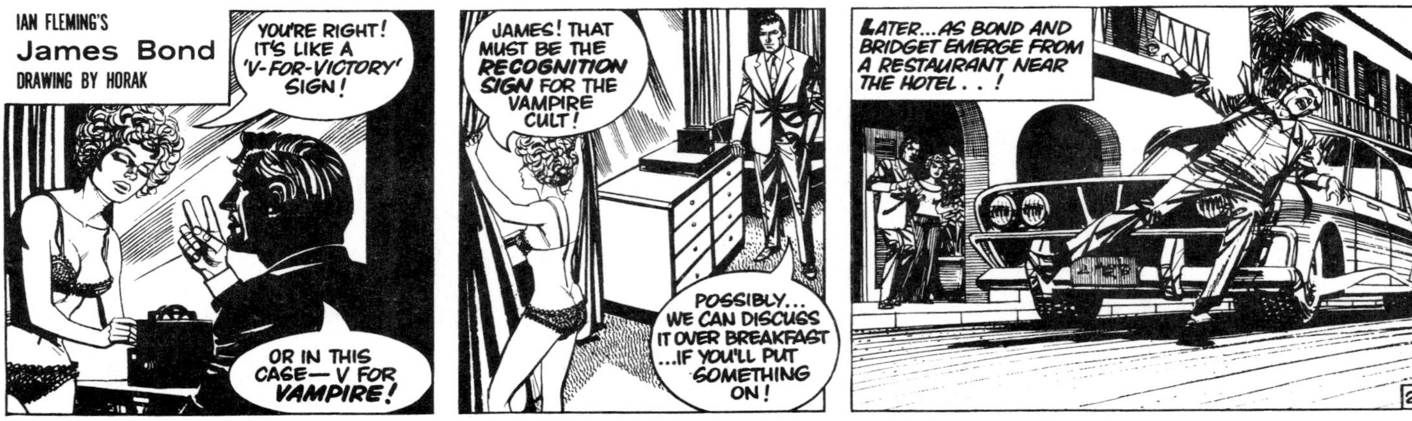
IAN FLEMING'S
James Bond
DRAWING BY HORAK
YOU'RE RIGHT! IT'S LIKE A 'V-FOR-VICTORY' SIGN!
OR IN THIS CASE— V FOR VAMPIRE!
JAMES! THAT MUST BE THE RECOGNITION SIGN FOR THE VAMPIRE CULT!
POSSIBLY... WE CAN DISCUSS IT OVER BREAKFAST ...IF YOU'LL PUT SOMETHING ON!
LATER... AS BOND AND BRIDGET EMERGE FROM A RESTAURANT NEAR THE HOTEL..!
2097

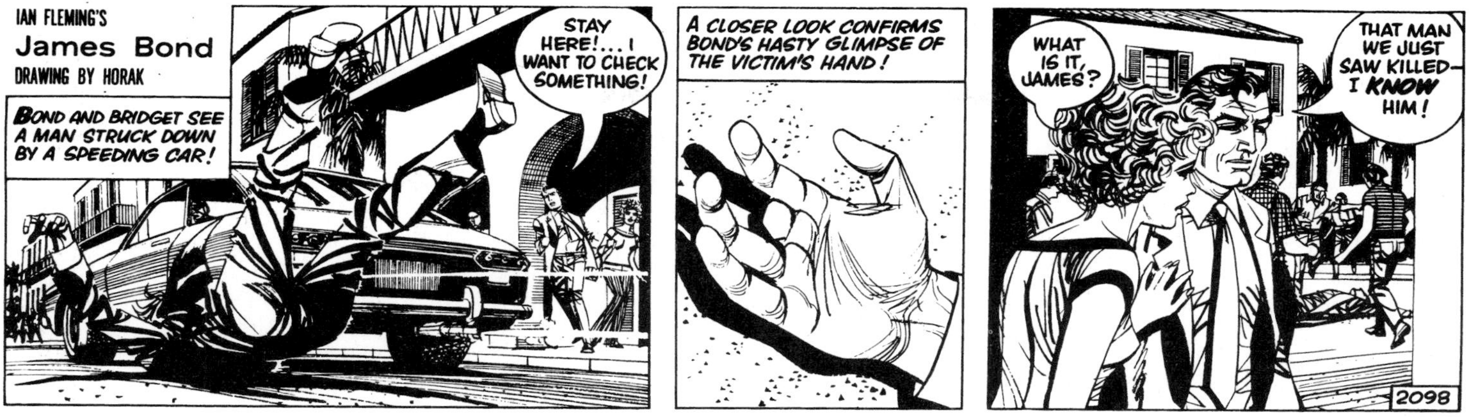
IAN FLEMING'S
James Bond
DRAWING BY HORAK
BOND AND BRIDGET SEE A MAN STRUCK DOWN BY A SPEEDING CAR!
STAY HERE!... I WANT TO CHECK SOMETHING!
A CLOSER LOOK CONFIRMS BOND'S HASTY GLIMPSE OF THE VICTIM'S HAND!
WHAT IS IT, JAMES?
THAT MAN WE JUST SAW KILLED— I KNOW HIM!
2098

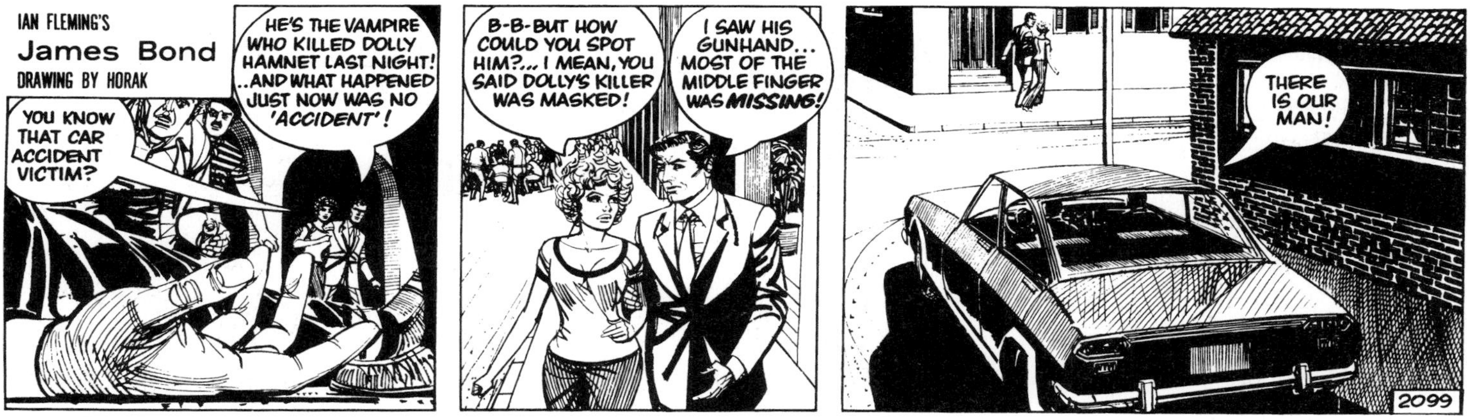
IAN FLEMING'S
James Bond
DRAWING BY HORAK
YOU KNOW THAT CAR ACCIDENT VICTIM?
HE'S THE VAMPIRE WHO KILLED DOLLY HAMNET LAST NIGHT! ..AND WHAT HAPPENED JUST NOW WAS NO 'ACCIDENT'!
B-B-BUT HOW COULD YOU SPOT HIM?... I MEAN, YOU SAID DOLLY'S KILLER WAS MASKED!
I SAW HIS GUNHAND... MOST OF THE MIDDLE FINGER WAS MISSING!
THERE IS OUR MAN!
2099

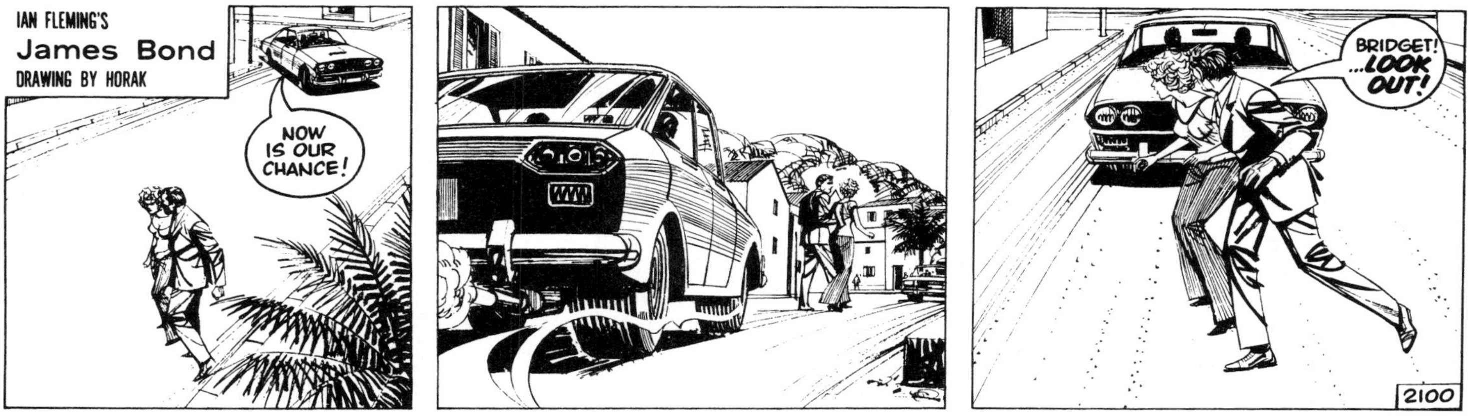
IAN FLEMING'S
James Bond
DRAWING BY HORAK
NOW IS OUR CHANCE!
BRIDGET! ...LOOK OUT!
2100

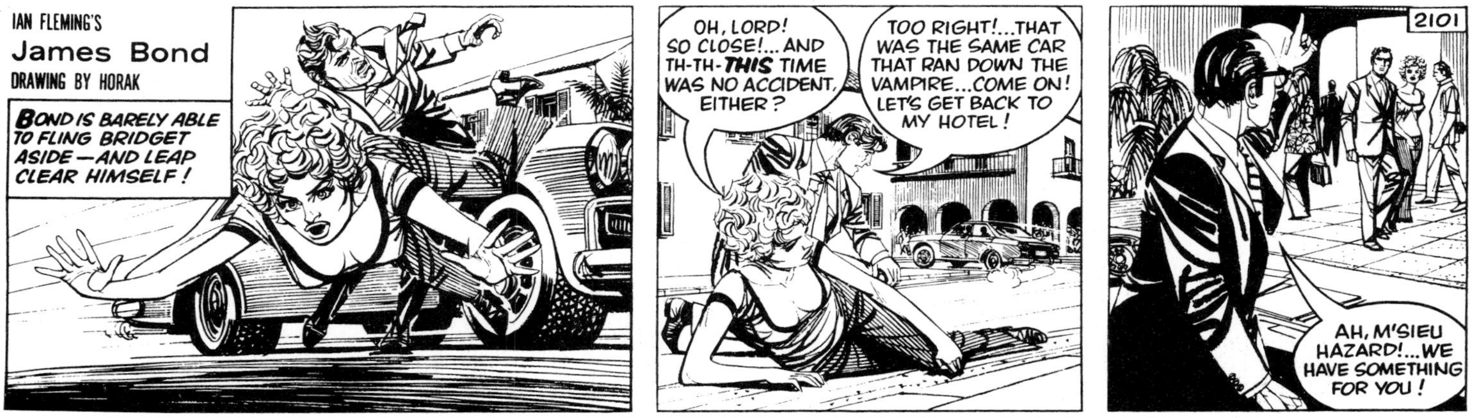
IAN FLEMING'S
James Bond
DRAWING BY HORAK
BOND IS BARELY ABLE TO FLING BRIDGET ASIDE—AND LEAP CLEAR HIMSELF!
OH, LORD! SO CLOSE!... AND TH-TH-THIS TIME WAS NO ACCIDENT, EITHER?
TOO RIGHT!...THAT WAS THE SAME CAR THAT RAN DOWN THE VAMPIRE...COME ON! LET'S GET BACK TO MY HOTEL!
2101
AH, M'SIEU HAZARD!... WE HAVE SOMETHING FOR YOU!

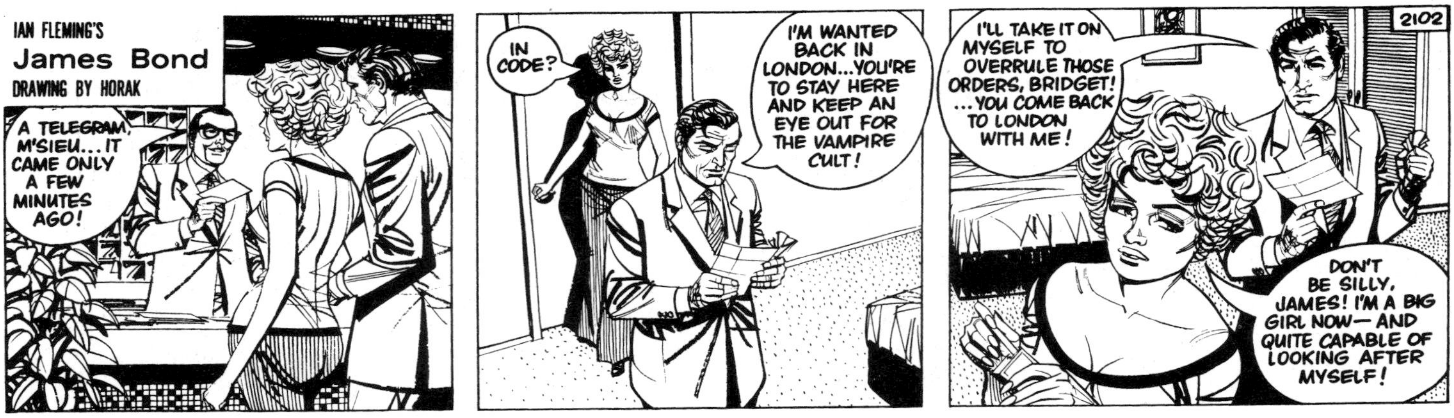
IAN FLEMING'S
James Bond
DRAWING BY HORAK
A TELEGRAM, M'SIEU... IT CAME ONLY A FEW MINUTES AGO!
IN CODE?
I'M WANTED BACK IN LONDON... YOU'RE TO STAY HERE AND KEEP AN EYE OUT FOR THE VAMPIRE CULT!
2102
I'LL TAKE IT ON MYSELF TO OVERRULE THOSE ORDERS, BRIDGET! ... YOU COME BACK TO LONDON WITH ME!
DON'T BE SILLY, JAMES! I'M A BIG GIRL NOW— AND QUITE CAPABLE OF LOOKING AFTER MYSELF!

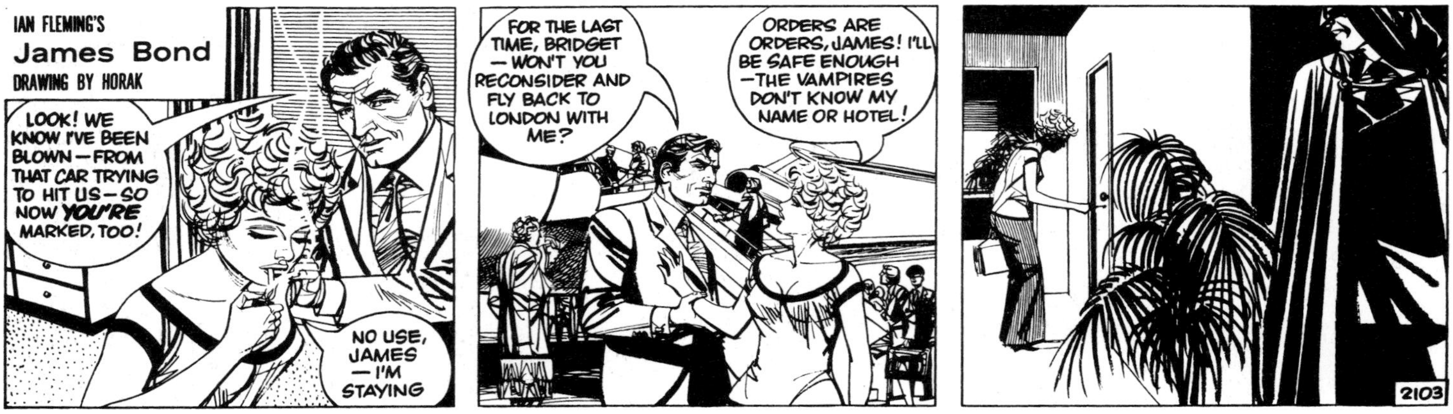
IAN FLEMING'S
James Bond
DRAWING BY HORAK
LOOK! WE KNOW I'VE BEEN BLOWN—FROM THAT CAR TRYING TO HIT US—SO NOW YOU'RE MARKED, TOO!
NO USE, JAMES —I'M STAYING
FOR THE LAST TIME, BRIDGET —WON'T YOU RECONSIDER AND FLY BACK TO LONDON WITH ME?
ORDERS ARE ORDERS, JAMES! I'LL BE SAFE ENOUGH —THE VAMPIRES DON'T KNOW MY NAME OR HOTEL!
2103

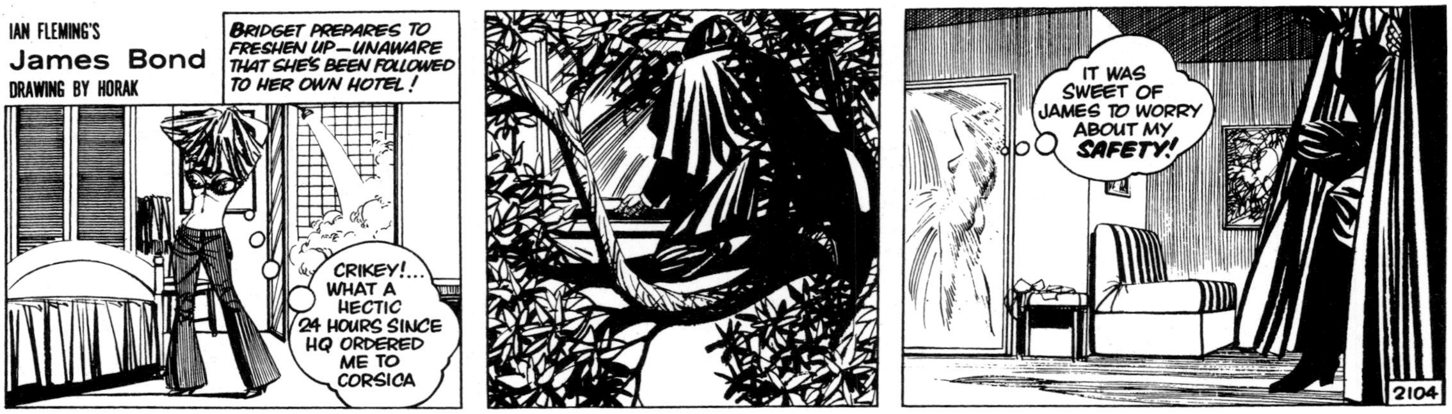
IAN FLEMING'S
James Bond
DRAWING BY HORAK
BRIDGET PREPARES TO FRESHEN UP—UNAWARE THAT SHE'S BEEN FOLLOWED TO HER OWN HOTEL!
CRIKEY!... WHAT A HECTIC 24 HOURS SINCE HQ ORDERED ME TO CORSICA
IT WAS SWEET OF JAMES TO WORRY ABOUT MY SAFETY!
2104

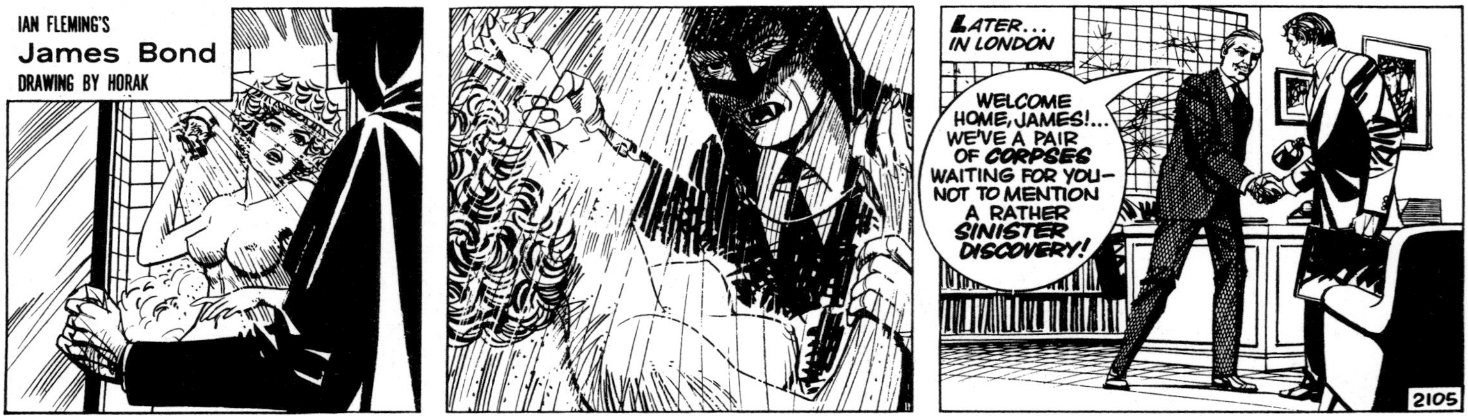
IAN FLEMING'S
James Bond
DRAWING BY HORAK
LATER... IN LONDON
WELCOME HOME, JAMES!... WE'VE A PAIR OF CORPSES WAITING FOR YOU— NOT TO MENTION A RATHER SINISTER DISCOVERY!
2105

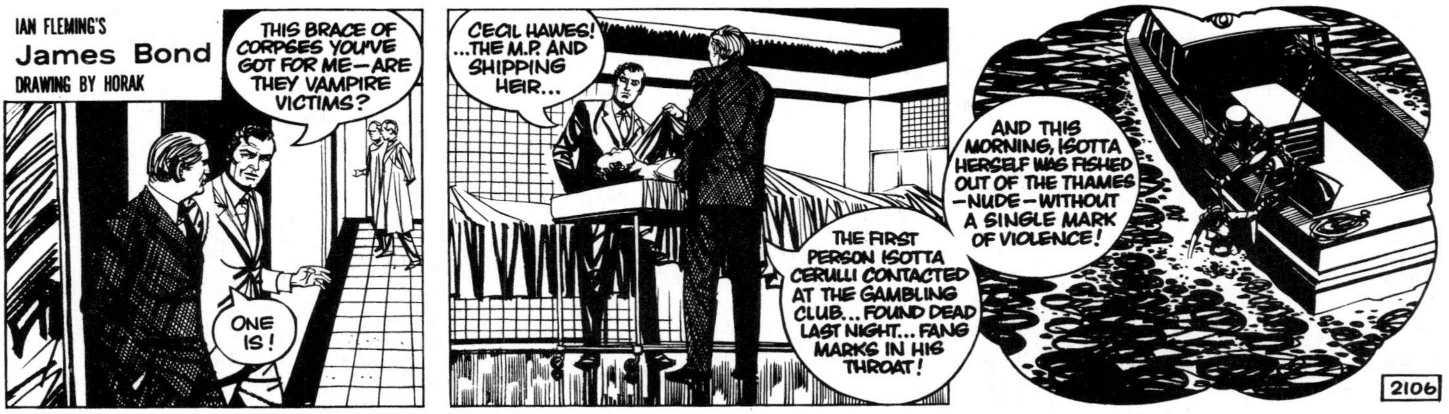
IAN FLEMING'S
James Bond
DRAWING BY HORAK
THIS BRACE OF CORPSES YOU'VE GOT FOR ME—ARE THEY VAMPIRE VICTIMS?
ONE IS!
CECIL HAWES! ...THE M.P. AND SHIPPING HEIR...
THE FIRST PERSON ISOTTA CERULLI CONTACTED AT THE GAMBLING CLUB... FOUND DEAD LAST NIGHT... FANG MARKS IN HIS THROAT!
AND THIS MORNING, ISOTTA HERSELF WAS FISHED OUT OF THE THAMES —NUDE—WITHOUT A SINGLE MARK OF VIOLENCE!
2106

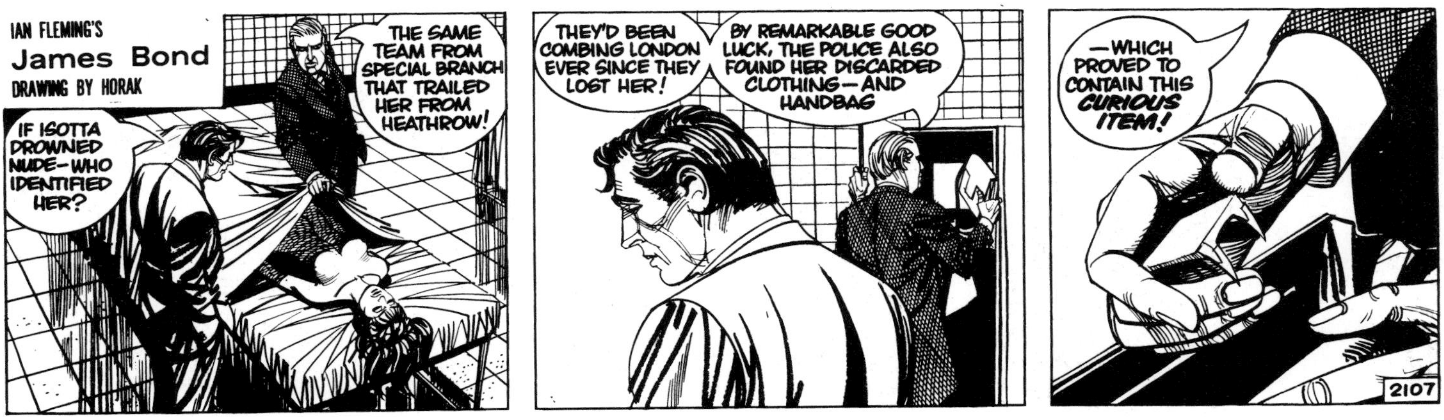
IAN FLEMING'S
James Bond
DRAWING BY HORAK
IF ISOTTA DROWNED NUDE—WHO IDENTIFIED HER?
THE SAME TEAM FROM SPECIAL BRANCH THAT TRAILED HER FROM HEATHROW!
THEY'D BEEN COMBING LONDON EVER SINCE THEY LOST HER!
BY REMARKABLE GOOD LUCK, THE POLICE ALSO FOUND HER DISCARDED CLOTHING—AND HANDBAG
—WHICH PROVED TO CONTAIN THIS CURIOUS ITEM!
2107

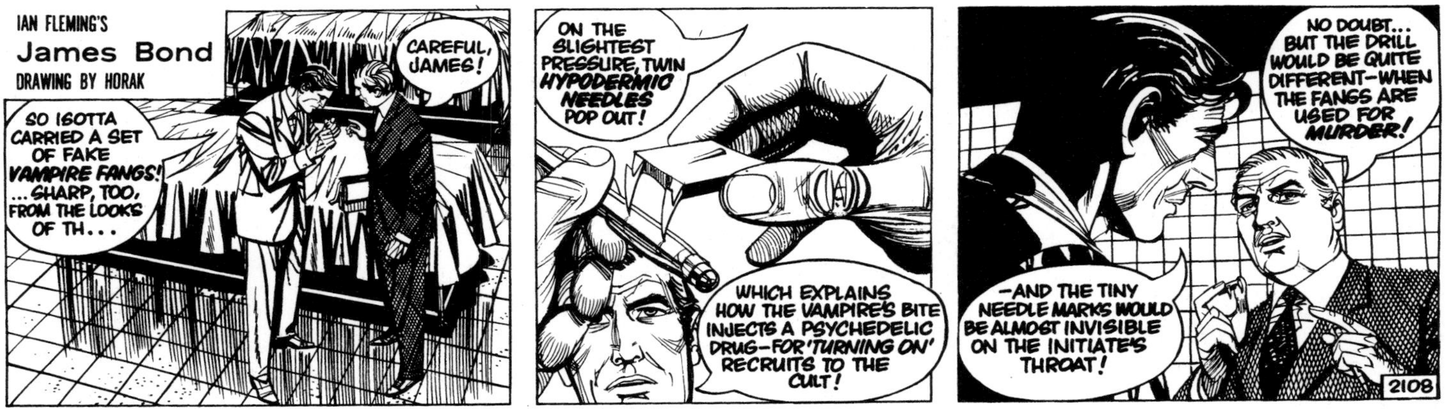
IAN FLEMING'S
James Bond
DRAWING BY HORAK
SO ISOTTA CARRIED A SET OF FAKE VAMPIRE FANGS! ... SHARP, TOO, FROM THE LOOKS OF TH...
CAREFUL, JAMES!
ON THE SLIGHTEST PRESSURE, TWIN HYPODERMIC NEEDLES POP OUT!
WHICH EXPLAINS HOW THE VAMPIRE'S BITE INJECTS A PSYCHEDELIC DRUG—FOR 'TURNING ON' RECRUITS TO THE CULT!
NO DOUBT... BUT THE DRILL WOULD BE QUITE DIFFERENT—WHEN THE FANGS ARE USED FOR MURDER!
—AND THE TINY NEEDLE MARKS WOULD BE ALMOST INVISIBLE ON THE INITIATE'S THROAT!
2108

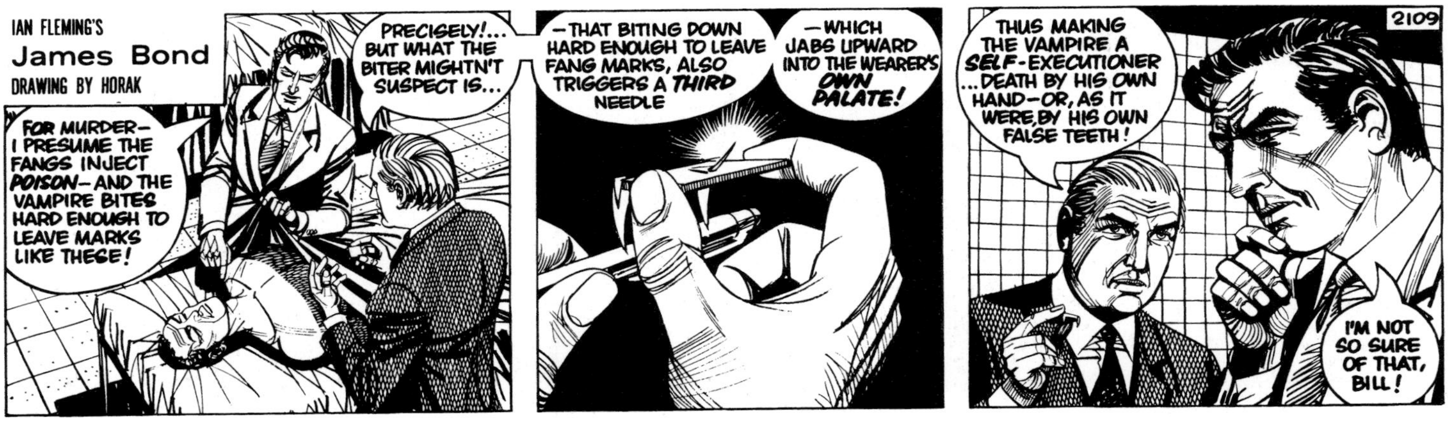
IAN FLEMING'S
James Bond
DRAWING BY HORAK
FOR MURDER— I PRESUME THE FANGS INJECT POISON—AND THE VAMPIRE BITES HARD ENOUGH TO LEAVE MARKS LIKE THESE!
PRECISELY!... BUT WHAT THE BITER MIGHTN'T SUSPECT IS...
—THAT BITING DOWN HARD ENOUGH TO LEAVE FANG MARKS, ALSO TRIGGERS A THIRD NEEDLE
—WHICH JABS UPWARD INTO THE WEARER'S OWN PALATE!
THUS MAKING THE VAMPIRE A SELF-EXECUTIONER ...DEATH BY HIS OWN HAND—OR, AS IT WERE, BY HIS OWN FALSE TEETH!
I'M NOT SO SURE OF THAT, BILL!
2109

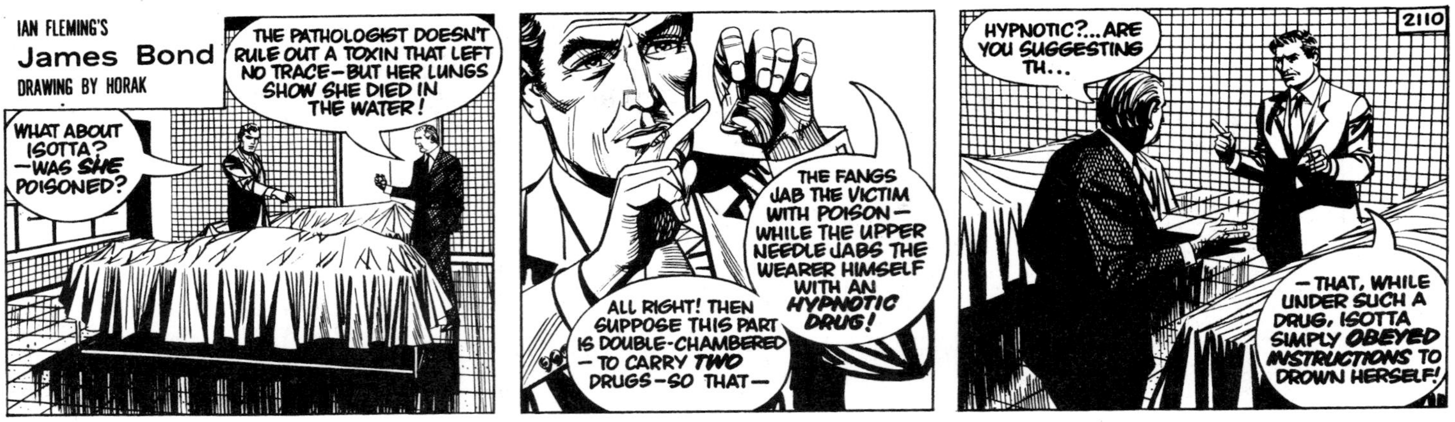
IAN FLEMING'S
James Bond
DRAWING BY HORAK
2110
WHAT ABOUT ISOTTA? —WAS SHE POISONED?
THE PATHOLOGIST DOESN'T RULE OUT A TOXIN THAT LEFT NO TRACE—BUT HER LUNGS SHOW SHE DIED IN THE WATER!
ALL RIGHT! THEN SUPPOSE THIS PART IS DOUBLE-CHAMBERED —TO CARRY TWO DRUGS—SO THAT—
THE FANGS JAB THE VICTIM WITH POISON—WHILE THE UPPER NEEDLE JABS THE WEARER HIMSELF WITH AN HYPNOTIC DRUG!
HYPNOTIC?...ARE YOU SUGGESTING TH...
—THAT, WHILE UNDER SUCH A DRUG, ISOTTA SIMPLY OBEYED INSTRUCTIONS TO DROWN HERSELF!

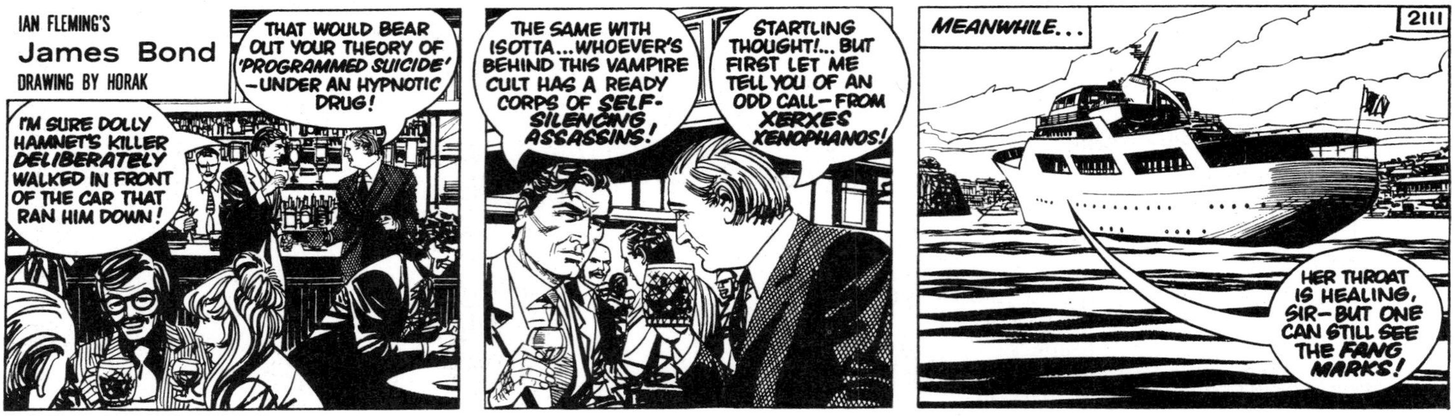
IAN FLEMING'S
James Bond
DRAWING BY HORAK
I'M SURE DOLLY HAMNET'S KILLER DELIBERATELY WALKED IN FRONT OF THE CAR THAT RAN HIM DOWN!
THAT WOULD BEAR OUT YOUR THEORY OF 'PROGRAMMED SUICIDE' —UNDER AN HYPNOTIC DRUG!
THE SAME WITH ISOTTA...WHOEVER'S BEHIND THIS VAMPIRE CULT HAS A READY CORPS OF SELF-SILENCING ASSASSINS!
STARTLING THOUGHT!... BUT FIRST LET ME TELL YOU OF AN ODD CALL—FROM XERXES XENOPHANOS!
MEANWHILE...
2111
HER THROAT IS HEALING, SIR—BUT ONE CAN STILL SEE THE FANG MARKS!

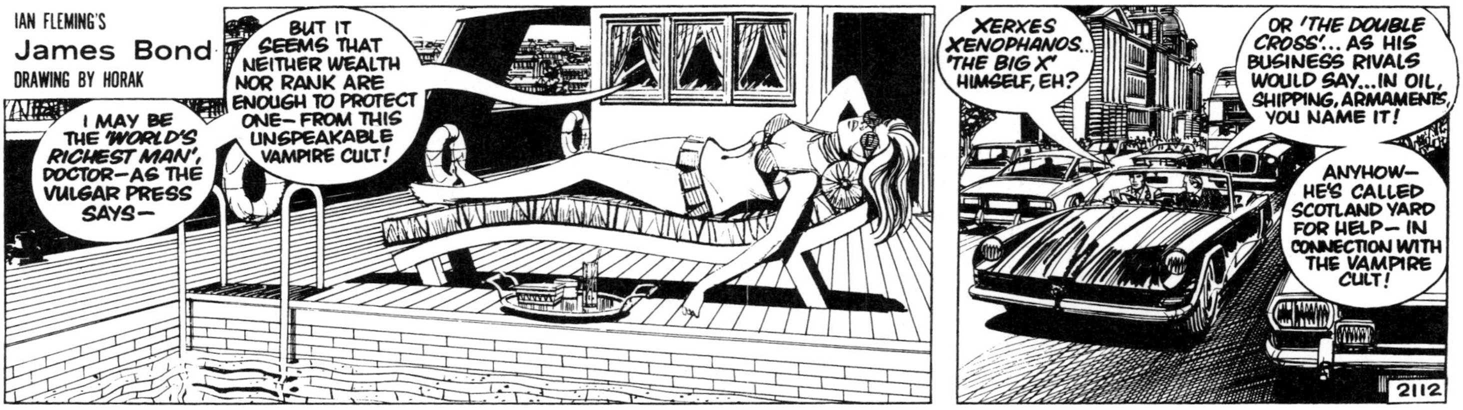
IAN FLEMING'S
James Bond
DRAWING BY HORAK
I MAY BE THE 'WORLD'S RICHEST MAN', DOCTOR—AS THE VULGAR PRESS SAYS—
BUT IT SEEMS THAT NEITHER WEALTH NOR RANK ARE ENOUGH TO PROTECT ONE—FROM THIS UNSPEAKABLE VAMPIRE CULT!
XERXES XENOPHANOS... 'THE BIG X' HIMSELF, EH?
OR 'THE DOUBLE CROSS'... AS HIS BUSINESS RIVALS WOULD SAY...IN OIL, SHIPPING, ARMAMENTS, YOU NAME IT!
ANYHOW—HE'S CALLED SCOTLAND YARD FOR HELP—IN CONNECTION WITH THE VAMPIRE CULT!
2112

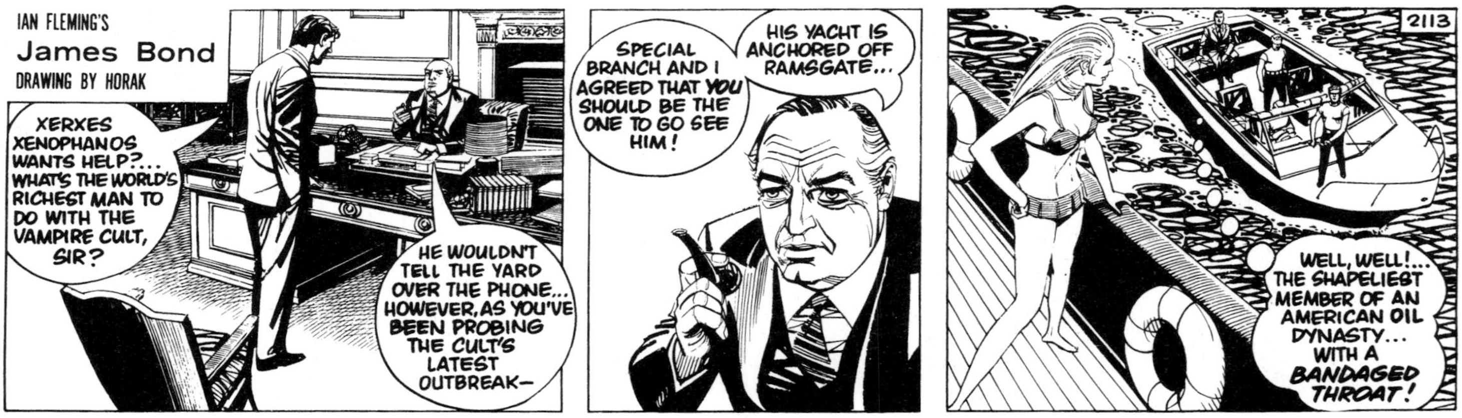
IAN FLEMING'S
James Bond
DRAWING BY HORAK
XERXES XENOPHANOS WANTS HELP?... WHAT'S THE WORLD'S RICHEST MAN TO DO WITH THE VAMPIRE CULT, SIR?
HE WOULDN'T TELL THE YARD OVER THE PHONE... HOWEVER, AS YOU'VE BEEN PROBING THE CULT'S LATEST OUTBREAK—
SPECIAL BRANCH AND I AGREED THAT YOU SHOULD BE THE ONE TO GO SEE HIM!
HIS YACHT IS ANCHORED OFF RAMSGATE...
2113
WELL, WELL!... THE SHAPELIEST MEMBER OF AN AMERICAN OIL DYNASTY... WITH A BANDAGED THROAT!

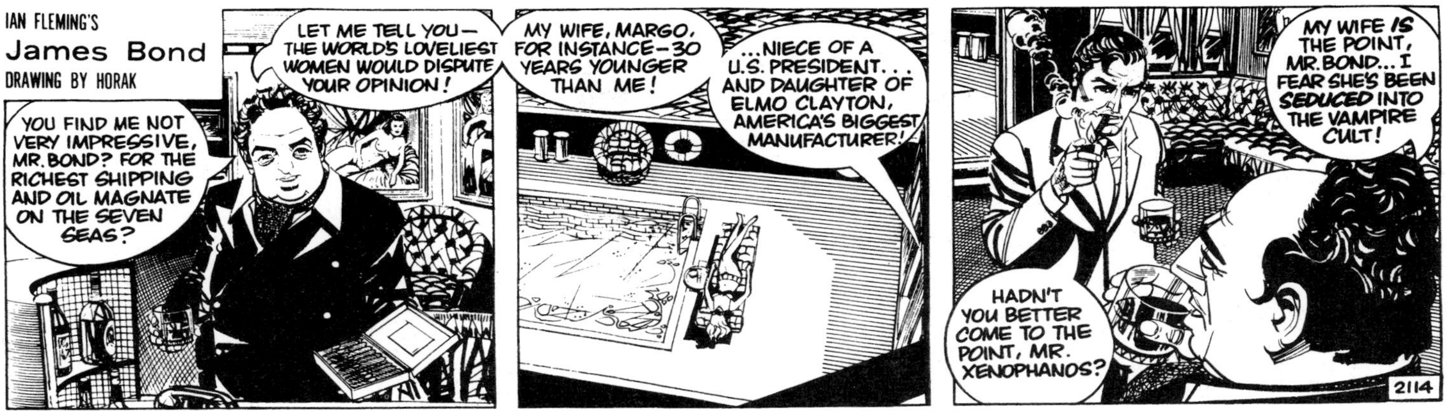
IAN FLEMING'S
James Bond
DRAWING BY HORAK
YOU FIND ME NOT VERY IMPRESSIVE, MR. BOND? FOR THE RICHEST SHIPPING AND OIL MAGNATE ON THE SEVEN SEAS?
LET ME TELL YOU— THE WORLD'S LOVELIEST WOMEN WOULD DISPUTE YOUR OPINION!
MY WIFE, MARGO, FOR INSTANCE—30 YEARS YOUNGER THAN ME!
...NIECE OF A U.S. PRESIDENT... AND DAUGHTER OF ELMO CLAYTON, AMERICA'S BIGGEST MANUFACTURER!
HADN'T YOU BETTER COME TO THE POINT, MR. XENOPHANOS?
MY WIFE **IS** THE POINT, MR. BOND... I FEAR SHE'S BEEN **SEDUCED** INTO THE VAMPIRE CULT!
2114

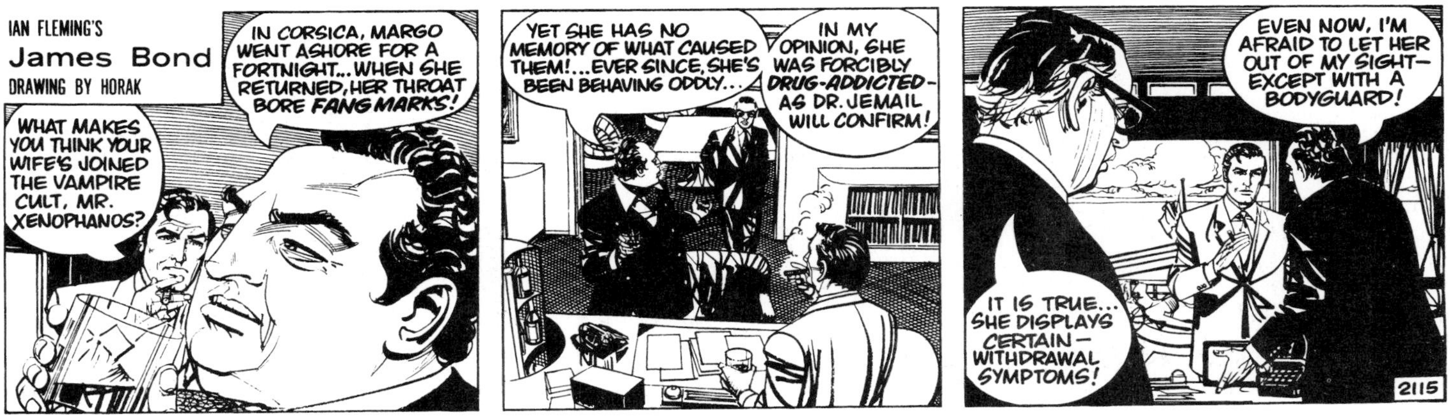
IAN FLEMING'S
James Bond
DRAWING BY HORAK
WHAT MAKES YOU THINK YOUR WIFE'S JOINED THE VAMPIRE CULT, MR. XENOPHANOS?
IN CORSICA, MARGO WENT ASHORE FOR A FORTNIGHT... WHEN SHE RETURNED, HER THROAT BORE **FANG MARKS**!
YET SHE HAS NO MEMORY OF WHAT CAUSED THEM!... EVER SINCE, SHE'S BEEN BEHAVING ODDLY...
IN MY OPINION, SHE WAS FORCIBLY **DRUG-ADDICTED**—AS DR. JEMAIL WILL CONFIRM!
IT IS TRUE... SHE DISPLAYS CERTAIN—WITHDRAWAL SYMPTOMS!
EVEN NOW, I'M AFRAID TO LET HER OUT OF MY SIGHT— EXCEPT WITH A BODYGUARD!
2115

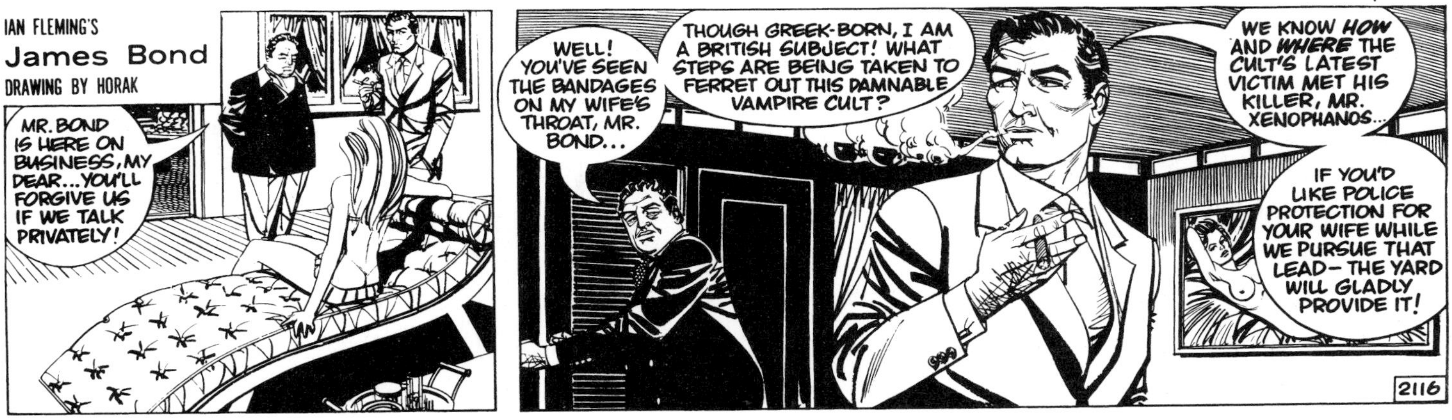
IAN FLEMING'S
James Bond
DRAWING BY HORAK
MR. BOND IS HERE ON BUSINESS, MY DEAR... YOU'LL FORGIVE US IF WE TALK PRIVATELY!
WELL! YOU'VE SEEN THE BANDAGES ON MY WIFE'S THROAT, MR. BOND...
THOUGH GREEK-BORN, I AM A BRITISH SUBJECT! WHAT STEPS ARE BEING TAKEN TO FERRET OUT THIS DAMNABLE VAMPIRE CULT?
WE KNOW **HOW** AND **WHERE** THE CULT'S LATEST VICTIM MET HIS KILLER, MR. XENOPHANOS...
IF YOU'D LIKE POLICE PROTECTION FOR YOUR WIFE WHILE WE PURSUE THAT LEAD—THE YARD WILL GLADLY PROVIDE IT!
2116

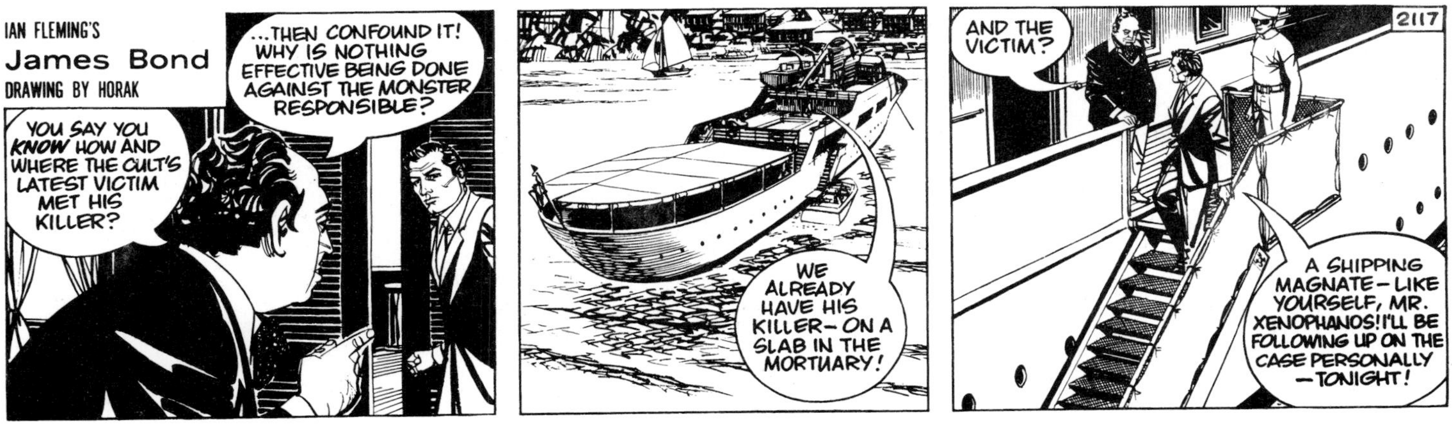
IAN FLEMING'S
James Bond
DRAWING BY HORAK
YOU SAY YOU **KNOW** HOW AND WHERE THE CULT'S LATEST VICTIM MET HIS KILLER?
...THEN CONFOUND IT! WHY IS NOTHING EFFECTIVE BEING DONE AGAINST THE MONSTER RESPONSIBLE?
WE ALREADY HAVE HIS KILLER—ON A SLAB IN THE MORTUARY!
AND THE VICTIM?
A SHIPPING MAGNATE—LIKE YOURSELF, MR. XENOPHANOS! I'LL BE FOLLOWING UP ON THE CASE PERSONALLY —TONIGHT!
2117

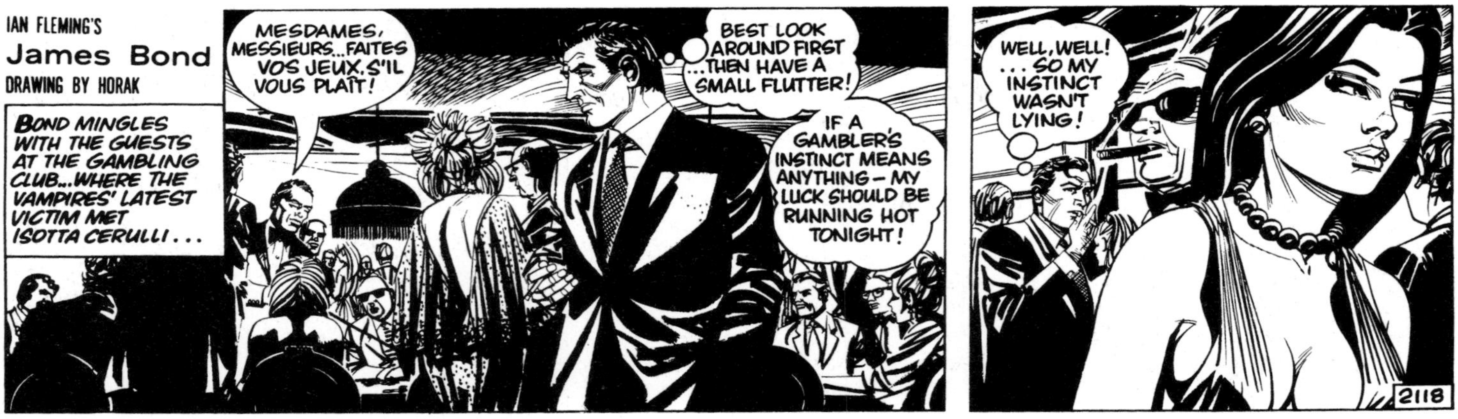
IAN FLEMING'S
James Bond
DRAWING BY HORAK
BOND MINGLES WITH THE GUESTS AT THE GAMBLING CLUB...WHERE THE VAMPIRES' LATEST VICTIM MET ISOTTA CERULLI...
MESDAMES, MESSIEURS...FAITES VOS JEUX, S'IL VOUS PLAÎT!
BEST LOOK AROUND FIRST ...THEN HAVE A SMALL FLUTTER!
IF A GAMBLER'S INSTINCT MEANS ANYTHING – MY LUCK SHOULD BE RUNNING HOT TONIGHT!
WELL, WELL! ...SO MY INSTINCT WASN'T LYING!
2118

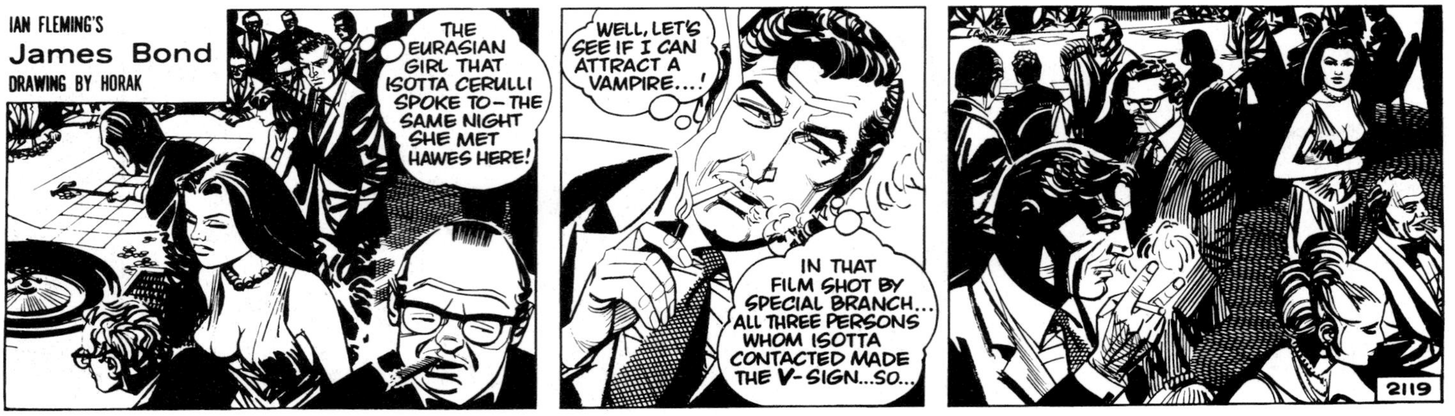
IAN FLEMING'S
James Bond
DRAWING BY HORAK
THE EURASIAN GIRL THAT ISOTTA CERULLI SPOKE TO – THE SAME NIGHT SHE MET HAWES HERE!
WELL, LET'S SEE IF I CAN ATTRACT A VAMPIRE...!
IN THAT FILM SHOT BY SPECIAL BRANCH... ALL THREE PERSONS WHOM ISOTTA CONTACTED MADE THE V-SIGN...SO...
2119

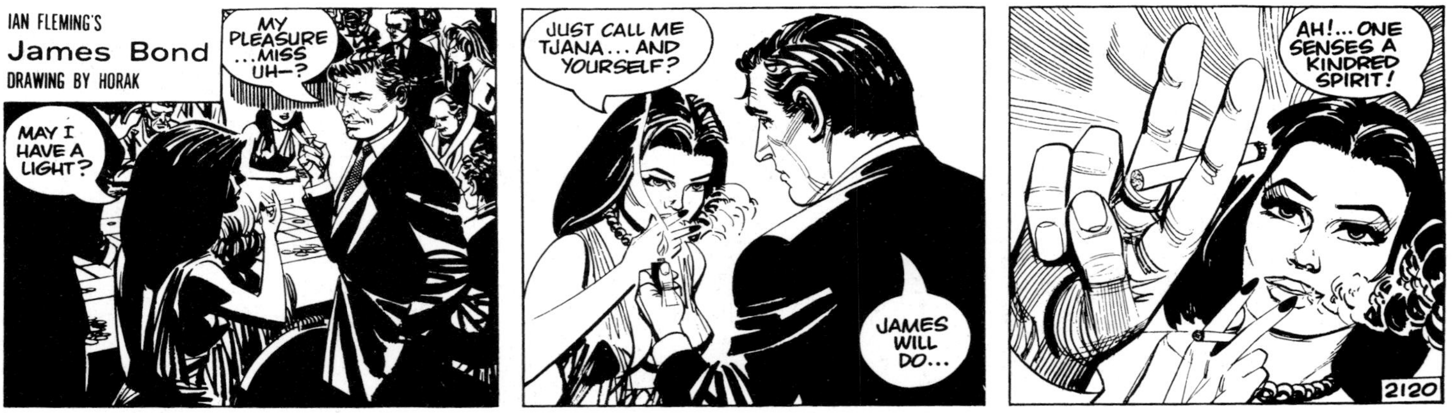
IAN FLEMING'S
James Bond
DRAWING BY HORAK
MAY I HAVE A LIGHT?
MY PLEASURE ...MISS UH–?
JUST CALL ME TJANA... AND YOURSELF?
JAMES WILL DO...
AH!... ONE SENSES A KINDRED SPIRIT!
2120

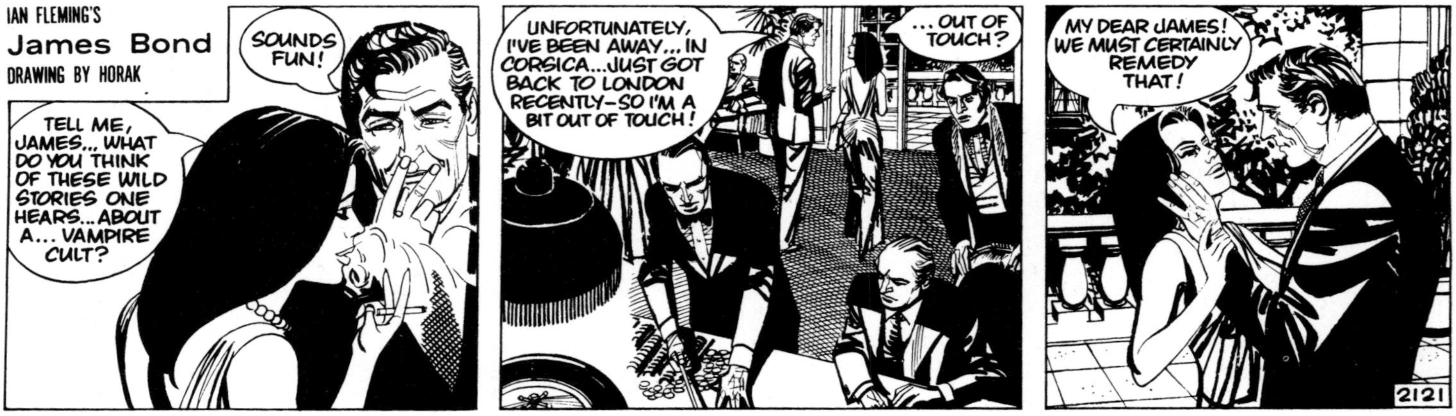
IAN FLEMING'S
James Bond
DRAWING BY HORAK
TELL ME, JAMES... WHAT DO YOU THINK OF THESE WILD STORIES ONE HEARS...ABOUT A... VAMPIRE CULT?
SOUNDS FUN!
UNFORTUNATELY, I'VE BEEN AWAY... IN CORSICA...JUST GOT BACK TO LONDON RECENTLY–SO I'M A BIT OUT OF TOUCH!
...OUT OF TOUCH?
MY DEAR JAMES! WE MUST CERTAINLY REMEDY THAT!
2121

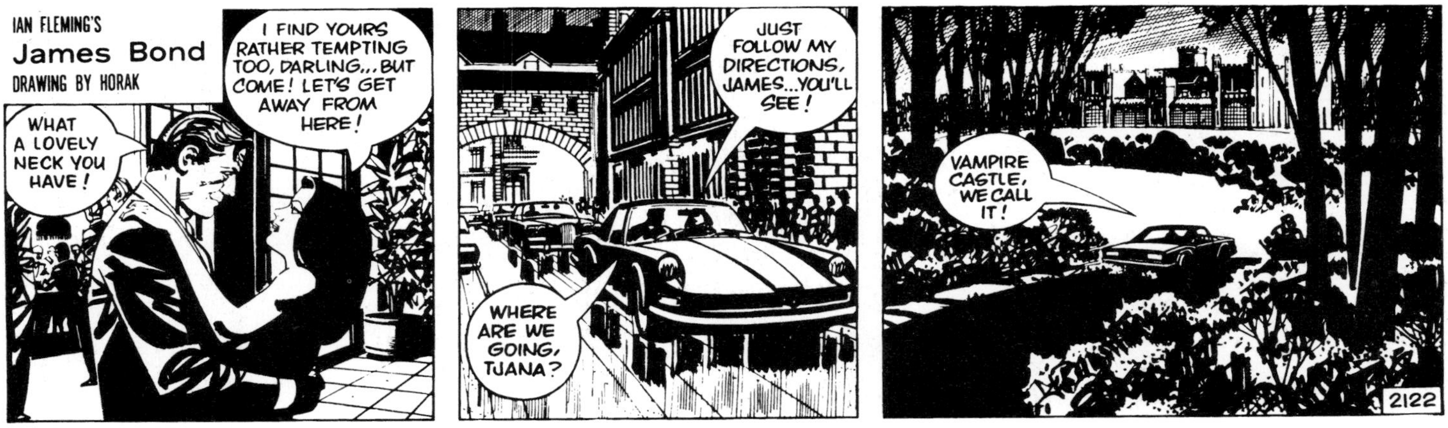
IAN FLEMING'S
James Bond
DRAWING BY HORAK
WHAT A LOVELY NECK YOU HAVE!
I FIND YOURS RATHER TEMPTING TOO, DARLING,.. BUT COME! LET'S GET AWAY FROM HERE!
JUST FOLLOW MY DIRECTIONS, JAMES... YOU'LL SEE!
WHERE ARE WE GOING, TJANA?
VAMPIRE CASTLE, WE CALL IT!
2122

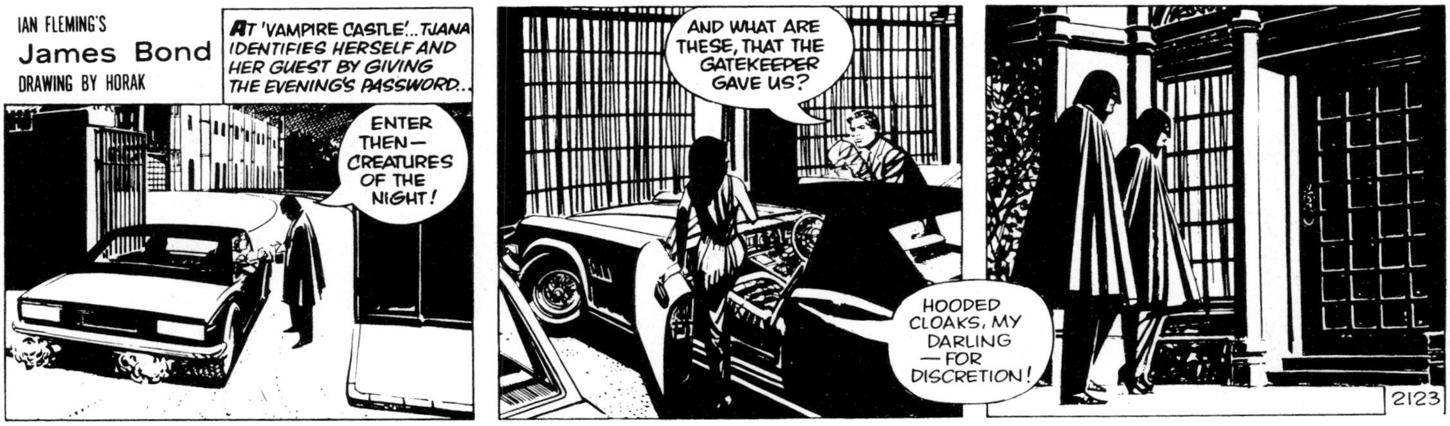
IAN FLEMING'S
James Bond
DRAWING BY HORAK
AT 'VAMPIRE CASTLE'... TJANA IDENTIFIES HERSELF AND HER GUEST BY GIVING THE EVENING'S PASSWORD...
ENTER THEN— CREATURES OF THE NIGHT!
AND WHAT ARE THESE, THAT THE GATEKEEPER GAVE US?
HOODED CLOAKS, MY DARLING —FOR DISCRETION!
2123

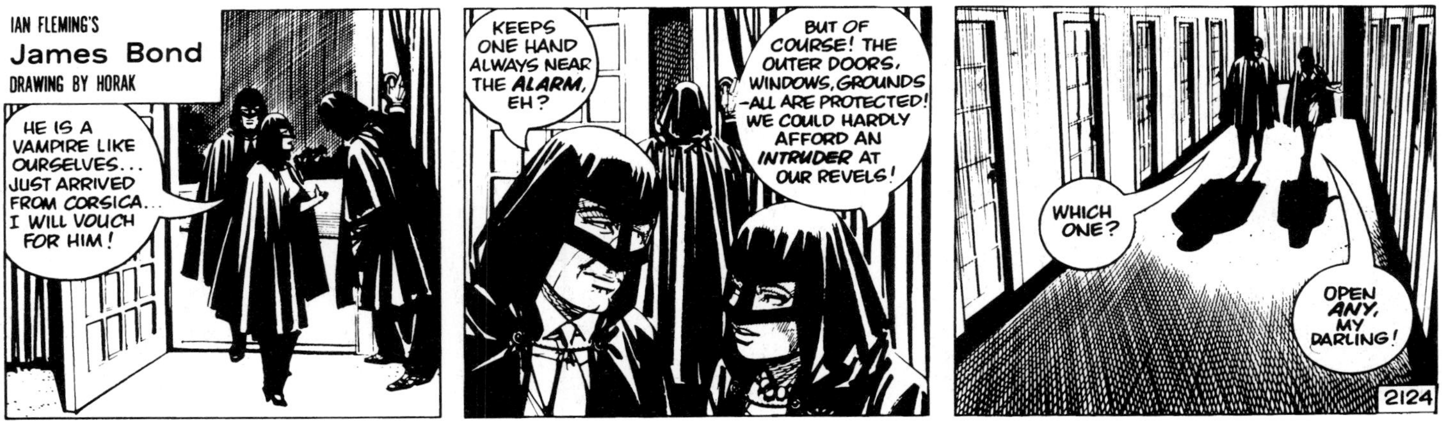
IAN FLEMING'S
James Bond
DRAWING BY HORAK
HE IS A VAMPIRE LIKE OURSELVES... JUST ARRIVED FROM CORSICA... I WILL VOUCH FOR HIM!
KEEPS ONE HAND ALWAYS NEAR THE ALARM, EH?
BUT OF COURSE! THE OUTER DOORS, WINDOWS, GROUNDS -ALL ARE PROTECTED! WE COULD HARDLY AFFORD AN INTRUDER AT OUR REVELS!
WHICH ONE?
OPEN ANY, MY DARLING!
2124

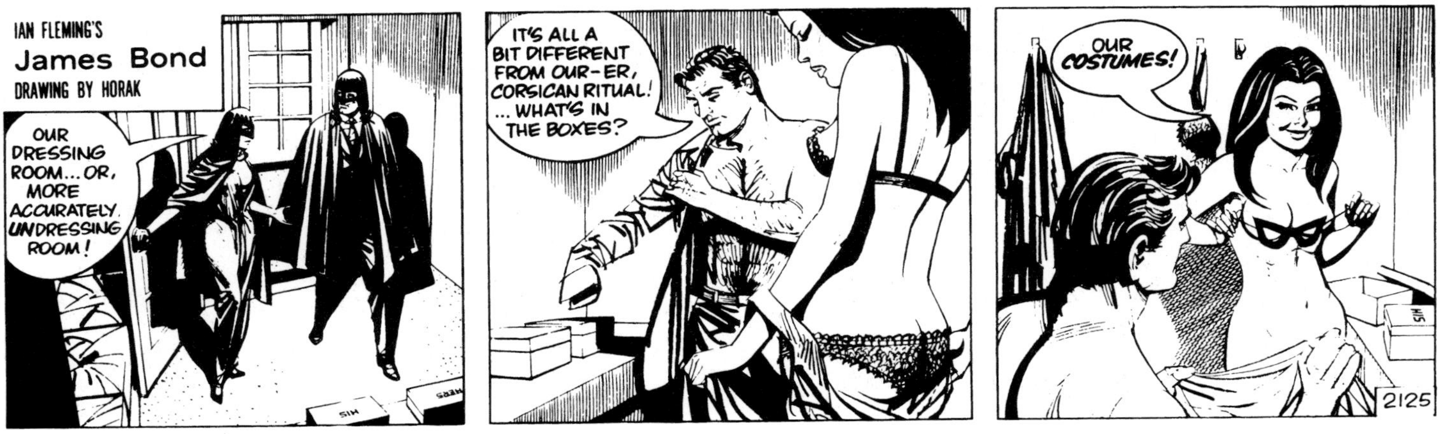
IAN FLEMING'S
James Bond
DRAWING BY HORAK
OUR DRESSING ROOM... OR, MORE ACCURATELY, UNDRESSING ROOM!
IT'S ALL A BIT DIFFERENT FROM OUR-ER, CORSICAN RITUAL! ... WHAT'S IN THE BOXES?
OUR COSTUMES!
2125

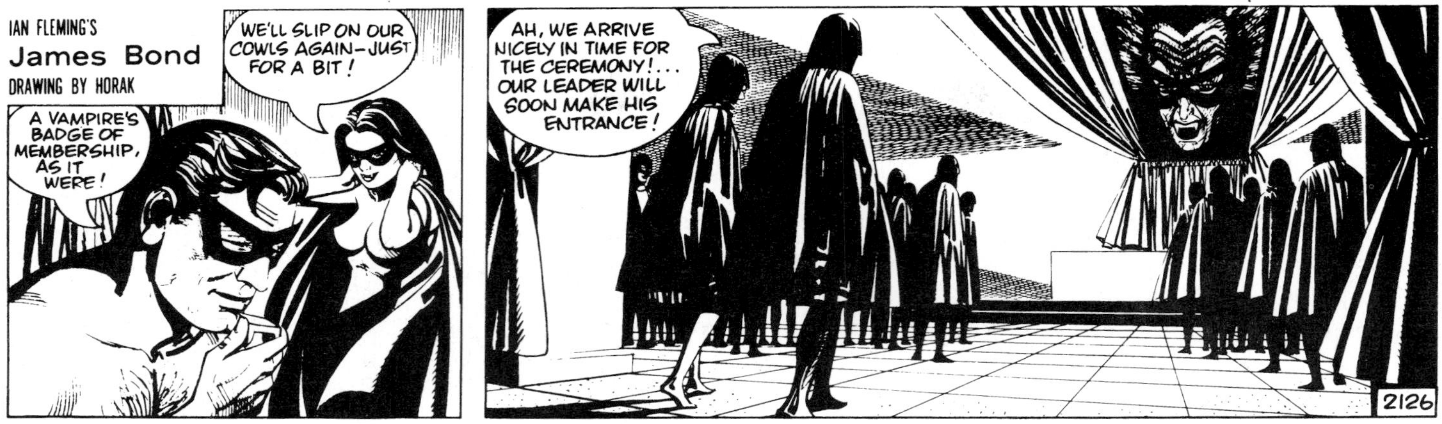
IAN FLEMING'S
James Bond
DRAWING BY HORAK
WE'LL SLIP ON OUR COWLS AGAIN–JUST FOR A BIT!
A VAMPIRE'S BADGE OF MEMBERSHIP, AS IT WERE!
AH, WE ARRIVE NICELY IN TIME FOR THE CEREMONY!... OUR LEADER WILL SOON MAKE HIS ENTRANCE!
2126

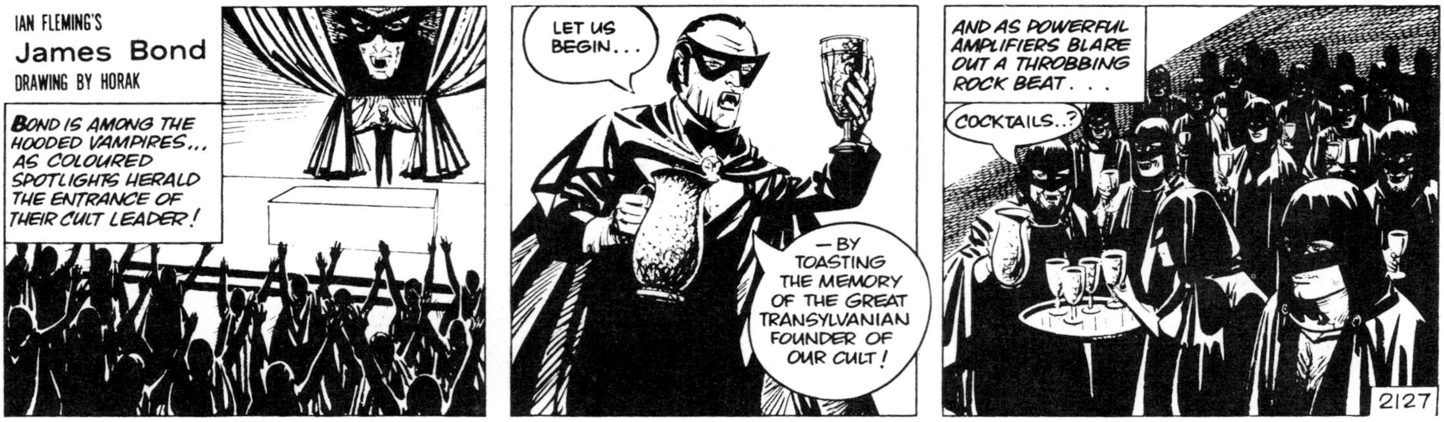
IAN FLEMING'S
James Bond
DRAWING BY HORAK
BOND IS AMONG THE HOODED VAMPIRES... AS COLOURED SPOTLIGHTS HERALD THE ENTRANCE OF THEIR CULT LEADER!
LET US BEGIN...
—BY TOASTING THE MEMORY OF THE GREAT TRANSYLVANIAN FOUNDER OF OUR CULT!
AND AS POWERFUL AMPLIFIERS BLARE OUT A THROBBING ROCK BEAT...
COCKTAILS..?
2127

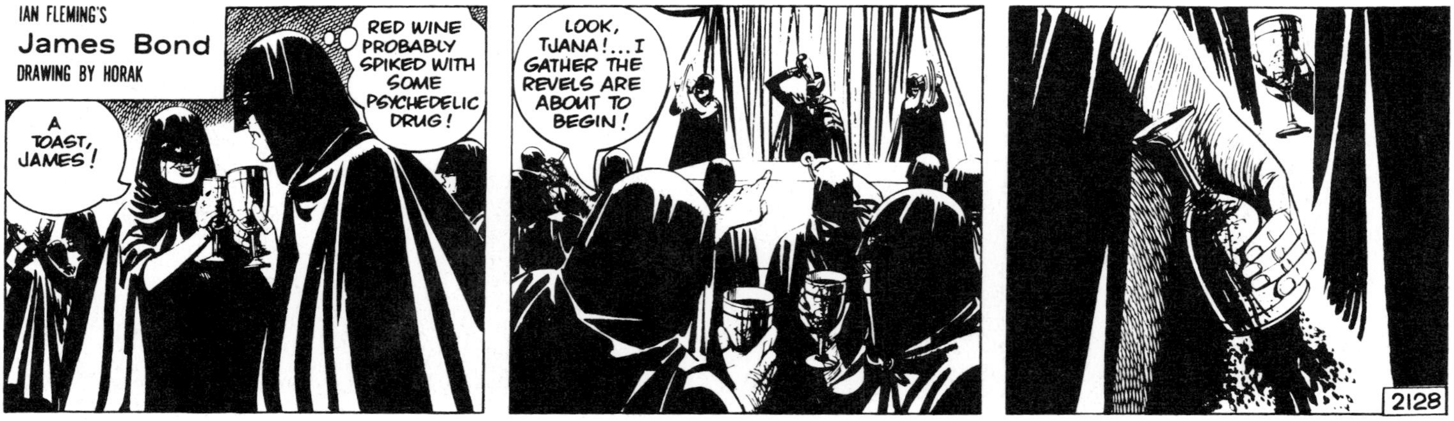
IAN FLEMING'S
James Bond
DRAWING BY HORAK
RED WINE PROBABLY SPIKED WITH SOME PSYCHEDELIC DRUG!
A TOAST, JAMES!
LOOK, TIJANA!... I GATHER THE REVELS ARE ABOUT TO BEGIN!
2128

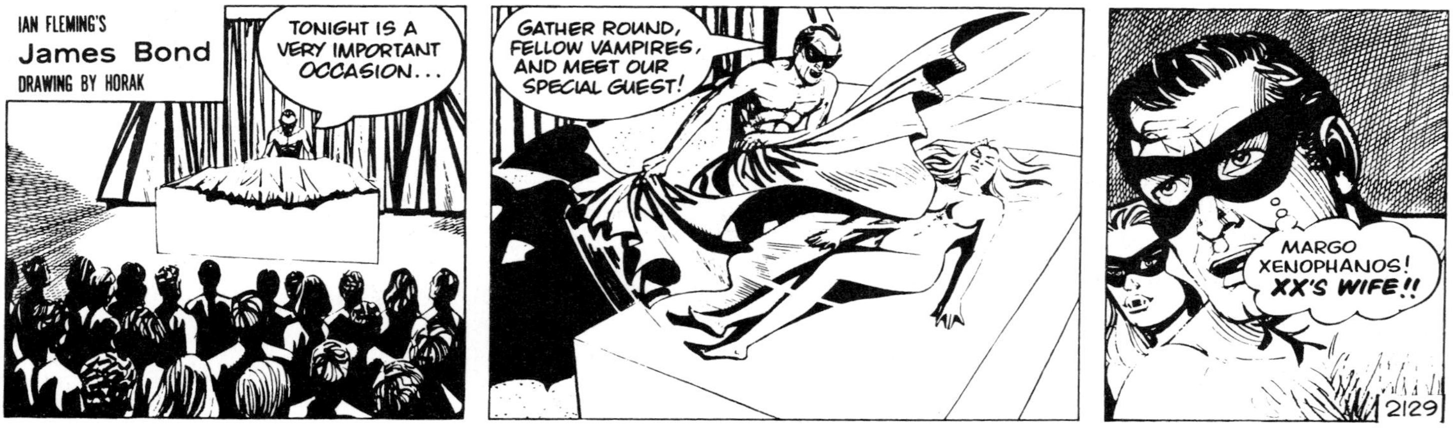
IAN FLEMING'S
James Bond
DRAWING BY HORAK
TONIGHT IS A VERY IMPORTANT OCCASION...
GATHER ROUND, FELLOW VAMPIRES, AND MEET OUR SPECIAL GUEST!
MARGO XENOPHANOS! XX'S WIFE!!
2129

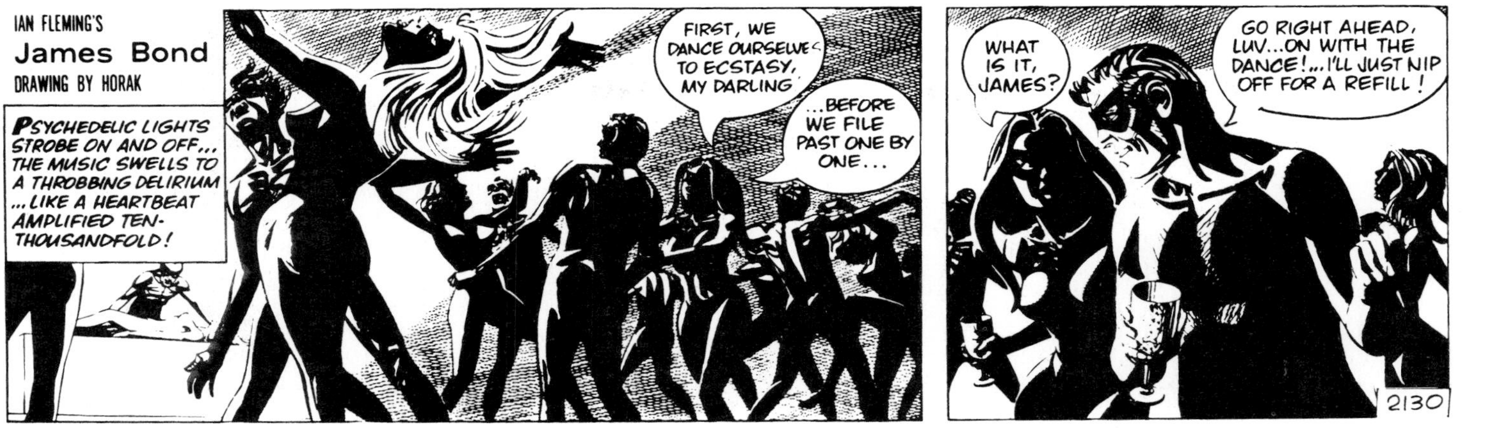
IAN FLEMING'S
James Bond
DRAWING BY HORAK
PSYCHEDELIC LIGHTS STROBE ON AND OFF... THE MUSIC SWELLS TO A THROBBING DELIRIUM ...LIKE A HEARTBEAT AMPLIFIED TEN-THOUSANDFOLD!
FIRST, WE DANCE OURSELVES TO ECSTASY, MY DARLING
...BEFORE WE FILE PAST ONE BY ONE...
WHAT IS IT, JAMES?
GO RIGHT AHEAD, LUV...ON WITH THE DANCE!...I'LL JUST NIP OFF FOR A REFILL!
2130

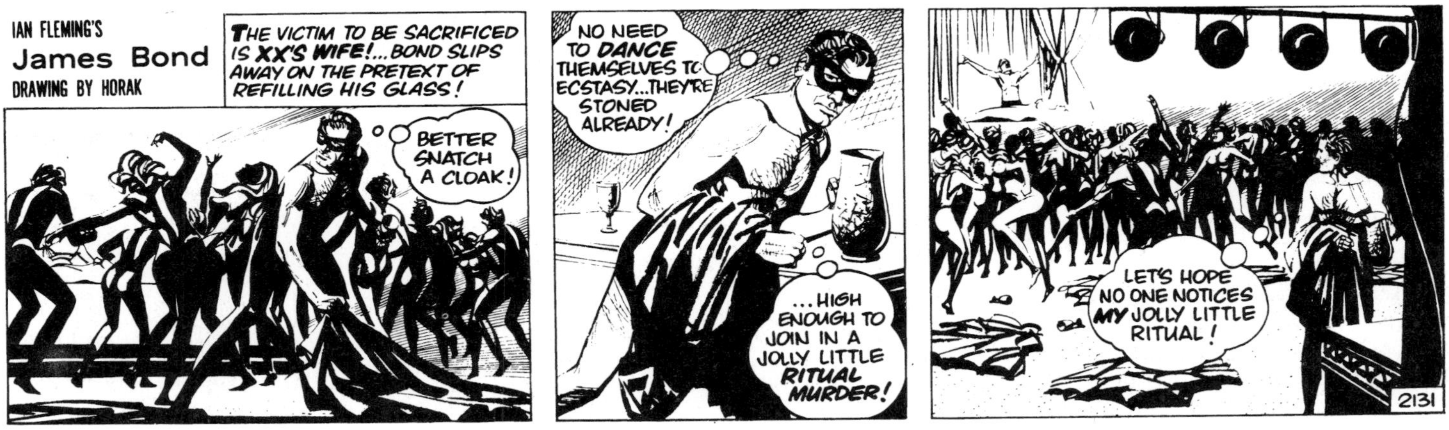
IAN FLEMING'S
James Bond
DRAWING BY HORAK
THE VICTIM TO BE SACRIFICED IS XX'S WIFE!...BOND SLIPS AWAY ON THE PRETEXT OF REFILLING HIS GLASS!
BETTER SNATCH A CLOAK!
NO NEED TO DANCE THEMSELVES TO ECSTASY...THEY'RE STONED ALREADY!
...HIGH ENOUGH TO JOIN IN A JOLLY LITTLE RITUAL MURDER!
LET'S HOPE NO ONE NOTICES MY JOLLY LITTLE RITUAL!
2131

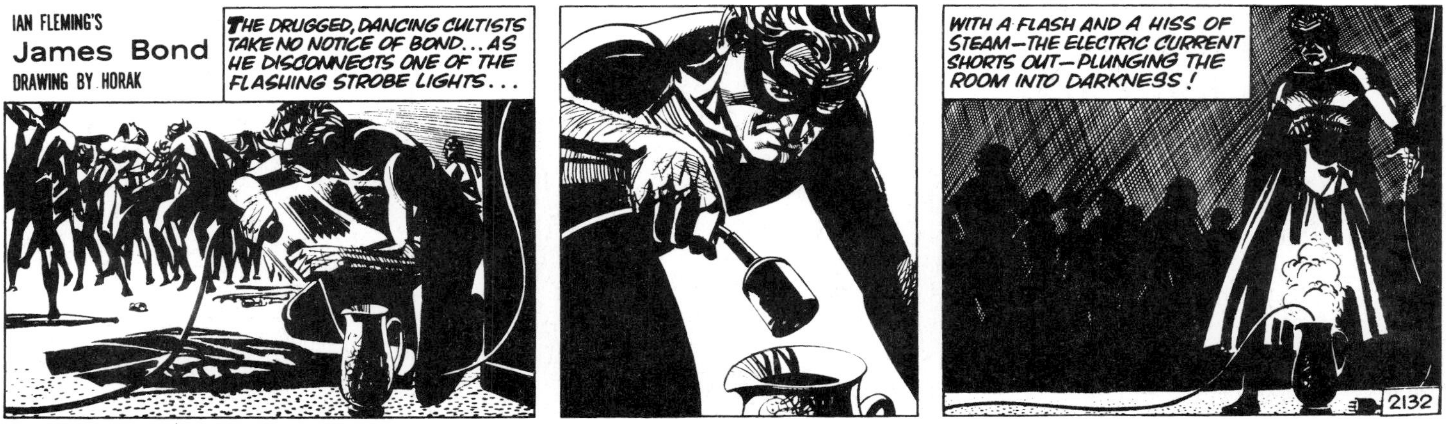
IAN FLEMING'S
James Bond
DRAWING BY HORAK
THE DRUGGED, DANCING CULTISTS TAKE NO NOTICE OF BOND...AS HE DISCONNECTS ONE OF THE FLASHING STROBE LIGHTS...
WITH A FLASH AND A HISS OF STEAM—THE ELECTRIC CURRENT SHORTS OUT—PLUNGING THE ROOM INTO DARKNESS!
2132

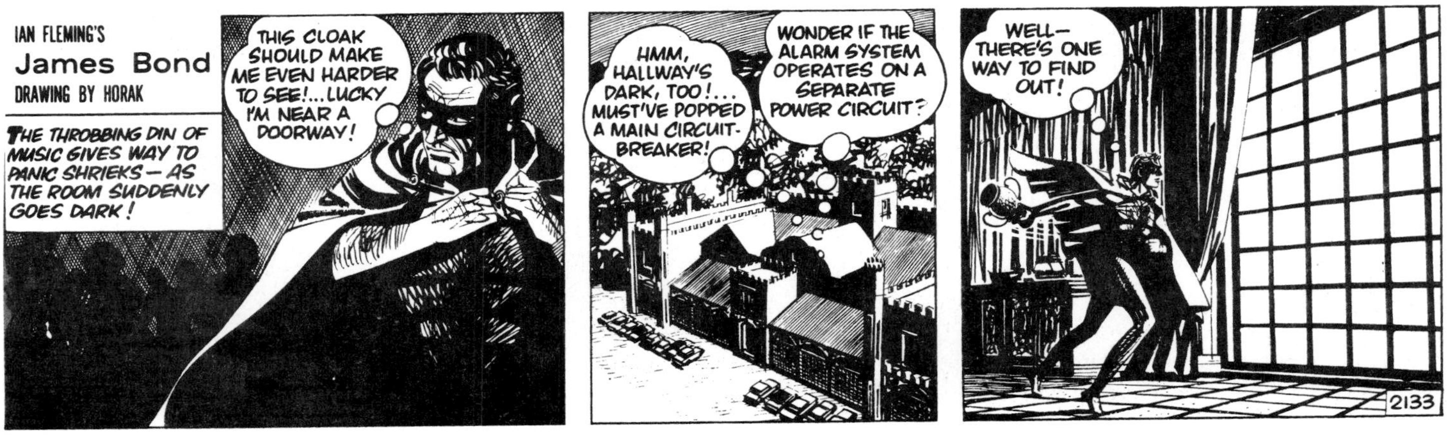
IAN FLEMING'S
James Bond
DRAWING BY HORAK
THE THROBBING DIN OF MUSIC GIVES WAY TO PANIC SHRIEKS — AS THE ROOM SUDDENLY GOES DARK!
THIS CLOAK SHOULD MAKE ME EVEN HARDER TO SEE!...LUCKY I'M NEAR A DOORWAY!
HMM, HALLWAY'S DARK, TOO!...MUST'VE POPPED A MAIN CIRCUIT-BREAKER!
WONDER IF THE ALARM SYSTEM OPERATES ON A SEPARATE POWER CIRCUIT?
WELL—THERE'S ONE WAY TO FIND OUT!
2133

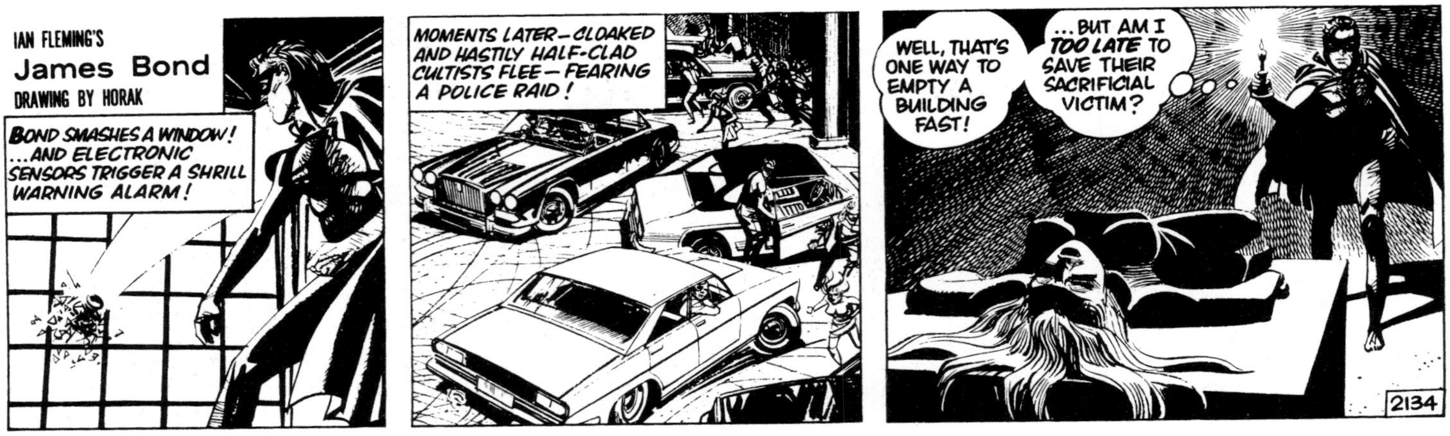
IAN FLEMING'S
James Bond
DRAWING BY HORAK
BOND SMASHES A WINDOW! ...AND ELECTRONIC SENSORS TRIGGER A SHRILL WARNING ALARM!
MOMENTS LATER—CLOAKED AND HASTILY HALF-CLAD CULTISTS FLEE—FEARING A POLICE RAID!
WELL, THAT'S ONE WAY TO EMPTY A BUILDING FAST!
...BUT AM I TOO LATE TO SAVE THEIR SACRIFICIAL VICTIM?
2134

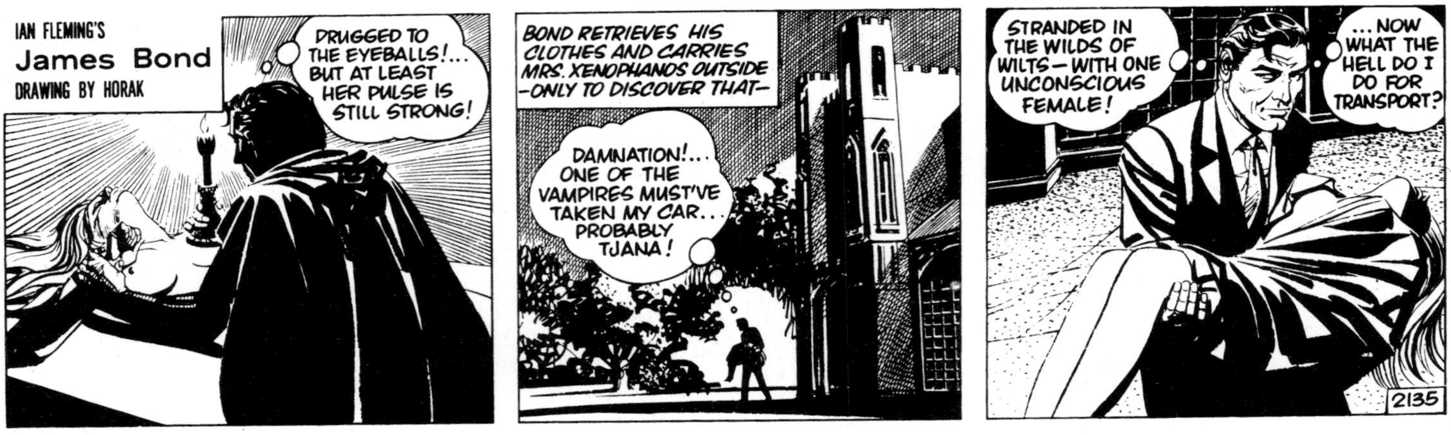
IAN FLEMING'S
James Bond
DRAWING BY HORAK
DRUGGED TO THE EYEBALLS!... BUT AT LEAST HER PULSE IS STILL STRONG!
BOND RETRIEVES HIS CLOTHES AND CARRIES MRS. XENOPHANOS OUTSIDE -ONLY TO DISCOVER THAT-
DAMNATION!... ONE OF THE VAMPIRES MUST'VE TAKEN MY CAR... PROBABLY TJANA!
STRANDED IN THE WILDS OF WILTS—WITH ONE UNCONSCIOUS FEMALE!
...NOW WHAT THE HELL DO I DO FOR TRANSPORT?
2135

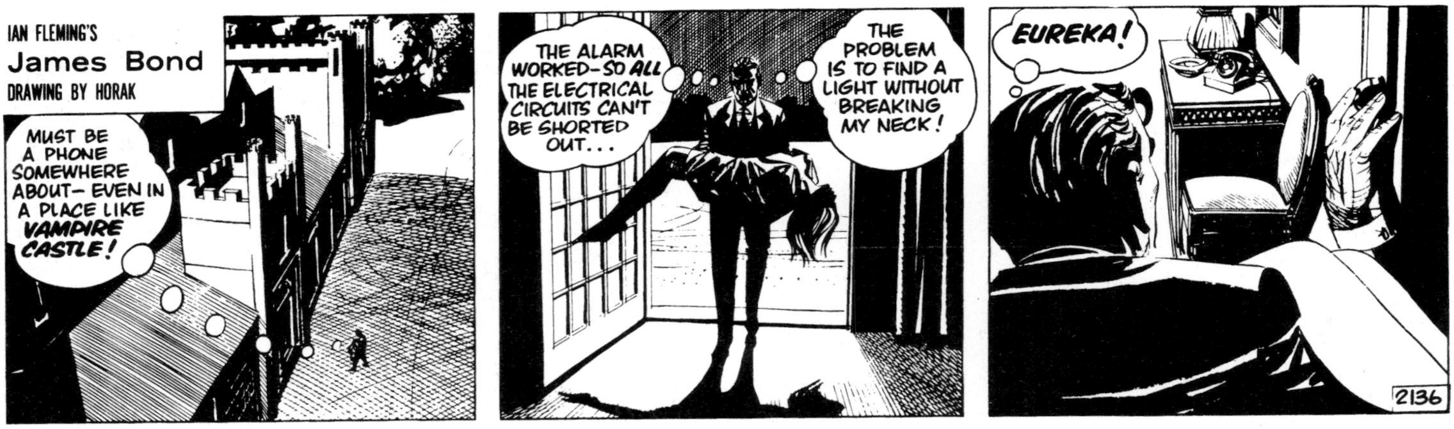
IAN FLEMING'S
James Bond
DRAWING BY HORAK
MUST BE A PHONE SOMEWHERE ABOUT- EVEN IN A PLACE LIKE VAMPIRE CASTLE!
THE ALARM WORKED—SO ALL THE ELECTRICAL CIRCUITS CAN'T BE SHORTED OUT...
THE PROBLEM IS TO FIND A LIGHT WITHOUT BREAKING MY NECK!
EUREKA!
2136

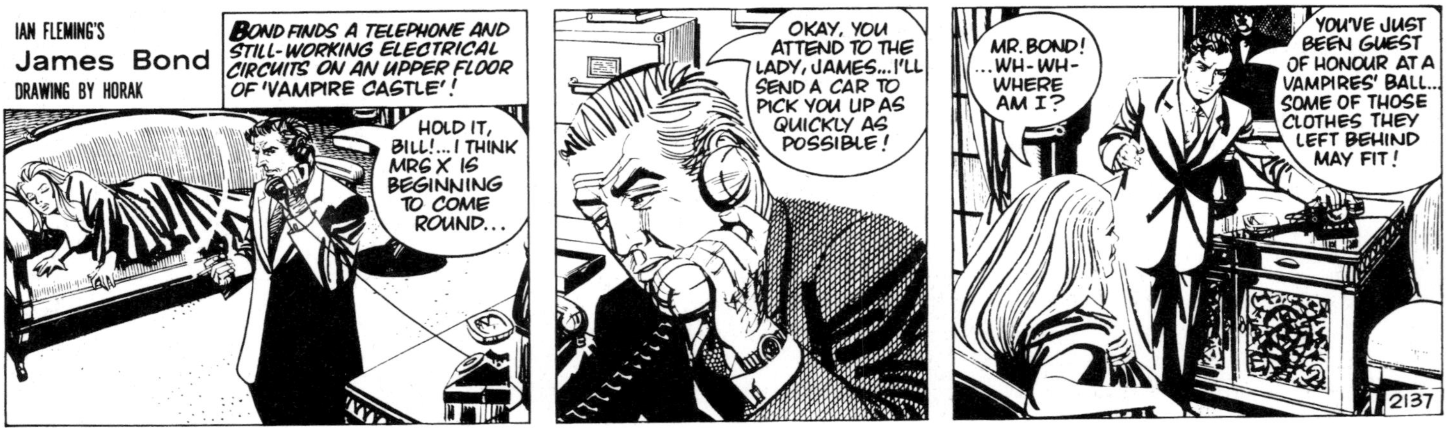
IAN FLEMING'S
James Bond
DRAWING BY HORAK
BOND FINDS A TELEPHONE AND STILL-WORKING ELECTRICAL CIRCUITS ON AN UPPER FLOOR OF 'VAMPIRE CASTLE'!
HOLD IT, BILL!...I THINK MRS X IS BEGINNING TO COME ROUND...
OKAY, YOU ATTEND TO THE LADY, JAMES...I'LL SEND A CAR TO PICK YOU UP AS QUICKLY AS POSSIBLE!
MR. BOND! ...WH-WH-WHERE AM I?
YOU'VE JUST BEEN GUEST OF HONOUR AT A VAMPIRES' BALL... SOME OF THOSE CLOTHES THEY LEFT BEHIND MAY FIT!
2137

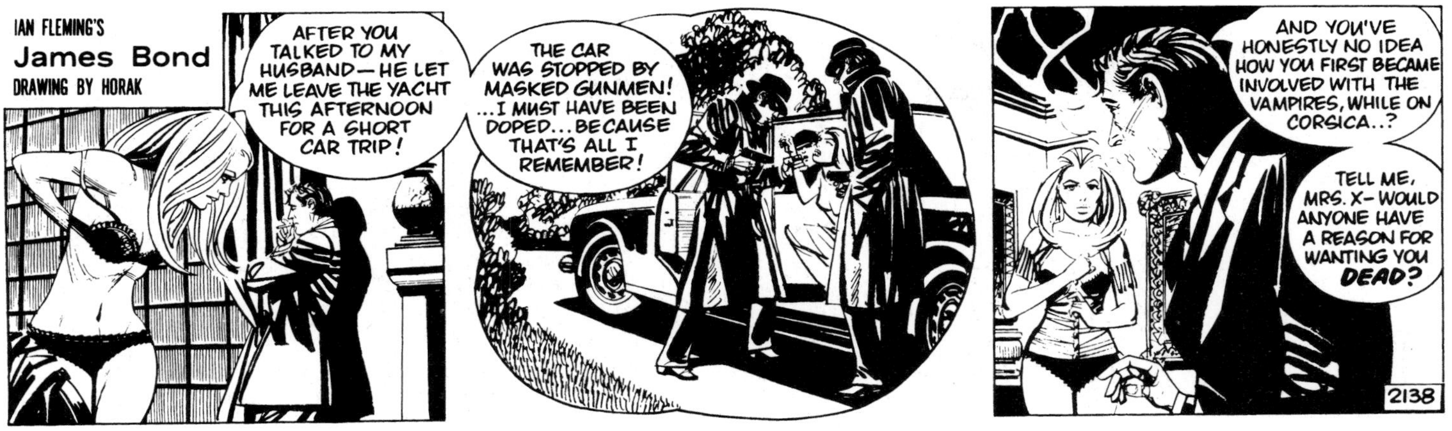
IAN FLEMING'S
James Bond
DRAWING BY HORAK
AFTER YOU TALKED TO MY HUSBAND—HE LET ME LEAVE THE YACHT THIS AFTERNOON FOR A SHORT CAR TRIP!
THE CAR WAS STOPPED BY MASKED GUNMEN! ...I MUST HAVE BEEN DOPED... BECAUSE THAT'S ALL I REMEMBER!
AND YOU'VE HONESTLY NO IDEA HOW YOU FIRST BECAME INVOLVED WITH THE VAMPIRES, WHILE ON CORSICA..?
TELL ME, MRS. X—WOULD ANYONE HAVE A REASON FOR WANTING YOU DEAD?
2138

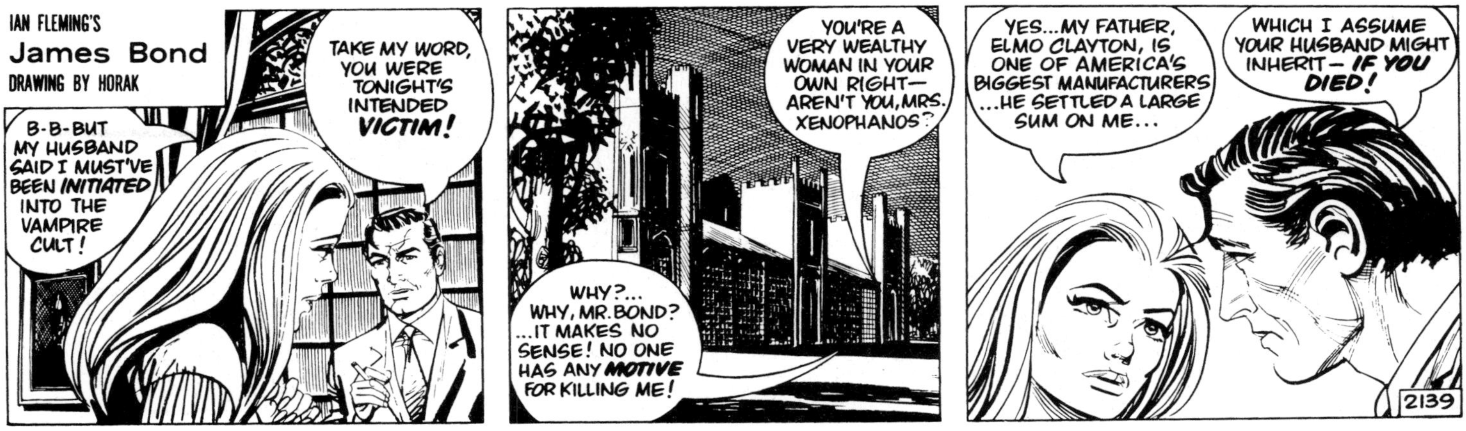
IAN FLEMING'S
James Bond
DRAWING BY HORAK
TAKE MY WORD, YOU WERE TONIGHT'S INTENDED VICTIM!
B-B-BUT MY HUSBAND SAID I MUST'VE BEEN INITIATED INTO THE VAMPIRE CULT!
YOU'RE A VERY WEALTHY WOMAN IN YOUR OWN RIGHT—AREN'T YOU, MRS. XENOPHANOS?
WHY?... WHY, MR. BOND? ...IT MAKES NO SENSE! NO ONE HAS ANY MOTIVE FOR KILLING ME!
YES... MY FATHER, ELMO CLAYTON, IS ONE OF AMERICA'S BIGGEST MANUFACTURERS ...HE SETTLED A LARGE SUM ON ME...
WHICH I ASSUME YOUR HUSBAND MIGHT INHERIT—IF YOU DIED!
2139

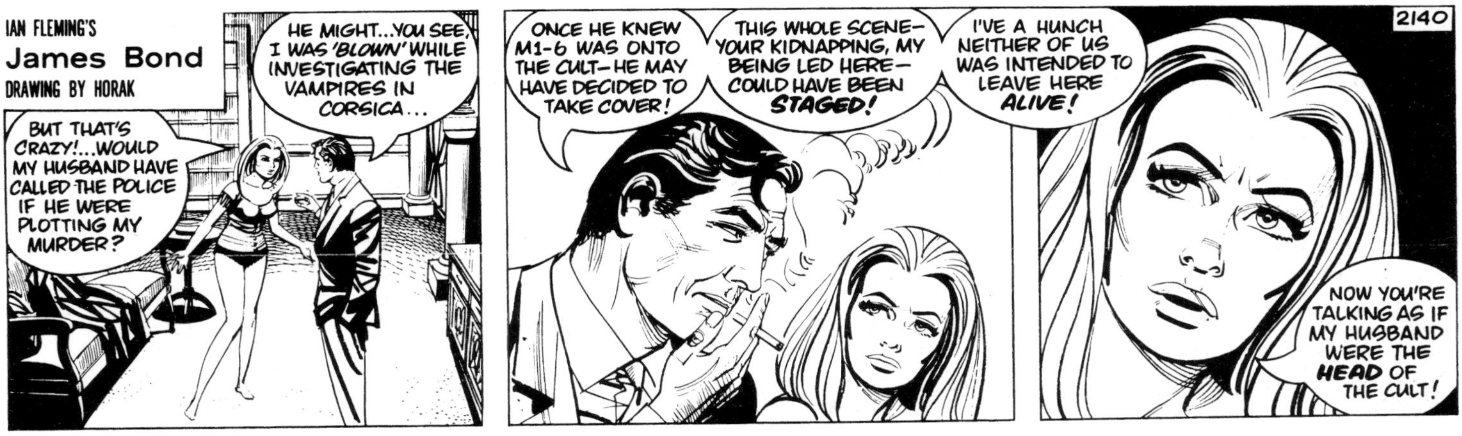
IAN FLEMING'S
James Bond
DRAWING BY HORAK
HE MIGHT... YOU SEE, I WAS 'BLOWN' WHILE INVESTIGATING THE VAMPIRES IN CORSICA...
BUT THAT'S CRAZY!... WOULD MY HUSBAND HAVE CALLED THE POLICE IF HE WERE PLOTTING MY MURDER?
ONCE HE KNEW M1-6 WAS ONTO THE CULT—HE MAY HAVE DECIDED TO TAKE COVER!
THIS WHOLE SCENE—YOUR KIDNAPPING, MY BEING LED HERE—COULD HAVE BEEN STAGED!
I'VE A HUNCH NEITHER OF US WAS INTENDED TO LEAVE HERE ALIVE!
2140
NOW YOU'RE TALKING AS IF MY HUSBAND WERE THE HEAD OF THE CULT!

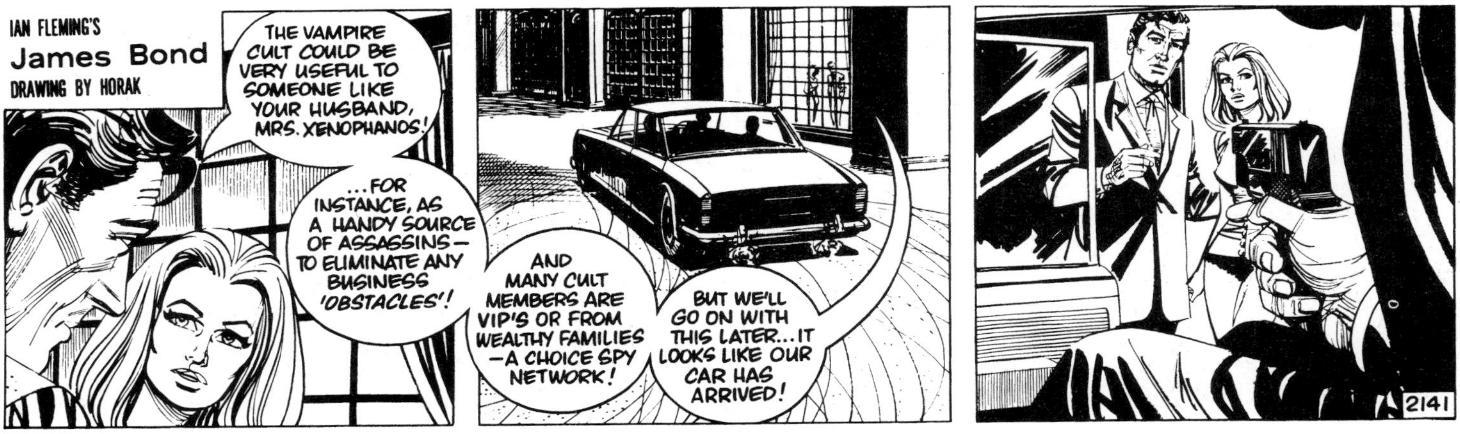
IAN FLEMING'S
James Bond
DRAWING BY HORAK
THE VAMPIRE CULT COULD BE VERY USEFUL TO SOMEONE LIKE YOUR HUSBAND, MRS. XENOPHANOS!
...FOR INSTANCE, AS A HANDY SOURCE OF ASSASSINS—TO ELIMINATE ANY BUSINESS 'OBSTACLES'!
AND MANY CULT MEMBERS ARE VIP'S OR FROM WEALTHY FAMILIES—A CHOICE SPY NETWORK!
BUT WE'LL GO ON WITH THIS LATER... IT LOOKS LIKE OUR CAR HAS ARRIVED!
2141

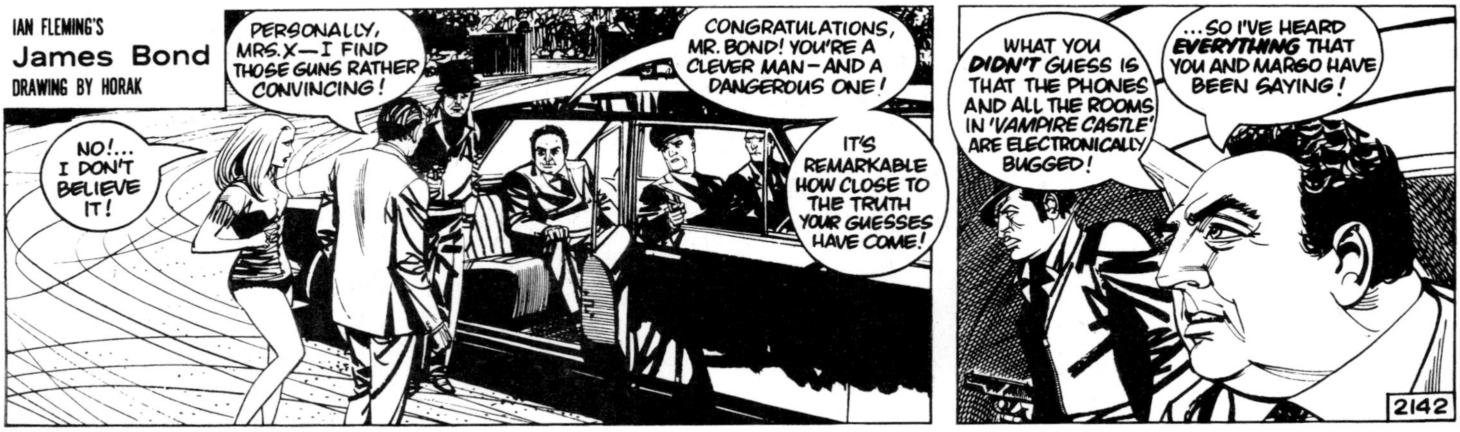
IAN FLEMING'S
James Bond
DRAWING BY HORAK
PERSONALLY, MRS. X—I FIND THOSE GUNS RATHER CONVINCING!
NO!... I DON'T BELIEVE IT!
CONGRATULATIONS, MR. BOND! YOU'RE A CLEVER MAN—AND A DANGEROUS ONE!
IT'S REMARKABLE HOW CLOSE TO THE TRUTH YOUR GUESSES HAVE COME!
WHAT YOU DIDN'T GUESS IS THAT THE PHONES AND ALL THE ROOMS IN 'VAMPIRE CASTLE' ARE ELECTRONICALLY BUGGED!
...SO I'VE HEARD EVERYTHING THAT YOU AND MARGO HAVE BEEN SAYING!
2142

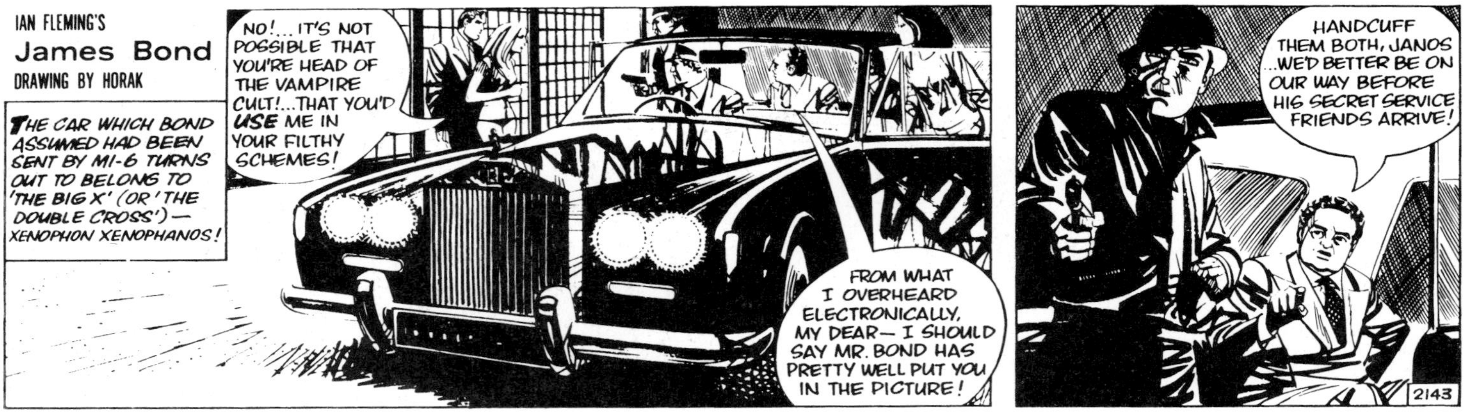
IAN FLEMING'S
James Bond
DRAWING BY HORAK
THE CAR WHICH BOND ASSUMED HAD BEEN SENT BY MI-6 TURNS OUT TO BELONG TO 'THE BIG X' (OR 'THE DOUBLE CROSS')—XENOPHON XENOPHANOS!
NO!... IT'S NOT POSSIBLE THAT YOU'RE HEAD OF THE VAMPIRE CULT!... THAT YOU'D USE ME IN YOUR FILTHY SCHEMES!
FROM WHAT I OVERHEARD ELECTRONICALLY, MY DEAR— I SHOULD SAY MR. BOND HAS PRETTY WELL PUT YOU IN THE PICTURE!
HANDCUFF THEM BOTH, JANOS ...WE'D BETTER BE ON OUR WAY BEFORE HIS SECRET SERVICE FRIENDS ARRIVE!
2143

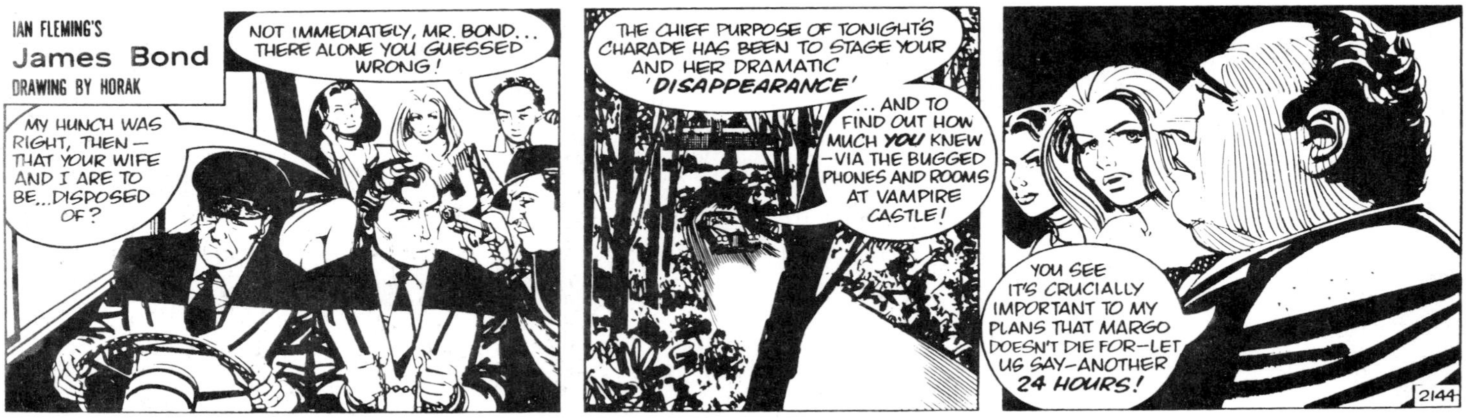
IAN FLEMING'S
James Bond
DRAWING BY HORAK
MY HUNCH WAS RIGHT, THEN— THAT YOUR WIFE AND I ARE TO BE... DISPOSED OF?
NOT IMMEDIATELY, MR. BOND... THERE ALONE YOU GUESSED WRONG!
THE CHIEF PURPOSE OF TONIGHT'S CHARADE HAS BEEN TO STAGE YOUR AND HER DRAMATIC 'DISAPPEARANCE'
...AND TO FIND OUT HOW MUCH YOU KNEW —VIA THE BUGGED PHONES AND ROOMS AT VAMPIRE CASTLE!
YOU SEE IT'S CRUCIALLY IMPORTANT TO MY PLANS THAT MARGO DOESN'T DIE FOR—LET US SAY—ANOTHER 24 HOURS!
2144

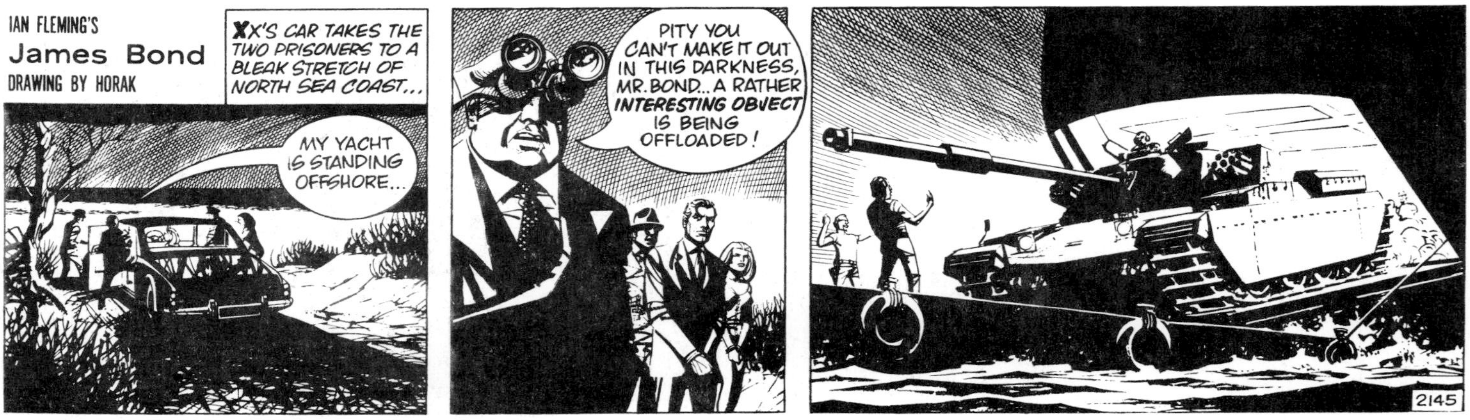
IAN FLEMING'S
James Bond
DRAWING BY HORAK
XX'S CAR TAKES THE TWO PRISONERS TO A BLEAK STRETCH OF NORTH SEA COAST...
MY YACHT IS STANDING OFFSHORE...
PITY YOU CAN'T MAKE IT OUT IN THIS DARKNESS, MR. BOND... A RATHER INTERESTING OBJECT IS BEING OFFLOADED!
2145

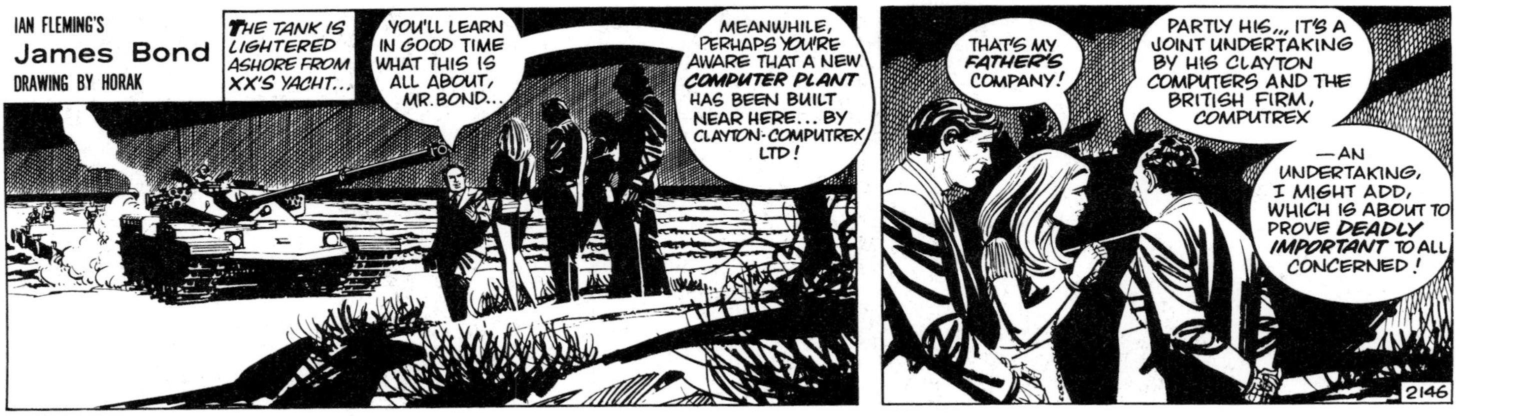
IAN FLEMING'S
James Bond
DRAWING BY HORAK
THE TANK IS LIGHTERED ASHORE FROM XX'S YACHT...
YOU'LL LEARN IN GOOD TIME WHAT THIS IS ALL ABOUT, MR. BOND...
MEANWHILE, PERHAPS YOU'RE AWARE THAT A NEW **COMPUTER PLANT** HAS BEEN BUILT NEAR HERE... BY CLAYTON-COMPUTREX LTD!
THAT'S MY **FATHER'S** COMPANY!
PARTLY HIS... IT'S A JOINT UNDERTAKING BY HIS CLAYTON COMPUTERS AND THE BRITISH FIRM, COMPUTREX
—AN UNDERTAKING, I MIGHT ADD, WHICH IS ABOUT TO PROVE **DEADLY IMPORTANT** TO ALL CONCERNED!
2146

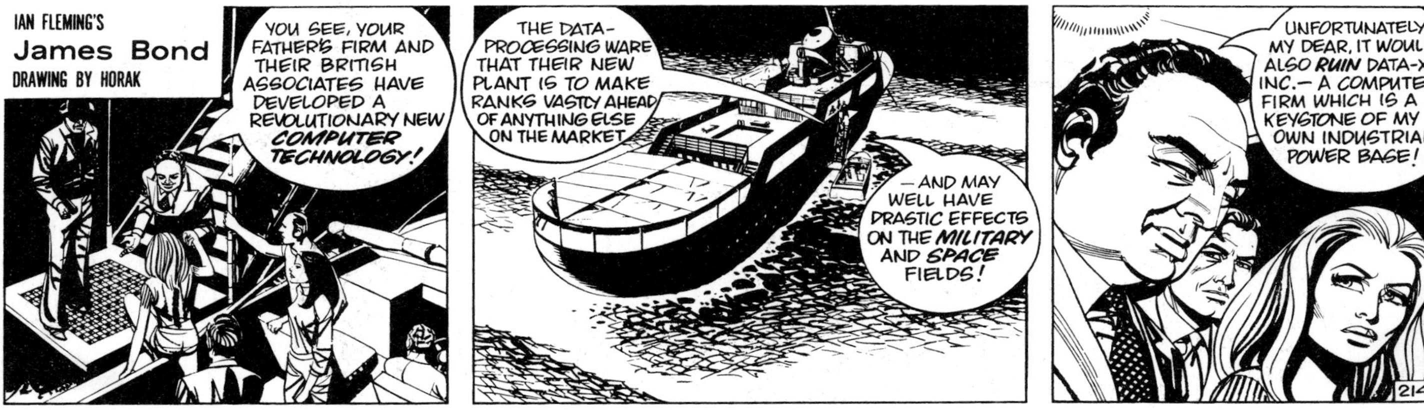
IAN FLEMING'S
James Bond
DRAWING BY HORAK
YOU SEE, YOUR FATHER'S FIRM AND THEIR BRITISH ASSOCIATES HAVE DEVELOPED A REVOLUTIONARY NEW **COMPUTER TECHNOLOGY!**
THE DATA-PROCESSING WARE THAT THEIR NEW PLANT IS TO MAKE RANKS VASTLY AHEAD OF ANYTHING ELSE ON THE MARKET
—AND MAY WELL HAVE DRASTIC EFFECTS ON THE **MILITARY** AND **SPACE** FIELDS!
UNFORTUNATELY, MY DEAR, IT WOULD ALSO **RUIN** DATA-X, INC.— A COMPUTER FIRM WHICH IS A KEYSTONE OF MY OWN INDUSTRIAL POWER BASE!
2147

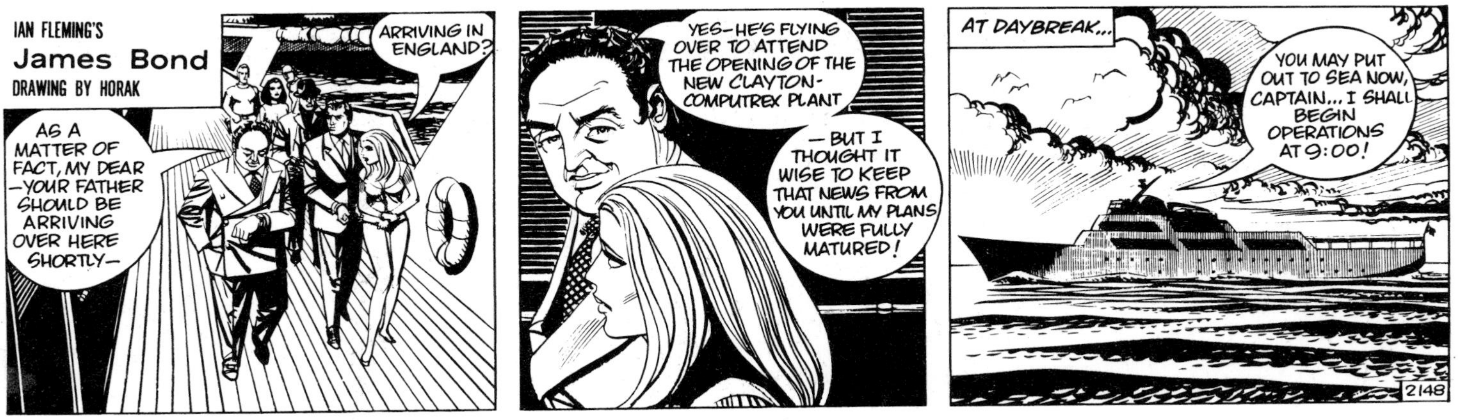
IAN FLEMING'S
James Bond
DRAWING BY HORAK
AS A MATTER OF FACT, MY DEAR —YOUR FATHER SHOULD BE ARRIVING OVER HERE SHORTLY—
ARRIVING IN ENGLAND?
YES—HE'S FLYING OVER TO ATTEND THE OPENING OF THE NEW CLAYTON-COMPUTREX PLANT
—BUT I THOUGHT IT WISE TO KEEP THAT NEWS FROM YOU UNTIL MY PLANS WERE FULLY MATURED!
AT DAYBREAK...
YOU MAY PUT OUT TO SEA NOW, CAPTAIN... I SHALL BEGIN OPERATIONS AT 9:00!
2148

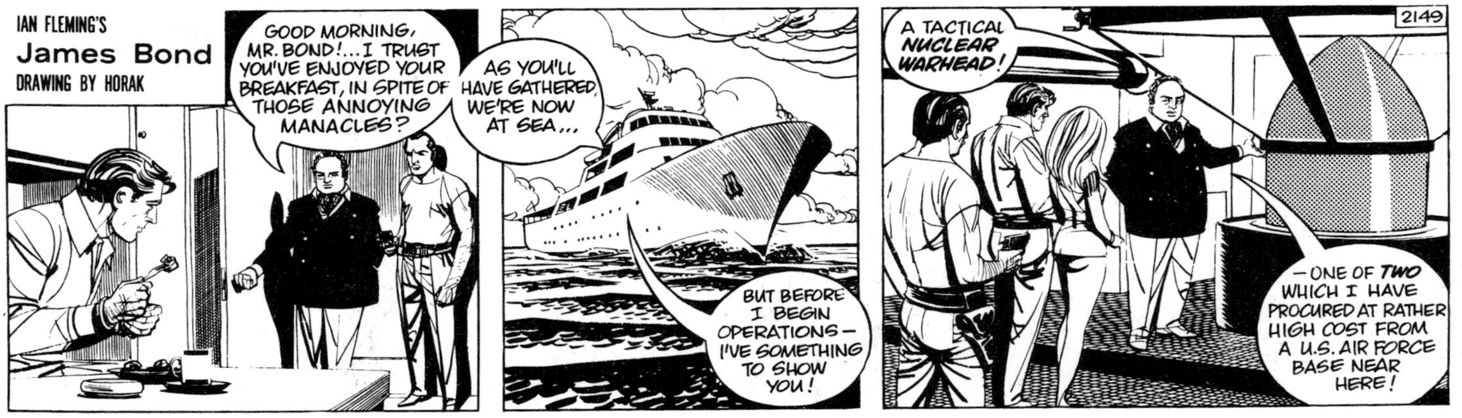
IAN FLEMING'S
James Bond
DRAWING BY HORAK
GOOD MORNING, MR. BOND!... I TRUST YOU'VE ENJOYED YOUR BREAKFAST, IN SPITE OF THOSE ANNOYING MANACLES?
AS YOU'LL HAVE GATHERED, WE'RE NOW AT SEA...
BUT BEFORE I BEGIN OPERATIONS—I'VE SOMETHING TO SHOW YOU!
2149
A TACTICAL **NUCLEAR WARHEAD!**
—ONE OF **TWO** WHICH I HAVE PROCURED AT RATHER HIGH COST FROM A U.S. AIR FORCE BASE NEAR HERE!

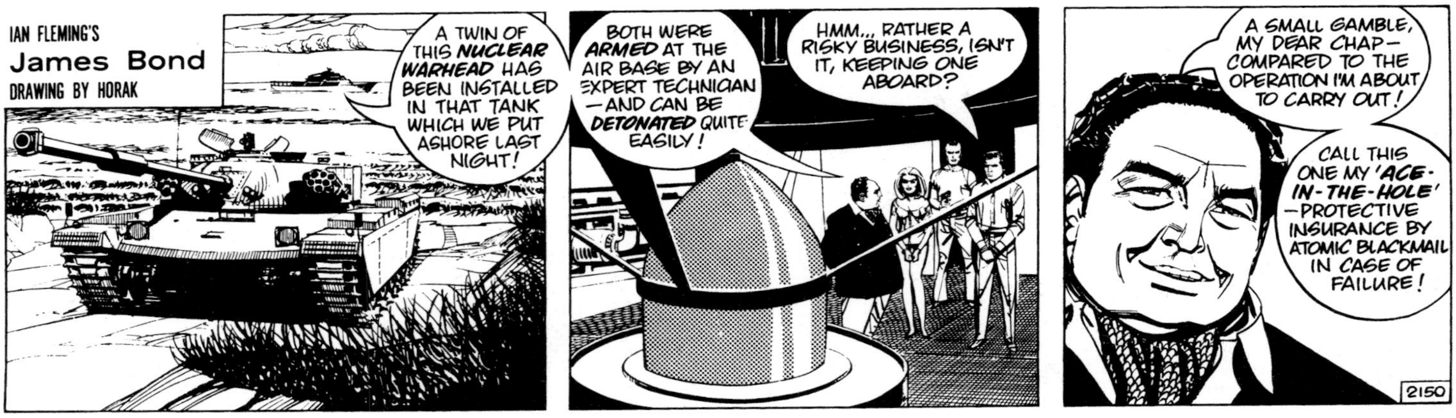
IAN FLEMING'S
James Bond
DRAWING BY HORAK
A TWIN OF THIS NUCLEAR WARHEAD HAS BEEN INSTALLED IN THAT TANK WHICH WE PUT ASHORE LAST NIGHT!
BOTH WERE ARMED AT THE AIR BASE BY AN EXPERT TECHNICIAN —AND CAN BE DETONATED QUITE EASILY!
HMM... RATHER A RISKY BUSINESS, ISN'T IT, KEEPING ONE ABOARD?
A SMALL GAMBLE, MY DEAR CHAP— COMPARED TO THE OPERATION I'M ABOUT TO CARRY OUT!
CALL THIS ONE MY 'ACE-IN-THE-HOLE' —PROTECTIVE INSURANCE BY ATOMIC BLACKMAIL IN CASE OF FAILURE!
2150

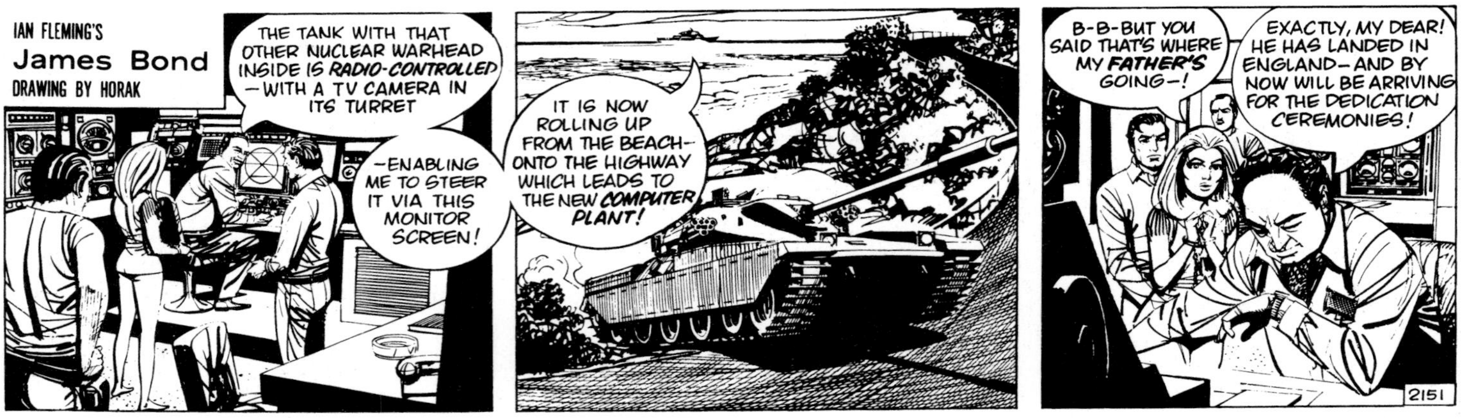
IAN FLEMING'S
James Bond
DRAWING BY HORAK
THE TANK WITH THAT OTHER NUCLEAR WARHEAD INSIDE IS RADIO-CONTROLLED —WITH A TV CAMERA IN ITS TURRET
—ENABLING ME TO STEER IT VIA THIS MONITOR SCREEN!
IT IS NOW ROLLING UP FROM THE BEACH ONTO THE HIGHWAY WHICH LEADS TO THE NEW COMPUTER PLANT!
B-B-BUT YOU SAID THAT'S WHERE MY FATHER'S GOING—!
EXACTLY, MY DEAR! HE HAS LANDED IN ENGLAND—AND BY NOW WILL BE ARRIVING FOR THE DEDICATION CEREMONIES!
2151

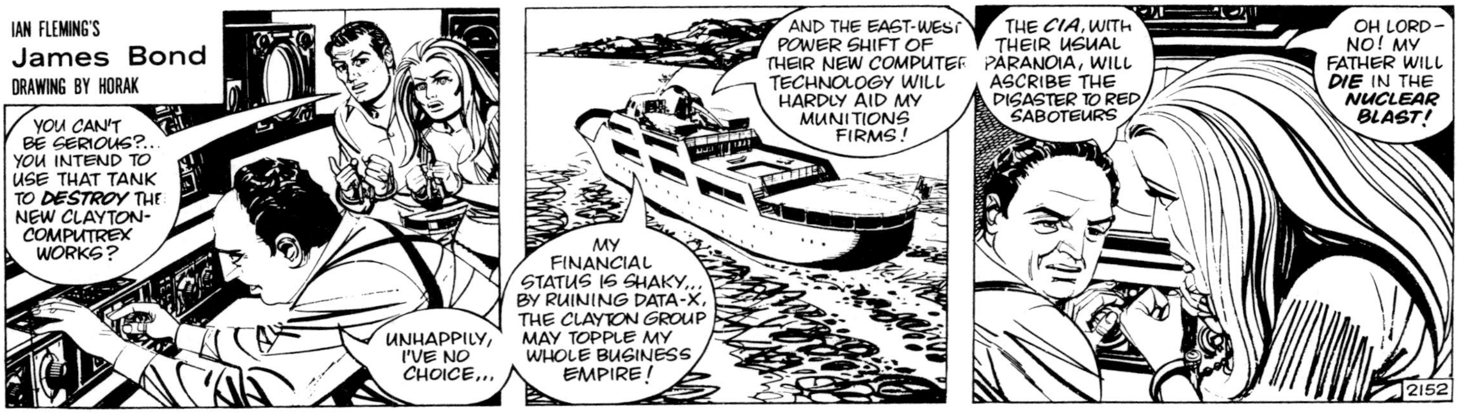
IAN FLEMING'S
James Bond
DRAWING BY HORAK
YOU CAN'T BE SERIOUS?.. YOU INTEND TO USE THAT TANK TO DESTROY THE NEW CLAYTON-COMPUTREX WORKS?
UNHAPPILY, I'VE NO CHOICE...
AND THE EAST-WEST POWER SHIFT OF THEIR NEW COMPUTER TECHNOLOGY WILL HARDLY AID MY MUNITIONS FIRMS!
MY FINANCIAL STATUS IS SHAKY... BY RUINING DATA-X, THE CLAYTON GROUP MAY TOPPLE MY WHOLE BUSINESS EMPIRE!
THE CIA, WITH THEIR USUAL PARANOIA, WILL ASCRIBE THE DISASTER TO RED SABOTEURS
OH LORD—NO! MY FATHER WILL DIE IN THE NUCLEAR BLAST!
2152

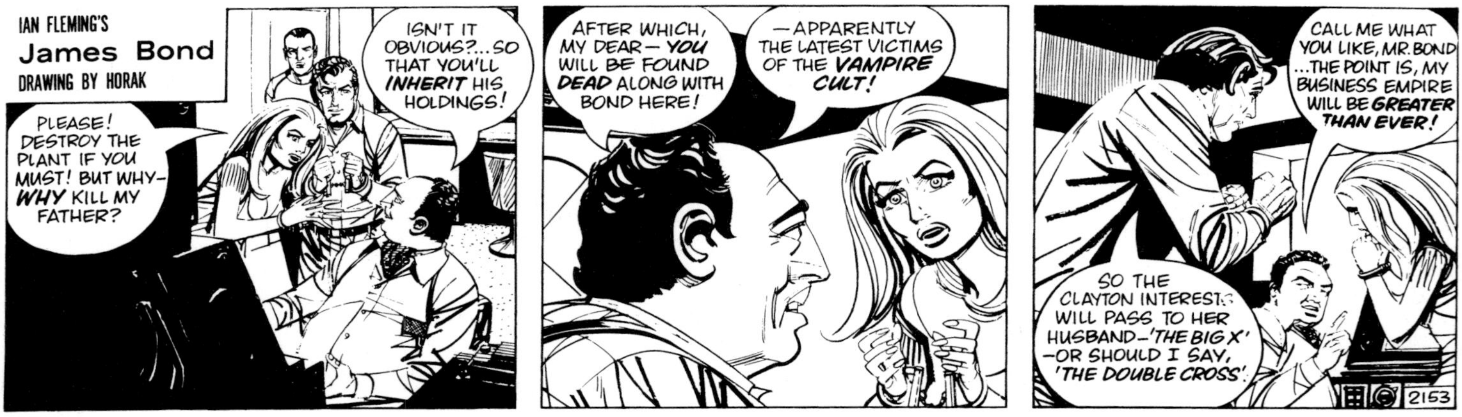
IAN FLEMING'S
James Bond
DRAWING BY HORAK
PLEASE! DESTROY THE PLANT IF YOU MUST! BUT WHY—WHY KILL MY FATHER?
ISN'T IT OBVIOUS?...SO THAT YOU'LL INHERIT HIS HOLDINGS!
AFTER WHICH, MY DEAR—YOU WILL BE FOUND DEAD ALONG WITH BOND HERE!
—APPARENTLY THE LATEST VICTIMS OF THE VAMPIRE CULT!
CALL ME WHAT YOU LIKE, MR. BOND ...THE POINT IS, MY BUSINESS EMPIRE WILL BE GREATER THAN EVER!
SO THE CLAYTON INTERESTS WILL PASS TO HER HUSBAND—'THE BIG X' —OR SHOULD I SAY, 'THE DOUBLE CROSS'.
2153

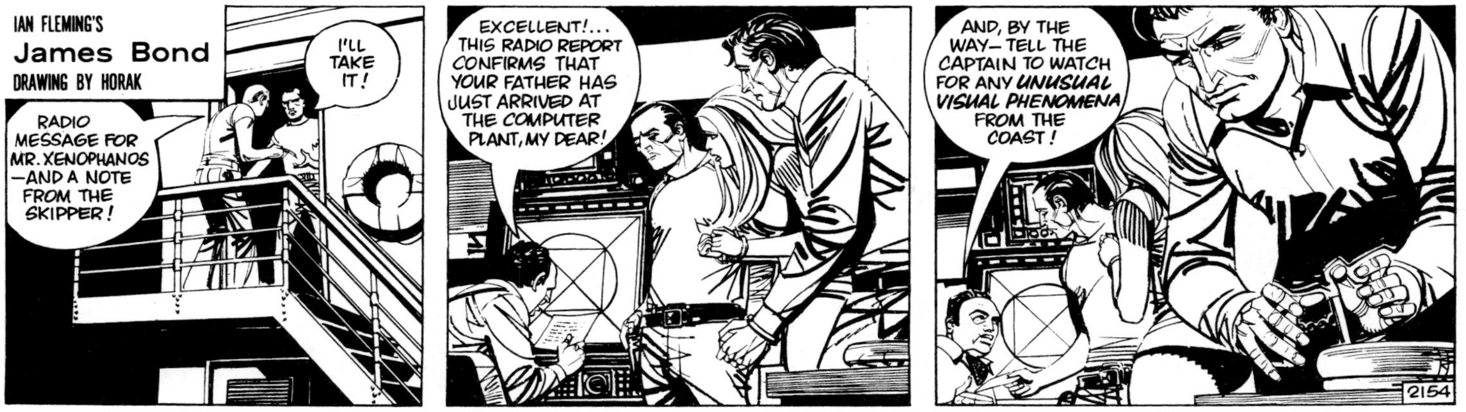
IAN FLEMING'S
James Bond
DRAWING BY HORAK
RADIO MESSAGE FOR MR. XENOPHANOS —AND A NOTE FROM THE SKIPPER!
I'LL TAKE IT!
EXCELLENT!... THIS RADIO REPORT CONFIRMS THAT YOUR FATHER HAS JUST ARRIVED AT THE COMPUTER PLANT, MY DEAR!
AND, BY THE WAY— TELL THE CAPTAIN TO WATCH FOR ANY UNUSUAL VISUAL PHENOMENA FROM THE COAST!
2154

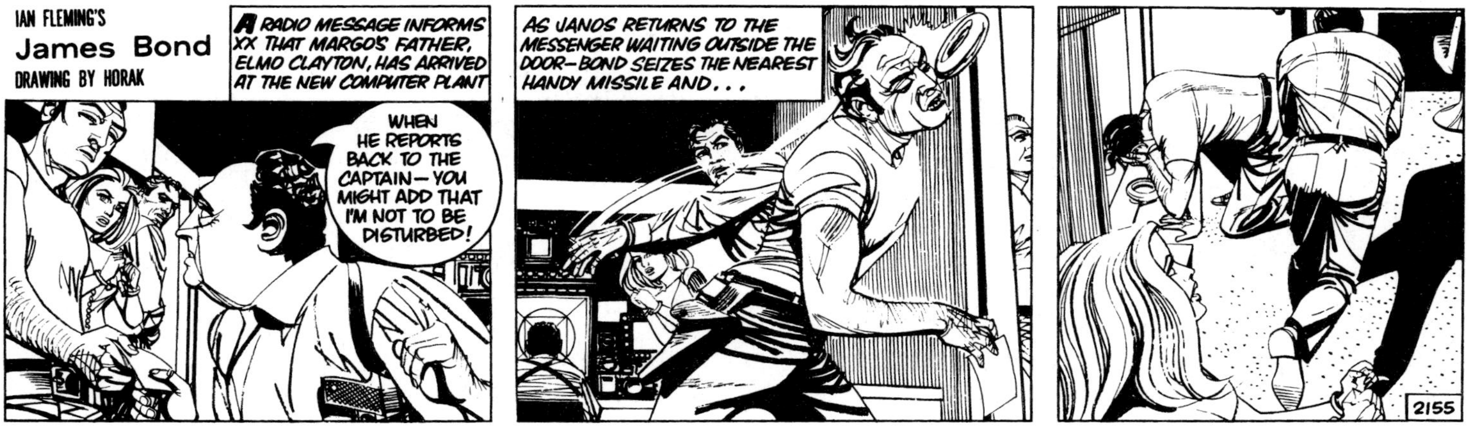
IAN FLEMING'S
James Bond
DRAWING BY HORAK
A RADIO MESSAGE INFORMS XX THAT MARGO'S FATHER, ELMO CLAYTON, HAS ARRIVED AT THE NEW COMPUTER PLANT
WHEN HE REPORTS BACK TO THE CAPTAIN— YOU MIGHT ADD THAT I'M NOT TO BE DISTURBED!
AS JANOS RETURNS TO THE MESSENGER WAITING OUTSIDE THE DOOR— BOND SEIZES THE NEAREST HANDY MISSILE AND...
2155

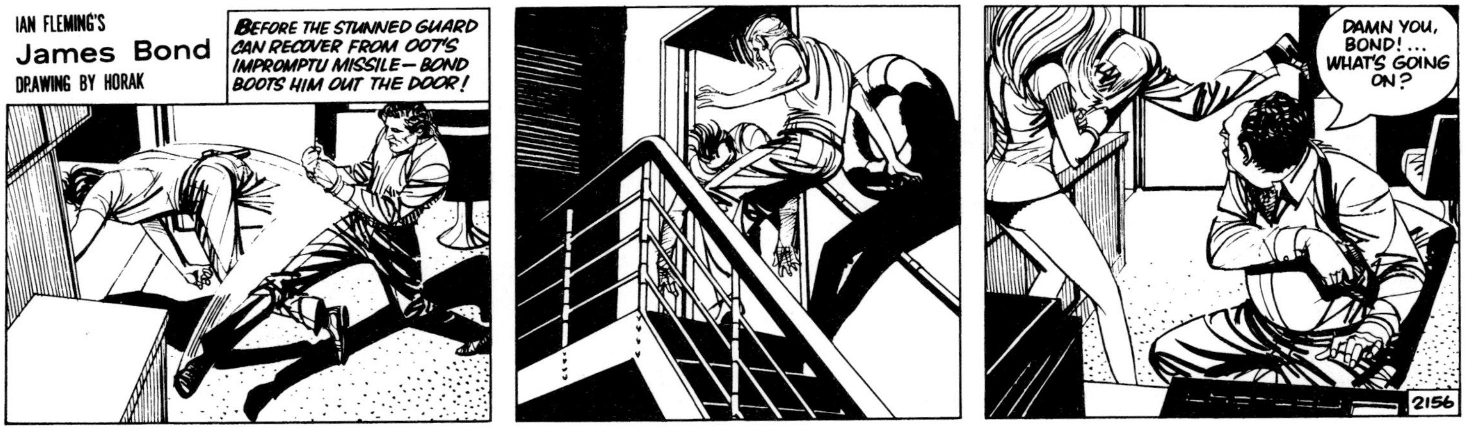
IAN FLEMING'S
James Bond
DRAWING BY HORAK
BEFORE THE STUNNED GUARD CAN RECOVER FROM OOT'S IMPROMPTU MISSILE— BOND BOOTS HIM OUT THE DOOR!
DAMN YOU, BOND!... WHAT'S GOING ON?
2156

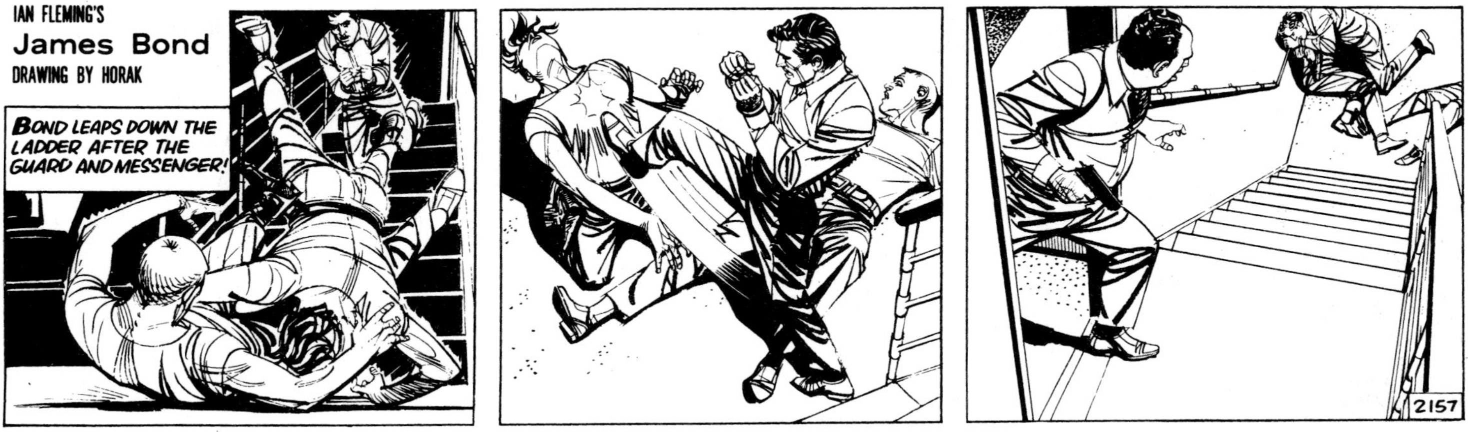
IAN FLEMING'S
James Bond
DRAWING BY HORAK
BOND LEAPS DOWN THE LADDER AFTER THE GUARD AND MESSENGER!
2157

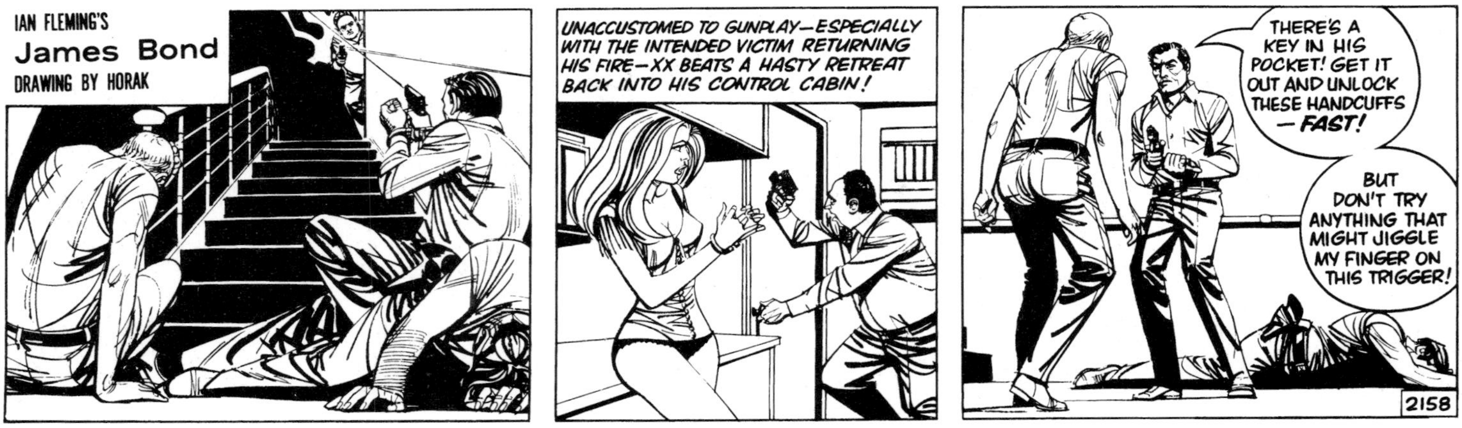
IAN FLEMING'S
James Bond
DRAWING BY HORAK
UNACCUSTOMED TO GUNPLAY—ESPECIALLY WITH THE INTENDED VICTIM RETURNING HIS FIRE—XX BEATS A HASTY RETREAT BACK INTO HIS CONTROL CABIN!
THERE'S A KEY IN HIS POCKET! GET IT OUT AND UNLOCK THESE HANDCUFFS —FAST!
BUT DON'T TRY ANYTHING THAT MIGHT JIGGLE MY FINGER ON THIS TRIGGER!
2158

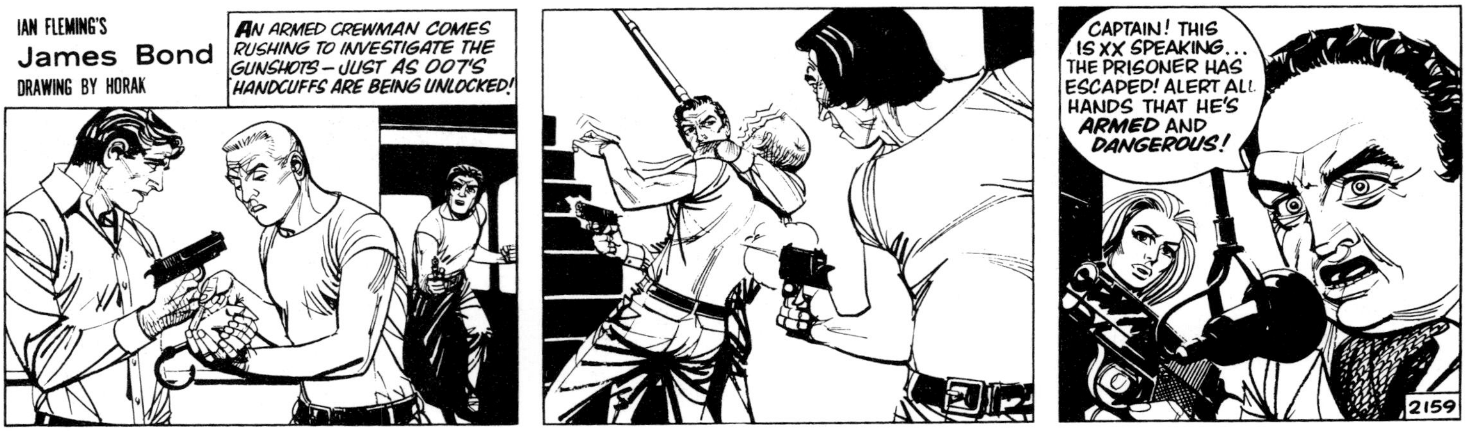
IAN FLEMING'S
James Bond
DRAWING BY HORAK
AN ARMED CREWMAN COMES RUSHING TO INVESTIGATE THE GUNSHOTS—JUST AS 007'S HANDCUFFS ARE BEING UNLOCKED!
CAPTAIN! THIS IS XX SPEAKING... THE PRISONER HAS ESCAPED! ALERT ALL HANDS THAT HE'S ARMED AND DANGEROUS!
2159

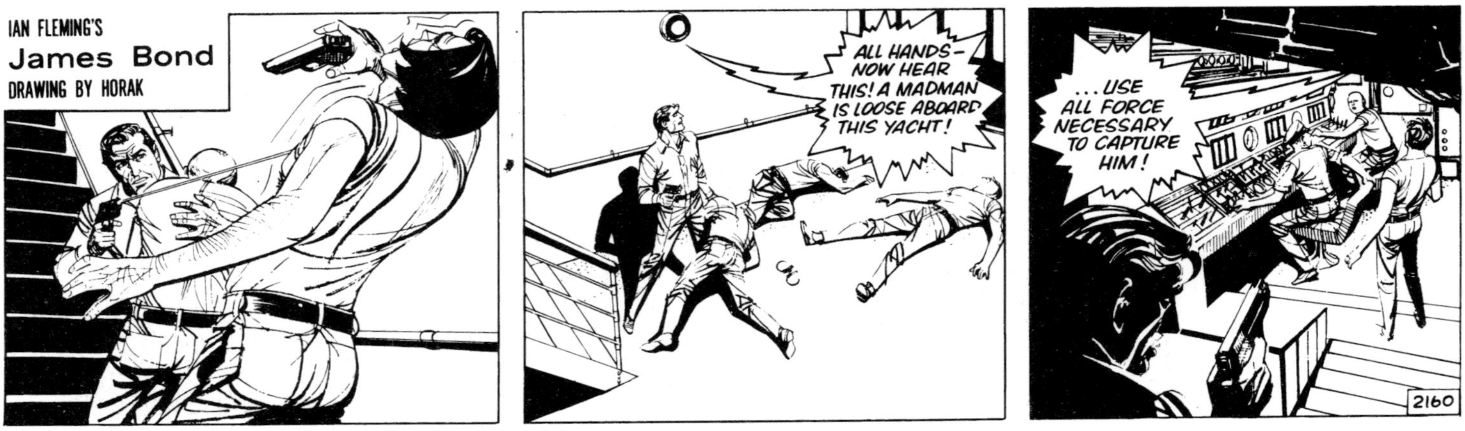
IAN FLEMING'S
James Bond
DRAWING BY HORAK
ALL HANDS—NOW HEAR THIS! A MADMAN IS LOOSE ABOARD THIS YACHT!
...USE ALL FORCE NECESSARY TO CAPTURE HIM!
2160

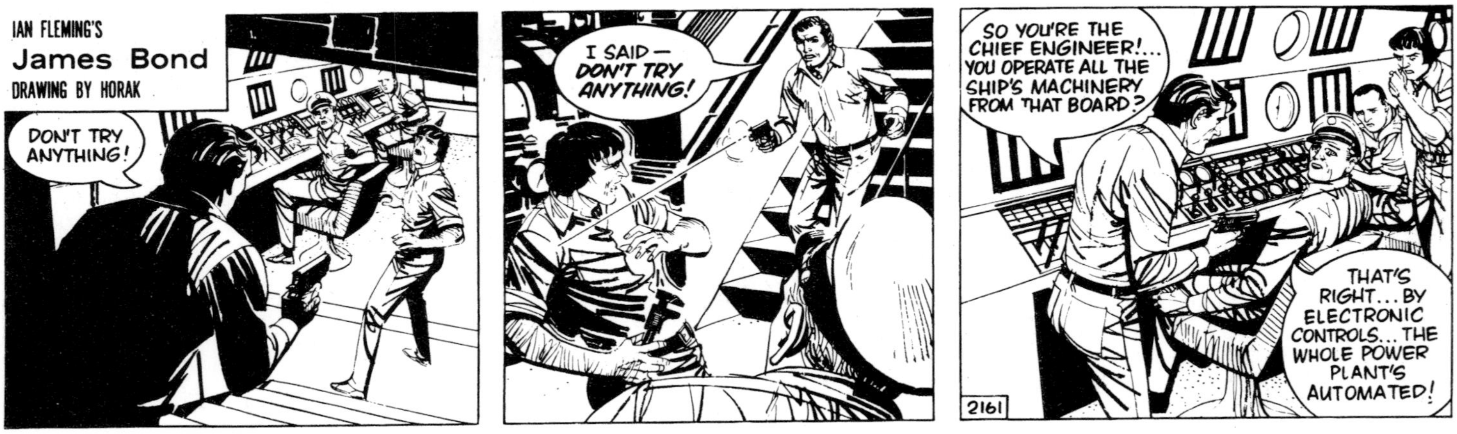
IAN FLEMING'S
James Bond
DRAWING BY HORAK
DON'T TRY ANYTHING!
I SAID—DON'T TRY ANYTHING!
SO YOU'RE THE CHIEF ENGINEER!... YOU OPERATE ALL THE SHIP'S MACHINERY FROM THAT BOARD?
THAT'S RIGHT... BY ELECTRONIC CONTROLS... THE WHOLE POWER PLANT'S AUTOMATED!
2161

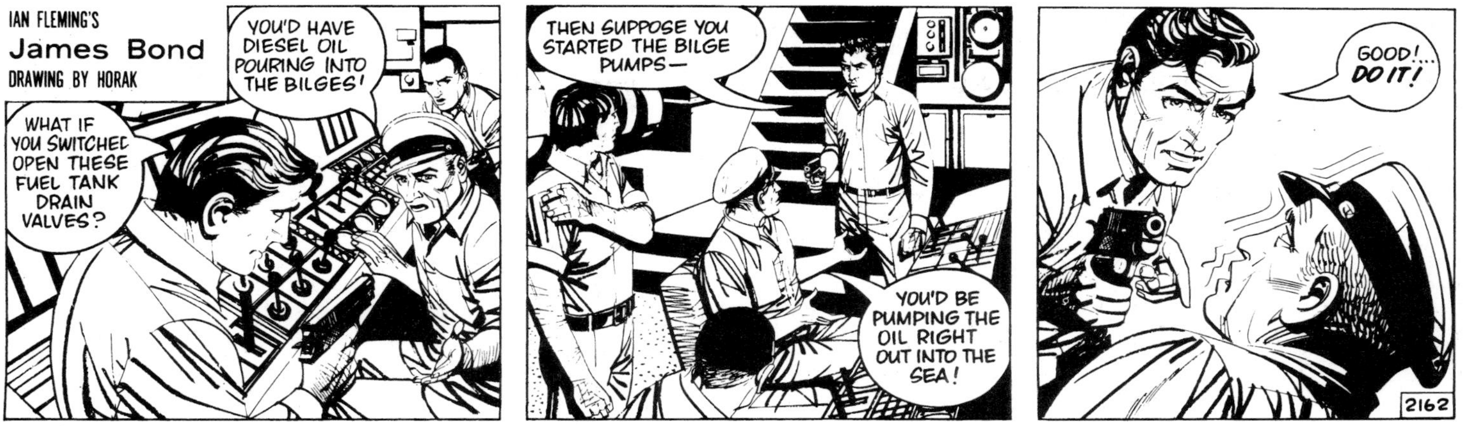
IAN FLEMING'S
James Bond
DRAWING BY HORAK
WHAT IF YOU SWITCHED OPEN THESE FUEL TANK DRAIN VALVES?
YOU'D HAVE DIESEL OIL POURING INTO THE BILGES!
THEN SUPPOSE YOU STARTED THE BILGE PUMPS—
YOU'D BE PUMPING THE OIL RIGHT OUT INTO THE SEA!
GOOD!... DO IT!
2162

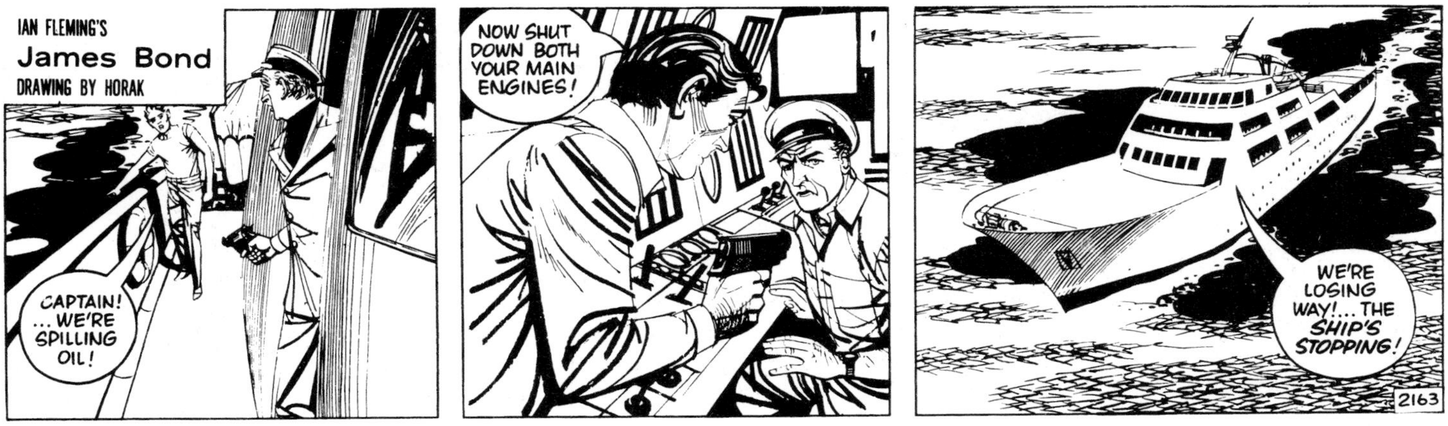
IAN FLEMING'S
James Bond
DRAWING BY HORAK
CAPTAIN! ... WE'RE SPILLING OIL!
NOW SHUT DOWN BOTH YOUR MAIN ENGINES!
WE'RE LOSING WAY!... THE SHIP'S STOPPING!
2163

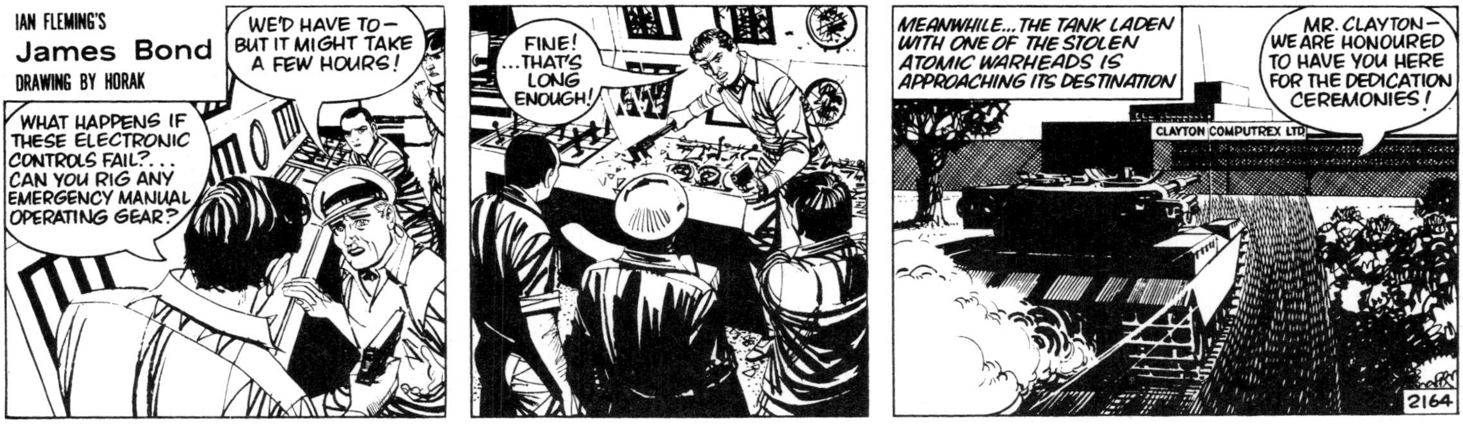
IAN FLEMING'S
James Bond
DRAWING BY HORAK
WHAT HAPPENS IF THESE ELECTRONIC CONTROLS FAIL?... CAN YOU RIG ANY EMERGENCY MANUAL OPERATING GEAR?
WE'D HAVE TO— BUT IT MIGHT TAKE A FEW HOURS!
FINE! ...THAT'S LONG ENOUGH!
MEANWHILE... THE TANK LADEN WITH ONE OF THE STOLEN ATOMIC WARHEADS IS APPROACHING ITS DESTINATION
MR. CLAYTON— WE ARE HONOURED TO HAVE YOU HERE FOR THE DEDICATION CEREMONIES!
CLAYTON COMPUTREX LTD
2164

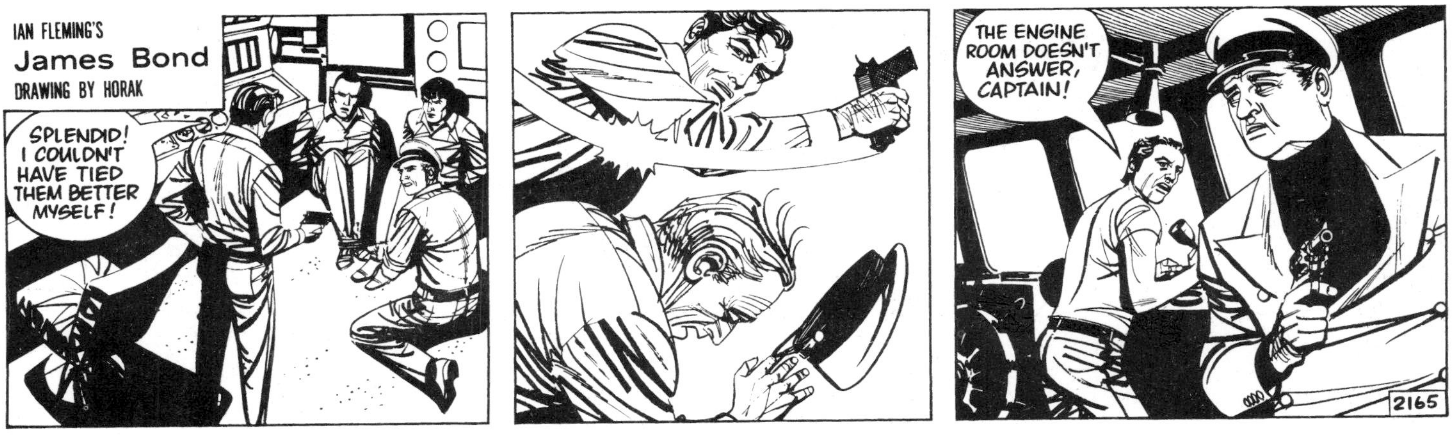
IAN FLEMING'S
James Bond
DRAWING BY HORAK
SPLENDID! I COULDN'T HAVE TIED THEM BETTER MYSELF!
THE ENGINE ROOM DOESN'T ANSWER, CAPTAIN!
2165

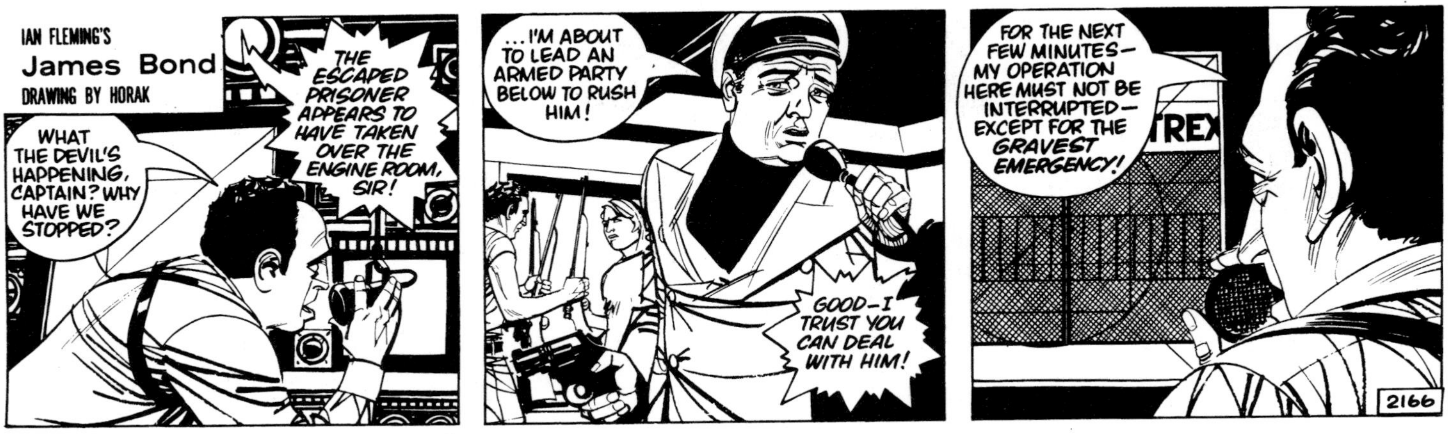
IAN FLEMING'S
James Bond
DRAWING BY HORAK
THE ESCAPED PRISONER APPEARS TO HAVE TAKEN OVER THE ENGINE ROOM, SIR!
WHAT THE DEVIL'S HAPPENING, CAPTAIN? WHY HAVE WE STOPPED?
...I'M ABOUT TO LEAD AN ARMED PARTY BELOW TO RUSH HIM!
GOOD—I TRUST YOU CAN DEAL WITH HIM!
FOR THE NEXT FEW MINUTES—MY OPERATION HERE MUST NOT BE INTERRUPTED—EXCEPT FOR THE GRAVEST EMERGENCY!
TREX
2166

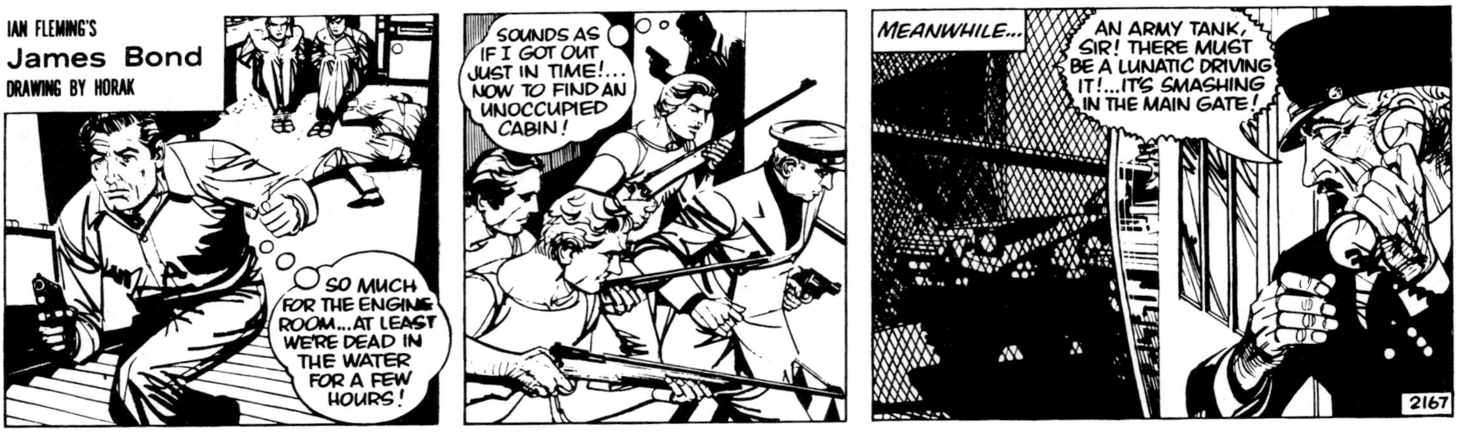
IAN FLEMING'S
James Bond
DRAWING BY HORAK
SO MUCH FOR THE ENGINE ROOM...AT LEAST WE'RE DEAD IN THE WATER FOR A FEW HOURS!
SOUNDS AS IF I GOT OUT JUST IN TIME!... NOW TO FIND AN UNOCCUPIED CABIN!
MEANWHILE...
AN ARMY TANK, SIR! THERE MUST BE A LUNATIC DRIVING IT!...IT'S SMASHING IN THE MAIN GATE!
2167

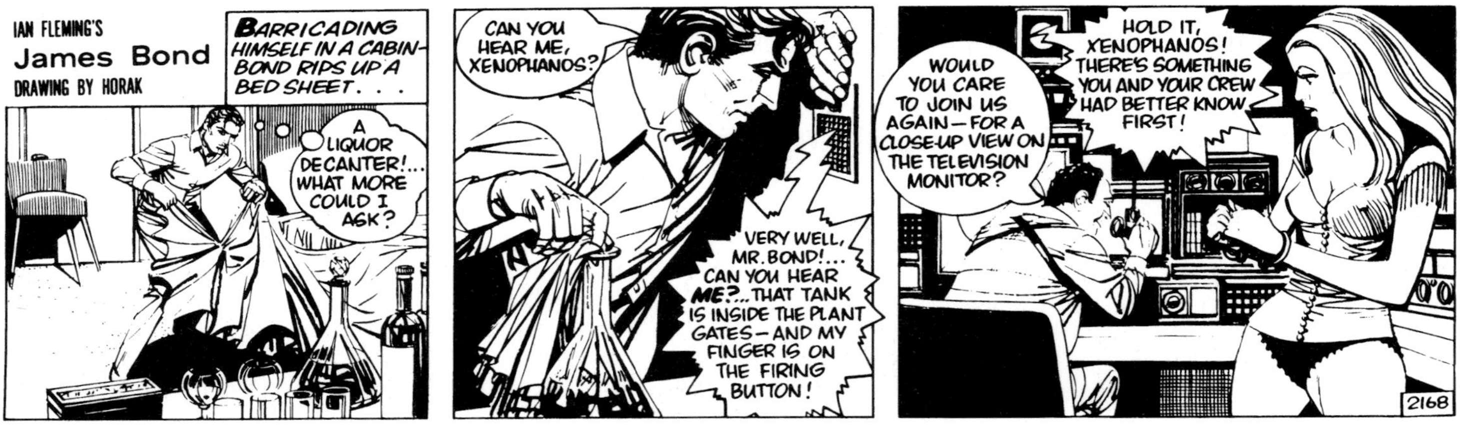
IAN FLEMING'S
James Bond
DRAWING BY HORAK
BARRICADING HIMSELF IN A CABIN-BOND RIPS UP A BED SHEET . . .
A LIQUOR DECANTER!... WHAT MORE COULD I ASK?
CAN YOU HEAR ME, XENOPHANOS?
VERY WELL, MR. BOND!... CAN YOU HEAR ME?... THAT TANK IS INSIDE THE PLANT GATES—AND MY FINGER IS ON THE FIRING BUTTON!
WOULD YOU CARE TO JOIN US AGAIN—FOR A CLOSE-UP VIEW ON THE TELEVISION MONITOR?
HOLD IT, XENOPHANOS! THERE'S SOMETHING YOU AND YOUR CREW HAD BETTER KNOW FIRST!
2168

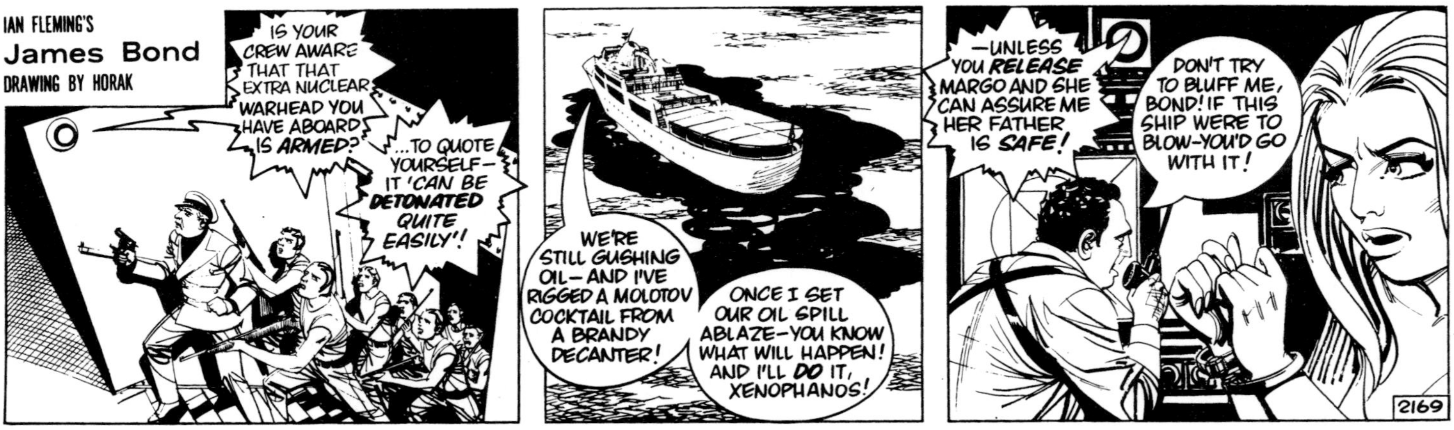
IAN FLEMING'S
James Bond
DRAWING BY HORAK
IS YOUR CREW AWARE THAT THAT EXTRA NUCLEAR WARHEAD YOU HAVE ABOARD IS ARMED?
...TO QUOTE YOURSELF—IT 'CAN BE DETONATED QUITE EASILY'!
WE'RE STILL GUSHING OIL—AND I'VE RIGGED A MOLOTOV COCKTAIL FROM A BRANDY DECANTER!
ONCE I SET OUR OIL SPILL ABLAZE—YOU KNOW WHAT WILL HAPPEN! AND I'LL DO IT, XENOPHANOS!
—UNLESS YOU RELEASE MARGO AND SHE CAN ASSURE ME HER FATHER IS SAFE!
DON'T TRY TO BLUFF ME, BOND! IF THIS SHIP WERE TO BLOW—YOU'D GO WITH IT!
2169

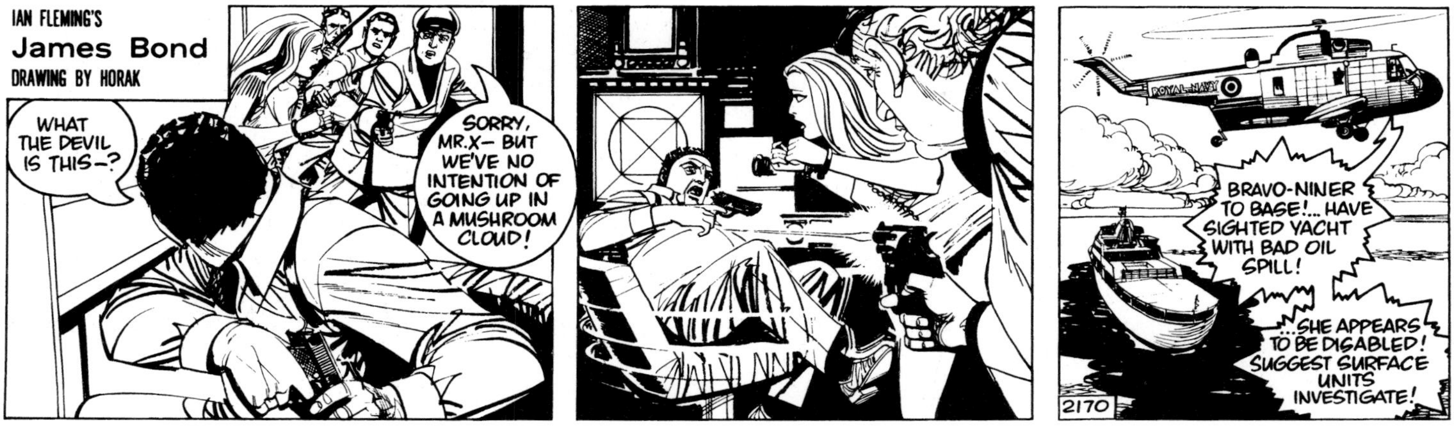
IAN FLEMING'S
James Bond
DRAWING BY HORAK
WHAT THE DEVIL IS THIS-?
SORRY, MR.X- BUT WE'VE NO INTENTION OF GOING UP IN A MUSHROOM CLOUD!
ROYAL NAVY
BRAVO-NINER TO BASE!... HAVE SIGHTED YACHT WITH BAD OIL SPILL!
...SHE APPEARS TO BE DISABLED! SUGGEST SURFACE UNITS INVESTIGATE!
2170

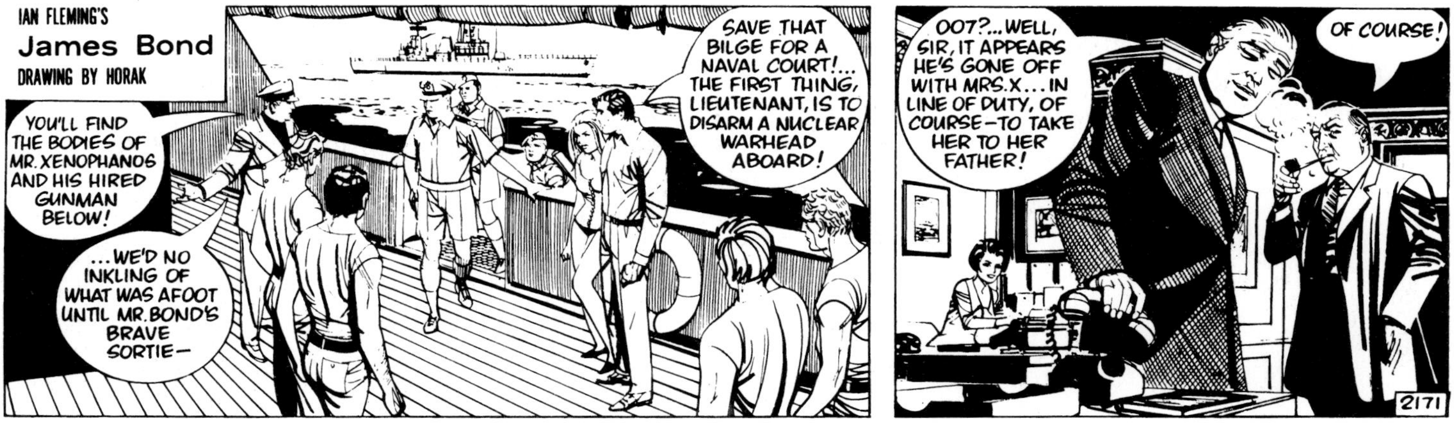
IAN FLEMING'S
James Bond
DRAWING BY HORAK
YOU'LL FIND THE BODIES OF MR. XENOPHANOS AND HIS HIRED GUNMAN BELOW!
...WE'D NO INKLING OF WHAT WAS AFOOT UNTIL MR. BOND'S BRAVE SORTIE-
SAVE THAT BILGE FOR A NAVAL COURT!... THE FIRST THING, LIEUTENANT, IS TO DISARM A NUCLEAR WARHEAD ABOARD!
007?...WELL, SIR, IT APPEARS HE'S GONE OFF WITH MRS.X... IN LINE OF DUTY, OF COURSE-TO TAKE HER TO HER FATHER!
OF COURSE!
2171

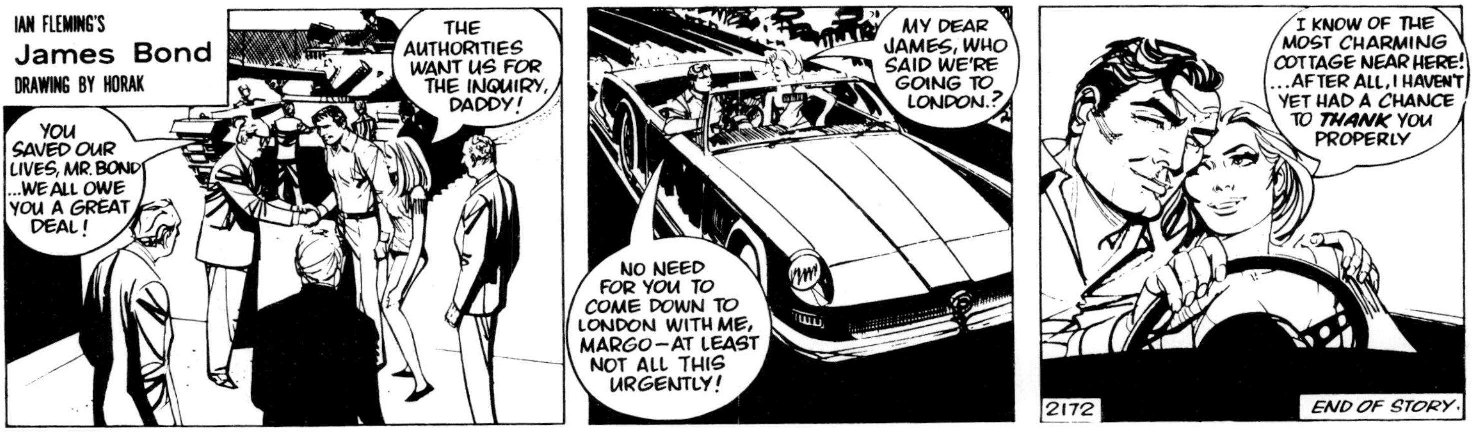
IAN FLEMING'S
James Bond
DRAWING BY HORAK
YOU SAVED OUR LIVES, MR. BOND ...WE ALL OWE YOU A GREAT DEAL!
THE AUTHORITIES WANT US FOR THE INQUIRY, DADDY!
MY DEAR JAMES, WHO SAID WE'RE GOING TO LONDON.?
NO NEED FOR YOU TO COME DOWN TO LONDON WITH ME, MARGO-AT LEAST NOT ALL THIS URGENTLY!
I KNOW OF THE MOST CHARMING COTTAGE NEAR HERE! ...AFTER ALL, I HAVEN'T YET HAD A CHANCE TO THANK YOU PROPERLY
2172
END OF STORY.

DIE WITH MY BOOTS ON

*D*ie With My Boots On — like so many original strips in the series — introduces James Bond into the story in a rather novel way. Jim Lawrence has certainly done a good job of keeping the plot moving quickly, but as a result, it certainly doesn't feel as in-depth as some of Lawrence's earlier work on the series; there isn't much in the way of plot, other than the change of a character's loyalties. Lawrence's grasp of Bond's character seems to suffer for the story's brevity, too, as he utters some of his poorest lines to date. However, Yaroslav Horak has — as always — done a fantastic job of depicting Bond's world richly and consistently throughout the story. The level of detailing allows the reader to understand exactly what is happening throughout, without being patronising.

Fans of the both the books and films will notice where Lawrence seems to have drawn his inspiration. Similarities can be drawn between *Die With My Boots On* and Fleming's *Live and Let Die*; we get a sense of 'New York soul', particularly when Smoky Turpin gives Bond his "Harlem Hotshots". It should be noted that towards the end of the strip's UK run, James Bond once again returned to cinema screens, this time played by Roger Moore in *Live and Let Die*.

Unlike the other comic strip adventures, *Die With My Boots On* lacks any real romantic inclinations between Bond and either of the female leads. Even at the end of the strip — where fans would normally expect to find Bond coming out 'on top' — there is no suggestion that he will this time...

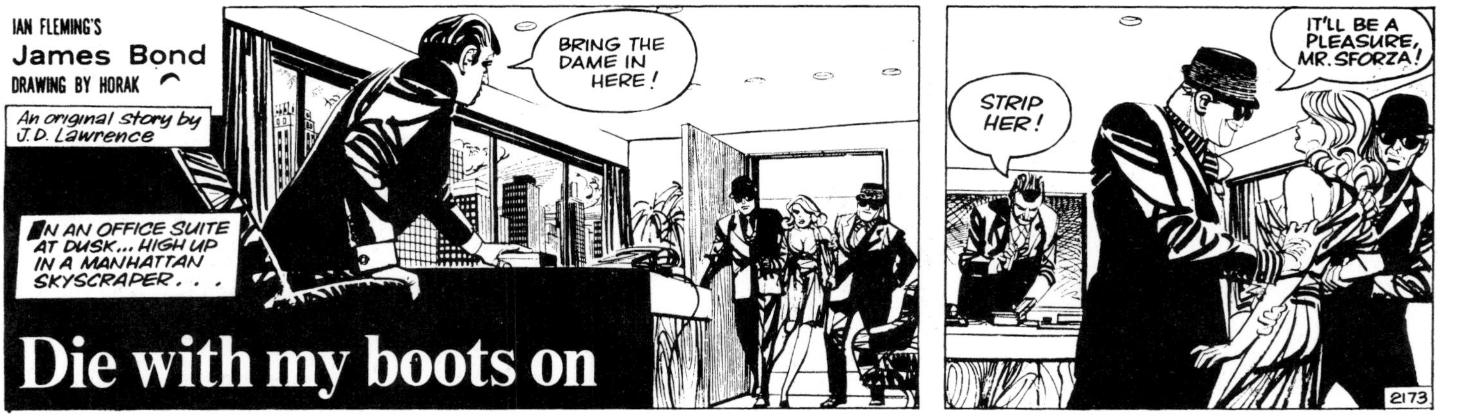
IAN FLEMING'S
James Bond
DRAWING BY HORAK
An original story by J.D. Lawrence
IN AN OFFICE SUITE AT DUSK... HIGH UP IN A MANHATTAN SKYSCRAPER...
BRING THE DAME IN HERE!
Die with my boots on
STRIP HER!
IT'LL BE A PLEASURE, MR. SFORZA!
2173

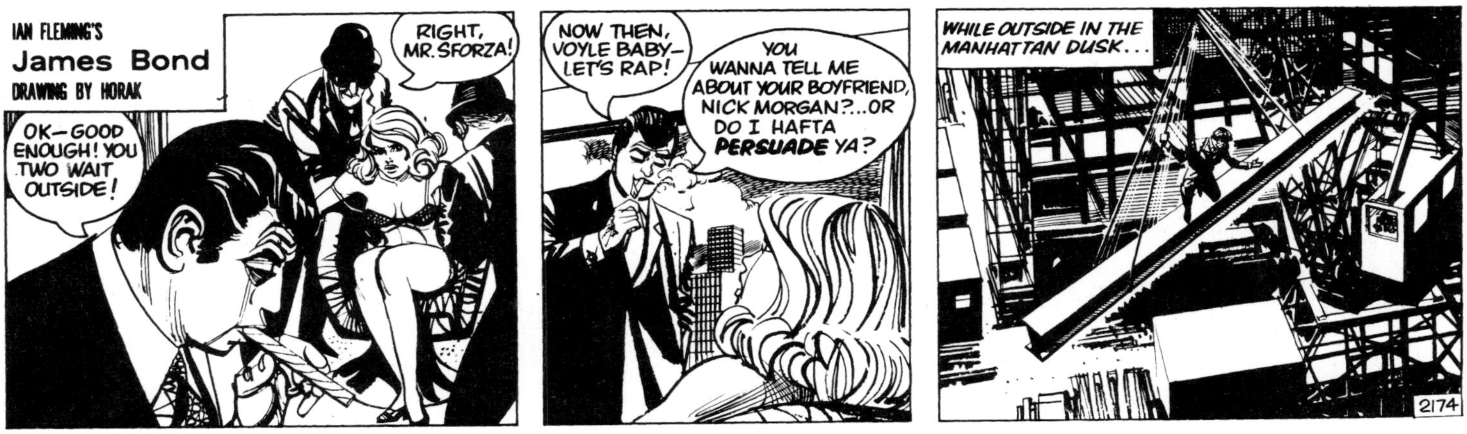
IAN FLEMING'S
James Bond
DRAWING BY HORAK
OK—GOOD ENOUGH! YOU TWO WAIT OUTSIDE!
RIGHT, MR. SFORZA!
NOW THEN, VOYLE BABY—LET'S RAP!
YOU WANNA TELL ME ABOUT YOUR BOYFRIEND, NICK MORGAN?...OR DO I HAFTA PERSUADE YA?
WHILE OUTSIDE IN THE MANHATTAN DUSK...
2174

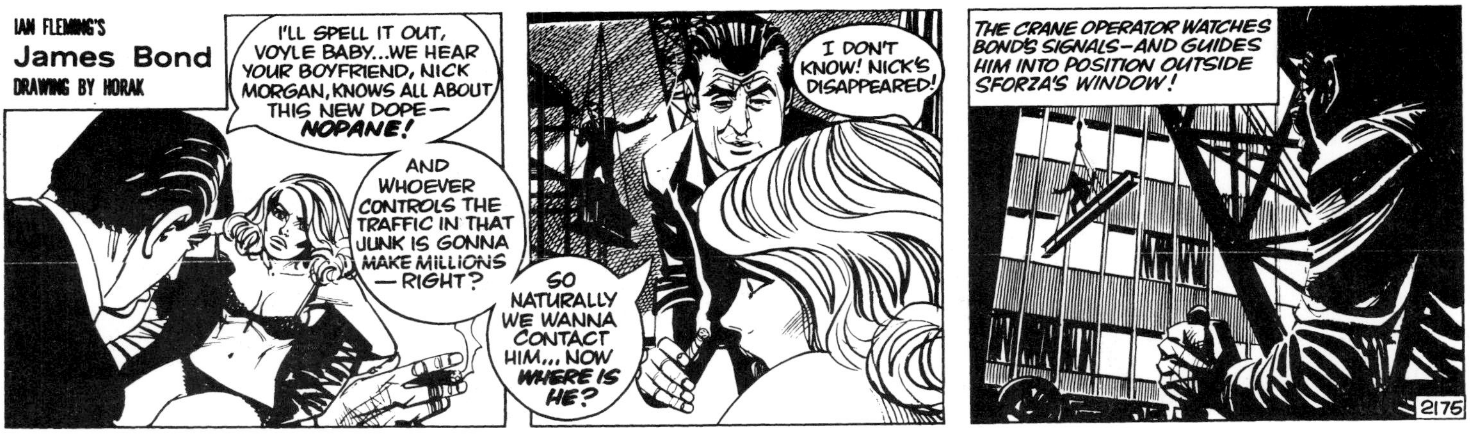
IAN FLEMING'S
James Bond
DRAWING BY HORAK
I'LL SPELL IT OUT, VOYLE BABY...WE HEAR YOUR BOYFRIEND, NICK MORGAN, KNOWS ALL ABOUT THIS NEW DOPE—NOPANE!
AND WHOEVER CONTROLS THE TRAFFIC IN THAT JUNK IS GONNA MAKE MILLIONS —RIGHT?
SO NATURALLY WE WANNA CONTACT HIM... NOW WHERE IS HE?
I DON'T KNOW! NICK'S DISAPPEARED!
THE CRANE OPERATOR WATCHES BOND'S SIGNALS—AND GUIDES HIM INTO POSITION OUTSIDE SFORZA'S WINDOW!
2175

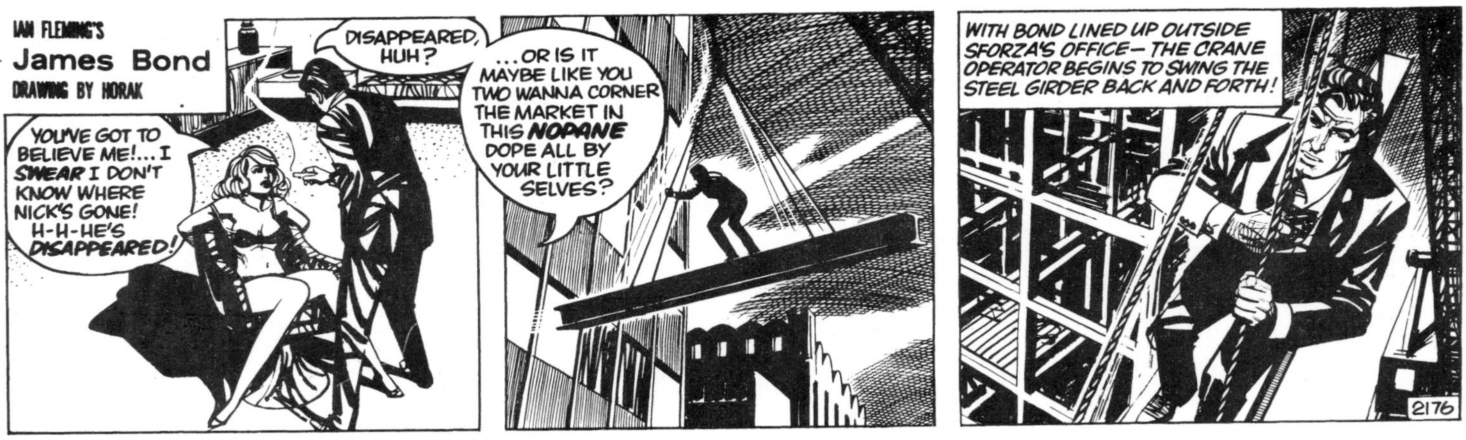
IAN FLEMING'S
James Bond
DRAWING BY HORAK
YOU'VE GOT TO BELIEVE ME!... I SWEAR I DON'T KNOW WHERE NICK'S GONE! H-H-HE'S DISAPPEARED!
DISAPPEARED, HUH?
...OR IS IT MAYBE LIKE YOU TWO WANNA CORNER THE MARKET IN THIS NOPANE DOPE ALL BY YOUR LITTLE SELVES?
WITH BOND LINED UP OUTSIDE SFORZA'S OFFICE—THE CRANE OPERATOR BEGINS TO SWING THE STEEL GIRDER BACK AND FORTH!
2176

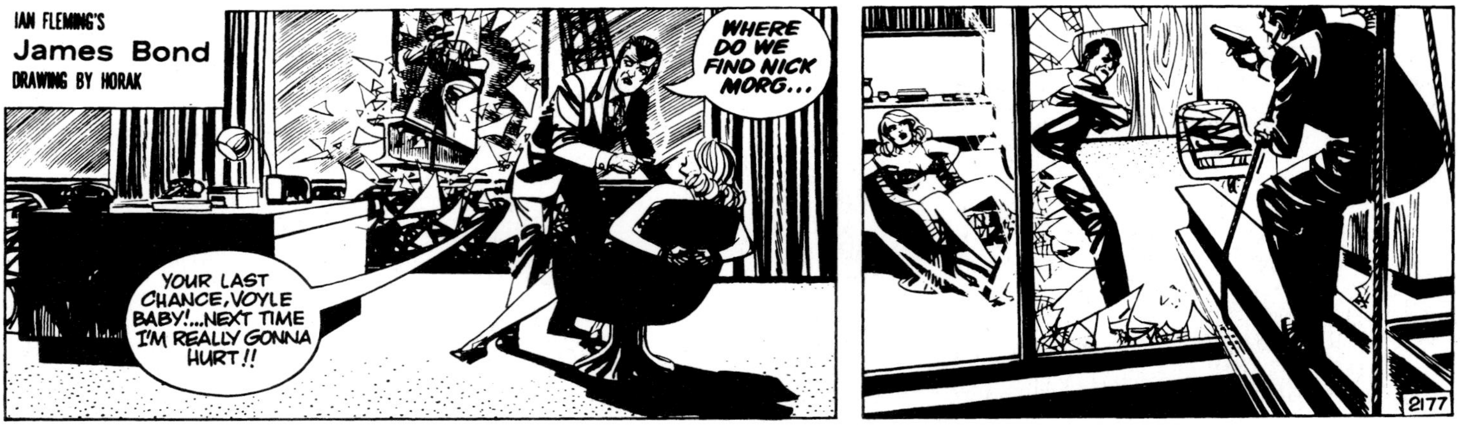
IAN FLEMING'S
James Bond
DRAWING BY HORAK
WHERE DO WE FIND NICK MORG...
YOUR LAST CHANCE, VOYLE BABY!...NEXT TIME I'M REALLY GONNA HURT!!
2177

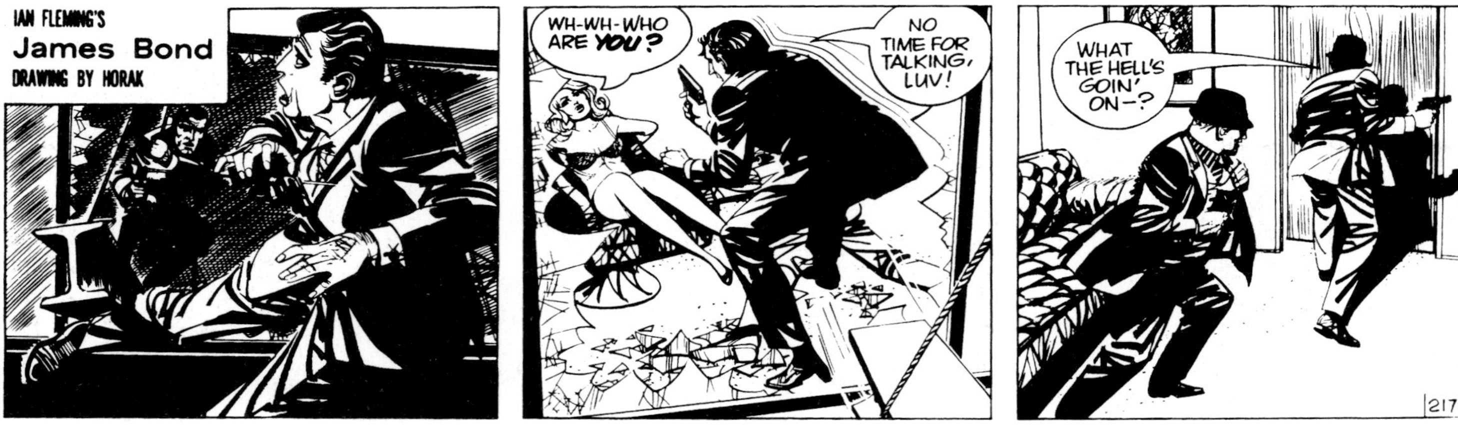
IAN FLEMING'S
James Bond
DRAWING BY HORAK
WH-WH-WHO ARE YOU?
NO TIME FOR TALKING, LUV!
WHAT THE HELL'S GOIN' ON-?
2178

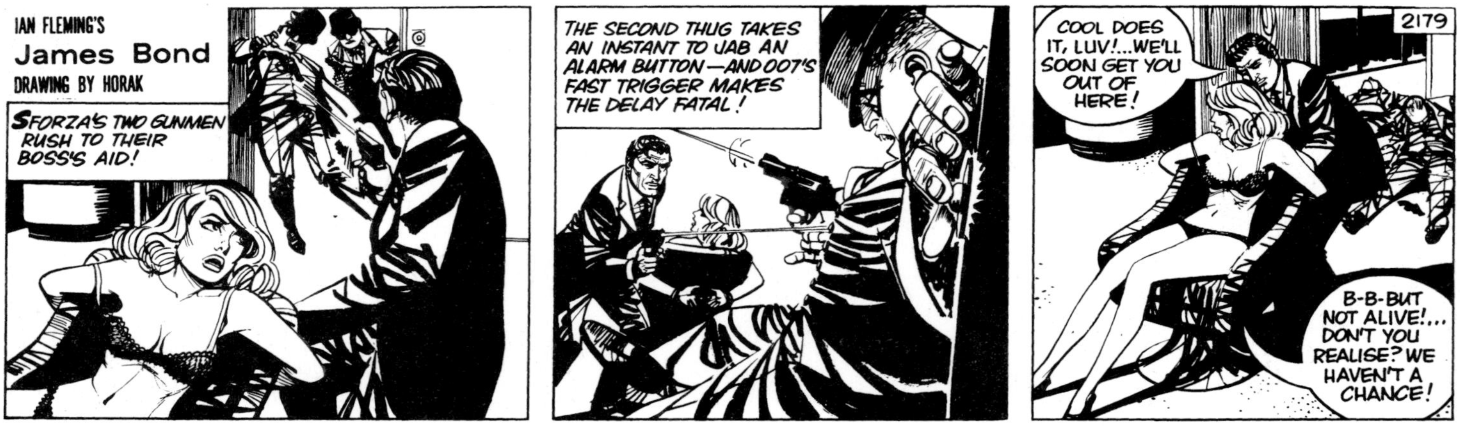
IAN FLEMING'S
James Bond
DRAWING BY HORAK
SFORZA'S TWO GUNMEN RUSH TO THEIR BOSS'S AID!
THE SECOND THUG TAKES AN INSTANT TO JAB AN ALARM BUTTON—AND 007'S FAST TRIGGER MAKES THE DELAY FATAL!
2179
COOL DOES IT, LUV!...WE'LL SOON GET YOU OUT OF HERE!
B-B-BUT NOT ALIVE!... DON'T YOU REALISE? WE HAVEN'T A CHANCE!

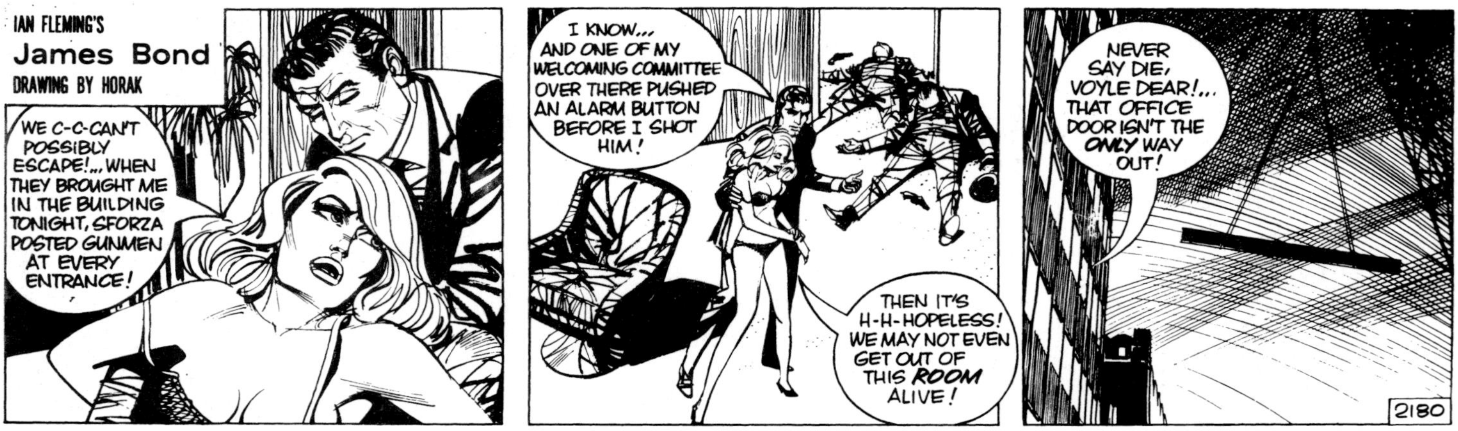
IAN FLEMING'S
James Bond
DRAWING BY HORAK
WE C-C-CAN'T POSSIBLY ESCAPE!... WHEN THEY BROUGHT ME IN THE BUILDING TONIGHT, SFORZA POSTED GUNMEN AT EVERY ENTRANCE!
I KNOW... AND ONE OF MY WELCOMING COMMITTEE OVER THERE PUSHED AN ALARM BUTTON BEFORE I SHOT HIM!
THEN IT'S H-H-HOPELESS! WE MAY NOT EVEN GET OUT OF THIS ROOM ALIVE!
NEVER SAY DIE, VOYLE DEAR!... THAT OFFICE DOOR ISN'T THE ONLY WAY OUT!
2180

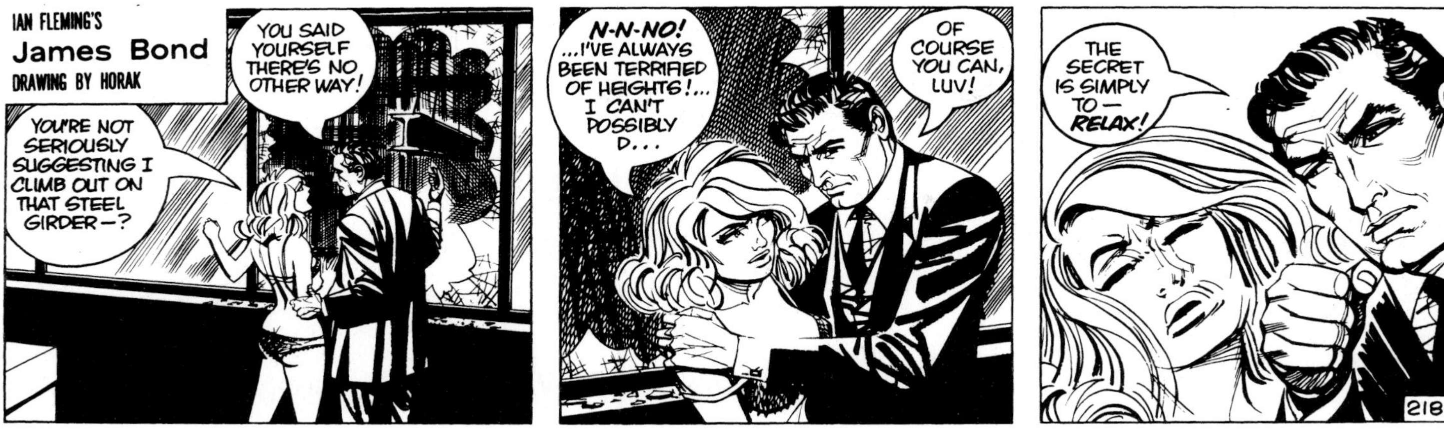
IAN FLEMING'S
James Bond
DRAWING BY HORAK
YOU'RE NOT SERIOUSLY SUGGESTING I CLIMB OUT ON THAT STEEL GIRDER—?
YOU SAID YOURSELF THERE'S NO OTHER WAY!
N-N-NO! ...I'VE ALWAYS BEEN TERRIFIED OF HEIGHTS!... I CAN'T POSSIBLY D...
OF COURSE YOU CAN, LUV!
THE SECRET IS SIMPLY TO— RELAX!
2181

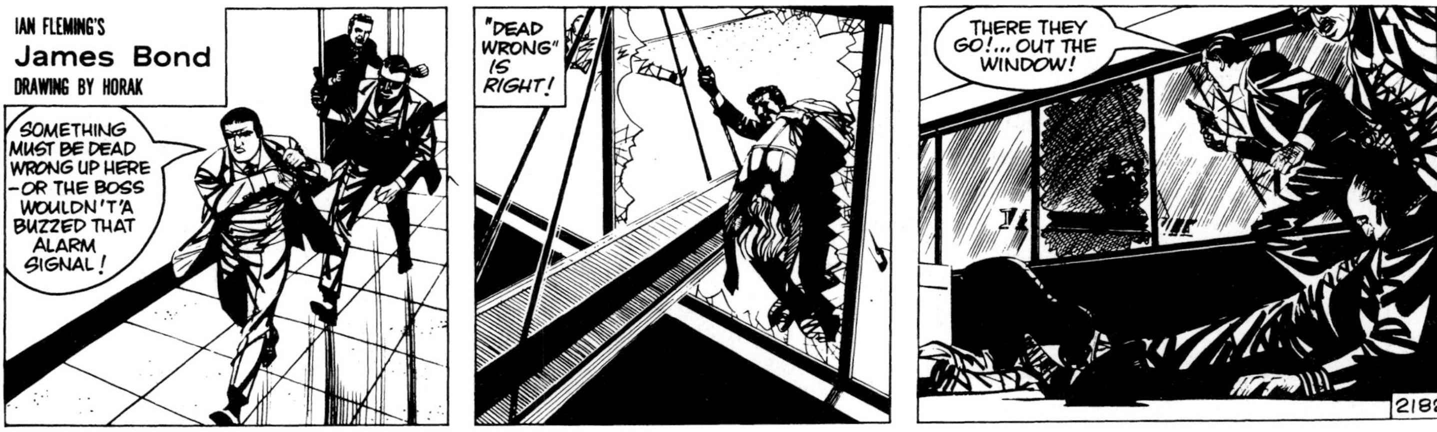
IAN FLEMING'S
James Bond
DRAWING BY HORAK
SOMETHING MUST BE DEAD WRONG UP HERE —OR THE BOSS WOULDN'T'A BUZZED THAT ALARM SIGNAL!
"DEAD WRONG" IS RIGHT!
THERE THEY GO!... OUT THE WINDOW!
2182

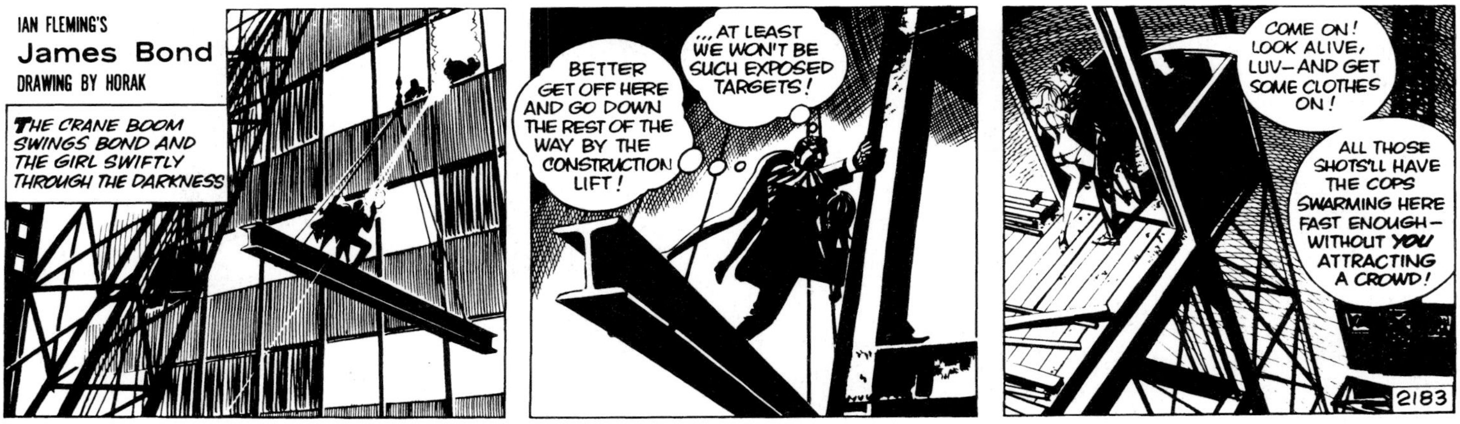
IAN FLEMING'S
James Bond
DRAWING BY HORAK
THE CRANE BOOM SWINGS BOND AND THE GIRL SWIFTLY THROUGH THE DARKNESS
BETTER GET OFF HERE AND GO DOWN THE REST OF THE WAY BY THE CONSTRUCTION LIFT!
...AT LEAST WE WON'T BE SUCH EXPOSED TARGETS!
COME ON! LOOK ALIVE, LUV—AND GET SOME CLOTHES ON!
ALL THOSE SHOTS'LL HAVE THE COPS SWARMING HERE FAST ENOUGH— WITHOUT YOU ATTRACTING A CROWD!
2183

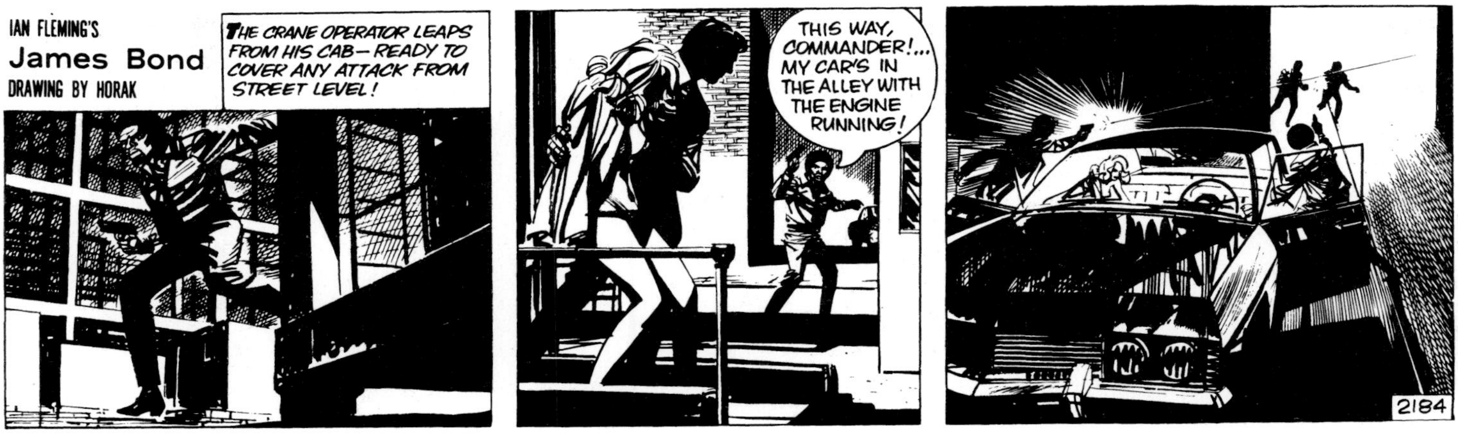
IAN FLEMING'S
James Bond
DRAWING BY HORAK
THE CRANE OPERATOR LEAPS FROM HIS CAB—READY TO COVER ANY ATTACK FROM STREET LEVEL!
THIS WAY, COMMANDER!... MY CAR'S IN THE ALLEY WITH THE ENGINE RUNNING!
2184

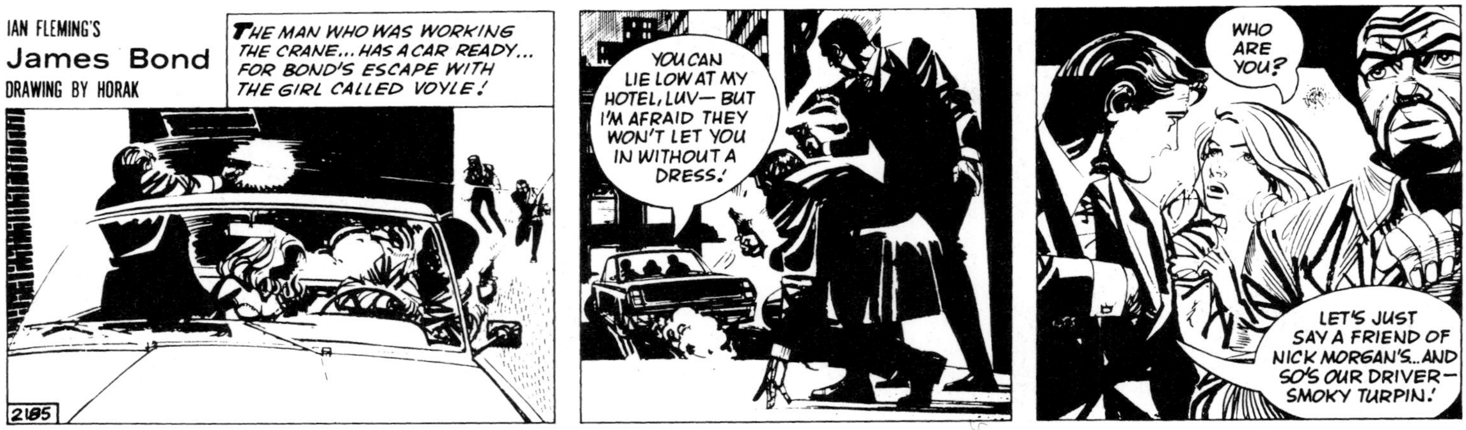
IAN FLEMING'S
James Bond
DRAWING BY HORAK
THE MAN WHO WAS WORKING THE CRANE... HAS A CAR READY... FOR BOND'S ESCAPE WITH THE GIRL CALLED VOYLE!
YOU CAN LIE LOW AT MY HOTEL, LUV— BUT I'M AFRAID THEY WON'T LET YOU IN WITHOUT A DRESS!
WHO ARE YOU?
LET'S JUST SAY A FRIEND OF NICK MORGAN'S... AND SO'S OUR DRIVER— SMOKY TURPIN!
2185

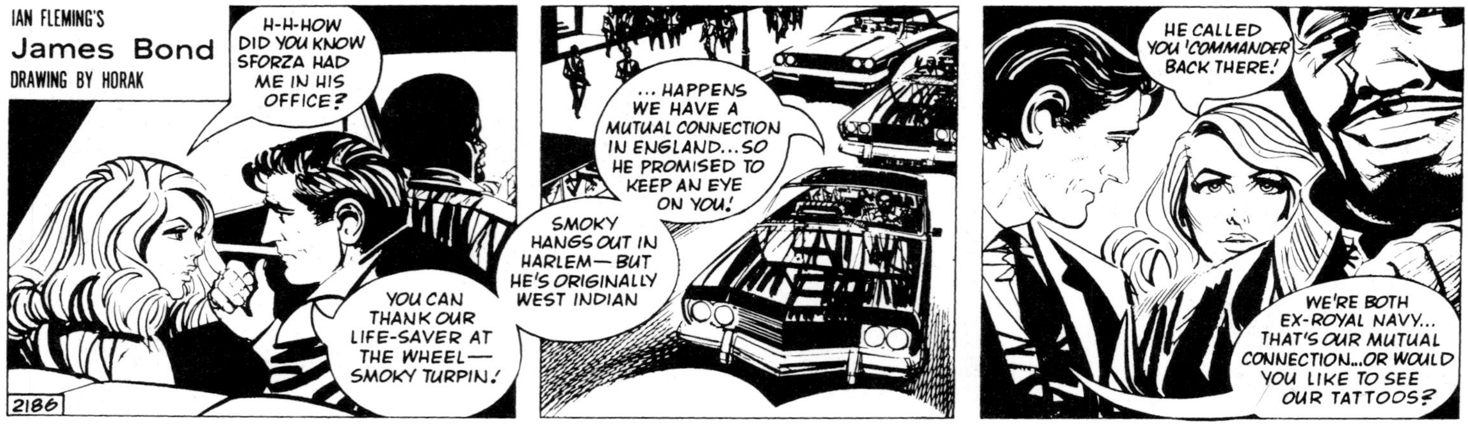
IAN FLEMING'S
James Bond
DRAWING BY HORAK
H-H-HOW DID YOU KNOW SFORZA HAD ME IN HIS OFFICE?
YOU CAN THANK OUR LIFE-SAVER AT THE WHEEL— SMOKY TURPIN!
... HAPPENS WE HAVE A MUTUAL CONNECTION IN ENGLAND... SO HE PROMISED TO KEEP AN EYE ON YOU!
SMOKY HANGS OUT IN HARLEM— BUT HE'S ORIGINALLY WEST INDIAN
HE CALLED YOU 'COMMANDER' BACK THERE!
WE'RE BOTH EX-ROYAL NAVY... THAT'S OUR MUTUAL CONNECTION... OR WOULD YOU LIKE TO SEE OUR TATTOOS?
2186

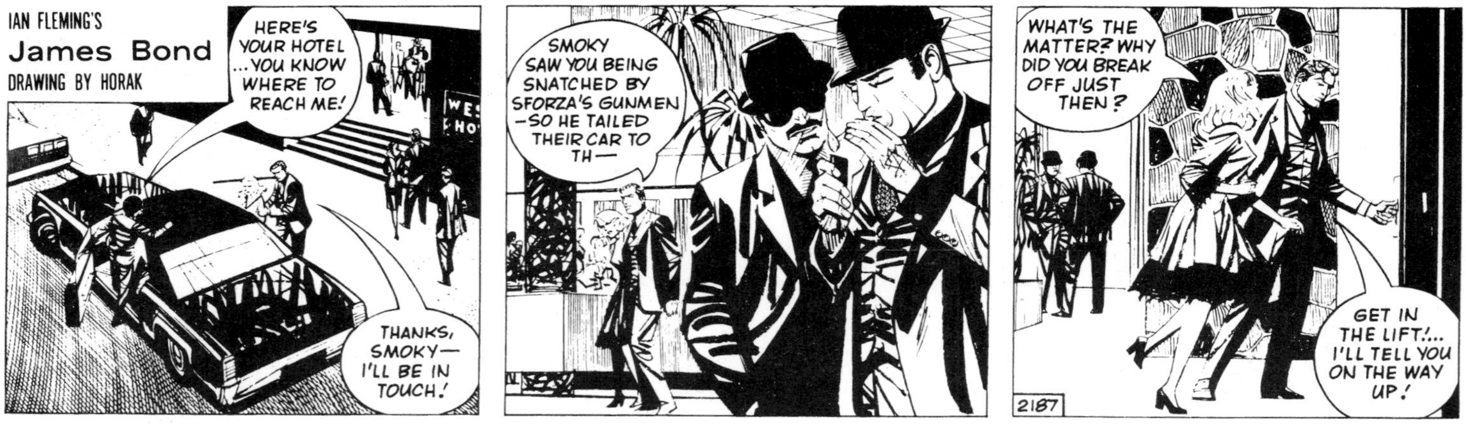
IAN FLEMING'S
James Bond
DRAWING BY HORAK
HERE'S YOUR HOTEL ...YOU KNOW WHERE TO REACH ME!
THANKS, SMOKY— I'LL BE IN TOUCH!
SMOKY SAW YOU BEING SNATCHED BY SFORZA'S GUNMEN —SO HE TAILED THEIR CAR TO TH—
WHAT'S THE MATTER? WHY DID YOU BREAK OFF JUST THEN?
GET IN THE LIFT!... I'LL TELL YOU ON THE WAY UP!
2187

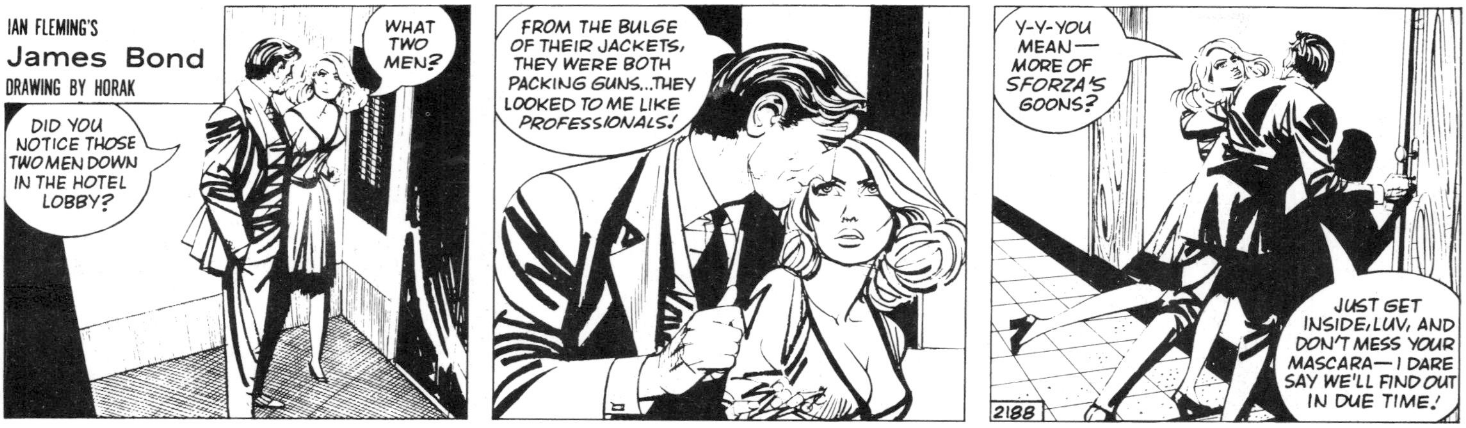
IAN FLEMING'S
James Bond
DRAWING BY HORAK
DID YOU NOTICE THOSE TWO MEN DOWN IN THE HOTEL LOBBY?
WHAT TWO MEN?
FROM THE BULGE OF THEIR JACKETS, THEY WERE BOTH PACKING GUNS... THEY LOOKED TO ME LIKE PROFESSIONALS!
Y-Y-YOU MEAN— MORE OF SFORZA'S GOONS?
JUST GET INSIDE, LUV, AND DON'T MESS YOUR MASCARA— I DARE SAY WE'LL FIND OUT IN DUE TIME!
2188

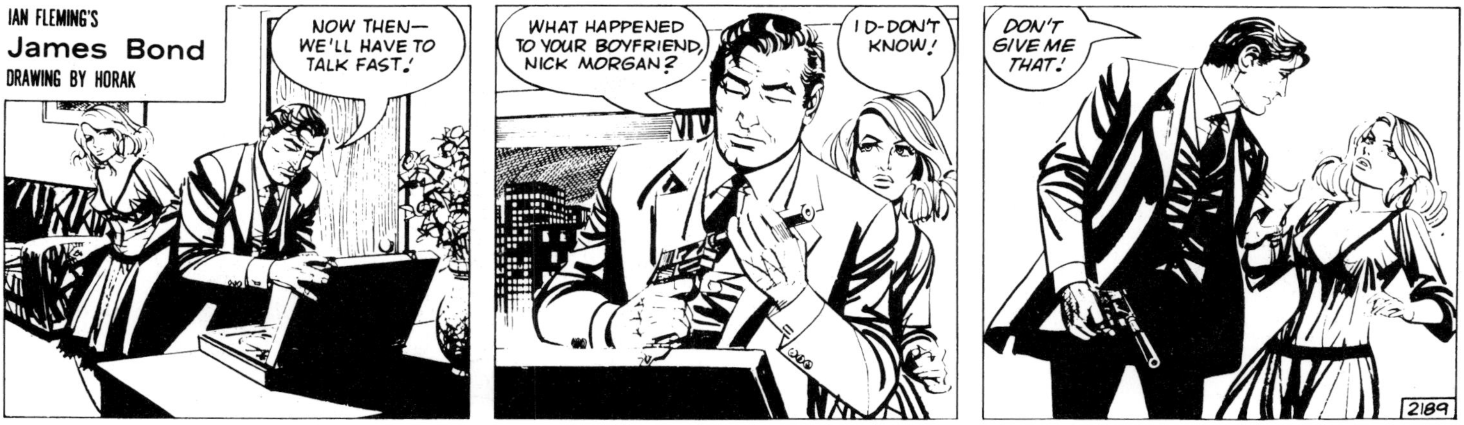
IAN FLEMING'S
James Bond
DRAWING BY HORAK
NOW THEN— WE'LL HAVE TO TALK FAST!
WHAT HAPPENED TO YOUR BOYFRIEND, NICK MORGAN?
I D-DON'T KNOW!
DON'T GIVE ME THAT!
2189

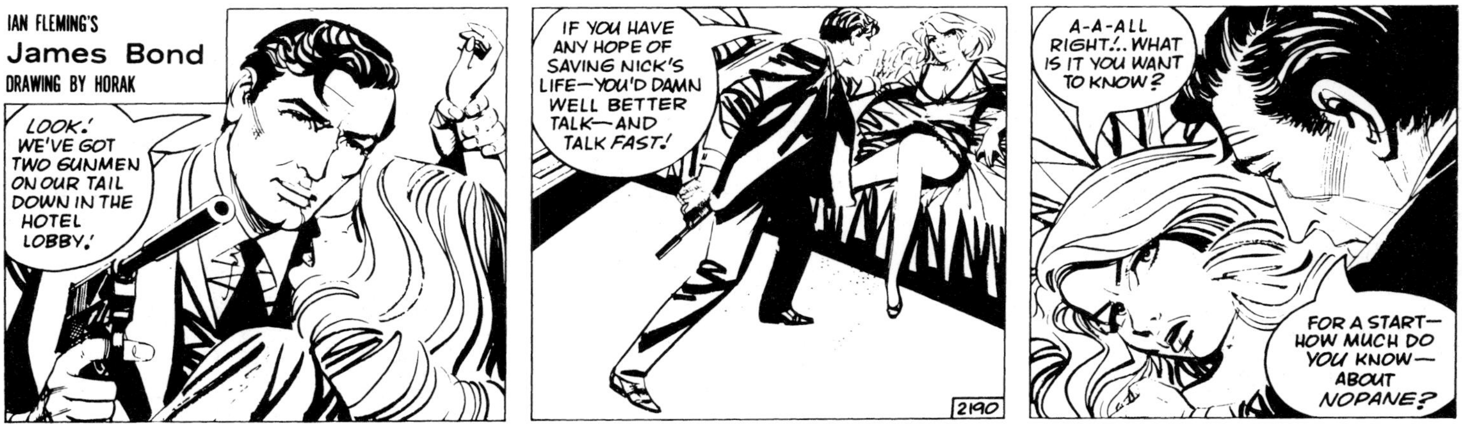
IAN FLEMING'S
James Bond
DRAWING BY HORAK
LOOK! WE'VE GOT TWO GUNMEN ON OUR TAIL DOWN IN THE HOTEL LOBBY!
IF YOU HAVE ANY HOPE OF SAVING NICK'S LIFE—YOU'D DAMN WELL BETTER TALK—AND TALK FAST!
2190
A-A-ALL RIGHT!.. WHAT IS IT YOU WANT TO KNOW?
FOR A START— HOW MUCH DO YOU KNOW— ABOUT NOPANE?

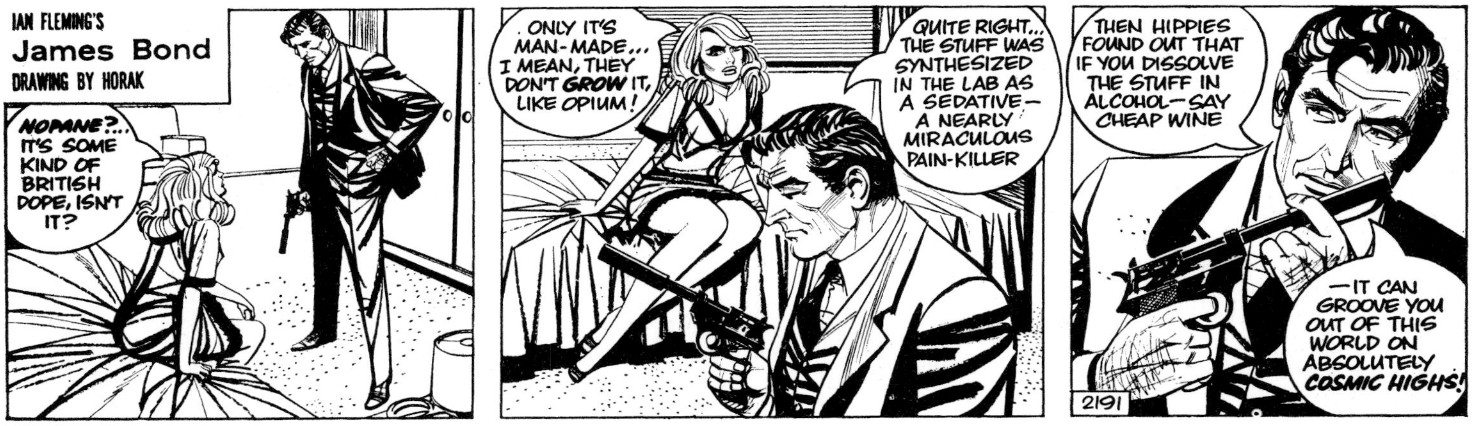
IAN FLEMING'S
James Bond
DRAWING BY HORAK
NOPANE?... IT'S SOME KIND OF BRITISH DOPE, ISN'T IT?
ONLY IT'S MAN-MADE... I MEAN, THEY DON'T GROW IT, LIKE OPIUM!
QUITE RIGHT... THE STUFF WAS SYNTHESIZED IN THE LAB AS A SEDATIVE— A NEARLY MIRACULOUS PAIN-KILLER
THEN HIPPIES FOUND OUT THAT IF YOU DISSOLVE THE STUFF IN ALCOHOL—SAY CHEAP WINE
—IT CAN GROOVE YOU OUT OF THIS WORLD ON ABSOLUTELY COSMIC HIGHS!
2191

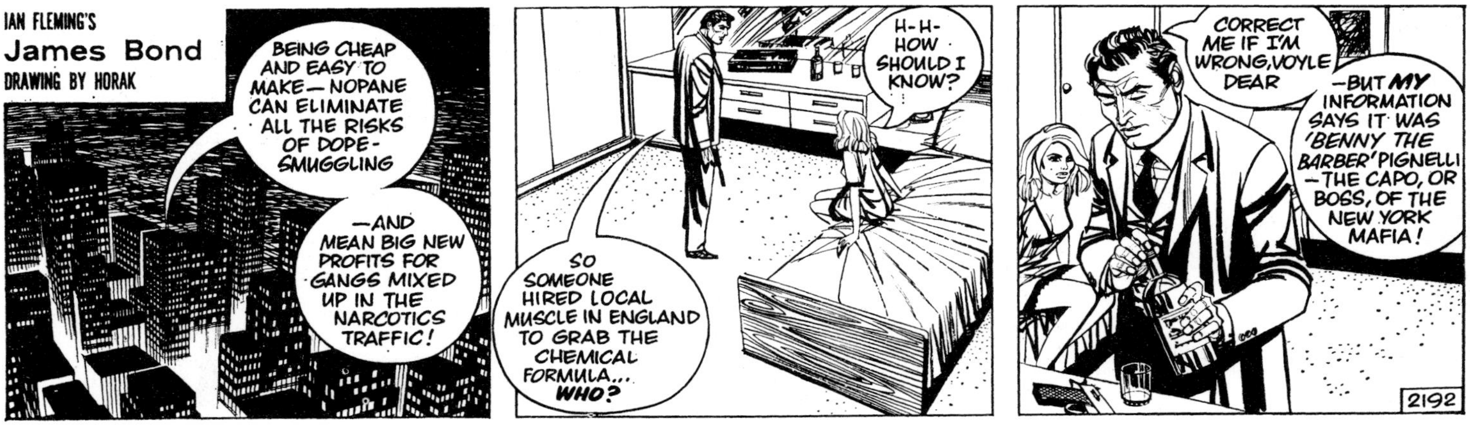
IAN FLEMING'S
James Bond
DRAWING BY HORAK
BEING CHEAP AND EASY TO MAKE— NOPANE CAN ELIMINATE ALL THE RISKS OF DOPE-SMUGGLING
—AND MEAN BIG NEW PROFITS FOR GANGS MIXED UP IN THE NARCOTICS TRAFFIC!
H-H-HOW SHOULD I KNOW?
SO SOMEONE HIRED LOCAL MUSCLE IN ENGLAND TO GRAB THE CHEMICAL FORMULA... WHO?
CORRECT ME IF I'M WRONG, VOYLE DEAR
—BUT MY INFORMATION SAYS IT WAS 'BENNY THE BARBER' PIGNELLI —THE CAPO, OR BOSS, OF THE NEW YORK MAFIA!
2192

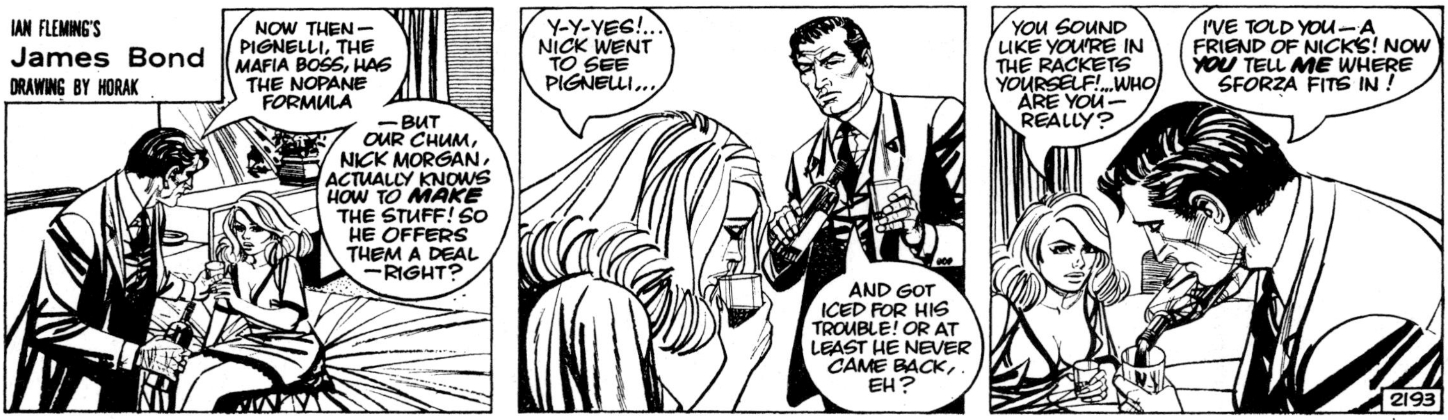
IAN FLEMING'S
James Bond
DRAWING BY HORAK
NOW THEN— PIGNELLI, THE MAFIA BOSS, HAS THE NOPANE FORMULA
—BUT OUR CHUM, NICK MORGAN, ACTUALLY KNOWS HOW TO MAKE THE STUFF! SO HE OFFERS THEM A DEAL —RIGHT?
Y-Y-YES!... NICK WENT TO SEE PIGNELLI...
AND GOT ICED FOR HIS TROUBLE! OR AT LEAST HE NEVER CAME BACK, EH?
YOU SOUND LIKE YOU'RE IN THE RACKETS YOURSELF!...WHO ARE YOU—REALLY?
I'VE TOLD YOU—A FRIEND OF NICK'S! NOW YOU TELL ME WHERE SFORZA FITS IN!
2193

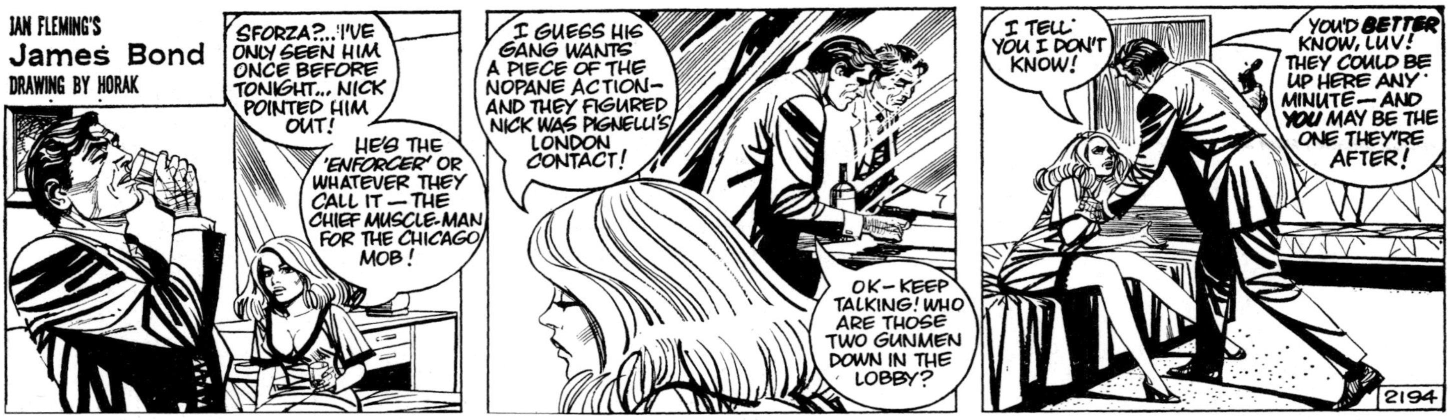
IAN FLEMING'S
James Bond
DRAWING BY HORAK
SFORZA?...I'VE ONLY SEEN HIM ONCE BEFORE TONIGHT... NICK POINTED HIM OUT!
HE'S THE 'ENFORCER' OR WHATEVER THEY CALL IT — THE CHIEF MUSCLE-MAN FOR THE CHICAGO MOB!
I GUESS HIS GANG WANTS A PIECE OF THE NOPANE ACTION— AND THEY FIGURED NICK WAS PIGNELLI'S LONDON CONTACT!
OK—KEEP TALKING! WHO ARE THOSE TWO GUNMEN DOWN IN THE LOBBY?
I TELL YOU I DON'T KNOW!
YOU'D BETTER KNOW, LUV! THEY COULD BE UP HERE ANY MINUTE—AND YOU MAY BE THE ONE THEY'RE AFTER!
2194

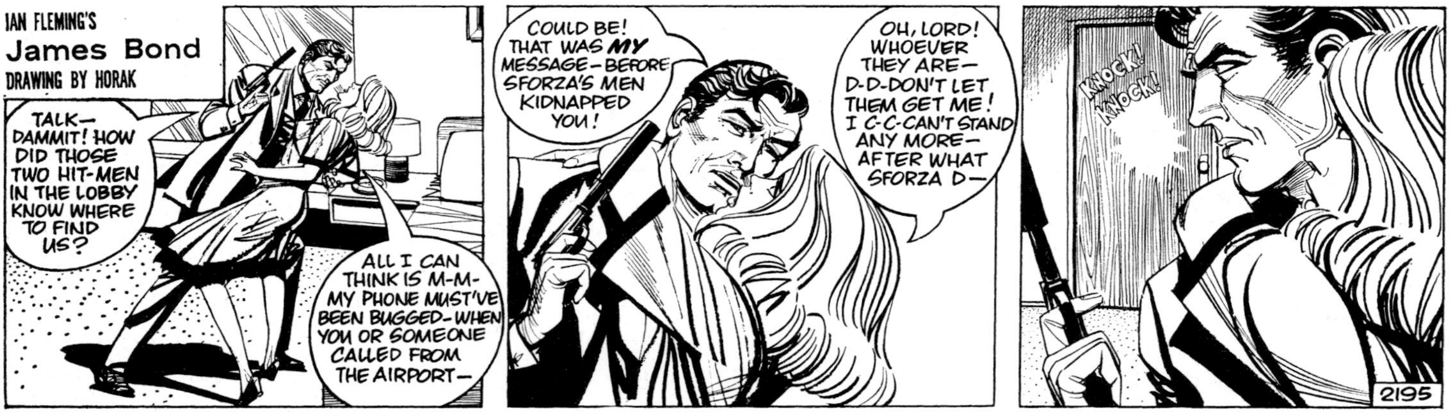
IAN FLEMING'S
James Bond
DRAWING BY HORAK
TALK— DAMMIT! HOW DID THOSE TWO HIT-MEN IN THE LOBBY KNOW WHERE TO FIND US?
ALL I CAN THINK IS M-M-MY PHONE MUST'VE BEEN BUGGED—WHEN YOU OR SOMEONE CALLED FROM THE AIRPORT—
COULD BE! THAT WAS MY MESSAGE—BEFORE SFORZA'S MEN KIDNAPPED YOU!
OH, LORD! WHOEVER THEY ARE— D-D-DON'T LET THEM GET ME! I C-C-CAN'T STAND ANY MORE— AFTER WHAT SFORZA D—
KNOCK! KNOCK!
2195

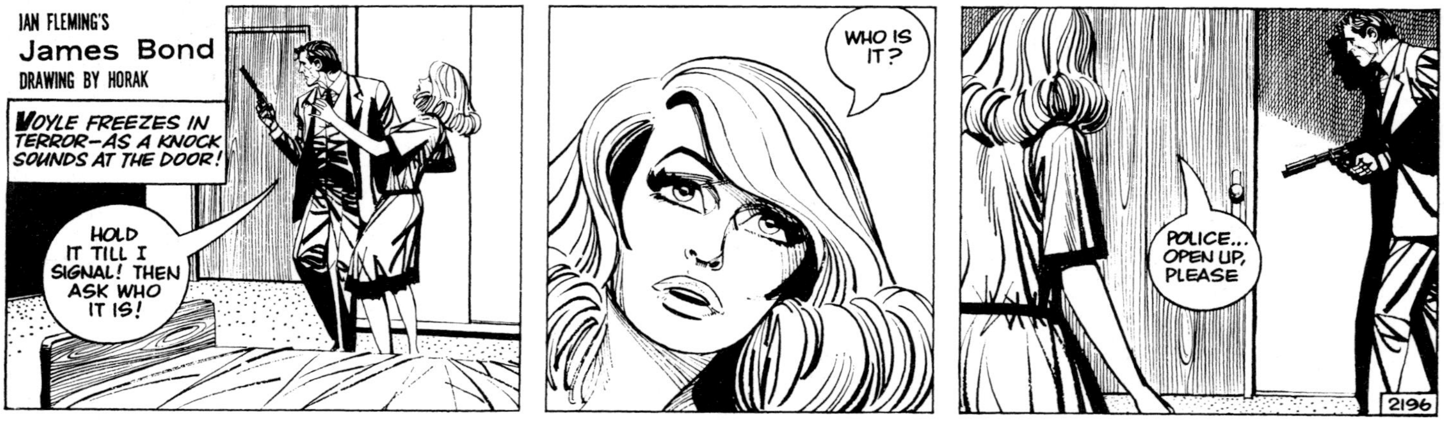
IAN FLEMING'S
James Bond
DRAWING BY HORAK
VOYLE FREEZES IN TERROR—AS A KNOCK SOUNDS AT THE DOOR!
HOLD IT TILL I SIGNAL! THEN ASK WHO IT IS!
WHO IS IT?
POLICE... OPEN UP, PLEASE
2196

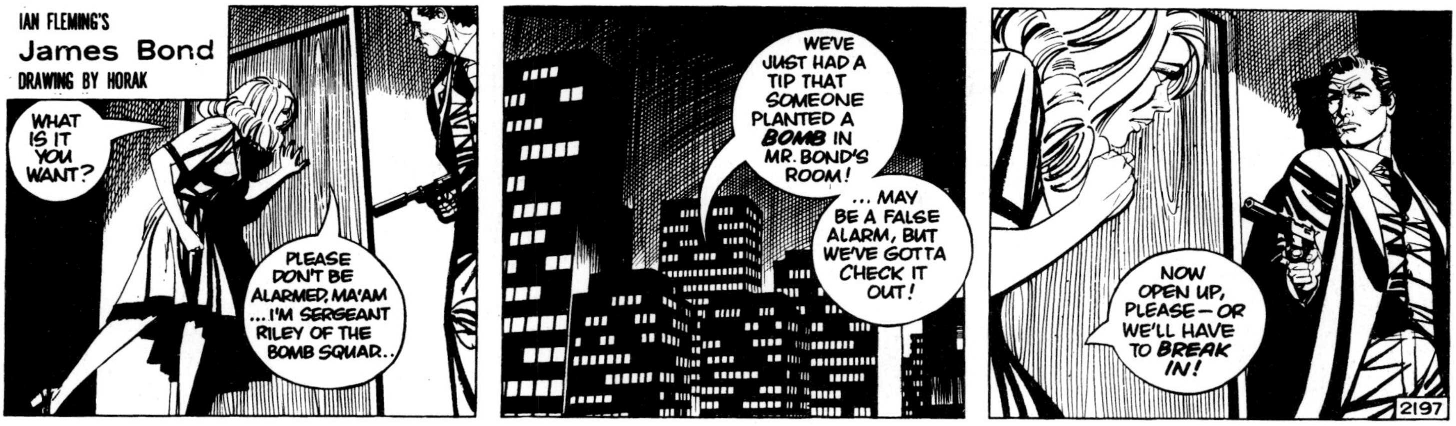
IAN FLEMING'S
James Bond
DRAWING BY HORAK
WHAT IS IT YOU WANT?
PLEASE DON'T BE ALARMED, MA'AM ...I'M SERGEANT RILEY OF THE BOMB SQUAD..
WE'VE JUST HAD A TIP THAT SOMEONE PLANTED A **BOMB** IN MR. BOND'S ROOM!
... MAY BE A FALSE ALARM, BUT WE'VE GOTTA CHECK IT OUT!
NOW OPEN UP, PLEASE—OR WE'LL HAVE TO **BREAK IN!**
2197

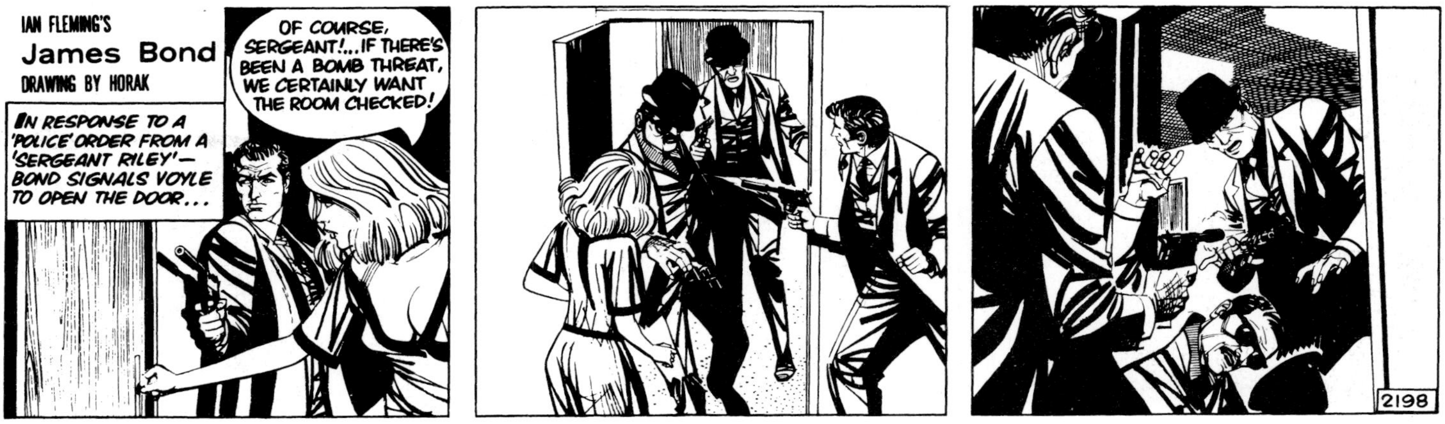
IAN FLEMING'S
James Bond
DRAWING BY HORAK
IN RESPONSE TO A 'POLICE' ORDER FROM A 'SERGEANT RILEY'—BOND SIGNALS VOYLE TO OPEN THE DOOR...
OF COURSE, SERGEANT!... IF THERE'S BEEN A BOMB THREAT, WE CERTAINLY WANT THE ROOM CHECKED!
2198

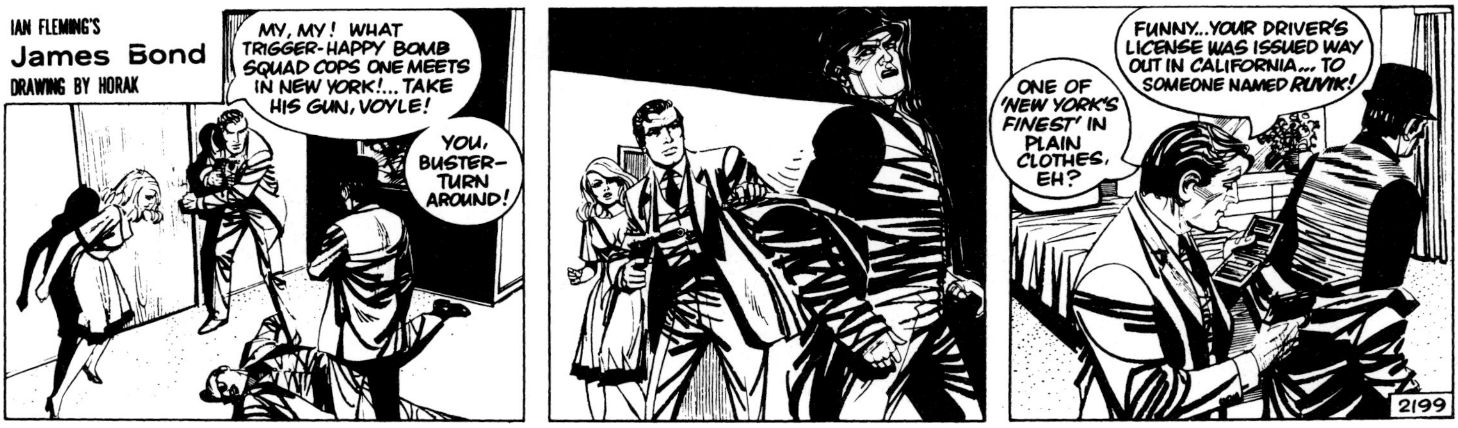
IAN FLEMING'S
James Bond
DRAWING BY HORAK
MY, MY! WHAT TRIGGER-HAPPY BOMB SQUAD COPS ONE MEETS IN NEW YORK!... TAKE HIS GUN, VOYLE!
YOU, BUSTER-TURN AROUND!
ONE OF 'NEW YORK'S FINEST' IN PLAIN CLOTHES, EH?
FUNNY.. YOUR DRIVER'S LICENSE WAS ISSUED WAY OUT IN CALIFORNIA... TO SOMEONE NAMED **RUVIK!**
2199

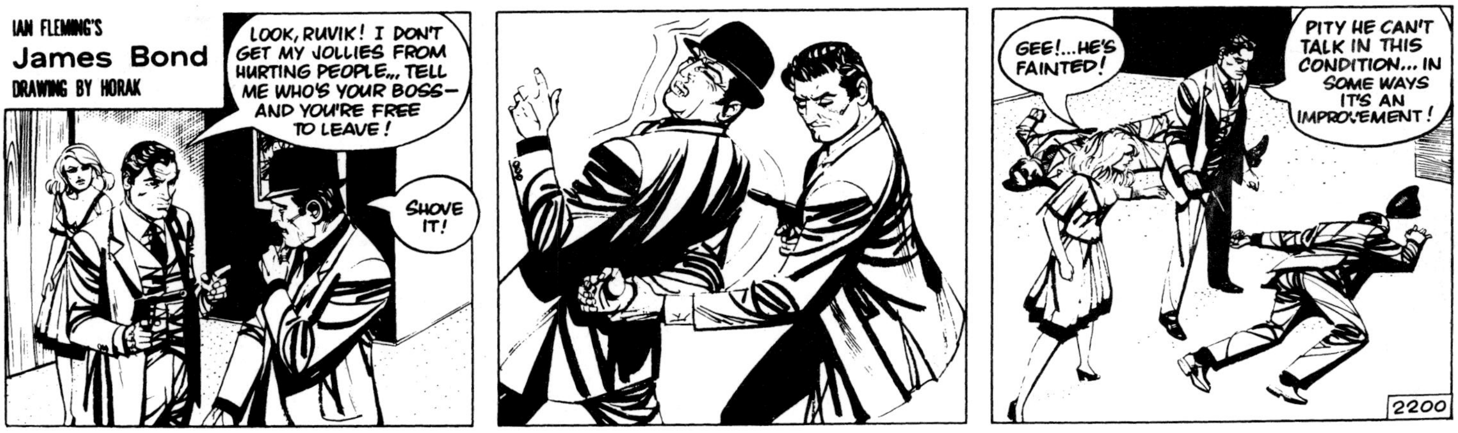
IAN FLEMING'S
James Bond
DRAWING BY HORAK
LOOK, RUVIK! I DON'T GET MY JOLLIES FROM HURTING PEOPLE... TELL ME WHO'S YOUR BOSS—AND YOU'RE FREE TO LEAVE!
SHOVE IT!
GEE!... HE'S FAINTED!
PITY HE CAN'T TALK IN THIS CONDITION... IN SOME WAYS IT'S AN IMPROVEMENT!
2200

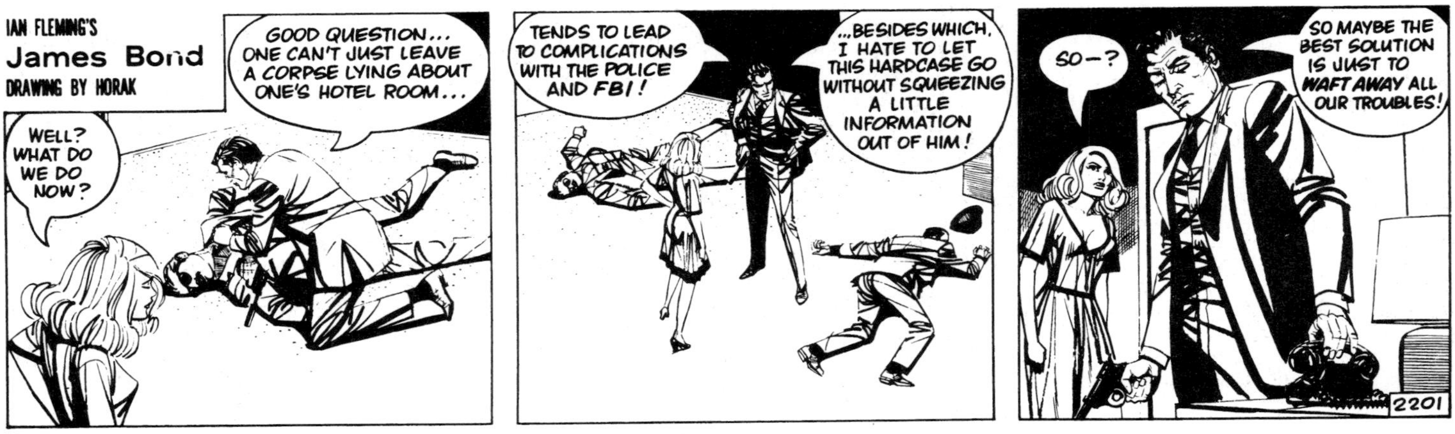

IAN FLEMING'S
James Bond
DRAWING BY HORAK
WELL? WHAT DO WE DO NOW?
GOOD QUESTION... ONE CAN'T JUST LEAVE A CORPSE LYING ABOUT ONE'S HOTEL ROOM...
TENDS TO LEAD TO COMPLICATIONS WITH THE POLICE AND FBI!
...BESIDES WHICH, I HATE TO LET THIS HARDCASE GO WITHOUT SQUEEZING A LITTLE INFORMATION OUT OF HIM!
SO–?
SO MAYBE THE BEST SOLUTION IS JUST TO WAFT AWAY ALL OUR TROUBLES!
2201

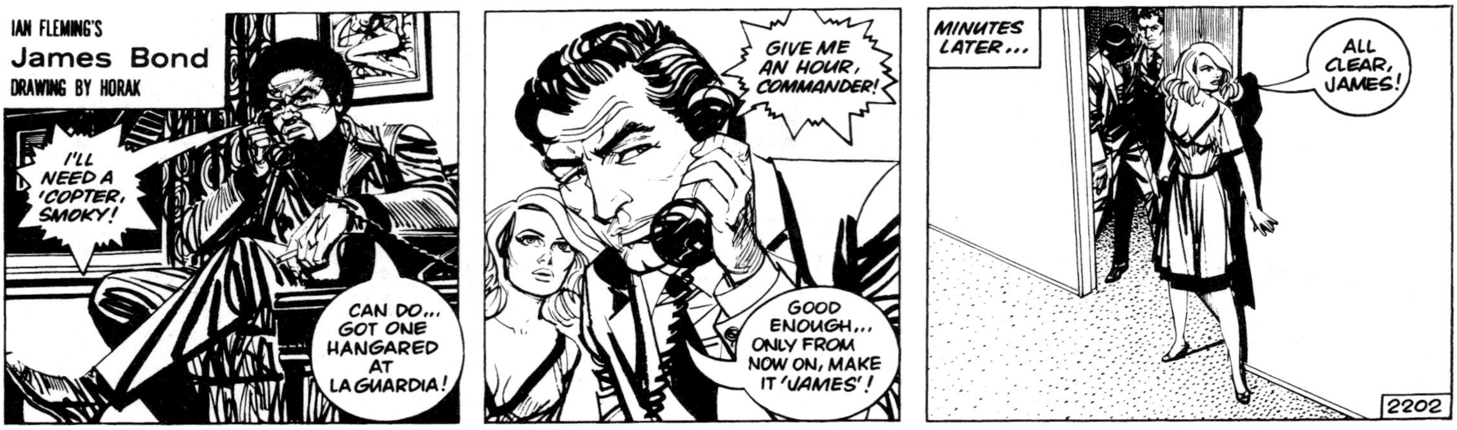

IAN FLEMING'S
James Bond
DRAWING BY HORAK
I'LL NEED A 'COPTER, SMOKY!
CAN DO... GOT ONE HANGARED AT LAGUARDIA!
GIVE ME AN HOUR, COMMANDER!
GOOD ENOUGH... ONLY FROM NOW ON, MAKE IT 'JAMES'!
MINUTES LATER...
ALL CLEAR, JAMES!
2202

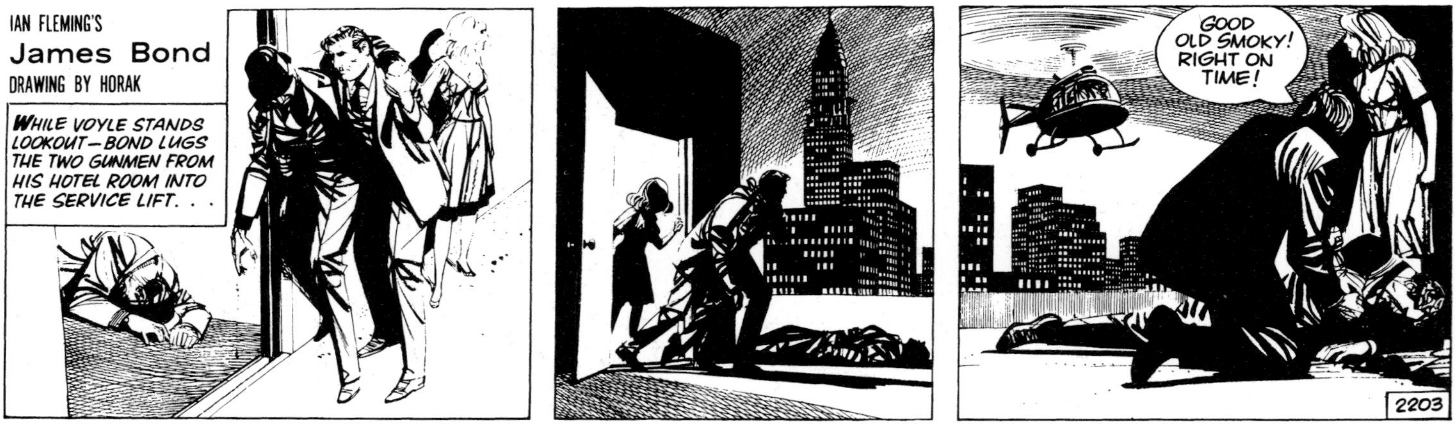

IAN FLEMING'S
James Bond
DRAWING BY HORAK
WHILE VOYLE STANDS LOOKOUT–BOND LUGS THE TWO GUNMEN FROM HIS HOTEL ROOM INTO THE SERVICE LIFT...
GOOD OLD SMOKY! RIGHT ON TIME!
2203

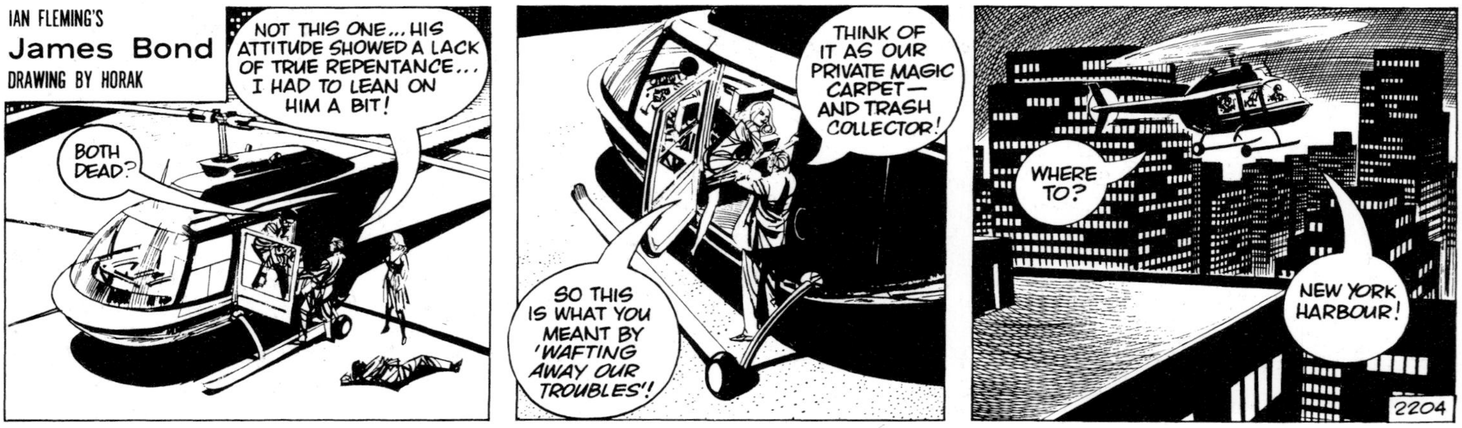

IAN FLEMING'S
James Bond
DRAWING BY HORAK
BOTH DEAD?
NOT THIS ONE... HIS ATTITUDE SHOWED A LACK OF TRUE REPENTANCE... I HAD TO LEAN ON HIM A BIT!
SO THIS IS WHAT YOU MEANT BY 'WAFTING AWAY OUR TROUBLES'!
THINK OF IT AS OUR PRIVATE MAGIC CARPET— AND TRASH COLLECTOR!
WHERE TO?
NEW YORK HARBOUR!
2204

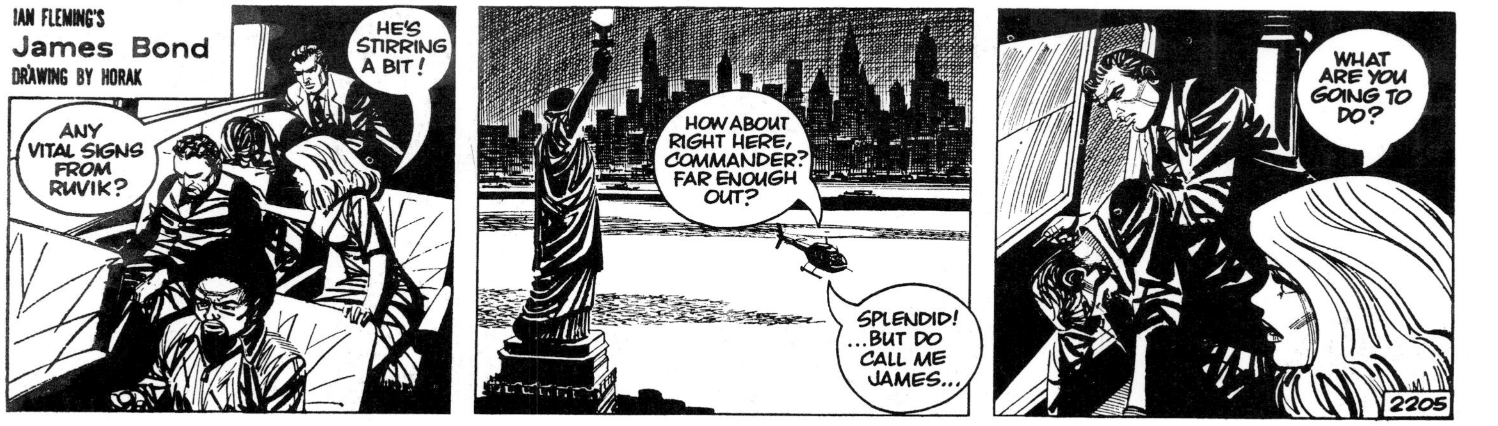
IAN FLEMING'S
James Bond
DRAWING BY HORAK
HE'S STIRRING A BIT!
ANY VITAL SIGNS FROM RUVIK?
HOW ABOUT RIGHT HERE, COMMANDER? FAR ENOUGH OUT?
SPLENDID! ...BUT DO CALL ME JAMES...
WHAT ARE YOU GOING TO DO?
2205

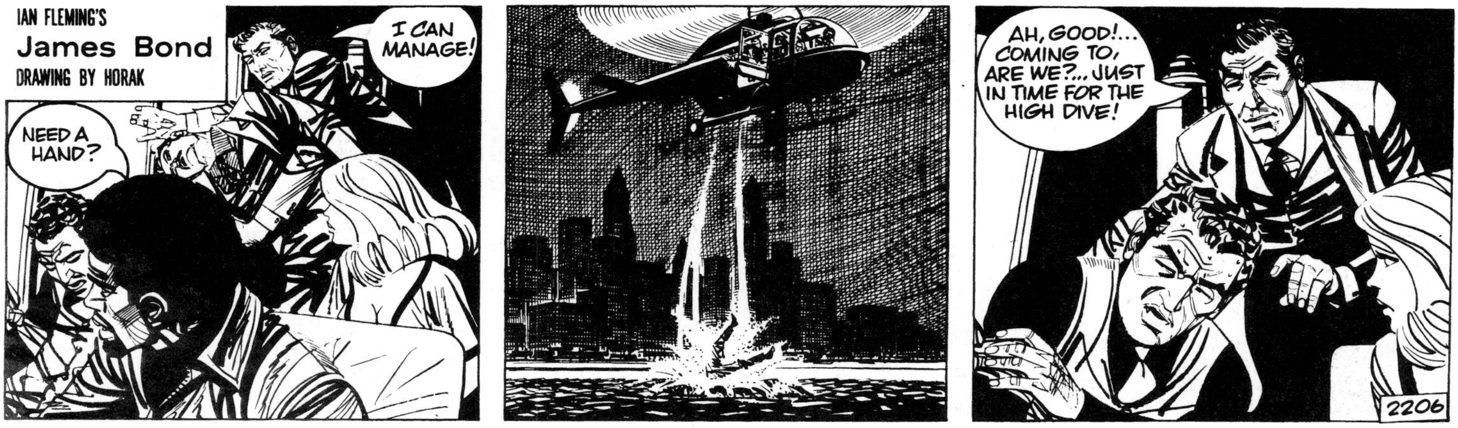
IAN FLEMING'S
James Bond
DRAWING BY HORAK
I CAN MANAGE!
NEED A HAND?
AH, GOOD!... COMING TO, ARE WE?... JUST IN TIME FOR THE HIGH DIVE!
2206

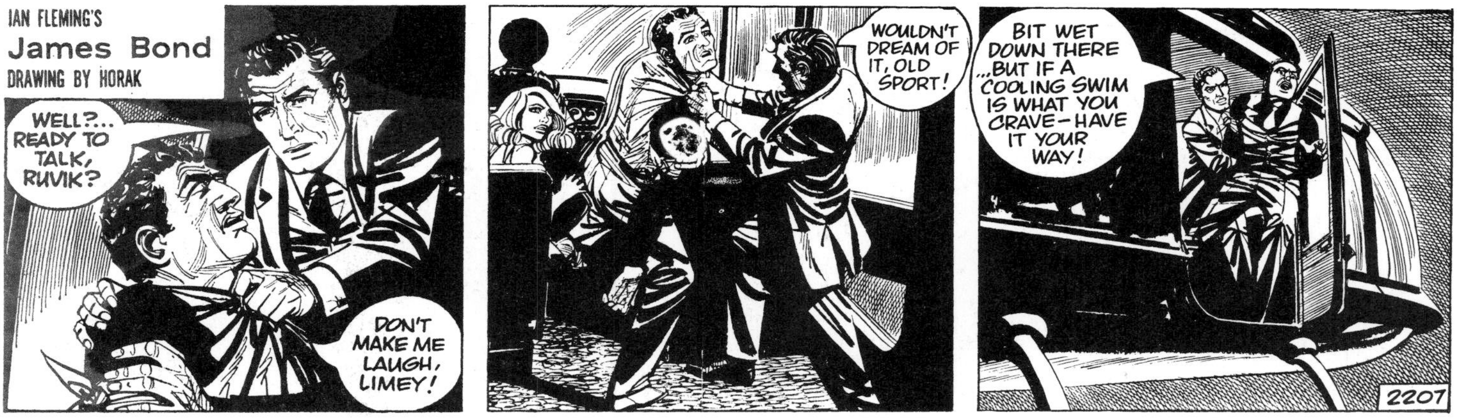
IAN FLEMING'S
James Bond
DRAWING BY HORAK
WELL?... READY TO TALK, RUVIK?
DON'T MAKE ME LAUGH, LIMEY!
WOULDN'T DREAM OF IT, OLD SPORT!
BIT WET DOWN THERE ...BUT IF A COOLING SWIM IS WHAT YOU CRAVE-HAVE IT YOUR WAY!
2207

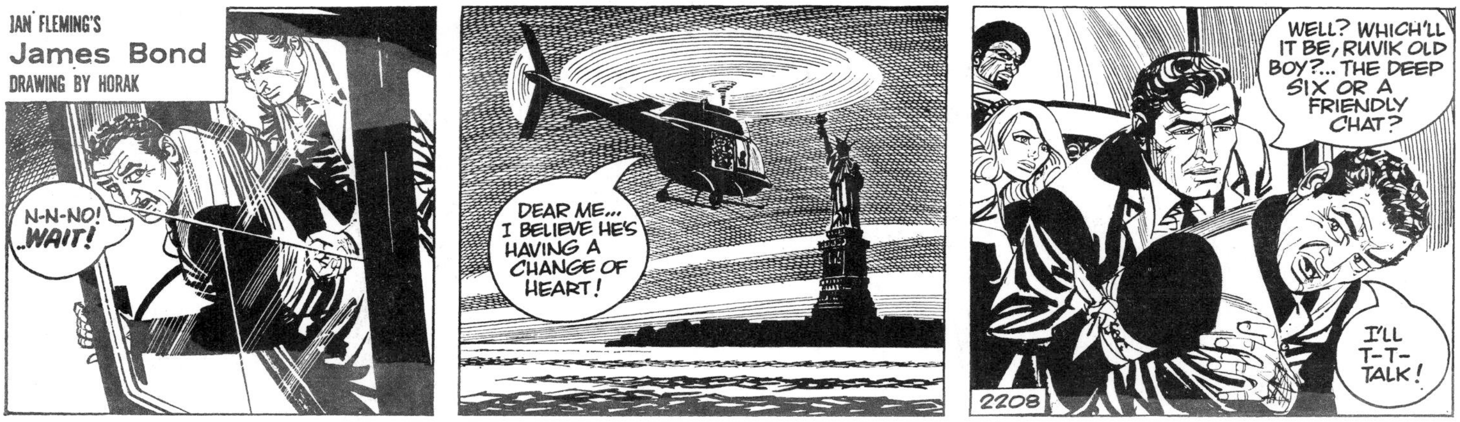
IAN FLEMING'S
James Bond
DRAWING BY HORAK
N-N-NO! ..WAIT!
DEAR ME... I BELIEVE HE'S HAVING A CHANGE OF HEART!
WELL? WHICH'LL IT BE, RUVIK OLD BOY?... THE DEEP SIX OR A FRIENDLY CHAT?
I'LL T-T-TALK!
2208

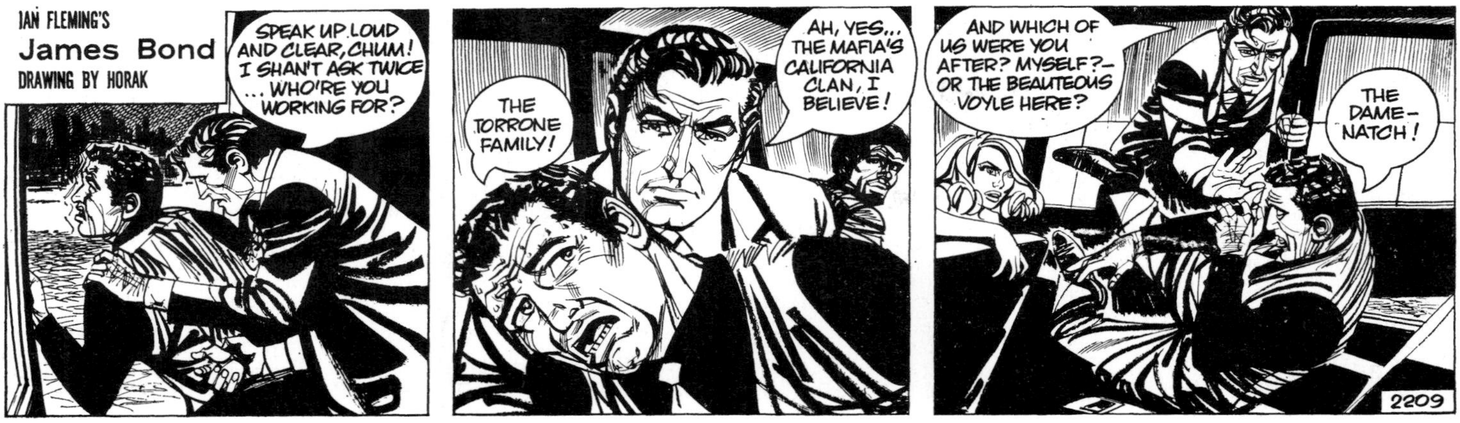
IAN FLEMING'S
James Bond
DRAWING BY HORAK
SPEAK UP. LOUD AND CLEAR, CHUM! I SHAN'T ASK TWICE ... WHO'RE YOU WORKING FOR?
THE TORRONE FAMILY!
AH, YES... THE MAFIA'S CALIFORNIA CLAN, I BELIEVE!
AND WHICH OF US WERE YOU AFTER? MYSELF?— OR THE BEAUTEOUS VOYLE HERE?
THE DAME-NATCH!
2209

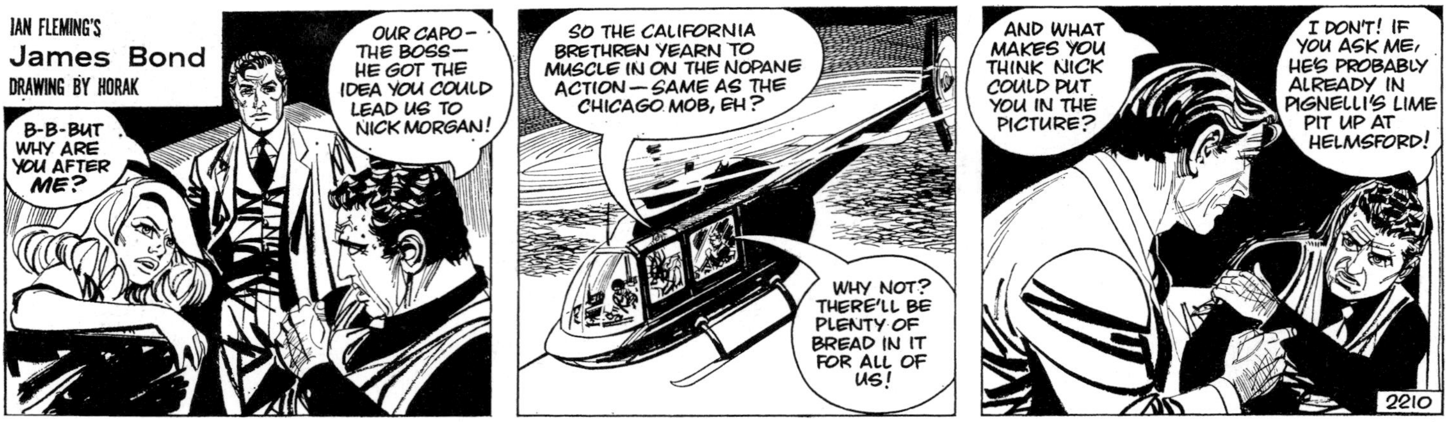
IAN FLEMING'S
James Bond
DRAWING BY HORAK
B-B-BUT WHY ARE YOU AFTER ME?
OUR CAPO-THE BOSS— HE GOT THE IDEA YOU COULD LEAD US TO NICK MORGAN!
SO THE CALIFORNIA BRETHREN YEARN TO MUSCLE IN ON THE NOPANE ACTION — SAME AS THE CHICAGO MOB, EH?
WHY NOT? THERE'LL BE PLENTY OF BREAD IN IT FOR ALL OF US!
AND WHAT MAKES YOU THINK NICK COULD PUT YOU IN THE PICTURE?
I DON'T! IF YOU ASK ME, HE'S PROBABLY ALREADY IN PIGNELLI'S LIME PIT UP AT HELMSFORD!
2210

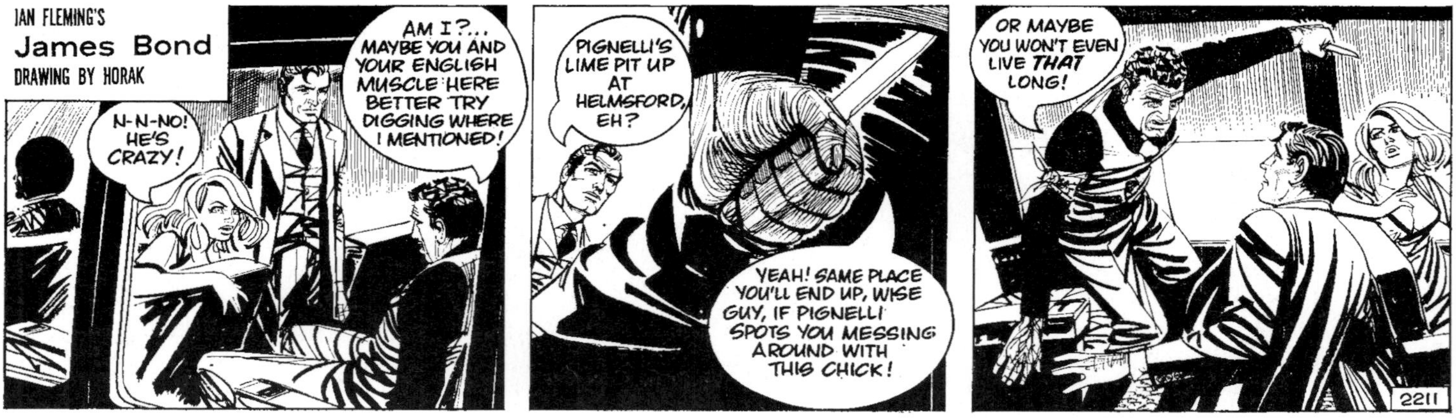
IAN FLEMING'S
James Bond
DRAWING BY HORAK
N-N-NO! HE'S CRAZY!
AM I?... MAYBE YOU AND YOUR ENGLISH MUSCLE HERE BETTER TRY DIGGING WHERE I MENTIONED!
PIGNELLI'S LIME PIT UP AT HELMSFORD, EH?
YEAH! SAME PLACE YOU'LL END UP, WISE GUY, IF PIGNELLI SPOTS YOU MESSING AROUND WITH THIS CHICK!
OR MAYBE YOU WON'T EVEN LIVE THAT LONG!
2211

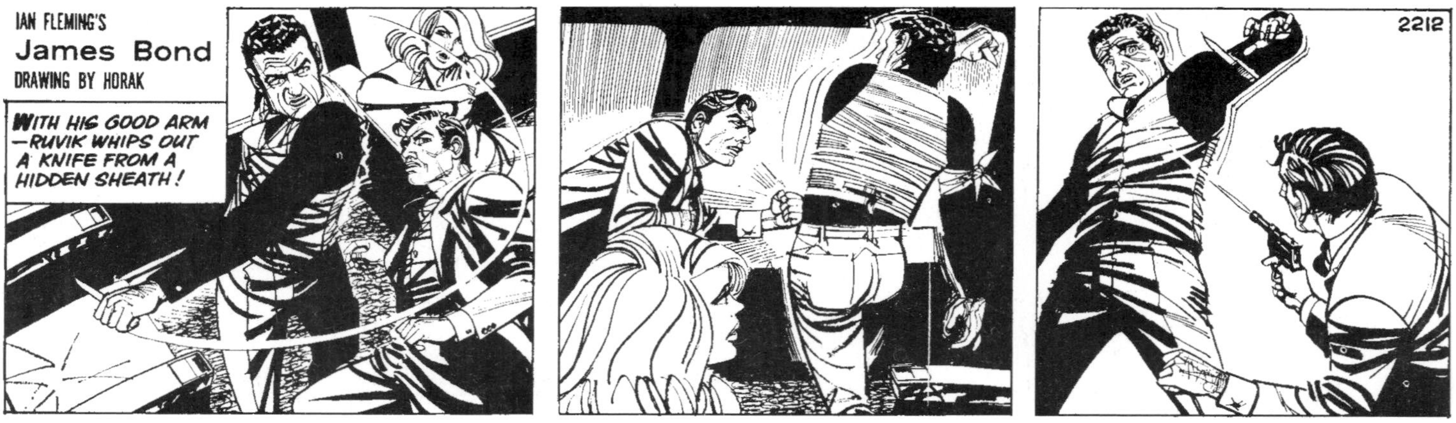
IAN FLEMING'S
James Bond
DRAWING BY HORAK
WITH HIS GOOD ARM —RUVIK WHIPS OUT A KNIFE FROM A HIDDEN SHEATH!
2212

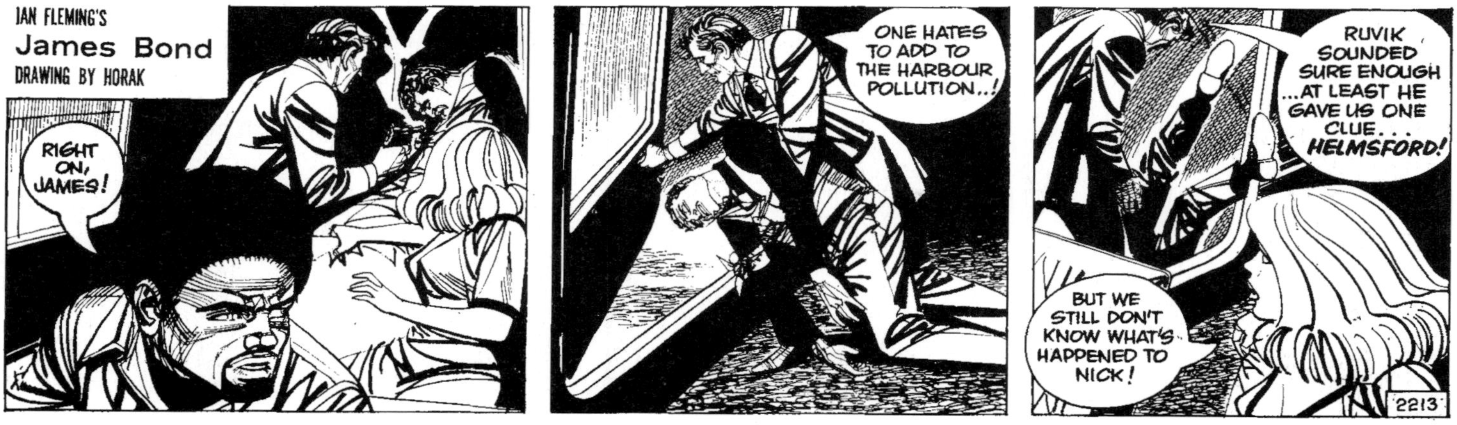
IAN FLEMING'S
James Bond
DRAWING BY HORAK
RIGHT ON, JAMES!
ONE HATES TO ADD TO THE HARBOUR POLLUTION..!
RUVIK SOUNDED SURE ENOUGH ...AT LEAST HE GAVE US ONE CLUE... HELMSFORD!
BUT WE STILL DON'T KNOW WHAT'S HAPPENED TO NICK!
2213

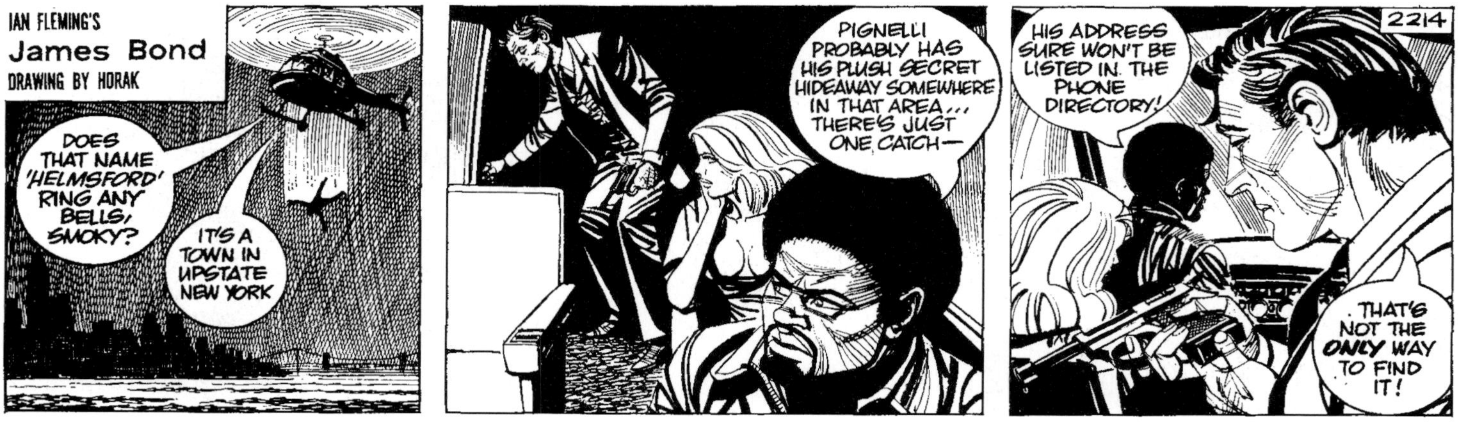
IAN FLEMING'S
James Bond
DRAWING BY HORAK
DOES THAT NAME 'HELMSFORD' RING ANY BELLS, SMOKY?
IT'S A TOWN IN UPSTATE NEW YORK
PIGNELLI PROBABLY HAS HIS PLUSH SECRET HIDEAWAY SOMEWHERE IN THAT AREA... THERE'S JUST ONE CATCH—
2214
HIS ADDRESS SURE WON'T BE LISTED IN THE PHONE DIRECTORY!
. THAT'S NOT THE ONLY WAY TO FIND IT!

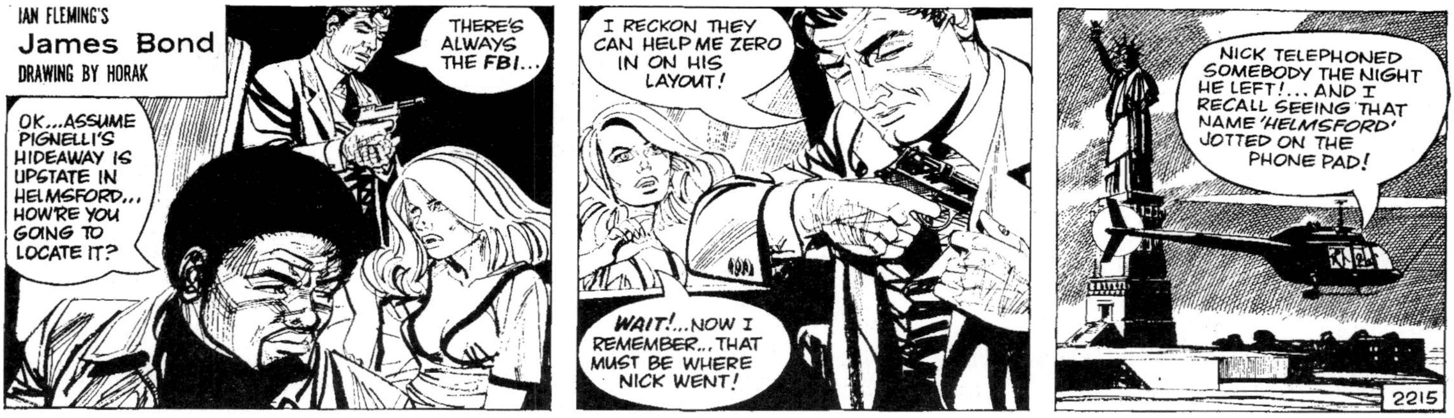
IAN FLEMING'S
James Bond
DRAWING BY HORAK
OK...ASSUME PIGNELLI'S HIDEAWAY IS UPSTATE IN HELMSFORD... HOW'RE YOU GOING TO LOCATE IT?
THERE'S ALWAYS THE FBI...
I RECKON THEY CAN HELP ME ZERO IN ON HIS LAYOUT!
WAIT!...NOW I REMEMBER... THAT MUST BE WHERE NICK WENT!
NICK TELEPHONED SOMEBODY THE NIGHT HE LEFT!... AND I RECALL SEEING THAT NAME 'HELMSFORD' JOTTED ON THE PHONE PAD!
2215

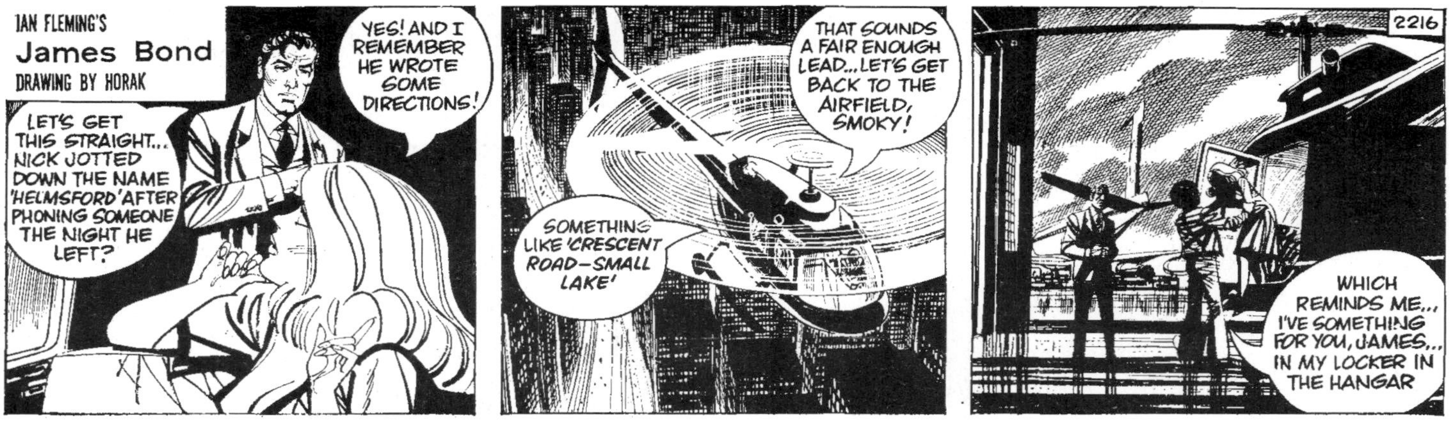
IAN FLEMING'S
James Bond
DRAWING BY HORAK
LET'S GET THIS STRAIGHT... NICK JOTTED DOWN THE NAME 'HELMSFORD' AFTER PHONING SOMEONE THE NIGHT HE LEFT?
YES! AND I REMEMBER HE WROTE SOME DIRECTIONS!
SOMETHING LIKE 'CRESCENT ROAD-SMALL LAKE'
THAT SOUNDS A FAIR ENOUGH LEAD...LET'S GET BACK TO THE AIRFIELD, SMOKY!
2216
WHICH REMINDS ME... I'VE SOMETHING FOR YOU, JAMES... IN MY LOCKER IN THE HANGAR

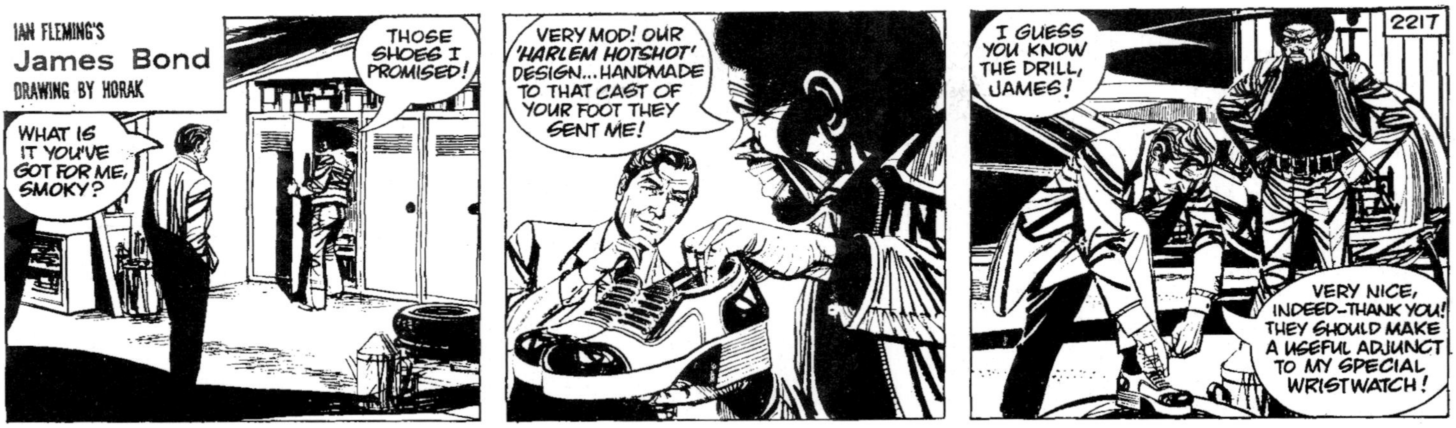
IAN FLEMING'S
James Bond
DRAWING BY HORAK
WHAT IS IT YOU'VE GOT FOR ME, SMOKY?
THOSE SHOES I PROMISED!
VERY MOD! OUR 'HARLEM HOTSHOT' DESIGN... HANDMADE TO THAT CAST OF YOUR FOOT THEY SENT ME!
2217
I GUESS YOU KNOW THE DRILL, JAMES!
VERY NICE, INDEED—THANK YOU! THEY SHOULD MAKE A USEFUL ADJUNCT TO MY SPECIAL WRISTWATCH!

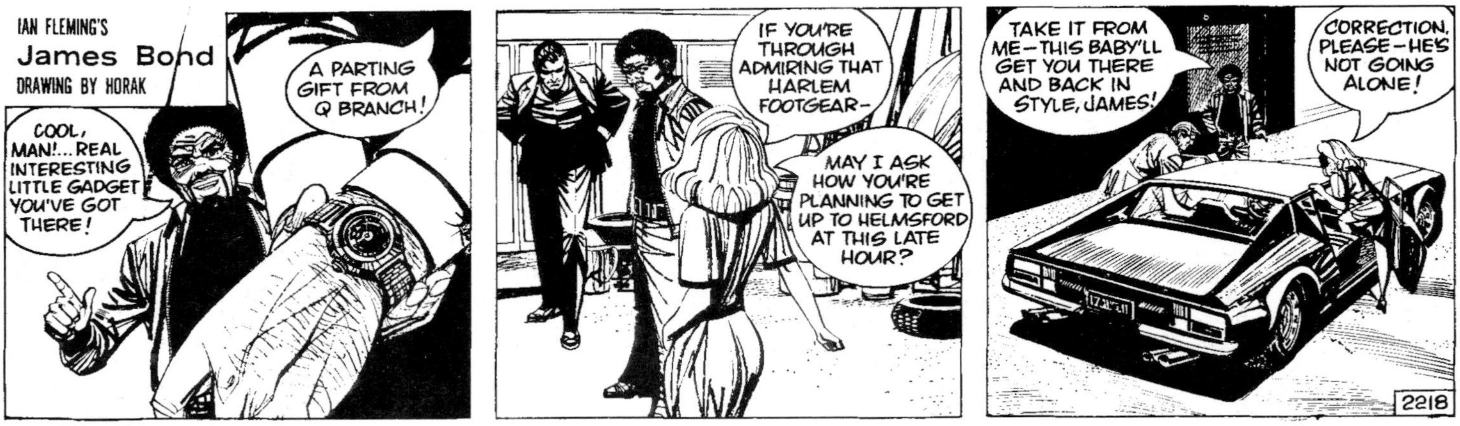
IAN FLEMING'S
James Bond
DRAWING BY HORAK
A PARTING GIFT FROM Q BRANCH!
COOL, MAN!... REAL INTERESTING LITTLE GADGET YOU'VE GOT THERE!
IF YOU'RE THROUGH ADMIRING THAT HARLEM FOOTGEAR—
MAY I ASK HOW YOU'RE PLANNING TO GET UP TO HELMSFORD AT THIS LATE HOUR?
TAKE IT FROM ME—THIS BABY'LL GET YOU THERE AND BACK IN STYLE, JAMES!
CORRECTION, PLEASE—HE'S NOT GOING ALONE!
2218

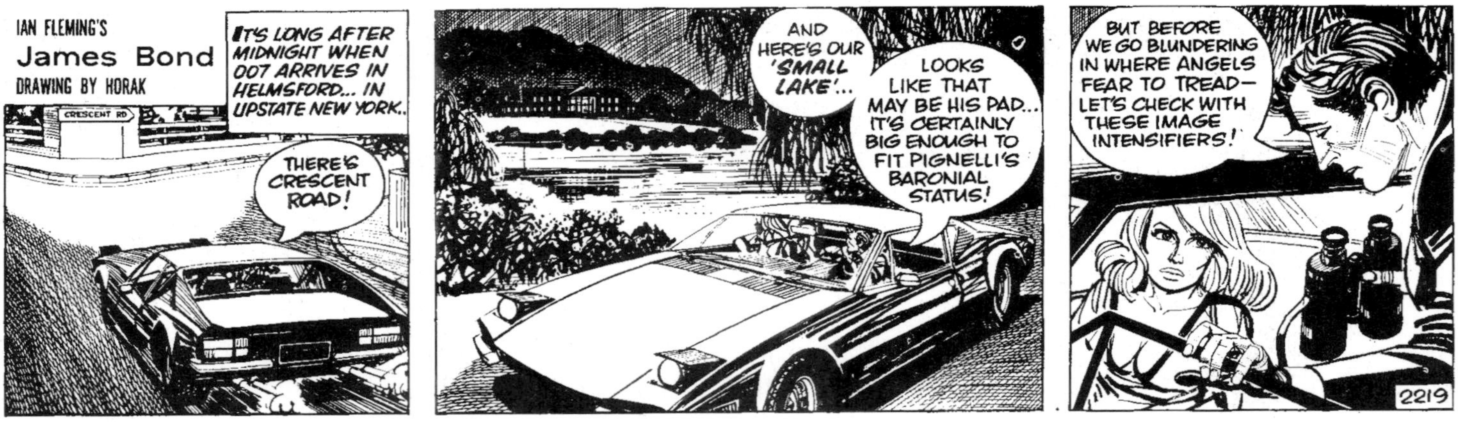
IAN FLEMING'S
James Bond
DRAWING BY HORAK
IT'S LONG AFTER MIDNIGHT WHEN 007 ARRIVES IN HELMSFORD... IN UPSTATE NEW YORK..
CRESCENT RD
THERE'S CRESCENT ROAD!
AND HERE'S OUR 'SMALL LAKE'...
LOOKS LIKE THAT MAY BE HIS PAD... IT'S CERTAINLY BIG ENOUGH TO FIT PIGNELLI'S BARONIAL STATUS!
BUT BEFORE WE GO BLUNDERING IN WHERE ANGELS FEAR TO TREAD—LET'S CHECK WITH THESE IMAGE INTENSIFIERS!
2219

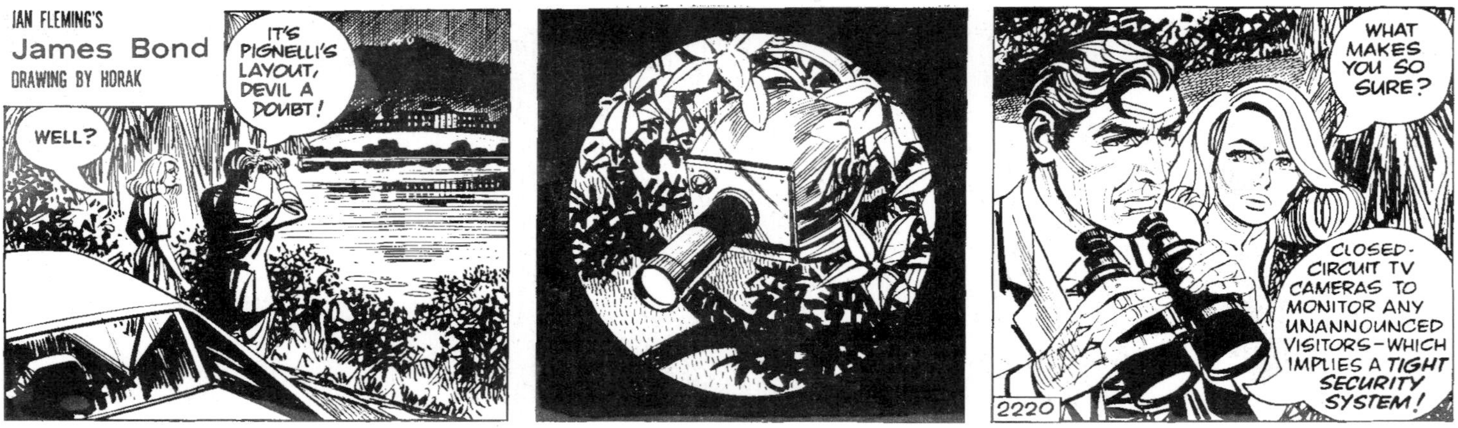
IAN FLEMING'S
James Bond
DRAWING BY HORAK
IT'S PIGNELLI'S LAYOUT, DEVIL A DOUBT!
WELL?
WHAT MAKES YOU SO SURE?
CLOSED-CIRCUIT TV CAMERAS TO MONITOR ANY UNANNOUNCED VISITORS—WHICH IMPLIES A TIGHT SECURITY SYSTEM!
2220

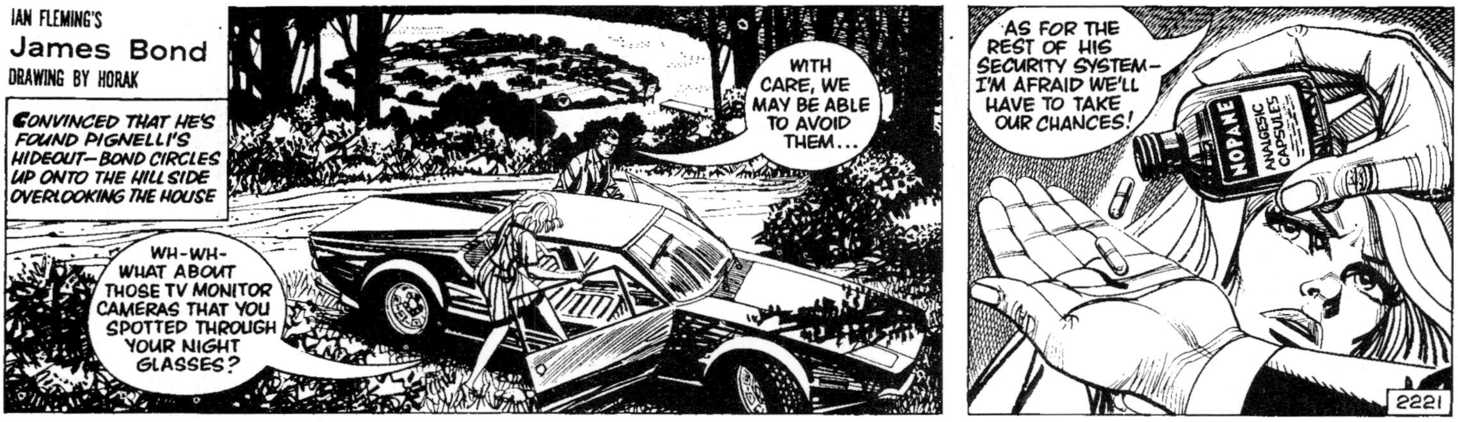
IAN FLEMING'S
James Bond
DRAWING BY HORAK
CONVINCED THAT HE'S FOUND PIGNELLI'S HIDEOUT—BOND CIRCLES UP ONTO THE HILL SIDE OVERLOOKING THE HOUSE
WH-WH-WHAT ABOUT THOSE TV MONITOR CAMERAS THAT YOU SPOTTED THROUGH YOUR NIGHT GLASSES?
WITH CARE, WE MAY BE ABLE TO AVOID THEM...
AS FOR THE REST OF HIS SECURITY SYSTEM—I'M AFRAID WE'LL HAVE TO TAKE OUR CHANCES!
NOPANE
ANALGESIC CAPSULES
2221

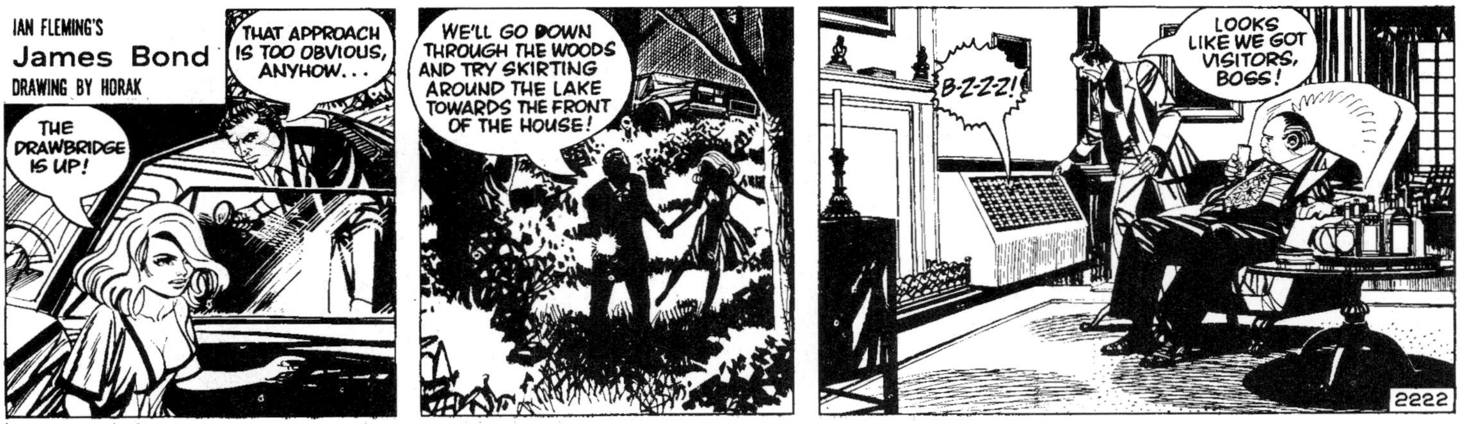
IAN FLEMING'S
James Bond
DRAWING BY HORAK
THAT APPROACH IS TOO OBVIOUS, ANYHOW...
THE DRAWBRIDGE IS UP!
WE'LL GO DOWN THROUGH THE WOODS AND TRY SKIRTING AROUND THE LAKE TOWARDS THE FRONT OF THE HOUSE!
B-Z-Z-Z!
LOOKS LIKE WE GOT VISITORS, BOSS!
2222

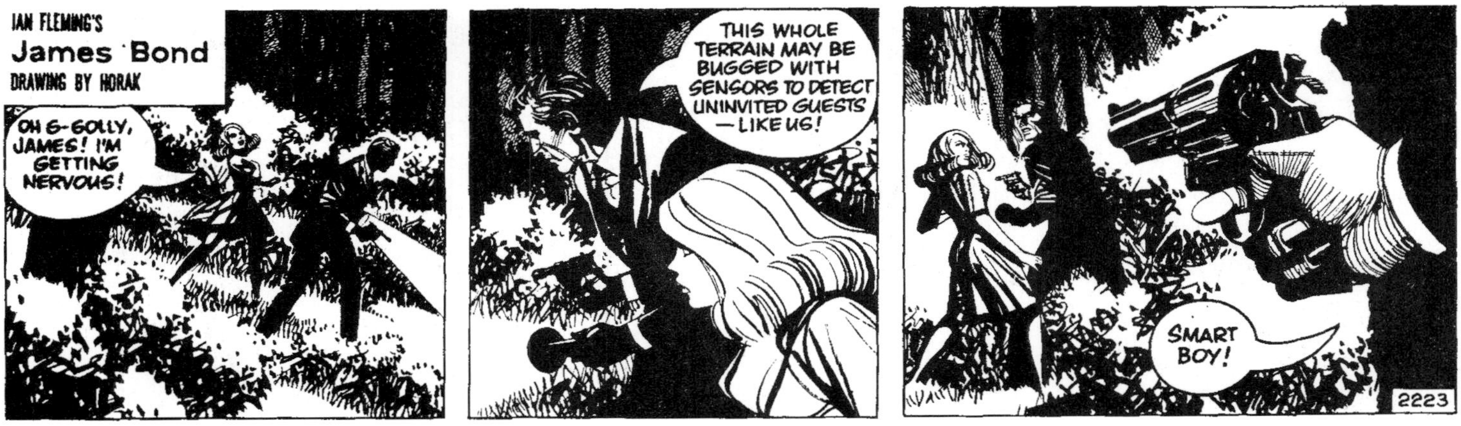
IAN FLEMING'S
James Bond
DRAWING BY HORAK
OH G-GOLLY, JAMES! I'M GETTING NERVOUS!
THIS WHOLE TERRAIN MAY BE BUGGED WITH SENSORS TO DETECT UNINVITED GUESTS —LIKE US!
SMART BOY!
2223

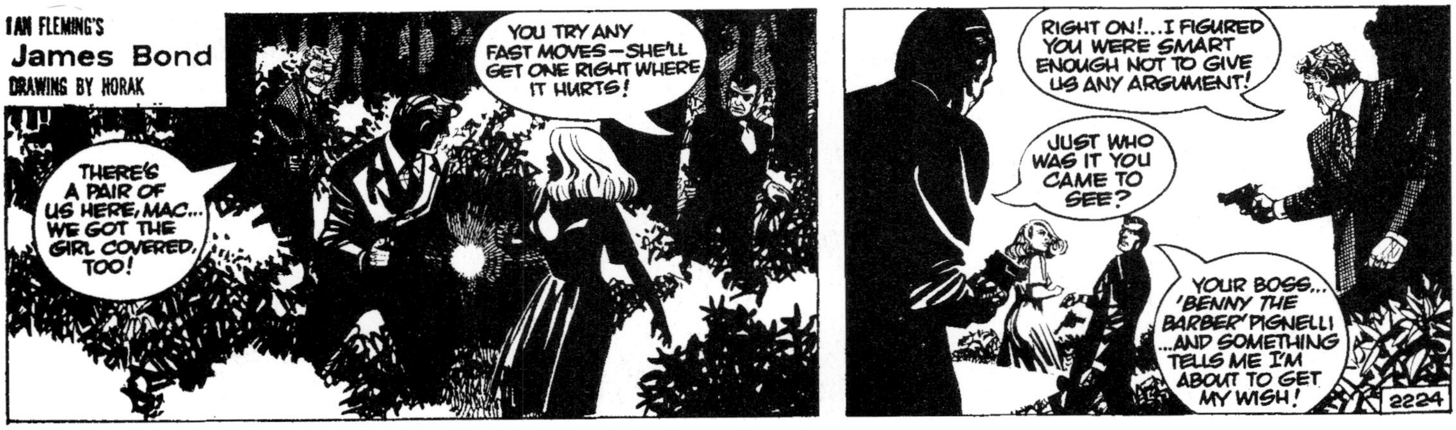
IAN FLEMING'S
James Bond
DRAWING BY HORAK
THERE'S A PAIR OF US HERE, MAC... WE GOT THE GIRL COVERED, TOO!
YOU TRY ANY FAST MOVES—SHE'LL GET ONE RIGHT WHERE IT HURTS!
RIGHT ON!...I FIGURED YOU WERE SMART ENOUGH NOT TO GIVE US ANY ARGUMENT!
JUST WHO WAS IT YOU CAME TO SEE?
YOUR BOSS... 'BENNY THE BARBER' PIGNELLI ...AND SOMETHING TELLS ME I'M ABOUT TO GET MY WISH!
2224

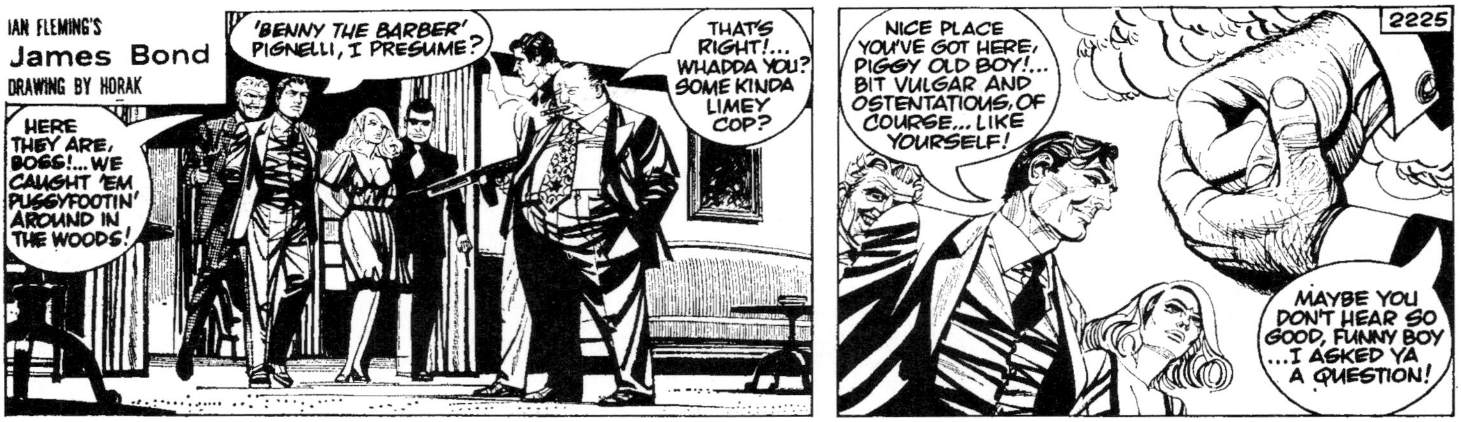
IAN FLEMING'S
James Bond
DRAWING BY HORAK
HERE THEY ARE, BOSS!... WE CAUGHT 'EM PUSSYFOOTIN' AROUND IN THE WOODS!
'BENNY THE BARBER' PIGNELLI, I PRESUME?
THAT'S RIGHT!... WHADDA YOU? SOME KINDA LIMEY COP?
2225
NICE PLACE YOU'VE GOT HERE, PIGGY OLD BOY!... BIT VULGAR AND OSTENTATIOUS, OF COURSE... LIKE YOURSELF!
MAYBE YOU DON'T HEAR SO GOOD, FUNNY BOY ...I ASKED YA A QUESTION!

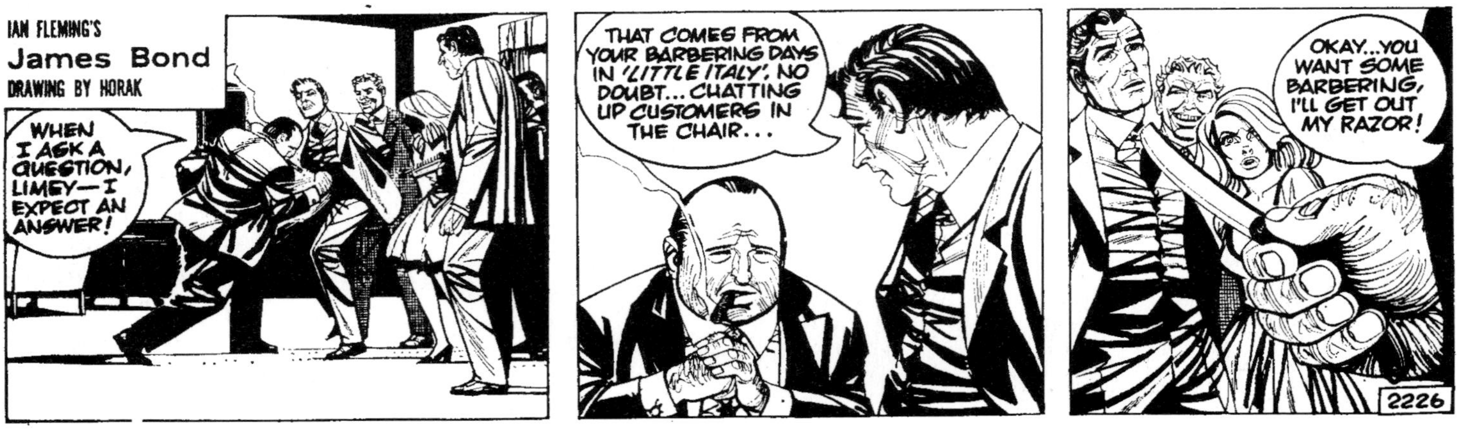
IAN FLEMING'S
James Bond
DRAWING BY HORAK
WHEN I ASK A QUESTION, LIMEY— I EXPECT AN ANSWER!
THAT COMES FROM YOUR BARBERING DAYS IN 'LITTLE ITALY', NO DOUBT... CHATTING UP CUSTOMERS IN THE CHAIR...
OKAY... YOU WANT SOME BARBERING, I'LL GET OUT MY RAZOR!
2226

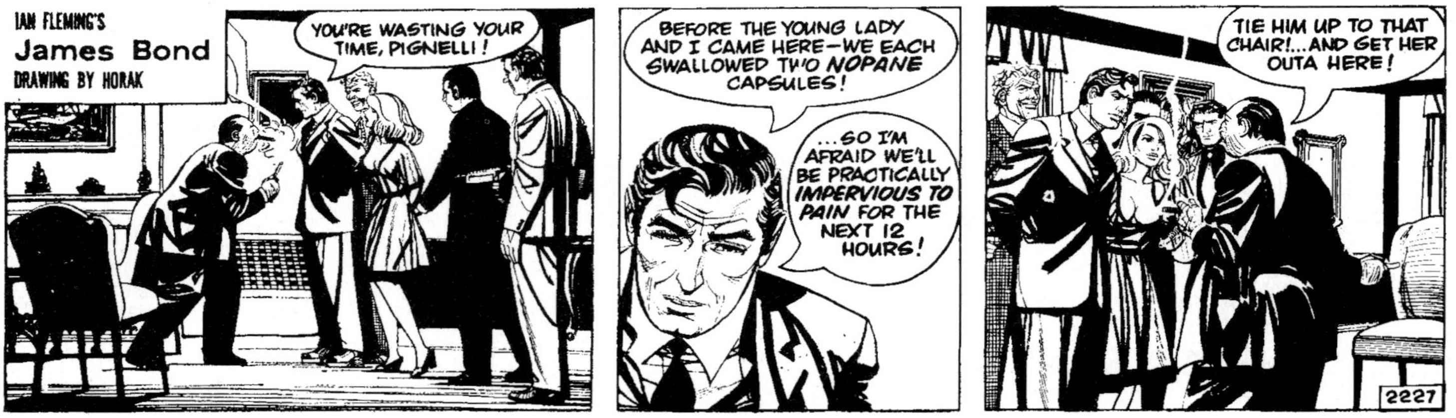
IAN FLEMING'S
James Bond
DRAWING BY HORAK
YOU'RE WASTING YOUR TIME, PIGNELLI!
BEFORE THE YOUNG LADY AND I CAME HERE—WE EACH SWALLOWED TWO NOPANE CAPSULES!
...SO I'M AFRAID WE'LL BE PRACTICALLY IMPERVIOUS TO PAIN FOR THE NEXT 12 HOURS!
TIE HIM UP TO THAT CHAIR!... AND GET HER OUTA HERE!
2227

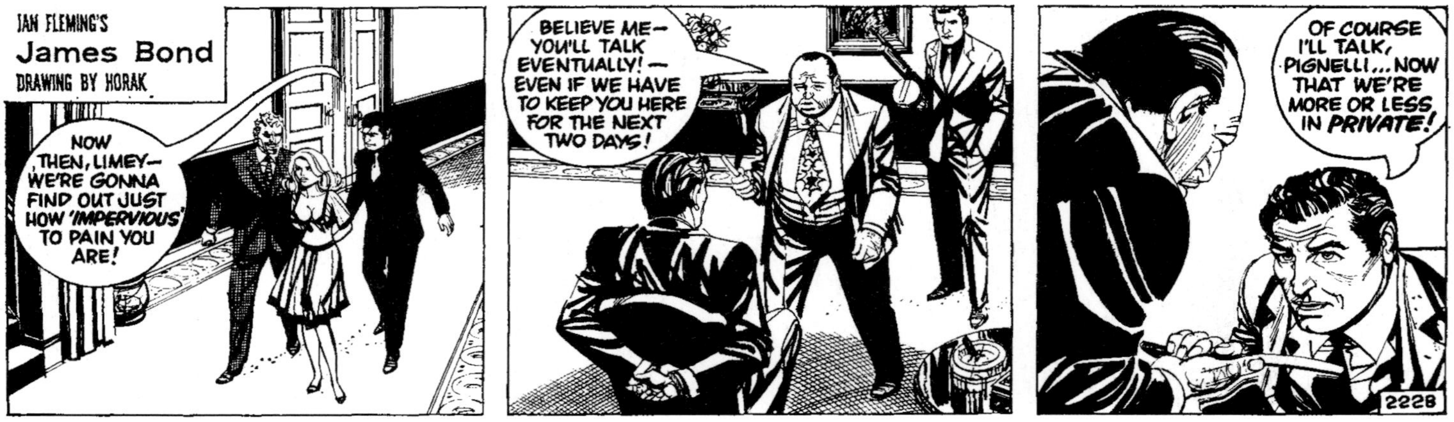
IAN FLEMING'S
James Bond
DRAWING BY HORAK
NOW THEN, LIMEY— WE'RE GONNA FIND OUT JUST HOW 'IMPERVIOUS' TO PAIN YOU ARE!
BELIEVE ME— YOU'LL TALK EVENTUALLY!— EVEN IF WE HAVE TO KEEP YOU HERE FOR THE NEXT TWO DAYS!
OF COURSE I'LL TALK, PIGNELLI... NOW THAT WE'RE MORE OR LESS IN PRIVATE!
2228

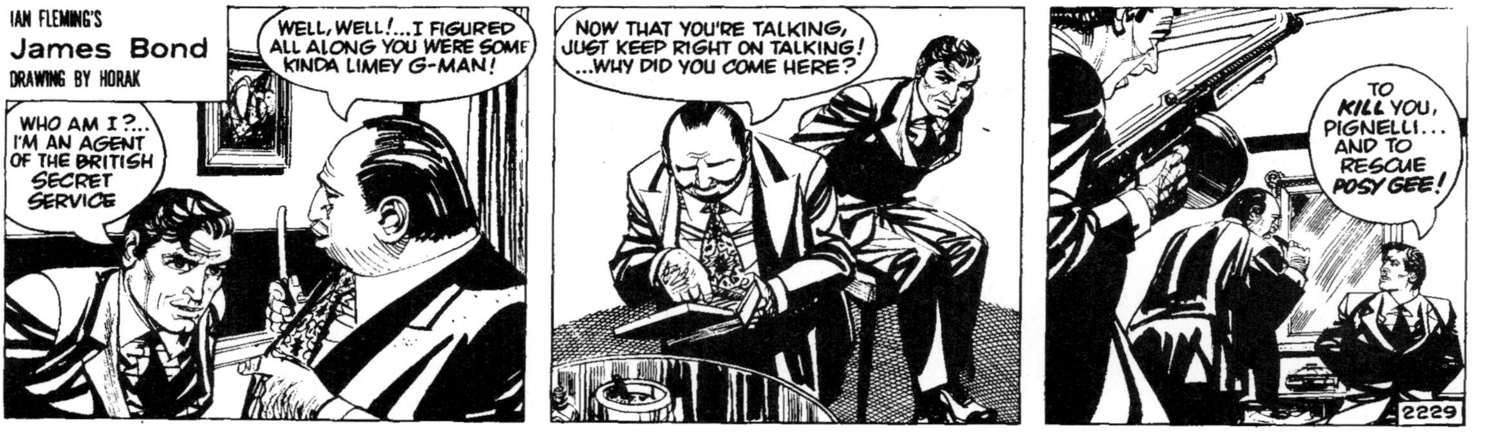
IAN FLEMING'S
James Bond
DRAWING BY HORAK
WHO AM I?... I'M AN AGENT OF THE BRITISH SECRET SERVICE
WELL, WELL!...I FIGURED ALL ALONG YOU WERE SOME KINDA LIMEY G-MAN!
NOW THAT YOU'RE TALKING, JUST KEEP RIGHT ON TALKING! ...WHY DID YOU COME HERE?
TO KILL YOU, PIGNELLI... AND TO RESCUE POSY GEE!
2229

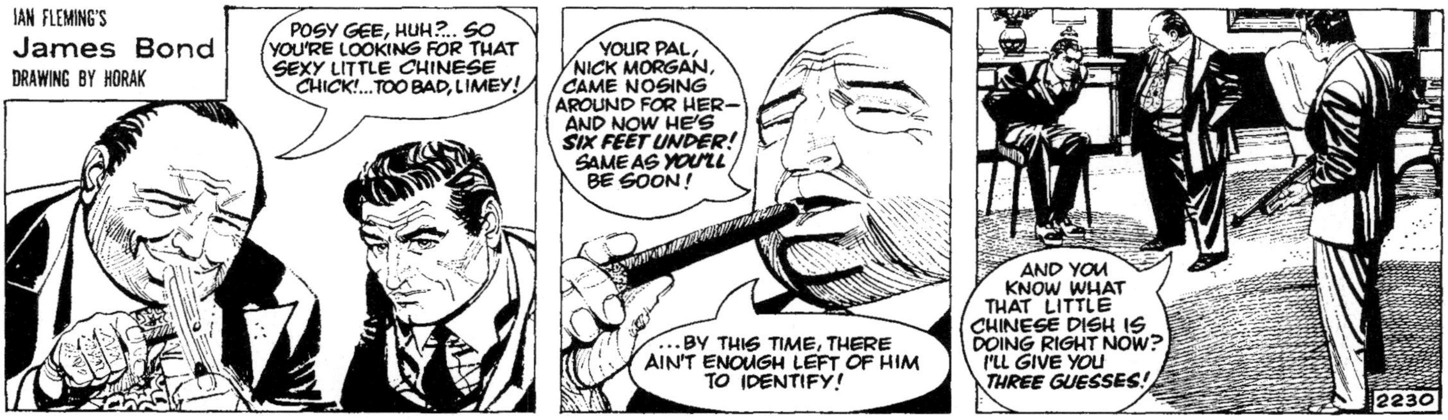
IAN FLEMING'S
James Bond
DRAWING BY HORAK
POSY GEE, HUH?... SO YOU'RE LOOKING FOR THAT SEXY LITTLE CHINESE CHICK!...TOO BAD, LIMEY!
YOUR PAL, NICK MORGAN, CAME NOSING AROUND FOR HER– AND NOW HE'S SIX FEET UNDER! SAME AS YOU'LL BE SOON!
...BY THIS TIME, THERE AIN'T ENOUGH LEFT OF HIM TO IDENTIFY!
AND YOU KNOW WHAT THAT LITTLE CHINESE DISH IS DOING RIGHT NOW? I'LL GIVE YOU THREE GUESSES!
2230

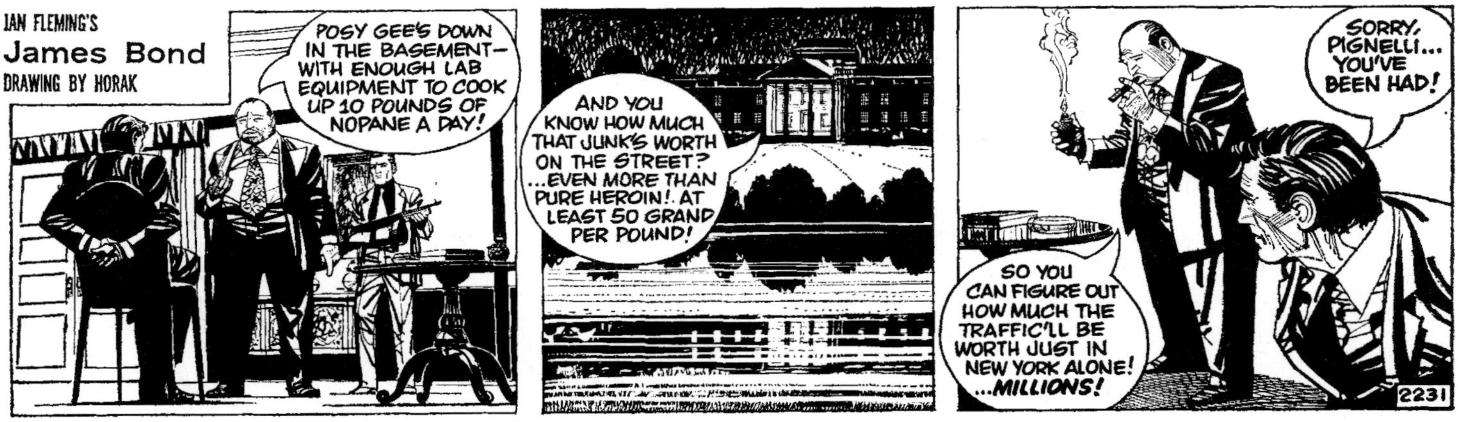
IAN FLEMING'S
James Bond
DRAWING BY HORAK
POSY GEE'S DOWN IN THE BASEMENT– WITH ENOUGH LAB EQUIPMENT TO COOK UP 10 POUNDS OF NOPANE A DAY!
AND YOU KNOW HOW MUCH THAT JUNK'S WORTH ON THE STREET? ...EVEN MORE THAN PURE HEROIN!. AT LEAST 50 GRAND PER POUND!
SO YOU CAN FIGURE OUT HOW MUCH THE TRAFFIC'LL BE WORTH JUST IN NEW YORK ALONE! ...MILLIONS!
SORRY, PIGNELLI... YOU'VE BEEN HAD!
2231

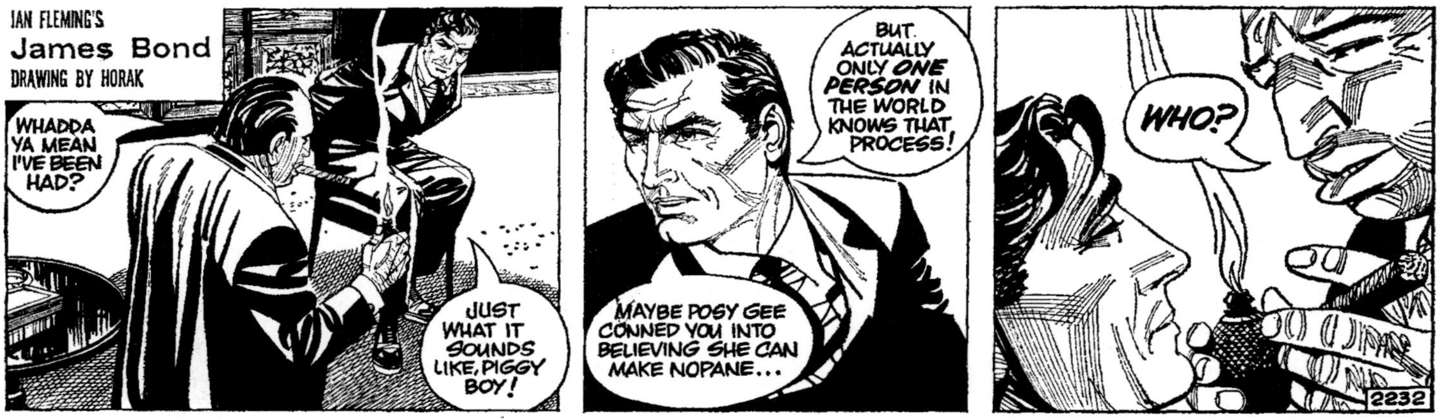
IAN FLEMING'S
James Bond
DRAWING BY HORAK
WHADDA YA MEAN I'VE BEEN HAD?
JUST WHAT IT SOUNDS LIKE, PIGGY BOY!
BUT ACTUALLY ONLY ONE PERSON IN THE WORLD KNOWS THAT PROCESS!
MAYBE POSY GEE CONNED YOU INTO BELIEVING SHE CAN MAKE NOPANE...
WHO?
2232

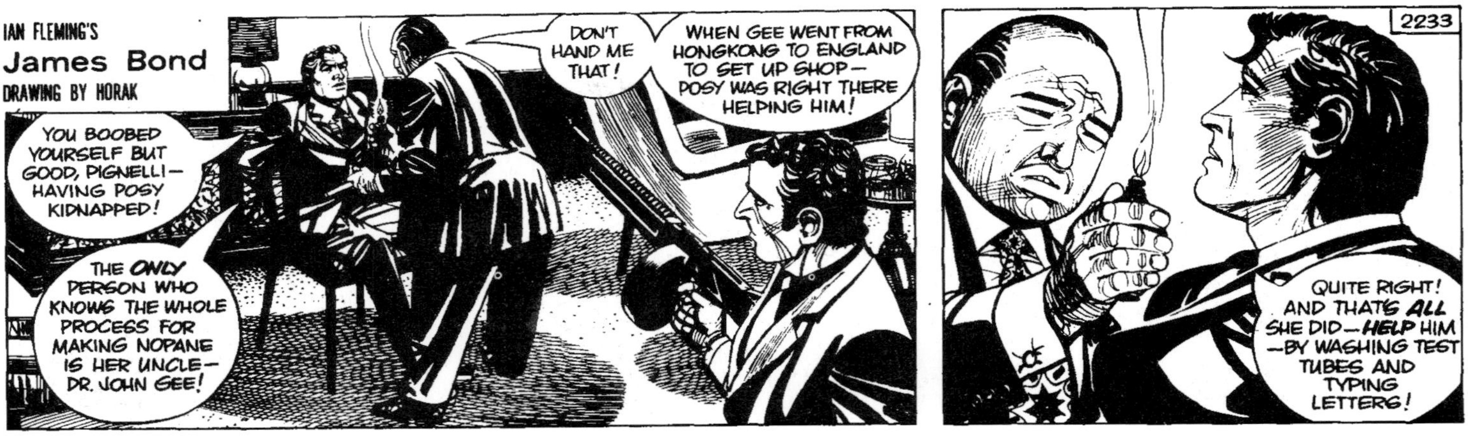
IAN FLEMING'S
James Bond
DRAWING BY HORAK
YOU BOOBED YOURSELF BUT GOOD, PIGNELLI—HAVING POSY KIDNAPPED!
THE ONLY PERSON WHO KNOWS THE WHOLE PROCESS FOR MAKING NOPANE IS HER UNCLE—DR. JOHN GEE!
DON'T HAND ME THAT!
WHEN GEE WENT FROM HONGKONG TO ENGLAND TO SET UP SHOP—POSY WAS RIGHT THERE HELPING HIM!
2233
QUITE RIGHT! AND THAT'S ALL SHE DID—HELP HIM—BY WASHING TEST TUBES AND TYPING LETTERS!

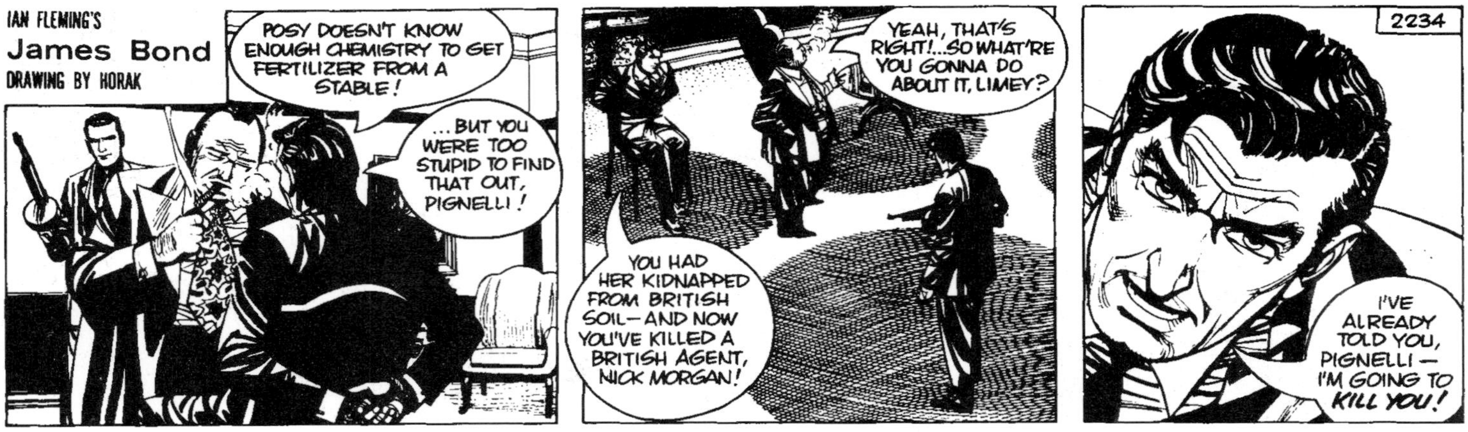
IAN FLEMING'S
James Bond
DRAWING BY HORAK
POSY DOESN'T KNOW ENOUGH CHEMISTRY TO GET FERTILIZER FROM A STABLE!
...BUT YOU WERE TOO STUPID TO FIND THAT OUT, PIGNELLI!
YEAH, THAT'S RIGHT!...SO WHAT'RE YOU GONNA DO ABOUT IT, LIMEY?
YOU HAD HER KIDNAPPED FROM BRITISH SOIL—AND NOW YOU'VE KILLED A BRITISH AGENT, NICK MORGAN!
2234
I'VE ALREADY TOLD YOU, PIGNELLI—I'M GOING TO KILL YOU!

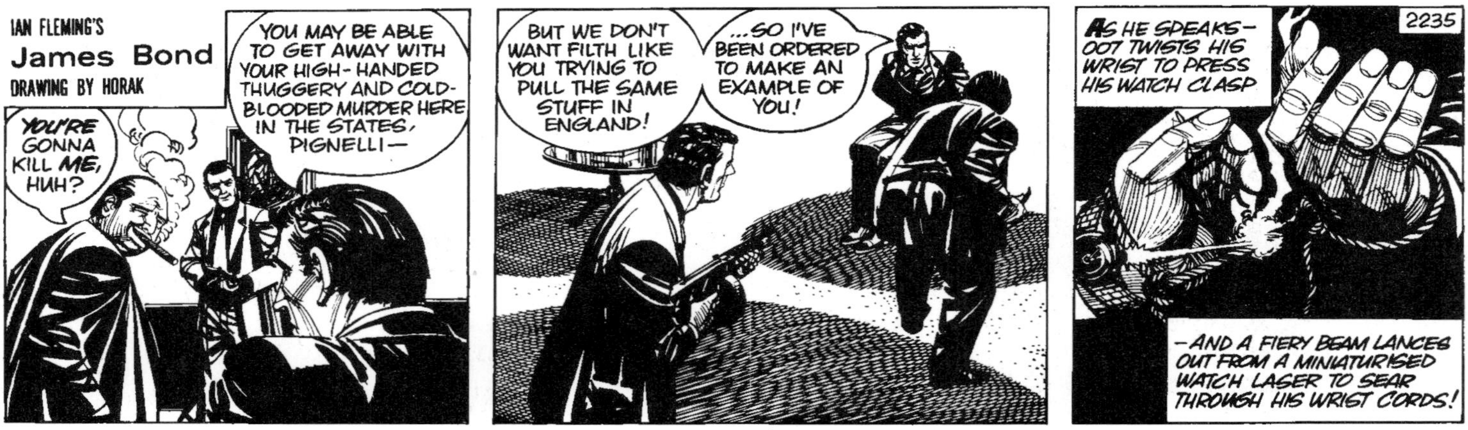
IAN FLEMING'S
James Bond
DRAWING BY HORAK
YOU'RE GONNA KILL ME, HUH?
YOU MAY BE ABLE TO GET AWAY WITH YOUR HIGH-HANDED THUGGERY AND COLD-BLOODED MURDER HERE IN THE STATES, PIGNELLI—
BUT WE DON'T WANT FILTH LIKE YOU TRYING TO PULL THE SAME STUFF IN ENGLAND!
...SO I'VE BEEN ORDERED TO MAKE AN EXAMPLE OF YOU!
2235
AS HE SPEAKS—007 TWISTS HIS WRIST TO PRESS HIS WATCH CLASP
—AND A FIERY BEAM LANCES OUT FROM A MINIATURISED WATCH LASER TO SEAR THROUGH HIS WRIST CORDS!

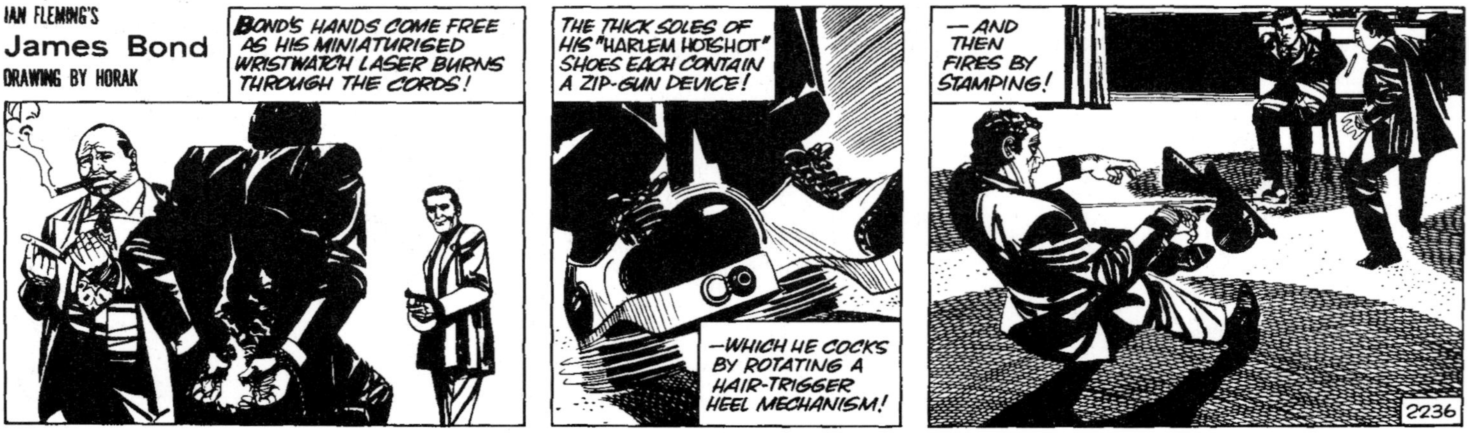
IAN FLEMING'S
James Bond
DRAWING BY HORAK
BOND'S HANDS COME FREE AS HIS MINIATURISED WRISTWATCH LASER BURNS THROUGH THE CORDS!
THE THICK SOLES OF HIS "HARLEM HOTSHOT" SHOES EACH CONTAIN A ZIP-GUN DEVICE!
—WHICH HE COCKS BY ROTATING A HAIR-TRIGGER HEEL MECHANISM!
—AND THEN FIRES BY STAMPING!
2236

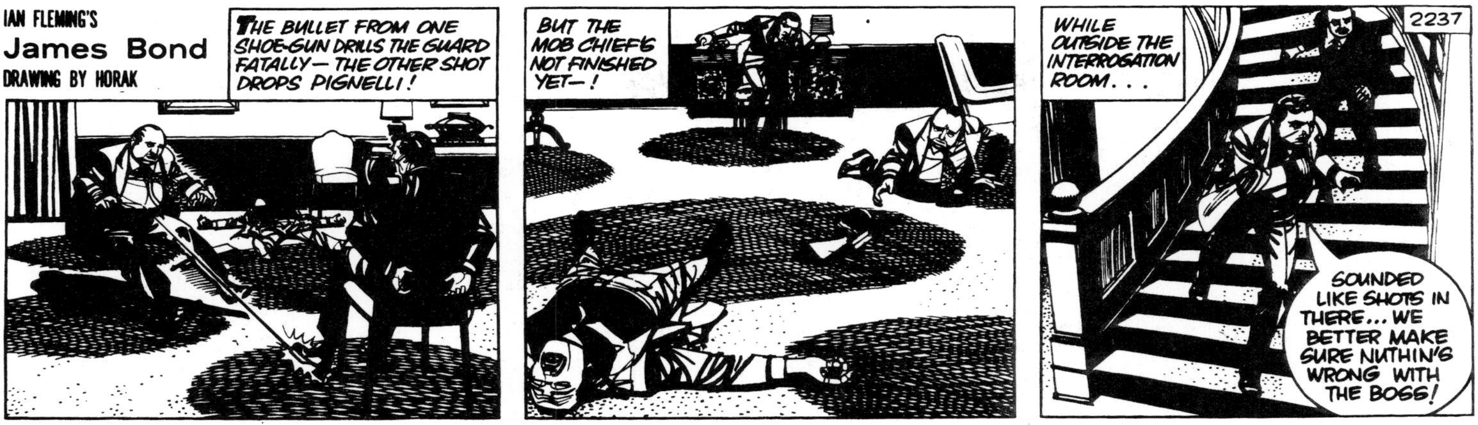
IAN FLEMING'S
James Bond
DRAWING BY HORAK
THE BULLET FROM ONE SHOE-GUN DRILLS THE GUARD FATALLY— THE OTHER SHOT DROPS PIGNELLI!
BUT THE MOB CHIEF'S NOT FINISHED YET—!
WHILE OUTSIDE THE INTERROGATION ROOM...
2237
SOUNDED LIKE SHOTS IN THERE... WE BETTER MAKE SURE NUTHIN'S WRONG WITH THE BOSS!

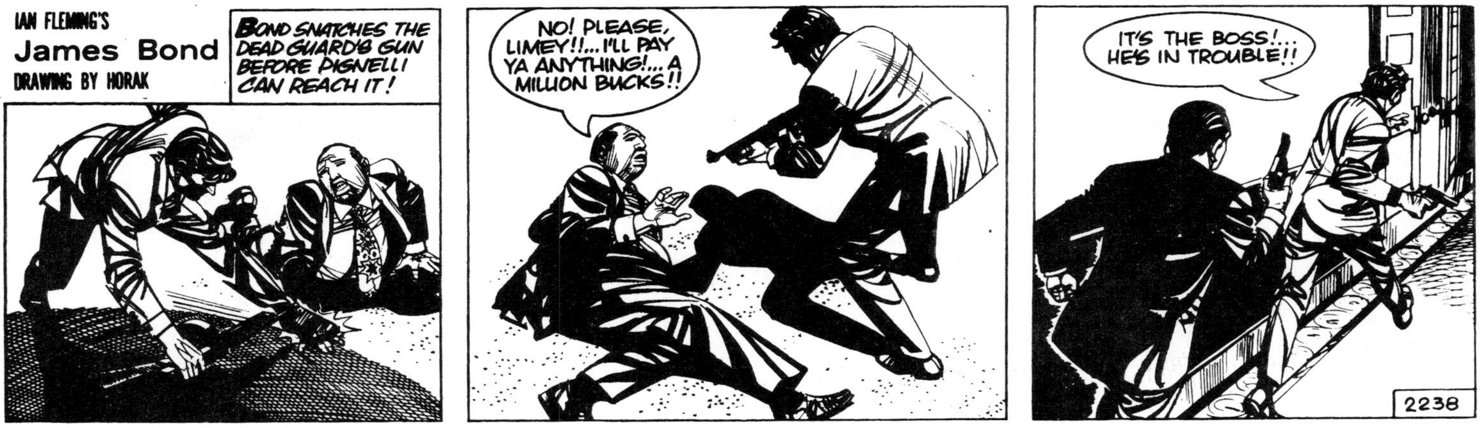
IAN FLEMING'S
James Bond
DRAWING BY HORAK
BOND SNATCHES THE DEAD GUARD'S GUN BEFORE PIGNELLI CAN REACH IT!
NO! PLEASE, LIMEY!!... I'LL PAY YA ANYTHING!... A MILLION BUCKS!!
IT'S THE BOSS!... HE'S IN TROUBLE!!
2238

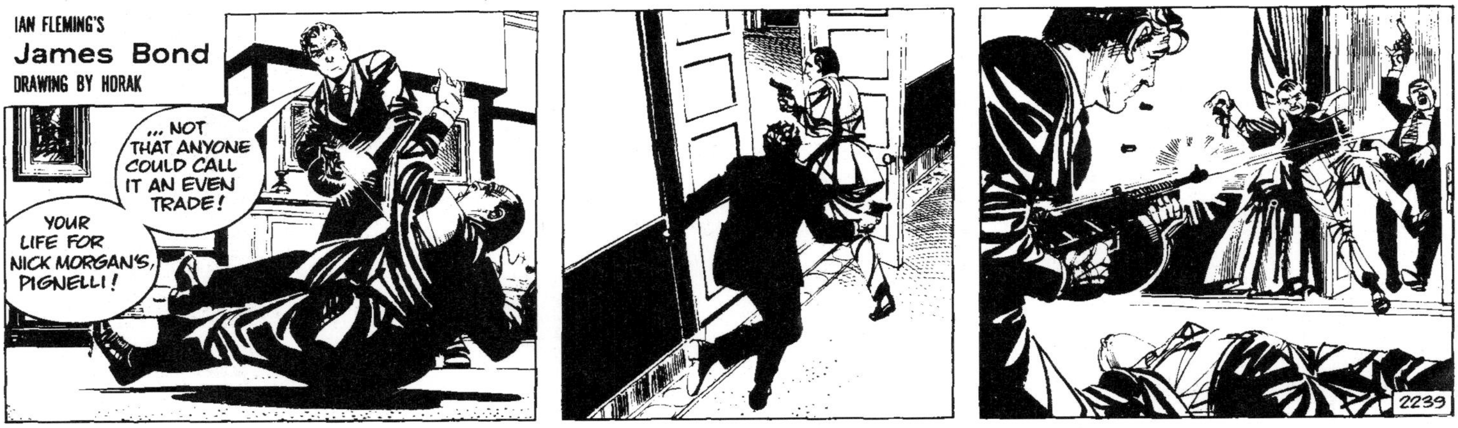
IAN FLEMING'S
James Bond
DRAWING BY HORAK
YOUR LIFE FOR NICK MORGAN'S, PIGNELLI!
... NOT THAT ANYONE COULD CALL IT AN EVEN TRADE!
2239

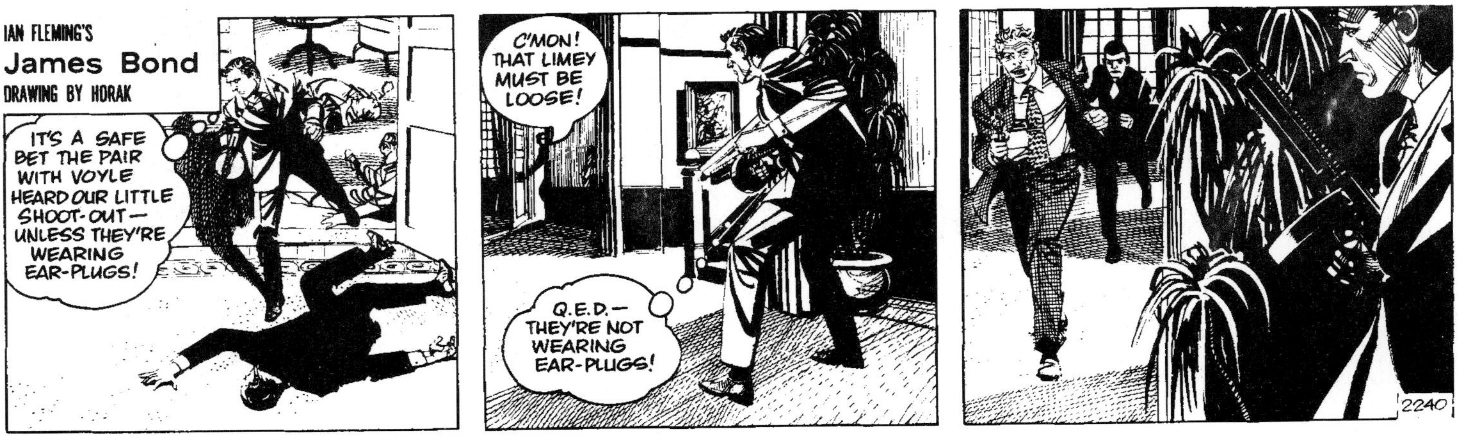
IAN FLEMING'S
James Bond
DRAWING BY HORAK
IT'S A SAFE BET THE PAIR WITH VOYLE HEARD OUR LITTLE SHOOT-OUT— UNLESS THEY'RE WEARING EAR-PLUGS!
C'MON! THAT LIMEY MUST BE LOOSE!
Q.E.D.— THEY'RE NOT WEARING EAR-PLUGS!
2240

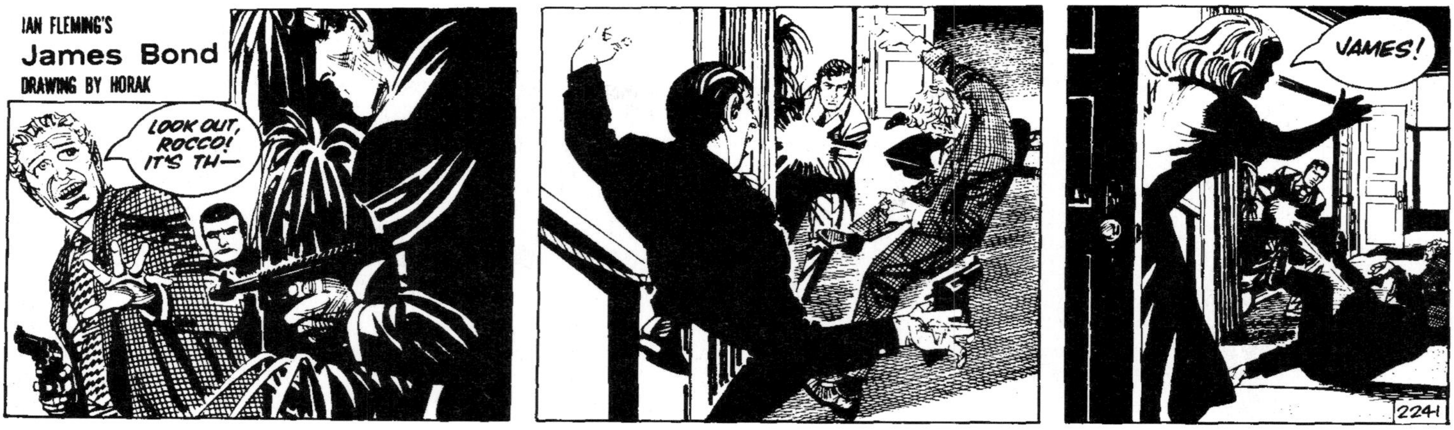
IAN FLEMING'S
James Bond
DRAWING BY HORAK
LOOK OUT, ROCCO! IT'S TH—
JAMES!
2241

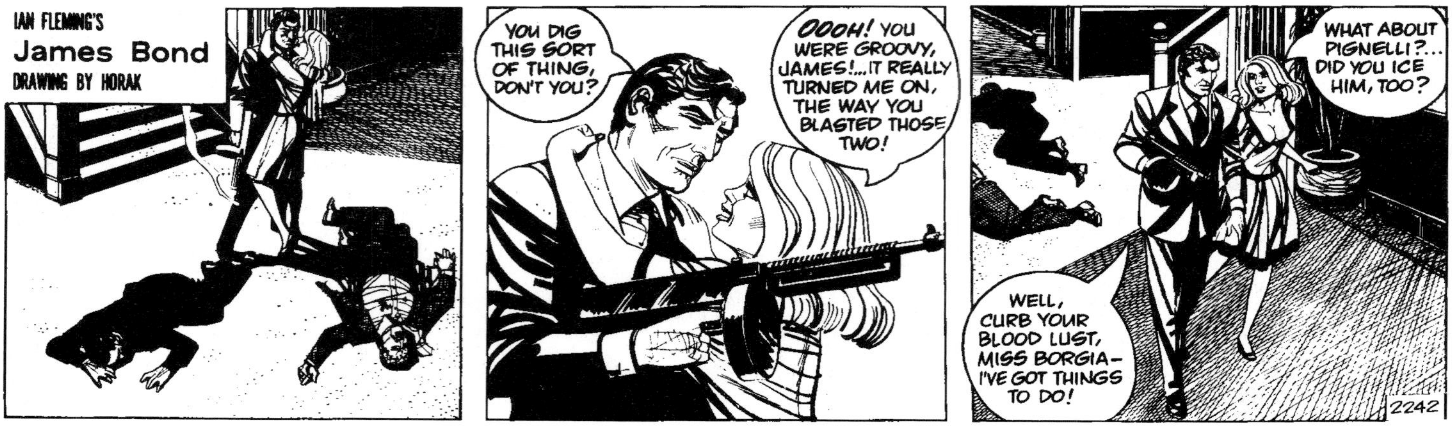
IAN FLEMING'S
James Bond
DRAWING BY HORAK
YOU DIG THIS SORT OF THING, DON'T YOU?
OOOH! YOU WERE GROOVY, JAMES!... IT REALLY TURNED ME ON, THE WAY YOU BLASTED THOSE TWO!
WHAT ABOUT PIGNELLI?... DID YOU ICE HIM, TOO?
WELL, CURB YOUR BLOOD LUST, MISS BORGIA- I'VE GOT THINGS TO DO!
2242

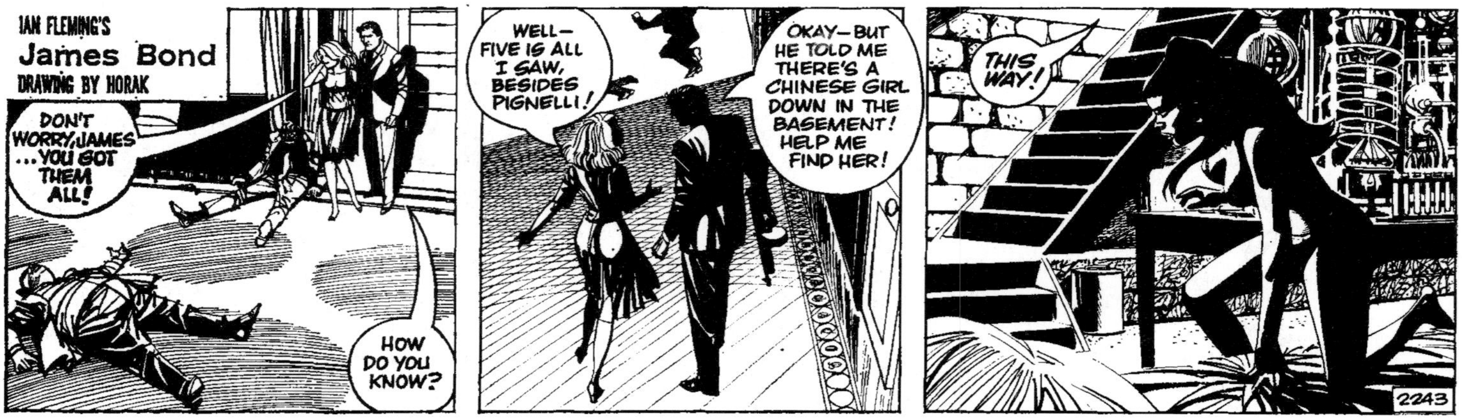
IAN FLEMING'S
James Bond
DRAWING BY HORAK
DON'T WORRY, JAMES ... YOU GOT THEM ALL!
HOW DO YOU KNOW?
WELL— FIVE IS ALL I SAW, BESIDES PIGNELLI!
OKAY—BUT HE TOLD ME THERE'S A CHINESE GIRL DOWN IN THE BASEMENT! HELP ME FIND HER!
THIS WAY!
2243

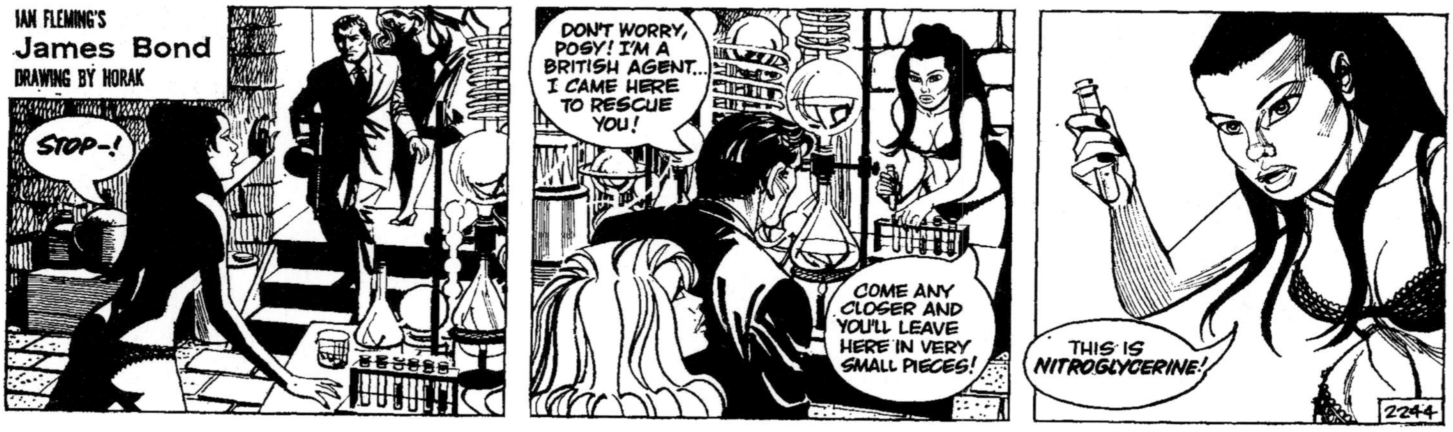
IAN FLEMING'S
James Bond
DRAWING BY HORAK
STOP-!
DON'T WORRY, POSY! I'M A BRITISH AGENT... I CAME HERE TO RESCUE YOU!
COME ANY CLOSER AND YOU'LL LEAVE HERE IN VERY SMALL PIECES!
THIS IS NITROGLYCERINE!
2244

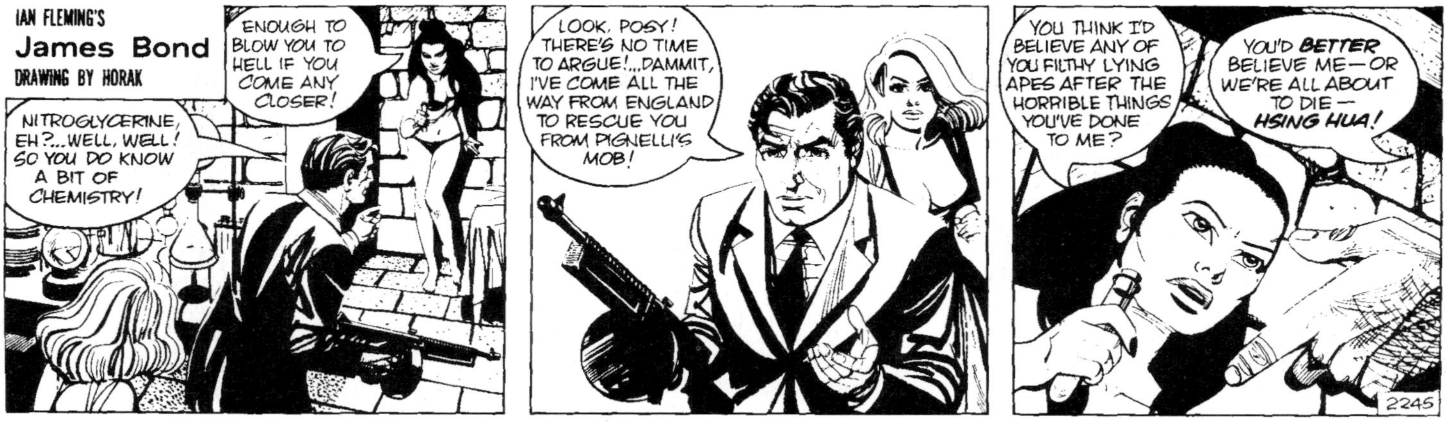
IAN FLEMING'S
James Bond
DRAWING BY HORAK
ENOUGH TO BLOW YOU TO HELL IF YOU COME ANY CLOSER!
NITROGLYCERINE, EH?... WELL, WELL! SO YOU DO KNOW A BIT OF CHEMISTRY!
LOOK, POSY! THERE'S NO TIME TO ARGUE!... DAMMIT, I'VE COME ALL THE WAY FROM ENGLAND TO RESCUE YOU FROM PIGNELLI'S MOB!
YOU THINK I'D BELIEVE ANY OF YOU FILTHY LYING APES AFTER THE HORRIBLE THINGS YOU'VE DONE TO ME?
YOU'D BETTER BELIEVE ME—OR WE'RE ALL ABOUT TO DIE— HSING HUA!
2245

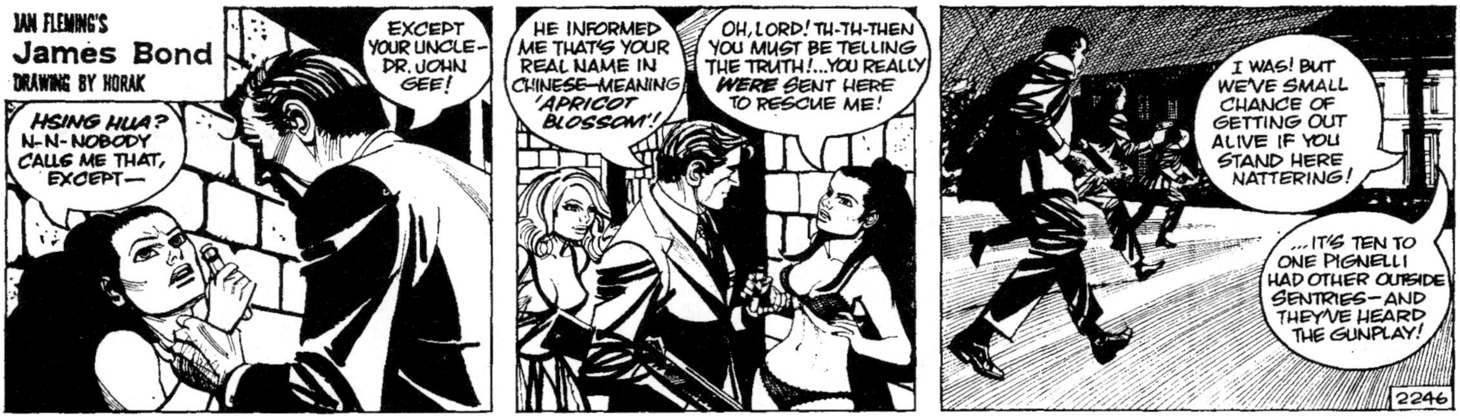
IAN FLEMING'S
James Bond
DRAWING BY HORAK
HSING HUA? N-N-NOBODY CALLS ME THAT, EXCEPT—
EXCEPT YOUR UNCLE- DR. JOHN GEE!
HE INFORMED ME THAT'S YOUR REAL NAME IN CHINESE—MEANING 'APRICOT BLOSSOM'!
OH, LORD! TH-TH-THEN YOU MUST BE TELLING THE TRUTH!... YOU REALLY WERE SENT HERE TO RESCUE ME!
I WAS! BUT WE'VE SMALL CHANCE OF GETTING OUT ALIVE IF YOU STAND HERE NATTERING!
...IT'S TEN TO ONE PIGNELLI HAD OTHER OUTSIDE SENTRIES—AND THEY'VE HEARD THE GUNPLAY!
2246

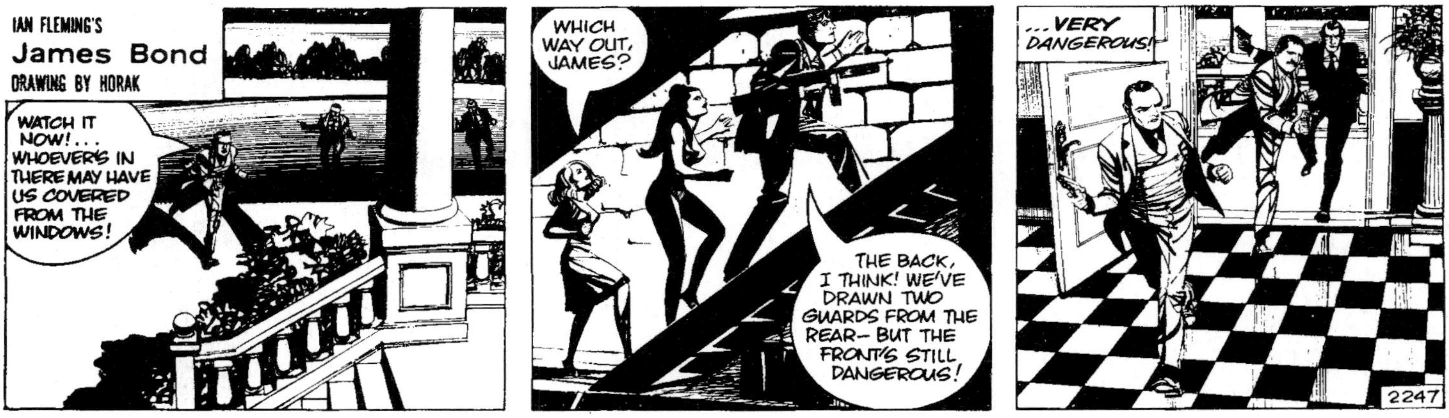
IAN FLEMING'S
James Bond
DRAWING BY HORAK
WATCH IT NOW!... WHOEVER'S IN THERE MAY HAVE US COVERED FROM THE WINDOWS!
WHICH WAY OUT, JAMES?
THE BACK, I THINK! WE'VE DRAWN TWO GUARDS FROM THE REAR- BUT THE FRONT'S STILL DANGEROUS!
...VERY DANGEROUS!
2247

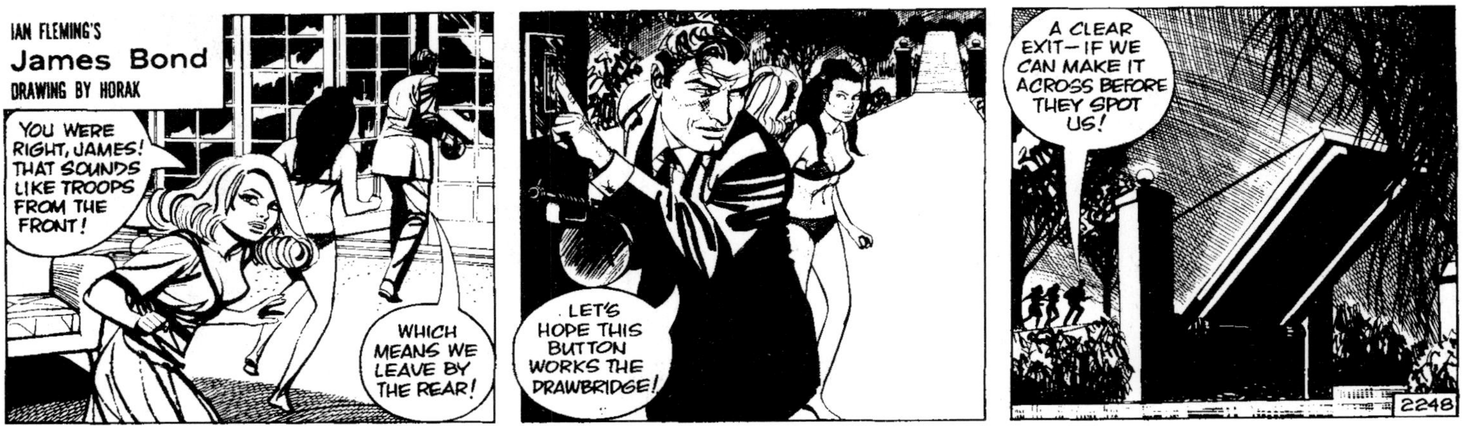
IAN FLEMING'S
James Bond
DRAWING BY HORAK
YOU WERE RIGHT, JAMES! THAT SOUNDS LIKE TROOPS FROM THE FRONT!
WHICH MEANS WE LEAVE BY THE REAR!
LET'S HOPE THIS BUTTON WORKS THE DRAWBRIDGE!
A CLEAR EXIT— IF WE CAN MAKE IT ACROSS BEFORE THEY SPOT US!
2248

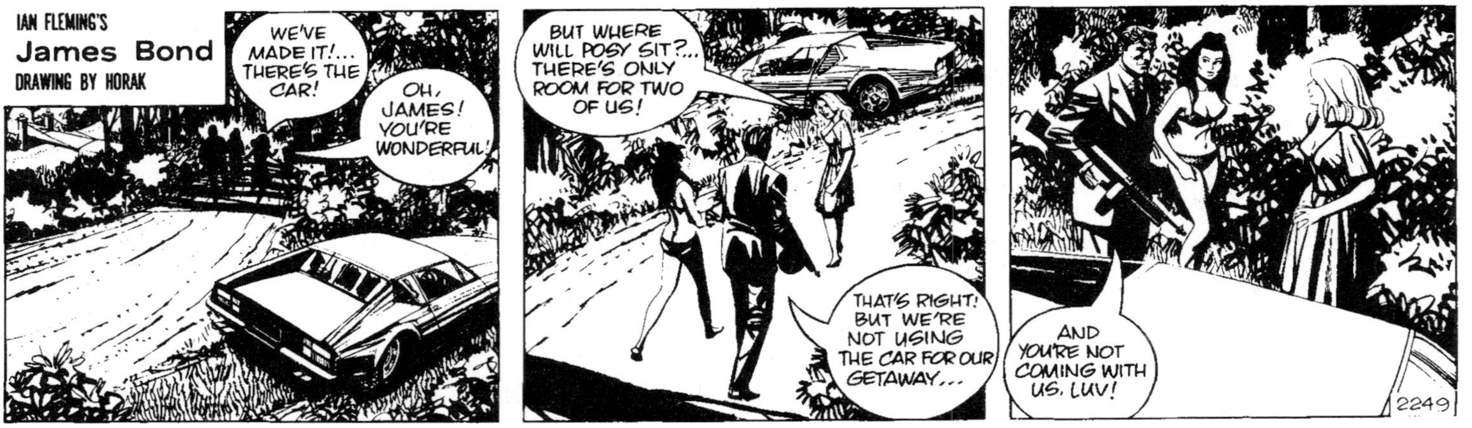
IAN FLEMING'S
James Bond
DRAWING BY HORAK
WE'VE MADE IT!... THERE'S THE CAR!
OH, JAMES! YOU'RE WONDERFUL!
BUT WHERE WILL POSY SIT?... THERE'S ONLY ROOM FOR TWO OF US!
THAT'S RIGHT! BUT WE'RE NOT USING THE CAR FOR OUR GETAWAY...
AND YOU'RE NOT COMING WITH US, LUV!
2249

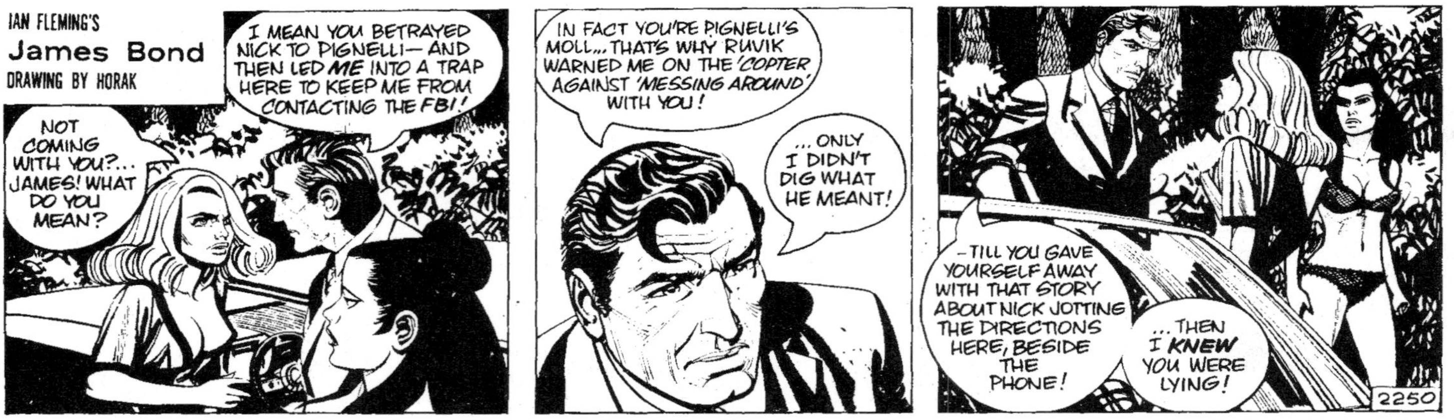
IAN FLEMING'S
James Bond
DRAWING BY HORAK
NOT COMING WITH YOU?... JAMES! WHAT DO YOU MEAN?
I MEAN YOU BETRAYED NICK TO PIGNELLI— AND THEN LED ME INTO A TRAP HERE TO KEEP ME FROM CONTACTING THE FBI!
IN FACT YOU'RE PIGNELLI'S MOLL... THAT'S WHY RUVIK WARNED ME ON THE 'COPTER AGAINST 'MESSING AROUND' WITH YOU!
...ONLY I DIDN'T DIG WHAT HE MEANT!
—TILL YOU GAVE YOURSELF AWAY WITH THAT STORY ABOUT NICK JOTTING THE DIRECTIONS HERE, BESIDE THE PHONE!
...THEN I KNEW YOU WERE LYING!
2250

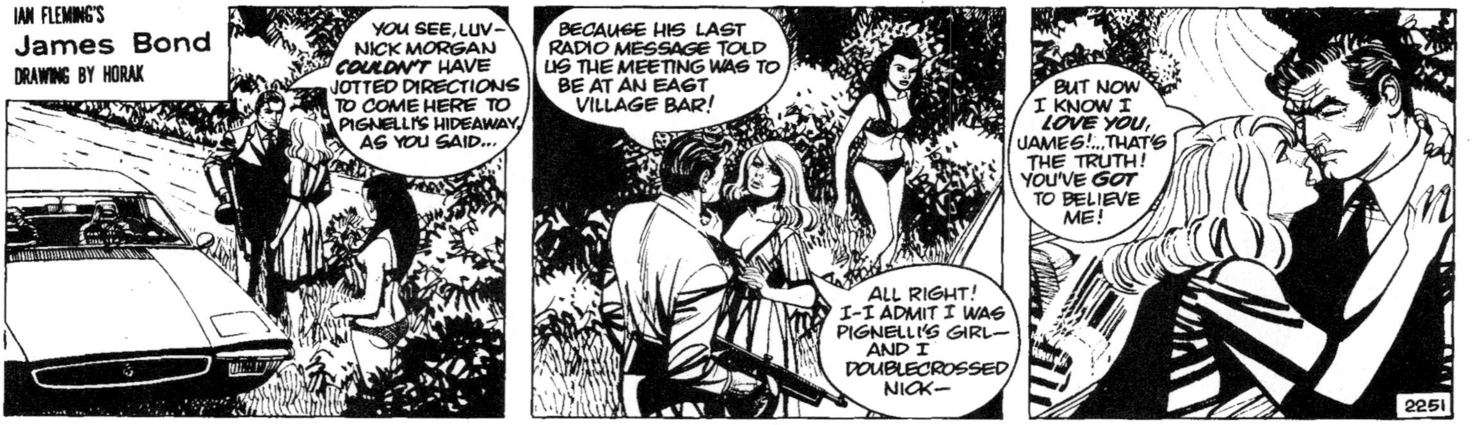
IAN FLEMING'S
James Bond
DRAWING BY HORAK
YOU SEE, LUV- NICK MORGAN COULDN'T HAVE JOTTED DIRECTIONS TO COME HERE TO PIGNELLI'S HIDEAWAY, AS YOU SAID...
BECAUSE HIS LAST RADIO MESSAGE TOLD US THE MEETING WAS TO BE AT AN EAST VILLAGE BAR!
ALL RIGHT! I-I ADMIT I WAS PIGNELLI'S GIRL— AND I DOUBLECROSSED NICK—
BUT NOW I KNOW I LOVE YOU, JAMES!... THAT'S THE TRUTH! YOU'VE GOT TO BELIEVE ME!
2251

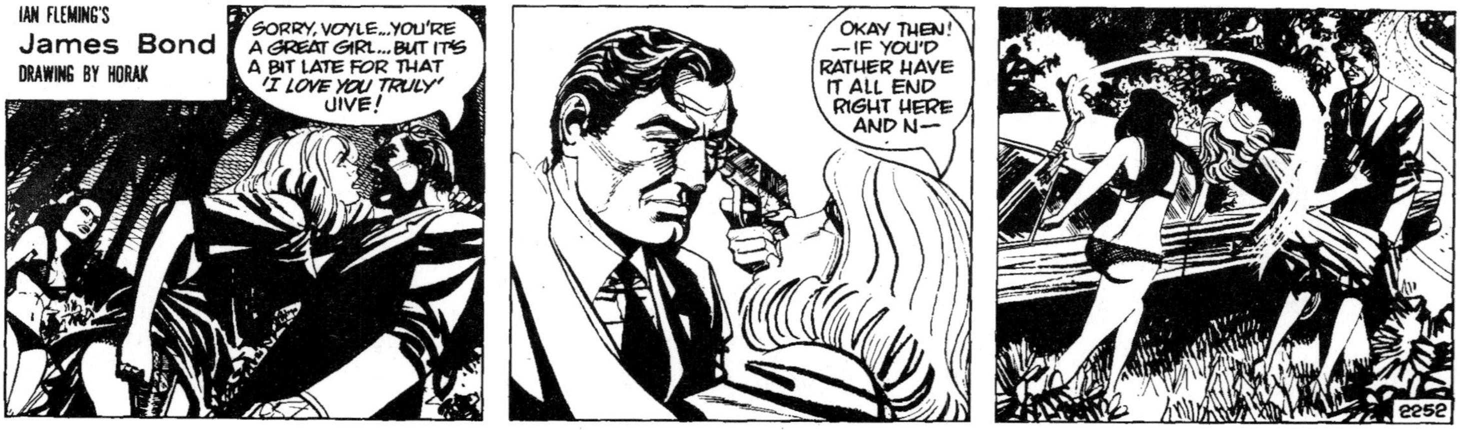
IAN FLEMING'S
James Bond
DRAWING BY HORAK
SORRY, VOYLE... YOU'RE A GREAT GIRL... BUT IT'S A BIT LATE FOR THAT 'I LOVE YOU TRULY' JIVE!
OKAY THEN! —IF YOU'D RATHER HAVE IT ALL END RIGHT HERE AND N—
2252

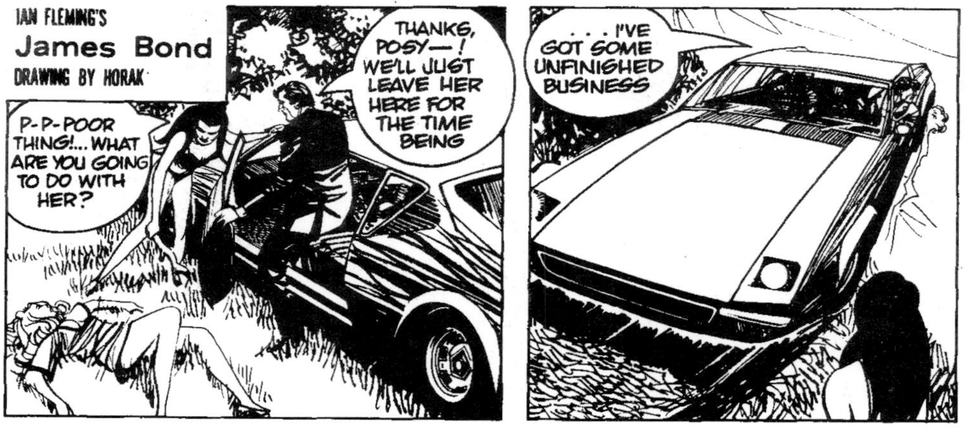
IAN FLEMING'S
James Bond
DRAWING BY HORAK
P-P-POOR THING!... WHAT ARE YOU GOING TO DO WITH HER?
THANKS, POSY—! WE'LL JUST LEAVE HER HERE FOR THE TIME BEING
. . . I'VE GOT SOME UNFINISHED BUSINESS
2253

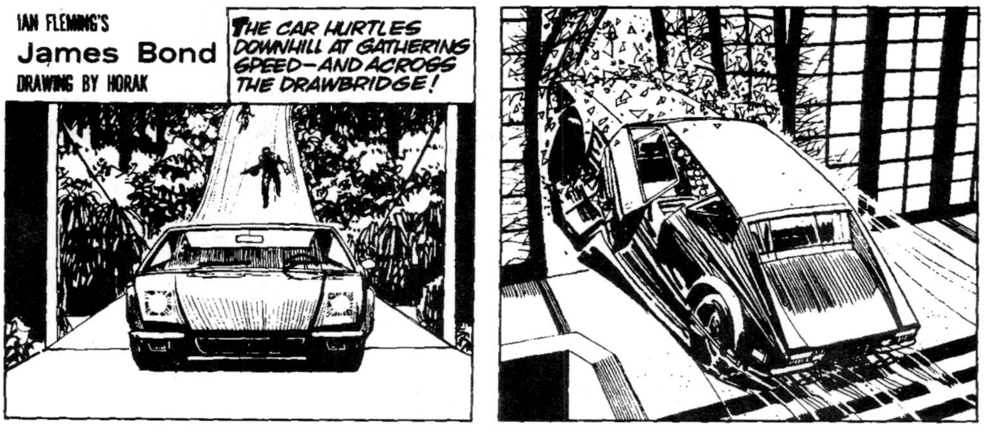
IAN FLEMING'S
James Bond
DRAWING BY HORAK
THE CAR HURTLES DOWNHILL AT GATHERING SPEED—AND ACROSS THE DRAWBRIDGE!
THERE'S THE B—!
GET HIM!
2254

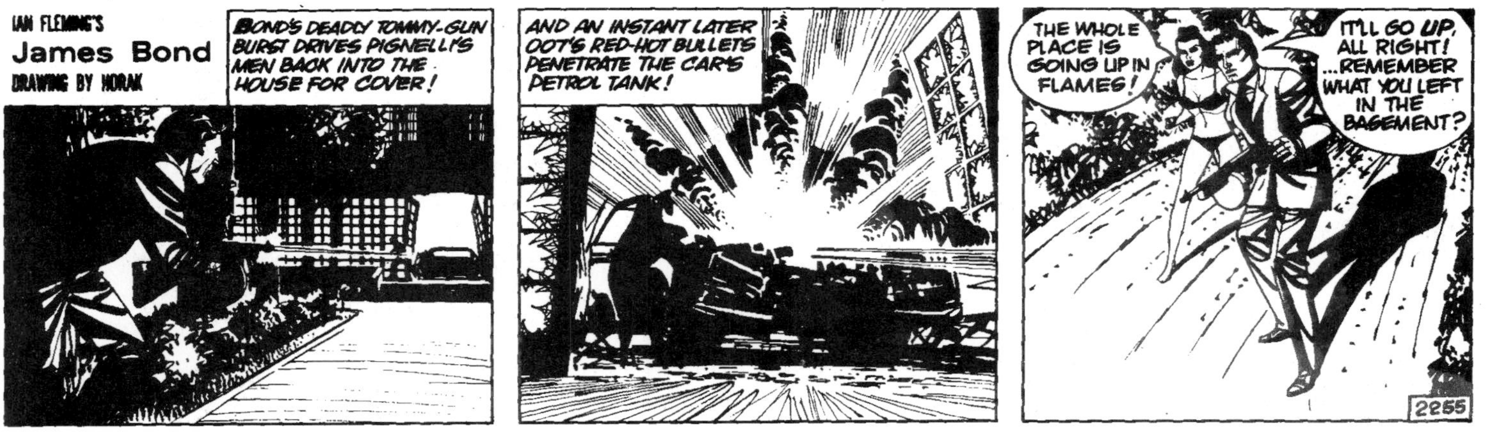
IAN FLEMING'S
James Bond
DRAWING BY HORAK
BOND'S DEADLY TOMMY-GUN BURST DRIVES PIGNELLI'S MEN BACK INTO THE HOUSE FOR COVER!
AND AN INSTANT LATER OOT'S RED-HOT BULLETS PENETRATE THE CAR'S PETROL TANK!
THE WHOLE PLACE IS GOING UP IN FLAMES!
IT'LL GO UP, ALL RIGHT! ...REMEMBER WHAT YOU LEFT IN THE BASEMENT?
2255

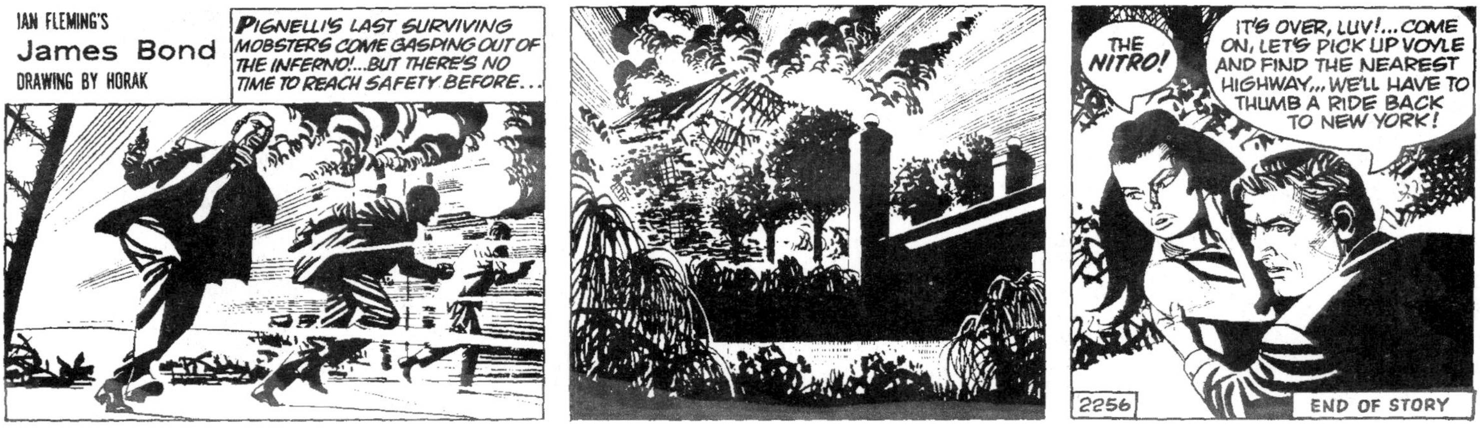
IAN FLEMING'S
James Bond
DRAWING BY HORAK
PIGNELLI'S LAST SURVIVING MOBSTERS COME GASPING OUT OF THE INFERNO!...BUT THERE'S NO TIME TO REACH SAFETY BEFORE . . .
THE NITRO!
IT'S OVER, LUV!...COME ON, LET'S PICK UP VOYLE AND FIND THE NEAREST HIGHWAY... WE'LL HAVE TO THUMB A RIDE BACK TO NEW YORK!
2256
END OF STORY

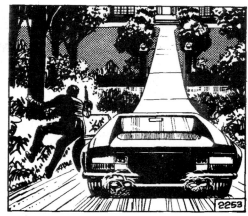

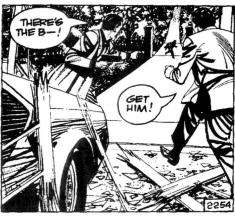

THE COMPLETE JAMES BOND SYNDICATED NEWSPAPER CHECKLIST

The following is a complete checklist of *James Bond* strips to have appeared in the *Express* newspapers and been syndicated in non-UK newspapers.

STORY	WRITER	ARTISTS	DATE	SERIAL No.
Serialised in the *Daily Express*				
Casino Royale	IF/AH	JM	7.7.58–13.12.58	1–138
Live and Let Die	IF/HG	JM	15.12.58–28.3.59	139-225
Moonraker	IF/HG	JM	30.3.59–8.8.59	226-339
Diamonds Are Forever	IF/HG	JM	10.8.59–30.1.60	340–487
From Russia With Love	IF/HG	JM	3.2.60–21.5.60	488–583
Dr. No	IF/PO	JM	23.5.60–1.10.60	584–697
Goldfinger	IF/HG	JM	3.10.60–1.4.61	698–849
Risico	IF/HG	JM	3.4.61–24.6.61	850–921
From A View To A Kill	IF/HG	JM	25.6.61–9.9.61	922–987
For Your Eyes Only	IF/HG	JM	11.9.61–9.12.61	988–1065
Thunderball	IF/HG	JM	11.12.61–10.2.62	1066–1128*

**Series aborted prematurely*

STORY	WRITER	ARTISTS	DATE	SERIAL No.
(Series Two)				
On Her Majesty's Secret Service	IF/HG	JM	29.6.64–17.5.65	1–274
You Only Live Twice	IF/HG	JM	18.5.65–8.1.66	275–475
(Series Three)				
The Man With the Golden Gun	IF/JL	YH	10.1.66–10.9.66	1–209
The Living Daylights	IF/JL	YH	12.9.66–12.11.66	210–263
Octopussy	IF/JL	YH	14.11.66–27.5.67	264–428
The Hildebrand Rarity	IF/JL	YH	29.5.67–16.12.67	429–602
The Spy Who Loved Me	IF/JL	YH	18.12.67–3.10.68	603–815
The Harpies	JL	YH	4.10.68–23.6.69	816–1037
River of Death	JL	YH	24.6.69–29.11.69	1038–1174
Colonel Sun	KA/JL	YH	1.12.69–20.8.70	1175–1393
The Golden Ghost	JL	YH	21.8.70–16.1.71	1394–1519
Fear Face	JL	YH	18.1.71–20.4.71	1520–1596
Double Jeopardy	JL	YH	21.4.71–28.8.71	1597–1708
Starfire	JL	YH	30.8.71–24.12.71	1709–1809
Trouble Spot	JL	YH	28.12.71–10.6.72	1810–1951
Isle of Condors	JL	YH	12.6.72–21.10.72	1952–2065
The League of Vampires	JL	YH	25.10.72–28.2.73	2066–2172
Die With My Boots On	JL	YH	1.3.73–18.6.73	2173–2256
The Girl Machine	JL	YH	19.6.73–3.12.73	2257–2407
Beware of Butterflies	JL	YH	4.12.73–11.5.74	2408–2541
The Nevsky Nude	JL	YH	13.5.74–21.9.74	2542–2655
The Phoenix Project	JL	YH	23.9.74–18.2.75	2656–2780
The Black Ruby Caper	JL	YH	19.2.75–15.7.75	2781–2897
Till Death Do Us Part	JL	YH	7.7.75–14.10.75	2898–2983
The Torch–Time Affair	JL	YH	15.10.75–15.1.76	2984–3060
Hot-Shot	JL	YH	16.1.76–1.6.76	3061–3178
Nightbird	JL	YH	2.6.76–4.11.76	3179–3312
Ape of Diamonds	JL	YH	5.11.76–22.1.77	3313–3437

STORY	WRITER	ARTISTS	DATE	SERIAL No.
Serialised in the *Sunday Express*				
(Series Four)				
When the Wizard Awakes	JL	YH	30.1.77–22.5.77	1–54
Syndicated strips not featured in newspapers in the UK				
Sea Dragon	JL	YH	not applicable	55–192
Death Wing	JL	YH	not applicable	193–354
The Xanadu Connection	JL	YH	not applicable	355–468
Shark Bait	JL	YH	not applicable	469–636
Serialised in the *Daily Star*				
(Series Five)				
Doomcrack	JL	HN	2.2.81–19.8.81	1–174
The Paradise Plot	JL	JM	20.8.81–4.6.82	175–378
Deathmask	JL	JM	7.6.82–8.2.83	379–552
Flittermouse	JL	JM	9.2.83–20.5.83	553–624
Polestar	JL	JM	23.5.83–15.7.83	625–719*

**Series stopped publishing in the* Daily Star *at 673*

STORY	WRITER	ARTISTS	DATE	SERIAL No.
Syndicated strips not featured in UK newspapers				
The Scent of Danger	JL	JM	not applicable	720–821
Snake Goddess	JL	YH	not applicable	822–893
Double Eagle	JL	YH	not applicable	894–965

GLOSSARY

KEY TO CREATORS

IF: IAN FLEMING
AH: ANTHONY HERN
HG: HENRY GAMMIDGE
PO: PETER O'DONNELL
JL: JIM LAWRENCE
KA: KINGSLEY AMIS (under pseudonym Robert Markham)
JM: JOHN MCLUSKY
YH: YAROSLAV HORAK
HN: HARRY NORTH

SERIAL NUMBERS

Each serial number represents a day. However, in Scotland, some strips were published in the *Daily Express* on days when there were Bank Holidays in England and Wales; these were designated by the suffix 'a' after the serial number on the strips.

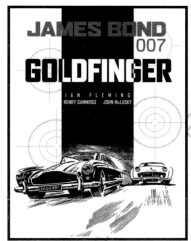
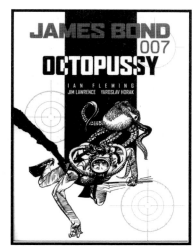

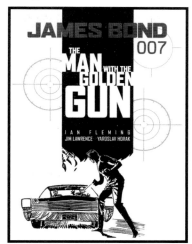
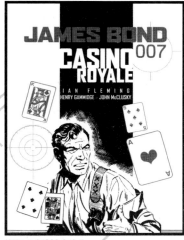
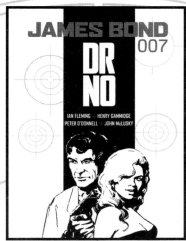

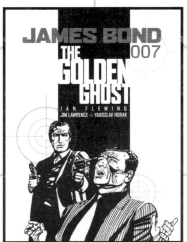

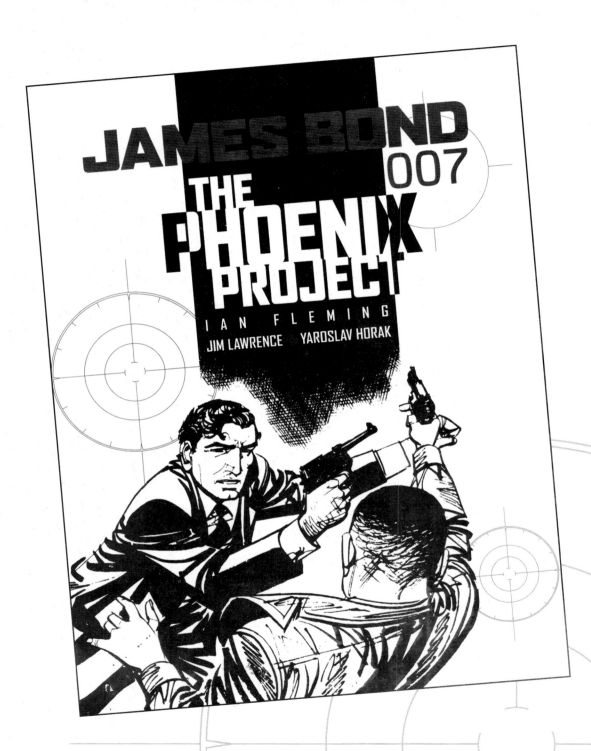